2315. (5 VOLS)

Doing Business in Asia

Asia Business Law Series

In cooperation with CCH Asia, Kluwer Law International is proud to present the *Asia Business Law Series*.

The *Asia Business Law Series* provides practical guidelines, legislation and case law, in order to help practitioners, policy makers and scholars understand how business is conducted in the rapidly growing Asian market.

1. *Tax Planning for Expatriates in China.* 2005. ISBN 90-411-2423-3

2. *China Master Tax Guide 2005.* 2005. ISBN 90-411-2424-1

3. *Investment in Greater China. Opportunities & Challenges for Investors.* 2005. ISBN 90-411-2425-X

4. *Foreign Exchange Control in China.* 2005. ISBN 90-411-2426-8

5. *Resolving Business Disputes in China.* 2005. ISBN 90-411-2416-0

6. *China Company Law Guide.* 2005. ISBN 90-411-2417-9 (2 Vols)

7. *China Business Law Guide.* 2005. ISBN 90-411-2418-7 (3 Vols)

8. *Doing Business in Asia.* 2005. ISBN 90-411-2420-9 (5 Vols)

9. *Employment Law Asia.* 2005. ISBN 90-411-2421-7 (5 Vols)

10. *Tax Planning & Compliance in Asia.* 2005. ISBN 90-411-2422-5 (6 Vols)

11. *China Intellectual Property Law Guide.* 2005. ISBN 90-411-2419-5

Doing Business in Asia

Volume I

First Edition

KLUWER LAW
INTERNATIONAL

A C.I.P. Catalogue record for this book is available from the Library of Congress.

ISBN 90-411-2420-9 (Set)
9888001136 (Vol. I)

Published by:
Kluwer Law International
P.O. Box 85889
2508 CN The Hague
The Netherlands
E-mail: sales@kluwerlaw.com
Website: http://www.kluwerlaw.com

Sold and distributed in North, Central and South America by:
Aspen Publishers Inc.
7201 McKinney Circle
Frederick, MD 21704
USA

Sold and distributed in Europe by:
Turpin Distribution Services Ltd.
Stratton Business Park
Pegasus Drive
Biggleswade
Bedfordshire SG18 8TQ
United Kingdom

This book was originally published by CCH Asia as the loose-leaf *Doing Business in Asia,*
ISBN 981-00-2799-0 (Set), ISBN 981-00-2191-7 (Vol.1), ISBN 981-00-2798-2 (Vol.2)

CCH Asia Pte Limited
11 Keppel Road
RCL Centre #11-01
Singapore 089057
E-mail: support@cch.com.sg
Website: http://www.cch.com.sg

Printed on acid-free paper

Printed in The Netherlands.

PAGE NUMBERING

The page numbers located at the top of each page, were previously used in the loose-leaf counterpart of this title for the purpose of filing new reports.

As a result you may notice gaps in the page numbering sequence. These are necessary in a loose-leaf reporting service. Where such a gap occurs, the next page number is provided between brackets.

Pages have also been numbered according to paragraphs. Gaps were originally left in the numbering sequence to enable new paragraphs to be added when these became necessary.

The numbers of the first new paragraph on the left page and the last new paragraph on the right page are indicated in bold type at the foot of those pages. These numbers are referred to in indexes and internal references.

GENERAL
TABLE OF CONTENTS

VOLUME I

	Page
Time Zones	3
Features of This Reporter	21
Loose-leaf Reports	24
Related CCH Publications	26
Index	101
Lines of Inquiry	1,001
Australia [AUS]	7,001
China [CHN]	13,001

VOLUME II

	Page
Hong Kong [HKG]	19,001
India [IND]	25,001
Indonesia [INS]	31,001

VOLUME III

	Page
Japan [JPN]	37,001
Korea [KOR]	43,001
Malaysia [MAL]	49,001

continued over ...

2

VOLUME IV

	Page
Myanmar [MYA]	55,001
Philippines [PHL]	61,001
Singapore [SGP]	67,001

VOLUME V

	Page
Taiwan [TWN]	73,001
Thailand [THA]	79,001
Vietnam [VIT]	85,001
Cumulative Index New Developments	100,001

Local standard time can be determined for any area in the world by adding one hour for each time zone counted in an easterly direction from one's own, or by subtracting one hour for each zone counted in a westerly direction.

TIME ZONES

INTERNATIONAL DATE LINE

MONDAY

SUNDAY

Hawaii

Fiji

New Zealand

−10hr 30m

−9hr 30m

PNG

Australia

USSR

Japan

Korea

Taiwan

Mongolia

China −8hr

Hong Kong

Philippines

Vietnam

Laos

Cambodia

Myanmar

Thailand

Malaysia

Singapore −7hr 30m

Indonesia

India

Pakistan

Afghanistan

Iran

4 PM | 5 PM | 6 PM | 7 PM | 8 PM | 9 PM | 10 PM | 11 PM | Midnight | 1 AM | 2 AM | 3 AM

Features of the Reporter

General arrangement .... ¶1   Report numbers .... ¶7
Lines of Inquiry .... ¶2   Index .... ¶8
Countries .... ¶3   Cumulative Index ●
Coloured tabs .... ¶4   New Developments .... ¶9
Paragraph numbers .... ¶5   How to find information .... ¶10
Page numbers .... ¶6

¶1   General arrangement

Doing Business in Asia is a two-volume loose-leaf Reporter designed to meet the needs of companies wishing to do business in Asia, and their professional advisers. The contents of *Doing Business in Asia* is divided into sections.

The first section is called the "Lines of Inquiry" and contains a series of questions. The sections following the first section cover countries. Each country section consists of the answers to the questions posed in the "Lines of Inquiry". Each section is discussed in more detail below.

¶2   Lines of Inquiry

The first section of the Reporter sets out the lines of inquiry which must be followed by corporations and their advisers who plan to do business in a foreign country. This has been done in a series of questions termed "Lines of Inquiry". The questions are grouped into topics and each topic has an Introduction which explains the significance of the questions and the reasoning behind them.

Each question has a paragraph number and a brief heading. The questions are not repeated in the country sections of the Reporter, but each answer has the same paragraph number and heading as the question — with the addition of the particular country's prefix for example THA ¶35-001 for paragraph 35-001 of commentary on Thailand.

¶3   Countries

These sections of the Reporter consist of answers to the questions posed in the Lines of Inquiry. The answers for each country are contained in a separate tab, marked with the name of the country for easy reference.

Each answer has the same paragraph number and heading as the question it answers. To prevent confusion each country has a prefix which appears before every paragraph number in the tab, for example, THA for Thailand, INS for Indonesia.

¶4   Coloured tabs

The Reporter contains a number of divisions, each marked distinctively by a coloured tab card. The tab cards give a summary title for the contents of each division. Each tab division has it own table of contents. Some of the paragraphs listed in the table of contents have their own additional, more detailed table of contents.

¶5   Paragraph numbers

Each question in the "Lines of Inquiry" has it own paragraph number, for example, ¶25-100. Each answer to a question has the same paragraph number as the question, with the country's prefix attached. While page numbers may change as the Reporter is updated and expanded, the paragraph numbers do not. Gaps have been left in the numbering sequence to enable new paragraphs to be added if these become necessary.

The numbers of the first new paragraph on the left page, and the last new paragraph on the right page are indicated in bold type at the foot of those pages, for example,

¶30-001

¶6   Page numbers

Page numbers, located at the top of each page, are used only for the purpose of filing new reports.

You may notice gaps in the page numbering sequence. These are necessary in a loose-leaf reporting service. Where such a gap occurs, CCH tells you what the next page number should be, for example,

[Next page is 6,051]

¶7   Report numbers

You may notice small numbers appearing at the top left-hand corner of right hand pages, for example,

2-6-91

This identifies each page in the Reporter with the report by which it was added. "2-6-91" simply means that the page was inserted by Report No. 2, dated the sixth month (June) of 1991. Should old and new pages ever become mixed, this information will readily enable you to separate the old from the new. Where there is no report number, it means the page was part of the original compilation of the *Doing Business in Asia* Reporter.

¶8   Index

The index to the Lines of Inquiry is situated behind the red "Index" tab card at the front of the Reporter.

The answers to each question differ greatly in length and complexity from one country to another according to the importance and development of the topic in that country. For this reason each country has its own index which appears at the front of that country's tab division.

A "Latest Additions to Index" is located before each country's index. The "Latest Additions to Index" contains entries for new or revised material and must be consulted in conjunction with the index. The entries in the "Latest Additions to Index" are periodically incorporated into the index to bring it completely up to date.

Index references are to paragraph numbers and not page numbers.

¶5

¶9   Cumulative Index ● New Developments

The red tab marked "Cumulative Index ● New Developments" is located near the back of the Reporter.

The "New Developments" section contains the latest information on topics relevant to the information contained in the Reporter.

The Cumulative Index provides the link between reports of new developments and the existing commentary. After reading a paragraph in the commentary, always check the first column in the Cumulative Index to see if that ¶ number appears. If that ¶ number does appear, there will be a cross-reference to the relevant New Developments item. A check of the Cumulative Index will thus clearly show whether there have been any new developments affecting a paragraph of the basic commentary since its last revision.

Items appearing in "New Developments" are incorporated into the commentary throughout the year. Once a New Developments item has been incorporated into the commentary, the relevant Cumulative Index entry to that item is deleted. If the item affects more than one part of the commentary, the Cumulative Index entries are removed progressively as each part of the commentary is updated. Even though an item has been fully incorporated into the commentary, and all Cumulative Index entries to that item removed, it may be that the item will remain physically in New Developments for some time. That item and all other "dead" items are physically removed whenever there is a consolidated reprint of the relevant part of New Developments.

Remember — after you have referred to the appropriate paragraph of the commentary, always check that paragraph number in the Cumulative Index to see if there are any New Developments.

¶10   How to find information

There are two basic ways in which to find information in the Reporter:

● For general enquiries through the "Lines of Inquiry",

— consult the Index in the red "Index" tab which will direct you to a paragraph in the Lines of Inquiry;

— read the paragraph and then turn to the same paragraph number in the appropriate country's tab;

— read the paragraph;

— check the Cumulative Index for new developments.

● For specific information about a country,

— consult the Index in the front of the country's tab division;

— read the paragraph referred to;

— check the Cumulative Index for new developments.

Loose leaf Reports

New reports .... ¶11   Report summaries .... ¶13
Filing new reports .... ¶12   Help in filing .... ¶14

¶11   New reports

At least four times a year CCH will send you Reports consisting of new loose-leaf pages. These are accompanied by filing instructions explaining which pages to remove and which new pages to insert.

To keep your Reporter up to date, Reports should be filed as soon as possible after the receipt of new pages.

To miss filing new pages is to render your Reporter inadequate.

¶12   Filing new reports

Each Report is accompanied by a numbered Filing Instruction Sheet with filing instructions for new pages. The Filing Instruction Sheet also carries a date which allows a check of the date to which the information in the volume is current.

Once the new pages have been inserted, the Filing Instruction Sheet itself should be filed under the pink tab card marked "Last Report Filing Instructions".

Before inserting the pages of a new Report always check the number of the last Filing Instruction Sheet.

This will ensure that no Reports remain unfiled.

The small numbers at the top of each right hand page near the rings of the binder indicate the number of the Report which inserted that page. For example,

2-6-91

This indicates that the page was inserted by Report No. 2 issued in the sixth month (June) of 1991.

¶13   Report summaries

Every loose-leaf report mailed to subscribers is accompanied by a summary. The summary is not for filing in the Reporter.

¶14   Help in filing

The Filing Instruction Sheet which lies on the top of the loose-leaf pages of each Report gives specific instructions for filing the loose-leaf pages of that Report in the compilation volume. Below are more general directions on report filing:

- *Opening the 5-ring binder.* To file the sheets, you are of course required to open the rings of the binder. If the binder is new and you have not already done so, first

¶11

remove the small cardboard wedge that was inserted near the base of the binder for shipment purposes only. To open the binder, lay it flat upon the desk and pull the lever towards you. To close the binder, push the lever back to ensure that it "clicks" and so is properly locked. During filing there is no need to "click" it every time — only when the last filing step has been completed.

- *Before you file any report.* Always check under the pink "Last Report Filing Instructions" tab to ensure that you are filed right up to date. The number of the last report filed in your volume appears on the last Filing Instruction Sheet filed in that tab division. This ensures that no report remains unfiled.

- *Filing.* The filing instructions are on the Filing Instruction Sheet. Put this filing sheet to one side for easy reference and file the remaining loose-leaf pages in accordance with the instructions given. The instructions require you to remove certain pages from the binder and insert certain pages.

- *Page numbering.* Sometimes more pages are inserted than removed; sometimes the opposite occurs. There are often gaps in the page numbering sequence. This allows for "growth" in the Reporter. Where a gap occurs there is a statement of the number of the next page at the top of the preceding page. Note that the number in large bold face type at the top corner of each page is the page number; a number at the foot of a page will be to a paragraph (¶) of comment located on the page. *The pages removed from the Reporter are of no value and should be destroyed when filing is completed.* The last step in filing always requires you to take the filing sheet page and use it to replace the previous filing sheet in the "Last Report Filing Instructions" tab division. This enables you to check that your filing is up to date. There should only be one filing sheet in the Reporter at any time.

- *Comparing old and new pages.* The small numbers at the top of each right-hand page (near the hole for the binder rings) indicate the number of the report which inserted that page, with the month and year of issue. This enables you to distinguish a "new" from an "old" page should they become intermixed.

RELATED CCH PUBLICATIONS

Australian Business Advisers Guide
Australian Business Law
The Australian and New Zealand Small Business Manual

China Business Law Guide
China Laws for Foreign Business
    — Business Regulation
    — Taxation & Customs
    — Special Zones & Cities
Copyright Law in China

Hong Kong Company & Practice
Hong Kong Revenue Legislation
Hong Kong Master Tax Guide

International Offshore Financial Centres
International Tax Planning Manual — Corporations
International Tax Planning — Expatriates & Migrants

Japan Business Law Guide
Japan Employers' Handbook

Malaysian Companies & Securities Legislation
Malaysian and Singapore Company Law & Practice
Malaysian & Singapore Company & Securities Law Cases
Malaysian Employers' Handbook
Malaysian Employment Legislation
Malaysian Master Tax Guide

Singapore Employers' Handbook
Singapore Employment Legislation
Singapore Master Tax Guide
Singapore Goods and Services Tax Guide
Singapore Revenue Legislation

Vietnam Business Law Guide

CCH also publishes *Doing Business in Europe* and *Doing Business in Eastern Europe*.

INDEX

Table of Contents

Page

Latest Additions to Index 151
Index 201

See also Index at p. 201

LATEST ADDITIONS TO INDEX
LINES OF INQUIRY

As additional questions are added to the Lines of Inquiry, relevant index entries may appear in the first instance on these pages until such time as they can be incorporated into the principal index. These "Latest Additions" should always be consulted together with the principal index.

Paragraph

A

Aircraft
arrest 80-005
security interests 75-301

Arrests
aircraft
– law governing 80-005
vessels
– law governing 80-005

Assets
classes of assets
– floating securities 75-511

B

Banking facilities
currency exchange 75-205
exchange rate risk 75-205

Bankruptcy
validity of security interests 75-515

Bankruptcy law 30-114

Borrowers
creditors' rights
– priority re security interests 75-504
property
– interest in 75-502
– security for finance 75-502
security for finance
– possession, retention of 75-514

Borrower's interest
security for finance 75-513

C

Capital expenditure
finance 75-111

Capital markets
international 75-003

Chattels
security interests 75-301

Paragraph

Commercial rights
security interests 75-301

Covenants 75-204

Credit institutions
self-regulation 75-105

Currency exchange 75-205
banking facilities 75-205

D

Dangerous substances
movement, law governing 80-004
pollution, law governing 80-004
storage, law governing 80-004

Development
financing 75-004

Dividends
recipient non-resident, how taxed 75-112

Documents
security for finance 75-503

E

Employees
local — see Local employees

Equity issues
foreign companies 75-103

Equity-loan ratios
foreign 75-011
local 75-011

Exchange rate risk 75-205
banking facilities 75-205

Exports
financing 75-005

Export credits insurance 85-000

Export licences
shipbuilders 80-011

See also Index at p. 201

Paragraph

F

Finance
capital expenditure 75- 111
working capital 75- 111

Finance companies 75-001

Financial institutions
finance, raising of
– forms 75-002
– terms 75-001
international capital markets,
    access to 75-003
investing money, customary
    terms 75-201; 75-202
lending money, customary
    terms 75-201; 75-202
self-regulation 75-105
specialised institutions
– development 75-004
– exports 75-004
– investment 75-004
types 75-001

Financial ratios 75-204

Financing
control 75-101–75-112
development 75-004
exports 75-005
investment 75-004
law governing 75-211
terms — see Terms of financing

Financing arrangements
insurance required 85-004

Financing guarantees
shipbuilding 80-011

Floating securities
assets, classes of 75-511

Foreign companies
equity issues 75- 103

Foreign insurance companies
operation within host country 85-000

G

Government creditors
priority re security interests 75-504

Government financing agencies 75-001

Grants
shipbuilding 80-011

Guarantees
security for finance 75-522

Paragraph

Guarantee insurance
shipbuilders 80-011

H

Hazardous substances
movement, law governing 80-004
storage, law governing 80-004

I

Immovables
security interests 75-301

Industrial property
security interests ....75 -301

Insurance
brokers, specification of 85-001
compulsory 85-011
death of employee 85-012
disablement of employee 85-012
export credits 85-000
financing arrangements 85-004
local employees 85-012
payments 85-014
premium rates 85-013
product liability 85-000; 85-021
range available 85-003
resident brokers, use of 85-001
resident underwriters, use of 85-001
state-owned brokers, use of 85-001
state-owned underwriters, use of 85-001
system 85-000

Insurance brokers
resident 85-001
specification on use 85-001
state-owned 85-001

Insurance claims
proceeds
– remittance 85-014
– transfer 85-000

Insurance companies 75-001
choice, legislation affecting 85-013
foreign — see Foreign insurance companies

Insurance industry
regulation 85-000

Insurance underwriters
classes 85-002
resident 85-001
specification on use 85-001
state-owned 85-001

Intangible movables
security interests 75-301

See also Index at p. 201

Paragraph

Intellectual property
security interests 75-301

International capital markets
access 75-003

International conventions
goods, movement of 80-003

International finance or aid agencies 75-001

Interest
recipient non-resident, how taxed 75- 112

Interest rates
calculation 75-203
financing 75-203
nature 75-203

Inventory
security for finance
– problems 75-503
security interests ....75 -301

Investment
financing 75-004

Investing money
customary terms 75-201; 75-202

Inward transport
law governing 80-001

J

Joint obligations
security for finance 75-522

L

Land
security interests 75-301

Laws
dangerous substances
– movement 80-004
– pollution 80-004
– storage 80-004
financing 75-211
goods
– movement 80-002
– storage 80-002
hazardous substances
– movement 80-004
– storage 80-004
insurance companies, choice of 85-013
inward transport 80-001
noxious substances
– movement 80-004
– storage 80-004
outward transport 80-001
shipping 80-001

Paragraph

shipping register, creation of 80-012
transport 80-001

Lenders
security for finance
– assignment free of borrower's interest 75-513
– enterprise sold as going concern 75-515
– realisation 75-515
– realisation proceeds 75-513
security interests, transfer of 75-521

Lending money
customary terms 75-201; 75-202

Loan finance
sources — see Sources of loan finance

Local equity capital
raising of, control 75-103
– discretionary...............................75-104
– statutory agencies 75-104

Local employees
death, insurance against 85-012
disablement, insurance against 85-012
insurance 85-012
retirement benefits 85-012

Local stock exchange
control 75-103

M

Maritime law 80-000

Merchant banks 75-001

Money-lenders 75-001

Mortgages
ships under construction 80-011

Mortgage insurance
security for finance 75-503

Motor vehicles
security for finance
– problems 75-503
security interests 75-301

Movement of goods 80-000
international conventions 80-003
law governing 80-002

N

Non-residents
dividends, taxation of 75-112
interest, taxation of 75-112

Noxious substances
movement, law governing 80-004
storage, law governing 80-004

Paragraph

O

Outward transport
law governing 80-001

P

Patents
security interests 75-301

Performance bonds
shipbuilders 80-011

Pollution
dangerous substances 80-004

Premium rates
insurance 85-013

Private commercial banks 75-001

Private development finance
institutions 75-001

Product liability insurance 85-000; 85-021

Property
dealings with same property
– priority re security interests 75-504
security for finance
– borrower's interest 75-502; 75-513
– identification 75-501
security interests 75-301
securities over same property
– limit 75-505
– priority re security interests 75-504

Protection
security interests 75-503

R

Registrable securities
security for finance
– problems 75-503

Registration
documents re security for finance 75-503
security interests 75-503
ships under construction, rights in 80-011
transaction re security for finance 75-503

Registration charges
security for finance 75-524

Retirement benefits
employees 85-012

S

Security for finance 75-301–75-525
acceptable securities 75-523

Paragraph

assignment free of borrower's
interest 75-513
borrower's interest 75-513
choice, influence of tax implications 75-525
creation, formalities 75-503
disposal by borrower 75-513
further advances 75-512
further securities, creation by
borrower 75-513
guarantees 75-522
inventory 75-503
joint obligations 75-522
mortgage insurance 75-503
motor vehicles 75-503
personal security 75-522
possession, retention by borrower ..75-514
proceeds of realisation
– borrower's claim......................75-513
– secured party's rights 75-513
property, identification of 75-501
realisation by lender 75-515
– receivership 75-515
remedy 75-515
registrable securities 75-503
registration
– charges 75-524
– documents 75-503
– failure to register 75-503
– security interest 75-503
– time limits 75-503
– transaction 75-503
suretyship 75-522
validity in bankruptcy 75-515

Security interests 75-204
aircraft 75-301
chattels 75-301
commercial rights 75-301
immovables 75-301
industrial property 75-301
intangible movables 75-301
intellectual property 75-301
inventory 75-301
land 75-301
lenders, transfer of interests 75-521
limit against one property 75-505
motor vehicles 75-301
patents 75-301
prior interests, determination of 75-504
preservation 75-503
priority 75-515
– dealings with same property 75-504
– government creditors 75-504
– securities over same property 75-504
– rights of general creditors 75-504
– tax liens 75-504

Paragraph

– workmen's liens 75-504
property 75-301
protection 75-503
registration 75-503
statutory immovables 75-301
tangible movables 75-301
trade marks 75-301

Security rights
recognised forms 75-401

Ships — see also **Vessels**
under construction
– mortgages 80-011
– registration of rights 80-011

Shipbuilders
guarantee insurance 80-011
performance bonds 80-011
regulation 80-011

Shipbuilding
companies 80-011
contract 80-011
export licence requirements 80-011
financing guarantees 80-011
grants 80-011
subsidies 80-011
suppliers' credits 80-011

Shipbuilding companies
regulation 80-011

Shipping
law governing 80-001

Shipping companies
operation 80-000

Shipping opportunities 80-000

Shipping register
creation, law governing 80-012

Sources of loan finance
control
– discretionary 75-102
– how exercised 75- 102
– statutory agencies 75-102
criteria for regulation 75-101

Statutory agencies
raising of local equity capital,
control of 75-104
sources of loan finance, control of 75-102

Statutory immovables
security interests 75-301

Stock exchanges 75-001

Storage of goods
law governing 80-002

Paragraph

Subsidies
shipbuilding 80-011

Supplier's credits
shipbuilding 80-011

Suretyship
security for finance 75-522

T

Tangible movables
security interests 75-301

Tax liens
priority re security interests 75-504

Tax treaties 35-001

Taxation
dividends to non-residents 75-112
interest to non-residents 75- 112

Terms of financing
covenants 75-204
currency exchange 75-205
exchange rate risk 75-205
financial ratios 75-204
interest rates 75-203
security interests 75-204

Time limits
security for finance, registration of 75-503

Trade marks
security interests 75-301

Trading houses 75-001

Transactions
security for finance 75-503

Transport
law governing 80-001

Treaties
tax 35-001

U

Underwriters
insurance 85-001

V

Vessels
arrest 80-005

W

Working capital
finance..75-111

Workmen's liens
priority re security interests................75-504

See also Latest Additions to Index at p. 151

INDEX

LINES OF INQUIRY

Paragraph

A

Accelerated depreciation allowance 35-513
  applicability 35-514

Accounts
  certification 35-103
  requirements re business profits
    tax 35-104
  requirements re company tax 35-103
  statutory
  – non-resident companies to file 30-103

Accounting
  methods 35-000
  standards 35-000

Accounting profession
  skills 35-000

Acquisition of land
  compensation upon acquisition 25-123
  power of government 25-122

Administration
  incentives, disincentives and controls on
    foreign investment 45-113

Advertising
  laws governing advertising of
    products 45-306

Advisory fees
  remittance 55-011

Aliens
  tax certificate 35-105

Alternative dispute resolution 70-000

Annual leave 60-004

Anti-dumping duties 50-000
  requirements 50-025

Appeals
  rights re detained goods 50-031

Approvals
  exports 50-003
  imports 50-001
  transfer of rights in land 25-102

Arbitral tribunals
  basis of jurisdiction 70-112
  foreign lawyers, status of 70-135

Paragraph

Arbitration 20-000
  amiable composition 70-132
  arbitral institutions, availability 70-000
  arbitrators, appointment of 70-122
  assistance from outside jurisdiction 70-141
  choice of applicable law 70-121
  choice of procedural law 70-115
  confidentiality of proceedings 70-143
  courts' assistance 70-114
  delays 70-125
  expense 70-124
  foreign companies' participation 70-133
  foreign lawyers, arbitration 70-135
  in third country 70-145
  industrial disputes, settlement of 60-011
  international and domestic arbitration
    distinguished 70-111
  international arbitration rules 70-104
  language of proceedings 70-142
  link to international regime 70-000
  recognised arbitration centres 70-302
  review by court 70-131
  rules of natural justice 70-134
  special procedures for certain
    disputes 70-144
  special provisions re clauses 70-103
  system 70-101
  tribunals' basis of jurisdiction 70-112
  United Nations Model Law 70-105
  venue 70-122

Arbitration clauses
  effectiveness 70-103

Arbitrators
  appointment 70-122
  internationally acceptable 70-303
  rules governing choice 70-123

Assessment
  executives
  – basis of tax 35-105

Assets
  expropriation 20-204
  guarantees against expropriation 45-114
  payment for shares 30-104

Asian Development Bank (ADB)
  membership 20-101

See also Latest Additions to Index at p. 151

Paragraph

Auditor
accounts, certification of 35-103

B

Bank accounts
non-residents
– control of accounts by exchange control
   authorities 55-022

Bank overdraft
rates of interests 55-022

Bearer shares
subsidiaries 30-104

Board of directors
powers 30-112
subsidiary
– number of nationals on board 30-104

Books
requirements 35-103

Branch profits
remittance 55-011

Breach of contract
remedies 30-016

Business
basic framework 45-000
effect on environment 25-212
micro-environment 45-000
regulation 45-000
restrictions re foreign control 50-005

Business activities
disincentives imposed on certain
   activities 45-004
general economic and political
   organisation ....,.......... 45-000
incentives offered ....,.......... 45-003
licensing 45-001–45-002
non-resident
– special provisions........................... 45-305
registration 45-001–45-002

Business organisation
forms 30-000
tax liability 35-102

Business profits
accounting base 35-000
taxation 35-101

Business profits tax
imported goods 35-104
imposition 35-104
levy 35-104
rate 35-104
registration requirements 35-104
returns, filing of 35-104

C

Capital
flow 35-000
raising
– restrictions 55-022
repatriation 55-005
– restrictions on 55-041

Capital gains
taxing, method of 35-401

Capital gains tax
offset of capital losses against
   revenue gains 35-403
offset of revenue losses against
   capital gains 35-404
roll-overs 35-402

Capital losses
offset against revenue gains 35-403

Character merchandising
protection 65-002

Charges
transfer of rights in land 25-102

Citizenship
labour laws, effect on 60-001

Civil law 20-000

Civil procedure
foreign companies 70-003
rules
– ascertainment re dispute settlement........ 70-004
– evidence outside jurisdiction............... 70-012
– interlocutory relief.......................... 70-011
– service and execution of process
   outside jurisdiction......................... 70-004

Collective bargaining
industrial disputes, settlement of 60-011

Commercial contracts
law, principles relevant 30-013
remedies 30-013
settlement outside courts 30-013

Commercial law
codification 30-002
distinction with contract law 30-000
historical sources 30-001
institutions, special rules 30-014
remedies granted 30-016
sources 30-000

Commercial organisations
forms 30-101

Commercial profits — see **Business profits**

Common law 20-000

Paragraph

Companies
constructive ownership 35-103
contracts, etc., prescribed requirements 35-103
depreciation allowances 35-103
foreign ownership, percentage of 30-111
managing structures 30-112
rate of tax 35-103
registration requirements 35-103
types distinguished in tax law 35-103
various forms
– establishment of branch 30-104
– time to set up............................... 30-104

Company law 30-101–30-113

Company tax
companies distinguished 35-103
credits, treatment of 35-103
depreciation allowances 35-103
fiscal year 35-103
levy 35-103
losses, treatment of 35-103
profits
– accumulated 35-103
rate 35-103

Compensation
acquired land 25-123
injury at work 60-004

Computer software
protection 65-002

Conciliation 20-000; 70-000
appointment of conciliators 70-203
disadvantages 70-224
dispute resolution 70-201
enforcement of settlement 70-211
industrial disputes, settlement of 60-011
restrictions on types of disputes 70-223
special rules governing proceedings 70-204

Conciliators
appointment 70-203
internationally acceptable 70-303

Consumer contracts
treatment 30-011

Consumer protection
laws 45-301

Contracts
breach, penalty for 30-000
government contracts 30-004
consumer contracts 30-011
penalty for breach 30-000
performance under changed
   circumstances 30-017
provisions for forms of dispute resolution . 70-222
standardised 30-015

Paragraph

terms
– review 30-017
– when power to review arises 30-017
trade contracts — see Trade contracts
"unfair" contracts, review of 45-307
with foreign entities 30-005

Contract law
codification 30-002
distinction with commercial law 30-000
historical sources 30-001
institutions, special rules 30-014
sources 30-000

Controls
foreign investment
– administration of controls 45-113
– nature of controls........................... 45-113
– types of controls 45-112
price control — see Price control

Conventions
International Centre for the Settlement
   of Investment Disputes Convention 20-203
international labour organisation 60-035
New York Convention on the Recognition
   and Enforcement of Foreign Arbitral
   Awards 20-102

Copyright
licences 45-304
protection 65-002
system 65-000

Countervailing duties 50-000
requirements 50-025

Court
assistance in arbitration process 70-114
basis of jurisdiction re dispute
   settlement 70-001
dispute resolution 70-000
language used 70-022
power of intervention in dispute
   resolution 70-214
power to review contract terms 30-017
review of arbitral proceedings and
   awards 70-131

Credits
tax treatment 35-103

Currency
convertibility 55-000
loans, currency to use 55-104
restrictions on remittance 55-013

Customary law 20-000

Customs duties
rates 50-012
time of payment 50-032

See also Latest Additions to Index at p. 151

Paragraph

D

Deductions
expenses
– export opportunities, exploration of 35-515

Defective products
liability for injury 30-012

Definitions
foreign businessman 45-103
foreign investor 45-103
royalty 35-211

Depreciation allowances 35-103

Designs
licences 45-304

Directors
minimum shareholder's qualification 30-104

Disclosure
non-resident company
– name and percentage shareholding 30-104

Dispute resolution
actions against government
– choice of forum 70-402
– enforcement of orders....................... 70-403
alternative methods 70-000; 70-201
– basis of jurisdiction 70-205
– disadvantages................................. 70-224
– enforcement of settlement................... 70-211
– special rules governing proceedings 70-204
appointment of conciliators and
mediators 70-203
choice of applicable law 70-213
confidentiality of proceedings 70-215
courts' power of intervention 70-214
domestic 70-223
foreign judgments, enforcement of 70-000
forms
– provisions in contract 70-222
framework 70-301–70-304
government, status of 70-401
institutions available 70-000
international 70-223
international agreements 70-000
international conventions 70-202; 70-301
internationally acceptable arbitrators 70-303
joint methods 70-225
local advisers, availability of 70-304
procedural law 70-000
recognised arbitration centres 70-302
regime 35-000
right of representation 70-212
special rules for foreign participation 70-221
substantive law 70-000

Paragraph

Disincentives
business activities 45-004
foreign investment
– administration of disincentives 45-113
– nature of disincentives....................... 45-113
– particular geographical areas 45-105
– particular industries 45-111
– types of disincentives 45-112

Disputes
arbitrability
– exceptions.................................... 70-113
types restricted for conciliation 70-223
types restricted for mediation 70-223

Dispute settlement
arbitration 70-101–70-145
basis of courts' jurisdiction 70-001
choice of applicable law 70-013
choice of forum 70-014
collection of evidence outside
jurisidiction 70-012
costs and delay re litigation 70-015
enforcement and execution of
judgments 70-023
foreign companies' status 70-002
foreign judgments, recognition of 70-024
foreign lawyers' status 70-025
interlocutory relief, availability of 70-011
rules of civil procedure and evidence 70-004
security for costs 70-021
service and execution of process
outside jurisdiction 70-005
special procedures for certain disputes 70-031

Dispute settlement mechanism
arbitration 20-000
conciliation 20-000
freedom of choice 20-014
litigation 20-000

Dividends
control 45-201
remittance 55-011

Documents
confidentiality 70-143
non-resident companies to file 30-103

Domestic law
tax credit provision 35-002

Domicile
tax liability, effect on 35-102

E

Economy
nature 45-000
state monopolies 20-005

Ded

See also Latest Additions to Index at p. 151

Paragraph   Paragraph

Employees
annual leave 60-004
compensation for injury at work 60-004
legal relationship with employer 60-003
lock-out 60-022
minimum wage 60-004
purchased business
– purchaser's obligations to existing
employees 60-025
severance pay 60-004
sick leave 60-004
strike 60-022

Employer organisations
government, institutional links 60-021
trade unions, institutional links 60-021

Employer-employee relationship ...60-000; 60-003

Employers
additional obligations to employees 60-031
legal relationship with employee 60-003
lock-out employees, right to 60-022

Employment
required balance of race or nationality 60-034
terms and conditions 60-000

Entry of goods
by-law 50-015
concessional 50-015

Environment
detriment upon establishment of
business 25-212
environmental assessment
– governmental requirements 25-203
environmental controls
– nature 25-211
– regulation 25-202
environmental restrictions affecting
land use 25-201

Evidence
collection outside jurisdiction
– allowability in dispute settlement 70-012

Exchange control
administering authorities
– transactions requiring approval 55-022
administering body 55-002
administration 55-000
applicable law 55-001
application of laws to various
countries 55-004
breach of law
– consequences 55-034
exemptions 55-031
foreign-controlled companies
– place of incorporation 55-024
formalities 55-033

laws
– treatment of residents and
non-residents 55-000
local participation, effect of 55-025
objectives of policies 55-003
regulations
– taxation considerations 55-042
residents and non-residents distinguished .. 55-023
structure, purposes and procedures 55-000

Exchange rate
differing rates applicable 55-021
host country's currency 55-015
method of fixing 55-015

Excise tax 35-301

Exclusive dealing
controls over contracts 45-303

Executives
basis of assessment 35-105
foreign executive
– work permits or visas 60-033
origin/source of income 35-105
power to make regulations 20-005
rate of tax 35-105

Exemptions
exchange control 55-031
price control 45-203

Expatriate personnel
pension fund contributions
– remittance 55-032
personal savings
– remittance 55-032

Expenses
arbitration 70-124
export opportunities, exploration of
– deductibility of expenses 35-515
industrial property rights, protection of 65-015

Export allowances
applicability 35-505
industries excluded 35-511

Export incentives 35-504

Export processing zones 35-512

Exporters
penalty on breach of code 50-024

Exports
approvals 50-003
control by licensing procedures 50-000
international treaties 50-023
letters of credit 50-003
licences 50-003
permits 50-003
rate of exchange applicable 55-021

See also Latest Additions to Index at p. 151

Exports — continued   **Paragraph**

restrictions 50-003
special tariff treatment 50-014
taxes 50-013

Expropriation
compensation for 20-205
guarantees against 20-205

Extra-territorial effect
laws re trade contracts 45-303

F

Fees
non-resident company, registration of 30-103
subsidiaries, incorporation of 30-104

Filing
income tax return 35-103
returns re business profits tax 35-104

Fiscal year
company tax 35-103
determination 35-004

Foreign businesses — see **Foreign investors**

Foreign businessman
definition 45-103

Foreign companies
carrying on business, permissibility 30-102
carrying on business
  without registration 30-102
civil procedure in litigation 70-003
dispute resolution procedures 70-221
incorporation of subsidiary 30-102
participation in arbitral proceedings 70-133
registration 30-102
status in dispute settlement 70-002

Foreign-controlled businesses
special restrictions 50-005

Foreign-controlled companies
place of incorporation for exchange
  control purposes 55-024

Foreign currency
remittance 55-012
repatriation 20-204

Foreign entities
laws applicable 20-013; 30-000
requirements re contracts 30-005

Foreign exchange
control, extent of 55-000
forward market 55-035
remittance of funds 55-000

Foreign investments   **Paragraph**
controls
  – administration 45-113
  – nature 45-113
  – types 45-112
incentives and disincentives
  – administration 45-113
  – geographical areas 45-105
  – nature 45-113
  – particular industries 45-111
  – types 45-111
rate of exchange applicable 55-021
special economic zones 25-000
tax incentives 35-000

Foreign investors
definition 45-103
establishment of joint ventures 45-104
government guarantees 20-204
protection 20-205
skills, transfer to nationals 60-000
special controls 45-101
supervision of control and
  management 45-102
technology, protection of 65-000
special application of labour laws 60-032
treatment 20-000

Foreign judgments
enforcement 70-000
recognition 70-024

Foreign lawyers
partnerships with local lawyers 20-012
right of audience 20-012
right of practice 20-012
status 70-025
status before arbitral tribunal 70-135

Forward market
foreign exchange 55-035

Foreign-owned subsidiaries
dispute resolution procedures 70-221

Foreign ownership
percentage 30-111

Foreign personnel
taxation 35-000

Foreign transactions
applicable law 20-013

Foreign workers
visas 60-033
work permits 60-033

Foreigners
investments, protection of 20-201
occupation of land, restrictions of 25-000
restrictions on occupation of land 25-000

See also Latest Additions to Index at p. 151

Paragraph

Paragraph

Franchises
controls over contracts 45-303

Free trade zones 50-021

Fringe benefits
tax treatment 35-103

G

Geographical areas
incentives and disincentives re
foreign investment 45-105

Government
actions against government in dispute
resolution 70-402–70-403
approval
– licensing agreements re industrial
property............................... 65-011: 65-023
employer organisations, institutional
links 60-021
guarantees against expropriation
of assets 45-114
investment in local companies 30-105
organisation 20-005
party to ICSID or MIGA convention 70-404
powers of acquisition of land 25-122
status in dispute resolution 70-401
trade unions, institutional links 60-021

Government authority
right to share in profits 45-205

Government contracts
requirements 30-004

Government guarantees
foreign investors 20-204

Gross profits
basis of tax 35-104

Guarantees
expropriation of assets 45-114
remittance of amounts payable under
guarantee 55-011

H

Host country
currency
– differing rates of exchange 55-021
– fixing of exchange rate 55-015
import and export control policies,
objectives 50-011
international treaties relevant to import
and export 50-023
laws re exchange control 55-001
remittance of dividends, etc.,
attitude towards 55-011
remittance of foreign currency 55-012

repatriation of capital, attitute
towards 55-005

Host government
constitutional nature 20-000
international agreements 20-102
international banks, membership 20-101
powers 20-000
structure 20-000

Hours of work
control 60-005

House and land tax 35-301

I

Imports
approvals 50-001
detention of goods by administering
authority 50-031
international treaties 50-023
letters of credit 50-002
licences 50-001
permits 50-001
quotas 50-001
rates of customs duties 50-012
rates of exchange applicable 55-021
restrictions 50-001
taxes 50-013

Import-export
quantitative controls 50-000
quotas
– nature and extent of use 50-000
restrictions 50-000
tariffs 50-000

Import and export control policy
objectives 50-011

Imported goods
business tax 35-104
valuation 35-104

Importers
penalty on breach of code 50-024
special requirements 50-002

Incentives
establishment of non-polluting plants 25-205
foreign investment
– administration of incentives.............. 45-113
– nature of incentives 45-113
– particular geographical areas 45-105
– particular industries 45-111
– types of incentives...................... 45-112
investment
– repatriation of capital, restrictions
on 55-041

See also Latest Additions to Index at p. 151

Paragraph

Incentive legislation 45-003

Income
 flow 35-000

Income tax return
 filing 35-103

Industries
 incentives and disincentives re
 foreign investment 45-111

Industrial designs
 protection 65-002
 system 65-000

Industrial disputes
 settlement 60-011
 – customary method 60-013
 – parameters of legal system 60-012
 special procedures 70-031; 70-144

Industrial property
 disadvantages for non-residents 65-022
 international agreements 65-001
 licensing agreements
 – government approval 65-011; 65-023
 owners
 – protection 65-003
 – right to license or assign rights 65-011
 owners in other countries
 – rights 65-021
 protection 65-002
 – duration 65-004
 – expenses incurred 65-015
 registration
 – procedures 65-014
 – rights conferred by registration 65-013

Injuries
 general principles governing injury 45-302
 standard of care 45-302

Intellectual property — see also **Industrial
property**
 expert assistance, presence of 65-000
 international agreements, adherence to 65-000
 legal remedies, availability of 65-000
 protection, range available 65-000

Inter-company accounts
 with non-resident parent 55-022

Interest
 remittance 55-011

Interlocutory relief
 availability in dispute settlement 70-011

International agreements
 "choice of forum" clauses 20-000
 "choice of law" clauses 20-000
 industrial property 65-001

Paragraph

ratification and putting into effect 20-102
tax credit provisions 35-002

International Bank for Reconstruction and
 Development (IBRD)
 membership 20-101

International banks
 membership 20-101

International Centre for the Settlement
 of Investment Disputes (ICSID) 70-404
 convention 20-203
 membership 70-000
 ratification and putting into effect 20-102

International Chamber of Commerce
 conciliation rules 70-202

International Chamber of Commerce
 Rules 70-104

International conventions
 dispute resolution 70-301

International Labour Organisation Conventions
 ratification and putting into effect 60-035

International tax treaties 35-001

Investments
 exchange control exemptions available 55-031
 matters to consider 20-000
 technology 65-000

Investment disputes
 special procedures 70-031; 70-144
 joint trade agreements 20-202

Investment in local companies
 geographical limits 30-105
 government participation 30-105
 local ownership, extent of 30-105
 local staff, use of 30-105
 restrictions 30-105

Investment incentives
 repatriation of capital, restrictions
 on 55-041

Investment profits
 deduction for tax 35-212
 non-residents 35-203
 residents 35-203
 tax 35-201
 tax credits 35-202

Investment protection
 joint trade agreements 20-202
 treaties 20-201
 – multilateral 20-203

See also Latest Additions to Index at p. 151

	Paragraph		Paragraph

J

Joint trade agreements
investment disputes
– dispute resolution 20-202
– protection 20-202

Joint ventures
creation 30-000
establishment by foreign investors 45-104
powers 30-113
structure 30-113

Judgments
enforcement and execution 70-023
foreign judgments
– recognition 70-024

K

Know-how
licensing
– government approval 65-023

L

Labelling requirements 50-022; 65-024

Labour laws
administration 60-023
administrative control 60-024
citizenship, effect of 60-001
judicial control 60-024
legislative control 60-024
nationality, effect of 60-001
organisational structure 60-000
race, effect of 60-001
scope 60-000
special application to foreigners 60-032

Labour relations
organisational structure 60-000

Land
acquisition 25-000
– compensation 25-123
– power of government 25-122
agreements restricting use 25-115
cadastral survey 25-000
compensation for acquisition 25-000
environmental controls 25-000
environmental restrictions 25-201
freely alienable 25-000
identification 25-000
infrastructural facilities 25-000
occupation by foreigners
– restrictions 25-000
ownership — see Land ownership
pre-emptive rights 25-003
registration systems 25-000

restrictions on occupation by
foreigners 25-000
restrictions on transfer 25-003
rights in land — see Rights in land
rights of access 25-101
registration of security 25-105
security in land, registration 25-105
seizure in execution of judgment 25-125
survey 25-104
system of registration 25-112
taxes 25-000
transfer
– restrictions 25-003
use
– agreements restricting 25-115

Land ownership
absolute ownership 25-101
bar to claims 25-101
forms 25-001
private ownership 25-002
registration of rights 25-111
specific rights 25-113
taxes and rates 25-124

Land tenure
customary land rights 25-011
land ownership, forms of 25-001
local regulations 25-004
rights of land use, forms 25-001
special areas 25-005

Language
arbitration proceedings 70-142
litigation 70-022

Law
applicable law, determination 20-013
civil law 20-000
codification 20-003
commercial law — see Commercial law
common law 20-000
consumer protection 45-301
contract and commercial law
distinguished 30-003
contract law — see Contract law
customary law 20-000
language 20-011
sources 20-003
system, characterisation 20-001

Law-making bodies 20-004
main areas of power 20-004

Lawyers
foreign — see Foreign lawyers
language 20-011
partnerships 20-012
role 20-000

See also Latest Additions to Index at p. 151

	Paragraph

Lease
land use 25-101

Legal database 20-011

Legal profession — see also **Lawyers**
division 20-012
function 20-012
organisation 20-012
structure 20-012

Legal remedies
contracts 30-000

Legal systems
characterisation 20-000
civil law 20-000
common law 20-000
customary law 20-000
origin 20-002
socialist law 20-000
standardised contracts, use of 30-015

Legal texts
journals, etc., in English 20-011

Legislature
authority, limits of 20-005
functions 20-005

Letters of credit
exports 50-003
imports 50-002

Levy
business profits tax 37-104
company tax 35-103

Liability
injury caused by defective products 30-012

Liability to tax
activities/undertakings attracting
liability 35-102
determination 35-102
domicile, effect of 35-102
nationality, effect of 35-102
residence 35-102

Licences
business activities 45-001–45-002
exports 50-003
– regulation of licences 50-004
imports 50-001
– regulation of licences 50-004
statutory monopolies 45-304

Licence fees
remittance 55-011

Liquidation
provision 30-104
realisation of proceeds, remittance 55-005

	Paragraph

Litigation 20-000
civil procedure for foreign
companies 70-003
costs 70-000
costs and delay 70-015
language used 70-022

Loans
currency to use 55-014

Local advisers
dispute resolution
– availability of advisers 70-304

Local agents
appointment by non-resident companies ... 30-103

Local companies
merger 30-105
takeovers 30-105

Local consultant
local customs and practices 45-115

Local currency
remittance 55-012

Local customs and practices
local consultant 45-115

Local development tax 35-301

Local ownership
extent 30-105

Lock-outs
restriction on right 60-022

Lodgment of documents
non-resident companies 30-103

Losses
tax treatment 35-103

M

Machine rental
remittance 55-011

Management
subsidiaries
– percentage of nationals 30-104
foreign management
– work permits or visas 60-033

Management fees
remittance 55-011

Managing structures
companies 30-112

Mediation 70-000
appointment of mediators 70-203
disadvantages 70-224

Lea

See also Latest Additions to Index at p. 151

Paragraph

dispute resolution 70-201
enforcement of settlement 70-211
industrial disputes, settlement of 60-011
restrictions on types of disputes 70-223
special rules governing proceedings 70-204

Mediators
appointment 70-203
internationally acceptable 70-303

Mergers
controls over contracts 45-303
local companies 30-105

Minimum paid-up capital
subsidiary 30-104

Minimum wage 60-004

Ministry of Labour 60-023

Monopolisation
controls over contracts 45-303
industrial property, laws affecting rights ... 65-005

N

Nationality
dual 60-002
labour laws, effect on 60-001
laws
– basis 60-002
loss 60-002
required balance in employment 60-034
tax liability, effect on 35-102

Nationals
board of directors
– number of nationals 30-104
percentage
– management 30-104
– staff 30-104

Net profits
basis of tax 35-103

New industries
tax relief 35-501–35-503

**New York Convention on Recognition and
  Enforcement of Foreign Arbitral
  Awards** 70-102
ratification and putting into
  effect 20-102

Nominal capital
subsidiary 30-104

Nominees
shareholding in non-resident
  company 30-104

Non-polluting plants
incentives for establishing 25-205

Paragraph

Non-residents — see also **Aliens**
bank accounts
– control by exchange control
  authorities 55-022
disadvantages re industrial property 65-022
distinction from residents for exchange
  control purposes 55-023
investment profits 35-203
joint venture with residents 30-113
shareholding in subsidiaries 30-104
special provisions re business activities 45-305
tax certificate 35-105

Non-resident companies
documents to file 30-103
export allowances, applicability 35-505
local agents, appointment of 30-103
nominees, shareholding 30-104
registration 30-103
registration fees 30-103
shareholdings, disclosure of 30-104
special restrictions 45-204
statutory accounts, filing of 30-103
statutory approvals 30-103
statutory bodies exercising jurisdiction 30-103

O

OECD declaration
acceptance 20-103

Outward remittances
approval 35-204
form 35-205

P

Packaging
requirements 50-022

Partnerships
foreign and local lawyers 20-012

Passing off
industrial property, laws affecting
  rights 65-005
protection against 65-000

Patents
labelling requirements, effect on 65-024
licences 45-304
protection 65-002
system 65-000

Patent attorneys 65-012

Payroll tax 35-301

See also Latest Additions to Index at p. 151

Paragraph

Penalties
breach of contract 30-000
import and export 50-024
non-compliance with regulations re
   trade contracts 45-303

Pension fund contributions
remittance by expatriate personnel 55-032

Permits
exports 50-003
imports 50-001

Personal income tax
deductions allowed 35-105

Personal savings
remittance by expatriate personnel 55-032

Pioneer industry
incentives 45-003

Pollution
incentives for non-polluting plants 25-205
standards applicable 25-204

Pre-emptive rights
transfer of land 25-003

Price control
body exercising control
– composition.................................. 45-202
commodities subject to control 45-201
criteria for application 45-206
exemptions 45-203

Price discrimination
controls over contracts 45-303

Products
advertising and promotion
– laws governing.............................. 45-306
information standards 45-301
liability laws 30-000
packaging 30-000
safety standards 30-000; 45-301

Procedure for arbitration
whether ascertainable 70-115
whether variable 70-115

Profits
accumulation 35-103
control 45-201
– criteria for application 45-206
redistribution 35-103
remittance
– rate of exchange applicable 55-021
sharing
– right of government authority 45-205

Promotion
laws governing promotion of products 45-306

Paragraph

Q

Quotas
imports 50-001

R

Race
labour laws, effect on 60-001
required balance in employment 60-034

Rate of interest
bank overdraft 55-022

Registration
business activities 45-001–45-002
business profits tax 35-104
companies 35-103
importers 50-002
industrial property 65-014
– rights conferred by registration.......... 65-013
land registration system 25-112
non-resident company 30-102; 30-103
rights of land ownership 25-111
rights of land use 25-111
security in land 25-105

Registration fees
non-resident company 30-103

Regulations
power of executive to make 20-005

Remedies
breach of contract 30-016
commercial contracts 30-013
commercial law 30-016

Remittance
foreign currency 55-012
local currency 55-012
pension fund contributions by
   expatriate personnel 55-032
personal savings of expatriate
   personnel 55-032

Representation
dispute resolution 70-212

Resale price maintenance
controls over contracts 45-303

Residents — see also **Nationals**
definition 35-105
distinction from non-residents for exchange
   control purposes 55-023
investment profits 35-203
joint venture with non-residents 30-113

Residence
tax liability, effect on 35-102

See also Latest Additions to Index at p. 151

Paragraph

Revenue losses
offset against capital gains 35-404

Rights in land
customary land rights 25-011
determination 25-000
existing rights, ascertainment of 25-121
extent 25-114
incentives and disincentives 25-000
land use by lease 25-101
nature 25-101
restrictions on acquisition 25-103
specific rights 25-113
transfer 25-102

Roll-overs 35-402

Royalties
definition 35-211
remittance 55-011

Rules of natural justice
arbitral proceedings, applicability in 70-134

Rules of the London Court of International Arbitration 70-104

S

Sales tax 35-301

Severance pay 60-004

Sick leave 60-004

Silicon chips
protection 65-002

Shares
assets as payment 30-104
disposal, restrictions on 30-104
transfer to non-resident
– exchange control authorities' approval ... 55-022

Share capital
subsidiaries
– percentage held by non-residents 30-104

Share certificates
despatch out of host country
– exchange control authorities' approval ... 55-022

Shareholding
non-resident company
– percentage shareholding, disclosure of ... 30-104

Socialist law 20-000

Special economic zones
foreign investment 25-000

Paragraph

Special tax treatment
new industries 25-501–35-515
visiting industrial experts 35-105

Staff
subsidiaries
– percentage of nationals 30-104

Stamp duty 35-301

Standardised contracts
use of 30-015

State monopolies 20-005

Statutory accounts
non-resident companies to file 30-103
subsidiaries
– requirements 30-104

Statutory approvals
non-resident companies 30-103

Statutory monopolies
licences 45-304

Strikes
restriction on right 60-022

Subsidiaries
bearer shares 30-104
directors
– nationality requirements 30-104
directors' qualifications 30-104
establishment, requirements 30-104
incorporation fees 30-104
management
– nationality requirements 30-104
minimum paid-up capital 30-104
nominal capital 30-104
share capital
– percentage held by non-residents 30-104
statutory accounts, requirements 30-104

Superannuation fund contributions
remittance by expatriate personnel 55-032

Surveys
land 25-104

System of law
characterisation 20-001

T

Takeovers
local companies 30-105

Tariffs 50-000

Tariff agreements
exports 50-014

Paragraph

Taxes
criteria for relief 35-503
exports 50-013
imports 50-013
import and export, additional taxes 50-024
ownership of land 25-124
relief period 35-502

Tax credits
existence 35-002
investment profits 35-202
tax-sparing 35-002

Tax disputes
resolution, procedures 35-003
special procedures 70-031; 70-144

Tax incentives 35-000

Tax liabilities
payment, method of 35-005

Tax planning
transfer pricing 35-000

Tax relief
criteria 35-503
new industries 35-501–35-503

Tax system
structure 35-000

Taxation laws 35-000

Technology
investment 65-000
protection 65-000

Thin capitalisation rules 35-103

Trade contracts
advance authorisations or clearances 45-303
body exercising control
– composition.................................... 45-303
extra-territorial effect of laws 45-303
penalty for non-compliance 45-303
prohibition or regulation 45-303
validity 45-303

Trade names
protection 65-002

Trade secrets
protection 65-002

Trade unions
liabilities 60-015
employer organisations, institutional
links 60-021
government, institutional links 60-021
make-up 60-014
privileges 60-015
status 60-014

Trade marks
labelling requirements, effect on 65-024
licences 45-304
protection 65-002
system 35-000

Transfers
rights in land 25-102

Transfer pricing 35-000

Transport tax 35-301

Treaties
international treaties relevant to import
and export 50-023
investment protection 20-201

Treaty obligations 20-000; 20-101–20-103

U

Unfair competition
industrial property, laws affecting rights ... 65-005

Unfair trading practices 45-000

Unitary tax 35-000
imposition 35-302

United Nations Committee on International Trade Law
conciliation rules 70-202

United Nations Committee on International Trade Law Rules 70-104

Utility model
system 65-000

V

Value added tax 35-301

Visas
foreign workers, etc. 60-033

Visiting industrial experts
special tax treatment 35-105

W

Wages
control 60-005

War risk
compensation 20-204

Warranty
laws prohibiting exclusion 45-301

Work hours — see Hours of work

Work permits
foreign workers, etc. 60-033

LINES OF INQUIRY

Table of Contents

	Page
Introduction	1,051
Abbreviations	1,101

	Paragraph
An overview (the system of law and government, and the organisation of the legal profession)	¶20-000
Land tenure — the site of the investment	¶25-000
The structure of the investment — (contract, commercial and company law)	¶30-000
Taxation	¶35-000
Regulation of business — general and special (incentives and disincentives)	¶45-000
Import and export controls	¶50-000
Exchange control — the movement of money	¶55-000
Labour and nationality laws	¶60-000
Intellectual property	¶65-000
Settlement of disputes	¶70-000
The sources, regulation of, and securities for local finance	¶75-000
Movement of goods (transport and shipping)	¶80-000
Insurance	¶85-000

Introduction

These lines of inquiry should be followed by anyone planning to do business in the countries covered as well as by their advisers. The Lines of Inquiry are based on a booklet published by the Trade Law Committee of the Law Council of Australia.

The Lines of Inquiry serve as an introductory test to this publication on doing business in a number of Asian countries, and provide a common format for the separate national studies. The questions are divided into sections by topic. Each section is headed by an introduction explaining the significance of the questions and the reasoning behind them. Knowing the ultimate aim of the question enables the reader to pursue the line of inquiry further if the particular situation demands.

The topics are broad but the questions are very specific. Not all lines of inquiry or all questions on any given topic will be relevant to any particular operation. The variable factors are innumerable; apart from the nature of the product or operation, there is the nature and condition of the investor and the nature and extent of the intended presence to be considered.

It is important to recognise that a major legal concern of a foreign operator is the interaction of the foreign legal system with the law of the home country. Much effort needs to be put into identifying the harmony or disharmony of the different systems to enable the construction of an operation that will accord with and derive the maximum benefit from both the host and home systems of law. The areas of taxation and exchange control are obvious major areas in which this reconciliation of two systems must take place. Reference to two systems presupposes a very basic operation, and there may be many more legal systems involved.

The questions each have a paragraph number and a heading. The questions are not repeated in the answers, but the heading and paragraph number is the same in each country — with each country's prefix inserted before the paragraph number to avoid confusion.

ABBREVIATIONS

LINES OF INQUIRY

GATT ....General Agreement on Tariff and Trade
ICC ....International Chamber of Commerce
ICSID ....International Centre for the Settlement of Investment Disputes
ILO ....International Labour Organisation
MIGA ....Multilateral Investment Guarantee Agency
OECD ....Organisation for Economic Cooperation and Development
UNCITRAL .....United Nations Committee on International Trade Law

AN OVERVIEW (THE SYSTEM OF LAW AND GOVERNMENT, AND THE ORGANISATION OF THE LEGAL PROFESSION)

Introduction .... ¶20-000
System of law .... ¶20-001
Origin of legal system .... ¶20-002
Sources of law .... ¶20-003
Law-making bodies .... ¶20-004
Organisation of government .... ¶20-005
Language of the law .... ¶20-011
Structure of legal profession .... ¶20-012
Determination of applicable law .... ¶20-013
Choice of method and forum .... ¶20-014
Treaty obligations .... ¶20-101
Guarantees and incentives .... ¶20-201

¶20-000 INTRODUCTION

This section of the Lines of Inquiry is concerned to identify the legal and governmental environment of the host country in which the investing business will be operating. The business is moving into the economic territory of a foreign country and, therefore, must expect that to a large degree it will be subject to that country's laws and to its governmental supervision or control. Investors need to know whether they can have confidence in both the legal and political systems. Although in few countries they would today have reason to fear a hostile environment, they need the assurance of legal and political stability in which they can operate their businesses. Motives for entering the host country may occasionally have a philanthropic or altruistic aspect, but the primary purpose is always to make profits. They need to know that the legal and political systems will be supportive of what they regard as their legitimate commercial objectives; that they can operate their business profitably; and that they can withdraw those profits to use elsewhere if they wish.

A first step for any investor trying to understand the legal system in the potential host country is to place it on the world's spectrum of different legal systems. There is a broad but generally accepted characterisation of legal systems into major legal "families". These are:

common law: originating in England and carried to most of the countries colonised by England;

civil law: of continental Europe, based on Roman law, codified by both France and Germany and spread as a version of either the French or German codes to most countries other than common law or socialist;

socialist: normally close to the civil law in concept and structure but reflecting a different economic philosophy; and *customary law:* religious (e.g. Islamic) or personal (e.g. *adat*), usually existing alongside a common law or civil law system.

If investors understand the general characteristics of each of the "families", they have a short cut to dealing with the host country. Most countries have adopted formally either the common law or the French or German civil law. In some cases, this was through settlement; in others, through conquest; and in others, law was adopted apparently voluntarily, although with the objective of removing foreign concessions and enclaves. Some codes are eclectic, drawing on both the French and German systems; whilst others draw also on the common law, either as a reflection of a chequered colonial past or as part of a genuine desire to incorporate the more desirable features of each system. It is tempting but dangerous, however, to assume that because a country may have adopted a German system, it can therefore be equated with German law. Law is a cultural phenomenon, and the same law will not merely be interpreted differently by different cultures but may be seen as serving quite disparate purposes. The investor should be aware of this phenomenon, and also should be concerned to investigate the continuing nature of reception or influence from the parent country to the host country.

The first point of reference for the investor is to identify at the outset the character of the legal system of the host country. This must be done first because it is necessary to know what the law is and also whether the law of the host country has the necessary degree of sophistication to support the investment or other business operation, so that the legitimate objectives of the investor can be reasonably capable of being realised. It is also necessary to know how, if at all, the law can be changed. Changes in the law of the host country can be beneficial or detrimental to the investment. It may be in some cases that investors would seek changes in the law of the host country to suit their needs, as a condition of their entry into the country. But having been assured of an acceptable legal environment, the investor may also be anxious to insulate itself from changes in the law. It has to be said that this can rarely be achieved. An investor should look for a country that has sufficient settled methods of changing the law to ensure the absence of arbitrariness or surprise. Hence, it is important to examine the constitutional nature of the host government, its agencies and its powers.

The host government — structure and powers

It is accepted today, as a corollary of sovereignty and national independence, that it is the prerogative of the host government to determine whether or not it will admit foreign investment, and to formulate conditions governing its form and the manner of its operation. This prerogative may be exercised as part of a general control of investment, both domestic and foreign, or there may be a separate regime for foreign investment superimposed upon the general regime applying to all investment and contained in separate laws and administered by separate institutions. It is generally acknowledged that there are internationally recognised minimum standards relating to the treatment of foreign investors. While there may be disagreement about the precise limits of these standards, their existence is not really in dispute and should be reflected in whatever legal regime of the host country affects foreign investors and businesses.

Thus there are many questions the investor should seek to have answered. What is the nature of the investment regime? What are the requirements and the procedures?

¶20-000

How do we determine the "nationality of the investment"? What are the incentives and the disincentives? What multilateral conventions may be relevant, and are there any bilateral agreements which will provide protection for the investor?

Many of these issues are dealt with in subsequent sections of this work and are important for determining how to enter the host country and how secure the investment will be. The questions in this section are concerned with identifying the decision makers and the scope of their powers and authorities. Who can approve and authorise the investment? Who will control or regulate it? Who can give assurances about the permissible scope of its operations? Who can change the rules, and in what circumstances and what ways? The adviser will be confronted with a mix of treaties and agreements, constitutions, economic plans, statutes, administrative directions, guidelines, regulations, and policy statements. A course must be charted through this but the major concern is that the processes of government should be apparent and predictable.

Treaty obligations

In many instances there may be treaties or conventions to which the host country is a party and which will bind the host government to accord certain standards of treatment to the foreign investor. These may be multilateral (e.g. under the aegis of the United Nations, the Hague Conference or the World Bank); or they may be bilateral trade or investment protection agreements or tax treaties between the investor's government and the host. Many of these will in effect provide guarantees by the host government for the benefit of the investor, and will thus raise the question of their enforceability. This again becomes an important line of inquiry to put to legal advisers in both the investing and the host countries.

The role of lawyers

What sort of advice can investors expect from lawyers? Can the lawyer in the investor's country answer all these questions in so far as they relate to the law of the host country? Can the investors' lawyers provide appropriate legal services to their clients in the host country? Investors must ascertain their lawyer's status to enter and undertake work of a professional legal nature in the host country. But no matter what degree of recognition is given to the lawyer's professional status by the host country, investors will inevitably need the advice of properly qualified lawyers or other professionals in the host country itself.

Investors should not assume that they will find direct professional counterparts to lawyers in the host country. They may be faced with several organisations purporting to offer legal advice or to perform what they would regard as professional services, particularly notaries. Just as a foreign business investing in a country like Australia would need to have explained the relation of solicitors and barristers (in each state) and the relation of both of them to other professionals, such as accountants or other business or financial consultants, so the investor needs to understand the roles of different categories of professionals in the host state. It is important not to be misled by labels. The fact that there is a body of professionals in the host country called "lawyers" does not mean that they perceive their professional role in the same way as people called "lawyers" in other countries.

Another important issue which needs to be addressed is the extent of independence from the government of the host state that legal and accounting professionals in that country are permitted to enjoy. To what extent are the interests of the investors paramount for those in the host country who may be retained to advise it?

Choice of law and choice of forum

The result of the researches of investors and lawyers into the matters canvassed in these lines of inquiry must be a decision as to whether investors can rely on the fairness, impartiality, and sophistication of the law and the civil process of the host country, or whether they should seek to have some other law govern its activities and some forum other than the courts of the host country determine any disputes that may arise. Perhaps the two most important clauses in any international agreement are the "choice of law" and "choice of forum" clauses. In so far as investors have engaged physically in commercial activities within the jurisdiction of the host country, they have brought themselves within the legal regime of that country and the jurisdiction of its courts. They will need to ask how much autonomy that jurisdiction will accord foreign investors to choose a governing law different from that of the host state, and how much autonomy there is to choose a different dispute settlement mechanism, whether by conciliation, arbitration, or litigation outside the host state.

Certainly investors will be met by a considerable body of law that is mandatory; but there may be areas where it is possible to negotiate the application of a different law, whether the law of the investors' country or a "neutral" system. There may be an option to arbitrate disputes as an alternative to litigation, but the institutions that will conduct the arbitration and the site of the arbitration may be more difficult to agree on. If litigation or arbitration takes place outside the host country, investors will need to know whether any judgment or award will be recognised and enforced within the host country.

These are areas in which multilateral agreements under the auspices of the United Nations and the World Bank are providing valuable alternative regimes.

¶20-001 SYSTEM OF LAW

How is the system of law characterised; e.g. common law, civil law, socialist law, Islamic law, customary law, a mixed system?

¶20-002 ORIGIN OF LEGAL SYSTEM

From which system of law and from which country was the law derived? To what extent is it still dependent on its source as a matter of law or tradition or practice?

¶20-003 SOURCES OF LAW

Is the law principally found in statutory or non-statutory sources? Are any parts of the law codified?

¶20-001

¶20-004   LAW-MAKING BODIES

What are the law-making bodies (federal, state and local)? What are their main areas of power?

¶20-005   ORGANISATION OF GOVERNMENT

What are the broad functions and limits of authority, both legal and practical, of the legislature, executive and judiciary? To what extent can the executive make regulations? What, if any, areas of the economy are state monopolies?

¶20-011   LANGUAGE OF THE LAW

What is the language of the law and of the lawyers? Are there available reports, journals, texts on this legal system (in English or at all)? Is there any material on legal database?

¶20-012   STRUCTURE OF LEGAL PROFESSION

What is the organisation, division and function of the legal profession? Is its organisation and training modelled on any other legal system? What is its standing? To what extent do foreign lawyers have a right of practice? Are they restricted to home state law or can they also advise on local or any other law? Do they have a right of audience before courts or other tribunals in the country? Can they form partnerships with local lawyers?

¶20-013   DETERMINATION OF APPLICABLE LAW

How do courts or tribunals in the country determine the law applicable to dealings with foreign entities or transactions which have some foreign element? In particular, to what extent do the parties have freedom to choose the law applicable to their particular transaction, and to what extent and on what basis is the choice of law prescribed?

¶20-014   CHOICE OF METHOD AND FORUM

To what extent do the parties have freedom to choose between litigation and other forms of dispute settlement, and to what extent can they choose courts or tribunals in other countries?

Treaty obligations

Membership of international   International agreements .... ¶20-102
banks .... ¶20-101   OECD declaration .... ¶20-103

¶20-101   MEMBERSHIP OF INTERNATIONAL BANKS

Is the host government a member of the International Bank for Reconstruction and Development or the Asian Development Bank or any other regional bank? To what extent does it adhere to these banks' policies?

¶20-102   INTERNATIONAL AGREEMENTS

Has the host government ratified and put into effect such international agreements as those governing the International Centre for the Settlement of Investment Disputes and the New York Convention on the Recognition and Enforcement of Foreign Arbitral Awards?

¶20-103   OECD DECLARATION

Has the OECD Declaration on International Investment and Multinational Enterprises been expressly accepted?

Guarantees and incentives

Investment protection   Government guarantees for
treaties .... ¶20-201   foreign investors .... ¶20-204
Joint trade agreements .... ¶20-202   Protection for foreign
Multilateral investment   investors .... ¶20-205
protection treaties .... ¶20-203

¶20-201   INVESTMENT PROTECTION TREATIES

Are there any treaties which provide protection for the investments of foreigners?

¶20-202   JOINT TRADE AGREEMENTS

Are there any joint trade agreements which provide a method of protection or dispute resolution in relation to investment disputes?

¶20-101

¶20-203 MULTILATERAL INVESTMENT PROTECTION TREATIES

Is there any relevant multilateral treaty applicable to investment protection such as the International Centre for the Settlement of Investment Disputes Convention?

¶20-204 GOVERNMENT GUARANTEES FOR FOREIGN INVESTORS

Are specific government guarantees available for foreign investors? If so, what matters are covered by such guarantees, e.g. expropriation of assets, blockage of the repatriation of foreign currency and compensation for war risk?

¶20-205 PROTECTION FOR FOREIGN INVESTORS

Do particular laws of the host country give protection? For example, some countries' constitutions contain guarantees against expropriation or of due compensation for expropriation. In other cases, laws dealing with joint ventures or the encouragement of foreign investment contain similar forms of protection.

LAND TENURE — THE SITE OF THE INVESTMENT

Introduction .... ¶25-000
Land tenure .... ¶25-001
Rights in land .... ¶25-101

¶25-000 INTRODUCTION

This section is concerned with the physical presence of the investor in the host country.

The investment will need land — a site from which it can carry on its business. This may be the site of a factory, or of a quarry or mine or plantation or farm, or of an office block or a showroom or shop. It is necessary, therefore, at an early stage to enquire whether the investor can acquire such rights in land and buildings that will ensure it has sufficient security to carry on its business operations for the period of the investment.

The first problem may be a very basic one of the identification of the land in question. Has there been a cadastral survey which is not only reliable but is accepted as authoritative in the host country?

If the land is identified, the next issue is the scheme of rights that may be available in or over that land. Are they the rights familiar to the Western systems of common and civil law? Or are they native customary rights? In some cases it may be found that native customary land rights interact with Western rights, and this is a matter that must be investigated to ensure that this interaction is compatible with the use of the land by investors for the purposes of the investment.

It will be important for investors that, on the termination of the investment, the land can be sold for full value. Hence it is necessary to establish at the outset that land is freely alienable or, if it is not, what restrictions exist. At the same time investors need to know what powers exist, and in what bodies, to acquire the land compulsorily; and, if it can be so acquired, whether fair compensation is payable.

What is the extent of those rights that can exist in or over land? Some legal systems have separate systems of rights affecting land and buildings. It is necessary to ask, therefore, whether rights of ownership or use in connection with the land extend also to buildings on the land and other fixtures and crops and accretions, or whether a separate system of rights exists for buildings and structures. Similarly, do land rights extend also to minerals under the land; and do they extend to water on or under, or even close by, the land?

It is important to enquire whether there is an adequate system for the identification of rights in connection with any piece of land. Registration systems may come in many forms. They may provide for the registration of the land and of title and other interests in the land; in particular, it is important to know whether the registration system (if any) adequately records encumbrances, charges, and security interests. In some cases documents are registered, and it is necessary to enquire what documents are affected. Registration systems also vary concerning the place of registration, whether it is local or central, the duration of registration, and the consequences of failure to register.

What taxes, rates, and other charges or responsibilities affect the owner or occupier of the land? To what extent are these a matter of central or of local government? And, as with so many issues, how does one find out?

Is the land properly served with infrastructural facilities adequate for the needs of investors? These include water, electricity, and access to transport. The converse question must also be asked: is there adequate and assured access to the land for investors? Also, is there a sufficiently skilled labour force nearby from which investors can recruit? Can they provide appropriate accommodation near the site for expatriate staff which they may need to import?

In many cases, investors will find that there are restrictions on the occupation of land by foreigners, whether for business or dwelling purposes. Exemptions from these restrictions may have to be especially negotiated.

It may be that the host country as a matter of policy tries to direct different forms of investment to different parts of the country, and uses a system of incentives and disincentives (particularly relating to land rights) in order to achieve this. It may have established special areas or enclaves for foreign investment, variously known as industrial estates, special economic zones, etc. Areas such as these are likely to provide all infrastructural facilities that may be required, and also enable the foreign business to acquire rights of land use within that area on concessional terms. Also they may, by physically insulating the area from the rest of the country and its economy, provide a customs free zone in which investors can import materials and components without duty or licence and subsequently export the finished product, again without regulation or the minimum of regulation.

Finally, in most countries there are likely to be environmental controls affecting the use of land or requiring the restoration of the condition of the land on the termination of the enterprise. These environmental controls will need to be investigated.

Land tenure

Forms of land tenure .... ¶25-001   Local regulations .... ¶25-004
Private ownership of land .... ¶25-002   Special areas .... ¶25-005
Restrictions on transfer of   Customary land rights .... ¶25-011
   land .... ¶25-003

¶25-001   FORMS OF LAND TENURE

What forms of rights of land use or ownership exist?

¶25-002   PRIVATE OWNERSHIP OF LAND

To what extent is private ownership of land recognised?

¶25-003   RESTRICTIONS ON TRANSFER OF LAND

Is all land freely transferable in all parts of the country or are there any restrictions on alienability, including pre-emptive rights in favour of any person or any group of persons?

¶25-004   LOCAL REGULATIONS

How far are rights of land use or ownership in different areas of the country regulated by:

(a) codes, special laws, and statutes;

(b) customary or unwritten law?

¶25-005   SPECIAL AREAS

Are there any areas where a special system of law applies, such as:

(a) a special or localised domestic law;

(b) a system of foreign law; or

(c) industrial estates or export processing zones?

¶25-011   CUSTOMARY LAND RIGHTS

If native customary laws or rights of land use are recognised:

(a) are they recognised in a systematised form of customary law or based on traditional rights;

(b) is it difficult to ascertain customary laws or the nature of traditional rights;

(c) how settled are the customary laws; and any traditional rights;

(d) are customary rights, laws or traditions administered or controlled by any special tribunal, court or other organisation (including the government or government agencies);

(e) do customary laws, rights or traditions extend to or affect any other forms of use rights; and

(f) is land held on any kind of ownership or right of use subject to claim, compulsory acquisition or ownership, or other rights by or on behalf of the native peoples?

Rights in land

Nature of rights in land .... ¶25-101
Transfer of rights in land .... ¶25-102
Restrictions on acquisition of
  rights in land .... ¶25-103
Land surveying .... ¶25-104
Registration of security in
  land .... ¶25-105
Registration of rights of land use
  and ownership .... ¶25-111
System of land registration ..... ¶25-112
Specific rights .... ¶25-113
Extent of rights in land .... ¶25-114
Agreements restricting land
  use .... ¶25-115
Ascertainment of existing
  restrictions .... ¶25-121
Powers of acquisition of land ... ¶25-122

Compensation for acquired
  land .... ¶25-123
Taxes and rates .... ¶25-124
Seizure of land in execution of
  judgment .... ¶25-125
Environmental restrictions ..... ¶25-201
Regulation of environmental
  controls .... ¶25-202
Governmental requirements for
  environmental assessment ... ¶25-203
Pollution standards .... ¶25-204
Incentives for non-polluting
  plants .... ¶25-205
Nature of controls .... ¶25-211
Detriment to the environment .. ¶25-212

¶25-101   NATURE OF RIGHTS IN LAND

In respect of each form of land use or ownership in use in the country, what rights of land use or ownership can exist? In particular:

  (a) is absolute ownership available;

  (b) if absolute ownership is not available, what rights of land use by lease are available and, if any, from whom;

  (c) are there any restrictions on the term, the rental, transferability, or other terms or conditions in such leases;

  (d) are there sufficient rights of access to land, including rights to traverse other land, and rights to use roads, waterways, ports, harbours, etc.;

  (e) are claims relating to land use or ownership barred or extinguished by lapse of time and, if so, what is the period of time?

¶25-102   TRANSFER OF RIGHTS IN LAND

How are rights of land use or ownership acquired and transferred; is this a slow or lengthy process? In particular:

  (a) is the transfer of these rights usually done by legal professionals and, if not, by whom;

  (b) are costs or charges of transfer regulated and, if so, what is the approximate cost;

  (c) must the transactions be in any particular form; and

¶25-101

(d) are any approvals (governmental or otherwise) required in order to acquire or dispose of any interest in land:

   (i) generally;

   (ii) to any particular individuals or groups of peoples;

   (iii) in relation to transfers by any particular individuals or groups of peoples; or

   (iv) in relation to any size or term of land holding?

¶25-103 RESTRICTIONS ON ACQUISITION OF RIGHTS IN LAND

Are there any restrictions on the acquisition of those rights by reason of the nationality or corporate status of a person seeking them (e.g. foreign ownership restrictions or restrictions on corporations owning land)?

¶25-104 LAND SURVEYING

Is all land properly surveyed and mapped, and are there any difficulties or excessive costs in relation to surveying land generally or in particular localities?

¶25-105 REGISTRATION OF SECURITY IN LAND

Are rights of land use or ownership by way of security registrable? If so, where, centrally or locally? How long does it take to effect registration?

¶25-111 REGISTRATION OF RIGHTS OF LAND USE AND OWNERSHIP

Are rights of land use and ownership registrable; and, if so, is the system of registration based on registration of:

(a) ownership;

(b) transactions;

(c) documents; or

(d) a combination of (a) to (c)?

¶25-112 SYSTEM OF LAND REGISTRATION

In relation to any land registration system:

(a) does the registration system provide any governmental or other guarantee against errors or fraud in relation to the system;

(b) what interests can exist that are not shown in the register; and

(c) is there a need to investigate rights of land use or ownership prior to the date of registration?

¶25-113   SPECIFIC RIGHTS

Do the different forms of land use or ownership carry the right to:

(a) groundwater or other water rights;

(b) oil or gas;

(c) gold; or

(d) any other minerals?

¶25-114   EXTENT OF RIGHTS IN LAND

How far do rights of land use or ownership extend? Do they include:

(a) crops;

(b) fixtures, including buildings; and

(c) any other rights and, if so, what are those rights?

¶25-115   AGREEMENTS RESTRICTING LAND USE

Can land use be restricted by agreement? If so, are such agreements enforceable only by the parties thereto? If not, by whom?

¶25-121   ASCERTAINMENT OF EXISTING RESTRICTIONS

Can existing rights and restrictions be reliably ascertained by search or inspection?

¶25-122   POWERS OF ACQUISITION OF LAND

What powers of acquisition of land exist, whether by the government or any other organisation or individuals for its or their own purposes; or by the government on behalf of any person or organisation?

¶25-123   COMPENSATION FOR ACQUIRED LAND

If land is acquired:

(a) is there any constitutional or legislative entitlement to compensation;

(b) how is compensation assessed, on what basis and by whom; and

(c) in the event of there being any dispute in relation to compensation payable, how is the dispute resolved?

¶25-113

¶25-124 TAXES AND RATES

Are there any taxes, rates or any other payments connected with the ownership, occupation and use of land and, if so:

(a) does non-payment give rise to any right of seizure by the taxing authority;

(b) is information in respect of taxes and any existing liability readily obtainable;

(c) is information on taxes, etc., that is obtained provided in a form that is final and conclusive against the taxing authority;

(d) are there any accrued liabilities in relation to taxes affecting land that would not be shown by the usual searches; and

(e) are any taxes levied on land other than on a single holding basis and, if so, on what basis?

¶25-125 SEIZURE OF LAND IN EXECUTION OF JUDGMENT

Do the courts or any other tribunal have power to order seizure and sale of land in execution of judgments or orders or in enforcement of interim orders at any other stage of proceedings?

¶25-201 ENVIRONMENTAL RESTRICTIONS

Are there any laws restricting the setting up or operation of businesses or factories based on the protection of the environment in the host country?

¶25-202 REGULATION OF ENVIRONMENTAL CONTROLS

(a) Which body regulates environmental controls, and how is it composed?

(b) What are the penalties for non-compliance and who is entitled to enforce the controls?

¶25-203 GOVERNMENTAL REQUIREMENTS FOR ENVIRONMENTAL ASSESSMENT

What are the governmental requirements for environmental assessment (whether imposed by statute or by way of approval)?

¶25-204 POLLUTION STANDARDS

If controls are imposed on the pollution of air, land and water, what standards are applicable? Are discharges allowed, but with qualitative or quantitative limits?

[Next page is 1,761]

¶25-205   INCENTIVES FOR NON-POLLUTING PLANTS

(a) Are there incentives for establishing non-polluting plants in normally pollution-creating activities?

(b) What form do the incentives, if any, take?

¶25-211   NATURE OF CONTROLS

Must it be ensured, before the commencement of a business activity, that environmental requirements are fulfilled, or are the controls punitive in effect, operating only after the establishment of a business venture?

¶25-212   DETRIMENT TO THE ENVIRONMENT

Is detriment to the environment a factor which an authority is required to take into account when deciding whether to allow the establishment of a business or the acquisition of any existing business, or any other government approvals?

THE STRUCTURE OF THE INVESTMENT — (CONTRACT, COMMERCIAL AND COMPANY LAW)

Introduction .... ¶30-000
Historical sources of contract and commercial law ..... ¶30-001
Codification of law .... ¶30-002
Distinction between contract and commercial law .... ¶30-003
Requirements for government contracts .... ¶30-004
Requirements for contracts with foreign entities .... ¶30-005
Treatment of consumer contracts .... ¶30-011
Liability for injury caused by defective products .... ¶30-012
Methods of settlement outside court system .... ¶30-013
Special rules for institutions .... ¶30-014
Use of standardised contracts .... ¶30-015
Remedies under the commercial law .... ¶30-016
Performance of contracts under changed
    circumstances .... ¶30-017
Company law .... ¶30-101

¶30-000 INTRODUCTION

This section of the Lines of Inquiry is concerned with the laws of the host country that will govern the business activities of the investor. These laws regulate the form that the investment should take and the mandatory requirements that may govern both the structure and the activities of the business.

The sources of contract and commercial laws

It is necessary firstly to investigate the nature of the sources of the contract and commercial law of the host country. These may be entirely indigenous, although this is unlikely. It is probable that the basic legal system will be derived from a common law or one of the civil law systems, including socialist law, although with some local gloss in the form both of interpretation and of local special statutes or regulations. There may also be an element of customary law, which may be based on localities or may be personal. Where there are special statutes dealing with foreign investment and business activities, it is important to bear in mind that these statutes may be supplemented, and in some cases even substantially altered, by "implementing regulations".

It will be necessary to establish to what extent the parent law still exercises an influence in the host country. It is possible that there will be a continuing reception of law from the parent, either automatic or because there is a tradition of emulating in the host country new laws of the parent. In addition to this, or alternatively, there may be a continuing influence that is purely personal or cultural, based on a tradition of dependence on legal scholarship of the host country.

In modern times, when a great deal of international private law and transnational law is being unified or harmonised in the form of international conventions, it is necessary to enquire which of these conventions will apply to the business activities intended to be carried on in the host country.

The distinction between contract and commercial law

The commercial laws of all countries are built on the foundation of contract law. However, some systems — particularly the common law systems — do not draw formal distinctions between contract law and commercial law or between the general body of contract law and the law applicable to special types of contracts. Other systems — particularly in the civil law — do draw clear distinctions between their contract and commercial law, to the extent that they may be located in separate Codes and have separate applications. In these cases it is necessary to enquire what factors attract the application of the Commercial Code. It may depend on the nature of the transaction or upon the identity of the parties.

Mandatory or dispositive nature of the law

It is important to ascertain to what extent application of the law is mandatory and to what extent the parties can dispense with it and make their own rules in their contracts. The law may provide for standardised transactions in which the function of the law is simply to facilitate contract negotiation and drafting by implementing the presumed intention of the parties, leaving them free to exclude its application if they so wish and to manifest a different contractual intent. Alternatively, the law may, as a matter of economic, social or political expediency, prescribe the content of certain transactions in a manner which gives the parties little or no freedom of choice.

The content of the host country's law

Investors and their advisers will need to investigate the content of the host country's law so far as it will apply to and affect the business activities of the investors. In this area, two matters call for special attention. First, if the investor will be engaged in marketing products in the host country, the extent and nature of the product liability laws of the host country must be investigated. These extend not only to regulations governing the safety, packaging or description of the product, but also to the liability regime to which the investor will be exposed for any damage or loss that the product may cause. This is a major concern. The liability may be confined by notions of contract and of privity; or it may be a matter of statutory regulation and of statutory obligations and liabilities. Liability may be based on motions of fault, proved or presumed, or it may be strict liability independent of any proof of fault or blame.

Secondly, it is desirable to investigate the range of legal remedies that may be available to the investor personally or against him or her in actions brought by those with whom he or she deals. What are the remedies? What is their order of priority? Are they available as rights or are they discretionary? Are penalties regarded as a legitimate sanction in the case of breach of contractual or other obligations, or are they disallowed as being unconscionable? If they are disallowed, what circumstances determine this? If they are permissible, are there any legal requirements which must be satisfied to establish their legitimacy?

Special legal regimes

In many legal systems there will be separate laws or different applications of the law to different categories of business entities or to different types of transactions. Hence, enquiry should be made as to whether the host government is subject to the same laws and procedures as the non-governmental or foreign entity. In particular, there may be restrictions on the extent to which the host government can bind itself by contract so as to affect its future executive discretion; but the difference may go far beyond this and establish a quite different legal regime for transactions in which the government or a government entity is a party.

There may be separate laws or entire separate regimes governing the "foreign sector" of the host economy, however that may be defined. This may be part of a deliberate strategy to derive the advantages that can flow from providing, in some form of legal enclave, a familiar system of laws for the foreign entrepreneur, whilst endeavouring to insulate the domestic economy from these foreign influences, whether they be economic, commercial or political.

In the same way, legal regimes affecting consumer transactions may vary from those governing business or "commercial" transactions. The investor may, as a commercial entity, attract the application of one regime in its business operations but another regime when it markets its products in the country.

Just as the content of the law may differ depending on the categorisation of the parties or the transaction, so may its enforcement. There may be special courts or tribunals for different entities, including the government, and there may be a special range of remedies.

It is necessary for investors and their advisers to make a projection of all the investors' likely activities in order to determine the range of laws which may affect them.

Business organisation

One of the most pressing problems to investigate will concern the forms of business organisation permitted in the host country and the relative attraction or otherwise of their legal, financial and commercial incidents. It is important to remember in performing this task that similar words are often used in different countries to describe institutions that may have superficial resemblance; but that the use of labels in this fashion often conceals significant differences. For example, in many jurisdictions a partnership is not a separate legal entity from the partners who compose it, but in others a partnership is capable of having separate legal personality.

We are not concerned here simply with the company law of the host country. The issue is what forms of business organisation are open to the foreign investor and which of them will best suit his activities. The answer to the latter part of this question will often be found to turn on the taxation implications both in the host country and in the investor's country.

The investor is presumably concerned to establish a commercial presence in the host country. There is a wide range of possible forms of commercial establishment. These range from agencies of various sorts (and it must be remembered that the concept of agency itself may differ substantially from country to country) to branch operations as a foreign company, contractual joint ventures with local or possibly other foreign partners, the creation of new joint venture corporate entities, and the establishment of a wholly-owned subsidiary.

The enquiry into which of these are available will then turn to the approvals that may be necessary to establish them, the formalities of establishment, and the accounting, reporting, supervisory, and other regulatory requirements that will affect them. The governing and managing structures will also need to be examined.

An alternative to establishing a new entity in the host country might be the takeover of an existing host-country enterprise or the investment in a local enterprise. The conditions and machinery for any such operation will need to be closely scrutinised. There will probably also be requirements of local equity or of host government participation. It may also be necessary to engage local staff, and it may not always be possible to dismiss them.

¶30-001　HISTORICAL SOURCES OF CONTRACT AND COMMERCIAL LAW

From what system of law is the contract and commercial law derived, or what system of law or country has influenced its development? To what extent does that influence still persist? Is there a continuing reception in either legal or factual terms?

¶30-002　CODIFICATION OF LAW

To what extent is the contract and commercial law codified either in codes or in particular statutes or special laws and regulations? To what extent do international treaties override this law? To what extent is the law mandatory or to what extent can the parties exclude or vary it by contract?

¶30-003　DISTINCTION BETWEEN CONTRACT AND COMMERCIAL LAW

Is there a formal distinction between contract and commercial law? If so, on what basis is the distinction drawn (e.g. the nature of the transaction or the identity and character of the parties) and what is the significance and effect of that distinction?

¶30-004　REQUIREMENTS FOR GOVERNMENT CONTRACTS

Is there a separate legal regime for government contracts or contracts to which government or government agencies may be parties? If so, what is the basis of the distinction and what are its major characteristics?

¶30-005　REQUIREMENTS FOR CONTRACTS WITH FOREIGN ENTITIES

Is there a separate legal regime for contracts with foreign entities? If so, what is the basis of the distinction and its major characteristics?

¶30-001

¶30-011   TREATMENT OF CONSUMER CONTRACTS

Is there a separate legal regime for consumer contracts? If so, what is the basis of the distinction and what are its major characteristics?

¶30-012   LIABILITY FOR INJURY CAUSED BY DEFECTIVE PRODUCTS

To what extent are sellers, distributors, importers, and manufacturers (local or foreign) liable for injury caused by defective products? Does their liability, if any, depend on privity of contract, and is it strict liability or is it based on fault?

¶30-013   METHODS OF SETTLEMENT OUTSIDE COURT SYSTEM

To what extent are the formal principles of law relevant to commercial contracts? To what extent are there commercial remedies and methods of settlement outside courts?

¶30-014   SPECIAL RULES FOR INSTITUTIONS

To what extent are ordinary rules of contract or commercial law varied in relation to particular institutions or kinds of entities such as companies, banks or foreign investors?

¶30-015   USE OF STANDARDISED CONTRACTS

To what extent are standardised contract transactions permissible under the legal system? To what extent are such standard contracts used? To what extent is it permissible to include in contracts clauses for exemption from liabilities which would otherwise arise or to limit the extent of those liabilities?

¶30-016   REMEDIES UNDER THE COMMERCIAL LAW

To what extent are the remedies granted by the system of commercial law atypical of the system on which it is founded? What are the principal remedies for breach of contract? To what extent are they discretionary? To what extent will the law uphold penalties in contracts?

¶30-017   PERFORMANCE OF CONTRACTS UNDER CHANGED CIRCUMSTANCES

What, if any, legal principles govern the effect of changed circumstances on contract performance? Do courts or other bodies have the power to review contract terms? If so, on what grounds and in what circumstances?

Company law

Forms of commercial
  organisations .... ¶30-101

Foreign companies .... ¶30-102

Registration of non-resident
  companies .... ¶30-103

Requirements for establishment
  of subsidiaries .... ¶30-104

Investment in local
  companies .... ¶30-105

Percentage of foreign
  ownership .... ¶30-111

Types of governing and
  managing structures .... ¶30-112

Structure and powers of
  joint venture .... ¶30-113

¶30-101   FORMS OF COMMERCIAL ORGANISATIONS

What forms of commercial organisation exist, with or without limited liability?

¶30-102   FOREIGN COMPANIES

Can a foreign company carry on business in this country? In particular, can or should it:

(a) register as a non-resident company;

(b) incorporate a subsidiary under the law of the host country to operate in that country;

(c) carry on business as an agency or branch without registration or incorporation in that country?

¶30-103   REGISTRATION OF NON-RESIDENT COMPANIES

On the registration of a non-resident company, what are the formal requirements, and in particular:

(a) what fees are payable, and do they vary according to the amount of the nominal or issued capital of the non-resident company and does the fee increase after registration if such capital is increased;

(b) is it necessary for a non-resident to file statutory accounts;

(c) is it necessary to appoint a local agent and what are the qualifications of such an agent;

(d) is it necessary to file initially any documents other than evidence of incorporation and a copy of the charter of such non-resident; in particular, is it necessary to file any copies of mortgages or charges executed outside the country which could affect assets within the country and, if so, are any duties payable upon such filing;

(e) is it necessary to obtain government or any other statutory approvals (generally or relating only to foreign investment);

(f) what statutory bodies exercise jurisdiction over companies?

¶30-104 REQUIREMENTS FOR ESTABLISHMENT OF SUBSIDIARIES

What are the formal requirements for the establishment of a wholly or partly owned subsidiary; and in relation to the subsidiary:

(a) what are the fees or duties payable to the government of the host country on incorporation of such a company and upon the increase of capital, and are there any recurring fees;

(b) how many of the board of directors are required to be residents or nationals;

(c) what percentage of management or staff must be residents or nationals;

(d) what percentage of the share capital may be held by non-residents;

(e) can the shares be bearer shares;

(f) must all the company's nominal capital be issued, and are there any minimum paid-up capital requirements;

(g) is there a minimum shareholder's qualification in the case of directors;

(h) what time would be required to set up the various forms of companies;

(i) can a branch of such company be established;

(j) must statutory accounts be published, must they be audited, and what additional information must be disclosed (e.g. directors' and senior executives' remuneration);

(k) must the name and percentage shareholding of the non-resident company be disclosed;

(l) can the shares held by the non-resident company be held by nominees;

(m) what kinds of assets may be used as payment for shares and, where shares are allotted for a consideration other than cash, is there any independent examination of the value of assets so applied;

(n) what are the provisions relating to voluntary and involuntary liquidation;

(o) are there restrictions on the disposal of shares?

¶30-105 INVESTMENT IN LOCAL COMPANIES

(a) What restrictions are there on investment in existing local companies, including takeovers and mergers by the acquisition of shares or other means?

(b) Are there any policies or guidelines as to matters such as the extent of local ownership which it would be advisable to comply with? What favourable or unfavourable treatment may follow?

(c) Is government participation envisaged by equity ownership, managerial capacity or any other form?

(d) Will the host country limit the geographical area of the operation of the enterprise?

(e) Is there a requirement to use local staff or contractors or sub-contractors?

¶30-111 PERCENTAGE OF FOREIGN OWNERSHIP

Does the percentage of foreign ownership affect the status of the company?

¶30-112 TYPES OF GOVERNING AND MANAGING STRUCTURES

What governing and managing structures are available and, in particular, are the powers of the board limited or full?

¶30-113 STRUCTURE AND POWERS OF JOINT VENTURE

(a) If the operation should take the form of a contractual joint venture between residents and non-residents which is not registered, are there any legislative requirements that will affect the non-resident participants in the venture?

(b) Where the joint venture involves the creation of a new joint enterprise or company, to what extent should the structure of the joint venture be dealt with in the constitutional documents of the company or enterprise, and to what extent in a joint venture agreement?

(c) Is there any restriction or control on the power to enter into an agreement with another company or group of persons relating to the management of the affairs of the company?

¶30-114 BANKRUPTCY LAW

What are the regulations governing bankruptcy?

(a) who can be made a bankrupt?

(b) who is entitled to issue a bankruptcy petition?

(c) what is the most common method of petitioning bankruptcy?

(d) what are the consequences of an undischarged bankrupt?

TAXATION

Introduction .... ¶35-000
General taxation .... ¶35-001
Commercial and business profits .... ¶35-101
Investment profits .... ¶35-201
Miscellaneous taxes .... ¶35-301
Capital gains tax .... ¶35-401
Tax incentives .... ¶35-501

¶35-000   INTRODUCTION

This section is concerned with the incidents and the effect of the taxation laws of the host country and their interaction with other systems imposing a liability to tax. It covers all major forms of taxation and is not limited merely to taxation of income and taxation of corporate persons.

Many of the major decisions of the investor will be tax-driven so an understanding of the impact of the tax system is central to the whole process of investment. In turn, for the host country, the taxation system is a major means of articulating and implementing its policies towards the economic sectors of which the investor forms a part and the whole process of investment. This policy aspect of taxation law means that there may not necessarily be a coherent and organised system of tax laws, but often merely a collection of disparate laws and regulations and practices.

The understanding of tax law is eased by a growing common international vocabulary. It is based to a large extent on the network of international bilateral tax treaties between both capital importing and capital exporting countries, especially those prominent in seeking and making foreign investment. It is important to take into account not only tax treaties between the countries of the investor and the host country, but also with those countries where income may arise or flow as part of basic tax planning processes. The granting of foreign tax credits and the compatibility of systems of tax law, and the regulation of undesirable tax planning devices such as transfer pricing must be considered within this particular framework. The concepts and language of the treaty system may be further developed by domestic law.

This section therefore examines basic questions of the structure of the tax system and compiles all the forms of business and commercial profit taxes that might be relevant to an investor, including the taxation of foreign personnel who may be required to work in the host country for a period of time. The flow of income and capital in and out of the country, whether as interest, dividends, royalties or repatriated capital, warrants special attention.

The section also canvasses some particular problems of foreign investors, such as unitary tax and tax incentives. These raise issues which require thorough examination. If the host country grants tax incentives by way of inducement to the foreign investor, and those incentives are not recognised by the investor's home country, i.e. are not tax-sparing, then the value of the incentives is wholly eliminated. Many foreign investment regimes make the granting of such incentives conditional on their recognition by the investor's home country. The necessity for this compatibility between the two tax systems is one reason why tax incentives are being used less as a means of encouragement of foreign investment. The means of establishing the amount of the income earned by the foreign investor when it is part of a transnational group of companies is also contentious. Even if there is no unitary tax, it is necessary to have an agreed accounting base for the business profits attributable to the activities of that enterprise and taxable as such.

In developing the answers to these issues, attention needs to be paid to two particular aspects that may cause confusion. These may be costly and time consuming, and adversely affect the position and standing of the investor. The first is the extent to which, in particular systems or countries, a peculiar and local definition has been given to some legal or accounting concept that is widely used elsewhere. Examples such as ''permanent establishment'', ''business expense'' or ''profit'' readily spring to mind. In this context, it is important to examine the methods and standards of accounting employed within the host country, as well as the skills of the accounting profession, otherwise the determination of taxable income may be such as to neutralise any tax benefits or incentives that may have been accorded to the investor. The requirements by taxing authorities of specific documentation and usual methods of substantiation of claims should also be clarified. Otherwise assumptions made by the investor and based on other systems and a lack of familiarity of local practice may cause needless difficulty. In all cases, access to local professional accounting skills, knowledge of local sources of authoritative information, and an effective and acceptable tax dispute resolution regime can do much to minimise the inevitable problems that arise in adapting an investment to a new tax regime.

General taxation

International tax treaties .... ¶35-001   Fiscal year .... ¶35-004

Existence of tax credits .... ¶35-002   Method of payment of tax

Procedures for resolving tax   liabilities .... ¶35-005

   disputes .... ¶35-003

¶35-001   INTERNATIONAL TAX TREATIES

To what international agreements relating to multilateral or bilateral tax is the host government a party?

¶35-002   EXISTENCE OF TAX CREDITS

Is there any provision in international agreements or in the domestic law of the country to enable credit to be given for tax paid, either inside or outside the country? Do any credits give recognition to exemptions from tax liability (tax-sparing credits)?

¶35-003 PROCEDURES FOR RESOLVING TAX DISPUTES

Are there any special institutions or procedures for the resolution of tax disputes?

¶35-004 FISCAL YEAR

Is there a general fiscal year? If not, how is each relevant fiscal year determined?

¶35-005 METHOD OF PAYMENT OF TAX LIABILITIES

Is there a generally prescribed mode of payment of tax liabilities? If not, how is the mode of payment determined?

Commercial and business profits

Taxation of commercial and business profits .... ¶35-101
Taxable activities and undertakings .... ¶35-102
Details of tax on companies ..... ¶35-103
Details of business profits tax .. ¶35-104
Taxation of executives .... ¶35-105

¶35-101 TAXATION OF COMMERCIAL AND BUSINESS PROFITS

What direct and indirect forms of taxation on commercial and business profits exist, such as tax on profits of companies or other forms of business organisation, business profits tax, income tax, etc.

¶35-102 TAXABLE ACTIVITIES AND UNDERTAKINGS

What activities or undertakings attract the liability to tax? In particular, is it the nationality, domicile or residence of a business organisation, whether conducted inside or outside the country? If nationality, domicile or residence are relevant, how are they determined?

¶35-103 DETAILS OF TAX ON COMPANIES

If there is a tax on companies or other business organisations:

(a) what is the rate of tax;

(b) does the tax law distinguish between private and public companies or between manufacturing companies, mining and petroleum companies, and service-providing companies such as banks; if so, in what way;

(c) is there any tax differential between companies controlled or owned by non-residents and companies controlled or owned by residents;

(d) is there any differential between businesses carried on by non-residents (e.g. a branch profits tax) and businesses carried on by residents;

(e) what are the prescribed requirements for keeping books, accounts and supporting documents;

(f) what accounts are required to be submitted to the revenue department;

(g) are these required to be certified by an auditor;

(h) what are the registration requirements in relation to companies under the tax law;

(i) is company tax levied on net profits;

(j) what depreciation allowances are there;

(k) is depreciation allowed in respect of:

    (i) plant and equipment;

    (ii) buildings;

(l) what is the tax treatment in respect of losses;

(m) can losses and credits be carried forward, and, if so, for what period;

(n) is there any provision for carry back of losses and credits and, if so, for what period;

(o) may any fiscal year be selected;

(p) when must an income tax return be filed;

(q) are companies required to withhold personal income tax in relation to salary and other compensation paid to their employees; how are ''fringe benefits'' taxed;

(r) if so, when must such returns be filed;

(s) is there any provision in the relevant tax law for constructive ownership (if, for example, more than 50% of the entire capital of the company is owned by one person or company);

(t) are there any tax consequences if profits are accumulated or redistributed or re-invested;

(u) are there any thin capitalisation rules?

¶35-104   DETAILS OF BUSINESS PROFITS TAX

If there is a business profits tax:

(a) how is it levied, and in particular is it levied on gross profits;

(b) upon what categories of business is such tax levied;

(c) upon whom is the tax imposed;

(d) what is the rate of tax;

(e) what are the registration requirements;

(f) what accounting records are required to be kept;

(g) how often must returns be filed;

(h) is there a business tax on imported goods;

(i) if so, how are goods valued for such purpose;

(j) is there any regulation of, or control over, the invoice value of goods in transactions between related companies or commercial organisations, either within or outside the host country?

¶35-105   TAXATION OF EXECUTIVES

Taxation of executives:

(a) what is the rate of tax;

(b) what is the basis of assessment; e.g., is it based on residence or is it based on the place where services are performed;

(c) what is a resident for the purposes of the relevant tax law;

(d) is it material that the salary is paid outside the host country;

(e) in what circumstances will income derived from outside the host country be subject to tax;

(f) what deductions are allowed in relation to personal income tax;

(g) is it necessary for an alien or non-resident to obtain a tax certificate and, if so, in what circumstances;

(h) is there any special taxation treatment given to visiting industrial experts?

Investment profits

Taxes on investment profits .... ¶35-201
Tax credits .... ¶35-202
Treatment of residents and
   non-residents .... ¶35-203
Approval of outward
   remittances .... ¶35-204
Form of outward remittances .. ¶35-205
Meaning of "royalty" .... ¶35-211
Must tax be deducted from
   investment profits? .... ¶35-212

¶35-201   TAXES ON INVESTMENT PROFITS

Are there any taxes payable on profits of the investment, e.g. on dividends, interest, and royalties, licence, rental, and other fees? If so, what attracts the liability to tax?

¶35-202   TAX CREDITS

Are any credits given for taxes previously paid on the profits from which the dividends were declared?

¶35-203   TREATMENT OF RESIDENTS AND NON-RESIDENTS

Is any distinction drawn between the taxation of payments to or by residents or non-residents?

¶35-204   APPROVAL OF OUTWARD REMITTANCES

Is approval of outward remittances dependent on accounting for or paying tax liabilities?

¶35-205   FORM OF OUTWARD REMITTANCES

Is an actual transfer of funds required for the incurring of any tax liability, or can a remittance be made merely by book entries?

¶35-211   MEANING OF "ROYALTY"

What is comprehended within local regulation or understanding of "royalty"?

¶35-212   MUST TAX BE DEDUCTED FROM INVESTMENT PROFITS?

Is it possible to provide by agreement between the parties that investment profits shall be paid or remitted without deduction of tax and that the party remitting shall be responsible for the payment of any tax on such profits?

Miscellaneous taxes

Miscellaneous taxes .... ¶35-301   Unitary tax .... ¶35-302

¶35-301   MISCELLANEOUS TAXES

Are there any other taxes or duties that will affect the business, its directors and employees? What attracts liability for that tax? What are the rates of tax? In particular, is there any:

(a) stamp duty;

(b) excise tax;

(c) local development tax;

(d) house and land tax;

(e) tax on sale of goods or services;

(f) value added tax;

(g) transport tax; or

(h) payroll or other employment tax?

¶35-302   UNITARY TAX

Does the host country or jurisdiction impose a unitary tax?

¶35-204

Capital gains tax

Method of taxing capital
gains .... ¶35-401
Roll-overs .... ¶35-402
Offset of capital losses against
revenue gains .... ¶35-403

Offset of revenue losses against
capital gains .... ¶35-404

¶35-401   METHOD OF TAXING CAPITAL GAINS

How are capital gains taxed?

¶35-402   ROLL-OVERS

What roll-overs apply?

¶35-403   OFFSET OF CAPITAL LOSSES AGAINST REVENUE GAINS

Can capital losses be offset against revenue gains?

¶35-404   OFFSET OF REVENUE LOSSES AGAINST CAPITAL GAINS

Can revenue losses be offset against capital gains?

Tax incentives

Tax relief for new
industries .... ¶35-501
Period of tax relief .... ¶35-502
Criteria affecting relief .... ¶35-503
Existence and nature of export
incentives .... ¶35-504
Applicability of export
allowances .... ¶35-505
Industries excluded from export
allowances .... ¶35-511

Export processing zones .... ¶35-512
Accelerated depreciation
allowance .... ¶35-513
Applicability of accelerated
depreciation allowance .... ¶35-514
Deductibility of expenses
incurred exploring export
opportunities .... ¶35-515

¶35-501   TAX RELIEF FOR NEW INDUSTRIES

Does the host country give special tax treatment to new industries? If so, what is the nature of such tax relief?

¶35-502　PERIOD OF TAX RELIEF

For what period does tax relief extend?

¶35-503　CRITERIA AFFECTING RELIEF

Does tax relief depend on:

(a) the product or industry sought to be established;

(b) the siting of the industry or factory; or

(c) the employment of local staff or contractors?

¶35-504　EXISTENCE AND NATURE OF EXPORT INCENTIVES

Are there any export incentives? If so, are they by way of allowance and is such allowance related to increases in exports, the level of wages paid or the amount of local materials used?

¶35-505　APPLICABILITY OF EXPORT ALLOWANCES

Are non-resident companies excluded from export allowances?

¶35-511　INDUSTRIES EXCLUDED FROM EXPORT ALLOWANCES

Are certain industries excluded from export allowances?

¶35-512　EXPORT PROCESSING ZONES

Are there export processing zones?

¶35-513　ACCELERATED DEPRECIATION ALLOWANCE

Is there any provision for accelerated depreciation allowance?

¶35-514　APPLICABILITY OF ACCELERATED DEPRECIATION ALLOWANCE

What qualifications are necessary to obtain such accelerated depreciation allowance?

¶35-515　DEDUCTIBILITY OF EXPENSES INCURRED EXPLORING EXPORT OPPORTUNITIES

Are there special deductions from taxable income for expenses incurred for the purpose of seeking opportunities for exports of products manufactured in the host country?

¶35-502

REGULATION OF BUSINESS — GENERAL AND SPECIAL (INCENTIVES AND DISINCENTIVES)

Introduction .... ¶45-000
Licensing and registration of business activities .... ¶45-001
Granting and nature of licence or registration .... ¶45-002
Incentive legislation .... ¶45-003
Disincentives or restrictions on certain
    business activities .... ¶45-004
Special regulation of foreign investment .... ¶45-101
Price and profit controls .... ¶45-201
Unfair trading practices and consumer protection .... ¶45-301

¶45-000 INTRODUCTION

This section explores the basic framework for business; first, in the context of the general economic and political organisation of all business activity, and second by an examination of the particular place of the non-national or non-resident within the general framework for all business. Although most foreign investment is, by its nature, long-term, this section examines the legal framework for business at the time that the investment is established — and assumes that these questions are being asked by a potential investor, rather than by an on-going business. More than in other areas, these are Lines of Inquiry which open up areas of investigation which will vary greatly from one country to another and, within countries, from time to time, as political and economic changes occur.

The fundamental questions relate to the nature of the economy — and examine where it lies on the spectrum between command and unregulated economies. They investigate rights of establishment across all sectors of activity. An examination of closed spheres of activity leads naturally to an examination of the place of the non-national. To what extent are there areas of economic or geographical activity closed or limited in access to foreigners? It is important to see whether basic protections of the business activity of the foreigner are in place. To what extent are non-nationals obliged to use particular vehicles of activity, or have approved partners, including government or government agencies? This also has a positive aspect, in that some spheres of activity might be encouraged through tax or other kinds of incentives or support. In so far as these relate to tax, reference should be made to the taxation section.

The micro-environment for business is also examined — so that the intervention and regulation of terms and practices of business must be considered. It may be institutional or transactional: it may be enforced administratively or judicially; it may relate generally to prices or to other terms. In many cases, the degree of regulation may differ significantly depending on whether the transactions are viewed as commercial or as consumer transactions. Although this is a common phenomenon, the ways in which the distinctions are drawn will vary greatly from one country to another; making assumptions about regulation can be very unwise.

In all cases of regulation, it is important that the criteria, the procedures, and the underlying policies should be transparent and exposed to scrutiny and review. The intending participant in business should be free to challenge decisions and procedures and the terms of regulation where they appear to depart from established laws and policies.

Finally, this section tackles the contentious and vast area of unfair trading practices, including monopolisation, market dominance, and transactional abuses. Although the theme of this section is the doing of business in a specified country, it also recognises that modern business, especially where it is part of a foreign investment, is of its nature transnational; and so, how far the legal regime for regulation of business within the host country extends to regulate business offshore is of critical importance.

¶45-001   LICENSING AND REGISTRATION OF BUSINESS ACTIVITIES

What requirements exist for the licensing and registration of business activities? Is there any supervision or control or any policy of regulation?

¶45-002   GRANTING AND NATURE OF LICENCE OR REGISTRATION

(a) Who grants the licence or registration?

(b) Is it available as of right (subject to a fee) or is it discretionary?

(c) If it is discretionary, on what principles is the discretion exercised?

¶45-003   INCENTIVE LEGISLATION

(a) Is there any pioneer industry or similar incentive legislation?

(b) If so, what type of incentives are offered to new businesses or the expansion of existing businesses?

(c) Are incentives tied to particular commodities or geographical areas or to export of the goods produced.

(d) Who administers the scheme?

(e) Are the incentives discretionary and, if so, on what principles is the discretion exercised?

¶45-004   DISINCENTIVES OR RESTRICTIONS ON CERTAIN BUSINESS ACTIVITIES

(a) Is there any economic legislation that imposes disincentives or restrictions on particular types of business activities?

(b) If so, what sort of disincentives or restrictions are imposed on the establishment of new businesses or the expansion of existing businesses?

¶45-001

(c) Are such disincentives or restrictions tied to particular commodities or particular localities?

(d) Who administers the scheme?

(e) Is the scheme discretionary and, if so, on what principles is the discretion exercised?

Special regulation of foreign investment

Special controls for foreign
  businesses or investors .... ¶45-101
Control of foreign investor ...... ¶45-102
Definition of foreign businessman
  or investor .... ¶45-103
Special regulations covering
  joint ventures .... ¶45-104
Incentives and disincentives for
  geographical areas .... ¶45-105

Incentives and disincentives for
  particular industries .... ¶45-111
Types of incentives, disincentives
  and controls .... ¶45-112
Nature of incentives, disincentives
  and controls .... ¶45-113
Guarantees against expropriation
  of assets .... ¶45-114
Retention of local consultant ... ¶45-115

¶45-101   SPECIAL CONTROLS FOR FOREIGN BUSINESSES OR INVESTORS

Are there any special laws, regulations or policies which create incentives or disincentives or impose particular controls on foreign businesses or investors?

¶45-102   CONTROL OF FOREIGN INVESTOR

What procedures exist for the supervision of control and management of the foreign investor?

¶45-103   DEFINITION OF FOREIGN BUSINESSMAN OR INVESTOR

What is the definition of a foreign businessman or investor?

¶45-104   SPECIAL REGULATIONS COVERING JOINT VENTURES

Are there any special regulations governing the establishment of joint ventures?

¶45-105   INCENTIVES AND DISINCENTIVES FOR GEOGRAPHICAL AREAS

Are any of the incentives and disincentives or special regulations referred to above limited to or excluded from particular geographical areas?

¶45-111　INCENTIVES AND DISINCENTIVES FOR PARTICULAR INDUSTRIES

Are any of the incentives, disincentives or special regulations referred to above limited to or excluded from particular industries? Do the incentives, disincentives or special regulations vary or cease depending on the stage of development of the business.

¶45-112　TYPES OF INCENTIVES, DISINCENTIVES AND CONTROLS

What types of incentives, disincentives or controls are available or imposed?

¶45-113　NATURE OF INCENTIVES, DISINCENTIVES AND CONTROLS

If any such incentives, disincentives or controls are available or imposed:

(a) who administers them;

(b) are they discretionary;

(c) if so, on what principles is the discretion exercised;

(d) how far is the potential tax liability of the venture a factor in the exercise of the discretion;

(e) can the legislation or regulation be changed and, if so, how;

(f) can the legislation or regulation be changed with retroactive effect; and

(g) are any incentives, disincentives or controls linked to other areas of general government economic policy?

¶45-114　GUARANTEES AGAINST EXPROPRIATION OF ASSETS

To what extent can the foreign investor obtain a guarantee from the government against expropriation of its assets?

¶45-115　RETENTION OF LOCAL CONSULTANT

Should a local consultant be retained for advice on local customs and practices?

Price and profit controls

Commodities subject to price
control .... ¶45-201
Price control body .... ¶45-202
Exemptions from price
control .... ¶45-203
Special restrictions for certain
companies .... ¶45-204

Right of government authority
to share in profits .... ¶45-205
Criteria for application of
controls .... ¶45-206

¶45-201   COMMODITIES SUBJECT TO PRICE CONTROL

Are the prices of all or any commodities or services subject to price control, and are any commodities subject to a maximum price? Are the profits or dividends of any enterprise subject to control?

¶45-202   PRICE CONTROL BODY

What body exercises price control and how is such a body composed?

¶45-203   EXEMPTIONS FROM PRICE CONTROL

Is it possible to obtain exemption from price control or to obtain authorisations for restrictive practices relating to prices?

¶45-204   SPECIAL RESTRICTIONS FOR CERTAIN COMPANIES

Are there any restrictions which apply only to certain companies or to non-resident companies?

¶45-205   RIGHT OF GOVERNMENT AUTHORITY TO SHARE IN PROFITS

Does any government authority have the right to participate in profits?

¶45-206   CRITERIA FOR APPLICATION OF CONTROLS

What are the criteria used for the application of any such controls and what are the penalties for infringement?

Unfair trading practices and consumer protection

Consumer protection laws ...... ¶45-301
General principles governing
   injuries .... ¶45-302
Prohibition or regulation of
   restraint of trade
   contracts .... ¶45-303
Licences under statutory
   monopolies .... ¶45-304

Special provisions relating to
   business activities of
   non-residents .... ¶45-305
Laws governing advertising and
   promotion of products .... ¶45-306
Review of "unfair" contracts .. ¶45-307

¶45-301   CONSUMER PROTECTION LAWS

(a) Are there any consumer protection laws?

(b) In particular, are there any product safety or product information standards?

(c) Are there any laws prohibiting the exclusion of warranties by contract or implying such warranties?

¶45-302   GENERAL PRINCIPLES GOVERNING INJURIES

What are the general principles governing products or other injury to persons or property? What standard of care is required?

¶45-303   PROHIBITION OR REGULATION OF RESTRAINT OF TRADE CONTRACTS

(a) Are there any laws prohibiting or regulating contracts, arrangements, understandings and combinations (collectively referred to as "contracts") in restraint of trade or commerce?

(b) In particular, what controls or regulations exist over contracts relating to:

   (i) exclusive dealing;

   (ii) monopolisation;

   (iii) mergers;

   (iv) franchises;

   (v) price discrimination; and

   (vi) resale price maintenance?

(c) What body exercises control, and how is it composed?

(d) What are the penalties or other sanctions for non-compliance? Who is entitled to enforce these laws?

(e) Are such contracts valid and enforceable?

(f) Is it possible to obtain advance authorisations or clearances for such contracts?

¶45-301

(g) To what extent do these laws have extra-territorial effect? In particular, do they apply to contracts made or performed outside the host country, but having an effect in that country?

¶45-304 LICENCES UNDER STATUTORY MONOPOLIES

Are licences under statutory monopolies (copyright, patents, designs and trademarks) recognised as exceptions to the laws regulating trade practices and antitrust?

¶45-305 SPECIAL PROVISIONS RELATING TO BUSINESS ACTIVITIES OF NON-RESIDENTS

Are there any special provisions dealing with the business activities of non-residents?

¶45-306 LAWS GOVERNING ADVERTISING AND PROMOTION OF PRODUCTS

Are there any laws or regulations which govern advertising or promotional statements about products?

¶45-307 REVIEW OF "UNFAIR" CONTRACTS

Are there any laws which allow courts or government agencies to review contracts or arrangements which are alleged to be "unfair" or "unconscionable".

IMPORT AND EXPORT CONTROLS

Introduction .... ¶50-000
Restrictions on import of goods .... ¶50-001
Special requirements for importers .... ¶50-002
Restrictions on export of goods .... ¶50-003
Regulation of export and import licences .... ¶50-004
Special restrictions relating to foreign control
     of business .... ¶50-005
Major objectives of host country .... ¶50-011
Rates of customs duties .... ¶50-012
Taxes .... ¶50-013
Tariff agreements .... ¶50-014
Concessional entry of goods .... ¶50-015
Free trade zones .... ¶50-021
Labelling and packaging requirements .... ¶50-022
International treaties .... ¶50-023
Penalties and additional taxes .... ¶50-024
Anti-dumping and countervailing duties .... ¶50-025
Power to detain goods .... ¶50-031
When is duty or tax payable? .... ¶50-032

¶50-000 INTRODUCTION

Most investment is trade-related. This section examines the nature and extent of restrictions on the movement of goods, whether it is the importation of equipment or goods for use in the investment, or the export of the product of the investment. In some cases, import-export may be a means of earning hard currency so as to support the other activities of the investment within the domestic markets of the country.

Many countries have used the ability to control exports by licensing procedures as a lever to ensure adherence to a range of policies, not all of which are related to trade. Similarly, a host country may guarantee immunity from export and import controls through the availability of export-processing zones where preferential regimes are established. This is a common and valuable incentive for businesses dependent on overseas markets for sources of raw material.

For these reasons, the rules of the host country on the movement of goods are of fundamental importance. The relation of local or domestic laws to the international trading system, with the GATT at its apex, is of prime importance to investors. This section sets out to explore questions through the whole import-export regime of the host country.

Issues which must be addressed include the types of regulation in use, the policies which lie behind the controls, and the liabilities which may be incurred for any breach of the regulations. The mechanism of the tariff, tariff levels, the existence of preferential tariffs for developing or other countries, and the conformity of local to international standards of customs classification and valuations are all examined.

The nature and extent of the use of quotas and other quantitative controls are explored. It is also necessary to look at trade barriers which are not at the borders, and consider non-tariff barriers, including labelling and anti-monopoly laws and other controls. Membership of GATT is forcing the abandonment of quantitative controls and the reduction and the progressive elimination of tariffs. To the extent that the host country has adopted the relevant codes, there are international obligations in relation to ensuring freedom from dumping and subsidies. To an increasing extent in world trade protectionism, the granting of subsidies, and predatory dumping, are political and economic issues of great controversy. Against that background, the policies and structure of anti-dumping mechanisms and the imposition of countervailing duties are significant for the investor and government alike, not only for the government of the host country, but also for that of the investor's country.

¶50-001 RESTRICTIONS ON IMPORT OF GOODS

What restrictions are there on the import of goods? What type of prohibitions are applicable — absolute, conditional or temporary — and what consequences follow? In particular, is the import of any goods prohibited, or prohibited from certain countries, or are quotas imposed or import licences, permits or approvals required?

¶50-002 SPECIAL REQUIREMENTS FOR IMPORTERS

Are there any other special requirements, such as the registration of importers; use of locally based trading agents or trading houses; establishment of local presence; the lodging of deposits in respect of imports or covering imports by letter of credit; or other financing arrangement?

¶50-003 RESTRICTIONS ON EXPORT OF GOODS

What restrictions are there on the export of goods? In particular, is the export of any goods prohibited, or prohibited to certain countries, or are export licences, permits or approvals required, or must they be covered by letters of credit or other financing arrangements?

¶50-004 REGULATION OF EXPORT AND IMPORT LICENCES

Who grants export and import licences, permits or approvals? Are they available as of right (subject to a fee) or are they discretionary? If they are discretionary, on what principle is the discretion exercised? Are the licences transferable? If a licence, permit or approval is refused, is there an appeal right? Will the administering authority issue the required permits, licences or approvals after the goods have been imported? If so, in what circumstances?

¶50-001

¶50-005   SPECIAL RESTRICTIONS RELATING TO FOREIGN CONTROL OF BUSINESS

Are there any special restrictions on foreign-controlled export or import businesses? Is any duty imposed by law or otherwise upon importers or exporters if an agent acts negligently or fraudulently?

¶50-011   MAJOR OBJECTIVES OF HOST COUNTRY

What are the major objectives which the host country has sought to attain in recent years through its import and export control policies? Have there been any important recent changes in those policies?

¶50-012   RATES OF CUSTOMS DUTIES

What are the rates of customs duties on the import of goods? Are preferences granted in respect of imports from certain countries? What exemptions are there either generally or where goods are imported for particular purposes?

¶50-013   TAXES

Are there any other taxes in respect of exports or imports?

¶50-014   TARIFF AGREEMENTS

Do exports from the host country enjoy special tariff treatment granted by any other and, if so, what countries?

¶50-015   CONCESSIONAL ENTRY OF GOODS

Is by-law entry or concessional entry of goods available so as to reduce in whole or in part the amount of customs duty or tax which is payable?

¶50-021   FREE TRADE ZONES

Are there any free trade zones? Are there any other incentives available for trade? What are the details of those incentives, including nature, eligibility requirements, duration and administering authorities?

¶50-022   LABELLING AND PACKAGING REQUIREMENTS

Are there any special requirements concerning labelling, packaging and other standards?

¶50-023 INTERNATIONAL TREATIES

What international treaties, conventions, protocols or arrangements are relevant to import and export in the host country?

¶50-024 PENALTIES AND ADDITIONAL TAXES

What penalties or additional taxes or duties may be levied if the host code is breached by importers or exporters? Is there any requirement that commercial trading and other documents be retained by importers, exporters or the persons engaging in trade? If so, where and for what length of time? What powers may the administering authorities exercise for the purpose of conducting inquiries — search, seizure, answering questions on oath or otherwise?

¶50-025 ANTI-DUMPING AND COUNTERVAILING DUTIES

Are there any special requirements dealing with anti-dumping and countervailing duties?

¶50-031 POWER TO DETAIN GOODS

Does the administering authority have power to detain goods or otherwise delay importations and clearances? If so, on what grounds will the powers be exercised and what appeal rights are available?

¶50-032 WHEN IS DUTY OR TAX PAYABLE?

At what time is customs duty or other tax payable? Is it at the point of importation, customs clearance or some other time? Can payment be deferred through bonding or storing in a licensed warehouse or can duties and taxes be paid on a periodic basis?

EXCHANGE CONTROL —
THE MOVEMENT OF MONEY

Introduction .... ¶55-000
Which laws apply to exchange control? .... ¶55-001
Who administers exchange control? .... ¶55-002
Major objectives of exchange control policies .... ¶55-003
Application of exchange control laws to
     various countries .... ¶55-004
Repatriation of capital .... ¶55-005
Remittance of dividends, etc. .... ¶55-011
Limit on amount of local currency and foreign
     currency to remit out of host country .... ¶55-012
Restrictions on remittance of currency .... ¶55-013
Currency to be used for loans .... ¶55-014
Method of fixing exchange rate of host
     country's currency .... ¶55-015
Differing rates of exchange for host
     country's currency .... ¶55-021
Transactions requiring approval from
     exchange control authorities .... ¶55-022
Tests for distinguishing residents from non-residents .. ¶55-023
Distinctions between foreign-controlled companies
     incorporated inside or out of the host country ...... ¶55-024
Effect of local participation on exchange controls ...... ¶55-025
Exchange control exemptions .... ¶55-031
Remittance from host country of personal savings and
     pension fund contributions by expatriate
     personnel .... ¶55-032
Exchange control formalities .... ¶55-033
Consequences of breach of exchange control law ...... ¶55-034
Forward market for foreign exchange .... ¶55-035
Restrictions on repatriation of capital during
     continuation of investment incentives .... ¶55-041
Taxation considerations in respect of
     exchange control regulations .... ¶55-042

¶55-000   INTRODUCTION

This section examines the structure, purposes, and procedures of exchange control. Exchange control is an area of activity in which the domestic and international regulation of currency transactions are linked if the host country is a member of the International Monetary Fund and is bound by the Bretton Woods Agreement. In practical terms, the relation of local and international capital markets is both affected and determined by the structure of exchange control. Exchange control usually reflects immediately the current economic policy objectives of government generally and in relation to transnational business activities in the host country.

The first questions therefore examine the fundamental questions of structure and procedure and its relation to government policy and objectives. The nature of the currency and whether it is freely convertible will dictate both the long-term issues of repatriation of capital and remittance of profit, and also the routine transactions of sale, loan and guarantee in relation to the investment. If the foreign exchange market is not a government monopoly, the scope for participation in that market and its range of activities should be investigated.

The basic procedures of exchange control administration must also be examined. The extent to which broad strategies of reporting (*ad hoc* or regularly) or approval (prior or subsequent) of transactions is required affects directly the manner of doing business on a regular basis.

Where approvals are required or foreign exchange is tightly controlled, the consequences of an inability to obtain approvals or exchange again will affect routine business transactions, and it is important that the allocation of this risk should be constantly borne in mind. Similarly, the effects of any breach of the law should be carefully considered.

The capacity to keep accounts in local and overseas currency inside and outside the country also has substantial implications for the keeping of accounts for taxation purposes, the planning of tax strategy for the investor, and the host country's concern to eliminate tax avoidance and to maximise the benefits of foreign investment. In some countries, the exchange control law and practice differs depending on the nationality or residence of the participants in the transaction. The scope of activities of the non-national or resident subject to regulation is usually greater, and reference should also be made to the effect of regulation through exchange control on the general aspects of regulation of business. Sometimes, exemptions or particular benefits will be part of an incentive package for the investor, either as a matter of the application of the general law or as a matter of individual negotiation. Most of the problems encountered by the investor, but not always all the advantages, will be shared by non-nationals employed by the investor in the host country, who wish to deal in foreign exchange, in particular to deal with inward and outward remittance of funds.

¶55-001   WHICH LAWS APPLY TO EXCHANGE CONTROL?

Which laws of the host country apply to exchange control? ("Exchange control" should be read to include all the matters referred to in this section.)

¶55-002   WHO ADMINISTERS EXCHANGE CONTROL?

Which authority or authorities administer exchange control? What discretionary powers do they have, and on what principles do they exercise them? In particular, are issues of tax avoidance or minimisation relevant in the exercise of the discretion?

¶55-001

¶55-003 MAJOR OBJECTIVES OF EXCHANGE CONTROL POLICIES

What are the major objectives which the host country has sought to attain in recent years through its exchange control policies? Have there been any important recent changes in those policies?

¶55-004 APPLICATION OF EXCHANGE CONTROL LAWS TO VARIOUS COUNTRIES

Do the exchange control laws apply uniformly in relation to all countries outside the host country?

¶55-005 REPATRIATION OF CAPITAL

What is the attitude of the host country to repatriation of capital? Is advance approval given or, if it is not, is repatriation of capital allowed in practice? Are any conditions attached to permissions to repatriate? In the event of liquidation of the enterprise, can realisation of proceeds be remitted out of the host country?

¶55-011 REMITTANCE OF DIVIDENDS, ETC.

What is the attitude of the host country to the remittance of dividends, branch profits, interest, royalties, advisory fees, licence fees, management fees, machine rental and amounts payable under guarantee?

¶55-012 LIMIT ON AMOUNT OF LOCAL CURRENCY AND FOREIGN CURRENCY TO REMIT OUT OF HOST COUNTRY

What controls are there on the enterprise obtaining in the host country, and are there any likely limits on its ability to obtain:

(a) currency of the host country; and

(b) foreign currencies to remit out of the host country?

¶55-013 RESTRICTIONS ON REMITTANCE OF CURRENCY

Are there any restrictions on the persons to whom, places to which, or purposes for which currency may be remitted?

¶55-014 CURRENCY TO BE USED FOR LOANS

Is there any restriction on loans being made in a currency other than a currency of the host country?

¶55-015 METHOD OF FIXING EXCHANGE RATE OF HOST COUNTRY'S CURRENCY

How is the exchange rate of the currency of the host country fixed in relation to other currencies? Is it fixed in relation to a particular currency or currencies? Does it float or is it allowed to fluctuate within certain margins? Has the exchange rate been stable and, if not, what has been the pattern over recent years? Under what authority can rates of exchange be varied?

¶55-021 DIFFERING RATES OF EXCHANGE FOR HOST COUNTRY'S CURRENCY

(a) Does the host country use more than one rate of exchange? If so, what rates of exchange apply:

    (i) to bringing investments or borrowings into the host country;

    (ii) to remitting profits;

    (iii) to imports and exports of various classes of goods; and

    (iv) to other transactions?

(b) Is there any difference in exchange rates according to the class or classes of person involved?

¶55-022 TRANSACTIONS REQUIRING APPROVAL FROM EXCHANGE CONTROL AUTHORITIES

What types of transactions require approval by the exchange control authorities? In particular:

(a) Does the allotment or transfer of shares to a non-resident or the despatch of share certificates out of the host country require approval?

(b) Do the exchange control authorities control the debiting and crediting of bank accounts of non-residents?

(c) Are inter-company accounts allowed with non-resident parent or associated companies to minimise the necessity for transfers of funds? If so, what transactions may be entered in these accounts and what restrictions are there?

(d) What restrictions are there on contracts of various kinds between the enterprise and residents and non-residents, or between non-residents where the transactions are connected with the host country?

(e) Are there any restrictions on borrowing or otherwise raising capital inside or from outside the host country? What are the rates of interest on bank overdraft and other loans?

¶55-023 TESTS FOR DISTINGUISHING RESIDENTS FROM NON-RESIDENTS

What are the tests for distinguishing residents and non-residents for exchange control purposes?

¶55-024 DISTINCTIONS BETWEEN FOREIGN-CONTROLLED COMPANIES INCORPORATED INSIDE OR OUT OF THE HOST COUNTRY

What distinctions are made for exchange control purposes between a foreign-controlled company incorporated in the host country and a company incorporated outside the host country?

¶55-025 EFFECT OF LOCAL PARTICIPATION ON EXCHANGE CONTROLS

Do exchange controls vary according to the extent of local participation in the enterprise?

¶55-031 EXCHANGE CONTROL EXEMPTIONS

Are special exchange control exemptions available for particular types of investments?

¶55-032 REMITTANCE FROM HOST COUNTRY OF PERSONAL SAVINGS AND PENSION FUND CONTRIBUTIONS BY EXPATRIATE PERSONNEL

What is the attitude of the host country to the remittance out of the host country of personal savings and contributions to pension and superannuation funds by expatriate personnel of the enterprise and of contributions to such funds by the enterprise for the benefit of expatriate personnel? What limits are there on local or foreign currency which may be taken into or out of the host country by employees of the enterprise or their families?

¶55-033 EXCHANGE CONTROL FORMALITIES

What general formalities must be complied with in relation to exchange control?

¶55-034 CONSEQUENCES OF BREACH OF EXCHANGE CONTROL LAW

What are the consequences of breaches of the exchange control laws? What penalties are there? Are contracts or other transactions invalidated if there is failure to obtain exchange control approval?

¶55-035   FORWARD MARKET FOR FOREIGN EXCHANGE

Is there a forward market for foreign exchange?

¶55-041   RESTRICTIONS ON REPATRIATION OF CAPITAL DURING CONTINUATION OF INVESTMENT INCENTIVES

Is there any restriction on the ability to repatriate capital or remit profits during the continuation of investment incentives?

¶55-042   TAXATION CONSIDERATIONS IN RESPECT OF EXCHANGE CONTROL REGULATIONS

Are taxation considerations relevant to the administration of the exchange control regulations?

LABOUR AND NATIONALITY LAWS

Introduction .... ¶60-000
Effect of nationality, citizenship and race on
    labour laws .... ¶60-001
Basis of nationality law .... ¶60-002
Nature of relationship between employer and
    employee .... ¶60-003
Conditions guaranteed to employees .... ¶60-004
Control of wages and hours .... ¶60-005
Settlement of industrial disputes .... ¶60-011
Parameters of legal system of industrial
    dispute settlement .... ¶60-012
Customary method of settling industrial disputes .... ¶60-013
Status and make-up of trade unions .... ¶60-014
Liabilities and privileges of trade unions................. ¶60-015
Institutional links between government,
    trade unions and employer organisations .... ¶60-021
Right to strike or lock out .... ¶60-022
Administration of labour law .... ¶60-023
Legislative control of labour law .... ¶60-024
Obligations of purchaser to employees .... ¶60-025
Additional obligations of employers .... ¶60-031
Special application of labour laws to foreigners .... ¶60-032
Work permits or visas for foreign workers,
    executives and management .... ¶60-033
Required balance of race or nationality .... ¶60-034
International Labour Organisation conventions .... ¶60-035

¶60-000 INTRODUCTION

This section examines the scope of labour law and labour relations and the institutions that are significant in its organisation. It looks first to review the area generally, and then to see whether any special regime has been developed for those involved in the establishment or operation of a foreign investment. In many countries, there may be a marked contrast between the unregulated general aspects of labour law and labour relations, and the control that is exercised in relation to a foreign employer. Some of these concerns are those of the foreign investor who may seek conditions to which it is accustomed in its home country, especially in relation to negotiation of terms and conditions of employment. Some are public concerns of government, for, in many cases, the transfer of skills to nationals employed by foreign investors is one of the primary reasons for seeking the activity of the foreign investor. The need for the foreign investor may determine the extent to which that investment might seek special privileges and exemptions, for example in relation to the freedom to bring in foreign employees to work within the investment; and to settle the terms of their employment, not only in relation to the employer, but more generally their rights and privileges within the country. There are marked overlaps here with other sections, notably taxation, the regulation of business, and exchange control.

The organisational structure of labour law and labour relations is significant. The Lines of Inquiry call for not merely a statement of the formal structure, but also for an evaluation of its practical importance in the face of the customary practice and legal culture of employer-employee relations, and relations between them and government. This is relevant particularly to the resolution of disputes, as well as to more general aspects of terms and conditions of employment. The extent to which these are governed by general provisions or by particular regimes is important. The criteria for particular regimes may include the race or nationality of the employee and the investor-employer and the sector of the economy in which the enterprise operates. Although the issue of nationality is important throughout the whole of the investment process, it is often of particular significance in employment, and this is why it receives specific attention in this section.

The place of trade unions calls for special examination within this framework. It is one area where assumptions imported by the investor from its home country might warrant careful reassessment.

The extent to which any of these matters are resolved solely by internal laws and policies and ideologies or by the necessity to adhere to international conventions such as those of the International Labour Organisation or other bilateral agreements is significant. It is part of a larger investigation of the general state of maturity of the labour law of the host country and its particular relation to the aims and objectives of foreign investment in general and any enterprise in particular.

¶60-001   EFFECT OF NATIONALITY, CITIZENSHIP AND RACE ON LABOUR LAWS

Are laws relating to nationality, citizenship and race of either natural or juristic persons relevant to carrying on business or to the application of general labour laws?

¶60-002   BASIS OF NATIONALITY LAW

(a) What is the general basis of the nationality law: birth, blood or registration? Is naturalisation or adoption possible?

(b) In what circumstances will nationality be lost?

(c) Is dual nationality possible?

¶60-003   NATURE OF RELATIONSHIP BETWEEN EMPLOYER AND EMPLOYEE

What is the nature of the legal relationship between employer and employee?

¶60-001

¶60-004 CONDITIONS GUARANTEED TO EMPLOYEES

What legal guarantees are afforded to employees: minimum wage, compensation for injury at work, sick leave, annual leave, severance pay?

¶60-005 CONTROL OF WAGES AND HOURS

To what extent are wages and hours the subject of control, and by whom is this control exercised?

¶60-011 SETTLEMENT OF INDUSTRIAL DISPUTES

What legal measures are available to assist in the settlement of industrial disputes? Is the system one of mediation, conciliation and arbitration, collective bargaining, or a combination of these?

¶60-012 PARAMETERS OF LEGAL SYSTEM OF INDUSTRIAL DISPUTE SETTLEMENT

What are the parameters of the legal system of industrial dispute settlement — is there conciliation and arbitration and/or collective bargaining over all aspects of the employment relationship, or are some areas excluded?

¶60-013 CUSTOMARY METHOD OF SETTLING INDUSTRIAL DISPUTES

Aside from the formal legal rules, what means are customarily used for the settlement of industrial disputes?

¶60-014 STATUS AND MAKE-UP OF TRADE UNIONS

What is the legal status of trade unions and employer organisations? Are such organisations developed along industry or craft lines?

¶60-015 LIABILITIES AND PRIVILEGES OF TRADE UNIONS

What are the possible liabilities of such organisations? Do they have any exemptions of privileges, such as immunity for legal action in industrial disputes?

¶60-021 INSTITUTIONAL LINKS BETWEEN GOVERNMENT, TRADE UNIONS AND EMPLOYER ORGANISATIONS

What are the institutional links and controls between government and trade unions and employer organisations?

¶60-022 RIGHT TO STRIKE OR LOCK OUT

Is there any restriction on the right to strike or to lock out employees?

¶60-023   ADMINISTRATION OF LABOUR LAW

What organisations or agencies are set up to supervise and administer the labour law of the country? Is there a Ministry of Labour and, if so, what is its position in the administrative hierarchy?

¶60-024   LEGISLATIVE CONTROL OF LABOUR LAW

Generally, to what extent is labour law the subject of legislative, judicial or administrative control? To what extent is this subject to scrutiny by government or labour agencies?

¶60-025   OBLIGATIONS OF PURCHASER TO EMPLOYEES

What are the obligations of a purchaser of a business to the existing employees in that business who are offered or not offered new employment by the purchaser?

¶60-031   ADDITIONAL OBLIGATIONS OF EMPLOYERS

What other obligations do employers have to their employees not otherwise covered by the foregoing paragraphs?

¶60-032   SPECIAL APPLICATION OF LABOUR LAWS TO FOREIGNERS

To what extent are foreign investors in a special position with relation to any application of the law relating to nationality or to labour laws? Are there any particular requirements for training schemes for local employees?

¶60-033   WORK PERMITS OR VISAS FOR FOREIGN WORKERS, EXECUTIVES AND MANAGEMENT

What is the law relating to work permits or visas for foreign workers or for foreign executives or management? Are there any time limits? Can they be negotiated with the relevant authority?

¶60-034   REQUIRED BALANCE OF RACE OR NATIONALITY

Is a foreign investor required to maintain any balance of race or nationality at all levels of employment, including management?

¶60-035   INTERNATIONAL LABOUR ORGANISATION CONVENTIONS

Has the country ratified and put into effect any conventions of the International Labour Organisation (ILO)?

¶60-023

Intellectual Property

International agreements .... ¶65-001

Domestic legislation .... ¶65-002

Copyright .... ¶65-003

Trademarks .... ¶65-004

Patents .... ¶65-005

Industrial designs .... ¶65-011

Trade secrets .... ¶65-012

Circuit layouts .... ¶65-013

Plant varieties .... ¶65-014

Unfair competition .... ¶65-015

Geographical indications .... ¶65-018

Registration procedures .... ¶65-021

Transfers and licensing agreements .... ¶65-022

Compulsory licenses .... ¶65-023

Table of fees .... ¶65-024

Disadvantages for non-residents .... ¶65-025

Enforcement .... ¶65-031

¶65-001   INTERNATIONAL AGREEMENTS

To which international agreements relating to industrial property or the repression of unfair competition is the host government a party?

¶65-002   DOMESTIC LEGISLATION

What domestic legislation has been enacted pursuant to treaty obligations? What existing legislation is available for the protection of intellectual property? What industrial property is protected? For example, is there separate legislation covering trademarks, patents, copyright, trade names, trade secrets, industrial designs, computer software, silicon chips, character merchandising? To what extent is industrial property protected by non-statutory general law, eg passing off? What are the new bills and amendments (if any) at the time of writing?

¶65-003   COPYRIGHT

What kinds of works are copyrightable? What are the legal rights of the copyright holder/owner and what kind of protection is available? Are there any other ownership issues in the jurisdiction — for example, the government and the creator's rights to ownership or use. What is the duration of copyright protection? How long does the protection continue and can it be extended for an additional period? What are the remedies available and the penalties for infringement of copyright?

¶65-004   TRADEMARKS

What are the guidelines for registrable/unregistrable trademarks? To what extent are labelling requirements affected by trademarks? What is the duration of trademark protection? How long does the protection continue and can it be extended for an additional period? What are the remedies available and the penalties for infringement of trademark?

¶65-005   PATENTS

What kinds of inventions are patentable? Are there any circumstances that may allow the postponement, non-registration, acquisition or use without permission of patents? For example, the government may by presidential decree postpone the registration of a patent in the interest of public health or national development. What are the rights of prior inventors and patent-holders? To what extent are labelling requirements affected by patents? What is the duration of patent protection? What are the remedies available and the penalties for infringement of patent?

¶65-011   INDUSTRIAL DESIGNS

What is the definition of an "industrial design"? What are the rights of the design owner and are there any exceptions to the rule? What is the duration of protection, how long does the protection continue and can it be extended for an additional period? What are the remedies available and the penalties for infringement of industrial design?

¶65-012   TRADE SECRETS

What kinds of information are considered "trade secrets" and is there any legislation protecting trade secrets? What are the rights of the trade secret owner? What are the remedies available and the penalties for infringement of trade secret?

¶65-013   CIRCUIT LAYOUTS

What are the rights of the circuit layout holder? What is the duration of circuit layout protection? How long does the protection continue and can it be extended for an additional period? What are the remedies available and the penalties for infringement of circuit layout?

¶65-014 PLANT VARIETIES

Is there any protection for plant varieties in the jurisdiction? If there is none, how does the protection of plant varieties relate to the international agreement(s) that the jurisdiction country is a party?

¶65-015 UNFAIR COMPETITION

Are there any laws relating to unfair competition, monopolisation, passing off, etc which may affect the rights in relation to industrial property?

¶65-018 GEOGRAPHICAL INDICATIONS

Is the country party to the 1994 Agreement on Trade-Related Aspects of Intellectual Property Rights? What protection does geographical indications offer in the country? What is the minimum amount of protection? How are protection rights affected if a geographical indication is not registered? For how long is the protection period? Are there any exceptions to the protection afforded by geographical indications in the country?

¶65-021 REGISTRATION PROCEDURES

Do all rights require registration in order to be adequately protected? To the extent that registration is optional, what additional rights does registration give? Does an owner of industrial property outside the country have any rights against a person who has registered similar industrial property in the country? Is there a profession of patent attorneys or similar body, or do legal attorneys handle industrial property matters?

What are the procedures for registration or whatever other means are necessary for obtaining protection?

¶65-022 TRANSFERS AND LICENSING AGREEMENTS

How are intellectual property rights transferred and are any guarantees required? For instance, the transfer of trademark rights may require a guarantee that the quality of services will be continued.

Does the registered or other owner of industrial property have the right to license or assign rights in respect of that property? Is government approval required for licensing agreements? What limitations are there on assignment and licensing of industrial property rights? Do owners or originators of industrial property in other countries have any special rights and if so, what is the procedure for taking advantage of these rights? Is there a profession of patent attorneys or similar body, or do legal attorneys handle industrial property matters?

¶65-023 COMPULSORY LICENSES

When and how are compulsory licences granted? Is it necessary to obtain government approval for licensing know-how?

¶65-024   TABLE OF FEES

What are the expenses of:

- obtaining protection; and
- maintaining that protection?

¶65-025   DISADVANTAGES FOR NON-RESIDENTS

Is a non-resident at a disadvantage over a resident in registering and protecting property? Is it necessary or desirable to have an agent in the country or to be using the industrial property in question in the country?

¶65-031   ENFORCEMENT

What kind of enforcement (eg injunctions, damages, account of profits, etc) are available? In practice, how effective is the enforcement of industrial property protection in the jurisdiction?

SETTLEMENT OF DISPUTES

Introduction .... ¶70-000
Basis of courts' jurisdiction .... ¶70-001
Status of foreign companies .... ¶70-002
Civil procedure for foreign companies .... ¶70-003
Rules of civil procedure and evidence .... ¶70-004
Service and execution of process outside jurisdiction .. ¶70-005
Availability of interlocutory relief .... ¶70-011
Collection of evidence outside the jurisdiction .... ¶70-012
Choice of applicable law .... ¶70-013
Choice of forum .... ¶70-014
Costs and delay associated with litigation .... ¶70-015
Security for costs .... ¶70-021
Language of courts .... ¶70-022
Enforcement and execution of judgments .... ¶70-023
Recognition of foreign judgments .... ¶70-024
Status of foreign lawyers .... ¶70-025
Special procedures for certain disputes .... ¶70-031
Arbitration .... ¶70-101
Conciliation, mediation and alternative
        dispute resolution .... ¶70-201
Framework for dispute resolution .... ¶70-301
Position of government .... ¶70-401

¶70-000   INTRODUCTION

Few issues are more important to the investor than the anticipation of future disputes and the possible means of their resolution. The foreign investor needs to know very clearly what institutions are available in the host country for dispute resolution and the processes which are followed in those institutions. The identification, even as a group, of those who will resolve the disputes is crucial. The investor also needs to know which rules would govern the choice of institution and the procedural and substantive law which would be applied within the chosen institution. All of these determine the acceptability of these regimes. If they are not acceptable, then, to the extent that this is feasible, the search for an alternative means and venue of settlement will begin. This section sets out to answer those questions.

The first part of the section deals with the courts and examines such issues as the basis upon which courts will accept jurisdiction, the procedural rules which are applied in the courts, the rules for bringing parties before the courts, and the language which will be employed in the courts, which is of vital importance, since working in a foreign language may be a distinct handicap. The costs of litigation are also of primary relevance.

Finally, the section examines the processes for enforcing foreign judgments within the host country if it is possible to obtain a judgment elsewhere and pursue a defendant to the host country.

The second part asks similar questions in relation to the arbitration process, which has become the major commercial alternative to litigation. Modern contracts tend to nominate arbitration as the preferred dispute resolution process and so it is important to discover whether the host country has a readily available arbitration system. It is also important to know whether the host country has linked itself to the evolving international regime for arbitration and has agreed to abide by the UNCITRAL model arbitration law, the UNCITRAL model arbitration rules, and the New York Convention for the Recognition and Enforcement of Foreign Arbitral Awards. This section sets out to explore those issues. The section also enquires whether there are established arbitral institutions which may offer the foreign investor competent arbitrators and competent legal assistance. Matters such as confidentiality, cost, speed, and finality, are all basic to the arbitration process and are explored through the domestic rules of the host country.

A third part deals with the rapidly evolving processes of alternative dispute resolution. Since the countries of Asia have been renowned for their reluctance to resort to litigation in commercial matters, this section focuses on alternative processes and institutions which might be available to foreign investors. The processes of conciliation and mediation are of particular concern.

More general issues which are relevant to these three major alternatives, litigation, arbitration, and alternative dispute resolution, relate to the importance of international agreements in the host country, the availability and quality of third parties who may assist in dispute resolution, and the availability and quality of domestic legal assistance. Foreign investors are also usually most interested in knowing whether they can bring with them legal assistance from their home country and so the host country rules in this area are analysed in this section.

Finally, the foreign investor may often find itself in conflict with the host government and so it is important to know in advance whether the government is subject to the law and legal institutions in its own area. In particular, membership of the host country of the International Centre for the Settlement of Investment Disputes (ICSID) under the auspices of the World Bank will give access to an external venue for dispute resolution agreed in advance of any dispute, frequently as a condition of entry of a foreign investment to the host country.

The detailed questions set out in this section are designed to throw light on the available process for dispute resolution and indicate where competent assistance may be obtained.

¶70-001   BASIS OF COURTS' JURISDICTION

On what basis do courts exercise jurisdiction?

¶70-002   STATUS OF FOREIGN COMPANIES

Are there any special rules relating to the capacity of foreign companies and foreign-owned subsidiaries to sue and be sued in the courts of the host country?

¶70-003   CIVIL PROCEDURE FOR FOREIGN COMPANIES

Are there any special rules governing civil procedure in litigation in which foreign companies and foreign-owned subsidiaries are involved?

¶70-004   RULES OF CIVIL PROCEDURE AND EVIDENCE

Are the rules of civil procedure and evidence easily ascertainable? Where are they to be found?

¶70-005   SERVICE AND EXECUTION OF PROCESS OUTSIDE JURISDICTION

Do the rules of civil procedure and evidence provide for service and execution of process outside the jurisdiction?

¶70-011   AVAILABILITY OF INTERLOCUTORY RELIEF

Do the rules of civil procedure and evidence provide for interlocutory relief?

¶70-012   COLLECTION OF EVIDENCE OUTSIDE THE JURISDICTION

Do the rules of civil procedure and evidence allow parties to obtain evidence outside the jurisdiction?

¶70-013   CHOICE OF APPLICABLE LAW

To what extent are parties free to choose the law which will be applied by the courts in settlement of the dispute?

¶70-014   CHOICE OF FORUM

To what extent are parties free to choose the forum for the dispute?

¶70-015   COSTS AND DELAY ASSOCIATED WITH LITIGATION

What order of costs and delay are involved in bringing or defending legal action?

¶70-021   SECURITY FOR COSTS

In what circumstances may security for costs be required or obtained?

¶70-022   LANGUAGE OF COURTS

In what language will the litigation be conducted?

¶70-023   ENFORCEMENT AND EXECUTION OF JUDGMENTS

What is the procedure for enforcement and execution of judgments?

¶70-024   RECOGNITION OF FOREIGN JUDGMENTS

On what basis will foreign judgments be recognised and enforced?

¶70-025   STATUS OF FOREIGN LAWYERS

What is the status of foreign lawyers before the courts?

¶70-031   SPECIAL PROCEDURES FOR CERTAIN DISPUTES

Are there any particular procedures for particular types of disputes, e.g. tax disputes, industrial disputes, investment disputes, etc.

Arbitration

Arbitration system .... ¶70-101
New York Convention on
  Recognition and Enforcement
  of Foreign Arbitral
  Awards .... ¶70-102
Special provisions required for
  arbitration clauses .... ¶70-103
International arbitration
  rules .... ¶70-104
United Nations Model Law ..... ¶70-105
Distinction between
  international and domestic
  arbitration .... ¶70-111
Tribunals' basis of
  jurisdiction .... ¶70-112
Exceptions .... ¶70-113
Courts' assistance in
  arbitration process .... ¶70-114
Choice of procedural law .... ¶70-115
Choice of applicable law .... ¶70-121
Specification of appointment of
  arbitrators, etc. .... ¶70-122

Rules governing choice of
  arbitrators .... ¶70-123
Expense of arbitration .... ¶70-124
Delays in arbitration .... ¶70-125
Review by court .... ¶70-131
Arbitration by amiable
  composition .... ¶70-132
Participation by foreign
  companies .... ¶70-133
Rules of natural justice .... ¶70-134
Status of foreign lawyers .... ¶70-135
Assistance from outside
  jurisdiction .... ¶70-141
Language of proceedings .... ¶70-142
Confidentiality of
  proceedings .... ¶70-143
Special procedures for
  certain disputes .... ¶70-144
Arbitration in third country .... ¶70-145

¶70-101   ARBITRATION SYSTEM

Is there a system of arbitration? If so, is it regulated by any legislation, ethical rules or by any group or association?

¶70-102   NEW YORK CONVENTION ON RECOGNITION AND ENFORCEMENT OF FOREIGN ARBITRAL AWARDS

Is the host country a party to the New York Convention on the Recognition and Enforcement of Foreign Arbitral Awards? Are there any other rules governing the recognition and enforcement of foreign arbitral awards?

¶70-103   SPECIAL PROVISIONS REQUIRED FOR ARBITRATION CLAUSES

Should any special provision be included in an arbitration clause to ensure the effectiveness of the clause or the enforcement of any award?

¶70-104   INTERNATIONAL ARBITRATION RULES

Are the International Chamber of Commerce (ICC) Rules, United Nations Committee on International Trade Law (UNCITRAL) Rules or the Rules of the London Court of International Arbitration acceptable? If not, is the procedure for arbitration ascertainable, and how far can it be varied by stipulation of the parties?

¶70-105   UNITED NATIONS MODEL LAW

To what extent is the UNCITRAL Model Law applicable in whole or in part? Is its application or non-application, in whole or in part, subject to the agreement of the parties?

¶70-111   DISTINCTION BETWEEN INTERNATIONAL AND DOMESTIC ARBITRATION

Is there a distinction made between international and domestic commercial arbitration? If so, how are the terms defined?

¶70-112   TRIBUNALS' BASIS OF JURISDICTION

What is the basis of jurisdiction of arbitral tribunals?

¶70-113   EXCEPTIONS

Are there any exceptions to the arbitrability of disputes?

¶70-114   COURTS' ASSISTANCE IN ARBITRATION PROCESS

To what extent are the courts empowered to provide assistance to the arbitrators or in relation to the arbitration process, including enforcement? In particular, to what extent is assistance available in terms of interim or conservatory measures?

¶70-115   CHOICE OF PROCEDURAL LAW

(a) How far are the parties free to stipulate the procedural law to be applied by the arbitral tribunal in the settlement of the dispute?

(b) Is the procedure for arbitration ascertainable, and how far can it be varied by stipulation of the parties or as a result of their choice of procedural law?

¶70-121   CHOICE OF APPLICABLE LAW

How far are the parties free to stipulate the law to be applied by the arbitral tribunal to the substance of the dispute?

¶70-104

¶70-122 SPECIFICATION OF APPOINTMENT OF ARBITRATORS, ETC.

Is it necessary or desirable to specify the method of appointment of arbitrators or the place of arbitration?

¶70-123 RULES GOVERNING CHOICE OF ARBITRATORS

Are there any special rules governing choice of arbitrators?

¶70-124 EXPENSE OF ARBITRATION

Is the expense of arbitration likely to be less or greater than that of litigation?

¶70-125 DELAYS IN ARBITRATION

What delays and costs are involved in the settlement of disputes by arbitration?

¶70-131 REVIEW BY COURT

To what extent are arbitral proceedings and awards subject to stay and review by the courts?

¶70-132 ARBITRATION BY AMIABLE COMPOSITION

To what extent is arbitration by amiable composition permissible?

¶70-133 PARTICIPATION BY FOREIGN COMPANIES

Are there any special rules relating to the participation in arbitral proceedings of foreign companies and foreign-owned subsidiaries?

¶70-134 RULES OF NATURAL JUSTICE

Are the rules of natural justice applicable to arbitral proceedings? If so, are mediation, conciliation or any alternative dispute resolution procedures available which are compatible with these rules so that dispute resolution other than by arbitration may be simultaneously pursued?

¶70-135 STATUS OF FOREIGN LAWYERS

What is the status of foreign lawyers before the arbitration tribunal?

¶70-141 ASSISTANCE FROM OUTSIDE JURISDICTION

Are experienced arbitrators available in the host country, and what are the rules about obtaining assistance from outside, including visas and the admission of witnesses?

¶70-142   LANGUAGE OF PROCEEDINGS

In what language would an arbitration be conducted? Is it desirable to agree upon a language in advance?

¶70-143   CONFIDENTIALITY OF PROCEEDINGS

To what extent are the proceedings confidential? How can parties protect the confidentiality of documents disclosed?

¶70-144   SPECIAL PROCEDURES FOR CERTAIN DISPUTES

Are there any particular procedures for particular types of disputes, e.g. tax disputes, industrial disputes, investment disputes, etc.

¶70-145   ARBITRATION IN THIRD COUNTRY

If an arbitration is to be held in a third country (other than that of either party), is any particular place preferable for arbitration proceedings? Is any place outside the host country more likely to be acceptable for arbitration proceedings, e.g. London or Paris?

Conciliation, mediation and alternative dispute resolution

Alternative methods of
  dispute resolution .... ¶70-201
International conventions .... ¶70-202
Appointment of conciliators and
  mediators .... ¶70-203
Special rules governing
  proceedings .... ¶70-204
Basis of jurisdiction .... ¶70-205
Enforcement of settlement ...... ¶70-211
Right of representation .... ¶70-212
Choice of applicable law .... ¶70-213
Courts' power of intervention .. ¶70-214
Confidentiality of proceedings .. ¶70-215
Special rules for foreign
  participation .... ¶70-221
Provisions in contract for
  forms of dispute resolution ... ¶70-222
Restrictions on types of
  disputes for conciliation,
  etc. .... ¶70-223
Disadvantages of conciliation,
  etc. .... ¶70-224
Joint methods of dispute
  resolution .... ¶70-225

¶70-201   ALTERNATIVE METHODS OF DISPUTE RESOLUTION

Is dispute resolution by conciliation, mediation or other alternative dispute resolution methods available? If so, is it regulated by any legislation, ethical rules or by any group or association?

¶70-202   INTERNATIONAL CONVENTIONS

Is the host country a party to any international convention concerning conciliation, mediation and other forms of dispute resolution? Are the conciliation rules of the

International Chamber of Commerce or United Nations Committee on International Trade Law (UNCITRAL) available?

¶70-203 APPOINTMENT OF CONCILIATORS AND MEDIATORS

Are there any special rules governing appointment and choice of conciliators or mediators?

¶70-204 SPECIAL RULES GOVERNING PROCEEDINGS

Are there any special rules governing conciliation, mediation or other proceedings?

¶70-205 BASIS OF JURISDICTION

What is the basis of jurisdiction, e.g. by the consent of the parties or by direction or regulation?

¶70-211 ENFORCEMENT OF SETTLEMENT

What is the basis of enforcement of settlement achieved by conciliation, mediation or other alternative dispute resolution?

¶70-212 RIGHT OF REPRESENTATION

Can the parties be represented and, if so, by legal or other representatives?

¶70-213 CHOICE OF APPLICABLE LAW

Are the parties free to specify the system of substantive or procedural law within which conciliation, mediation or other alternative dispute resolution methods are to take place?

¶70-214 COURTS' POWER OF INTERVENTION

To what extent is the process subject to the control of the courts, and when, and in what form, may court intervention (if any) take?

¶70-215 CONFIDENTIALITY OF PROCEEDINGS

To what extent are the proceedings confidential? How can the parties protect the confidentiality of documents disclosed?

¶70-221 SPECIAL RULES FOR FOREIGN PARTICIPATION

Are there any special rules relating to the participation in dispute resolution procedures of foreign companies and foreign-owned subsidiaries?

¶70-222   PROVISIONS IN CONTRACT FOR FORMS OF DISPUTE RESOLUTION

What provisions should be inserted in contract documents for dispute resolution by conciliation, mediation or other alternative dispute resolution? What matters should be covered, e.g. place, choice of conciliator or mediator, venue, procedure to be adopted?

¶70-223   RESTRICTIONS ON TYPES OF DISPUTES FOR CONCILIATION, ETC.

Are there any restrictions on the type of disputes that can be dealt with by conciliation, mediation or other forms of alternative dispute resolution? Is a distinction made between international and domestic dispute resolution?

¶70-224   DISADVANTAGES OF CONCILIATION, ETC.

What disadvantages are there in using conciliation, mediation or alternative dispute resolution, e.g. if the parties fail to achieve a settlement or other resolution of the dispute apart from time delay, what disadvantages are there?

¶70-225   JOINT METHODS OF DISPUTE RESOLUTION

Can conciliation, mediation or other forms of alternative dispute resolution be pursued simultaneously with arbitral proceedings or does this present difficulties, particularly in relation to the rules of natural justice, if applicable to arbitral proceedings?

Framework for dispute resolution

International conventions .... ¶70-301
Recognised arbitration
  centres............................ ¶70-302
Internationally acceptable
  arbitrators .... ¶70-303
Availability of local advisers .... ¶70-304

¶70-301   INTERNATIONAL CONVENTIONS

What international conventions are applicable?

¶70-302   RECOGNISED ARBITRATION CENTRES

Is there a recognised international commercial arbitration or dispute resolution centre in the jurisdiction?

¶70-303   INTERNATIONALLY ACCEPTABLE ARBITRATORS

Are there internationally acceptable arbitrators, conciliators and mediators available in the jurisdiction?

¶70-304 AVAILABILITY OF LOCAL ADVISERS

Are there appropriate legal or other advisers and representatives available within the jurisdictions?

Position of government

Status of government .... ¶70-401   Enforcement of orders .... ¶70-403
Choice of forum .... ¶70-402   International conventions........ ¶70-404

¶70-401 STATUS OF GOVERNMENT

Under its own law, can the government claim immunity from suit, whether judicial or arbitral, in respect of actions arising out of:

(i) governmental guarantees;

(ii) government agencies;

(iii) joint ventures with government participation; or

(iv) other commercial activities of government?

¶70-402 CHOICE OF FORUM

Is there any restriction on the choice of forum for actions against the government?

¶70-403 ENFORCEMENT OF ORDERS

Are there any limitations on the remedies or enforcement of orders for payment of damages or other actions if an action is successful against the government?

¶70-404 INTERNATIONAL CONVENTIONS

Is the government a party to the ICSID or MIGA conventions?

THE SOURCES, REGULATION OF, AND SECURITIES FOR LOCAL FINANCE

Introduction .... ¶75-000
Identification of sources .... ¶75-001
Control of financing .... ¶75-101
Terms of financing .... ¶75-201
Legal securities for finance .... ¶75-301

¶75-000 INTRODUCTION

This section deals with the raising of debt and equity capital within the host country. The funding of the capital of the enterprise, including its working capital both on establishment and subsequently is a fundamental issue in foreign investment. If there is no adequate local capital market, or one to which foreign investors are denied access wholly or in part, the investor faces a major deterrent. Furthermore, the capacity in the foreign investor to divest itself of equity in favour of local investors depends on the existence of a local stock exchange or similar institution.

The section examines the legal framework for the local capital market, with particular reference to the regulatory regime, and its impact on the raising of finance for the investment. Access to the international capital market from within the host country must be considered, particularly the question of any impediments for the investor. Specialised financing institutions for particular areas of investment activity are also relevant, particularly in some developing countries. There is some discussion of taxation, but reference should also be made to the sections on taxation and on the regulation of business generally and for foreign investment in particular.

There are also important aspects of practice to be considered, in terms of the customary means and terms of obtaining finance, as distinct from the institutions that exist.

The terms on which loan capital can be raised will depend on whether that loan is secured or unsecured. To some extent, the identity of the borrower as well as the particular market or transaction may determine this issue, but the availability of an adequate system of securities, and the current practice as to terms and conditions is a major factor for both financier and investor. An examination of this context of secured transactions involves a survey of real and personal security interests, the manner of formation, realisation including priorities, and systems of registration. Again issues of taxation and current practice are of critical importance.

Identification of sources

Types of local financial
  institutions .... ¶75-001
How do financial institutions
  raise and supply finance? .... ¶75-002
Methods used to access
  international capital
  markets .... ¶75-003

Specialised institutions for
  investment and
  development .... ¶75-004
Specialised institutions for
  financing exports .... ¶75-005
Local and foreign equity-loan
  ratios .... ¶75-011

¶75-001   TYPES OF LOCAL FINANCIAL INSTITUTIONS

Which of the following kinds of institutions exist:

(a) government and semi-government financing agencies, whether banking or non-banking;

(b) private commercial banks, whether local or foreign, and with full or limited banking privileges;

(c) private development finance institutions, whether local or foreign, and with full or limited banking privileges;

(d) merchant banks;

(e) stock exchanges;

(f) finance companies;

(g) money-lenders;

(h) trading houses giving credit;

(i) insurance companies;

(j) international finance or aid agencies;

(k) local corporations, whether equity, debt or joint venture participation?

¶75-002   HOW DO FINANCIAL INSTITUTIONS RAISE AND SUPPLY FINANCE?

In what form and on what terms do they raise and supply finance?

¶75-003   METHODS USED TO ACCESS INTERNATIONAL CAPITAL MARKETS

Is there an established practice of local entities accessing the international capital markets (e.g. Asian Dollar and Eurodollar or U.S. markets)?

¶75-001

Sources, regulation of, and securities
for local finance
3,543

¶75-004   SPECIALISED INSTITUTIONS FOR INVESTMENT AND DEVELOPMENT

Are there any specialised institutions established for the financing of specific types of investment or development?

¶75-005   SPECIALISED INSTITUTIONS FOR FINANCING EXPORTS

Are there any specialised institutions established for the financing of exports (either governmental or non-governmental)?

¶75-011   LOCAL AND FOREIGN EQUITY-LOAN RATIOS

What are the local requirements concerning proportions of local and foreign equity-loan ratios?

Control of financing

Criteria for regulation of
  sources of loan finance .... ¶75-101
Manner in which sources of
  loan finance controlled .... ¶75-102
Regulations covering raising of
  local equity capital .... ¶75-103
Manner of regulating raising of
  local equity capital .... ¶75-104

Self-regulation by credit and
  financial institutions .... ¶75-105
Methods used for raising
  capital .... ¶75-111
Taxation of dividends or interest
  to non-residents .... ¶75-112

¶75-101   CRITERIA FOR REGULATION OF SOURCES OF LOAN FINANCE

Is regulation and control of sources of loan finance achieved by reference to type of institution, the purpose of credit, lender credit or vendor credit?

¶75-102   MANNER IN WHICH SOURCES OF LOAN FINANCE CONTROLLED

By whom and how is such control exercised? In particular, is it achieved by statute of general or particular application? Are there any statutory agencies that apply those controls? How far are such controls discretionary and where does the discretion reside?

¶75-103   REGULATIONS COVERING RAISING OF LOCAL EQUITY CAPITAL

What regulation, control and procedures exist for the raising of equity capital locally? What control and supervision of the local stock exchange exists? What practice exists for foreign companies undertaking equity issues?

¶75-104 MANNER OF REGULATING RAISING OF LOCAL EQUITY CAPITAL

By whom and how is such control exercised? In particular, is it achieved by statute of general or particular application? Are there any statutory agencies that apply those controls? How far are such controls discretionary and where does the discretion reside?

¶75-105 SELF-REGULATION BY CREDIT AND FINANCIAL INSTITUTIONS

To what extent do credit and financial institutions regulate or police their own activities through professional or voluntary or non-government associations?

¶75-111 METHODS USED FOR RAISING CAPITAL

What methods are most often used locally to raise finance for capital expenditure and working capital?

¶75-112 TAXATION OF DIVIDENDS OR INTEREST TO NON-RESIDENTS

What taxes (e.g. withholding taxes) apply to the payment of dividends or interest to non-resident persons?

Terms of financing

Customary terms for lending or investing money .... ¶75-201

Flexibility of customary terms for lending or investing money .... ¶75-202

Interest rates .... ¶75-203

Covenants, financial ratios and security interests .... ¶75-204

Local arrangements concerning currency exchange and rates .... ¶75-205

Which law governs financing? .. ¶75-211

¶75-201 CUSTOMARY TERMS FOR LENDING OR INVESTING MONEY

Are there customary terms on which local institutions will lend or invest money, and are copies of such terms and conditions available?

¶75-202 FLEXIBILITY OF CUSTOMARY TERMS FOR LENDING OR INVESTING MONEY

To what extent are those terms the product of mandatory statutory rules, government policy directives, or internal policy decisions? How far are they amenable to change?

¶75-104

¶75-203   INTEREST RATES

What are the rates of interest? Are they fixed or variable? How are they calculated?

¶75-204   COVENANTS, FINANCIAL RATIOS AND SECURITY INTERESTS

What covenants, financial ratios or security interests are customarily sought by local lenders or investors?

¶75-205   LOCAL ARRANGEMENTS CONCERNING CURRENCY EXCHANGE AND RATES

What arrangements concerning currency exchange and exchange rate risk are typically included in financing? What local banking facilities exist to cater for such matters? Are there local laws or regulations that impact on negotiated arrangements on these matters?

¶75-211   WHICH LAW GOVERNS FINANCING?

What provisions relating to governing laws and submission to jurisdiction are customary in financing?

Legal securities for finance

Security interests in
  property .... ¶75-301

Recognised forms of
  security rights .... ¶75-401
Security rights .... ¶75-501

¶75-301   SECURITY INTERESTS IN PROPERTY

Can security interests be taken in the following forms of property:

(a) immovables or statutory immovables (land and registrable chattels);

(b) tangible movables (chattels, inventory, motor vehicles, aircraft, etc.);

(c) intangible movables (commercial rights, patents and trade marks, industrial and intellectual property rights, etc.)?

¶75-401   RECOGNISED FORMS OF SECURITY RIGHTS

In respect of each of the above forms of property, what form of security rights is recognised; e.g. is it based on transfer, charge, lease, etc.?

Security rights

Can subject property be readily identified? .... ¶75-501

Can borrower's interest be readily identified? .... ¶75-502

Formalities for creation of security .... ¶75-503

Priority of security interests ...... ¶75-504

Number of security interests against one property .... ¶75-505

Floating securities over classes of assets .... ¶75-511

Securities for further advances .... ¶75-512

Is the continuing interest of the borrower recognised and protected? .... ¶75-513

Retention of possession by borrower .... ¶75-514

Realisation of security by lender .... ¶75-515

Transferability of lender's security .... ¶75-521

Forms of personal security .... ¶75-522

Acceptable securities .... ¶75-523

Charges for registration of securities .... ¶75-524

Tax implications and choice of security .... ¶75-525

¶75-501 CAN SUBJECT PROPERTY BE READILY IDENTIFIED?

Can property which is subject to security be readily identified, e.g. through registration?

¶75-502 CAN BORROWER'S INTEREST BE READILY IDENTIFIED?

Can the borrower's interest in that property be readily identified? Are there problems associated with a mingling of such property not subject to the interest?

¶75-503 FORMALITIES FOR CREATION OF SECURITY

What formalities are required for the creation of each type of security?

(a) Can each of the security interests referred to above be registered? If so, where — centrally or locally or both? How long does it take to register the security? Is there any form of mortgage insurance? What special problems do certain kinds of property offered as security present, e.g. inventory, registrable securities, motor vehicles, etc.?

(b) What is registered — documents or the security interest, or the transaction?

(c) Are there any time limits for registration?

(d) What are the consequences of registration or failure to register?

(e) Is there any form of protection for security interests other than by registration, e.g. the lodging of caveats?

(f) What action, if any, must be taken to preserve a security interest?

¶75-501

¶75-504   PRIORITY OF SECURITY INTERESTS

What is the priority of the above security interests against:

(a) other securities over the same property;

(b) other dealings with the same property;

(c) rights of general creditors of the borrower;

(d) persons or bodies having the benefit of statutory preferred rights (e.g. government creditors, tax liens, workmen's liens, etc.);

(e) what procedures exist to determine the existence of prior interests;

both inside and outside bankruptcy and liquidation?

¶75-505   NUMBER OF SECURITY INTERESTS AGAINST ONE PROPERTY

Can further security interests be created over the same property?

¶75-511   FLOATING SECURITIES OVER CLASSES OF ASSETS

Is it possible to create a floating security over a class of assets or all the assets of the borrower? What is the status of after acquired property? Can it be done only in the case of certain classes of assets or certain types of borrower? What is the relationship between the holder of a prior perfected interest and the interest of a subsequent lender who perfects an interest in such assets?

¶75-512   SECURITIES FOR FURTHER ADVANCES

Will each of the securities listed above secure further advances?

¶75-513   IS THE CONTINUING INTEREST OF THE BORROWER RECOGNISED AND PROTECTED?

Is the continuing interest of the borrower in the property recognised and protected, especially:

(a) Can the borrower create further securities in or dispose of property subject to the security interest?

(b) Subject to (a) above, does the borrower have a claim on the proceeds of any realisation of the property by the lender? What are the secured party's rights with respect to proceeds?

(c) Can the lender assign or charge the property, otherwise than on default, free of the borrower's interest?

¶75-514   RETENTION OF POSSESSION BY BORROWER

Does the borrower, as long as he/she is not in default, retain possession of the property with power to use and exploit its economic value? What restrictions may the parties by agreement impose on such use? What property must be transferred to the lender to create a secured interest?

¶75-515   REALISATION OF SECURITY BY LENDER

Can the lender realise the security speedily and effectively on default by the borrower? In particular:

(a) what, if any, court procedures are required to enable him to do so;

(b) is the security valid in bankruptcy, and to what extent does it enjoy priority and preference over other claims;

(c) is the lender who has realised security accountable for the surplus and can he/she recover a deficit;

(d) can the lender sell the enterprise as a going concern rather than be obliged to divide up assets for individual sale; and

(e) is the remedy or receivership or receivership and management available?

¶75-521   TRANSFERABILITY OF LENDER'S SECURITY

Is the lender's security interest freely transferable?

¶75-522   FORMS OF PERSONAL SECURITY

What forms of personal security by way of suretyship or guarantee or joint obligations are:

(a) available;

(b) in use?

¶75-523   ACCEPTABLE SECURITIES

Which of all the securities listed above are regarded as acceptable by local and other financiers?

¶75-524   CHARGES FOR REGISTRATION OF SECURITIES

What charges are made on the registration of securities?

¶75-525   TAX IMPLICATIONS AND CHOICE OF SECURITY

Is the choice of security affected by tax implications?

MOVEMENT OF GOODS
(TRANSPORT AND SHIPPING)

Introduction .... ¶80-000
Laws relating to inward and outward transport .... ¶80-001
Laws relating to movement and storage of goods .... ¶80-002
International conventions .... ¶80-003
Laws relating to movement of dangerous substances .. ¶80-004
Arrest of vessels, etc. .... ¶80-005
Regulation of shipbuilding industry .... ¶80-011
Laws relating to shipping register .... ¶80-012

¶80-000   INTRODUCTION

Investments which are linked to international trade raise many issues about the facilities to move goods to and from the host country. This section poses questions to determine whether the host country operates its own shipping companies and whether those companies are the beneficiaries of any special advantages offered by the host government. The questions link the host country system to the detailed international regime of maritime law. The remedies specifically available against ships are analysed. There are some detailed questions about the shipbuilding industry within the host country which may be of direct concern to some investors.

Overall the questions in this section are designed to give the investor a basis of comparison between shipping opportunities offered by the home government and the host country.

¶80-001   LAWS RELATING TO INWARD AND OUTWARD TRANSPORT

Which laws of the host country regulate inward and outward transport and/or shipping?

¶80-002   LAWS RELATING TO MOVEMENT AND STORAGE OF GOODS

What laws of the host country apply to the movement and storage of goods and/or persons into, out of and/or within that country by all modes of transport?

¶80-003   INTERNATIONAL CONVENTIONS

(a) Are any international conventions relating to the movement of goods and/or persons into, out of and/or within that country by all modes of transport adopted into domestic legislation of the host country? Specify such conventions.

(b) Specify the relevant law of the host country in respect of each such convention referred to in (a) above and whether such convention applies compulsorily to that movement.

¶80-004 LAWS RELATING TO MOVEMENT OF DANGEROUS SUBSTANCES

What laws of the host country apply to the domestic and/or international movement and storage of dangerous, hazardous and noxious substances and to the pollution of the environment by such substances?

¶80-005 ARREST OF VESSELS, ETC.

Does the law of the host country provide for arrest of vessels, aircraft and/or other property? If so, specify such law and the grounds upon which such arrests are effected.

¶80-011 REGULATION OF SHIPBUILDING INDUSTRY

In respect of shipbuilding within the host country:

(a) What shipbuilding companies carry on business in the host country?

(b) What law of the host country regulates shipbuilders?

(c) What law of the host country deals with the following issues:

    (i) export licence requirements;

    (ii) requirements as to the governing law of the shipbuilding contract;

    (iii) financing guarantees;

    (iv) suppliers' credits;

    (v) subsidies or grants;

    (vi) registration of rights in ships under construction;

    (vii) mortgages on ships under construction;

    (viii) performance bonds by builder; and

    (ix) guarantee insurance by the builder?

¶80-012 LAWS RELATING TO SHIPPING REGISTER

Specify the laws of the host country relating to the creation of a shipping register and of the registration requirements.

INSURANCE

Introduction .... ¶85-000
Use of state-owned or resident brokers .... ¶85-001
Classes of insurance underwriters .... ¶85-002
Available range of insurance .... ¶85-003
Insurance required for financing arrangements .... ¶85-004
Compulsory insurance .... ¶85-011
Insurance of local employees .... ¶85-012
Legislation affecting choice of insurance company ..... ¶85-013
Application for insurance payments .... ¶85-014
Product liability insurance .... ¶85-021

¶85-000 INTRODUCTION

A specialist area for investment, as well as a crucial service for the general investor, is the insurance industry, including reinsurance facilities. The questions in this section are designed to acquaint the potential investor with the host country's insurance system and the government role in regulating the insurance industry. In particular, the questions ask whether foreign insurance companies may operate within the host country and address the types of insurance which are available for the benefit of a business conducted by the foreign investor.

The questions also address whether proceeds of insurance claims may be freely transferred out of the country and whether the host country provides product liability insurance cover for the benefit of exporters to the host country, as well as export credits insurance for exporters from the host country.

Since the insurance industry is often protected by the host government, there is a clear relationship between the material in this section and in the section on the regulation of business.

¶85-001 USE OF STATE-OWNED OR RESIDENT BROKERS

Is it compulsory to use a state-owned or resident broker or underwriter in the host country for any classes of insurance?

¶85-002 CLASSES OF INSURANCE UNDERWRITERS

What classes of insurance underwriters operate in the host country? Do any of them enjoy any particular advantage or disadvantage under the law of the host country?

¶85-003 AVAILABLE RANGE OF INSURANCE

Is insurance readily available to cover all kinds of loss of or damage to property, whether of the enterprise or other persons, employer's liability, loss of profits, liability to members of the public for injury, and life insurance?

[End of Tab Division]

¶85-004   INSURANCE REQUIRED FOR FINANCING ARRANGEMENTS

What risks would it be prudent, or are required by financing arrangements, to insure against?

¶85-011   COMPULSORY INSURANCE

Are there any risks against which it is compulsory to insure?

¶85-012   INSURANCE OF LOCAL EMPLOYEES

Is it usual to insure any particular classes of local employees against death or disablement or to provide retirement benefits for them? If so, what types and levels of insurance or retirement benefits are usual, and is it usual to provide retirement benefits, through insurance? What facilities are there for arranging such insurance or benefits?

¶85-013   LEGISLATION AFFECTING CHOICE OF INSURANCE COMPANY

What legislation or regulations are there in the host country with respect to insurance having important effects for the enterprise? Are there any laws as to premium rates or which affect the ability of the enterprise to insure with the company of its choice whether inside or outside the host country?

¶85-014   APPLICATION FOR INSURANCE PAYMENTS

Are any procedures required for the application for payments? Can the proceeds of insurance claims be freely remitted?

¶85-021   PRODUCT LIABILITY INSURANCE

Is product liability insurance cover available?

AUSTRALIA

Department of Business Law and Taxation

MONASH UNIVERSITY, MELBOURNE

Clayton, Victoria 3168

Australia

Tel: 61 3 9905 9100

Fax: 61 3 9905 9111

DIRECTORY OF EDITORS

INTRODUCTION, AN OVERVIEW, LAND TENURE, THE STRUCTURE OF THE INVESTMENT, INTELLECTUAL PROPERTY, SETTLEMENT OF DISPUTES, REGULATION OF LOCAL FINANCE, AND INSURANCE

Paul Latimer

Associate Professor of Law

Department of Business Law and Taxation

Monash University, Melbourne

Author of Australian Business Law

Published annually by CCH Australia Ltd since 1981

Paul.Latimer@buseco.monash.edu.au

REGULATION OF BUSINESS, IMPORT AND EXPORT CONTROLS, EXCHANGE CONTROL, LABOUR AND NATIONALITY LAWS, AND MOVEMENT OF GOODS

Alice de Jonge

Lecturer in Law

Department of Business Law and Taxation

Monash University, Melbourne

Alice.DeJonge@buseco.monash.edu.au

TAXATION

Ken Devos

Lecturer in Taxation

Department of Business Law and Taxation

Monash University, Melbourne

Ken.Devos@buseco.monash.edu.au

Table of Contents

Paragraph

An overview (the system of law and government) ... AUS ¶20-001

Land tenure — the site of the investment .... AUS ¶25-001

The structure of the investment .... AUS ¶30-001

Taxation .... AUS ¶35-001

Regulation of business .... AUS ¶45-001

Import and export controls .... AUS ¶50-001

Exchange control — the movement of money .... AUS ¶55-001

Labour and nationality laws .... AUS ¶60-001

Intellectual property .... AUS ¶65-001

Settlement of disputes .... AUS ¶70-001

Regulation of local finance .... AUS ¶75-001

Movement of goods (transport and shipping) .... AUS ¶80-001

Insurance .... AUS ¶85-001

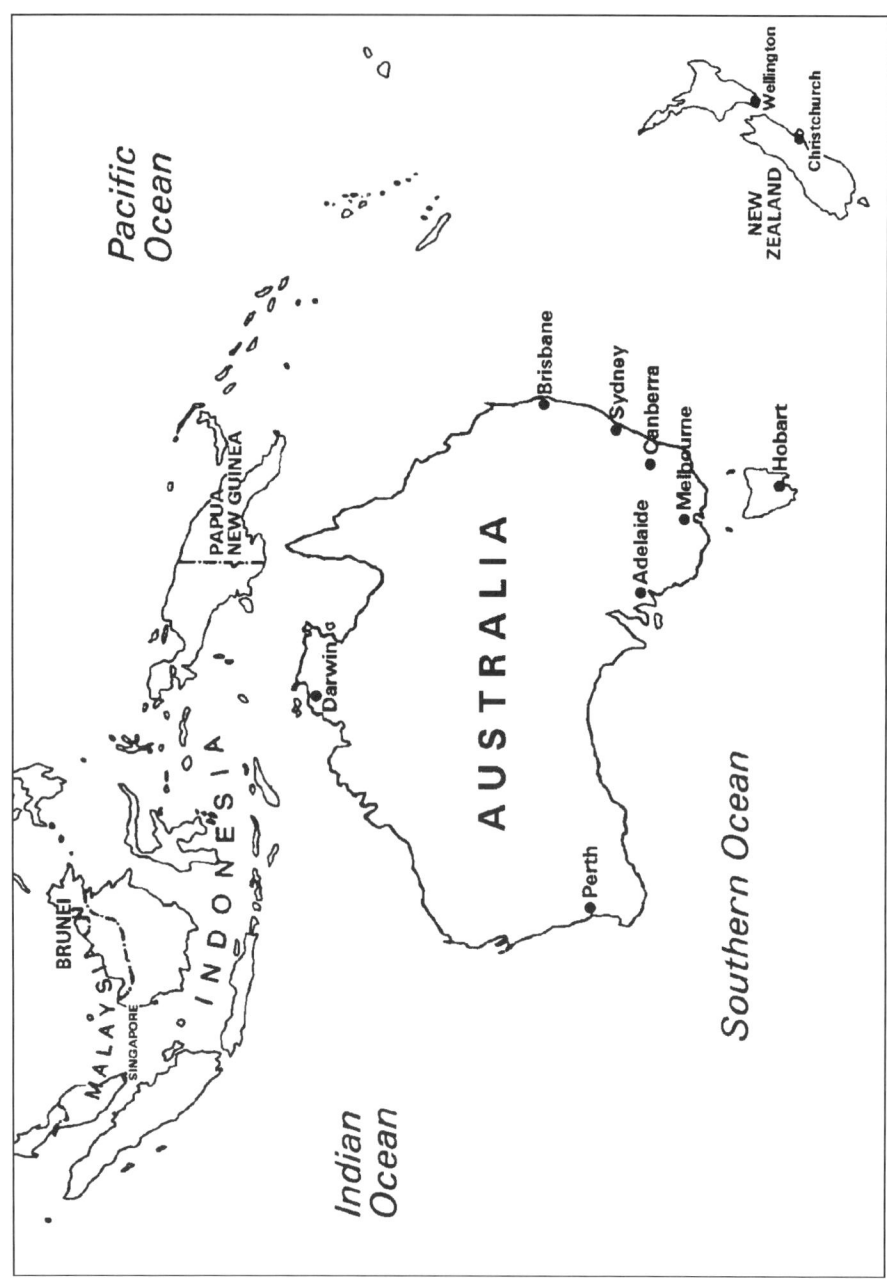

Statistical Summary

AUSTRALIA	
People	
Population (2001):	19.4 million
Ethnic groups:	Caucasians 95%, Asian 4%, Aborigines & others 1.6%
Language(s):	English, native languages
Geography	
Land area:	7.68 million sq km
Climate:	North tropical, south temperate
Average temperature:	4°C to 28°C (up to 50°C in the interior)
Government	
Government type:	Federal Parliamentary State
Head of State:	Queen Elizabeth II
Head of government:	Prime Minister John Howard
Exchange rate:	AUS$1 = US$0.61 (March 2003)
Economy (2001)	
GDP (US$ billion)	368.6
Growth rate (%)	2.4%
Employment by sector (%)	
Services	47.06
Wholesale/retail	20.52
Manufacturing	13.8
Construction	7.24
Agriculture	4.91
Other	6.64
Trade (2001)	
Total exports (US$ million):	68.8
Total imports (US$ million):	70.2
Leading three export items:	Leading three export markets:
1. Coal	1. Japan
2. Gold	2. US
3. Wool & other animal hair	3. Korea
Leading three import items:	Leading three import markets:
1. Machinery & transport	1. US
2. Computers	2. Japan
3. Telecom equipment and parts	3. China

ABBREVIATIONS — AUSTRALIA

AAT	Administrative Appeals Tribunal
ACCC	Australian Competition and Consumer Commission
ACDC	Australasian Commercial Disputes Centre
ACICA	Australasian Centre for International Commercial Arbitration
ACT	Australian Capital Territory (capital: Canberra)
ACTU	Australian Council of Trade Unions
ADG Code	Australian Code for the Transportation of Dangerous Goods by Road and Rail
ADR	Alternative dispute resolution
AIRC	Australian Industrial Relations Commission
AISN	Australian Investment Scheme Number
APEC	Asia Pacific Economic Cooperation
APRA	Australian Prudential Regulation Authority
ARBN	Australian Registered Body Number
ASIC	Australian Securities and Investments Commission
ASX	Australian Stock Exchange
ATAC	Australia Transport Advisory Council
ATO	Australian Taxation Office
AUSTRAC	Australian Transaction Reports and Analysis Centre
AUSTRADE	Australian Trade Commission
CFC	controlled foreign corporations
Cth or Cwth	Commonwealth
EFIC	Export Finance and Insurance Corporation
FCT	Federal Commissioner of Taxation. See ATO
FIRB	Foreign Investment Review Board
GATT	General Agreement on Tariffs and Trade
ICSID	International Convention on Settlement of Investment Disputes
ILO	International Labour Organisation
IMF	International Monetary Fund
IMO	International Maritime Organisation
IPPA	Investment Promotion and Protection Agreement
ITR	Integrated Tourism Resorts
ITSA	Insolvency and Trustee Service Australia
MIGA	Multilateral Investment Guarantee Agency

OECD	Organisation for Economic Cooperation and Development
PAYE	Pay as you earn
SFE	Sydney Futures Exchange
SMART	Sydney Maritime Arbitration Rules and Terms
TPA	Trade Practices Act 1974 (Cth)
TRIPs	Trade-Related Aspects of Intellectual Property Rights
UNCITRAL	United Nations Committee on International Trade Law
USL	Uniform Shipping Laws
WIPO	World Intellectual Property Organisation
WTO	World Trade Organisation

LATEST ADDITIONS TO INDEX

AUSTRALIA

As additional information is added to the "Australia" tab, relevant index entries may appear in the first instance on this page until such time as they can be incorporated into the principal index. These "Latest Additions" should always be consulted together with the principal index.

The principal Index is currently up-to-date.

INDEX

AUSTRALIA

Paragraph

A

Accelerated depreciation allowance.....AUS 35-513
applicability ....AUS 35-514

Accounts
non-resident companies ....AUS 30-103
subsidiaries ....AUS 30-104

Accounting period
fiscal year...AUS 35-103

Acquisition
rights in land
– restrictions ....AUS 25-103
shares
– local companies ....AUS 30-105
urban real estate ....AUS 45-111

Advertising
laws governing....................................AUS 45-306

Agreements
land use, restricting.............................AUS 25-115

Air transportation
carriage of goods
– law governing ....AUS 80-002
dangerous substances,
movement of....................................AUS 80-004
international conventions.....................AUS 80-003
law governing ....AUS 80-001

Alternative methods
dispute resolution.......... AUS 70-201; AUS 70-211
– applicable law ....AUS 70-213
– disadvantages..................................AUS 70-224
– joint methods ....AUS 70-225

Amiable composition
arbitration...AUS 70-132

Anti-dumping duty
imports...AUS 50-025

Anton Piller order
settlement of dispute ....AUS 70-005

Applicable law
arbitration...AUS 70-121
conciliation ....AUS 70-213
determination ....AUS 20-013
dispute resolution
– alternative method ....AUS 70-213
mediation ....AUS 70-213
settlement of dispute...........................AUS 70-013

Paragraph

Appointments
arbitrators...AUS 70-122
conciliators ....AUS 70-203
mediators ....AUS 70-203

Arbitral awards
foreign ....AUS 70-102
review by court...................................AUS 70-131

Arbitral proceedings — see **Arbitration**

Arbitral tribunal
basis of jurisdiction.............................AUS 70-112
procedural law ....AUS 70-115

Arbitration
amiable composition............................AUS 70-132
applicable law.....................................AUS 70-121
assistance from outside jurisdiction.....AUS 70-141
centres, recognised ....AUS 70-302
clauses, special provisions...................AUS 70-103
confidentiality of proceedings ....AUS 70-143
court's assistance ....AUS 70-114
delays...AUS 70-125
dispute resolution ....AUS 20-014
exceptions..AUS 70-113
expenses...AUS 70-124
foreign lawyers, status ....AUS 70-135
foreign participation ....AUS 70-133
industrial dispute settlement...............AUS 60-012
international and domestic
distinguished...................................AUS 70-111
joint with conciliation.........................AUS 70-225
joint with mediation............................AUS 70-225
language of proceedings ....AUS 70-142
local advisers ....AUS 70-304
New York Convention.........................AUS 70-102
procedural law, choice.........................AUS 70-115
review by court...................................AUS 70-131
rules of natural justice ....AUS 70-134
system..AUS 70-101
third country ....AUS 70-145
UNCITRAL rules .... AUS 70-103; AUS 70-104;
AUS 70-105

Arbitrators
appointments ....AUS 70-122
choice, rules governing........................AUS 70-122
internationally acceptable...................AUS 70-303

Arrest
vessels..AUS 80-005

Paragraph

Asia Pacific Economic Council
membership.............................AUS 20-101

Asian Development Bank
membership.............................AUS 20-101

Assessable income
definition...............................AUS 35-101

Assets
capital gains tax ....AUS 35-401
floating securities.................AUS 75-511
foreign investors
– expropriation.....................AUS 45-114
roll-overs.............................AUS 35-402

Australian Maritime Safety
Authority..............................AUS 80-011

Australian stock exchange
equity capital, raising of ....AUS 75-103

Australian takeover law
takeovers.............................AUS 30-105

Authorisation
price control........................AUS 45-202
restraint of trade..................AUS 45-303

B

Bankruptcy law......................AUS 30-114

Banks
contract and commercial law
– application ....AUS 30-014
foreign investment incentives.............AUS 45-111

Basis of assessment
salary.................................AUS 35-105

Basis of jurisdiction
arbitral tribunal ....AUS 70-112
conciliation ....AUS 70-205
courts ....AUS 70-001
mediation ....AUS 70-205

Bearer shares
subsidiary companies...........AUS 30-104

Borrower
security interests, retention of.............AUS 75-514

Borrower's interest
security interests
– identification....................AUS 75-502
– whether recognised and protected.....AUS 75-513

Breach
exchange control law ....AUS 55-034

Business activities
disincentives ....AUS 45-004
environmental requirements ....AUS 25-211
licence...............................AUS 45-001

Paragraph

– granting.............................AUS 45-002
non-residents
– provisions ....AUS 45-305
registration..........................AUS 45-001
– granting.............................AUS 45-002
restrictions ....AUS 45-004

Business expenses
allowable deductions ....AUS 35-101

Business profits
taxation ....AUS 35-101; AUS 35-104

C

Capital
raising, method of................AUS 75-105
repatriation..........................AUS 55-005

Capital gains
income tax ....AUS 35-401
offset of revenue losses........AUS 35-404
roll-overs............................AUS 35-402

Capital gains tax...................AUS 35-401

Capital losses
offset against revenue gains.............AUS 35-403

Carriage of goods
air
– law governing ....AUS 80-001; AUS 80-002

Cash transaction
remittance
– restrictions ....AUS 55-013

Character merchandising
copyright............................AUS 65-003

Charges
registration.........................AUS 75-502
security interests
– creation, formalities..........AUS 75-503

Circuit layouts ....AUS 65-013
disadvantages for non-residents..........AUS 65-025
exclusive right ....AUS 65-013
protection...........................AUS 65-013
silicon chips........................AUS 65-013

Citizenship
acquisition ....AUS 60-002
labour laws.........................AUS 60-001
loss of ....AUS 60-002

Civil aviation
foreign investment incentives.............AUS 45-111

Civil procedure
foreign companies
– industrial dispute ....AUS 70-003
rules
– industrial dispute ....AUS 70-004

See also Latest Additions to Index at p. 7,051

	Paragraph		Paragraph
Codification of law	AUS 30-002	licensing agreement	AUS 65-022
		transfers	AUS 65-022
Collective bargaining			
industrial dispute settlement	AUS 60-012	**Concessional entry**	AUS 50-015
Commercial law		**Conciliation**	
application re institutions	AUS 30-014	applicable law	AUS 70-213
codification	AUS 30-002	basis of jurisdiction	AUS 70-205
contract law distinguished	AUS 30-003	confidentiality	AUS 70-215
historical sources	AUS 30-001	disadvantages	AUS 70-224
remedies	AUS 30-016	industrial dispute settlement	AUS 60-012
		– enforcement of	AUS 70-211
Commercial organisations		joint with arbitration	AUS 70-225
forms	AUS 30-101	local advisers	AUS 70-304
Commercial profits		representation	AUS 70-212
taxation	AUS 35-101	rules governing	AUS 70-204
		types of disputes, restrictions on	AUS 70-223
Commodities			
price control	AUS 45-201	**Conciliators**	
		appointment	AUS 70-203
Commonwealth taxes	AUS 35-301		
		Confidentiality	
Companies		arbitral proceedings	AUS 70-143
constructive ownership	AUS 35-103	conciliation proceedings	AUS 70-215
contract and commercial law		mediation proceedings	AUS 70-215
– application	AUS 30-014		
distinction between public and		**Constructive ownership**	
private	AUS 35-103	companies	AUS 35-103
establishment	AUS 30-105	**Consumer contracts**	
foreign ownership		law governing	AUS 30-011
– percentage	AUS 30-111		
income tax	AUS 35-102	**Consumer protection**	
investments	AUS 30-105	law governing	AUS 45-301
law governing	AUS 30-101	**Contracts**	
managing structure	AUS 30-112	consumer — see Consumer contracts	
price fixing		court's jurisdiction	AUS 70-001
– restrictions	AUS 45-204	damages	AUS 30-016
private — see Private companies		foreign entities	
public — see Public companies		– requirements	AUS 30-005
subsidiary — see Subsidiaries		government — see Government contracts	
tax file number	AUS 35-103	performance under changed	
tax losses	AUS 35-103	circumstances	AUS 30-017
tax rate	AUS 35-103	remedies	AUS 30-016
thin capitalisation rules	AUS 35-103	restraint of trade	
undistributed profits tax	AUS 35-103	– prohibition	AUS 45-303
		standardised form, use of	AUS 30-015
Compensation		unfair	
land acquisition	AUS 25-123	– review of	AUS 45-307
seamen	AUS 80-001		
		Contract law	
Compulsory licenses		application re institutions	AUS 30-014
industrial property	AUS 65-023	codification	AUS 30-002
Computer software		commercial law distinguished	AUS 30-003
copyright	AUS 65-003	historical sources	AUS 30-001
disadvantages for non-residents	AUS 65-025	**Contractual dispute**	
licensing agreement	AUS 65-022	arbitration, exceptions	AUS 70-113
transfers	AUS 65-022		
		Conveyancing fees	
Copyright		rights in land, transfer	AUS 25-102
disadvantages for non-residents	AUS 65-025		
international agreement	AUS 65-001		

	Paragraph
Copyright	AUS 65-003
character merchandising	AUS 65-003
computer software	AUS 65-003
Copyright Act	AUS 65-003
duration	AUS 65-003
exclusive right	AUS 65-003
performers' protection	AUS 65-003
protection	AUS 65-003
Costs	
arbitration	AUS 70-124
litigation	
– settlement of dispute	AUS 70-015
rights in land, transfer	AUS 25-102
Countervailing duty	
imports	AUS 50-025
Courts	
arbitration process	AUS 70-114
basis of jurisdiction	AUS 70-001
dispute resolution	
– power of intervention	AUS 70-214
language in use	AUS 70-022
review	
– arbitration process	AUS 70-131
Covenants	AUS 75-204
Credit	
self-regulation	AUS 75-105
Currency	
remittance	AUS 55-012
– restrictions	AUS 55-013
used for loans	AUS 55-014
Custom duties	AUS 35-301
rates	AUS 50-012
time for payment	AUS 50-032
Customary land rights	AUS 25-011

D

Damages	
contracts	AUS 30-016
Dangerous substances	
movement of	
– law governing	AUS 80-004
Deductions	
depreciation allowances	AUS 35-103
income tax	AUS 35-105
investment profits	AUS 35-212
tax losses	AUS 35-103
Defective products	
injuries, liability for	AUS 30-012
Definitions	
assessable income	AUS 35-101

	Paragraph
copyright	AUS 65-003
domestic arbitration agreement	AUS 70-111
foreign interest	AUS 45-103
public companies	AUS 35-103
royalty	AUS 35-211
trademarks	AUS 65-004
Delays	
arbitration	AUS 70-125
litigation	AUS 70-015
Designs — see **Industrial designs**	
Development	
financing	AUS 75-004
financial institutions	AUS 75-004
Directors	
qualification	
– subsidiaries	AUS 30-104
subsidiaries	
– nationality	AUS 30-104
Disincentives	
business activities	AUS 45-004
foreign investment	AUS 45-111; AUS 45-112; AUS 45-113
geographical areas	AUS 45-105
Disputes	
government contracts	AUS 30-004
Dispute resolution — see also **Settlement**	
of dispute	AUS 70-031
alternative method	AUS 70-201
– disadvantages	AUS 70-224
– restrictions	AUS 70-223
applicable law	AUS 70-213
arbitration	AUS 20-014
centres, recognised	AUS 70-302
choice of method	AUS 20-014
courts' intervention	AUS 70-214
foreign participation	AUS 70-211
forms, provisions in contract	AUS 70-222
governing centres	AUS 20-014
international conventions	AUS 70-202; AUS 70-301
joint methods	AUS 70-225
local advisers	AUS 70-304
settlement, enforcement of	AUS 70-211
special procedures	AUS 70-144
Dividends	
franked	AUS 35-202
non-residents	
– withholding tax	AUS 75-112
non-resident companies	
– withholding tax	AUS 35-103
remittance	AUS 55-011
tax credit	AUS 35-202
withholding tax	AUS 35-201; AUS 55-011

Paragraph

Documents
non-resident companies,
– registration ....AUS 30-103

Domestic arbitration
definition..AUS 70-111

Domestic legislation
industrial property................................AUS 65-002

Double tax agreements..........................AUS 35-001
tax credits...AUS 35-002

Double taxation
international treaties ....AUS 35-001

E

Easements
land ....AUS 25-001

Employees
conditions guaranteed ....AUS 60-004
insurance...AUS 85-012
leave, types of.......................................AUS 60-004
obligations of employer ....AUS 60-025
– additional ....AUS 60-025
redundancy provisions..........................AUS 60-004
relationship with employer ....AUS 60-003
remuneration
– fringe benefits tax ....AUS 35-301
– tax withheld ....AUS 35-103
retirement provisions ....AUS 60-004
subsidiaries
– nationality ....AUS 30-104
superannuation......................................AUS 85-012
wages ....AUS 60-004
– control of...AUS 60-005
working hours ....AUS 60-004
– control of...AUS 60-005

Employers
fringe benefits tax ....AUS 35-301
obligations to employees ....AUS 60-025
– additional ....AUS 60-025
"pay as you earn"
– tax withheld ....AUS 35-103
payroll tax...AUS 35-301
relationship with employee...................AUS 60-003
superannuation guarantee scheme ....AUS 85-012
tax liabilities
– method of payment ....AUS 35-005

Employment
foreign lawyers ....AUS 20-012
foreign workers.....................................AUS 60-033

Enforcement
industrial property................................AUS 65-031

Environment
detriment...AUS 25-212

Paragraph

Environmental assessment
governmental requirements ....AUS 25-203

Environmental controls
administration.......................................AUS 25-202
penalties
– non-compliance ....AUS 25-202
regulation..AUS 25-202

Environmental impact
assessment ....AUS 25-203
business, establishment of ....AUS 25-211

Environmental restrictions
law governing..AUS 25-201

Equity-capital
raising of
– administering body ....AUS 75-104
– law governing ....AUS 75-103

Equity-loan ratios
financial institutions ....AUS 75-011
foreign ....AUS 75-011
local ....AUS 75-011

Equipment
depreciation allowances.......................AUS 35-103

Evidence
collection outside jurisdiction ....AUS 70-012

Exchange control — see also **Foreign exchange**
administering body ....AUS 55-002
breach of law ....AUS 55-034
exemptions...AUS 55-031
foreign-controlled companies
– place of incorporation.......................AUS 55-024
formalities...AUS 55-033
laws governing......................................AUS 55-001
– application to foreign countries.......AUS 55-004
local participation, effect....................AUS 55-025
policy objectives...................................AUS 55-003
regulations
– tax considerations ....AUS 55-042
residents and non-residents,
distinction ....AUS 55-023
transactions requiring approval ....AUS 55-022

Exchange rate
differing rates.......................................AUS 55-021
method of fixing ....AUS 55-015

Excise duties...AUS 35-301

Executives
tax rates...AUS 35-105

Exemptions
acquisitions of urban land....................AUS 45-111
exchange control...................................AUS 55-031
price control..AUS 45-203

Paragraph

Expatriates
pension fund contributions,
remittance of ....AUS 55-032
personal savings, remittance of ....AUS 55-032

Expenses
arbitration..AUS 70-124
export opportunities, exploring of ....AUS 35-515

Exports
exploring opportunities
– expenses deductible ....AUS 35-515
financing ....AUS 75-005
foreign-controlled ....AUS 50-005
free trade zones ....AUS 50-021
law governing ....AUS 50-003
restrictions ....AUS 50-003
tariff agreements ....AUS 50-014

Export allowances
applicability ....AUS 35-505
industries excluded ....AUS 35-511

Export controls
objectives...AUS 50-011

Export incentives...............................AUS 35-504

Export licence
application ....AUS 50-004

Export processing zones....................AUS 35-512

F

Farming
foreign investment incentives ....AUS 45-111

Federal court system ....AUS 70-001

Federal parliament
election of members..............................AUS 20-004
law-making body ....AUS 20-004

Fees
industrial property................................AUS 65-024
registration
– non-resident companies ....AUS 30-103
– subsidiaries ....AUS 30-104

Financial institutions
equity-loan ratios ....AUS 75-011
exports, financing ....AUS 75-005
finance, raising of ....AUS 75-002
finance, supply of ....AUS 75-002
investment, financing...........................AUS 75-004
self-regulation ....AUS 75-105
sources of loan finance
– control...AUS 75-101
types...AUS 75-001

Financial ratios ....AUS 75-204

Financing
control.......................... AUS 75-101– AUS 75-112

Paragraph

law governing ....AUS 75-211
raising of
– financial institutions ....AUS 75-002
terms ....AUS 75-201– AUS 75-211

Financing arrangements
insurance..AUS 85-004

Fiscal year ....AUS 35-004; AUS 35-103

Floating charges
assets, classes of ....AUS 75-511

Foreign arbitral awards....................AUS 70-102

Foreign borrowings
currency to use.....................................AUS 55-014

Foreign companies ....AUS 30-102
accounts..AUS 30-103
arbitral proceedings ....AUS 70-133
civil procedure
– industrial dispute ....AUS 70-003
dispute resolution ....AUS 70-211
dividends
– withholding tax.................................AUS 35-103
local agent..AUS 30-103
rate of tax...AUS 35-103
registration.................. AUS 30-102; AUS 30-103;
                                              AUS 45-001
– documents to file ....AUS 30-103
– government approval ....AUS 30-103
registration fees ....AUS 30-103
status in dispute settlement..................AUS 70-002
subsidiaries — see Subsidiaries

Foreign-controlled business
restrictions ....AUS 50-005

Foreign-controlled companies
place of incorporation
– exchange control laws ....AUS 55-024

Foreign corporations — see Foreign companies

Foreign currency
borrowings in.......................................AUS 75-205
remittance ....AUS 55-012

Foreign entities
contracts..AUS 30-005

Foreign exchange — see also Exchange control
forward market ....AUS 55-035
tax considerations ....AUS 55-042

Foreign interests
definition ....AUS 45-103
examination ....AUS 45-102

Foreign investments
control..AUS 55-031
disincentives .... AUS 45-111; AUS 45-112;
                                              AUS 45-113

Exp

Paragraph

government's policy ....AUS 20-205
incentives .... AUS 45-111; AUS 45-112;
AUS 45-113
special control ....AUS 45-101

Foreign Investments Review Board
foreign ownership ....AUS 25-103

Foreign investors
contract and commercial law
– application ....AUS 30-014
control ....AUS 45-102
expropriation of assets ....AUS 45-114
geographical areas ....AUS 45-104
government guarantees ....AUS 20-204
local consultant ....AUS 45-115
protection ....AUS 20-205

Foreign judgments
enforcement ....AUS 70-024
recognition ....AUS 70-024

Foreign lawyers
arbitral proceedings ....AUS 70-135
employment ....AUS 20-012
status ....AUS 70-025

Foreign ownership
percentage
– status of company ....AUS 30-111

Foreign participation
arbitral proceedings ....AUS 70-133
dispute resolution ....AUS 70-211

Foreign workers
visas ....AUS 60-033
work permits ....AUS 60-033

Foreigners
labour laws ....AUS 60-032
land ownership ....AUS 25-103

Forms
dispute resolution
– provisions in contract ....AUS 70-222
rights in land, transfer of ....AUS 25-102

Forum
action against government ....AUS 70-402
settlement of dispute ....AUS 70-014

Forward market
foreign exchange ....AUS 55-035

Franchise
sole trader ....AUS 30-101

Free trade zones ....AUS 50-021

Freehold estate .... AUS 25-001; AUS 25-101

Fringe benefits tax ....AUS 35-301

Paragraph

G

General Agreement on Tariffs and Trade
membership ....AUS 20-202

General Interest Charge ....AUS 35-005

Geographical areas
disincentives ....AUS 45-105
incentives ....AUS 45-105

Goods
custom duties ....AUS 35-301
excise duties ....AUS 35-301
labelling and packaging
requirements ....AUS 50-022
price control ....AUS 45-201
sales tax ....AUS 35-301
security interests
– creation ....AUS 75-503
– registration ....AUS 75-503

Goods and Services Tax ....AUS 35-301

Government
action against ....AUS 70-401
– choice of forum ....AUS 70-402
– enforcement of orders ....AUS 70-403
– international conventions ....AUS 70-404
environmental assessment ....AUS 25-203
foreign investment policy ....AUS 20-205
immunity from suit ....AUS 70-401
institutional link with trade union ....AUS 60-021
land acquisition ....AUS 25-122
organisation ....AUS 20-005
profit sharing ....AUS 45-205
registration of foreign companies ....AUS 30-103
status in dispute settlement ....AUS 70-401

Government contracts
requirements ....AUS 30-004

Government guarantees
foreign investors ....AUS 20-205

Government participation
investment in local companies ....AUS 30-105

H

Harmonized tariff ....AUS 50-012

Historical sources
commercial law ....AUS 30-001
contract law ....AUS 30-001

Host country
exchange rate
– differing rates ....AUS 55-021
– method of fixing ....AUS 55-015
objectives ....AUS 50-011

Paragraph

I

Imports
anti-dumping duty .... AUS 50-025
concessional duty .... AUS 50-015
controls, objectives .... AUS 50-011
countervailing duty .... AUS 50-025
foreign-controlled .... AUS 50-005
free trade zones .... AUS 50-021
law governing .... AUS 50-001
penalties .... AUS 50-024
restrictions .... AUS 50-001
sales tax .... AUS 35-301
seizure .... AUS 50-031
tariff agreements .... AUS 50-014
taxes .... AUS 50-013
– additional .... AUS 50-024
– time for payment .... AUS 50-032

Import licence .... AUS 50-002
application .... AUS 50-004
goods imported .... AUS 50-002

Importers
requirements .... AUS 50-002

Incentives
foreign investment .... AUS 45-111; AUS 45-112;
                                           AUS 45-113
geographical areas .... AUS 45-105
law governing .... AUS 45-003
non-polluting plants .... AUS 25-205

Income tax — see also **Tax**
administration .... AUS 35-003
assessable income .... AUS 35-101
basis of assessment .... AUS 35-105
capital gains .... AUS 35-401
deductions .... AUS 35-105
non-residents .... AUS 35-102
payments, method of .... AUS 35-005
rates
– companies .... AUS 35-103
residence .... AUS 35-105
residents .... AUS 35-102
returns .... AUS 35-103
royalty income .... AUS 35-201

Industrial designs .... AUS 65-011
disadvantages for non-residents .... AUS 65-025
duration .... AUS 65-011
exclusive right .... AUS 65-011
international agreements .... AUS 65-001
licensing agreement .... AUS 65-022
registration .... AUS 65-021
transfers .... AUS 65-022

Industrial dispute
resolution .... AUS 70-031
settlement .... AUS 60-011

– customary method .... AUS 60-012
– parameters of legal system .... AUS 60-012

Industrial property
circuit layouts .... AUS 65-013
compulsory licenses .... AUS 65-023
copyright .... AUS 65-003
disadvantages for non-residents .... AUS 65-025
domestic legislation .... AUS 65-002
enforcement .... AUS 65-031
fees .... AUS 65-024
industrial designs .... AUS 65-011
labelling requirements .... AUS 65-031
license .... AUS 65-023
patents .... AUS 65-005
plant varieties .... AUS 65-014
registration .... AUS 65-021
trade marks .... AUS 65-004
trade secrets .... AUS 65-012
transfers .... AUS 65-022
unfair competition .... AUS 65-015

Industrial tribunal
labour law
– control .... AUS 60-024

Industries
export allowances, exclusion from ...... AUS 35-511
tax relief .... AUS 35-501

Injuries
defective products
– liability .... AUS 30-012
law governing .... AUS 45-302

Instruments of transfer
stamp duty .... AUS 35-301

Insurance
available range .... AUS 85-003
compulsory .... AUS 85-011
employees .... AUS 85-012
financing arrangements .... AUS 85-004
law governing .... AUS 85-001
proceeds of claims .... AUS 85-014
product liability .... AUS 85-021
resident brokers, use of .... AUS 85-001
state-owned brokers, use of .... AUS 85-001
workers compensation .... AUS 85-011

Insurance company
law governing .... AUS 85-013

Insurance underwriters
classes of .... AUS 85-002

Integrated circuits
international agreements .... AUS 65-001

Intellectual property — see **Industrial property**

Interests
land .... AUS 25-001

Paragraph

withholding tax.....................................AUS 35-201
non-residents
– withholding tax...............................AUS 75-112

Interest rates ....AUS 75-203

Interlocutory relief
industrial dispute..............................AUS 70-011

International agreements
Berne Convention ....AUS 65-001
domestic legislation ....AUS 65-001
host country signatory ....AUS 20-102
industrial property.............................AUS 65-001
TRIPs..AUS 65-001
WIPO Treaty......................................AUS 65-001

International banks
membership...AUS 20-101

International capital markets
access..AUS 75-003

**International commercial
arbitration**...AUS 70-101

International conventions ....AUS 50-023
air transportation...............................AUS 80-003
action against government..................AUS 70-404
dispute resolution......... AUS 70-202; AUS 70-301
industrial property.............................AUS 65-001
shipping ....AUS 80-003

**International Labour Organisation
Conventions** ....AUS 60-035

International tax treaties ....AUS 35-001

International treaties...........................AUS 50-023
host country signatory ....AUS 20-102

Investing money
customary terms..................................AUS 75-201
– flexibility ....AUS 75-202
financial institutions ....AUS 75-004
financing...AUS 75-004

Investments
local companies ....AUS 30-105

Investment disputes
resolution ....AUS 70-031

Investment incentives..........................AUS 45-003
repatriation of capital........................AUS 55-041

Investment profits
tax deduction ....AUS 35-212
taxes..AUS 35-201

Investment protection treaties.............AUS 20-201
multilateral...AUS 20-203

J

Joint trade agreements..........................AUS 20-202

Joint ventures
special regulations ....AUS 45-104
structure..AUS 30-113

Judgments
enforcement
– settlement of dispute.......................AUS 70-023
execution
– land seizure.....................................AUS 25-125
foreign — see Foreign judgments

Jurisdiction
arbitration
– outside jurisdiction ....AUS 70-141
arrest of vessels.................................AUS 80-005
foreign judgment, enforcement...........AUS 70-024

L

Labelling requirements
industrial property ....AUS 65-031
prescribed goods.................................AUS 50-022

Labour law
administration.....................................AUS 60-023
citizenship, effect of ....AUS 60-001
foreigners..AUS 60-032
legislative control ....AUS 60-024
nationality, effect of...........................AUS 60-001
race, effect of.....................................AUS 60-001
system governing................................AUS 60-001

Land
acquisition
– compensation...................................AUS 25-123
– powers of...AUS 25-122
customary rights ....AUS 25-011
easements..AUS 25-001
foreign ownership ....AUS 25-103
freehold estate...............AUS 25-001; AUS 25-101
law...AUS 25-001
– special areas....................................AUS 25-005
leasehold estate.............AUS 25-001; AUS 25-101
local regulations ....AUS 25-004
mortgages ....AUS 25-001
profits ;aga prendre...........................AUS 25-001
rates..AUS 25-124
registration, system of........................AUS 25-112
restrictive covenants ....AUS 25-001
rights — see Rights in land
rights of access ....AUS 25-101
security interests
– creation..AUS 75-503
security rights ....AUS 25-105
seizure
– execution of judgment.....................AUS 25-125
surveys..AUS 25-104
transfers
– restriction..AUS 25-003

	Paragraph
Land ownership	AUS 25-001
absolute	AUS 25-101
private	AUS 25-002
registration of rights	AUS 25-111
specific rights	AUS 25-113
Land tax	AUS 25-124; AUS 35-301
Land tenure	
forms	AUS 25-001
Land titles	
registration	AUS 75-502
Land use	AUS 25-001
agreement restricting	AUS 25-115
registration of rights	AUS 25-111
Language in use	
arbitration	AUS 70-142
courts	AUS 70-022
law	AUS 20-011
Laws	
advertising	AUS 45-306
air transportation	AUS 80-001
applicable	
– determination	AUS 20-013
bankruptcy	AUS 30-114
banks	AUS 30-101
carriage of goods	AUS 80-001
citizenship	AUS 60-002
commercial — see Commercial law	
companies	AUS 30-101
– managing structure	AUS 30-112
consumer contract	AUS 30-011
consumer protection	AUS 45-301
contract — see Contract law	
dangerous substances,	
movement of	AUS 80-004
employment of labour	AUS 60-001
environmental restrictions	AUS 25-201
equity-capital, raising of	AUS 75-103
exchange control	AUS 55-001
– application to foreign countries	AUS 55-004
exports	AUS 50-003
financing	AUS 75-211
foreign investors	AUS 30-101
imports, restrictions	AUS 50-001
injuries	AUS 45-302
insurance	AUS 85-001
insurance company	AUS 85-013
investment incentives	AUS 45-003
joint venture	AUS 30-113
land	AUS 25-001
– local regulations	AUS 25-004
– special areas	AUS 25-005
language in use	AUS 20-011
liquidation	AUS 30-104
movement of goods	AUS 80-002
promotions	AUS 45-306
seamen	AUS 80-001
shipping	AUS 80-001; AUS 80-002
shipping register	AUS 80-012
sources — see Sources of law	
system — see System of law	
storage of goods	AUS 80-002
Law-making bodies	AUS 20-004
Law practice	
certificate	AUS 20-012
licence	AUS 20-012
Lawyers	
practising certificate	AUS 20-012
qualification	AUS 20-012
Leasehold estate	AUS 25-001; AUS 25-101
Leaves	
employees	AUS 60-004
Legal profession	
structure	AUS 20-012
Legal system	
industrial dispute settlement	AUS 60-012
origin	AUS 20-002
Lender	
security interests	
– realisation of	AUS 75-515
– transferability	AUS 75-521
Lending money	
customary terms	AUS 75-201
– flexibility	AUS 75-202
Liability	
injury by defective products	AUS 30-012
Licences	
business activities	AUS 45-001
– granting	AUS 45-002
compulsory	AUS 65-023
computer software	AUS 65-022
copyright	AUS 65-022
import — see Import licence	
industrial designs	AUS 65-022
law practice	AUS 20-012
nature of	AUS 45-002
patents	AUS 65-022
performers' protection	AUS 65-022
plant breeder's rights	AUS 65-022
silicon chips	AUS 65-022
statutory monopolies	AUS 45-304
trade marks	AUS 65-022
trade names	AUS 65-022
trade secrets	AUS 65-022
Litigation	
dispute settlement	AUS 70-001

	Paragraph
– costs	AUS 70-015
– delay	AUS 70-015
Liquidation	
law governing	AUS 30-104
Loans	
currency to use	AUS 55-014
financial institutions, role of	AUS 75-002
interest rate	AUS 75-002
Loan finance	
sources — see Sources of loan finance	
Local advisers	
arbitration	AUS 70-304
conciliation	AUS 70-304
dispute resolution	AUS 70-304
Local agents	
non-resident companies	AUS 30-103
Local consultants	
foreign investors	AUS 45-115
Local councils	
election of members	AUS 20-004
law-making body	AUS 20-004
Local ownership	
investment in local companies	AUS 30-105
Local participation	
exchange controls, effect	AUS 55-025
Lock-out	
right to	AUS 60-022
Losses	
citizenship	AUS 60-002

M

Managing structures	
companies	AUS 30-112
Mareva injunction	
arrest of vessels	AUS 80-005
settlement of dispute	AUS 70-011
Mediation	
applicable law	AUS 70-213
basis of jurisdiction	AUS 70-205
confidentiality	AUS 70-215
disadvantages	AUS 70-224
enforcement of settlement	AUS 70-211
joint with arbitration	AUS 70-225
representation	AUS 70-212
rules governing	AUS 70-204
types of disputes, restrictions on	AUS 70-223
Mediators	
appointment	AUS 70-203

	Paragraph
Mining	
foreign investment incentives	AUS 45-111
Mining projects	
guidelines	AUS 45-104
Miscellaneous tax	AUS 35-301
Monopolisation	
prohibition	AUS 45-303
Mortgages	
land	AUS 25-001
Motor vehicles	
registration	AUS 75-502
security interests	
– creation	AUS 75-503
Movement of goods	
law governing	AUS 80-002
Multilateral treaties	AUS 20-102
Municipal rates	
land	AUS 25-124

N

Nationality	
balance in employment	AUS 60-034
basis of law	AUS 60-002
directors	
– subsidiaries	AUS 30-104
dual	AUS 60-002
employees	
– subsidiaries	AUS 30-104
labour laws	AUS 60-001
loss of	AUS 60-002
Native Title Act	
customary land rights	AUS 25-011
New York Convention	
arbitration	AUS 70-102
Newspaper	
foreign investment incentives	AUS 45-111
Non-polluting plants	
incentives	AUS 25-205
Non-residents	
Australian-sourced income	
– income tax	AUS 35-105
business activities	
– provisions	AUS 45-305
franked dividend	AUS 35-202
income tax	AUS 35-102
industrial property	
– disadvantages	AUS 65-025
residents distinguished	AUS 55-023

Non-residents — continued   **Paragraph**
royalty income
– income tax.......................................AUS 35-201
shareholdings in subsidiaries...............AUS 30-104
withholding tax....................................AUS 75-112
tax treatment ....AUS 35-203

Non-resident companies — see **Foreign companies**

Non-residential real estate
guidelines..AUS 45-104

O

**Organisation for Economic Cooperation and
Development**
membership..AUS 20-103

Outward remittances
approval ....AUS 35-204
form ....AUS 35-205

Overseas defendant
court's jurisdiction..............................AUS 70-001

P

Packaging requirements
prescribed goods..................................AUS 50-022

Partnerships
law governing ....AUS 30-101
taxable income.....................................AUS 35-101

Patents...AUS 65-005
disadvantages for non-residents...........AUS 65-025
exclusive rights....................................AUS 65-005
innovation patent.................................AUS 65-005
international agreements.......................AUS 65-001
licensing agreement ....AUS 65-022
protection...AUS 65-005
registration .... AUS 65-021; AUS 75-502
standard patent....................................AUS 65-005
transfers...AUS 65-022

"Pay as you earn" (PAYE)
tax withheld ....AUS 35-103

Payroll tax..AUS 35-301

Penalties
environmental controls
– non-compliance ....AUS 25-202
imports...AUS 50-024
restraint of trade.................................AUS 45-303
pollution..AUS 25-202

Pension fund contributions
remittance by expatriates ....AUS 55-032

Performers' protection
copyright..AUS 65-003
disadvantages for non-residents..........AUS 65-025
international agreements.......................AUS 65-001

Paragraph
licensing agreement.............................AUS 65-022
transfers ....AUS 65-022

Personal savings
remittance by expatriates.....................AUS 55-032

Personal security
forms of ....AUS 75-522

Plant
depreciation allowances.......................AUS 35-103
non-polluting
– incentives...AUS 25-205

Plant breeder's rights...........................AUS 65-014
disadvantages for non-residents...........AUS 65-025
exclusive right ....AUS 65-014
international agreements.......................AUS 65-001
licensing agreement.............................AUS 65-022
protection...AUS 65-014
registration ....AUS 65-021
transfers ....AUS 65-022

Pollution
dangerous substances,
movement of.....................................AUS 80-004
law governing ....AUS 25-201
penalties...AUS 25-202
standards..AUS 25-204

Price control
application ....AUS 45-206
body administering...............................AUS 45-203
commodities ....AUS 45-201
exemptions...AUS 45-203
restrictions for certain companies........AUS 45-204

Procedures
specific disputes...................................AUS 70-144
taxation disputes ....AUS 70-031

Product liability insurance ....AUS 85-021

Profits
government participation......................AUS 45-205

Profits à prendre
land..AUS 25-001

Promotions
law governing ....AUS 45-306

Proper law
settlement of dispute...........................AUS 70-013

Property
security interests ....AUS 75-301

Proprietary companies
law governing ....AUS 30-101
disposal of shares................................AUS 30-104

Protection
circuit layouts ....AUS 65-013
copyright..AUS 65-003

Paragraph

patents......................................AUS 65-005
plant breeder ....AUS 65-014
trade secrets ....AUS 65-012
trademarks...............................AUS 65-004

Public companies
definition................................AUS 35-103
law governing ....AUS 30-101
private companies distinguished..........AUS 35-103

R

Race
balance in employment.........................AUS 60-034
labour laws................................AUS 60-001

Radio
foreign investment incentives..............AUS 45-111

Rates of tax
custom duties ....AUS 50-012
executives ....AUS 35-105
fringe benefits tax ....AUS 35-301
land ....AUS 25-124
sales tax..................................AUS 35-301

Redundancy provisions
employees...............................AUS 60-004

Reform
corporate law ....AUS 30-101

Refund
sales tax...................................AUS 50-013

Registration
business activities ....AUS 45-001
– granting.................................AUS 45-002
fees
– non-resident companies ....AUS 30-103
– subsidiaries ....AUS 30-104
foreign companies......... AUS 30-102; AUS 45-001
industrial property...................AUS 65-021
industrial designs ....AUS 65-021
land
– security rights ....AUS 25-105
– system...............................AUS 25-112
land ownership.........................AUS 25-103
– rights ....AUS 25-111
land use, right of ....AUS 25-111
nature of...................................AUS 45-002
non-resident companies ....AUS 30-103
– documents to be filed ....AUS 30-103
– government approval ....AUS 30-103
patents...................................AUS 65-021
plant breeder's rights ....AUS 65-021
security interests .... AUS 75-501; AUS 75-502
ships......................................AUS 80-012
trade marks..............................AUS 65-021

Paragraph

Regulations
business activities
– non-residents....................AUS 45-305
environmental control..............AUS 25-202
export and import licences........AUS 50-004
joint venture...........................AUS 45-104
shipbuilding industry.............AUS 80-011

Remedies
commercial law......................AUS 30-016
contracts...............................AUS 30-016

Remittances
currency
– restrictions ....AUS 55-013
dividends ....AUS 55-011
foreign currency....................AUS 55-012
local currency ....AUS 55-012
pension fund contributions
– expatriate personnel...........AUS 55-032
personal savings
– expatriate personnel...........AUS 55-032

Remuneration
employees
– tax withheld ....AUS 35-103
executives
– income tax ....AUS 35-105
fringe benefits tax ....AUS 35-301

Repatriation of capital ....AUS 55-005
restrictions ....AUS 55-041

Representation — see **Right of representation**

Reserve Bank of Australia
exchange control
– administration of................AUS 55-002
– policies.............................AUS 55-003

Residents
income tax ....AUS 35-102
non-residents distinguished ....AUS 55-023
tax treatment.........................AUS 35-203

Restraint of trade
administration of trade practices........AUS 45-303
authorisation ....AUS 45-303
extraterritorial effect.............AUS 45-303
penalties...............................AUS 45-303
prohibition ....AUS 45-303

Restrictive covenants
land ....AUS 25-001

Restrictive trade practices — see
Restraint of trade

Retirement provisions
employees.............................AUS 60-004

Revenue gains
offset of capital losses...........AUS 35-403

Paragraph

Revenue losses
offset against capital gains.................AUS 35-404

Rights in land
acquisition, restrictions.......................AUS 25-103
ascertainment....................................AUS 25-121
extension...AUS 25-114
extinction of rights.............................AUS 25-101
nature of..AUS 25-101
transfer...AUS 25-102
– conveyancing fees..........................AUS 25-102
– prescribed form..............................AUS 25-102

Right of access...................................AUS 25-101

Right of commons
land..AUS 25-001

Right of representation
conciliation..AUS 70-212
mediation..AUS 70-212

Roll-overs
capital gains......................................AUS 35-402

Royalty
definition...AUS 35-211
non-residents
– income tax.....................................AUS 35-201

Rules
arbitrators, choice of..........................AUS 70-122
conciliation..AUS 70-204
mediation..AUS 70-204

Rules of civil procedure
industrial dispute...............................AUS 70-004
interlocutory relief.............................AUS 70-011

Rules of natural justice.......................AUS 70-005
arbitral proceedings...........................AUS 70-134

S

Salaries
basis of assessment...........................AUS 35-105
payroll tax...AUS 35-301

Sales tax..AUS 35-301
imports..AUS 50-013
time for payment...............................AUS 50-032

Seamen
compensation....................................AUS 80-001
law governing....................................AUS 80-001

Securities
acceptable securities..........................AUS 75-523
registration charges............................AUS 75-524
types of
– tax implication................................AUS 75-525

Security for costs
settlement of dispute.........................AUS 70-021

Paragraph

Security interests................................AUS 75-204
borrower's interest
– identification...................................AUS 75-501
– whether recognised and protected....AUS 75-513
company charges...............................AUS 75-503
creation, formalities............................AUS 75-503
further advances................................AUS 75-512
land..AUS 75-503
lender's security, transfer of...............AUS 75-521
number against one property...............AUS 75-505
priority..AUS 75-504
property...AUS 75-301
property subjected, identification.......AUS 75-501
realisation by lender...........................AUS 75-515
recognised forms................................AUS 75-401
registration....................AUS 75-501; AUS 75-502
retention by borrower.........................AUS 75-514
ships...AUS 75-503

Security rights
land
– registration....................................AUS 25-105
recognised forms................................AUS 75-401

Seizure
imports..AUS 50-031
land
– execution of judgment....................AUS 25-125

Self-employed
tax liabilities, payment of...................AUS 35-005

Settlement of dispute — see also
Dispute resolution
applicable law....................................AUS 70-013
– choice..AUS 70-121
arbitration — see Arbitration
commercial disputes...........................AUS 30-013
conciliation
– enforcement...................................AUS 70-211
contractual disputes...........................AUS 30-013
evidence, collection of........................AUS 70-012
execution outside jurisdiction..............AUS 70-005
foreign companies, status...................AUS 70-002
foreign judgment, enforcement...........AUS 70-024
foreign lawyers, status........................AUS 70-025
forum..AUS 70-104
government's status............................AUS 70-401
interlocutory relief.............................AUS 70-011
judgments, enforcement.....................AUS 70-023
litigation...AUS 70-001
– costs..AUS 70-015
– delay..AUS 70-015
mediation
– enforcement...................................AUS 70-211
procedural law, applicability...............AUS 70-115
rules of civil procedure.......................AUS 70-004
rules of evidence................................AUS 70-004

Paragraph

security for costs .... AUS 70-021
service outside jurisdiction .... AUS 70-005

Services
jurisdiction .... AUS 70-005
price control .... AUS 45-201

Shares
acquisition
– local company .... AUS 30-105

Shareholdings
subsidiaries
-- non-residents .... AUS 30-104

Ships
registration .... AUS 75-502; AUS 80-012
security interests
– creation .... AUS 75-503

Shipbuilding industry
regulatory bodies .... AUS 80-011

Shipping
dangerous substances,
movement of .... AUS 80-004
international convention .... AUS 80-003
law governing .... AUS 80-001; AUS 80-002

Shipping register
law governing .... AUS 80-012

Silicon chips
circuit layouts .... AUS 65-013
licensing agreement .... AUS 65-022
transfers .... AUS 65-022

Sole trader
franchise .... AUS 30-101
law governing .... AUS 30-101

Sources of law .... AUS 20-003

Sources of loan finance
control .... AUS 75-101; AUS 75-102

Specific rights
land ownership .... AUS 25-113

Staff
investment in local companies .... AUS 30-105

Stamp duty .... AUS 35-301
rights in land, transfer of .... AUS 25-102

State parliaments
election of members .... AUS 20-004
law-making body .... AUS 20-004

State taxes .... AUS 35-301

Statutory monopolies
licence .... AUS 45-304

Storage of goods
law governing .... AUS 80-002

Paragraph

Strikes
industrial dispute settlement .... AUS 60-013
right to .... AUS 60-022

Subsidiaries
accounts .... AUS 30-104
bearer shares .... AUS 30-104
directors' nationality .... AUS 30-104
directors' qualification .... AUS 30-104
employees, nationality .... AUS 30-104
establishment
– requirements .... AUS 30-104
nominal capital .... AUS 30-104
registration fees .... AUS 30-104
shareholdings by non-residents .... AUS 30-104

Superannuation
employees .... AUS 85-012

Surface transportation
dangerous substances, movement of .... AUS 80-004

Surveys
land .... AUS 25-104

System of law .... AUS 20-001

T

Takeovers
Australian Takeover Law .... AUS 30-105
investment in local companies .... AUS 30-105

Tariff agreements
import-export .... AUS 50-014

Tax — see also Income tax
additional
– imports .... AUS 50-024
depreciation allowances .... AUS 35-103
documentary evidence .... AUS 35-103
imports .... AUS 50-013
– time for payment .... AUS 50-032
investment profits .... AUS 35-201
land .... AUS 25-124
miscellaneous .... AUS 35-301

Tax considerations
exchange control regulations .... AUS 55-042

Tax credits .... AUS 35-202
existence .... AUS 35-002

Tax incentives .... AUS 35-501– AUS 35-515

Tax liabilities
method of payment .... AUS 35-005

Tax losses .... AUS 35-103

Tax rate — see Rates of Tax

Tax relief
criteria affecting .... AUS 35-503

Tax relief — continued   **Paragraph**

new industries ....AUS 35-501
period ....AUS 35-502

Tax returns ....AUS 35-103

Tax sparing credit ....AUS 35-002

Tax treatment
distinction between resident and
non-resident ....AUS 35-203

Taxable income
computation ....AUS 35-101

Taxation disputes
resolution
– procedures .... AUS 35-003; AUS 70-031;
AUS 70-144

Television
foreign investment incentives ....AUS 45-111

Thin capitalisation rules ....AUS 35-103
foreign borrowings ....AUS 55-014
foreign control ....AUS 55-024

Third country
arbitration ....AUS 70-145

Torrens system
land
– registration ....AUS 25-104
– transfer of ....AUS 25-105

Tort
court's jurisdiction ....AUS 70-001
law governing ....AUS 45-302

Trade marks ....AUS 65-004
disadvantages for non-residents ....AUS 65-025
exclusive right ....AUS 65-004
international agreements ....AUS 65-001
licensing agreement ....AUS 65-022
protection ....AUS 65-004
registration ....AUS 65-021
transfers ....AUS 65-022
registration ....AUS 75-502

Trade names
licensing agreement ....AUS 65-022
transfers ....AUS 65-022

Trade Practices Commission ....AUS 45-303

Trade secrets ....AUS 65-012
civil remedies ....AUS 65-012
duration ....AUS 65-012
licensing agreement ....AUS 65-022
protection ....AUS 65-012
transfers ....AUS 65-022

Trade unions
institutional link with government ....AUS 60-021
liabilities and privileges ....AUS 60-014

Paragraph

make-up ....AUS 60-014
status ....AUS 60-014

Transfers
computer software ....AUS 65-022
copyright ....AUS 65-022
industrial designs ....AUS 65-022
land
– restrictions ....AUS 25-003
patents ....AUS 65-022
performers' protection ....AUS 65-022
plant breeder's rights ....AUS 65-022
rights in land ....AUS 25-102
– conveyancing fees ....AUS 25-102
– prescribed form ....AUS 25-102
silicon chips ....AUS 65-022
trade marks ....AUS 65-022
trade names ....AUS 65-022
trade secrets ....AUS 65-022

Trusts
taxable income ....AUS 35-101

U

Undistributed profits tax ....AUS 35-103

Unfair competition
industrial property ....AUS 65-015

Unfair contracts
review of ....AUS 45-307

Unitary tax ....AUS 35-302

**United Nations Committee on International
Trade Law (UNCITRAL)**
arbitration .... AUS 70-103;AUS 70-104;
AUS 70-105
conciliation .... AUS 70-103; AUS 70-104;
AUS 70-105

Urban real estate
acquisitions ....AUS 45-111
foreign investment incentives ....AUS 45-111

V

Vessels
arrest ....AUS 80-005

Visas
foreign workers ....AUS 60-033

W

Wages
control ....AUS 60-005
basis of assessment ....AUS 35-105
employees ....AUS 60-004
payroll tax ....AUS 35-301

Paragraph

Water rates
land ....AUS 25-124

Withholding tax
dividends....................... AUS 35-201; AUS 55-011
– non-residents....................................AUS 75-112
– non-resident companies ....AUS 35-103
interest ....AUS 35-201
– non-residents....................................AUS 75-112
unfranked dividends ....AUS 35-202

Work permits
foreign workers...................................AUS 60-033

Paragraph

Workers compensation
insurance.......................AUS 85-011; AUS 85-012

Workers' compensation insurance
employers' obligation..........................AUS 60-031

Working hours
control...AUS 60-005
employees..AUS 60-004

World Bank
membership ....AUS 20-101

INTRODUCTION

Australia is the world's largest island; it lies between the South Pacific and Indian Oceans. It has a land mass almost as great as the USA (excluding Alaska) and is about 50% bigger than Europe (excluding Russia).

Australia has been populated for at least 50,000 years. The indigenous or the "first" Australians arrived after a sea voyage of about 60km, making this probably the world's earliest sea-borne migration.

Spanish, Portuguese and Dutch sailors sighted the Australian coast in the 16th and 17th centuries. The Dutch explored the western coast, but the major voyages of discovery were by the British. As a result of Captain James Cook's voyages in the second half of the 18th century, possession of the whole of the eastern coast of Australia on behalf of the British was taken in 1770. Formal possession on behalf of the British Crown was taken of the whole of the eastern part of the continent and Tasmania by Captain Arthur Phillip in 1788 when he settled in Sydney with convicted prisoners (convicts) to establish an overseas jail or convict colony.

By the middle of 1829, Australia had become a dependency of the United Kingdom.

The early colonists — both convicts and the small number of free settlers — brought with them the common law of England which applied as much as was possible in a convict colony. This was important as convicts became free citizens when their sentences expired. The common law laid the foundations for the development of trade and commerce in the colonies. An Act of the UK parliament in 1828 provided that "all laws and statutes in force within the realm of England on 25 July 1828 should be applied in the administration of justice in the courts of New South Wales and Van Diemen's Land [Tasmania] so far as the same could be applied within those colonies".

At first, the laws of the colony were made and administered by naval and military Governors appointed by the British government, but gradually power shifted to legislative bodies (legislative council) which gradually developed the principles of responsible government as seen in the British parliament. Civil courts were established from the beginning and local legal professions grew in response to the growth in trade and commerce.

During the 19th century, the continent was settled at separate places along its foreshores, and in turn the main settlements developed into separate colonies. So by the end of that century the continent plus Tasmania was divided into six self-governing British colonies.

Those colonies united to form the Commonwealth of Australia which was proclaimed on 1 January 1901. From that date, the description of the six colonies was changed to that of States.

Under the Australian constitution, the legislative power of the Commonwealth of Australia is vested in the Commonwealth (or "federal" or "national") Parliament based in Canberra, and the extent of the legislative power of the Commonwealth parliament and those of the six State parliaments is defined in the Australian and State constitutions respectively.

Australia has a population of approximately 19 million. This population is largely concentrated in two coastal regions — the larger number live in the south east stretching from South Australia, through Victoria, Tasmania, and New South Wales to Queensland, and the smaller number live in the south-west of Western Australia.

The official language of Australia is English.

Originally, Australia's main industries were in the rural sector led by wheat and wool. Since World War II, manufacturing and mining has developed so that iron ore, coal and bauxite, plus wool and wheat, today represent Australia's major exports. Increasingly, Australia is exporting services such as education and e-commerce.

An Overview (The System of Law and Government)

System of law .... AUS ¶20-001

Origin of legal system .... AUS ¶20-002

Sources of law .... AUS ¶20-003

Law-making bodies .... AUS ¶20-004

Organisation of government .... AUS ¶20-005

Language of the law .... AUS ¶20-011

Structure of legal profession .... AUS ¶20-012

Determination of applicable law .... AUS ¶20-013

Choice of method and forum .... AUS ¶20-014

Treaty obligations .... AUS ¶20-101

Guarantees and incentives .... AUS ¶20-201

AUS ¶20-001   SYSTEM OF LAW

When the British government established a colony for convicts in New South Wales in 1788 to ease pressure on overcrowded British jails, the occupied land was considered by current constitutional theory not to be owned by any group or state and no recognised legal system was considered to exist. It was only after *Mabo's case* in the High Court of Australia in 1992 (*Mabo v Queensland (No 2)* (1992) 175 CLR 1) that aboriginal occupation of Australia for thousands of years was recognised by the Australian legal system, especially in the area of land law.

Formal possession on behalf of the British Crown of the eastern part of the Australian continent and Tasmania was taken on 7 February 1788, and through the 19th century the whole territory now known as Australia was settled in six areas which were colonies of the United Kingdom. Some of the colonies such as New South Wales and Tasmania were settled by the British as convict colonies (or prisons) for the British; some like South Australia and Victoria were never convict colonies.

The laws in force in England at the date of that first British settlement were taken to be the laws of the colonies on the basis that the colonies were "settled" by the British. Accordingly, the first British settlers in Australia carried with them as their common law birthright so much of the existing English common law as was applicable to their situation and to the conditions in the new colony.

In 1828, the British parliament passed the *Australian Courts Act* which had the effect of proclaiming that English law existing up to 1828 was in force in Australia (at that time, New South Wales and Tasmania) as far as it could apply to the conditions of the colonies. Accordingly, the law that was immediately applied in the Australian colonies comprised:

- case law and custom, known as "common law" (which includes both "law" and "equity"); and
- English statute law.

The law developed an Australian "accent" over time as it was applied to the special circumstances which arose within the colonies. The growth of a uniquely Australian body of law was advanced by the establishment of responsible government within each of the colonies and the creation of local parliaments which passed local laws. However, as with most common law jurisdictions, the law remained, and even today remains, largely English in character and content with some American aspects.

In 1901, the six colonies federated under the name "Commonwealth of Australia" and a federal system of government was adopted. Australia now consist of six States and two Territories. Each State and Territory has its own parliament. There is also the Commonwealth (or national, central, or federal) parliament, the legislative powers of which are set out in the Australian Constitution. Broadly speaking, the Commonwealth parliament is empowered to make laws about matters which are of national concern such as trade and commerce among the States, external affairs, currency, weights and measures and communications.

The States and Territories can make laws about any matter except those falling under Commonwealth jurisdiction and in the event of an inconsistency between a Commonwealth law and a State or Territory law, the Commonwealth law prevails.

Australia has a common law system based on a mixture of case law and statute law, and recognising the multicultural nature of modern Australian society, there is recognition of customary aboriginal law, canon law, Jewish law and Muslim law.

AUS ¶20-002   ORIGIN OF LEGAL SYSTEM

By the end of the nineteenth century, the continent of Australia had been divided into six self-governing colonies, namely New South Wales, Victoria, Queensland, South Australia, Western Australia and Tasmania.

The six British colonies agreed among themselves in 1901, with the agreement of the United Kingdom, to federate under the name "Commonwealth of Australia", based on the Australian Constitution. The Commonwealth of Australia consisted of the former six colonies, now called "States" and the Northern Territory. The Australian Capital Territory (ACT) became part of the Commonwealth when it was created a few years later. The ACT is the location of Canberra (first settled in mid-1920s), Australia's national or federal capital city.

Under sec. 51 of the Australian Constitution, the Commonwealth (or "federal" or "national") parliament is able to make laws on most matters of national importance such as:

- international trade and commerce;
- inter-State trade and commerce;

- taxation;

- post, telegraph and "other like services" (now including e-commerce);

- defence;

- currency;

- banking;

- bankruptcy and insolvency;

- copyrights, patents, designs and trademarks;

- corporations;

- immigration;

- external affairs;

- matters referred to the Commonwealth by the States (such as power over corporations referred in 2001); and

- matters incidental to the above.

Some of the powers of the Commonwealth government exist alongside those of the six State and the two Territory governments. This means that laws in relation to those matters may be made by the Commonwealth, or by the States or Territories. In the event of inconsistency, the Commonwealth law will prevail and the State or Territory law will be invalid under sec. 109.

In all matters not otherwise specifically vested in the Commonwealth government by the Constitution, the Australian State and Territory governments have independent jurisdiction. State and Territory laws apply normally only to persons who are residents of the State or Territory concerned and to things located in, or events occurring within, the State or Territory.

The common law is uniform throughout Australia, although statute law may vary between the States and Territories in matters of detail. Attempts are made, where possible, for uniform laws in areas of State and Territory jurisdiction especially in matters of national importance such as Australia's almost uniform fair trading law, consumer credit laws or partnership laws. In 1992, a *Mutual Recognition Act* was passed by the Commonwealth Parliament and by the parliaments of each State and Territory by which the Commonwealth and the States and Territories agreed to establish a scheme for the mutual recognition of regulatory standards for goods and occupations throughout Australia.

AUS ¶20-003   SOURCES OF LAW

The sources of law in Australia are legislation (or statutes or Acts of Parliament) passed by the Commonwealth, State and Territory parliaments and case law, the decisions of judges in the various Australian courts and tribunals at Commonwealth or State/Territory level.

AUS ¶20-004   LAW-MAKING BODIES

There are three levels of law-making in Australia: the Commonwealth parliament in Canberra, State/Territory parliaments and local government in cities, towns and in the shires of rural and regional Australia.

Federal parliament

The federal legislative power is vested by the Australian Constitution in the Commonwealth (or "Federal") parliament, where the laws are enacted in the name of the Sovereign, the Senate (the upper house), and the House of Representatives (the lower house). The subjects with respect to which the Commonwealth parliament is empowered to make laws are, as noted above at AUS ¶20-002, set out in the Constitution.

Refer to the federal government homepage at fed.gov.au.

State/Territory parliaments

Each State or Territory parliament has power to govern and pass laws generally (but subject to the Australian Constitution) in and for their respective State/Territory in all cases whatsoever. The power of the States to make laws was enhanced in 1986 by the enactment by the Commonwealth parliament of the *Australia Act 1986*. Subject to certain limitations, the States may alter, repeal, or vary their Constitutions.

Where a law of a State/Territory is inconsistent with a law of the Commonwealth parliament, the latter law prevails and the former law is, to the extent of the inconsistency, invalid under sec. 109 of the Constitution.

All State and Territory Parliaments have an upper house (Legislative Council) and a lower house (Legislative Assembly) (except Queensland, the Australian Capital Territory and the Northern Territory which are unicameral).

Local councils

Australia is divided into local government districts called cities, municipalities and shires, all of which get their authority from statutes passed by the State or Territory parliament.

Franchise

Members of the federal and State/Territory parliaments and local government councils are elected by universal suffrage. Voting is compulsory for Australian citizens from the age of 18.

AUS ¶20-005   ORGANISATION OF GOVERNMENT

For the organisation of its governments at Commonwealth and State/Territory level, Australia has adopted the Westminster system of responsible government.

The power of government is not absolute due to the "separation of powers" among the three branches of government:

(1) The legislature makes the laws. At the Commonwealth level, the executive government (i.e. the Cabinet presided over by the Prime Minister) exercises a

controlling influence over the House of Representatives in respect of its agenda. The principal factors are that:

— the government is drawn from the legislature;

— to continue in office, the government depends on the support of the majority of the Members of the House of Representatives; and

— the party system and its rules of discipline help the government to maintain its majority.

The same system exists at State and Territory level. Executive power is exercised by the Cabinet which is headed by the Premier (or the Chief Minister in the two Territories), who is the leader of the majority party in the lower house of parliament.

(2) The executive (civil service) administers the laws.

(3) The judiciary interprets, applies and enforces the laws.

Under the separation of powers, no one person or group controls all three branches of government.

The seat of government is the national or State/Territory capital, as follows:

• Commonwealth of Australia	Canberra
• New South Wales	Sydney
• Victoria	Melbourne
• South Australia	Adelaide
• Western Australia	Perth
• Queensland	Brisbane
• Tasmania	Hobart
• Australian Capital Territory	Canberra
• Northern Territory	Darwin

AUS ¶20-011   LANGUAGE OF THE LAW

English is the language of the law in Australia. Australia is a multi-cultural country where many Asian languages are spoken and court interpreters are available for those who do not speak English.

Australian legislation, cases and legal literature are published by companies such as CCH Australia Ltd, and much Australian law is now available on the Internet at sites such as the following:

General:

Austlii — www.austlii.edu.au

CCH — www.cch.com.au

LexisNexis Butterworths — www.butterworths.com.au

Lawbook Company — www.lbc.com.au

Thomson's FindLaw Australia — www.au.findlaw.com

By jurisdiction:

Commonwealth — www.lawsearch.gov.au, or

Commonwealth — http://scaleplus.law.gov.au

New South Wales — www.nsw.gov.au

Victoria — www.dms.dpc.vic.gov.au

Queensland — www.legislation.qld.gov.au

South Australia — www.sacentral.sa.gov.au/government/parliament_sa

Western Australia — www.slp.wa.gov.au/statutes/swans.nsf

Tasmania — www.thelaw.tas.gov.au

ACT — www.legislation.act.gov.au

Northern Territory — www.nt.gov.au/lant

Many issues discussed in this Tab can be updated from Australian law firm websites such as those of:

Allens Arthur Robinson — www.aar.com.au

Deacons — www.deacons.com.au

Freehills — www.freehills.com.au

Mallesons Stephen Jaques — www.mallesons.com

AUS ¶20-012   STRUCTURE OF LEGAL PROFESSION

The structure of the legal profession in Australia was originally modelled on that of England. Now, only New South Wales and Queensland retain a divided profession under which a lawyer may practise as a barrister or solicitor, but not as both a barrister and solicitor. In those two States, solicitors are those practitioners who maintain offices to which members of the public may go for legal advice for a fee on a whole range of matters. However, solicitors have the right of audience in court and some maintain an advocacy practice. Traditionally barristers specialise in advice, opinions and advocacy in court and do not do the work done by solicitors. Barristers can only act for a client on the instructions of a solicitor but in some jurisdictions, individuals (including patent attorneys and tax accountants) can instruct barristers directly without needing to go through a solicitor.

In all States and Territories (except New South Wales and Queensland), the legal profession is fused, which means that a legal practitioner may act as both a barrister and a solicitor. However, for reasons of efficiency and specialisation, separate bars exist in many jurisdictions which in theory have a fused profession such as in Canberra and in some regional centres.

In some jurisdictions in Australia, judges and barristers (including a solicitor appearing as a barrister) robe in the traditional wigs and gowns. Judges of the High Court wear American-inspired gowns and no wigs.

The legal profession is generally controlled by Law Societies (solicitors) or Bar Councils (barristers), which are self-regulatory professional bodies. All of these societies and councils are members of the Law Council of Australia.

To become a legal practitioner in Australia, an aspiring lawyer must first fulfil the educational requirements — normally a law course at a university leading to the degree of LL.B., followed by ''articles of clerkship''or a short professional practice or skills course — and must then be admitted to practice by the applicant's State or Territory Supreme Court. There are about 30 law schools in Australian universities. These can be accessed via www.austlii.edu.au under the education icon.

The right to practise as a solicitor is given by a license, usually called a practising certificate, by the relevant law society. It is an offence for a person to act as a solicitor without having the appropriate practising certificate, or to perform certain legal work for a fee unless the person is a legal practitioner (this term is defined as the holder of a current practising certificate). The Australian legal profession is gradually moving to the concept of a ''travelling'' practising certificate, and in the near future a lawyer in one State/Territory will have the right to practise in another State/Territory.

Foreign lawyers living in Australia may be entitled to practise foreign law in Australia or may be employed by Australian solicitors to practise foreign law, but are not themselves entitled to act as, or to hold themselves out as, Australian solicitors. For example, the details for the State of Victoria are set out at on the Legal Practice Board's homepage at www.lpb.vic.gov.au.

Refer also to the Law Council of Australia homepage at www.lawcouncil.asn.au.

AUS ¶20-013   DETERMINATION OF APPLICABLE LAW

Australian law falls within the Anglo-American model and rests on the basis that the parties may expressly select the law that will govern the contract.

The parties to a contract may determine for themselves what the proper law of the contract will be, provided that their expressed intention is *bona fide* and legal, and provided there is no reason for avoiding their choice on the general rules of public policy. However, on public policy grounds, a mandatory law of the forum cannot be set aside by a choice of law designed to take the transaction outside the limits of its operation.

AUS ¶20-014   CHOICE OF METHOD AND FORUM

Alternative dispute resolution (''ADR'') is an alternative to the court system involving commercial arbitration and/or mediation.

ADR encourages disputants to reach their own solution and the role of the third party is to facilitate the disputants to reach a solution.

The power to regulate arbitration and other forms of dispute resolution lies principally with the States, unless Australia's treaty obligations call for or require federal legislation. All States and Territories have adopted a more or less identical model arbitration law (called the *Commercial Arbitration Act*).

The *International Arbitration Act 1974* (Cth) governs international commercial disputes unless expressly excluded by the parties.

The major centres of ADR are:

• the Australian Centre for International Commercial Arbitration www.acica.com.au; the Centre is affiliated with the Institute of Arbitrators and Mediators Australia); and

• the Australian Commercial Disputes Centre (available at www.acdcltd.com.au).

Both Centres operate Australia-wide.

See further AUS ¶70-001 ''Settlement of Disputes''. The subject is dealt with in detail in *Doyles Dispute Resolution Practice — Asia Pacific*, CCH International Limited.

TREATY OBLIGATIONS

Membership of international
    banks .... AUS ¶20-101
International agreements .. AUS ¶20-102

OECD declaration .... AUS ¶20-103

AUS ¶20-101   MEMBERSHIP OF INTERNATIONAL BANKS

Australia is a member of the World Bank, the Asian Development Bank (ADB), the International Bank for Reconstruction and Development (IBRD) and the Asia Pacific Economic Cooperation (APEC). Australia supports these international financial and development initiatives.

APEC was established in 1989 in response to the growing interdependence among Asia-Pacific economies. It originally commenced as an informal dialogue group and has since become the primary regional vehicle for promoting open trade and practical economic cooperation in the region. Its goal is to advance Asia-Pacific economic dynamism and foster a sense of community. Today, APEC's 21 member economies have a combined Gross Domestic Product of over US$18 trillion in 1999 and 43.85% of global trade.

Further details are available on APEC's home page at www.apecsec.org.sg.

AUS ¶20-102   INTERNATIONAL AGREEMENTS

Australia has ratified and implemented the *Convention on the Recognition and Enforcement of Foreign Arbitral Awards* (the ''New York Convention'') by the *International Arbitration Act 1974* (see AUS ¶70-102).

Australia has ratified and implemented:

AUS ¶20-101

the Convention on the Recognition and Enforcement of Foreign Arbitral Awards (the "New York Convention") by the International Arbitration Act 1974 (see AUS ¶70-102), and

International Convention on the Settlement of Investment Disputes between States and Nationals of Other States 1965 (the "ICSID" or the "Washington Convention") by the ICSID *Implementation Act* 1990.

Australia has also implemented:

- the United Nations Commission on International Trade Law (UNCITRAL) Model Law on International Commercial Arbitration (the "Model Law") (by the *International Arbitration Amendment Act* 1989); and

- the United Nations Convention on Contracts for the International Sale of Goods 1980 (CISG).

AUS ¶20-103 OECD DECLARATION

As a member of the Organisation for Economic Cooperation and Development (OECD), Australia is a party to the OECD Declaration on International Investment and Multinational Enterprises in 1976. In general terms, this declares that member countries should give foreign-controlled enterprises within their country treatment that is consistent with international law and that is no less favourable than that given to domestic enterprises. The Declaration contains non-binding principles and does not override Australian law. See further www.firb.gov.au.

GUARANTEES AND INCENTIVES

Investment protection treaties .... AUS ¶20-201	Government guarantees for foreign investors .... AUS ¶20-204
Joint trade agreements ...... AUS ¶20-202	Protection for foreign investors .... AUS ¶20-205
Multilateral investment protection treaties .... AUS ¶20-203	

AUS ¶20-201 INVESTMENT PROTECTION TREATIES

Australia has a strong commitment to the freedom of international capital flows. Australia has acceded to the OECD Acts in force including the *Code of Liberalisation of Capital Movements* and the *Code of Liberalisation of Current Invisible Operations* through accession in 1971.

AUS ¶20-202 JOINT TRADE AGREEMENTS

In addition to the multi-lateral agreements outlined at AUS ¶20-102, AUS ¶20-103 and AUS ¶20-201, Australia is also a party to bilateral Investment Promotion and Protection Agreements ("IPPAs") with a number of countries. IPPAs provide a clear statement of principles relating to the protection of investments, combined with rules to enhance the effectiveness of these principles in a bilateral context.

The IPPAs involve the giving of ''most favoured nation'' commitments in regard to matters such as the admission and subsequent treatment of foreign investment, the giving of guarantees about expropriation/nationalisation and the establishment of mechanisms for resolving disputes over investment matters.

Australia has signed IPPAs with many countries, including China, Hong Kong, India, Indonesia, Laos, Papua New Guinea, Pakistan, Philippines and Vietnam.

Australia has also entered free trade agreements with:

*   New Zealand (Closer Economic Relations, CER, 1983);
*   Singapore (Free Trade Agreement, SAFTA, 2003);
*   Thailand (Closer Economic Relations, 2003); and
*   the USA (Free Trade Agreement, 2004).

Australia has signed agreements to further strengthen bilateral economic relations with:

*   Japan (the Australia-Japan Trade and Economic Framework, 2003, building on earlier agreements going back to 1957), and
*   China (the Australia-China Trade and Economic Framework, 2003).

See further www.firb.gov.au; www.dfat.gov.au.

AUS ¶20-203   MULTILATERAL INVESTMENT PROTECTION TREATIES

Apart from the OECD and conventions on dispute resolution, Australia is not a member of any multilateral investment protection arrangements.

AUS ¶20-204   GOVERNMENT GUARANTEES FOR FOREIGN INVESTORS

The Australian government welcomes foreign investment but, apart from such general guarantees as are contained in the OECD Guidelines for Multilateral Enterprises which form an integral part of the OECD's Declaration on International Investment, Australia has not established a systematic framework for government guarantees for foreign investors.

AUS ¶20-205   PROTECTION FOR FOREIGN INVESTORS

The Australian government's policy is to encourage direct foreign investment consistent with the needs of the Australian community, including the expansion of private investment, the development of internationally competitive and export-oriented industries and the creation of employment opportunities.

Administration of the policy is based on guidelines rather than inflexible rules: it is practical and non-discriminatory.

Restrictions are applied in a few areas (for example, developed residential real estate) where the government considers that there are few benefits to the Australian community from foreign investment. In the industry sector, proposals over certain amounts are to be notified to the Foreign Investment Review Board and are approved unless judged contrary to the national interest.

In the application of foreign investment policy, the government seeks the cooperation of foreign investors. As part of this process of cooperation, and in its role of maintaining awareness of the activities of foreign-controlled corporations operating in Australia, the Foreign Investment Review Board welcomes opportunities to discuss with foreign companies their operations and plans for investment in Australia. Usually, such discussions take place on an informal basis during the course of the consideration of particular proposals.

The government also directs the attention of foreign investors to the OECD Guidelines for Multinational Enterprises. The Guidelines form an integral part of the OECD Declaration on International Investment, with which Australia has associated itself, and the government seeks the cooperation of foreign companies operating in Australia to observe them.

Special taxation controls apply to the financing of foreign investments in Australian companies and businesses to ensure that foreign investors do not, through the structuring of their investments, obtain a taxation advantage not available to local investors.

See details at www:firb.gov.au

Land Tenure — The Site of the Investment

Land tenure .... AUS ¶25-001

Rights in land .... AUS ¶25-101

LAND TENURE

Forms of land tenure .... AUS ¶25-001

Private ownership of land . AUS ¶25-002

Restrictions on transfer of
   land .... AUS ¶25-003

Local regulations .... AUS ¶25-004

Special areas .... AUS ¶25-005

Customary land rights: "Native
   title" .... AUS ¶25-011

AUS ¶25-001   FORMS OF LAND TENURE

Australian law making is shared between three levels of government — the Commonwealth government, the governments of the States and Territories and local government (AUS ¶20-001 to AUS ¶20-002).

Land law (or real property law) in Australia is regulated by the States and Territory governments under legislation such as the *Real Property Act 1900* (NSW) and the *Land Title Act 1994* (Qld).

About 95% of Australian land titles are held under Torrens title, with a small number held under general law (common law) or old system title, and with the recognition of native title in some situations (AUS ¶25-011):

- The Torrens system is the name given to the system of land ownership under which land ownership passes not by the execution of deeds but by the registration of title and dealings on a public register maintained by a government department (called, for example, the Land Titles Office). Torrens title overcomes the difficulties of conveyancing and proof of land ownership which may arise under general law or old system title.

- Ownership of land under general law or old system title is proved by tracing ownership back to an unchallengeable beginning, originally meaning back to a grant of land by the Crown, but now in most jurisdictions meaning proof of ownership going back 30 years to a good root of title.

Although the Commonwealth government is not authorised to make laws about land or property generally under the Australian Constitution (AUS ¶20-002), land use and ownership is affected by a number of Commonwealth laws such as laws concerning trade practices, divorce and family relationships, bankruptcy, the environment, sexual and racial discrimination, foreign ownership of land and acquisition of land by the Commonwealth government.

The regulation of land use and ownership in Australia is, therefore, affected by regulation by Australia's three levels of government.

AUS ¶25-002   PRIVATE OWNERSHIP OF LAND

Australian land law is based on the private ownership of land, with many restrictions and controls.

Land law provides for the method of acquisition and disposal of land, the use to which it can be put, the owner's entitlement to things found on it or in it, the extent to which the owner can protect his or her interest, the payment of various rates and taxes in respect of the land, and various other lesser interests in the land which interfere with the owner's free use and enjoyment of it.

AUS ¶25-003   RESTRICTIONS ON TRANSFER OF LAND

In general, land is freely transferable in Australia according to the respective State and Territory laws.

However, restrictions do apply to certain land transfers. For example, the consent of the relevant government minister is required before a person can validly transfer Crown land or land used for mining. There is also Commonwealth legislation which regulates foreign investment in Australia and this legislation stipulates that the approval of the federal Treasurer is required for certain land transactions (see AUS ¶25-103, AUS ¶55-001 and AUS ¶55-031). Further, the right of Australia's indigenous people to the use and enjoyment of certain land is protected by "native title" legislation throughout Australia (see also AUS ¶25-011). Such legislation typically provides that parcels of Crown land may be vested in aboriginal organisations which then hold the land on trust for the aboriginal inhabitants.

AUS ¶25-004   LOCAL REGULATIONS

As mentioned at AUS ¶25-001, Australian land law is made up of common law principles and statute law. Australian land law is administered by the government of each State and Territory. However, as these laws all derive from the same Anglo-Australian legal tradition, the principles of land law are essentially uniform throughout Australia. Partly due to the authoritative decision-making by the High Court of Australia, the case law principles of common law and equity are virtually the same in each State and Territory.

In addition, throughout Australia there is legislation dealing with town planning, protection of the environment and land use, the conveyancing of property and the registration of interests in land.

AUS ¶25-002

AUS ¶25-005 SPECIAL AREAS

There are no areas in Australia where a special domestic law or system of foreign land law applies; nor are any industrial estates or export processing zones subject to special land law rules.

AUS ¶25-011 CUSTOMARY LAND RIGHTS

Each State of Australia has legislation concerning aboriginal land rights, but the most direct legislation was passed by the Commonwealth government for the Northern Territory in 1976.

In 1992, the High Court of Australia in *Mabo's case* (1992) 175 CLR 1 recognised Aboriginal customary rights or "native title" to land for the first time. The High Court held that when the British Crown acquired sovereignty over Australia in 1788, the ownership of the Crown was subject to the "interests and rights of indigenous inhabitants in land whether communal, group or individual, possessed under the traditional laws acknowledged by and the traditional customs observed by the indigenous inhabitants."

The Commonwealth government responded with the *Native Title Act 1993* (Cth) which recognises native title rights and sets down the basic principles in relation to native title in Australia. Some State and Territory governments have enacted complementary legislation. Native title or "native title rights and interests" is defined in the Act to mean "the communal, group or individual rights and interests of Aboriginal peoples or Torres Strait Islanders in relation to land or waters" and includes hunting, gathering and fishing rights.

The *Native Title Act* validates:

- "past acts" — those before 1994 — which include freehold estate and certain leases such as commercial leases, agricultural leases and pastoral leases.

- "intermediate period acts" — those from 1994 to 1996 — the period between the commencement of the original *Native Title Act* and the second High Court native title case, the Wik case. This validates action taken by governments and others because of the legitimate and reasonable assumption that the act, such as a pastoral lease, extinguished native title.

Note however, that the native title holders may be entitled to compensation despite the extinguishment of their interest. Mining leases granted by the Commonwealth or States do not extinguish native title but rather the native title interest is subject to the lease.

Further details are set out on the National Native Title homepage at www.nntt.gov.au.

RIGHTS IN LAND

Nature of rights in land ..... AUS ¶25-101   **Transfer of rights in land** .. AUS ¶25-102

AUS ¶25-011

Restrictions on acquisition of
rights in land .... AUS ¶25-103

Land surveying .... AUS ¶25-104

Registration of security in
land .... AUS ¶25-105

Registration of rights of land
use and ownership .... AUS ¶25-111

System of land
registration .... AUS ¶25-112

Specific rights .... AUS ¶25-113

Extent of rights in land ...... AUS ¶25-114

Agreements restricting land
use .... AUS ¶25-115

Ascertainment of existing
restrictions .... AUS ¶25-121

Powers of acquisition of
land .... AUS ¶25-122

Compensation for acquired
land .... AUS ¶25-123

Taxes and rates .... AUS ¶25-124

Seizure of land in execution of
judgment .... AUS ¶25-125

Environmental
restrictions .... AUS ¶25-201

Regulation of environmental
controls .... AUS ¶25-202

Governmental requirements for
environmental
assessment .... AUS ¶25-203

Pollution standards .... AUS ¶25-204

Incentives for non-polluting
plants .... AUS ¶25-205

Nature of controls .... AUS ¶25-211

Detriment to the
environment .... AUS ¶25-212

AUS ¶25-101   NATURE OF RIGHTS IN LAND

Australian land law reflects its English origins. Individuals own estates in land, the more important of which are freehold and leasehold estates.

A freehold estate, or an estate in "fee simple", is absolute and unlimited ownership of land.

A leasehold estate is an estate in land which is held for a specified duration, as discussed below. The lessee, or "tenant", holds the estate for the period of the lease. The tenant is entitled to exclusive possession of the land during the period of the lease.

Apart from estates, the law recognises other interests in land. Like estates in land, these interests are said to "run with" the land and so bind successors in title. The more important of these interests are described below.

Mortgages

In the case of land under general law or old system title, a mortgage is an interest in land taken by a lender to secure repayment of the moneys lent.

In the case of land under Torrens title, a mortgage usually takes the form of a statutory charge over the borrower's land. The charge must be registered on the certificate of title of the borrower's land at the Land Titles Office. This gives the charge priority over later interests and alerts any person dealing with the land of the lender's interest in the land.

AUS ¶25-101

Easements

An easement is a proprietary right vested in an owner of land to use the lands of another. An easement is more than a personal right and may be enforced against third parties. The right exists so that the owner can effectively use and enjoy his or her own land. Examples of easements include rights of way, easements of support, easements to drain water and easements to preserve the passage of light and air to the land.

Restrictive covenants

A restrictive covenant is a right to prevent others from using land in specified ways. Like an easement, a restrictive covenant exists so that the person having the benefit of it can gain better use of his or her own land. For example, a restrictive covenant may restrict or regulate development on the land in order to preserve an adjoining landowner's view or to maintain the appearance of the neighbourhood. Restrictive covenants are interests in land which bind successors in title.

Profits à prendre or "right of common"

A *profit à prendre* or a right of common is a right to enter the land of another and take from the land. Unlike easements and restrictive covenants (except those created by statute), the person having the right need not own adjoining land or any land at all. Rights to take wood, to quarry stone and cut turf are examples of *profits à prendre.*

Equitable estates and interests

Equity law may recognise estates and other interests in land when the law does not. For example, a land transaction may be held to be enforceable even though the legal requirements for enforceability have not been observed and a legal owner may, in certain circumstances, be regarded as holding his or her land on trust for another person.

Contractual rights to use land

It is possible to acquire a right to use land according to ordinary contractual principles. That is, the right to the land may be a personal right instead of an interest in land and therefore it does not bind successors in title.

A licence is an example of a right to use land. Unlike a lease, a licence does not give the licensee a right to exclusive possession of the land. The owner retains possession but gives the licensee the right to enter and perhaps the right to occupy the land. Because a licence is not a proprietary right, it does not bind a successor to title.

Leases

Under a lease, a person (lessee or tenant) takes a leasehold estate from the owner of the land (the lessor or landlord).

Although there are many covenants or terms implied in a lease by both statute law and common law, the rights and obligations of the landlord and tenant are usually governed by express covenants which they themselves have agreed while negotiating the lease.

There is an ever-increasing range of statutory controls over the relationship of landlord and tenant in Australia. The broad aim of much of this legislation is to overcome the injustices which occur when the respective bargaining positions of the parties to the lease transaction are unequal. For example:

- Residential leases are regulated by residential tenancies legislation in most jurisdictions, with disputes dealt with by residential tenancies tribunals.

- Business leases may be re-opened and rewritten under sec. 51AC of the *Trade Practices Act 1974* (Cth) (as from 1998) if there is evidence of "unconscionable" conduct. Factors indicating unconscionable conduct include the relative strengths of the bargaining positions of the supplier and the business consumer, the "fine print" and the tactics at the pre-contract negotiations. This is discussed further at the Australian Competition and Consumer Commission website at www.accc.gov.au.

- In New South Wales, business and retail shop leases are also regulated by the *Contracts Review Act 1980* (NSW). Under this Act, contracts may be rewritten or set aside if they operate unfairly or if, in general, the circumstances surrounding their execution were unjust. (Under sec. 109 of the Australian Constitution, the *Trade Practices Act* [a Commonwealth Act] will predominate if there is any inconsistency with the *Contracts Review Act* [a State Act].)

Sublease

A person may take a leasehold estate from an existing tenant under a sublease. The term of a sublease must be shorter than the term of the headlease. If it is not, then the transaction does not create a sublease and instead creates an assignment of the headlease.

It is theoretically possible for leasehold estates to be held by an unlimited number of subtenants, although in practice an interest beyond that of one subtenant is rarely created.

Rights of access

Local governments in Australia have the power to set aside land for roads which may be used by the public at large. Waterways may also be used by the public at large.

In cases where land cannot be reached by some public thoroughfare, it may be necessary to obtain an easement over adjoining land (see AUS ¶25-101). Sometimes, parcels of land become landlocked, such as when the owner of the land sells all the land around it. The law may, in those circumstances, imply an easement of necessity for the benefit of the landowner if there is evidence of a common intention among the parties to preserve a right of way.

Extinction of rights

Limitation statutes throughout Australia impose time limits on the commencing of proceedings. The rationale for these statutes is that there comes a time when it is a lesser evil to deprive a delaying plaintiff of his or her cause of action than to upset the status quo. The limitation statutes apply to actions for the recovery of interests in land.

Taking New South Wales as an example, a person who occupies land to the exclusion of the true owner for a continuous period of 12 years — or, in the case of land owned by the Crown, 30 years — acquires an estate in fee simple and the title of the original true owner to the land is extinguished.

AUS ¶25-102   TRANSFER OF RIGHTS IN LAND

Legislation in each of the six States and the Northern Territory regulates the Torrens system of land transfer. This applies to a large proportion of land in Australia. (All land in Canberra and the Australian Capital Territory is leasehold from the Commonwealth government.) A standard form of contract for sale records the parties' agreement. It contains a provision that a purchaser should submit a transfer to the vendor for signing. Registration of the transfer vests title to the land in the purchaser.

Solicitors have a monopoly on conveyancing in some jurisdictions, but for example in New South Wales, Victoria, South Australia and Western Australia, there are licensed, non-legally qualified conveyancers who specialise in land transactions.

Costs of transfer

In addition to legal fees, the client must bear outgoings incurred on his or her behalf, namely, actual expenses such as search fees, survey fees and registration fees. Another cost is stamp duty — and as from 1 July 2000, goods and services tax (GST) on some transactions — which is payable on the transfer of any interest in land. Legislation prescribes the rate of stamp duty and GST and the person primarily liable to pay the duty applicable to a particular transaction.

Form of transfer

The form of transfer is prescribed by legislation. The property sold must be identified and the name of the parties and the amount of consideration must be stated. The transfer must also be properly executed by the owner and marked as to the payment of stamp duty.

Title is passed and priority guaranteed by registration. The title cannot be challenged except in exceptional circumstances such as fraud.

Approvals

No general approvals are required for the acquisition or disposition of interests in land, except those discussed at AUS ¶25-103.

Each jurisdiction has a Land Titles Office or equivalent. For example, further details are available from the NSW Land Titles Office's website at www.lpi.nsw.gov.au.

AUS ¶25-103   RESTRICTIONS ON ACQUISITION OF RIGHTS IN LAND

Foreign ownership

Queensland maintains a compulsory register of foreign ownership of land. The purpose of the register is to record, but not to prevent, ownership of land.

Foreign Investments Review Board (FIRB)

The Commonwealth government encourages foreign investment, including foreign investment in land and the economic benefits it brings so long as it is compatible with community interests. However, FIRB — a Commonwealth government agency — can block proposals it determines are "contrary to the national interest", including ownership of developed residential real estate to ensure that foreign investors operate in Australia as good corporate citizens.

Smaller proposals are exempt from notification and larger proposals will be approved unless judged contrary to the national interest. The screening process of FIRB enables comments to be obtained from the relevant parties and from other government agencies.

Government policy regarding real estate is to channel foreign investment to increase the number of residences and not to be speculative in nature.

FIRB requires notification of acquisitions of urban land (including interests which arise via leases, financing and profit sharing arrangements and the acquisition of interests in urban land corporations and trusts) by "foreign interests" that involve the acquisition of:

- developed non-residential commercial real estate where the property is subject to heritage listing, valued at AUS$5 million or more;
- developed non-residential commercial real estate, where the property is not subject to heritage listing, valued at AUS$50 million or more;
- accommodation facilities irrespective of value;
- vacant urban real estate irrespective of value;
- residential real estate irrespective of value;

or proposals where any doubt exists as to whether they are notifiable.

Proposed acquisition of residential real estate by foreign interests is exempt from examination in the case of foreign nationals purchasing as joint tenants with their Australian citizen spouse or foreign nationals who are holders of permanent residence visas or "special category visas".

Proposed acquisitions of real estate for development are normally approved subject to a specific condition requiring continuous construction to commence within 12 months.

Foreign interests are normally given approval to buy:

- vacant residential land where construction has not commenced on condition that continuous construction of a residence will be commenced within 12 months; and
- house and land packages, home units, townhouses, "off-the-plan" residences etc. under construction or newly constructed. "Off-the-plan" sales to foreigners are only permitted for new development projects or for extensively refurbished commercial structures which have been converted to residential on condition that no more than half the dwellings are sold to foreign interests.

Proposed acquisitions of residential property (both vacant land and existing dwellings) which are in an "Integrated Tourism Resort" (ITR) before September 1999 are exempt from examination by FIRB.

Foreign nationals temporarily resident in Australia continuously for more than 12 months may be given approval to purchase developed residential real estate for use as their principal place of residence while in Australia. Those include long-stay retirees on condition that the real estate is sold when the temporary resident visa expires, when they leave Australia or when the property is no longer used as their principal place of residence.

All other proposals by foreign interests to acquire developed residential real estate are examinable by FIRB and are not normally approved. This is exceptional in the case of foreign companies with an established substantial business in Australia buying for named senior executives resident in Australia for periods longer than 12 months, provided the accommodation is sold when no longer required for this purpose.

Proposed acquisitions of developed non-residential commercial real estate by foreign interests are normally approved by FIRB unless they are contrary to the national interest.

Proposed acquisitions of hotels and motels operating under one title are normally approved by FIRB unless considered contrary to the national interest under the tourism sector policy.

FIRB is discussed further at AUS ¶30-103.

Refer to the FIRB homepage at: www.firb.gov.au.

AUS ¶25-104   LAND SURVEYING

The Torrens system of land registration, which originated in Australia in 1858 (AUS ¶25-001), requires survey of registered land. Therefore, virtually all land in use in Australia is surveyed. Because of the extent of existing survey, a surveyor is usually able to tie in to an existing survey document, making survey in Australia cheaper and easier than in some jurisdictions in the Asian region.

AUS ¶25-105   REGISTRATION OF SECURITY IN LAND

The Torrens system of land transfer is a system of title by registration. The government authoritatively establishes title by setting up a register and guaranteeing that the person named as owner has a perfect title free from unregistered interests and subject only to encumbrances noted on the title. See AUS ¶25-001.

AUS ¶25-111   REGISTRATION OF RIGHTS OF LAND USE AND OWNERSHIP

The system of registration of rights of land use and ownership is efficient and is based on a combination of ownership, transactions and documents. Computerisation of the system has developed rapidly.

AUS ¶25-112   SYSTEM OF LAND REGISTRATION

The Torrens system of land ownership provides a government guarantee against error or fraud by the staff operating the system, and a guarantee against the fraud of anyone causing a loss of interest in title (AUS ¶25-001). Legal action is no longer required in order to obtain compensation. An error by a solicitor in dealing with a land transaction can be claimed by the client against the compulsory insurance for solicitors imposed by the relevant State or Territory Law Society.

The system used in Australia is designed to record any legal interest in land on the register. The relatively few sources of interest which can exist without being shown on the land titles register can be checked by a solicitor or land conveyancer practising in the jurisdiction. For example, a person's equitable interest in land cannot be registered, but a caveat may be lodged which prohibits the registration of any instruments that do not take into account the equitable interest (e.g. a person may have an equitable interest as beneficiary under a will or a trust).

There are rules regarding priority of interests which operate to determine whether one unregistered interest prevails over another conflicting unregistered interest in the same land:

- one cannot give what one does not have (the "nemo dat" rule) — if A has sold land to B, a later purported sale by A to C is void under the general law. However, if the conveyance to C is bona fide and for valuable consideration by C, and is registered by C before the sale to B is registered, C's interest is effective and gains priority over B's interest.

- the person who is first in time has the stronger legal claim (the "qui prior est" rule).

- where the equities are equal, the law prevails.

There is still some land in some Australian jurisdictions which is recorded in a deed registry system under the general law or old system title. This land must be searched to establish a good root of title. In New South Wales, Queensland, Tasmania and Victoria, a purchaser need not search beyond the statutory period for the commencement of title which is 30 years unless the purchaser actually makes investigations or inquiries into matters prior to that period.

AUS ¶25-113   SPECIFIC RIGHTS

Ownership of land includes the land and fixtures to that land including, for example, a building and things attached to buildings like an electrical system wired in a building and a satellite dish on that land. The owner of land theoretically has rights to all the airspace above and all the ground space below that land. However, legislation has limited the extent of these rights.

While it is possible to sell airspace above land, the marketability of that airspace may be limited as a result of town planning controls set down by local government (municipal and shire councils) which regulate such matters as building heights.

Under the surface, land ownership is limited by mining legislation which vests minerals such as gold, silver and petroleum in the government (Crown). Certain mining rights can be acquired by statutory grant from the government and override the title of the owner. Ground water legislation gives control and use of ground water to the government.

AUS ¶25-113

AUS ¶25-114 EXTENT OF RIGHTS IN LAND

The sale of residential homes usually comprises the sale of the land and improvements (houses and outbuildings) and may include household effects. Fixtures, plants and crops pass with the land unless expressly excluded.

AUS ¶25-115 AGREEMENTS RESTRICTING LAND USE

It is possible to restrict the use of land by agreement. A landowner may confer on another person an interest in his or her land. This will have the effect of interfering with the landowner's ability to use and enjoy his or her land. A person who acquires an interest in land has a proprietary interest and will be able to enforce that interest against the landowner's successors in title.

A landowner may also confer on another person a mere contractual right to use the land in some specified manner. If there is no agreement to the contrary, such a right is not enforceable against future owners of the land.

The main types of interests in land and contractual rights to use land are discussed at AUS ¶25-101.

AUS ¶25-121 ASCERTAINMENT OF EXISTING RESTRICTIONS

Interests in Torrens title land may be protected by registration at the Land Titles Office and can usually be checked by searching the Torrens title register. If the relevant interest has not been registered, it might be disclosed by a caveat on the title to the land. Otherwise, the rules on priority of interests in land will generally operate to determine whether that unregistered interest will prevail over any subsequently acquired interest (see AUS ¶25-112). There may be remedies for breach of contract against a landowner who fails to disclose any unregistered interests affecting his or her land.

The existence of interests in old system or general law land may be determined by searching the various documents which establish the title of the owner. Such interests should also be recorded in a register administered by the Land Titles Office/Registrar of Titles in each State or Territory.

AUS ¶25-122 POWERS OF ACQUISITION OF LAND

The Commonwealth and each of the State and Territory governments have the power to compulsorily acquire land. This authority is usually delegated to public sector groups such as publicly owned utilities, local government (for local government services such as local roads, water, gas and electrical reticulation, sewage systems), transportation authorities and to the private sector for the acquisition of utility easements where utilities are privately owned.

AUS ¶25-123 COMPENSATION FOR ACQUIRED LAND

The Commonwealth government is required under the Australian Constitution to provide compensation for land taken. State and Territory governments will normally provide compensation for land compulsorily acquired, the value of which is established by negotiation between the acquiring authority and the owner. The date for valuation is the date of acquisition by the acquiring authority. Valuation includes improvements, immovables and actual and potential use other than the specific use which is the subject of the acquisition. If negotiation fails, the matter can be litigated. Expert valuers are usually used by both sides.

AUS ¶25-124   TAXES AND RATES

The standard contract for sale provides that council and water rates as well as land tax and goods and services tax (GST, from 1 July 2000), if payable, will be apportioned between the vendor and purchaser on settlement so that each party pays its own share.

Water and local government (municipal) rates are assessed at a flat rate based on land value and are payable quarterly. Legislation treats these rates as a charge on the land. Unpaid rates may be recovered from the person liable (i.e. the owner of the land) in any court having jurisdiction. A certificate stating the amount outstanding can be obtained from the relevant authority and is conclusive regarding the matters contained in it. A person who disposes of land remains liable for these rates until the necessary notice of transfer is given to the relevant authority.

Local government authorities have the power to sell the land if there has been default in payment of municipal rates for a certain period. These powers have not been conferred on water authorities.

Land tax is levied annually on the unimproved value of all land which is not exempt land and which is owned by the taxpayer at midnight on the day immediately preceding the year for which tax is assessed. It is a first charge on the land in priority to all other encumbrances. The purchaser must make an allowance for the vendor's liability for land tax on the basis of a notional calculation determined by treating the specific land as the only property owned by the vendor. The purchaser can determine whether the land is subject to a charge by applying for a certificate from the land tax authority. The certificate is conclusive only in favour of a purchaser.

AUS ¶25-125   SEIZURE OF LAND IN EXECUTION OF JUDGMENT

A creditor who obtains a judgment against a debtor in respect of a debt may apply to the relevant court for the issue of a writ of execution. In general, a writ of execution directs the court sheriff to seize the judgment debtor's property and then sell it to pay the judgment debt. As long as the debt exceeds a specified amount, the judgment debtor's land is generally available to the court sheriff under a writ of execution.

A judgment creditor wishing to have the judgment debt satisfied from the proceeds of sale of the judgment debtor's land must, in the case of Torrens title land, ensure that the writ of execution is recorded by the Registrar of Titles (see AUS ¶25-001). If this is not done, the court sheriff or other relevant court officer will be unable to effectively transfer title to the purchaser.

AUS ¶25-201   ENVIRONMENTAL RESTRICTIONS

Australia has a Commonwealth, State and Territory approach to environmental legislation and administration where each jurisdiction has its own planning and pollution statutes. Under sec 109 of the Australian Constitution, Commonwealth law prevails in the event of any inconsistency with a State law.

The Commonwealth government has passed the *Environment Protection and Biodiversity Conservation Act 1999* (Cth). This aims to implement the principles of ecologically sustainable development through the adoption of an efficient environmental impact assessment and approval process, and to introduce an improved, integrated framework for the conservation and sustainable use of Australia's biodiversity.

In New South Wales, for example, planning is covered by the *Environmental Planning and Assessment Act 1979* and the *Local Government Act 1993*. The South Australian legislation is the *Environment Protection Act 1993* (SA).

In most jurisdictions, there are many pollution statutes covering clean air, clean waters, noise control, environmentally hazardous chemicals, ozone protection, marine pollution and dangerous goods and waste disposal as well as a number of industry statutes.

AUS ¶25-202   REGULATION OF ENVIRONMENTAL CONTROLS

Each jurisdiction has a body or bodies responsible for environmental administration. In most jurisdictions, this body is known as the Environment Protection Authority. The planning statutes are usually administered in part by local governments. (The planning statutes are relevant to pollution law since guidelines for development require industry to meet pollution standards.)

Penalties for non-compliance

Penalties, in broad terms, can take many forms in pollution control. There are financial penalties and jail terms, loss of licences, clean-up costs, loss of business and the risk of adverse publicity.

In recent times, there has been a growing trend to impose substantial financial penalties. Maximum licence fees have been increased to reflect the quantities of waste generated by large industrial premises. In certain circumstances, directors and managers may be personally liable for offences committed by the company. In some circumstances, occupiers may be liable for clean-up costs even though they did not cause the pollution.

AUS ¶25-203   GOVERNMENTAL REQUIREMENTS FOR ENVIRONMENTAL ASSESSMENT

Commonwealth government provisions dealing with environmental impact assessments can be found in the Commonwealth legislation mentioned at AUS ¶25-201. These provisions apply to developers who need Commonwealth approval in the area of its jurisdiction for a particular development. Responsibility also rests with the individual States and Territory governments.

In New South Wales, the *Environmental Planning and Assessment Act 1979* contains procedures for the environmental assessment of proposed activities. The consent authority (usually the local council) must examine specified considerations when it determines an application for development. Conditions may be imposed on the development to ease any adverse environmental impact. In certain circumstances, it is also necessary to prepare and submit an Environmental Impact Statement.

AUS ¶25-204   POLLUTION STANDARDS

There are specific standards in Australia for discharges into the air (including carbon monoxide, lead and and ozone); discharges into water; waste disposal; site contamination; and handling, transport and storage practices. Due to the increasing severity of penalties for non-compliance with standards imposed, some industries have implemented a pollution compliance or due diligence program. This informs directors and senior management of potential risks and measures by which compliance may be ensured.

AUS ¶25-205   INCENTIVES FOR NON-POLLUTING PLANTS

There are few specific incentives for industries to establish non-polluting activities. The thrust of most State and Territory legislation is to provide a deterrent system by the imposition of heavy penalties.

Australia is moving towards further use of taxation and economic incentives as a method of non-pollution environmental regulation. Initiatives include taxes to curb environmental abuse, tax credits, land tax reductions with respect to conservation values of agricultural land, environmental taxes, incentives for renewable energy and special-purpose tax subsidies for promoting environmental goals. For example, there is full taxation deductibility for expenditure for land degradation control. Land degradation expenditure can be claimed for controlling pests and weeds on land used for primary production.

AUS ¶25-211   NATURE OF CONTROLS

Before the commencement of business activity, certain environmental requirements must be met. These vary from jurisdiction to jurisdiction. Controls also continue to operate after the establishment of a business venture (see AUS ¶25-202).

AUS ¶25-212   DETRIMENT TO THE ENVIRONMENT

The environment is a major concern in assessing investment proposals in Australia although, as already noted at AUS ¶25-201, this is dealt with on a jurisdiction to jurisdiction basis. The emphasis will therefore vary between jurisdictions. A growing public concern in all environmental issues is leading to stronger controls and heavier penalties and fees.

Selection of further reading

Commonwealth Department of the Environment and Heritage: http://www.deh.gov.au/index.html

Environment Protection Authority (NSW): www.epa.nsw.gov.au

Environment Protection Authority (Victoria): www.epa.vic.gov.au

Department of Natural Resources and Environment (Victoria): www.nre.vic.gov.au

Department of Natural Resources (Queensland): www.dnr.qld.gov.au

The Structure of the Investment

Historical sources of contract and commercial law .... AUS ¶30-001

Codification of law .... AUS ¶30-002

Distinction between contract and commercial law .... AUS ¶30-003

Requirements for government contracts .... AUS ¶30-004

Requirements for contracts with foreign entities .... AUS ¶30-005

Treatment of consumer contracts .... AUS ¶30-011

Liability for injury caused by defective products .... AUS ¶30-012

Methods of settlement outside court system .... AUS ¶30-013

Special rules for institutions .... AUS ¶30-014

Use of standardised contracts .... AUS ¶30-015

Remedies under the commercial law .... AUS ¶30-016

Performance of contracts under changed
   circumstances .... AUS ¶30-017

Company law .... AUS ¶30-101

AUS ¶30-001   HISTORICAL SOURCES OF CONTRACT AND COMMERCIAL LAW

Australia's contract and commercial law is derived from the English common law tradition. Imperial statutes of the British parliament in the early nineteenth century extended to, and were in force in, the original six British colonies in Australia to the extent that they could apply to the conditions of those colonies. When they started passing local laws, these colonies had a tradition of paralleling changes made to the law in England. This tradition continued after the colonies became largely self-governing in the second half of the nineteenth century. It continued with some exceptions even after the colonies became States in the Commonwealth of Australia in 1901 up until the time when the Australian common law really started developing with uniquely Australian legislation from about the 1960s, and especially from the 1970s with legislation such as the *Trade Practices Act 1974* (Cth).

The *Commonwealth of Australia Constitution Act 1900*, drafted in Australia by the "fathers of federation" in the 1890s but enacted as a statute of the British parliament, vested in the new Commonwealth of Australia Parliament a number of areas of jurisdiction which affect contract and commercial law such as the power over inter-State "trade and commerce" and the power over corporations. These Commonwealth powers have been the basis for the expansion of the Commonwealth government into areas previously considered to be matters of State and Territory law (see AUS ¶20-002).

In practical terms, Australian contract and commercial law is now dominated by "Commonwealth", "federal", "national" or "Australian" legislation of the Commonwealth Parliament in Canberra passed for Australia-wide application such as the *Trade Practices Act 1974* (Cth) and the *Corporations Act 2001* (Cth).

AUS ¶30-002   CODIFICATION OF LAW

Codification of law is rare in Australia. Neither contract law nor commercial law is codified. The principles of contract law are mostly set out by judges in their judgments, based upon accepted contractual principles. The task of consolidating and analysing these judgments has been largely performed by academic writers and commentators in textbooks and other publications

However, many statutes of both the Commonwealth and State/Territory parliaments affect aspects of contract, commercial and company law, sometimes with far reaching effects. A statute sometimes provides the basis in the most significant areas of commercial law.

Industry codes of conduct exist in areas such as banking, electronic banking and insurance. The Franchising Code has legal recognition and can be enforced under the *Trade Practices Act* (see AUS ¶30-101).

AUS ¶30-003   DISTINCTION BETWEEN CONTRACT AND COMMERCIAL LAW

There is no formal distinction between contract law and commercial law in Australia and the formal rules of contract apply to all commercial transactions. Contract law is a sub-set of commercial law like company law and partnership law.

There are special rules under legislation such as the *Trade Practices Act* and the equivalent State and Territory fair trading legislation for contracts involving consumers (see AUS ¶30-011).

Many areas of what is referred to as commercial law could be viewed as relating to specialised contracts, such as sale of goods, banking and insurance. Other areas, such as trade practices law and consumer credit law, modify contract law.

AUS ¶30-004   REQUIREMENTS FOR GOVERNMENT CONTRACTS

There is no separate regime for government contracts in Australia, and in court the government is a litigant like any other party. Disputes relating to government contracts are heard in the ordinary civil courts.

AUS ¶30-005   REQUIREMENTS FOR CONTRACTS WITH FOREIGN ENTITIES

There is no separate legal regime for contracts with foreign entities, though the proper law of the contract may be a relevant factor in such contracts. Any barriers to contracts with foreign entities exist separately from contract law, such as those that are based on restrictions on foreign investment or from customs laws relating to prohibited imports.

AUS ¶30-011   TREATMENT OF CONSUMER CONTRACTS

There is no separate legal regime for consumer contracts and these are dealt with at several levels:

- At the most general level is Australia's single most important business law section, sec. 52 of the *Trade Practices Act 1974* of the Commonwealth (which is parallelled in the equivalent Fair Trading Acts of all six States and two Territories).

  Section 52, headed "misleading or deceptive conduct", prohibits "conduct that is misleading or deceptive or is likely to mislead or deceive." Breach of sec. 52 gives the right to private legal action for remedies including damages.

- The *Trade Practices Act* (and State/Territory equivalents) also prohibits some "sharp practices" such as:

  - false or misleading representations, for example, with respect to standard, quality, approval, affiliation, place of origin and the effect of exclusions, conditions or warranties (sec. 53 — sec. 53C);
  - offering gifts and prizes (sec. 54);
  - bait advertising (sec. 56);
  - referral selling (sec. 57);
  - accepting payment without intending or being able to supply as ordered (sec. 58);
  - misleading representations about business activities (sec. 59);
  - harassment and coercion (sec. 60); and
  - pyramid selling (sec. 61).

  Breach of these sections give rise to private legal action for remedies including damages. These sections have criminal parallels in Part VC (Offences), breach of which can lead to prosecution by the ACCC. For example, the criminal offence equivalent of sec. 53 is sec. 75AZC.

- At the next level are provisions in legislation that apply to particular consumer contracts. These range from the fairly general, relating to contracts for the sale of goods and services, to the more particular, as in statutes that relate to consumer credit and insurance. For example, a business may qualify as a "consumer" under sec. 4B of the *Trade Practices Act 1974* (Cth) and State/Territory equivalents and thereby be able to enforce rights under consumer protection laws such as the *Sale of*

Goods Act's non-excludable implied terms of description, fitness for purpose and merchantability.

Refer to the ACCC site at www.accc.gov.au for further information.

All States and Territories make special provision for the resolution of consumer contracts by specialist tribunals such as Small Claims Tribunals. There is usually a limit on the value of contracts that these tribunals can consider.

AUS ¶30-012   LIABILITY FOR INJURY CAUSED BY DEFECTIVE PRODUCTS

Liability for injury caused by defective products in Australia is regulated by at least seven different areas of law. These date from different periods and focus on different aspects of defective products. The remedies are not exclusive and an injury caused by a defective product may give rise to several of these remedies:

- liability under the tort of negligence, established by the House of Lords in *Donoghue v. Stevenson* in 1932;

- liability for damages for breach of contract with the retailer, or possibly the manufacturer if the plaintiff has a contract with the manufacturer;

- liability of the retailer for breach of contractual terms implied by the *Trade Practices Act 1974* (Cth) (sec. 69 to 72) and/or the *Sale of Goods Act* of the States and Territories. There are five statutory "sale of goods" implied terms — title, description, fitness for purpose, merchantability and sale by sample. If there is a contract between buyer and manufacturer, the buyer may also sue the manufacturer under this law;

- statutory liability of the manufacturer (if there is no privity of contract) for unsuitable goods, false descriptions, unmerchantable quality and/or non-correspondence with samples under Part V Division 2A (sec. 74B to 74E) of the *Trade Practices Act* and other statutes in some jurisdictions;

- statutory liability of the manufacturer for defective goods under Part VA of the *Trade Practices Act* — "goods have a defect if their safety is not such as persons are generally entitled to expect" (sec. 75AC);

- liability for breach of a product safety standard and/or a product information standard under sec. 65C to 65D of the *Trade Practices Act*; and

- liability for "misleading or deceptive" conduct under sec. 52 of the *Trade Practices Act* and State/Territory equivalents.

This liability can be insured against under product liability insurance: AUS ¶85-021.

AUS ¶30-013   METHODS OF SETTLEMENT OUTSIDE COURT SYSTEM

As explained at AUS ¶30-003, the law of contract is a sub-set of commercial law. Therefore, the formal principles of law apply to commercial contracts as they do to other contracts.

As a response to the expense and delay involved in the settlement of contractual disputes by the ordinary civil courts, Australia has developed alternative dispute resolution (ADR) remedies and methods of settlement outside courts. These are dealt with at AUS ¶70-101.

AUS ¶30-014   SPECIAL RULES FOR INSTITUTIONS

As a general principle, the ordinary rules of contract and commercial law apply in relation to particular institutions such as companies, banks and foreign investors.

Some institutions (such as government or public sector corporations) and bodies (such as local government councils) may be restricted by their constitutional documents — such as the statute by which they are set up — in respect of the types of contracts they may enter. Companies in the private sector are not so restricted and have the same contractual capacity as a natural person.

Foreign investors are subject to Australian law for dealings in Australia.

AUS ¶30-015   USE OF STANDARDISED CONTRACTS

There is widespread use of standardised written contracts in Australia which sometimes use exemption clauses to limit liability. However, the courts often scrutinise these clauses closely and may use legalistic interpretive techniques to minimise their effect in appropriate cases.

The Commonwealth government and most States and Territories have passed legislation giving the courts power to prevent parties from relying on clauses in contracts where this reliance is regarded as:

- misleading or deceptive;
- based on a false representation; or
- unconscionable.

The courts may declare a contract "unconscionable" if it can be shown that a person with superior bargaining power has taken advantage of that power.

In addition to unconscionable conduct at common law, unconscionable conduct is now also enforceable under Part IVA of the *Trade Practices Act 1974* (Cth) in three situations:

- The Act prohibits engaging in conduct that is unconscionable "within the meaning of the unwritten law" of the States and Territories (sec. 51AA) ie, unconscionability according to current case law.
- The Act also prohibits engaging in conduct with a consumer that is unconscionable. It then sets out a checklist of what may be unconscionable (sec. 51AB):
    "— the relative strengths of the bargaining positions of the corporation and the consumer;
    — whether, as a result of conduct engaged in by the corporation, the consumer was required to comply with conditions that were not reasonably necessary for the protection of the legitimate interests of the corporation;

— whether the consumer was able to understand any documents relating to the supply or possible supply of the goods or services;

— whether any undue influence or pressure was exerted on, or any unfair tactics were used against, the consumer; and

— the amount for which, and the circumstances under which, the consumer could have acquired identical or equivalent goods or services from a person other than the corporation.'' (sec. 51AB(2))

- The Act prohibits unconscionable conduct in business transactions (sec. 51AC).

Breach of sec. 51AA, 51AB and/or 51AC may give rise to remedies under the *Trade Practices Act* such as damages and injunction.

Exclusion clauses purporting to exclude the implied conditions of description, fitness for purpose and merchantability in consumer contracts are ''void'' under sec. 68 of the *Trade Practices Act 1974* (Cth) and State/Territory equivalents and may lead to damages under sec. 53(g) and penalties under the equivalent sec. 75AZC(1)(k).

AUS ¶30-016   REMEDIES UNDER THE COMMERCIAL LAW

Remedies under Australian commercial law are the same as those in other common law jurisdictions: damages for breach of contract, and the discretionary remedies of rescission, specific performance, injunction, Mareva order (to preserve assets: AUS ¶70-011), Anton Piller order (to obtain evidence: AUS ¶70-011) and restitution.

The measure of damages in contract is the monetary amount which will compensate the innocent party for the loss of the bargain. It is based on the English principle of *Hadley v. Baxendale* ((1854) 156 ER 145) which is based on the concepts of foreseeability and actual knowledge. The guilty party must compensate the innocent party for:

- the damage that flows ''naturally'' or in the ''usual course of things'', and also for

- such damages ''as may reasonably be supposed to have been in contemplation of both parties, at the time when they made the contract''. There is a limitation of remoteness which the court can use to restrict damages on the ground that the harm complained of is too remote from the guilty action, and a general principle that the innocent party must take reasonable steps to mitigate the loss suffered.

The courts will uphold liquidated damages clauses as long as these represent a reasonable estimate of the loss and not a penalty.

AUS ¶30-017   PERFORMANCE OF CONTRACTS UNDER CHANGED CIRCUMSTANCES

Australian jurisdictions recognise the common law principle of termination of contact by frustration by statute in three jurisdictions (the *Frustrated Contracts Act 1959* (Vic); the *Frustrated Contracts Act 1978* (NSW) and the *Frustrated Contracts Act 1988* (SA)) or by the common law — that performance of the contract under the changed circumstances would be something fundamentally different from what had been anticipated. However, the courts are less willing than American courts to apply this doctrine when what has changed is the economic setting of the contract.

COMPANY LAW

Forms of commercial
   organisations .... AUS ¶30-101

Foreign companies .... AUS ¶30-102

Registration of non-resident
   companies .... AUS ¶30-103

Requirements for establishment
   of subsidiaries .... AUS ¶30-104

Investment in local
   companies .... AUS ¶30-105

Percentage of foreign
   ownership .... AUS ¶30-111

Types of governing and
   managing structures ..... AUS ¶30-112

Structure and powers of joint
   venture .... AUS ¶30-113

Bankruptcy Law .... AUS ¶30-114

AUS ¶30-101   FORMS OF COMMERCIAL ORGANISATIONS

Both incorporated and unincorporated commercial organisations exist in Australia.

Sole trader

The simplest commercial organisation is the unincorporated sole trader. The sole trader does not have the benefit of limited liability, and, although not regulated by the *Corporations Act 2001* (Cth), the sole trader is still subject to a wide range of other legislative controls (such as labour laws, land use laws, tax laws, consumer protection law, competition law and, in the case of certain occupations, licensing laws).

Franchise

Franchises are governed by sections of many Acts such as the *Trade Practices Act 1974* (Cth), the common law principles of contract, fiduciaries and so on, and as from 1998, the Franchising Code of Conduct.

The Franchising Code is "prescribed" by the *Trade Practices Act*, which makes compliance mandatory. The remedies of the Act apply to breaches of the Code such as injunctions, corrective advertising, damages, enforceable undertakings and orders to rewrite contracts.

The Franchising Code is available at the Attorney-General's legislative database at: http://scaleplus.law.gov.au.

Partnership

The partnership is common in Australia and is primarily regulated by the *Partnership Act* of each State and Territory. These are essentially the same as the original *English Act*, with the main difference being the section numbering in some jurisdictions.

(Most section numbers of the NSW Act and the SA Act are the same as those in the *English Act*.)

Unlike a company, a partnership is not a separate legal entity, and no formal agreement is necessary to establish the relationship of partnership. The Act defines a partnership as a "relation which subsists between persons carrying on a business in common with a view of profit". It is open to the courts to imply such an agreement and to find that a partnership exists as a matter of law even if the parties had planned otherwise.

The States of Victoria, New South Wales, Tasmania, Western Australia and Queensland have each introduced a form of limited liability partnership.

Companies

There are a number of ways in which business entities in Australia can be incorporated:

- Unincorporated associations, incorporated associations and co-operatives. The latter two are usually non-profit organisations incorporated under State or Territory legislation.

- Public sector corporations, usually tied to government in some way, can be important in the commercial sphere. They are usually incorporated under legislation specific to the particular corporation. However, with the many recent "privatisations" in the areas such as telecommunications, transport and utilities, the number of public sector corporations has fallen.

- Private sector companies are usually incorporated under the *Corporations Act 2001* (Cth), a Commonwealth (or federal or national) legislation which replaced the previous State- and Territory-based corporate regulation on 15 July 2001 following agreement by Australia's six State governments to "refer" their power to regulate companies to the Commonwealth government. Under the *Corporations Act*, most Australian companies enjoy limited liability (indicated by the inclusion of the word "Limited" or the abbreviation "Ltd" in a company's name). There is also a category of unlimited companies under the *Corporations Act*.

Companies under the *Corporations Act* are subdivided into companies limited by shares, companies limited by guarantee, companies with unlimited liability and no-liability companies.

Companies under the *Corporations Act* can also be divided into private companies (known as "proprietary" companies [Pty Ltd]) and public companies (Ltd). Proprietary companies may not approach the public for funds by way of share issues or debt. In return, the disclosure and reporting requirements on proprietary companies are less onerous. Proprietary companies must also place limits on the transferability of their shares.

Public companies may seek funds from the public by way of the issue of shares or debt. They have more stringent reporting and disclosure requirements under the *Corporations Act*. For instance, non-public price sensitive information held by listed companies (and certain other entities) must be disclosed immediately. Public companies seek listing on the Australian Stock Exchange will be subject to the even more onerous operating rules (listing rules) of ASX. These are set out at www.asx.com.au.

Corporate law reform

From through the 1990s, Australian company law has been undergoing a process of updating and reform to improve Australia's global competitiveness, its ability to attract investment and the follow-on increase in economic and employment growth in response to changes in the business world. Amendments include:

- Changes to insider trading laws (1991).
- Prohibitions on a public company giving benefits to directors and other related parties (1992).
- Indemnification of directors and enhanced disclosure by companies (1994)
- Simplification (1995) and the *Company Law Review Act 1998* (Cth), which

rewrotmany of the core provisions of Australian company law. The major areas affected by the Act cover areas dealing with company formation, company administration, meetings, share capital and financial statements and audit.

- The *Managed Investments Act 1998* (Cth) improved the regulation of collective investments, with the introduction of Chapter 5C into the *Corporations Act*.

More recent changes include:

- The *Financial Sector Reform (Amendments and Transitional Provisions) Act 1998* (Cth) expanded the jurisdiction of the then Australian Securities Commission (ASC) into ASIC (Australian Securities and Investments Commission), with increased jurisdiction in the financial sector including powers over investments such as insurance.
- The *Financial Sector Reform (Amendments and Transitional Provisions) Act (No. 1) 1999* (Cth) completed ASIC's coverage of the whole financial sector, including new jurisdiction over building societies, credit unions and friendly societies.
- The *CLERP Act 1999* . Changes brought about by the *Corporate Law Economic Reform Program Act 1999* (Cth) (''CLERP'') have included reformulating directors' duties and corporate governance, including the introduction of a business judgment rule; new laws dealing with takeovers (refer to www.takeovers.gov.au); and new laws to facilitate small business fund-raising by allowing issuers to raise up to:
  — AUS$2 million each year from up to 20 persons without issuing a prospectus or other disclosure document and to raise up to AUS$5 million under an offer information statement instead of a full prospectus.
- The *Corporation Act 2001* (Cth) and the *Australian Securities and Investments Commission Act 2001* (Cth), which came into effect in 2001, overcame the constitutional uncertainties surrounding the 1990 national scheme. The Acts were a result of a political breakthrough in 2000 when the six States and the Northern Territory agreed to put the national interest first by transferring their legal their powers over corporations to the Commonwealth by a referral of their powers to the Commonwealth under Constitution sec. 51(xxxvii). With its authority to legislate

confirmed by the referral of power, the Commonwealth passed the *Corporations Act 2001* (Cth) and related legislation. The *Corporations Act* repealed the former *Corporations Law* and re-enacted it as Commonwealth legislation.

- *Financial Services Reform Act 2001* (Cth).

This Act came into effect in 2002 to amend the *Corporations Act 2001* and the *Australian Securities and Investments Commission Act 2001*. It providesd for one-stop Australia-wide harmonised regulation for market integrity and consumer protection across the financial services industry including:

  — uniform regulation of all financial products;

  — a single licence called an Australian financial services licence (sec. 911A) for all financial services providers — those providing "financial product advice" (sec. 766B) — including extending licensing to many financial services providers who did not previously require licensing as a securities dealer or as an investment adviser such as insurance agents and brokers and superannuation advisers;

  — minimum standards of conduct for providers of financial services dealing with retail clients;

  — uniform disclosure obligations for all financial products provided to retail clients;

  — flexibility for authorisation of market operators (i.e. stock exchanges) under the name "an Australian market licence" (sec. 791A) and for clearing and settlement facilities; and

  — extending market and other misconduct provisions such as insider trading to apply to all financial products and markets.

Further information is available at the ASIC website at www.asic.gov.au under the Financial Services Reform icon.

ffi CLERP 8, which plans to amend the Corporations Act to adopt the UNCITRAL Model Law on cross-border insolvency. ffCLERP 9 on corporate disclosure, which plans increased disclosure including better disclosure of executive remuneration, increased auditor independence and increased protections from harassment for corporate whistleblowers.

Changes can be followed at:

ffi http://www.lipton-herzberg.com.au/law_reform.htm ffi Corporate Law Bulletin, available at http://cclsr.law.unimelb.edu.au

AUS ¶30-102   FOREIGN COMPANIES

A foreign company does not have to be re-incorporated in Australia and can carry on business in Australia if it is registered as a foreign company in Australia (sec. 601CD) or if it incorporates a subsidiary in Australia.

AUS ¶30-102

Registration as a foreign company

A "foreign company" is defined in sec. 9 of the *Corporations Act* as a body corporate incorporated outside Australia. The definition excludes an unincorporated body formed outside Australia.

AUS ¶30-103   REGISTRATION OF NON-RESIDENT COMPANIES

The authority for registering both local and foreign companies is the Australian Securities and Investments Commission (ASIC). This is an authority of the Commonwealth Government and has offices Australia-wide.

Refer to the ASIC homepage at www.asic.gov.au.

Telephone Infoline (Australia) 1 300 300 630.

Fees

There is a fee for the registration of a foreign company for the filing of an annual return or balance sheet and profit and loss account and for the filing of a range of other documents related to the conduct of the business of the foreign company.

Statutory accounts

A registered foreign corporation must, once every calendar year, and at intervals of not more than 15 months, lodge copies of its balance sheet, cash flow statement and profit and loss account for the last financial year. In addition, the company must lodge copies of other documents required by the law of its place of incorporation (sec. 601CK).

The Australian Securities and Investments Commission (ASIC) may require further documents and particulars where it believes that the documents lodged do not sufficiently disclose the company's financial position (sec. 601CK(3)). These requirements may not exceed the obligations on a public company incorporated under the *Corporations Act*.

Local agent of non-resident company

A registered foreign corporation must appoint at least one agent, and notify the appointment to ASIC.

The agent is answerable for doing everything that the *Corporations Act* requires the foreign company to do. The courts have a discretion whether to impose on the agent penalties imposed on the foreign corporation for breaches of the *Corporations Act*.

Documents to be filed for registration of non-resident company

Section 601CE of the *Corporations Act* requires an application for registration of a foreign company to be accompanied by the following documents:

- a certified copy of its current certificate of incorporation or registration in its place of origin, or an equivalent document;
- a certified copy of its constitution;
- a list of directors containing personal details equivalent to those required of directors of Australian companies;

- the documents relating to existing charges on property of the foreign company that would be required under the *Corporations Act* of an Australian company in relation to charges on its property;

- notice of the address of the company's registered office, or principal place of business, in its place of origin; and

- notice of the address of its registered office in Australia.

Government approvals

The Australian Securities and Investments Commission (ASIC) will register a foreign corporation and issue a registration number if the application is in proper form.

However, foreign investment in Australian companies, Australian businesses and Australian real estate is regulated by the Foreign Investment Review Board (''FIRB'' — a statutory authority) and by the Commonwealth government.

The setting up of a local company to acquire an Australian business or Australian urban real estate will not, by itself, be sufficient to avoid the foreign investment controls if the control of the company lies offshore. Acquisitions of companies and businesses with assets of more than AUS$50 million, proposals to establish new businesses involving a total investment of AUS$10 million or more and acquisitions of urban real estate are subject to a ''national interest'' test. This is determined by the Foreign Investment Review Board and the Commonwealth government (or federal) Treasurer. Many categories of proposed acquisition must be notified to FIRB for examination before implementation; in practice, non-examinable proposals are also referred to FIRB (see AUS ¶25-103).

Refer to the FIRB homepage at: www.treasury.gov.au.

Email: firb@treasury.gov.au.

Regulators

Although the main regulator of companies (including foreign companies) is ASIC, the jurisdiction of other regulators may be relevant, depending on the activities of the company, such as:

- the Australian Taxation Office: refer to the ATO at www.ato.gov.au; and

- the Australian Competition and Consumer Commission (ACCC): www.accc.gov.au. The ACCC regulates restrictive trade practices and anti-consumer behaviour.

AUS ¶30-104   REQUIREMENTS FOR ESTABLISHMENT OF SUBSIDIARIES

Australian courts and legislation treat subsidiary companies as separate from the holding company. Therefore, establishing a subsidiary is very similar to incorporating an independent company.

AUS ¶30-104

Fees

Registration fees are prescribed for incorporation, the filing of the annual return and accounts and for the filing of certain other documents related to the conduct of the company's business.

Nationality of directors

A proprietary company must have at least one director under the *Corporations Act*. For a public company, three directors are required of which two must be resident of Australia (*Corporations Act* sec. 201A).

Nationality of employees

There is no requirement for any percentage of management or staff to be resident or nationals of Australia.

Shareholdings by non-residents

There is no requirement in the *Corporations Act* that shares in an Australian company be held by residents. There may, however, be restrictions in specific industries, like broadcasting.

Bearer shares

Shares in Australian companies are issued in register form and most are held in uncertificated or paper-free form under the electronic CHESS (the Clearing House Electronic Subregister System). CHESS is the computer system that operates as:

- a clearing house, by transferring the title or legal ownership of shares between buyer and seller; and
- a subregister, by electronically registering ownership of shares in ASX listed companies.

Refer to the ASX homepage at: www.asx.com.au.

Nominal capital

It is not necessary for all of the company's authorised capital to be issued, nor is there any minimum nominal paid-up capital.

The concept of nominal or authorised capital was abolished for new companies in 1998. For companies formed after 1998, there is no longer a requirement that the company must include in its constitution a statement indicating the amount of its authorised share capital.

Directors' qualifications

There are no minimum shareholder qualifications required in the case of directors. The grounds for disqualification of directors are age, in that persons under the age of 18 or, in respect of public companies or subsidiaries of public companies, over the age of 72 years may not be appointed or act as directors. This upper limit can be waived by the members with a three-quarters majority. There is no upper age limit for directors of proprietary companies.

ASIC has the power to disqualify persons from managing a corporation for such matters as conviction of an offence, breaching a civil penalty provision, insolvency and non-payment of debts and repeated contraventions of the law (*Corporations Act* Part 2D.6 Disqualification from Managing Corporations).

Time

Many advisers in Australia, such as lawyers and accountants, have incorporated "shelf" companies, which may be purchased by clients.

Branches

Branch offices may be established elsewhere in Australia. The legislative requirement is that there be one registered office to which all communications may be addressed and which has minimum hours of opening.

Statutory accounts

All companies in Australia must maintain written financial records that correctly record and explain their transactions and financial position and performance and enable true and fair financial statements to be prepared and audited (sec. 286). However, the extent of the accounts required and the necessity for an audit vary between categories of company, the criterion being the vulnerability of the investing public. The lightest burden falls on the "small proprietary company" (previously called an "exempt proprietary company") and the heaviest on the public company listed on the Australian Stock Exchange (ASX) or other stock exchange.

The financial records can be kept in any language/electronic form so long as a translation into English/hard copy can be made available within a reasonable time if requested.

Shareholdings of non-resident companies

There is no requirement that the name and percentage shareholding of any non-resident company be disclosed.

Nominees

Shares may be held by nominees or trustees.

Payment for shares

There is no barrier to the payment in kind for shares, or, more technically, for a consideration other than in cash.

Liquidation

The *Corporations Act* provides various possibilities for the winding up of a company:

* winding up in insolvency;
* winding up by the court on other grounds; and
* voluntary winding up, for example, by a scheme of arrangement under which creditors may allow a company to continue trading.

Disposal of shares

Proprietary companies are required to place restrictions on the transfer of their shares because it must have no more than 50 non-employee shareholders. This is not the case with public companies.

AUS ¶30-105   INVESTMENT IN LOCAL COMPANIES

Acquisition of shares

See AUS ¶30-103 under "Government approvals".

Takeovers

Takeovers are regulated in an effort to ensure that takeovers occur in "an efficient, competitive and informed market". In particular, the *Corporations Act* aims to ensure that the directors and shareholders:

- know the identity of the bidder;
- have a reasonable time to consider the proposal;
- are given enough information to enable them to assess the merits of the proposal; and
- have reasonable and equal opportunity to participate in the benefits of the takeover.

These are the four "Eggleston principles" — set out in sec. 602, which form the basis of Australian takeover law.

Australian takeover law

Chapter 6 of the *Corporations Act* prohibits the acquisition of shares above a limit of 20% unless there is a takeover bid — either an on-market purchase (for quoted securities only) or and an off-market purchase (for quoted or unquoted securities).

Section 611 then provides permissible methods by which the 20% threshold may be exceeded:

- Acceptance of a take-over offer;
- On-market purchase of convertible securities during the bid period;
- Acceptance of scrip offered as takeover consideration;
- Lenders: acquisition by a receiver, or by a receiver and manager, under a mortgage, charge or other security;
- Approval by resolution of the target company;
- Where the target company is newly formed, if it has not started to carry on business and has not borrowed any money;
- Exemption for creeping acquisition: 3% creep in six months;
- Dividend reinvestment;
- Initial public offering (IPO) fund-raising;
- Underwriting of fund-raising;
- Acquisition through a listed company;

- Acquisition through a will or other operation of law;
- Acquisition that results from an auction of forfeited shares;
- Acquisition that results from a compromise, arrangement, liquidation or buy-back; and
- Acquisition made in a manner prescribed by Regulations under the *Corporations Act*.

  See further www.takeovers.gov.au.

Local ownership

There are no policies or guidelines which govern the extent of local ownership which is necessary in establishing a new company.

Government participation

Government participation is rare in Australia, either through equity ownership, managerial capacity or other form. Indeed, in recent years, governments have sold their business interests in banking, telecommunications and utilities.

Geographical limits

Companies in Australia are not limited as to the geographical area in which they may operate. The *Corporations Act* purports to have extra-territorial application in some areas such as the prohibition of insider trading.

Local staff

There is no legal requirement to use local staff, contractors or subcontractors.

AUS ¶30-111   PERCENTAGE OF FOREIGN OWNERSHIP

The percentage of foreign ownership does not affect the status of a company in Australia.

AUS ¶30-112   TYPES OF GOVERNING AND MANAGING STRUCTURES

Australian company law follows English traditions closely and gives pre-eminence to the board of directors in the governing and managing of companies.

As from 1998, companies are no longer required to have a constitution in the form of a memorandum or articles of association. Companies can choose to have a constitution or to be governed by the "replaceable rules" as set out in the *Corporations Act*. The replaceable rules deal with such matters as directors, directors' meetings, meetings of members, the company secretary, inspection of books, shares and the transfer of shares.

For an existing company, its current memorandum and articles of association may make up the constitution, or the company may choose to adopt some or all of the replaceable rules in the *Corporations Act*.

Shareholders do have the right to call general meetings. Under the *Corporations Act*, directors must convene a general meeting within 21 days and hold it within two months

— on the requisition of a member or members holding, in total, at least 5% of voting rights, or on the requisition of not less than 100 members entitled to vote at the meeting (sec. 249D).

AUS ¶30-113   STRUCTURE AND POWERS OF JOINT VENTURE

The concept of the joint venture is well-established in Australian law in areas such as mining, property development and sharefarming.

The legislative requirements that will affect a non-resident corporate participant in a joint venture are those that relate to the registration of foreign corporations doing business in Australia (see AUS ¶30-103), or that relate to foreign investment (see AUS ¶45-004 to AUS ¶45-104).

As mentioned above, business structures such as joint ventures in Australia need not be registered with any government — except for corporations and business names.

The structure of a joint venture would normally be set out in the joint venture agreement rather than in the constitutional documentation of any company that might be formed for the purpose of the joint venture.

The law of business structures in Australia is regulated by contract law and there are few restrictions on what may be contracted. If a company is chosen, the extent to which these arrangements must be set out in the company's constitutional documents will require close compliance with the requirements of the *Corporations Act*.

AUS ¶30-114   BANKRUPTCY LAW

In Australia, the bankruptcy of natural persons is governed by the *Bankruptcy Act 1966* (Cth). The *Corporations Act* contains similar provisions relating to the insolvency and winding up of companies.

Bankruptcy is administered by the Insolvency and Trustee Service Australia within the Commonwealth Attorney-General's Department.

Refer to its homepage at http://www.itsa.gov.au.

More information is available on the website of the Insolvency Practitioners Association of Australia at www.ipaa.com.au.

Natural persons

A debtor who becomes aware that he or she is unable to pay their debts as and when they fall due may inform their creditors so that they may take appropriate action. Alternatively, the debtor may petition the court to become a bankrupt. A failure to take one of these steps may cause the debtor to commit an act of bankruptcy which would entitle their creditors to present a bankruptcy petition against the debtor.

Once declared bankrupt, all the debtor's property (including certain ''after-acquired'' property) vests in a trustee in bankruptcy. The trustee collects and sells the bankrupt's property so that it may be distributed to the creditors. A bankrupt's assets are to be distributed among their unsecured creditors evenly and fairly so that no one unsecured creditor has preference or priority over another unsecured creditor. In contrast, secured creditors may be paid out of their security.

Where a creditor is aware that a debtor is unable to pay his or her debts as and when they fall due and the creditor receives payment or takes security for payment from the debtor, the payment or security may be void under the provisions of the *Bankruptcy Act* if the debtor later becomes bankrupt. If found to be void, the payment or security will have to be returned to form part of the debtor's estate available to the creditors generally.

Providing a bankrupt has committed no wrongful act, he or she is entitled to be discharged from bankruptcy at the earliest opportunity after a proper investigation of their affairs.

Once discharged, a bankrupt is free from all of his or her previous debts. However, discharge from bankruptcy does not release the bankrupt from certain liabilities such as debts incurred by fraud, maintenance agreements in family law and pecuniary penalties such as those under the *Corporations Act*.

There are provisions in the *Bankruptcy Act* which allow a debtor in financial difficulties to enter into various arrangements to overcome their difficulties:

- a Part IX ''debt agreement'' — a simple, no cost alternative to bankruptcy for low income debtors with few assets and small debts; and

- a composition or arrangement with creditors without sequestration. The composition or arrangement is called a ''Part X Arrangement'' and is binding on the debtor and his or her creditors.

An undischarged bankrupt faces many limitations such as the loss of most property, inability to obtain credit, inability to carry on a business without disclosing their status of bankruptcy and inability to be a director of a company.

Companies

It is usual for a security over a company's assets to contain a power authorising the secured creditor to appoint a receiver to realise the secured property or, in some cases (for instance where the security is a charge over the company's undertaking) to manage the company's business temporarily for the purpose of better realising the assets. The receivership provisions in the *Corporations Act* cover mortgagees and their agents.

Creditors of all insolvent companies who believe that with a little more time the company could trade out of its difficulties may agree that:

- the company be placed into voluntary administration under Part 5.3A of the *Corporations Act*. The directors, liquidators or secured lenders may appoint an administrator to help a struggling company trade out of its financial difficulties The administrator controls the company under administration in place of the directors who cease to hold office; and

- the company be wound up in insolvency (Part 5.4). There are deeming provisions in the *Corporations Act* which prescribe circumstances where a company is deemed to be ''unable to pay its debts'' and thereby open to an order of winding up.

The court has a discretion to grant the order. If the court grants the application, a liquidator is appointed to the company who assumes control of the company's property in substitution for the directors.

The *Corporations Act* contains provisions in Part 5.7B dealing with voidable transactions, similar to those under the *Bankruptcy Act*, which render void or voidable the following payments made to a creditor during a certain period prior to the date of the filing of the application for winding up:

- unfair preferences;
- non-commercial transactions;
- insolvent transactions;
- unfair loans to a company such as pre-liquidation loans at high interest designed to defeat unsecured creditors;
- voidable transactions;
- floating charges created within six months before the relation-back day;
- the company be wound up on other grounds such as on an application by ASIC that the company cannot pay its debts and be wound up (Part 5.4A); and
- the company be wound up under Part 5.6.

Creditors are required to lodge proofs of their debts and secured creditors have the option of realising, valuing or relinquishing their security. Where liabilities exceed assets, shareholders in a company limited by shares, guarantee or shares and guarantee are required to contribute to the extent of the amount unpaid on the shares held or the amount of the guarantee or both.

Upon completion of the winding up, the liquidator may apply to the court for an order that he be released and also that the company be dissolved.

Directors' duty to prevent insolvent trading

The *Corporations Law* aims to protect creditors from being presented with an empty shell by lifting the "corporate veil" to place a statutory duty on directors to prevent insolvent trading and to hold them personally liable for company debts incurred while insolvent (sec. 588G).

Taxation

General taxation .... AUS ¶35-001

Commercial and business profits .... AUS ¶35-101

Investment profits .... AUS ¶35-201

Miscellaneous taxes .... AUS ¶35-301

Capital gains tax .... AUS ¶35-401

Tax incentives .... AUS ¶35-501

GENERAL TAXATION

International tax treaties ... AUS ¶35-001

Existence of tax credits ...... AUS ¶35-002

Procedures for resolving tax disputes .... AUS ¶35-003

Fiscal year .... AUS ¶35-004

Method of payment of tax liabilities .... AUS ¶35-005

AUS ¶35-001   INTERNATIONAL TAX TREATIES

Australia is party to a number of bilateral international agreements designed to overcome double taxation. Many of these agreements follow the OECD Model Convention on Income and Capital.

Each of the double tax agreements currently in force in Australia allocates, between the contracting countries, rights to tax business and commercial profits of enterprises. They also deal with the taxation of various forms of passive investment income such as dividends, interest, and royalties and certain forms of income from real property.

The taxation of income from the provision of the personal services of individuals resident in one contracting country, but performed in the other, is also covered in each of the agreements. Special arrangements are made concerning the taxation of certain visiting taxpayers including academic staff, teachers, students and government employees.

The agreements also deal with the problems of dual residency, government pensions and annuities and taxation of profits of air and sea carriers.

Most of Australia's agreements contain an article dealing with "other income". This includes income not expressly covered by any other article of the agreement. This income is generally taxable only in the country of residence of the recipient unless it is sourced in, or connected with a permanent establishment (affixed place of business, through which the business of the enterprise is wholly or partly carried on) in, the other country.

Presently Australia has concluded comprehensive double tax agreements with the following countries:

- Argentina
- Austria
- Belgium
- Canada
- China
- Czech Republic
- Denmark
- Fiji
- Finland
- France
- Germany
- Greece
- Hungary
- India
- Indonesia

- Ireland
- Italy
- Japan
- Kiribati
- Korea
- Malaysia
- Malta
- Mexico
- Netherlands
- New Zealand
- Norway
- Papua New Guinea
- Philippines
- Poland
- Romania

- Russia
- Singapore
- Slovak Republic
- Spain
- Sri Lanka
- South Africa
- Sweden
- Switzerland
- Taiwan
- Thailand
- United Kingdom
- United States of America
- Vietnam

A comprehensive agreement with Greece is awaiting signatures. Other proposed DTAs currently being negotiated and/or finalised for signature include, Chile and Turkey. Protocols to the DTA's with the United States and Malaysia have come into force, and legislation has been passed to implement new DTA's with the united Kingdom and Mexico. The Joint Standing Committee on Foreign Affairs, Defence and Trade has called on the government to give priority to the negotiation of DTAs with South American countries.

A decision of the High Court of Australia, *Minister of State for Immigration and Ethnic Affairs v. Ah Hin Teoh*, appears to confirm that where there is conflict between a provision in the domestic law and a provision in a double tax treaty or other treaty or convention relating to taxation which Australia has signed, the ambiguity should be resolved in favour of the provision in the treaty.

The case also decided that, where there is ambiguity in the meaning of a treaty, it should be resolved in a way that is consistent with model tax conventions signed by Australia.

The Government has completed conducting a review of Australia's international tax regime.

In particular, in the 2003/04 Budget the government said that it broadly supported moving towards a more "residence" based treaty policy instead of the current model based on source. It noted that a key element in achieving this would involve reducing withholding tax rates consistent with the direction set in the US protcol. See www.taxboard.gov.au.

AUS ¶35-001

AUS ¶35-002   EXISTENCE OF TAX CREDITS

In all Australian double tax agreements, the taxpayer's country of residence must give credit for certain taxes paid in the other country on particular types of income. This mechanism is designed to prevent double taxation. However, under sec 6AB(5A) of the ITAA 1936 the "false Tax Credit Rule", a taxpayer is not entitled to a credit for foreign tax where the tax is refunded to the taxpayer or to another person. All taxpayers can carry excess foreign tax credits forward for a maximum of five years for application against tax payable on foreign income of the same class. Excess credits must be utilised in the order in which they arise and may be transferred within company groups up to 1 July 2003. (Transfers after 1 July 2003 are governed by the new consolidations regime.)

Australia's domestic tax laws also provide Australian residents credits for foreign tax paid (regardless of any double tax agreement relief). The self-assessment system requires taxpayers to self-determine their tax credit entitlements. This usually necessitates documentary evidence to be kept.

AUS ¶35-003   PROCEDURES FOR RESOLVING TAX DISPUTES

The administration of income tax is the responsibility of the Federal Commissioner of Taxation ("Commissioner"). Both individuals and entities (such as companies and superannuation funds) are required to "self-assess" their income tax liability, i.e. they are generally required to determine their own annual tax liability. However, disputes may arise in various ways, e.g. as the result of a tax audit by the Commissioner or a mistake by the taxpayer.

In order to contest a tax assessment, a taxpayer may raise an objection against the assessment with the Commissioner. If the taxpayer is not satisfied with the Commissioner's decision on the objection, the taxpayer may appeal directly to the Administrative Appeals Tribunal on a question of fact, which has the power to remake the Commissioner's decision. A taxpayer that is dissatisfied with the decision of the Tribunal may then appeal to the Federal Court on questions of tax law only. Where the amount of tax in dispute is less than AUS$5,000, the Small Taxation Claims Tribunal will, in most cases, be a more suitable forum. The Australian Taxation Office (ATO) also has a Problem Resolution Service, which handles complaints that have not been resolved through the normal channels. If further information is required by the taxpayer to assist in solving any dispute, the taxpayer may make a request under the *Freedom of Information Act 1982*.

If unclear as to the application of a tax law, a taxpayer may apply to the Commissioner for a private ruling in relation to the way in which the tax law or tax laws apply to the taxpayer in respect of a year of income in relation to an arrangement.

In addition, the Commissioner may make public rulings which, if favourable to taxpayers, are effectively binding on the Commissioner, i.e. the Commissioner must assess a taxpayer in accordance with the law or the public ruling, whichever is the more favourable.

The ATO has also issued Practice Statements to supplement the public rulings system. These provide direction to the ATO staff on the approaches to be taken in performing their duties. Significantly, all private rulings (with taxpayer identifiers deleted) are now published on a public database, and advance opinions are no longer available except in limited circumstances. From February 2001, the ATO began issuing a new type of public ruling called, "class rulings". These rulings provide advice to an entity about the application of a tax law to specific class of persons in relation to a particular arrangement.

The ATO has released guidelines on the circumstances in which mediation may be used to resolve disputes rather than negotiation or litigation and these are contained in PS 2002/9. See (www.ato.gov.au/content.asp?=/content/Professionals/code_settlement.htm).

AUS ¶35-004   FISCAL YEAR

The Australian financial year is 1 July to 30 June. It is possible with the approval of the Commissioner to adopt, for taxation purposes, a substituted accounting period to the standard year ending 30 June.

AUS ¶35-005   METHOD OF PAYMENT OF TAX LIABILITIES

The system for the payment and collection of income taxes from 1 July 2000 is the PAYG (Pay As You Go) system. The first part of this system is the PAYG instalment system, which can be found in Pt 2-10 of Schedule 1 of the *Taxation Administration Act 1953*. Basically, the instalment system replaces the previous provisional tax and company tax instalment systems. It is designed to match the payment of tax to the earning of the associated income but does not effect the due date of lodgement of the taxpayer's income tax return.

The second part is the PAYG withholding system that is found in Pt 2-5 of Schedule 1 of the *Tax Administration Act 1953*. The withholding system replaces PAYE, PPS, RPS and imposes new withholding requirements in relation to; labour hire arrangements, work or services where it is agreed that withholding will occur and a supply where no ABN (Australian Business Number) has been quoted.

The PAYG withholding system is intended to provide more certainty as to which payments are subject to withholding at source and is designed to standardise and simplify withholding arrangements. It is proposed that deferred company instalment arrangements will be modified to reflect the extended due dates available to a "deferred BAS payer" for reporting quarterly BAS/IAS obligations. The due dates for reporting quarterly BAS/IAS obligations for taxpayers other than monthly GST reporters has been extended to 28 October, February, April and July.

Tax on Australian-sourced dividend, interest and royalty income derived by non-residents is generally deducted at source (see AUS ¶35-201). At present, separate taxation payments will still be made for personal income tax, fringe benefits tax and superannuation, which is all self-assessed. However, there could be scope to include these income tax liabilities as part of the PAYG system in the future.

During 2002 and 2003 the government enacted four instalments of legislation that now comprise the new Consolidations regime. The new legislation introduces new rules for consolidated groups and members of consolidated entry consolidated groups. These rules provide for wholly-owned group entities to be treated as a single group from 1 July 2002, for the purposes of determining income tax liability, and as such impact upon the operation of the PAYG instalment system.

General Interest Charge (GIC)

Under sec. 8AAC of the TAA 1953, a tax-deductible general interest charge is imposed upon late payment of tax.

The GIC will apply to late payment of a range of taxes, including the following:

- income tax;
- company tax instalments;
- withholding tax;
- franking deficit tax;
- deficit deferral tax;
- franking additional tax;
- fringe benefits tax;
- sales tax;
- superannuation guarantee charge;
- superannuation contributions tax; and
- termination payments tax.

GIC also applies to:

- late payment, underpayment or non-payment of deductions under the pay-as-you-earn scheme;
- reportable tax; and
- withholding tax systems by either private concerns or government instrumentalities.

New penalties have also been introduced for failing to notify the Commissioner of Taxation of the source of deductions or provide a reconciliation statement of source deductions made under the PAYG system.

COMMERCIAL AND BUSINESS PROFITS

Taxation of commercial and business profits .... AUS ¶35-101	Details of tax on companies .... AUS ¶35-103
Taxable activities and undertakings .... AUS ¶35-102	Details of business profits tax .... AUS ¶35-104
	Taxation of executives .... AUS ¶35-105

AUS ¶35-101   TAXATION OF COMMERCIAL AND BUSINESS PROFITS

Income tax is assessed under the *Income Tax Assessment Act 1997*, on "taxable income" regardless of whether the taxpayer is an entity or an individual. Taxable income is computed by deducting from "assessable income" all "deductions".

Included in assessable income are general business income and commercial profits and also "net capital gains" realised on certain property acquired after 19 September 1985 (see AUS ¶35-401).

Certain profits and items of revenue recognised in the accounts of a corporation effectively may not be assessable in a particular year. Unrealised profits recognised in accounts, such as profits on the revaluation of assets, may not be included in assessable income until they are realised. Franked dividends received by a resident corporation from a resident corporation, will be assessable income of the recipient and they will receive a franking rebate/tax offset equal to the amount of franking credit post 1 July 2002. These credits are refundable if not utilised against tax payable, from the 2000-2001 year onwards.

Business expenses that are not capital outgoings or expenses incurred in deriving exempt income, are generally allowable deductions. Other business expenses that are not deductible, include, income tax. A separate tax, called "fringe benefits tax" is levied on employers in respect of non-cash employee remuneration (see AUS ¶35-301).

Current legislation provides that expenses against current revenue will not be deductible until the relevant outgoing is incurred. Also, allowable expenses against foreign-sourced income cannot be deducted against income from other sources, but may be carried forward and offset against future income from the same source.

Non-resident shareholders, lenders and investors deriving Australian-sourced dividends, interest and royalties are generally not subject to the foregoing rules. Tax is paid on dividend, interest and royalty income of non-residents under a withholding tax regime (see AUS ¶35-201).

Partnerships and trusts

Taxpayers deriving income in partnership are required to include in their assessable income their respective shares of the taxable income of the partnership. Beneficiaries of trust estates are required to include in their assessable income the amount of the taxable

AUS ¶35-101

income of the trust estate to which they are respectively entitled. Where there is an amount of taxable income of a trust estate to which no beneficiary is entitled, the trustee may be assessed at a penalty rate of tax. Where there is a non-resident beneficiary entitled to income of the trust, the trustee is required to pay on behalf of the beneficiary the tax in respect of that income.

AUS ¶35-102   TAXABLE ACTIVITIES AND UNDERTAKINGS

Income tax is payable by both residents and non-resident taxpayers. Resident taxpayers are taxed in Australia on their worldwide income. Non-resident taxpayers are subject to tax in Australia on income from Australian sources only. Residence of individuals can be determined through four alternative tests offered in sec 6(1) of *ITAA36*. These include:

- residence according to ordinary concepts;
- domicile test;
- 183-day rule; or
- superannuation test.

An individual who does not satisfy at least one of these tests is a non-resident. However, in determining residency for tax purposes, the fact that a taxpayer does not have a usual place of abode in Australia does not necessarily mean that the taxpayer must have a usual place of abode somewhere else. (See AUS ¶35-105 in the case of *Subrahmanyam 2001 ATC 2177*.)

A taxpayer resident in a country with which Australia has a comprehensive double tax agreement, however, will only be subject to tax on business and commercial profits if the taxpayer carries on business in Australia through a "permanent establishment".

A corporation is a resident for tax purposes if it is incorporated in Australia. A corporation will also be an Australian resident if, although not incorporated in Australia, it carries on business in Australia and:

- central management and control of the company is carried on in Australia; or
- the voting power of the company is controlled by Australian residents.

In the case of dual residency, Australia's DTAs generally assign residence for individuals based on where they have their permanent home or closer personal or economic relations. For companies, Australia's DTAs refer to the place of effective management or in some cases place of incorporation as determinative of residence.

AUS ¶35-103   DETAILS OF TAX ON COMPANIES

Tax rate

A tax rate of 30% will be operative for the 2003/2004 year. There is no tax on undistributed profits of companies.

Distinctions between companies

There is a distinction between "public" and "private" companies for certain purposes. A company, which is not a public company, is a private company. The definition of a public company includes a company listed on a stock exchange at the end of the year, and a subsidiary of a public company.

Special deductions for expenditure are directed at specific industries, which effectively distinguish taxpayers carrying on business in those industries. Targeted industries include those companies engaged in mining, and those engaged in mineral exploration and prospecting. Measures such as an exemption from withholding tax for interest on borrowings of "offshore banking units" are directed at financial institutions.

Tax differentials for companies controlled by non-residents

The rate of tax payable on the worldwide income of an Australian resident company is the same regardless of whether it is controlled by resident or non-resident shareholders.

However, dividends payable to non-residents will be subject to withholding tax, whereas resident shareholders will be assessed at their ordinary tax rates. Where an imputation credit is attached to a dividend paid to a non-resident, the dividend will be free of withholding tax (see AUS ¶35-201). When the dividend is paid to a resident company, with an imputation credit, it effectively becomes tax-free.

An additional range of payments made to foreign residents in the course of an enterprise may become subject to withholding tax from 1 July 2003. The relevant types of payment and the rates of withholding will be prescribed by regulation after consultation with effected groups as they are identified as representing a compliance risk. According to the *Ralph Business Review*, the types of payments that could be targeted include; rents, gains on the realisation of assets and income from the provision of services.

The payment must be of such a kind that it could reasonably be related to assessable income of foreign residents. Amounts withheld will be available as a credit against final tax assessment. Withholding may also apply to payments received by an entity on behalf of a foreign resident. An exemption may apply if a non-resident can show that it has an established history of compliance with Australian tax obligations.

Documentation

All taxpayers carrying on business in Australia are required to maintain, in English, documentary evidence of all transactions or acts adequate to determine liability under the *Income Tax Assessment Act*. These records must be maintained for a period of at least five years.

Tax returns

Income tax returns are required to be lodged annually. Under the self-assessment system, companies are required to lodge returns and generally pay their tax through the PAYG Instalment system under Part 2-10 of the *Tax Administration Act 1953*.

There is no requirement for income tax returns to be certified by an auditor.

AUS ¶35-103

Registration requirements

A corporation is required to apply to the Australian Taxation Office to obtain a "tax file number" in order to lodge tax returns under the self-assessment system. All business will also require an ABN (Australian Business Number).

Company tax

Income tax is charged on "taxable income", determined under the *Income Tax Assessment Act*, and not on net profit according to ordinary accounting principles.

Depreciation allowances

Tax deductions are allowable for the depreciation of income-producing plant and equipment. The cost of depreciable plant and equipment is deductible over their effective life. Deductions similar to depreciation are also available for certain capital expenditure on income-producing buildings.

In addition, there are deductions similar to depreciation available for certain forms of intellectual property, and for capital expenditure incurred by taxpayers engaged in certain mining and mineral exploration activities.

In its response to the Ralph Review of Business Taxation, the Government has introduced a Uniform Capital Allowance system, which is based on the effective life of assets. The new system applies to assets commenced to be constructed or acquired under contracts, on or after 1 July 2001 and to black hole expenses incurred, such as site preparation costs, feasibility study costs and environmental assessment costs to be written off as "pooled project expenditure", on or after 1 July 2001.

The Commissioner has also updated the effective life of certain depreciating assets as from 1 July 2002, including assets used in the gas and oil industry, cars, aeroplanes and helicopters.

Small business taxpayers will still be more favourably treated under the current and new provisions having access to accelerated depreciation, balancing adjustment offsets and certain pooling arrangements. In particular, small business taxpayers that elect to enter the Simplified Tax System from 1 July 2001 have access to an immediate write-off for depreciating assets costing less than AUS$1,000 and a simple pooling facility for other depreciating assets.

Tax losses

Tax losses may be carried forward indefinitely, but may not be carried back to be offset against income of prior years. Corporate tax losses of prior years remain deductible, subject to continuity of the majority underlying interests in the company, or continuity by the company of the same business after any change in underlying ownership.

Domestic tax losses may be deducted from income of any source. Tax losses incurred in earning foreign-sourced income are only available to be deducted from income of the same class and from the same source.

After 1 July 2003 the group loss transfer rules generally cease to apply The Ralph Review of Business Taxation recommended that consolidated groups be allowed to choose the proportion of carry-forward losses to be deducted in a year. The consolidation regime applies from 1 July 2002. Companies may also use a global method of valuing assets for the purposes of the inter-entity loss multiplication provisions. Finally, the Government has provided tax relief for demergers (restructuring of the organisation) from 1 July 2002.

Fiscal year

Unless a "substituted accounting period" has been approved by the Commissioner of Taxation, the year of income of a company is the financial year ending 30 June. A substituted accounting period will generally be approved where there is a substantial business need. Australian resident subsidiaries of non-resident holding companies will usually be allowed to adopt, for tax purposes, the same accounting period as their holding companies.

Tax withheld from employee remuneration

Employers are required to withhold income tax from salary and wages paid to employees under the so-called "pay as you go" (PAYG) provisions. The PAYG system will also provide for tax to be withheld for certain payments made to contractors and workers in other particular industries. Employers are required to lodge Business Activity Statements on a monthly and/or quarterly basis.

Fringe benefits provided to employees are not treated as salary and wages but may be subject to "fringe benefits tax" in the hands of the employer. The employer will also pay all FBT obligations on a quarterly basis (see AUS ¶35-301).

Undistributed profits tax

In Australia, there is no longer a tax on the undistributed profits of a company.

Thin capitalisation

The thin capitalisation rules operate to deny deductions for interest incurred by resident taxpayers on "excess" debt owed to related non-resident lenders. These rules apply where there is 15%, or more, direct or indirect foreign control of the resident.

The excess debt in question is the amount by which debt owed to associated non-residents exceeds a multiple of equity in the resident borrower, attributable to non-resident associates. The ratio of allowable debt to equity is 6:1 where the resident is a financial institution, and 3:1 in all other cases.

As of 1 July 2001, the existing Thin Capitalisation rules have been strengthened. In particular, "total debt" as opposed to "foreign debt" will be used in measuring whether the thin capitalisation provisions have been breached. The rules will cover inward investment of foreign multinationals and outward investment of Australian-based multinationals, and include a "safe harbour" debt equity ratio of 3:1. Interest deductions will be denied to the extent that they exceed the ratio (unless an arms-length test applies). Separate rules will operate in respect of financial institutions. As a consequence of the introduction of the consolidation regime, where groups consolidate the thin capitalisation grouping rules apply to the head company. Where entities do not consolidate, the thin capitalisation grouping rules cease to operate from 1 July 2003.

AUS ¶35-103

Simplified imputation system

The Ralph Review of Business Taxation recommendation of a Simplified Imputation System became operational as from 1 July 2002. Under this regime, franking accounts are expressed in dollars of tax paid rather than the corresponding taxable income. Corporate tax entities that receive a franked dividend gross it up and receive an imputation credit and corresponding tax offset like individuals. Similarly, the Government has also accepted the recommendation to provide Australian companies with imputation credits for withholding tax paid by foreign companies on dividend distributions.

AUS ¶35-104   DETAILS OF BUSINESS PROFITS TAX

There is no distinct tax on business profits other than the income tax outlined above. There are, however, various measures in the income tax law to combat international transfer pricing. Where charges for goods and services are made between parties who are not dealing at arm's length, the Commissioner has power to impose arm's length charges for tax purposes. Challenging a transfer pricing determination on the basis that the Commissioner had acted in bad faith is only likely to succeed in extreme circumstances (*Daihatsu Australia 2001 ATC 4268*). However, the business taxation reforms propose that any double taxation arising from any transfer pricing adjustments should be avoided and administrative arrangements for transfer pricing should also be improved.

AUS ¶35-105   TAXATION OF EXECUTIVES

Tax rates

Cash remuneration of corporate executives is subject to tax at the rates applicable to individual taxpayers. Resident individual taxpayers are taxed on their worldwide incomes at progressive rates subject to a tax-free threshold. Australian-sourced income of non-resident individuals (which is not otherwise subject to withholding tax) is also subject to tax at progressive rates, but without the benefit of a tax-free threshold.

The maximum rate of tax is currently 47% on taxable income in excess of AUS$62,500 and the tax-free threshold is AUS$6,000. Residents are also required to pay a Medicare levy of 1.5% of their taxable income, which increases the maximum rate of tax to 48.5%.

Tax rates as from 1 July 2003	
Tax scale	
Taxable income (AUS$)	Tax rate (%)
up to 6,000	0
6,001 to 21,600	17
21,601 to 52,000	30
52,001 to 62,500	42
over 62,500	47

Basis of assessment

Under the Australian tax rules, the source of salary and wages income is usually taken to be the place where the employment services are performed. Unless a double tax agreement operates to modify these rules, non-residents are generally liable to tax on salary and wages in connection with services performed in Australia, regardless of where the salary or wages are paid. For trading stock and property, the source rule is generally where the contract was made. For interest payments, it is where the credit is provided, for dividends, it is the source of the profits out of which they are paid and for royalties it is where the property or intellectual rights are situated.

Residence

For tax purposes, an individual will be an Australian resident if the person's domicile is in Australia unless the Commissioner is satisfied that his permanent place of abode is outside Australia. A person who has been in Australia continuously or intermittently during more than one half of the year of income is also a resident unless the person's usual place of abode is outside Australia and the person does not intend to reside in Australia. In the case of *Subrahmanyam 2001 ATC 2177*, the taxpayer who resided in Australia for several years before her death was held not to be a resident as Australia was not her usual place of abode. Ultimately however the issue of residence is largely a question of fact and degree. (See AUS ¶35-102)

Deductions

Tax deductions are allowed for outgoings and losses to the extent that they are necessarily incurred in producing the taxpayer's assessable income and are not of a capital, private or domestic nature. However, deductions for outgoings incurred in producing foreign-sourced income of a resident taxpayer may only be offset against income of the same kind and from the same source.

Foreign-sourced income of a non-resident taxpayer is not assessable; therefore, expenses incurred in producing that income would not be deductible in Australia.

Resident and non-resident individual taxpayers may also be entitled to deductions for a variety of specific expenses, such as contributions to certain superannuation funds.

Corporate executives are not subject to tax on remuneration provided by way of non-cash benefits. Employers are, however, subject to tax on the value of non-cash benefits provided to employees, under the *Fringe Benefits Tax Assessment Act 1986*. There are certain exemptions that are particularly important to executives who are not permanently resident in Australia (see AUS ¶35-301).

There is no general exemption from Australian tax for visiting industrial experts.

Tax certificates

There is currently no requirement for non-residents to obtain tax certificates.

AUS ¶35-105

INVESTMENT PROFITS

Taxes on investment profits .... AUS ¶35-201	Form of outward remittances .... AUS ¶35-205	
Tax credits .... AUS ¶35-202	Meaning of "royalty" .... AUS ¶35-211	
Treatment of residents and non-residents .... AUS ¶35-203	Must tax be deducted from investment profits? .... AUS ¶35-212	
Approval of outward remittances .... AUS ¶35-204		

AUS ¶35-201   TAXES ON INVESTMENT PROFITS

Dividends, interest and royalties

In most situations, interest, dividends and royalties derived by non-residents from Australian investments are not assessable income under the ordinary income tax rules. Australian-sourced dividend, interest and royalty income derived by non-resident investors is, however, subject to a withholding tax.

Interest payable by a resident to a non-resident is subject to interest withholding tax. Interest withholding tax is imposed at the rate of 10% of the gross amount of the interest payable. The resident borrower, who is paying the interest, is liable to withhold the relevant amount of tax at source.

Dividends payable by an Australian resident company to a non-resident shareholder are subject to dividend withholding tax at the rate of 30% (or generally 15% where a double tax agreement applies) of the gross amount of the dividend payable. However, dividends, which are paid from "tax paid" profits of a resident company and carry an imputation credit (i.e. a "franked" dividend), are free of withholding tax to the extent of the imputation credit attaching to that dividend.

An exemption from withholding tax applies to the unfranked part of a dividend to the extent that a dividend consists of a "foreign dividend account" ("FDA") declaration amount. A FDA amount will generally arise where a company has received, on or after 1 July 1994, an amount from a foreign source, which is itself, exempted from tax or upon which a credit in respect of foreign tax has been granted.

Royalties paid by a resident to a non-resident are liable for withholding tax at the rate of 30% (or generally 10% where a double-tax agreement applies). However, royalties derived by a resident of a country with which Australia has a double tax agreement will not be subject to withholding tax where the royalties are connected with a business carried on through a permanent establishment in Australia. Such royalties are taxed as normal business profits. Other forms of Australian-sourced income of non-resident investors are subject to tax at the ordinary rates unless relief is available under a double tax agreement.

Every person in Australia holding moneys due to a non-resident who derives Australian source income or capital gains, or who is shareholder, debenture holder or depositor in a company deriving such income or capital gains, is deemed to be the non-residents agent. This ensures the collection of tax due by non-residents, particularly where they do not carry on business or furnish returns in Australia. As from 1 July 2002, temporary residents will be exempt from tax on their foreign source income, so as to encourage skill intensive businesses to locate in Australia. Likewise, foreign income accounts have been introduced into the non-resident withholding tax regime. From 1 July 2002, a special withholding tax applies to superannuation payments made to persons who entered Australia temporarily, on particular classes of visa and who subsequently left Australia permanently.

AUS ¶35-202   TAX CREDITS

Dividends paid by Australian resident companies from after-tax profits may be "franked". A franked dividend is a dividend, which is declared to have an imputation credit attached, reflecting tax paid by the company on the profits from which the dividend was paid. A dividend will not be franked if debited against a share capital account, share premium account or revaluation reserve. A franked dividend may be fully franked or partially franked.

A franked dividend, received by a non-resident shareholder, is free of dividend withholding tax to the extent that the dividend is franked. Unfranked dividends and that portion of a partially franked dividend, which is unfranked, is subject to withholding tax at the usual rate in the hands of the non-resident shareholder, unless specifically exempt.

AUS ¶35-203   TREATMENT OF RESIDENTS AND NON-RESIDENTS

The principal distinction between the tax treatment of resident and non-resident investors is that withholding tax does not ordinarily apply to dividend, interest and royalty income of resident investors. Residents therefore pay tax on investment income at the ordinary rates, without tax being collected at source. Residents are also able to claim tax deductions for outgoings and losses incurred in deriving dividend and interest income.

As part of the Business Tax reforms mentioned previously, in relation to foreign investment in Australia, a foreign income account will be established. This will provide relief from Australian dividend withholding tax on unfranked non-portfolio dividends paid to non-residents from foreign source income. This measure applies from 1 July 2001.

AUS ¶35-204   APPROVAL OF OUTWARD REMITTANCES

The responsibility to withhold tax from interest, dividends and royalties payable to non-resident lenders, shareholders and investors, rests with the resident borrower or company paying the interest, dividend or royalty, as mentioned previously . Withholding tax is due and payable within 21 days of the end of the month in which the remittance/crediting occurred.

No exchange control approval is required.

AUS ¶35-205   FORM OF OUTWARD REMITTANCES

The liability to tax on dividend, interest and royalty income derived by a non-resident from Australian sources arises when the income has been paid or "credited" to the non-resident taxpayer. Hence the liability to tax may arise before funds are actually transferred.

Liability to tax on other forms of investment income generally arises when it is paid to the non-resident taxpayer.

AUS ¶35-211   MEANING OF "ROYALTY"

A royalty is consideration for the use and exploitation of a right or some other form of property calculated by reference to the use actually made of the relevant right or property. Royalty is also defined for Australian tax purposes in virtually the same manner as defined in the OECD Model Convention and which is adopted in Australia's double tax agreements.

The definition of royalty includes a broad range of payments, such as payments for the use of copyrights, patents, commercial and scientific equipment, etc.; and payments for the use or supply of scientific, commercial and technical knowledge or information.

AUS ¶35-212   MUST TAX BE DEDUCTED FROM INVESTMENT PROFITS?

Withholding tax is payable on the gross amount of interest, dividends and royalties paid. There is, however, no withholding tax in respect of rents and capital gains. Although a resident paying an amount to a non-resident may be under an obligation to deduct the relevant amount of tax, the primary liability to tax remains that of the non-resident taxpayer who derives the income. This primary liability cannot be transferred by any agreement between the parties.

However, an obligation is placed upon an agent or trustee of a non-resident in Australia or a person having the receipt, control or disposal of moneys belonging to a non-resident to pay the tax which is or will become due by the non-resident.

Where interest is payable by a resident to a non-resident in relation to a loan of moneys over which a mortgage has been provided, a clause making the mortgagor/resident liable for income tax in respect of interest under the mortgage is void.

MISCELLANEOUS TAXES

Miscellaneous taxes .... AUS ¶35-301   Unitary tax .... AUS ¶35-302

AUS ¶35-301   MISCELLANEOUS TAXES

There is a range of taxes, in addition to income tax, imposed in Australia at both the federal and State levels. The principal taxes operating at each level, with their general application, are set out below.

Commonwealth taxes

Fringe benefits tax (FBT)

Employers who provide employee remuneration in the form of non-cash benefits are subject to "fringe benefits tax". Tax is assessed under the *Fringe Benefits Tax Assessment Act 1986* on the taxable value of "fringe benefits" provided during each year ending 31 March. The rate of FBT is currently 48.5% and is imposed upon the "tax-inclusive" value of the benefit. It is the employer, who is liable for the FBT. However, employers are entitled to a tax deduction in Australia for FBT paid. The calculation of the FBT since 1 July 2000 also takes into account the GST interaction, by providing a higher gross up and taxable value on benefits provided by employers who are able to claim input tax credits.

Concessions are available under the FBT for certain benefits provided to employees required to relocate because of their employment. Reasonable living-away-from-home allowances, including the cost of removal and various domestic establishment costs, such as connection of electricity and gas, are among the benefits which may be exempt from fringe benefits tax, where they arise because the employee has been required to move in order to carry out his employment duties.

Where the individual fringe benefits amount for an employee exceeds AUS$1,000 for the FBT year ending 31 March 2000 and onwards, this amount is the reportable fringe benefits amount to be included by the employer on the employee's payment summary.

Public benevolent institutions (PBI) are limited in the amount of concessional benefits that can be provided to employees. The rebate of tax that is allowed for PBI's for the FBT years commencing 1 April 2001 is limited to AUS$30,000. From 1 April 2003, a public hospital can access the FBT exemption for fringe benefits provided to employees up to AUS$17,000 cap, without being a (PBI). Generally, provisions relating to the collection and recovery of FBT have now been transferred to the *Tax Administration Act 1953*.

An FBT exemption for prescribed funds established to protect employee entitlements in the event of insolvency or to provide for entitlements, such as redundancy and long service leave, is effective as of 1 April 2003.

AUS ¶35-301   © **2004 CCH Asia Pte Limited**

Goods and Services Tax (GST)

A broad-based consumption tax, which aims to catch "private final consumption expenditure", has been operational as of 1 July 2000, replacing the wholesale sales tax system. A GST is charged on the supply of goods and services in Australia and on imported goods at the rate of 10%. Essentially, it is a value-added tax, where tax is paid at each step along the chain of transactions involving the goods or services until the end user is reached. Entities making taxable supplies will receive a credit for the GST paid on inputs. For entities with a turnover of less than AUS$1 million, they may elect to lodge GST returns on an annual basis. Likewise, monthly tax periods are no longer compulsory for entities with substituted accounting periods, particularly those with overseas parent companies.

Some of the categories of GST free supplies where no GST is payable on the supply but the entity is entitled to claim an input tax credit on any creditable acquisitions that relate to the supply include:

- health;
- education;
- childcare;
- government charges;
- exports;
- religious services;
- non-commercial activities of charities;
- international travel;
- food;
- water and sewerage; and
- sale of going concerns.

Customs and excise duties

In addition to the goods and services tax, there is also a complex customs and excise regime imposing duties on goods at different rates.

State taxes

Stamp duty

Stamp duty is a tax imposed in each of the States and Territories, principally on instruments executed in relation to various transactions such as the transfer of land, transfer of shares and taking security for financial accommodation. The rate of duty applicable will range depending on the nature of the transaction. Rewritten stamp duty legislation has applied in Victoria and Tasmania since 1 July 2001. Most States that have enacted new Duties Acts have significantly departed from the old legislation regarding the instruments and transactions liable to duty and various procedures in the payment of that duty. South Australia, WA and the NT are yet to replace the old legislation. In particular, stamp duty on transfers of listed marketable securities was abolished in all jurisdictions with effect from 1 July 2001. Lease duty in Victoria and franchise duty in NSW was also abolished since 1 July 2001. Bed taxes were abolished on 1 July 2001.

Payroll tax

Payroll tax is imposed in each of the States and Territories on employers. Employers are required to pay tax on the amount of salary and wages paid in excess of a threshold amount. Both the tax-free threshold and the rates of tax differ from State to State. The usual tax-free threshold is between AUS$500,000 and AUS$1,250,000 per year and the standard rate of payroll tax is between 4.75% to 6.85%. As of 1 January 2003, the rate is 5.25% in Victoria, 4.75% in Queensland, 5.67% in South Australia, 6.10% in Tasmania, and 6.2% in the Northern Territory.

For NSW from 1 July 2003 the exemption for lumpsum termination payments was removed, and taxable wages were extended to include certain trust distributions made in lieu of wages and remuneration by way of share plans and options and termination payments to non-executive directors. In NSW from 1 July 2003, fringe benefits will also be subject to payroll tax on the basis of the grossed-up value.

Land tax

Land tax is imposed in each of the States and Territories, generally on the unimproved value of land owned by the taxpayer. The tax payable is calculated by applying the appropriate rate of land tax to the taxable value. The rates of tax for 2004 for NSW for example, are nil up to AUS$317,000 and then AUS$100 + AUS1.7 cents for each AUS$1 in excess of AUS$317,000. In Victoria, the tax-free threshold was increased to AUS$150,000 for the 2003 land tax year and equalisation factors have been abolished and replaced with indexation factors. Other changes in thresholds and exemptions have occurred in Queensland, Western Australia, Tasmania and the Australian Capital Territory.

Superannuation Guarantee Charge

The Superannuation Guarantee (SG) scheme administered by the ATO requires employers to provide a minimum level of superannuation support for each of their employees, subject to limited exceptions. The SG Scheme applies from 1 July 2003 on a quarterly basis with the SG year divided into 4 quarters ending 30 September, 31 December, 31 March and 30 June. For 2003/04 and later years the required percentage of SG contributions for employees is 9% and the level of superannuation support provided for each employee is measured quarterly. Employers who have a SG shortfall are liable to a SG charge.

Workers' compensation levy

Principals and other persons to whom workers supply services are liable in each of the States and Territories to the payment of workers' compensation levy.

AUS ¶35-302 UNITARY TAX

There is no unitary tax imposed in Australia.

CAPITAL GAINS TAX

Method of taxing capital
  gains .... AUS ¶35-401

Roll-overs .... AUS ¶35-402

Offset of capital losses against
  revenue gains .... AUS ¶35-403

Offset of revenue losses against
  capital gains .... AUS ¶35-404

AUS ¶35-401 METHOD OF TAXING CAPITAL GAINS

The so-called "capital gains tax" is not a distinct tax from income tax. Since September 1985, certain realised capital gains are subject to income tax. Real gains realised by Australian resident taxpayers, from the disposal of assets acquired after 19 September 1985, are taxable capital gains, regardless of the location of the assets. Capital gains arising from the disposal of assets acquired before 20 September 1985 are not generally subject to capital gains tax.

The capital gains tax is designed to tax only real gains realised. This is achieved by increasing the cost of the asset to take account of inflation during the period the asset is held, thereby reducing the amount of the gain actually subject to tax. Alternatively, 50% of the nominal gain may be taken without any indexation providing certain conditions are satisfied. (see below).

Assets acquired by non-residents after 19 September 1985 will also be within the capital gains tax net if they are "taxable Australian assets". Taxable Australian assets include:

- land and buildings situated in Australia;

- shares in Australian resident private companies;

- shares in Australian resident public companies where at any time in the previous five years more than 10% of the shares were owned by the non-resident;

- an interest in an Australian resident trust estate;

- A 10% or greater unit-holding in an Australian unit trust; and

- property used in a business carried on by the non-resident taxpayer through a permanent establishment in Australia.

Assets subject to the capital gains tax include any form of property, with the exception of some motor vehicles. Exemptions are provided from capital gains tax for assets that form trading stock of a taxpayer, and for the taxpayer's main residence. Capital gains are not realised for tax purposes when a taxpayer dies.

When a non-resident taxpayer becomes an Australian resident, the taxpayer is deemed to have acquired, for their market value at that time, those assets actually acquired after 19 September 1985 which are not taxable Australian assets. Conversely, on becoming a non-resident, a taxpayer is deemed to have disposed of, for their market value at that time, all assets acquired after 19 September 1985 other than taxable Australian assets.

As a result of the Ralph Review of Business Taxation, there have been a number of changes to the law affecting the calculation and taxation of capital gains. These include:

- Indexation of the cost base for calculating capital gains tax for all taxpayers is frozen from 30 September 1999.

- Averaging of capital gains is no longer available to the disposal of assets after 21 September 1999.

- After 1 October 1999, capital losses can be offset against capital gains in the order favouring the taxpayer.

- Capital losses are to be offset against capital gains net of frozen indexation before being reduced and included in assessable income.

- 50% of the nominal gain post 21/9/99 can be used in calculating the capital gain.

Specifically where assets are acquired on or after 1 October 1999, and are held for at least one year, individuals will be taxed on half their capital gain. For assets acquired prior to 1 October 1999, and held for at least one year, individual taxpayers will have the choice of including in their assessable income, either half of the realised nominal gain or the whole of the difference between the disposal price and the frozen index cost base.

As a result of the Uniform Capital Allowances system, capital gains or losses can now arise where there is a balancing adjustment on a depreciating asset used for non-taxable purposes. There are also a number of capital gains tax concessions for small businesses provided certain conditions are satisfied.

AUS ¶35-402   ROLL-OVERS

"Roll-overs" are available to defer the realisation of assessable capital gains or the deductibility of capital losses. Where there is an event, which would otherwise realise a capital gain, roll-overs apply at the election of the taxpayer. Alternatively, where the event would otherwise have crystallised a capital loss, the taxpayer does not have an election to treat the transaction as a roll-over, and hence, the capital loss must be deferred. Generally, roll-overs apply where there is an event, which would otherwise realise a capital gain or capital loss but where there is no change in the underlying economic ownership of an asset. Rollover relief is also available to a fund that amends or replaces its trust deed in order to become an approved worker entitlement fund.

Hence, roll-overs are available for the transfer of assets within wholly owned corporate groups. They also apply where there is a reorganisation of the structure through which the asset is held, e.g. on transferring assets from a trust structure to a company, or from an individual to a company, where the underlying ownership of the asset is not affected.

However, from 1 July 2003, a wholly-owned group that does not choose to consolidate under the new consolidation regime will no longer be able to transfer assets between entities without triggering a capital gain. Nevertheless, capital gains tax relief and dividend exemption are available where a corporate or trust group restructures by splitting into two or more entities or groups under a demerger. This is as a result of the general value shifting regime that address both capital gains tax and revenue consequences, and applies from 1 July 2002.

The Ralph Review has also recommended that a "scrip for scrip" roll-over be introduced for takeovers where one of the entities was widely held (i.e. over 300 members where ownership interest is not concentrated in the hands of 20 or fewer individuals). The relief will be provided where there is an exchange of certain interests in companies or fixed trusts because of a takeover of at least 80% of the voting interests in the target entity (see ATO web site www.ato.gov.au).

There are also roll-over measures, which apply to some involuntary disposal of assets, such as in marriage breakdown. Where an asset is compulsorily acquired, lost or destroyed, roll-over relief will not be available if the replacement asset is a depreciating asset.

AUS ¶35-403 OFFSET OF CAPITAL LOSSES AGAINST REVENUE GAINS

Capital losses arising from the disposal of assets acquired after 19 September 1985 may only be offset against assessable capital gains. These capital losses are not deductible from other forms of assessable income. They may, however, be carried forward and offset against capital gains of future years. Capital losses realised from the disposal of assets acquired before 20 September 1985 are not available to be offset at all.

AUS ¶35-404 OFFSET OF REVENUE LOSSES AGAINST CAPITAL GAINS

Revenue losses and deductible outgoings may be offset against assessable capital gains after any capital losses available have been taken into account.

TAX INCENTIVES

Tax relief for new
industries .... AUS ¶35-501

Period of tax relief .... AUS ¶35-502

Criteria affecting relief ...... AUS ¶35-503

Existence and nature of export
incentives .... AUS ¶35-504

Applicability of export
allowances .... AUS ¶35-505

Industries excluded from export
allowances .... AUS ¶35-511

Export processing zones .... AUS ¶35-512

Accelerated depreciation
allowance .... AUS ¶35-513

Applicability of accelerated
depreciation allowance . AUS ¶35-514

Deductibility of expenses
incurred exploring export
opportunities .... AUS ¶35-515

AUS ¶35-501   TAX RELIEF FOR NEW INDUSTRIES

There is no special treatment under the income tax laws for new industries. Taxation concessions provided to facilitate the establishment of the regional headquarters ("RHQ") of multinational companies in Australia include an exemption from withholding tax for foreign source dividends passing through an Australian company, the inclusion in allowable deductions of business expenses incurred as a direct consequence of relocation. The Treasurer before making a determination that a company is an RHQ under the *Income Tax Assessment Act*, must consider various enumerated matters, including the extent to which the company's operations are located outside Australia, the costs and benefits to the Australian economy of a determination that a RHQ company exists, whether it is in the national interest that the company makes Australia its RHQ, and the commercial viability of the company in the long run.

A number of tax measures are designed to promote investment in specific industries. These include an exemption from interest withholding on borrowings of "offshore banking units", deductions for investments in Australian films, and deductions for investments in management and investment companies. A refundable tax offset for film production expenditure is also available to producers of foreign and Australian films that are completed after 3 September 2001. Black hole expenditures, which under previous law were not deductible, are now allowed to be expensed, amortised or capitalised as of 30 June 2000.

Concessional treatment is also provided in relation to expenditure incurred on research and development ("R&D") by a company incorporated in Australia and appropriately registered. Certain expenditure on approved R&D activities undertaken outside Australia will also be eligible for the concession. Concessions include a deduction of 125% (subject to a AUS$20,000 Threshold) for expenditure for R&D activities, including expenditure in respect of plant and equipment, which is wholly attributable to R&D, and an accelerated deduction in respect of expenditure on buildings wholly attributable to R&D. A premium rate of deduction of 175% is available to

AUS ¶35-501

companies that increase their level of R&D expenditure. Likewise, a new R&D rebate equivalent to the value of the R&D deduction will benefit small companies in loss situations. A number of measures have also been introduced to ensure that R&D deductions interact appropriately with the consolidation provisions. Since 1 July 2001, a deduction is available for certain project infrastructure expenditure that is not otherwise deductible.

As of 1 July 2002, R&D activities are not eligible to receive the concession unless they are carried on in accordance with the R&D plan. A company must prepare an R&D plan in accordance with guidelines issued by the R&D Board and have that plan approved before any of the core activities are undertaken. (See www.ausindustry.gov.au.) However, applications for R&D start grants and loans have reopened, following their suspension in April 2002.

As part of the Ralph Review of Business Tax, a foreign income account has been established. This will provide relief from Australian dividend withholding tax on unfranked non-portfolio dividends paid to non-residents from foreign source income, and applies as of 1 July 2000.

AUS ¶35-502 PERIOD OF TAX RELIEF

See AUS ¶35-501.

AUS ¶35-503 CRITERIA AFFECTING RELIEF

See AUS ¶35-501.

AUS ¶35-504 EXISTENCE AND NATURE OF EXPORT INCENTIVES

There are no special measures in the income tax law to promote exports or export industries.

However, an Export Market Development Grant is available upon application to the Australian Trade Commission in relation to eligible expenditure under the *Export Market Development Grants Act 1974*.

AUS ¶35-505 APPLICABILITY OF EXPORT ALLOWANCES

See AUS ¶35-504.

AUS ¶35-511 INDUSTRIES EXCLUDED FROM EXPORT ALLOWANCES

See AUS ¶35-504.

AUS ¶35-512 EXPORT PROCESSING ZONES

See AUS ¶35-504.

AUS ¶35-513 ACCELERATED DEPRECIATION ALLOWANCE

Since 1 July 2001 the Uniform Capital Allowance system applies and is effective for any plant constructed or acquired under a contract after 21 September 1999. Any plant and equipment acquired prior to this date could continue to be eligible under the accelerated depreciation system. Small businesses had the benefit of accelerated depreciation up until 1 July 2001. Since then, small business taxpayers may have opted to be part of the Simplified Tax System, which also provides concessional rates of depreciation for certain pooled assets. In particular, an immediate deduction is available for assets costing less than AUS$1,000 and the amount of any assessable balancing adjustment may be offset against replacement plant. The Commissioner of Tax has updated the effective life of certain depreciating assets as from 1 July 2002 and has raised the depreciation car cost limit for the first time since 1996/97 to AUS$57,009.

AUS ¶35-514 APPLICABILITY OF ACCELERATED DEPRECIATION ALLOWANCE

See AUS ¶35-513.

AUS ¶35-515 DEDUCTIBILITY OF EXPENSES INCURRED EXPLORING EXPORT OPPORTUNITIES

There are no specific measures to allow deductions for expenses incurred exploring export opportunities, which would not otherwise be deductible as ordinary business expenses.

See AUS ¶35-504.

Regulation of Business

Licensing and registration of business activities .... AUS ¶45-001

Granting and nature of licence or registration .... AUS ¶45-002

Incentive legislation .... AUS ¶45-003

Disincentives or restrictions on certain business .... AUS ¶45-004

Special regulation of foreign investment .... AUS ¶45-101

Price and profit controls .... AUS ¶45-201

Unfair trading practices and consumer protection ..... AUS ¶45-301

AUS ¶45-001   LICENSING AND REGISTRATION OF BUSINESS ACTIVITIES

The most general scheme for the registration of business activities is contained in the Commonwealth *Corporations Act 2001*. Companies must be registered with the Australian Securities and Investments Commission (ASIC). A foreign company must be registered under the *Corporations Act 2001* in order to carry on business in Australia. When applying for registration, the foreign company must:

- Reserve the company's name;
- Lodge with the ASIC a certified copy of its certificate of incorporation and constituent documents together with an application form setting out particulars relating to the company; and
- Appoint a local agent to represent the company in Australia.

If a company carries on a business in a name which is different to its company name, it must, in addition, register the business name with the appropriate State or Territory authority. These are: Registrar-General of Business Names (Australian Capital Territory), Department of Consumer Affairs (New South Wales), Office of Business Affairs (Northern Territory), Office of Consumer Affairs (Queensland), State Business and Corporate Affairs Office (South Australia), Corporate Affairs Office (Tasmania), Office of Fair Trading and Business Affairs (Victoria) and Business Names Registration Office (Western Australia).

Businesses which are not companies (e.g. sole traders and partnerships) are required to register their business name. The exception to this is if they conduct their activity only under the name of the person or persons involved (i.e. first name and surname, or initials and surname).

Registration or use of a business name does not create a legal entity (whereas registration of a company does) and does not allow the use of privileges to which a company is entitled, such as corporate tax rate or limited liability. A business name has no legal status. While the requirement to register business names is not provided for under the *Corporations Act 2001*, business names are still recorded in ASIC's National Names Index against which proposed new company and business names are checked.

A company name must indicate the company's legal status (proprietary or public), as well as the liability of its members. This will mean inclusion of one of the following:

- Proprietary Limited (Pty Ltd) — for proprietary companies with limited liability;
- Proprietary (Pty) — for unlimited proprietary companies;
- Limited (Ltd) — for public companies with limited liability; or
- No Liability (NL) — for unlimited public companies.

Each company is allocated a unique Australian Company Number upon registration. Where the company is issued an Australian Business Number (ABN), the number will be the nine-digit ACN with two additional leading digits resulting in an 11-digit number (e.g. ACN 12 456 789, new ABN 10 123 456 789). The Australian Business Number is a number which can be used for all dealings with the Australian Taxation Office (ATO), and most other government agencies at all levels, and is further explained herein.

A Registrable Australian Body is a body not already registered under the *Corporations Act 2001*. They can be a registered body that is not a company, recognised company, exempt authority or corporation sole; or an unregistered body having legal person status endowing it with certain rights and obligations (to sue or be sued, to hold property in the name of an officer of the body). Examples include Trading Co-operatives and Incorporated Associations. A foreign company is not a Registrable Australian Body, but is given an Australian Registered Body Number (ARBN).

An ARBN is also given to Registrable Australian Bodies carrying on or wishing to carry on business outside the state of Registration. Each is registered on a national basis and each is allocated a unique ARBN.

As well as incorporated bodies formed outside Australia, the term 'foreign company' also includes bodies registered in an external Territory of Australia, and unincorporated bodies (not including a corporation sole or exempt authority) with legal personality formed in an external Territory or outside Australia.

Managed Investment Schemes must be licensed and registered in a separate register, and each is allocated a unique Australian Investment Scheme Number (AISN).

Australian Business Number

As explained in AUS ¶50-013, Australia's system of indirect taxes has recently undergone a significant change. With effect from 1 July 2000, the Wholesales Sales Tax system has been replaced by a broad based Goods and Services Tax (GST). From this date onwards, with very few exceptions, all goods and services became subject to GST. To be part of the new tax system, all businesses operating and earning income in Australia should register for an Australian Business Number (ABN). This includes sole traders (e.g. contractors), bodies corporate, corporations, partnerships, unincorporated associations, charities, property landlords, trusts and superannuation funds.

The ABN is a unique identifier to enable businesses in Australia to deal with a range of government departments and agencies, including the Australian Taxation Office (ATO). In the case of businesses operating without an ABN, other businesses may have to deduct tax at the top tax rate (48.5%) from payments made to the unregistered business. The unregistered business would then have to wait until the end of the financial year to claim any taxation refund that may be due.

Having an ABN also entitles eligible businesses to claim certain government grants and rebates; for example, the grants that can be obtained under the government's new on-road diesel scheme. ABN registration can be done electronically through the business entry point at *www.business.gov.au*.

Any business having an annual turnover of more than AUS$50,000 (AUS$100,000 for non-profit bodies) must also register for GST. An ABN is needed to do this. The ABN will also be the GST registration number for the business. If the annual turnover is under these thresholds, the business *may* apply for GST if, for example, it wishes to claim back the GST paid on business inputs. Such businesses may also seek ABN registration even without applying for GST.

Further information on GST registration, the use of an ABN and other GST matters can be obtain from any branch of the ATO, through the ATO website and/or through the business entry point at *www.business.gov.au*.

Whether a business activity has to be licensed will depend on a variety of factors:

- the need for expertise;
- competence;
- safety or financial risks associated with the trade or profession;
- maintenance of ethical and professional standards; and
- consumer protection.

Legislation specifying licensing requirements is extensive. At the Commonwealth level, the *Corporations Act 2001*, together with the recent package of financial services reform acts passed by the government, contains requirements for the licensing of all financial service providers operating in Australia (securities dealers, investment advisers, brokers and advisers in the futures industry, etc).

The financial services reform legislation is administered by ASIC, and includes:

- *Financial Services Reform Act 2001*;
- *Financial Services Reform (Consequential Provisions) Act 2001*; and
- *Financial Services Reform (Consequential Provisions) Act 2002*.

Generally, the financial services reform legislation requires people who provide financial services to obtain an Australian financial services licence or become the representative of a licensee (depending on whether they are acting as a principal or a representative). Under the financial services reform legislation, a person provides financial services if they carry out certain activities (e.g. advising or dealing) in relation to "financial products".

Foreign financial service providers who provide services to Australian wholesale clients are required to comply with the licensing requirements under the *Corporations Act 2001*, unless they are specifically exempt. They will be exempt, for example, if ASIC has approved the overseas regulatory authority that regulates the foreign financial service provider and its activities in its home country. The exemption applies only to financial services provided that are the subject of the foreign regulation.

At State and Territory levels, there is usually a consolidated licensing authority, under the auspices of a department responsible for Consumer Affairs. Otherwise there can be a plethora of licensing bodies — for e.g. travel agents and builders. Professions are largely self-regulating through their professional bodies, although disciplinary committees and tribunals deal with misconduct and malpractice, and there is usually specific licensing legislation.

There are extensive controls on business activities that have or may have an environmental impact. These controls are mostly contained in State legislation. Typically, new development or significant alterations to existing development will be subject to an approval process in which the environment impact of the development must be considered. Many activities which cause pollution are also subject to further licensing or approval requirements. Pollution of air, land or water and the emission of excessive noise can be prohibited to varying degrees unless they are sanctioned by licence.

Licensing and other requirements or controls also apply to activities with dangerous goods, waste generation and waste disposal. Contravention of this legislation may result in prosecution and corporate criminal liability. In all States, directors and managers may also be prosecuted for offences.

AUS ¶45-002   GRANTING AND NATURE OF LICENCE OR REGISTRATION

Licensing and registration are by their nature and function discretionary, in that they imply the achievement of some minimum standard of accountability and expertise. Licences can be absolute or impose some restrictions on business activities. In practice, however, it could be said that registration is available as of right once the appropriate fee is paid, while licensing usually involves some exercise of discretionary power.

Whether a business requires a licence depends on the characteristics of the particular business activity (see AUS ¶45-001). Because of the constitutional distribution of legislative powers, business licences are issued by both State/Territory and Commonwealth governments. Specific advice should be obtained to assist in determining whether licences are required and who is the applicable granting authority.

The granting of occupational licences depends on a number of factors including the type of activity, educational and practical requirements, and the requirements of the relevant professional bodies. The granting of occupational licences is usually governed by an industry or professional group.

It should also be noted that if an application for registration or a licence is refused by a public authority, there are a number of administrative law mechanisms whereby that decision can be reviewed or appealed against. The Commonwealth legislation is the *Administrative Appeals Tribunal Act 1975* and the *Administrative Decisions (Judicial Review) Act 1977*. Each State and Territory also has legislation to facilitate appeals against administrative decisions made by a State or Territory authority.

AUS ¶45-002   © 2003 CCH Asia Pte Limited

AUS ¶45-003   INCENTIVE LEGISLATION

Incentive legislation exists, and is usually manifested in taxation concessions, or bounties, tied to particular industries. At Commonwealth level, it operates to encourage exports, to encourage development in specific fields, and to encourage foreign investment in particular areas. It also acts to protect business seen as fundamental to Australia's growth, such as the wool, wheat and mining industries. Research and development may attract tax concessions in accordance with sec. 73B of the *Income Tax Assessment Act*. It should be noted that research and development tax concessions may only be claimed by "eligible companies", which includes companies incorporated in Australia but does not include foreign companies, even if registered under the *Corporations Act 2001*.

As a further example of encouragement, Commonwealth legislation creating the Australian Trade Commission (AUSTRADE) empowers that Commission to promote access by Australian exporters to new markets. The Export Markets Development Grants Scheme is administered by AUSTRADE. There is an International Trade Enhancement Scheme for exporters. The Export Finance and Insurance Corporation (EFIC) provides insurance and finance facilities for Australian exporters. Differential tax or duty can come under the auspices of the *Customs Act*, or the *Excise Act*. Generous income tax provisions for exporting goods are provided through the *Income Tax Assessment Act*, GST-related legislation, bounties, export allowances, research and education subsidies.

There is not a single scheme, nor a single administering body. Rather, a variety of incentives exists, administered by a number of different statutory bodies at Commonwealth and State/Territory level.

At the Commonwealth level, Invest Australia is the national inward investment agency, set up by the Federal Government in 1997 to promote inward investment, with investment advisory specialists in 14 locations including New York, London, Paris, Frankfurt, Hong Kong, Singapore and Tokyo.

Invest Australia works with prospective investors to identify and access a range of government programs relevant to their needs, including research and development grants; export development; training and education support and infrastructure programs.

Invest Australia can provide financial assistance, in conjunction with State or Territory Governments, to eligible companies to undertake a pre-feasibility or feasibility study of a potential investment project. A grant of up to AUS$100,000 is available for any one study.

Through the Major Projects Facilitation service, Invest Australia provides the proponent with information, advice and support to assist with necessary government approvals. Invest Australia also identifies the sequence and timings for key approvals and the relevant government programs that may assist the project. Investors can apply to the Minister for Industry, Tourism and Resources for MPF status if their project:

- has a total capital expenditure of over AUS$50 million;
- needs Commonwealth Government approval(s); and
- is commercially ready to proceed through government approvals processes.

Invest Australia's Regional Headquarters Program is designed to encourage international firms to locate their regional headquarters and operating centres in Australia. The Program provides investors with access to tailored immigration agreements for streamlined immigration of expatriate employees and tax concessions for establishment costs. The RHQ Program is open to companies that are yet to locate in Australia or companies with an existing presence in Australia that are seeking to expand that office into a RHQ and cannot be utilised for recruiting people outside the company group.

Through the Strategic Investment Coordination process, the Strategic Investment Coordinator advises the Prime Minister and the Cabinet on requests for investment incentives. The Strategic Investment Coordinator is supported in this role by Invest Australia. Requests for incentives must address in detail the Strategic Investment Coordination criteria, and be accompanied by sufficient information in an acceptable form to facilitate assessment against the criteria. The project should have already been substantially developed and a decision made regarding potential location. To qualify, the project:

- Must provide significant net economic benefits to Australia;

- Must complement Australia's areas of competitive advantage;

- Would not occur in Australia without an incentive;

- Must be viable in the long term without subsidy; and

- Any incentive requested must be consistent with Australia's international obligations, including under WTO.

Decisions to grant or refuse a request for an incentive are entirely discretionary. The quantum and nature of an assistance or incentive provided by the government needs to be publicly disclosed, subject to an advanced pre-agreement between the Government and the proponent.

Local industry participation is encouraged and Invest Australia works with the Industrial Supplies Office Network (ISONET) to ensure that Australia's capital equipment and services capabilities are promoted in the design and development phases of major investment projects.

As part of the high priority placed on economic development of regional Australia, the Australian Government and Invest Australia launched a new project, Inside Intelligence, in July 2001. Inside Intelligence is an innovative business tool to help regional and rural communities identify existing investment strengths and resources and seek out appropriate and desirable foreign investment projects and partners.

For further information on Commonwealth and State/Territory incentive legislation and programs, the following are useful websites to visit:

http://www.investaustralia.gov.au   (Commonwealth)

http://www.invest.vic.gov.au   (Victoria)

http://www.development.tas.gov.au   (Tasmania)

http://www.sacentral.sa.gov.au	(South Australia)
http://www.bioinnovationsa.com.au	(South Australia)
http://www.backoffice-sa.com	(South Australia)
http://www.electronics-sa.com	(South Australia)
http://www.health-sa.net.au	(South Australia)
http://www.it-southaustralia.com.au	(South Australia)
http://www.sd.qld.gov.au	(Queensland)
http://www.otd.nt.gov.au	(Northern Territory)
http://www.aarc.com.au	
http://www.business.nsw.gov.au	(New South Wales)
http://www.business.act.gov.au	(Australian Capital Territory)

AUS ¶45-004 DISINCENTIVES OR RESTRICTIONS ON CERTAIN BUSINESS ACTIVITIES

Business activity is generally encouraged. Specifically, it is recognised at federal government level that successful trade in the Asia-Pacific region is vital to Australia's economic prosperity. Disincentives and restrictions are usually confined to industries which have an impact on national economic welfare. Examples are natural resources, such as coal and uranium, and minerals generally. Types of disincentive may take the form of prescribed Australian ownership or participation, or of more general policy considerations, or of specific reaction in sensitive areas, such as the ownership and development of urban land.

Geographic restrictions may be placed on certain business and professional activities by local government authorities. Expansion of business in some areas, such as the media or aviation, attract considerations of concentration of ownership.

The foreign investor should be aware of the regulatory activity of the Foreign Investment Review Board and the Australian Competition and Consumer Commission (ACCC). To take an example, the Commonwealth *Foreign Acquisitions and Takeovers Act 1975*, requires proposals to be put to the Foreign Investment Review Board on a wide range of investment propositions.

The *Trade Practices Act 1974* (Cth) (TPA) prohibits and restricts business practices that may lessen competition in trade and commerce and applies to virtually all businesses in Australia. The TPA covers anti-competitive market practices and mergers or acquisitions of companies which would have the effect of substantially lessening competition in a substantial market. The TPA merger provisions can also apply to transactions that occur outside Australia if they have the effect of substantially lessening competition in a substantial market in Australia.

The TPA also establishes a regime to facilitate access by third parties to certain facilities of national significance. This access regime is designed to encourage competition in related markets, such as electricity grids and natural gas pipelines.

An independent national statutory body, the Australian Competition and Consumer Commission (ACCC) deals with competition matters and is responsible for enforcement of the TPA.

It is also worth noting that in 1999, Australia and the USA formalised procedures for mutual cooperation and legal assistance between their respective antitrust authorities (the ACCC on the one hand, and the US Federal Trade Commission together with the US Department of Justice on the other). The aim is to improve the effectiveness, and broaden the scope of antitrust law investigation and enforcement in both countries.

SPECIAL REGULATION OF FOREIGN INVESTMENT

Special controls for foreign businesses or investors . AUS ¶45-101

Control of foreign investor .... AUS ¶45-102

Definition of foreign businessman or investor .... AUS ¶45-103

Special regulations covering joint ventures .... AUS ¶45-104

Incentives and disincentives for geographical areas .... AUS ¶45-105

Incentives and disincentives for particular industries ... AUS ¶45-111

Types of incentives, disincentives and controls .... AUS ¶45-112

Nature of incentives, disincentives and controls .... AUS ¶45-113

Guarantees against expropriation of assets . AUS ¶45-114

Retention of local consultant .... AUS ¶45-115

AUS ¶45-101   SPECIAL CONTROLS FOR FOREIGN BUSINESSES OR INVESTORS

In recognition of the contribution foreign investment has and can make to Australia's economic development and prosperity, the general approach of government policy is to welcome foreign investment. Legislation and policy provide for government scrutiny of many proposed foreign purchases of Australian business or real estate. Takeover legislation exists, and its application is not limited to purchase of shares in listed companies. It applies to acquisitions of securities in any unlisted company with more than 50 members. Broadly, the takeover laws prohibit any person from acquiring a relevant interest in issued voting shares in another company if that person's or someone else's voting power in that other company increases to more than 20%, except in certain specified circumstances (including where a takeover bid is made).

AUS ¶45-101

These laws also apply to "downstream acquisitions" (where, for example, a person acquires a majority holding in an unlisted company with less than 50 members, but that company in turn holds more than 20% of, say, a listed company or controls a listed company). Also, an acquisition of more than 20% of the voting shares in an upstream foreign company is taken to be an acquisition of any shares held by it in an Australian company, but the *Corporations Act* exempts the acquisition from the general prohibition where the foreign company is listed on a recognised foreign stock exchange.

The government (represented by the Treasurer) has a discretionary power under the *Foreign Acquisitions and Takeovers Act 1975* (the Act) to block proposals that are deemed contrary to national interests. In the exercise of this discretionary power, the Foreign Investment Review Board (FIRB) will advise the Treasurer. The Act also provides legislative backing for ensuring compliance with government regulations and policy.

In August-September 1999, the government announced a number of changes to its foreign investment policy (and the *Foreign Acquisitions and Takeovers Regulations*). The changes were designed to reduce notification obligations on business and to streamline the administration of foreign investment policy, while continuing to ensure that foreign investment was consistent with Australia's interests. The 1999 changes included an increase in the acquisition threshold for foreign investment in existing businesses. It also includes the removal of approval and notification requirements for acquisitions of residential property by a number of special categories of Australian visa holders through Australian-based companies and trusts.

A number of other modifications were also made to foreign investment policy relating to different forms of real estate. Most foreign investment proposals involve the purchase of real estate, and most will be approved so long as they serve to increase the overall supply of residences, and are not speculative in nature. Proposals for new developments are generally approve, but a much more restrictive policy applies in relation to already developed real estate.

AUS ¶45-102 CONTROL OF FOREIGN INVESTOR

Proposals which should be submitted for examination

The types of proposals by foreign interests to invest in Australia which require prior approval and should therefore be notified to the government are as follows:

- Acquisitions of substantial interests in existing Australian businesses with total assets over AUS$50 million or where the proposal values the business at over AUS$50 million;

- Proposals to establish new businesses involving a total investment of AUS$10 million or more;

- Portfolio investment in the media of 5% or more and all non-portfolio investments irrespective of size;

- Takeovers of offshore companies whose Australian subsidiaries or assets are valued at AUS$50 million or more, or account for more than 50% of the target company's global assets;

- Direct investment by foreign governments or their agencies irrespective of size;

- Acquisitions of interests in urban land (including interests arising through leases, financing and profit-sharing arrangements) and/or the acquisition of interests in urban land corporations and trusts that involve the:

  - acquisition of developed non-residential commercial real estate, where the property is not subject to heritage listing, valued at $50 million or more;

  - acquisition of accommodation facilities irrespective of value;

  - acquisition of vacant urban real estate irrespective of value;

  - acquisition of residential real estate irrespective of value; and

  - proposals where any doubt exists as to whether they are notifiable. It should be noted that funding arrangements that include debt instruments having quasi-equity characteristics will be treated as direct foreign investment.

This is a broad overview of the government's policy. See AUS ¶45-111 for a discussion of the special rules and exemptions which apply in particular industries. For recent developments in foreign investment policy, see the Australian Treasury foreign investment website at *www.treasury.gov.au*, from which most of information provided here has been adapted.

AUS ¶45-103 DEFINITION OF FOREIGN BUSINESS OR INVESTOR

Under the scheme discussed at AUS ¶45-101 and AUS ¶45-102, a foreign interest is described as:

- a natural person not ordinarily resident in Australia;

- a corporation in which a natural person not ordinarily resident in Australia or a foreign corporation holds a controlling interest;

- a corporation in which two or more persons, each of whom is either a natural person not ordinarily resident in Australia or a foreign corporation, hold an aggregate controlling interest;

- the trustee of a trust estate in which a natural person not ordinarily resident in Australia or a foreign corporation holds a substantial interest; or

- the trustee of a trust estate in which two or more persons, each of whom is either a natural person not ordinarily resident in Australia or a foreign corporation, hold an aggregate substantial interest.

A substantial foreign interest occurs when a single foreigner (and any associates) has 15% or more of the ownership or several foreigners (and any associates) have 40% or more in aggregate of the ownership of any corporation, business or trust.

AUS ¶45-103

A natural person who is a citizen of a foreign country is taken to be not ordinarily resident in Australia unless (a) that person has actually been in Australia for 200 days in the previous 12 months and (b) there is no legal limitation of that person remaining in Australia indefinitely.

AUS ¶45-104   SPECIAL REGULATIONS COVERING JOINT VENTURES

There are no special regulations governing the establishment of joint ventures. The Commonwealth government encourages the idea that Australians should have the opportunity to participate in the development of Australia's industries and natural resources.

AUS ¶45-105   INCENTIVES AND DISINCENTIVES FOR GEOGRAPHICAL AREAS

The government through the Foreign Investment Review Board does not limit foreign investors to any geographical area or promote any particular geographical area.

AUS ¶45-111   INCENTIVES AND DISINCENTIVES FOR PARTICULAR INDUSTRIES

In addition to the government's general policy regarding foreign investment outlined at AUS ¶45-102, there are special rules and restrictions that apply to foreign investments in particular sectors of the economy. Further details and information on recent developments can be found through the Australian Treasury foreign investment website at *http://www.treasury.gov.au*, from which most of the information provided here has been adapted.

Rural Businesses and Rural Land, Agricultural, Forestry, Fishing, Resource Processing, Oil and Gas, Mining, Manufacturing, Non-Bank Financial Institutions, Insurance, Sharebroking, Tourism, Most Other Services

Rural Land

Rural land is defined as land that is used wholly and exclusively for carrying on a substantial business of primary production. Acquisitions of vacant land that have rural zoning, 'hobby farms' and 'rural residential' blocks by foreign interests are included within the urban land category.

For proposals by foreign interests to invest in these sectors, all proposals above certain thresholds need prior notification and approval. Notification thresholds are over AUS$50 million for acquisitions of substantial interests in all existing businesses, AUS$10 million or more for the establishment of new businesses and AUS$50 million or more for offshore takeovers.

All tourism proposals which incorporate an accommodation facility, irrespective of value, need to be notified.

The government registers, but normally raises no objections to, proposals above the notification threshold where:

- the total assets of a target existing business falls below AUS$100 million in value; or
- the total proposed investment in a new business falls below AUS$100 million.

However, proposals in sensitive sectors (e.g. mining of scarce minerals, tourism), or those which raise specific national interest issues (e.g. uranium), will be subject to more detailed examination. Approval may be withheld, or made subject to restrictive conditions (e.g. conditions relating to required levels of Australian participation in a mining joint venture, and/or conditions relating to the environment).

Proposals to acquire an existing business having total assets of AUS$100 million or more, and proposals to establish a new business using total investment of AUS$100 million or more are fully examined, and will normally be approved unless contrary to the national interest. In practice, for those case where approval is made subject to specified conditions, such conditions relate almost entirely to the time period for real estate development or to environmental requirements.

Urban Land

Proposed acquisitions of residential real estate are exempt from examination in the case of purchases by:

- Australian citizens living abroad purchasing in their own name or through an Australian company or trust;
- foreign nationals purchasing as joint tenants with an Australian citizen spouse; and
- foreign nationals who hold permanent resident visas or hold, or are entitled to hold, a special category visa purchasing in their own name or through an Australian corporation or trust.

Proposed acquisitions of real estate development are normally approved subject to specific conditions requiring continuous substantial construction to commence within 12 months. The parties are also required to provide the date of completion and actual development expenditure once these are known.

In other cases, foreign interests are normally given approval to buy:

- Vacant residential land, including house and land packages where construction has not commenced (on condition that continuous construction of a dwelling is commenced within 12 months);
- House and land packages where construction has commenced, home units, townhouses etc; and
- 'Off the plan', in reference to property under construction or newly constructed but never occupied or previously sold. 'Off the plan' sales to foreign interests are only permitted for new development projects or extensively refurbished commercial structures which have been converted to residential. Sale is only permitted on condition that no more than half the dwellings in any one development are sold to foreign interests.

AUS ¶45-111

Proposed acquisitions of residential property (both vacant land and dwellings) which are within the bounds of a resort that the Treasurer has designated as an 'Integrated Tourism Resort' (ITR) prior to September 1999 are exempt from examination. For resorts designated as ITRs from September 1999, the exemption only applies to developed residential property which is subject to a long term (10 years or more) lease to the resort or hotel operator, making it available for tourist accommodation when not occupied by the owner.

All other property, including vacant land for development, within the ITR are subject to normal foreign investment restrictions. Strict conditions must be fully met to qualify for ITR status.

Foreign nationals, including long-stay retirees, temporarily resident in Australia continuously for more than 12 months, may be given approval to purchase developed residential real estate for use as their principal place of residence (i.e. not for rental purposes) while in Australia. A condition of such purchase is that the residence must be sold when the foreign nationals' temporarily residence visa expires, they leave Australia, or the property is no longer used as their principal place of residence.

All other proposals by foreign interests to acquire developed residential property are examinable and are not normally approved. Foreign companies that have an established substantial business in Australia are permitted to purchase real estate for use by named senior executives resident in Australia for periods longer than 12 months, provided the property is sold when no longer required for this purpose.

Whether a company is eligible, and the number of properties that can be acquired under this category, will depend on the extent of the foreign companies operations and assets in Australia. A company would not be eligible under this category, for example, if the property to be purchased represents a significant proportion of its assets in Australia. In the absence of special circumstances, a company will not be permitted to buy more than two houses under this category.

Proposed acquisitions of hotels and motels operating under one title are normally approved (unless considered contrary to the national interest) under the tourism sector policy. Proposed acquisitions of strata title hotel accommodation may be approved in certain designated hotels (see Urban Land policy above). Other accommodation facilities such as guesthouses, holidays flats, and undesignated strata titled hotels and motels are examined under policy applying to the residential real estate sector.

Banking and financial services

Foreign investment in the banking sector needs to be consistent with the *Banking Act 1959*, the *Financial Sector (Shareholdings) Act 1998* and Australian banking policy, including prudential requirements. Any proposed foreign takeover or acquisition of an Australian bank will be considered on a case-by-case basis and judged on its merits.

Foreign banks wishing to carry on banking business in Australia must obtain a banking authority issued by the Australian Prudential Regulatory Authority under the *Banking Act*, either to operate as a wholesale bank through an Australian branch or subsidiary or to conduct deposit-taking through an Australian incorporated subsidiary. The government will permit the issue of new banking authorities to foreign-owned banks where the Australian Prudential Regulation Authority (APRA) is satisfied that the bank and its home supervisor are of sufficient standing and where the bank agrees to comply with APRA's prudential supervision arrangements.

Foreign banks which do not wish to obtain a banking authority in Australia may operate a representative office in Australia for liaison purposes, but the activities of that office will be restricted.

Since November 1996, the provision of credit to individuals for personal, household or domestic purposes has been regulated by the *Uniform Consumer Credit Code*, which has been implemented in all Australian jurisdictions.

The *Financial Services Reform Act 2001* (Cth) commenced operation on 11 March 2002, and essentially removes the pre-existing dichotomy under the *Corporations Act* between regulation of securities (i.e. equities and debentures) and futures so that there is now a uniform approach (subject to exceptions) to the regulation of financial products. Key aspects of the FSR Act are:

- Uniform regulation of all financial products;
- A single licensing framework for providers of financial products;
- Minimum standards of conduct for financial service providers dealing with retail clients;
- Uniform disclosure requirements for all financial products (other than securities) provided to retail clients; and
- Flexibility for authorisation of market operators and clearing and settlement facilities.

Civil Aviation

Domestic Services

Foreign persons (including foreign airlines) can generally expect approval to acquire up to 100% of the equity in an Australian domestic airline, unless this is contrary to the national interest.

International Services

Foreign airlines can generally expect approval to acquire up to 25% of the equity in an Australian carrier (other than Qantas) individually or up to 35% in total aggregate foreign investment provided the proposal is not contrary to the national interest. In the case of Australia's national airline Qantas, total foreign ownership is restricted to a maximum of 49% in aggregate, with individual holdings limited to 25% and aggregate ownership by foreign airlines limited to 35%. In addition, a number of national interest criteria, relating to the nationality of board members and operational location of the enterprise, must be satisfied.

Airports

Foreign investment proposals for acquisitions of interests in Australian airports are subject to case-by-case examination in accordance with the standard notification requirements. In relation to the airports offered for sale by the Commonwealth, the

Airports Act 1996 stipulates a 49% foreign ownership limit, a 5% airline ownership limit and cross-ownership limits between Sydney Airport (together with Sydney West) and Melbourne, Brisbane and Perth airports.

Shipping

The *Shipping Registration Act 1981* requires that, for a ship to be registered in Australia, it must be majority Australian-owned, unless the ship is designated as chartered by an Australian operator.

Media

All direct (i.e. non-portfolio) proposals by foreign interests to invest in the media sector irrespective of size are subject to prior approval. Proposals involving portfolio share holdings of 5% or more must also be submitted for examination.

Restrictions on concentrations of ownership and on cross-ownership in the media have been eased, albeit slowly. While the government's approach has so far been that of extreme caution, the Australian Productivity Commission in April 2000 submitted a report to the government strongly recommending removal of current rules preventing media owners from owning more than a certain share of media outlets in a particular city. The Report, which contains the results of Commission's review of the broad range of laws and regulations governing the Australian media, also strongly recommends the abolition of restrictions on foreign investment in Australia's media.

Given the rapid globalisation and integration of different forms of media and telecommunications, the government is gradually coming to realise the impossibility of controlling the media/telecommunications sectors by controlling and restricting foreign ownership levels. Other methods of regulating these sectors (including various forms of cooperative arrangements between authorities in different nations), must be found, and as these are developed, restrictions on foreign ownership levels will almost inevitably disappear.

Broadcasting

Before being submitted for case-by-case examination and approval, proposals for foreign investment in an existing broadcasting service or in the establishment of a new one, the following criteria must be satisfied, in line with the *Broadcasting Services Act 1992* (BSA):

Foreign interests in commercial television broadcasting services continue to be limited to a 15% company interest for individuals and a 20% company interest in aggregate. A foreign person may not be in a position to control the holder of a commercial television broadcasting licence. No more than 20% of directors may be foreign persons.

For all subscription television broadcasting services licences, foreign interests are limited to a 20% interest for an individual and a 35% company interest in aggregate.

There are no foreign ownership or control limits on commercial radio or on other broadcasting services under the BSA.

Newspapers

Foreign investment in mass circulation national, metropolitan, suburban and provincial newspapers is restricted. All proposals by foreign interests to acquire an interest of 5% or more in an existing newspaper or to establish a new newspaper in Australia are subject to case-by-case examination. The maximum permitted aggregate foreign interest (non-portfolio) investment/involvement in national and metropolitan newspapers is 30% with any single foreign shareholder limited to a maximum interest of 25%; in which case unrelated foreign investment would be limited to a maximum aggregate shareholding (non-portfolio) of a further 5%. Aggregate foreign interest direct involvement (non-portfolio) in provincial and suburban newspapers is limited to less than 50%.

Telecommunications

Telstra Corporation Ltd (Telstra) is predominately owned by the Commonwealth government. Since October 1997, the government has partially privatised Telstra through the sale of 49.9% of its equity to institutional and individual investors. Aggregate foreign ownership of Telstra is restricted to 35% of that privatised equity and individual foreign investors are only allowed to acquire a holding of no more than 5% of total privatised equity.

Prior approval is required for foreign involvement in the establishment of new entrants to the telecommunications sector. Proposals above the notification thresholds will be dealt with on a case-by-case basis and will normally be approved unless judged contrary to the national interest.

Approval Period

Approval should only be sought for specific transactions which are expected to be completed in a timely manner. If an approved transaction does not proceed within 12 months and/or the parties enter into a new agreement, further approval must be sought. The time limit period for an approval may be varied where it can be shown that an extended period is fundamental to the success of a proposal and that extending the proposal does not involve an activity (e.g. real estate speculation) that would be contrary to the national interest.

AUS ¶45-112   TYPES OF INCENTIVES, DISINCENTIVES AND CONTROLS

The restrictions relate to permission to establish new businesses or to foreign investment in existing businesses. See AUS ¶45-004, AUS ¶45-101 and AUS ¶45-102.

AUS ¶45-113 NATURE OF INCENTIVES, DISINCENTIVES AND CONTROLS

See AUS ¶45-112.

AUS ¶45-114 GUARANTEES AGAINST EXPROPRIATION OF ASSETS

The government does not give guarantees against expropriation of a foreign investor's assets. Any expropriation, however, is required by the Australian Constitution to be on just terms and conditions.

AUS ¶45-115 RETENTION OF LOCAL CONSULTANT

Australian law, particularly relating to taxation law, administration of corporations and import and export are complex. Therefore, it may be advisable for a foreign investor to engage a local consultant. A wide range of specialist and skilled advice is available.

PRICE AND PROFIT CONTROLS

Commodities subject to price
control .... AUS ¶45-201

Price control body .... AUS ¶45-202

Exemptions from price
control .... AUS ¶45-203

Special restrictions for certain
companies .... AUS ¶45-204

Right of government authority
to share in profits ..... AUS ¶45-205

Criteria for application of
controls .... AUS ¶45-206

AUS ¶45-201 COMMODITIES SUBJECT TO PRICE CONTROL

Australia does not have a general system of price control for goods or services. The Australian government is thought not to have the power under Australian Constitution to introduce price control and the States and Territories have abandoned their schemes of control, introduced in wartime.

There are some, perhaps de facto, systems of control over particular goods and services where recommended rates of remuneration become the widely charged amount.

AUS ¶45-202 PRICE CONTROL BODY

The Australian government has established the Prices Surveillance Authority which inquires into prices, and price rises, for certain goods and services. Its declarations as to the levels that are justified operate only as recommendations but are normally adhered to. Other bodies make recommendations as to professional fees (e.g. doctors, lawyers, architects and real estate agents). These controls are usually on a State-by-State basis.

The *Competition Policy Reform Act 1995* abolishes both the Trade Practices Commission and the Prices Surveillance Authority. The powers and functions of these two bodies, plus some additional functions, are to be conferred on a new body, the Australian Competition and Consumer Commission.

AUS ¶45-203   EXEMPTIONS FROM PRICE CONTROL

Only a small number of categories of goods are subject to price recommendations. All other goods are exempt.

AUS ¶45-204   SPECIAL RESTRICTIONS FOR CERTAIN COMPANIES

As mentioned at AUS ¶45-203, authorisation for what would otherwise be seen as price fixing may be granted under the *Trade Practices Act* if the Australian Competition and Consumer Commission considers that the resulting public benefits would justify the authorisation (see AUS ¶45-303).

AUS ¶45-205   RIGHT OF GOVERNMENT AUTHORITY TO SHARE IN PROFITS

There are various government and semi-government authorities which participate in profits as commercial organisations.

AUS ¶45-206   CRITERIA FOR APPLICATION OF CONTROLS

See AUS ¶45-201 to AUS ¶45-205.

UNFAIR TRADING PRACTICES AND CONSUMER PROTECTION

Consumer protection laws   AUS ¶45-301

General principles governing
   injuries .... AUS ¶45-302

Prohibition or regulation of
   restraint of trade
   contracts .... AUS ¶45-303

Licences under statutory
   monopolies .... AUS ¶45-304

Special provisions relating to
   business activities of non-
   residents .... AUS ¶45-305

Laws governing advertising and
   promotion of products . AUS ¶45-306

Review of "unfair"
   contracts .... AUS ¶45-307

AUS ¶45-301   CONSUMER PROTECTION LAWS

Australia has a comprehensive code of consumer protection legislation, represented federally by the *Trade Practices Act 1974* and at State and Territory level by *Fair Trading Acts*. In addition, there are several statutes that contain more specific consumer protection, such as those relating to credit, door-to-door sales, and motor vehicle dealing.

Trade practices legislation prohibits conduct which is misleading or deceptive. Section 52 and equivalents in all States and Territories provide that:

"A corporation shall not, in trade or commerce, engage in conduct that is misleading or deceptive or is likely to mislead or deceive".

This is the most litigated section in all of Australian business law. It covers disputes across all areas of business including contract, negligence, banking, insurance etc. It is a civil section between person and person, providing remedies such as damages, injunctions, corrective advertising and court orders to rewrite contracts.

In addition, trade practices legislation provides for prosecution by the ACCC (with fines and even jail), and civil action, for:

- false or misleading representations, including in relation to land, employment and cash prices;
- offering gifts and prizes with the intention of not providing them;
- bait advertising;
- referral selling in some circumstances;
- accepting payment without intending or being able to supply as ordered;
- misleading representations about certain business activities;
- harassment and coercion in connection with the supply of goods or services; and
- pyramid selling.

This legislation is paralleled in the States and Territories.

Product liability law in Australia

Australia's product liability laws are made up of:

(1) liability under the tort of negligence;

(2) liability for damages for breach of contract with the retailer or possibly the manufacturer if there is a contract with the manufacturer;

(3) liability of the retailer for breach of contractual terms of merchantability, fitness for purpose etc implied by the *Trade Practices Act* and by the *Sale of Goods Act* in each jurisdiction based on the original UK model;

(4) statutory liability of the manufacturer (if there is no privity of contract) under Part V Div 2A of the *Trade Practices Act;*

(5) statutory liability for defective goods under Part VA. This new product liability scheme was added to the *Trade Practices Act* in 1992. Part VA headed "Liability of manufacturers and importers for defective goods" provides that a person who is injured or who suffers property damage as a result of a defective product has the right to compensation from the manufacturer without the need to prove negligence

on the part of the manufacturer. Once a causal link is established between the proper use of the product and the damage sustained, the onus then rests on the manufacturer to prove that the product was not defective. In other respects, the scheme largely derives from the European Community Directive.

(6) liability for breach of a product safety standard or a product information standard. Under Div 1A of Pt V of the *Trade Practices Act 1974*, secs. 65C and 65D prescribe compliance with safety and information standards respectively. Section 65E of the Act empowers the Minister to declare in the Government Gazette that a particular standard, for example a standard prepared by the Standards Association of Australia, is a product safety standard or a product information standard. The *Fair Trading Acts* in some of the States and Territories include similar provisions.

(7) liability for misleading or deceptive conduct under sec. 52 of the *Trade Practices Act* and equivalents in each State and Territory (above).

Both the *Trade Practices Act* and the *Fair Trading Acts* of the States and Territories contain provisions preventing the exclusion of warranties which they prescribe as implied in consumer transactions. Section 74K of the *Trade Practices Act*, for example, declares void any attempt to exclude liability attaching as a result of Div. 2A of the Act (no. (4) above). Similarly, attempts to exclude or modify the obligations imposed on sellers by Div. 2 of the Act (no. (3) above) are void under sec. 68.

Refer to the ACCC at *www.accc.gov.au*.

AUS ¶45-302 GENERAL PRINCIPLES GOVERNING INJURIES

General principles governing injury to persons or property encompass contract, tort and statute law, depending on the circumstances. At common law, the tort of negligence has developed a doctrine of foreseeability of harm based on the foresight of the reasonable person. Under the *Trade Practices Act 1974*, liability for damage caused by products is likely to be construed as a breach of a statutory duty following failure to satisfy one or more prescribed criteria. Whereas sale of goods legislation developed on the principles of contract law, under the *Trade Practices Act*, the existence of a contract is not necessary for actions against manufacture and importers.

AUS ¶45-303 PROHIBITION OR REGULATION OF RESTRAINT OF TRADE CONTRACTS

Restrictive trade practices

Part IV of the *Trade Practices Act 1974* prohibits the following restrictive trade practices:

(1) agreements affecting competition (horizontal agreements) — prohibited if it substantially lessens competition;

(2) horizontal price fixing — prohibited per se;

(3) covenants running with the land — prohibited if it substantially lessens competition;

AUS ¶45-302

(4)   covenants in relation to prices — prohibited if it substantially lessens competition;

(5)   primary boycotts with an exclusionary provision — prohibited per se;

(6)   secondary boycotts — prohibited if it substantially lessens competition;

(7)   misuse of market power — prohibited if it affects competition;

(8)   exclusive dealing — prohibited if it substantially lessens competition;

(9)   third line forcing — prohibited per se;

(10) resale price maintenance (vertical price fixing) — prohibited per se; and

(11) mergers — prohibited if it substantially lessens competition.

Contracts establishing franchises are permissible provided the agreement will not have a significant detrimental effect on competition in breach of any of the above or in breach of Part V of the Act dealing with consumer protection.

Authorisation

Contracts which breach the restrictive trade practices provisions are illegal, hence unenforceable.

The Australian Competition and Consumer Commission (the ACCC: see AUS ¶45-202) can grant to companies immunity from prosecution for some arrangements that would be in breach of the Act:

(1)   agreements affecting competition (horizontal agreements);

(8)   exclusive dealing;

(9)   third line forcing;

(10) resale price maintenance (vertical price fixing) — prohibited per se; and

(11) mergers — prohibited if it substantially lessens competition.

Broadly, the test is whether the agreement offers a greater benefit to the public than the detrimental effect of any lessening of competition that might result from the agreement. Inquiries about application for authorisation should be made to the Commission's office.

If a party is dissatisfied with a determination, application for review may be made to the Australian Competition Tribunal in accordance with sec. 101 of the Act.

Enforcement and penalties

An individual party may institute court proceedings to recover damages as a result of conduct contravening Pt IV of the *Trade Practices Act 1974*, which covers the restrictive trade practices under discussion here. Part VI of the Act details the enforcement and remedial provisions. The Minister responsible for the Australian Competition and Consumer Commission may institute proceedings on behalf of the Commonwealth for the recovery of pecuniary penalties for breaches of Pt IV. The proceedings are civil, not criminal, with the maximum penalty prescribed in sec. 76(1) for a body corporate being AUS$10 million. Also, by secs. 80 and 87, courts have a wide discretion to grant injunctions and make such other orders as are deemed appropriate.

Extraterritorial effect

By virtue of the power of the Commonwealth, and secs. 5 and 6 of the Act, these laws have some extraterritorial application to corporations and persons. Parts IV and V may extend to conduct outside Australia. Section 5(1) catches certain conduct outside Australia by companies (or persons residing in Australia) which carry on business in Australia, while sec. 5(2) catches conduct outside Australia related to the supply of goods or services to persons within Australia. Reference should be made particularly to sec. 47, which relates to exclusive dealing, and sec. 48, which deals with resale price maintenance. Both sections receive through sec. 5 the extended operation indicated above. There is precedent for an interpretation of sec. 5 as applying to conduct outside Australia which has the effect of reducing competition within Australia.

The extraterritorial consequences of legislation may be subject in certain circumstances to "blocking" legislation which protects citizens of one country from being subjected to particular laws of another country.

Administration of trade practices

The Australian Competition and Consumer Commission administers those provisions of the *Trade Practices Act* discussed here (see AUS ¶45-202). It is an independent statutory body comprising a Chairman and Deputy Chairman, Commissioners and other members appointed according to the Act.

While the sanction of litigated pecuniary penalties is provided for by the Act, the ACCC takes a positive view of the benefits of education and compliance agreements and programs.

Refer to the ACCC homepage at*www.accc.gov.au*.

The fair trading legislation of the States and Territories is administered through the relevant State and Territory consumer affairs department or sections, typically headed by a Commissioner for Consumer Affairs.

AUS ¶45-304   LICENCES UNDER STATUTORY MONOPOLIES

Licences granted in respect of copyright, patents, designs and trademarks receive statutory recognition through sec. 51(1) of the *Trade Practices Act 1974* as exceptions to laws regulating trade practices. Such licences can also be viewed positively as enhancing the protection of legitimate property interests essential to fair market-place practice.

AUS ¶45-305   SPECIAL PROVISIONS RELATING TO BUSINESS ACTIVITIES OF NON-RESIDENTS

The regulation of trade practices does not embody discrimination between the business activities of residents and non-residents. The extraterritorial effect of trade practices law is mentioned at AUS ¶45-303. At a general level, foreign business activity will not be impeded provided there is compliance with Australian regulations in the sphere of activity. Such regulations will usually be designed to ensure that national interest and development are not compromised. Non-resident business operations should be aware of prescriptive legislation and regulatory bodies, including the Foreign Investment Review Board, to which proposals are put in accordance with the *Foreign Acquisitions and Takeovers Act 1975*, and the requirements of the *Corporations Law*.

AUS ¶45-306   LAWS GOVERNING ADVERTISING AND PROMOTION OF PRODUCTS

Both the Commonwealth *Trade Practices Act* and the *Fair Trading Acts* of the States provide strong sanctions against misleading promotions and advertising. The general prohibition is against misleading conduct or representations, with some instances being specifically dealt with in legislation. For example, "bait and switch" advertising is prohibited, as are misleading representations as to the profitability or risk of a business enterprise.

The Australian Competition Consumer Commission and State departments of Consumer Affairs, or equivalent, monitor or advise on advertising. Regulation is largely self-administered within the relevant industries, but the Trade Practices Tribunal does authorise codes for bodies such as the Advertising Standards Council.

AUS ¶45-307   REVIEW OF "UNFAIR" CONTRACTS

Contracts can be found to be unconscionable at common law and according to statute. An environment creating an oppressive or unfair inequality in the bargaining and the agreement process is the usual context.

Numerous statutes allow courts or tribunals to review contracts on the basis of their being "unjust", "harsh", or "unconscionable":

- The *Trade Practices Act 1974* through secs. 51AA and 51AB, prohibits unconscionable conduct.
- The *Fair Trading Acts* of the States and Territories and the *Contracts Review Act 1980* (NSW) mirror those provisions.
- Provisions dealing with unconscionable conduct in business transactions were introduced to the *Trade Practices Act* in 1998 as sec. 51AC.

The legislation sets out tests of unconscionability such as:

- The relative strengths of the bargaining positions of the parties;
- Whether the consumer was able to understand the documents;
- Whether undue influence or pressure was exerted; and
- The comparable market price.

IMPORT AND EXPORT CONTROLS

Restrictions on import of goods .... AUS ¶50-001
Special requirements for importers .... AUS ¶50-002
Restrictions on export of goods .... AUS ¶50-003
Regulation of export and import licences .... AUS ¶50-004
Special restrictions relating to foreign control of
    business .... AUS ¶50-005
Major objectives of host country .... AUS ¶50-011
Rates of customs duties .... AUS ¶50-012
Taxes .... AUS ¶50-013
Tariff agreements .... AUS ¶50-014
Concessional entry of goods .... AUS ¶50-015
Free trade zones .... AUS ¶50-021
Labelling and packaging requirements .... AUS ¶50-022
International treaties .... AUS ¶50-023
Penalties and additional taxes .... AUS ¶50-024
Anti-dumping and countervailing duties .... AUS ¶50-025
Power to detain goods .... AUS ¶50-031
When is duty or tax payable? .... AUS ¶50-032

AUS ¶50-001   Restrictions on import of goods

Under Australian law, a range of legislation provides for the importation of certain goods to be prohibited either absolutely, or for a specified place or conditionally. This legislation includes the *Customs Act 1901*and related regulations; the *Commerce (Trade Descriptions) Act*; the *Trade Marks Act 1995*; the *Copyright Act 1968* and the *Quarantine Act 1908* and related regulations. There are no longer any quotas imposed on imports of any kind.

As part of the government's policy to reduce protection to local industry, over the past few years it has phased out all quantitative restrictions or controls on imports through tariff quotas.

The *Customs Act* provides a range of penalties for non-compliance with its requirements. All penalties are in addition to forfeiture of the goods.

AUS ¶50-002   Special requirements for importers

By virtue of the *Customs (Import Licensing) Regulations 1956*, certain goods can only be brought into Australia under a licence. Licensing imposes an absolute restriction on the quantity, weight or value of goods that may be imported in a certain period. Goods imported without a licence cannot be sold in the home market.

Where goods are subject to import controls under the *Customs (Prohibited Imports) Regulations*, the importer(s) must apply to the appropriate department or agency for permission to import, which must be obtained prior to the goods arriving in Australia. Failure to obtain the permission to import prior to the arrival of the goods may result in the forfeiture of the goods.

Trade Modernisation legislation passed both houses of parliament in June 2001. This entails a series of significant changes to the movement of cargo both into and out of Australia as part of Customs' modernisation of its cargo management systems under the government's Customs Cargo Management Re-engineering (CMR) project. The CMR project involves:

- A new open gateway communication system known as Customs Connect Facility (CCF);

- The merger of several computer systems into an Integrated Cargo System (ICS) that will replace earlier systems for the reporting and entry of imported goods;

- Tailored arrangements for low-risk importers and exporters under an accredited client program;

- Industry self-assessment of low-revenue, low-risk cargo; and

- Streamlined reporting mechanisms that combine cargo reports and declaration information.

Under the *Customs Legislation Amendment and Repeal (International Trade Modernisation) Act 2001*, the first phase of the CMR project commenced on 1 July 2002. This phase of the CMR project did not require significant procedural adjustments to importer operations. Rather, it simply served to build a legal basis for the operation of CMR, *inter alia*, by:

- introducing some new strict liability offences (for example, for false or misleading statements) and a new infringement notice scheme, to the extent it applies to those offences;

- enhancing Customs monitoring powers and other enforcement powers (eg to examine exports, to enter and search business premises);

- imposing some new document/record retention requirements — in general, importers, exporters, cargo handlers, cargo carriers and other persons causing goods to be imported must keep all related commercial documents for at least five years.

Importing goods

The final phase of the CMR project has now introduced significant changes to both the import cargo/vessel/aircraft reporting environment and the import declaration environment. All changes are scheduled to be fully in place by early 2005. The new compliance measures for reporting imported cargo are aimed at improving the quality and timeliness of cargo information provided to Customs, thereby allowing Customs to more easily identify high-risk cargo, particularly cargo that might contain illicit drugs. The legislation allows Customs officers to control the movement of goods if there are reasonable grounds to believe they have been incorrectly reported or if there are reasonable grounds to believe there has been a breach of the *Customs Act* or other Customs legislation.

There is also a new cost recovery system to support the other changes that have been made to the import and export processes. The *Depot Licensing Charges Amendment Act* and the *Import Processing Charges Act* are aimed at streamlining previously existing processes, removing the differentiation between the cost of transactions across different modes of transport and encouraging electronic lodgement of import declarations by means of a substantial price discount.

Vessel/Aircraft and cargo reporting

Impending arrival reports and *Actual arrival reports* (for both ships and aircraft carrying cargo) must be communicated electronically to Customs within prescribed times. This is mandatory whether the ship or aircraft is discharging cargo in Australia or not. Where cargo is to be discharged, a *Cargo Report* must be electronically communicated to Customs, prior to arrival at each intended port/airport of cargo discharge; again within prescribed times. *Cargo Reports* are also mandatory for in *transit* cargo, and must be communicated electronically prior to arrival at the first port/airport of arrival in Australia.

Cargo list reports for sea containers have replaced container lists and must also be reported electronically prior to arrival at port within prescribed times.

Reporting requirements also apply for under bond movement of goods in Australia.

Where sea freight containers are progressively unloaded from vessels in an Australia port, progressive discharge reports are required at the end of each three hour period. People unloading cargo from a ship or aircraft are required to lodge outturn reports to account for surplus or short-landed cargo. Break bulk and bulk cargo must be out-turned within five days of discharge. Stevedores must electronically communicate lists of re-stowed containers. Mandatory electronic out-turn reports must also be provided by all persons (eg stevedores, depot operators) in charge of a Customs place where goods enter Australia.

Importer obligations under the new legislative environment

The legislation sets out the time frames within which cargo information is to be provided to Customs.

Imported goods are now entered for home consumption or warehousing via a system of declarations. There are now three ways to declare imported goods for home consumption:

- Self-assessed clearance declaration (for low value goods);
- Import declaration; and
- Request for cargo release or RCR (for accredited clients).

Self assessed clearance (SAC) declarations

Goods with a Customs value equal to or below the entry threshold (currently AUD$250) must be "declared" on a Self Assessed Clearance (SAC) declaration. SACs only apply to the sea and air cargo environment (ie not to postal entry of goods), and can be "communicated" to Customs as either part of the cargo report or a separate declaration.

It is the role of the importer to self-assess the accuracy of information contained in an SAC before it is communicated to Customs. This includes any information that is communicated to Customs on behalf of an importer by a licensed customs broker.

SACs declared on a cargo report must meet certain threshold criteria, must not contain any alcohol or tobacco products and must not contain any prohibited or restricted items.

Separate SAC declarations (not forming part of a cargo report) can be lodged in either a short form or as a full declaration format. A short form SAC declaration is the most commonly required format, requiring minimal information for Customs to risk-assess the consignment. Short form SACs can include declaration lines if revenue is to be collected, such as for alcohol or tobacco products.

A full declaration format SAC mirrors the short form SAC and is submitted by an importer or their broker when further information is deemed necessary to enable the facilitated release of the consignment.

There is also a standard statement available for completing in the event that Unaccompanied Personal Effects (UPE) are brought into Australia. UPE statements can be lodged in either electronic format (via the Customs interactive website) or in manual format in person at a Customs counter or Australia Post Keypost outlets.

Import declarations

Goods with a Customs value above the entry threshold (in either the sea/air cargo environment or in the postal environment) must be "declared" on an import or warehouse declaration. There are three types of import declarations:

- Import declaration for home consumption goods;
- Warehouse declaration for entry into warehousing; and
- Warehouse declaration for entry into home consumption from warehousing.

A new type of declaration has now been introduced to allow a single communication to cover goods entered for home consumption and for warehousing.

All import declarations require the importer to provide detailed information regarding the goods covered by the declaration, including full valuation details for calculation of relevant duties and taxes. All valuations declared on an import declaration must be based on the relevant Incoterms 2000 term under which the goods were shipped.

Accredited client reporting

Certain importers and exporters who have demonstrated that they regularly provide accurate and timely information, consistently make revenue payments and pose a lesser risk to the Australian community will be allowed to become accredited clients. Accredited clients can negotiate individually tailored information contracts to meet their needs. Accredited clients are now able to have their goods cleared by facilitated means. This is via an electronically lodged Request for Cargo Release (RCR), that contains minimum information. Accredited clients must then submit a periodic declaration at the end of each month for all goods covered by RCRs lodged during that month.

AUS ¶50-003   Restrictions on export of goods

Restraints are maintained over goods exported from Australia. Export prohibitions and restrictions fall into three broad categories:

(1) The *Customs (Prohibited Exports) Regulations 1958* cover five broad classes of goods:

   a) Miscellaneous prohibited exports, the export of which is prohibited without permit from the relevant authority (includes items such as pornography and other objectionable items, asbestos and products containing asbestos, certain chemicals and chemical compounds, primary produce, toothfish, human

AUS ¶50-003

substances (including human blood, tissue and human embryos), biological substances, radioactive substances, rough diamonds, cat and dog fur);

b) Drugs and precursor substances, the export of which is prohibited unless Ministerial approval is obtained or the exporter is a licensed exporter;

c) Exportation of certain goods (mainly strategic, military type goods) to certain countries that are the subject of UN Security Council Resolutions is prohibited. Such countries currently include Rwanda, Sierra Leone, Afghanistan and Liberia;

d) Exportation of goods related to finance, defence and environment. Under this category, objectionable items related to finance such as counterfeit credit, debit and charge cards cannot be exported. Strategic and defence weapons, etc can only be exported with a licence or written permission from the Minister. Ozone-depleting substances, synthetic greenhouse gases or radioactive waste also cannot be exported unless a licence or written permission from the Minister has been obtained; and

e) The exportation of devices and documents relating to suicide is prohibited absolutely.

(2) The *Commerce (Trade Descriptions) Act 1905* prohibits the export of prescribed goods unless they are marked as specified in the appropriate regulations. The Act also prohibits the exportation of falsely marked goods.

(3) Bulk consignments of wine, brandy, grape spirit and wine-derived products cannot be exported unless a permit is first obtained from the Australian Wine and Brandy Corporation.

(4) Australian protected objects listed on the National Cultural Heritage Control List as Class A items (such as Victoria Cross medals awarded to Australian service personnel) are prohibited exports and cannot be exported under any circumstances. Objects listed as Class B (such as items of Australian Aboriginal and Torres Strait Islander heritage) may only be exported if a permit is granted under the *Movable Cultural Heritage Act 1986* by the Minister for the Environment and Heritage. The Department of the Environment and Heritage also issues permits for any exports of cetaceans (whales, dolphins and porpoises) or products derived from a cetacean.

(5) Animal and plant species and all products (including some medicinal products) manufactured from species listed in the appendices to the Convention on International Trade in Endangered Species (CITES) cannot be exported unless a special permit is first obtained from the Minister for the Environment and Heritage. Similar restrictions apply to the export of any Australian native animal or plant described in the List of Exempt Native Specimens.

AUS ¶50-004   Regulation of export and import licences

Import or Export licences and permits are only required where goods are subject to the *Customs (Prohibited Export) Regulations 1958*, the *Commerce (Imports) Regulations 1940* or other legislation regulating the import and/or export of goods.

Goods subject to import control, prohibition or restriction are many and varied. They include:

- Certain drugs and goods containing those drugs — hazardous and health related manufactured articles and substances;
- Animals and animal products — food and plant imports;
- Firearms — other weapons, including chemical weapons and chemicals which may have application in the production of chemical weapons;
- Other hazardous or dangerous goods such as toys or other products containing hazardous substances (lead, arsenic etc), and/or goods which do not meet safety manufacture and performance standards;
- Protected wildlife (animals) and related products;
- Protected cultural heritage items;
- Motor vehicles;
- Goods from certain countries; and
- Currency.

The Minister of the Department that is the relevant authority in respect of the restricted item (eg Department of Foreign Affairs and Trade, Department of Defence, Minister for Justice and Customs, Department of the Environment and Heritage etc) has a discretion to refuse to grant a licence or permit or to grant permission for export/import of the goods included in the application.

A person who is dissatisfied with a licensing or permit decision may request the Minister to review it. Appeals to the Administrative Appeals Tribunal are also available after a decision made by a Minister to refuse a licence or permit. Appeals to the Tribunal are governed by the *Administrative Appeals Tribunal Act 1975*. Further appeals are available under the *Administrative Decisions (Judicial Review) Act 1978* but such appeals must be based on one of the grounds set out in that Act.

AUS ¶50-005   Special restrictions relating to foreign control of business

There are no special restrictions on foreign-controlled export or import business.

AUS ¶50-011   Major objectives of host country

Australia's import and export controls can be generally regarded as seeking to achieve one or more of the following objectives:

- protection of local industry from anti-competitive conduct abroad;
- protection of the users of certain goods on health or safety grounds;
- protection of the community from the deleterious effect of drugs/weapons;
- environmental protection/conservation;
- consumer protection — packaging/marking requirements; and
- implementation of international commitments.

AUS ¶50-012   Rates of customs duties

The *Customs Tariff Act* constitutes the fulfilment of Australia's treaty obligation to implement the International Convention on the Harmonised Commodity Description and Coding System — the Harmonised Tariff.

AUS ¶50-005

The structure of the Tariff is significant as it provides, apart from the rates, substantive rules for its interpretation together with extensive other definitional provisions.

- The classifying of goods is achieved by determining which tariff item applies to the goods. However, it is the nature of the Tariff that goods may fall into two or more items across different Schedules. Being a taxing law, however, only one item can finally apply to the goods and this is achieved by the *Tariff Act* providing that it shall be the last classification in the tariff which is applicable.

Valuation

While there are several methods of valuing goods for Customs purposes, the method most applied (transaction value) is based on the price actually paid (or payable) for the imported goods subject to certain adjustments.

Valuation of imported goods can be complex and importers should seek advice from a Customs Information Centre. Further information on tariff valuation and tariff rates in general, as well as the addresses of the importers' closest Customs Information Centre(s) can be obtained by accessing the Customs department website at http://www.customs.gov.au.

Rules of Origin

Rules of Origin are the rules applied to determine from which country a good originates for international trade purposes.

Rules of origin are necessary for both preferential reasons i.e. determining eligibility for benefits such as reduced rates of duty, and non-preferential reasons such as the imposition of anti-dumping and countervailing duties, compliance with country of origin labelling requirements etc.

Australia is a signatory to bilateral trading agreements with New Zealand and Papua New Guinea, and most goods from those countries may be imported free of customs duty into Australia. In addition, goods from developing countries are also entitled to enter Australia at a preferential rate of duty, which is generally five percentage points lower than the general rate. To enter at preferential rates, goods must comply with certain rules of origin. Preference tariff arrangements are currently being adjusted for tariff items which are phasing down.

AUS ¶50-013   Taxes

With effect from 1 July 2000, the Wholesales Sales Tax (sales tax) system was replaced by a broad based Goods and Services Tax (GST). From this date onwards, with very few exceptions, all goods became subject to GST.

While the introduction of the GST system will have no effect on the determination of an importer's Customs duty liability, significant changes will occur to the rate, method of calculation and applicability of other taxes.

GST Calculation

As with the previous sales tax system, the first step in the GST assessment process is the calculation of duty against the Customs value. The duty is then added to the Customs value. Under GST, the amount paid or payable for international transport and insurance is then also added to arrive at the value of the taxable importation (VOTI). GST, at a rate of 10%, is then calculated against that figure.

GST is calculated as per the following example:

	AUS$
Customs value	1000
Duty @ 5%	50
Plus freight and insurance	150
VOTI	1200
GST @ 10%	120
Customs duty	50
GST	120
Total payable	170

For imports of motor vehicles and wine, the Luxury Car Tax or the Wine Equalisation Tax may also apply.

The Australian Business Number

Effective with the introduction of the GST, all importers must supply their Australian Business Number (ABN) when formally entering goods. Importers will need to be registered for GST purposes and have an ABN in order to obtain input tax credits or access the GST deferral scheme.

Further advice on GST matters, including registration, deferral and claiming of input credits can be obtained from any branch of the Australian Taxation Office (ATO).

AUS ¶50-014   Tariff agreements

Australia is a signatory to the General Agreement on Tariffs and Trade (GATT) which provides accepted advantages to member states. A GATT contracting party's fundamental obligation is to charge no more than its currently agreed maximum tariff rates on imports from other contracting parties and to accord no less favourable tariff treatment to imports from all other contracting parties.

Australia has also decided to accede to the United Nations Educational, Scientific and Cultural Organisation Agreement on the Importation of Educational, Scientific and Cultural Materials. Parties to this treaty, known as the Florence Agreement, undertake not to apply customs duties or other charges on educational, scientific or cultural goods.

Australia also has a bilateral agreement with New Zealand (the Closer Economic Relations Agreement). As a consequence, all tariffs, import licensing and quantitative restrictions and export incentives restricting trade between the two countries were removed from 1 July 1990.

Australian Harmonised Export Commodity Classification (AHECC)

Australian exporters can take advantage of the internationally agreed system of classifying goods in international trade (the Harmonised System). The Harmonised System standards form an important component of the AHECC system for exporters. The Australian Harmonised Export Commodity Classification (AHECC) is an eight-digit number used to classify goods for export. The first six digits are part of the international standard and the final two are specific to Australian exports. There are more than 5000 AHECC codes, so it is important to select the correct code when classifying goods. Customs provide a formal AHECC Hotline and Electronic Advisory Service. To access the new AHECC service, clients may complete an advice request pro forma available on the Customs Internet website (http://www.customs.gov.au). They may then email it to aheccadvice@customs.gov.auor fax it to a dedicated fax number. Alternatively they may call the Customs Information Centre on 1300 363 263 and ask to have the pro forma faxed or sent to them. There is also a CD-based learning tool, the AHECC guide, available by calling the Customs Information Centre on 1300 363 263 or by emailing information@customs.gov.au.

AUS ¶50-015   Concessional entry of goods

Customs administer a number of schemes that can be of benefit to importers, exporters and manufacturers. The schemes include allowing the importation of goods at free or at concessional deferment of duty payment. The following schemes are administered.

Export concessions: duty drawback

This scheme has an export assistance component. The scheme is designed to assist exporters to obtain a refund of customs duty paid on imported goods where those goods are exported unused since importation, or are first exhibited, treated, processed or incorporated in other goods and then exported. Applicants are required to register with Customs before claiming:

Customs warehouses: deferment of duty

This scheme provides the industry with a duty deferral facility whereby owners of imported goods may store their goods in licenced warehouses. The goods are held under Customs control until the owner is ready to enter the goods for home consumption (whereupon duty will be payable) or export the goods. Goods held in this manner are referred to as Under Bond Goods. Under Bond Goods may be exported or transferred, with permission, to another licenced warehouse without incurring duty liability. Warehouse licences are granted for storing goods generally or goods of a particular class and may restrict the manner in which the goods may be dealt with. Warehouses generally operate at the wholesale level with the exception of duty free shops which are warehouses that are specifically permitted to operate at the retail level.

Manufacturing in Bond.

Manufacturing in Bond (MiB) is a provision which allows the manufacturing of goods in a warehouse licenced by Customs, using imported components on which duty has not been paid. Applicants for MiB must first obtain approval from the Department of Industry, Science and Resources by demonstrating a clear intention to generate exports. Applicants will then need to satisfy Customs requirements for a warehouse licence to manufacture in bond. A firm with MiB approval will be able to import dutiable goods into a licenced warehouse free of duty as GST. If these goods are subsequently re-exported, either in their original or manufactured form, no duty or GST liability is incurred. Imports brought into the warehouse and subsequently 'entered for home consumption' (sold in the domestic market), incur a duty and GST liability at the time they leave the warehouse.

AUS ¶50-021　Free trade zones

There is only one free trade "zone" in Australia, the Trade Development Zone in Darwin in the Northern Territory. Similar in concept to duty free zones and export processing zones throughout the world, the Trade Development Zone provides for export manufacturers to process imported raw materials or components for export purposes, in an environment where there are preferential arrangements for sales tax, customs or excise duties.

AUS ¶50-022　Labelling and packaging requirements

The *Commerce (Trade Descriptions) Act* prohibits the export or import of prescribed goods unless they are marked as specified in the appropriate regulations. It also prohibits the export of any goods which are falsely marked.

A representation (particularly through labelling) that goods have a particular country of origin may provide certain marketing advantages to a company. Section 53(eb) was therefore included in the *Trade Practices Act 1974* in order to prohibit false or misleading representations concerning the origin of goods.

More generally, sec 52 of the *Trade Practices Act* also prohibits a corporation from engaging in conduct which is misleading or deceptive or which is likely to mislead or deceive. In 1998, the *Trade Practices Amendment (Country of Origin Representations) Act 1998* inserted a new Div 1AA into Part V of the *Trade Practices Act* to cure a number of uncertainties which had arisen in relation to determining the origin of goods and to ensure consistency in the treatment of origin claims. The general test for origin representations under Div 1AA is that the goods have been substantially transformed in a country and 50% or more of the cost of producing or manufacturing the goods is attributable to that country. The Division applies to all representations made in relation to the origin of goods, including "product of" or "produce of" representations and a number of prescribed logos. The Division ensures that so long as country of origin representations made about goods comply with its terms, then no contravention of sec 52, or of para 53(a) or (eb) or para 75AZC(1)(a) or (i) (which all deal with false or misleading representations) have occurred.

Commerce Trade Description

Importers are required to ensure that goods entering the commerce of Australia are correctly marked. Customs administers truth in labelling provisions which makes it an offence to knowingly apply, or for imported goods to carry, false trade descriptions.

A false trade description means any description which by addition, deletion or any other treatment is likely to mislead on matters such as weight, origin, manufacturer, preparation, contents, copyright, etc.

Trade description markings must be:

- in English;
- in prominent and legible characters;
- on a principal label or brand attached to the goods in a prominent position in a manner as permanent as is practicable; and
- in certain circumstances include the country of origin.

The *Commerce (Trade Descriptions) Act 1905* provides that any goods imported in contravention of any condition or regulation may be seized and forfeited to the crown.

Import Entry

A customs import entry must be lodged for goods above the following values:

- Postal: AUS$1,000 per consignment
- Non-postal: AUS$250 per consignment

Consignments valued at or below these amounts may be cleared on an approved form (from 2005 onwards, a Self Assessed Clearance declaration (SAC)) which is available at Customs offices or on the Customs website (www.customs.gov.au.)

Cost recovery charges apply for the processing of entries. The cost will depend on whether the entry is an electronic entry or a documentary (manual) entry.

Documentation

Usually, the minimum documentation required to be submitted with customs import declarations or SAC should include the relevant transport document (eg airway bill or bill of lading) and any other shipping documents (eg invoices, packing lists, insurance documents) relating to the shipment.

The *Customs Act 1901* requires importers to retain commercial documents relating to a transaction for five years from the date of entry. These documents may be required for Customs audit purposes. Failure to meet the requirement may attract a penalty.

Amendments to the *Customs Act* to come into full effect by early 2005 now incorporate stricter document and record retention requirements to allow for technological changes and to ensure that the accountability for accuracy and compliance with customs can easily be established. The obligation to retain commercial documents now includes everyone who causes cargo to be imported into and exported from Australia and persons who receive those goods (in Australia). An obligation to retain records has been introduced for people who communicate information to Customs to allow Customs to verify the content of the information.

AUS ¶50-023   International treaties

As a member of the World Trade Organisation (WTO), Australia is a signatory to all of the major Conventions coming under the purview of the WTO. The General Agreement on Tariffs and Trade 1994:

- The Agreement on Technical Barriers to Trade;
- The Agreement on Implementation of Article VI of the GATT 1994;
- The Agreement on Implementation of Article VII of the GATT 1994;
- The Anti-Dumping Code;
- The Import Licensing Procedures;
- The Agreement on Subsidies and Countervailing Measures;
- The Agriculture Agreements;
- The Agreement on Trade-Related Investment Measures;
- The Rules of Origin;
- The General Agreement on Trade in Services; and

- The Agreement on Trade-Related Aspects of Intellectual Property Rights.

Australia has also decided to accede to the Florence Agreement (see AUS ¶50-014) and is also a signatory to a large number of other conventions, including:

- Convention on International Trade in Endangered Species of Wild Fauna and Flora;
- The Chemical Weapons Convention (applicable as of 1997 and regulated by the Chemical Weapons Convention Office);
- Customs Convention on Containers;
- Customs Convention on the Temporary Importation of Private Road Vehicles;
- Customs Convention on the ATA Carnet for the Temporary Admission of Goods;
- Customs Convention Concerning Facilities for the Importation of Goods for Display or Use at Exhibitions, Fairs, Meetings and Similar Events; and
- International Convention on the Simplification and Harmonisation of Customs Procedures.

These conventions are supported by domestic customs laws, such as the *Customs (Prohibited export) Regulations 1958* and the *Commerce (Imports) Regulations 1940*.

AUS ¶50-024   Penalties and additional taxes

The *Customs Act* provides a wide range of penalties for non-compliance with its requirements. These range from administratively based penalties for the provision of incorrect information or omission of relevant information in the entry of goods for home consumption, to life imprisonment for the importation of commercial quantities of narcotic substances.

Any person who imports goods into Australia is obliged to keep all relevant ''commercial documents'' relating to the goods for a period of five years. This covers a broad range of documents which are usually created in the course of international sales and trade.

Under the Act, customs officers are empowered to search premises for, and inspect and copy, commercial documents relating to the entry of goods.

There is a new cost recovery system introduced under the *Depot Licensing Charges Amendment Act* and *Import Processing Charges Act*. These Acts new cost recovery arrangements to support changes to import and export processes under the CMR scheme. The new cost recovery system streamlines existing processes; removes the previously existing differentiation between the cost of transactions across different modes of transport and encourages the use of electronic document lodgments by offering substantial price discounts.

AUS ¶50-025   Anti-dumping and countervailing duties

Australian law gives effect to the provisions of the GATT 1994 relating to anti-dumping and countervailing duties.

Anti-dumping and countervailing duties are imposed under the *Customs Tariff (Anti-Dumping) Act* and relevant procedures and tests for determining whether either form of relief is permitted in a particular case are set out in Pt XVB of the *Customs Act*.

Review powers (concerning individual dumping and countervailing cases as well as policy issues referred for consideration) are given to the Anti-Dumping Authority under

AUS ¶50-024

the *Anti-Dumping Authority Act*. The Anti-Dumping Authority is obliged to have regard to the Australian government's policy in regard to anti-dumping matters and to Australia's obligations under the GATT not to use the imposition of duties under the *Anti-Dumping Act* to assist import competing industries in Australia or to protect industries in Australia from the need to adjust to changing economic conditions.

AUS ¶50-031   Power to detain goods

All imported goods must be entered before the expiry of the next day following their importation and if they are not, the Collector of Customs may require them to be placed in a warehouse and, failing their entry for home consumption or export from the warehouse, they may be sold. "Entry" refers to the administrative process of clearing the goods through Customs.

While most importers employ customs agents (customs brokers) to enter goods for clearance, the importer is always responsible for the correctness of the entry.

Customs may not capriciously delay or deny an owner authority to deal with goods simply because of a belief that Customs have not been fully advised about the goods by the owner.

Intellectual property rights and the power to detain

Customs are tasked with administering certain provisions of the *Copyright Act 1968*, the *Trade Marks Act 1995* and the *Sydney 2000 Games (Indicia and Images) Protection Act 1996* to protect intellectual property. These Statutes serve to protect the intellectual property rights of individuals, companies and corporations with regard to the unauthorised copying of copyright material, or the unauthorised use of a trademark or of words and/or images associated with the Olympic games.

In these Acts, the legislation establishes a scheme under which either the owner or authorised licencee can object to the importation of goods which allegedly infringe their intellectual property. Customs are authorised to act under this legislation once a Notice of Objection has been accepted. Its role is to enforce the protection of intellectual property at the Customs 'border'.

Customs have the power to seize imported goods which infringe intellectual property rights and to hold them for a specified period during which the objector must commence action in the Federal Court. Importers may, if they wish, forfeit infringing goods to Customs before legal action has commenced.

The issue of intellectual property rights enforcement at the Customs 'border' is complex because trademarks and copyright may exist in labels, logos and images as well as in more traditionally recognised works such as books, sound recordings, films, designs, computer software etc. These goods may also be subject to the truth in labelling provisions contained in the consumer protection legislation of the *Commerce (Trade Descriptions) Act 1905*.

Customs' role in the enforcement of intellectual property legislation is limited to imported goods which have not been released from Customs control. Copyright and trademark owners whose rights are infringed may also seek within the market place either a civil remedy or criminal prosecution. Civil litigation is the most common form of intellectual property rights enforcement. Effective criminal prosecution invariably requires police involvement, usually with the Australian Federal Police, although the relevant Acts do not name a specific enforcement agency other than Customs.

Part V, Div 7 (sec134-135AK inclusive) of the *Copyright Act* enables the owner of the copyright in copyright material to object to the importation into Australia of copies of the copyright material. The Division applies only to copies of copyright material if the making of the copy, if it had been carried out in Australia by the person importing the copy, constitutes an infringement of the copyright in the copyright material. In other words, copies of copyright material made in an overseas jurisdiction under licence or with the permission of the Australian copyright owner can be imported into Australia (parallel importing) quite legally. Notices of Objection are given to the Chief Executive Officer of Customs and remain in force for two years unless revoked or declared ineffective before then, or unless the relevant copyright in the copyright material expires before the end of the two years. Customs may seize copies of the copyright material in respect of which a Notice of Objection is in force. Seized copies may be forfeited to the Commonwealth and disposed of in accordance with the regulations, and an infringement notice issued to the importer/owner of the goods.

Part 13 (sec 131-142 inclusive) of the *Trade Marks Act* enables the registered owner (or the end user with consent of the registered owner) of a registered trademark to give to the Customs CEO a Notice objecting to the importation of goods that infringe the relevant trade mark. Part 13 applies to all imported goods manufactured outside Australia which have applied to them or in relation to them a sign that is, in the opinion of the Customs CEO, substantially identical with, or deceptively similar to, a registered trade mark in respect of which a Notice of Objection has been given.

When such goods become subject to the control of Customs, the Customs CEO *must* seize the goods unless he or she is satisfied that there are no reasonable grounds for believing that the notified trade mark is infringed by importation of the goods. Goods need not be seized, however, if the person or persons objecting to the import have not provided security in a sufficient amount to cover expenses incurred by the Commonwealth as a result of the seizure. As is the case under the *Copyright Act*, goods seized as being in breach of a registered trade mark may be forfeited and disposed of, and a notice of infringement may be issued to the owner of the goods. Civil remedies may also apply to enable the registered owner and/or authorised user of the relevant trade mark to obtain compensation from the importer found to be in breach of Part 13.

AUS ¶50-032   When is duty or tax payable?

Liability for the payment of customs duty, sales tax and goods and services tax arises upon the making of an entry for home consumption. Such liability is imposed on the owner of the goods.

Exchange Control — The Movement of Money

Which laws apply to exchange control? .... AUS ¶55-001

Who administers exchange control? .... AUS ¶55-002

Major objectives of exchange control policies .... AUS ¶55-003

Application of exchange control laws to various
    countries .... AUS ¶55-004

Repatriation of capital .... AUS ¶55-005

Remittance of dividends, etc. .... AUS ¶55-011

Limit on amount of local currency and foreign
    currency to remit out of host country .... AUS ¶55-012

Restrictions on remittance of currency .... AUS ¶55-013

Currency to be used for loans .... AUS ¶55-014

Method of fixing exchange rate of host country's
    currency .... AUS ¶55-015

Differing rates of exchange for host country's
    currency .... AUS ¶55-021

Transactions requiring approval from exchange
    control authorities .... AUS ¶55-022

Tests for distinguishing residents from non-residents .. AUS ¶55-023

Distinctions between foreign-controlled companies
    incorporated inside or out of the host country .... AUS ¶55-024

Effect of local participation on exchange controls ..... AUS ¶55-025

Exchange control exemptions .... AUS ¶55-031

Remittance from host country of personal savings and
    pension fund contributions by expatriate personnel . AUS ¶55-032

Exchange control formalities .... AUS ¶55-033

Consequences of breach of exchange control law ..... AUS ¶55-034

Forward market for foreign exchange .... AUS ¶55-035

Restrictions on repatriation of capital during
    continuation of investment incentives .... AUS ¶55-041

Taxation considerations in respect of exchange control
    regulations .... AUS ¶55-042

AUS ¶55-001   WHICH LAWS APPLY TO EXCHANGE CONTROL?

Before December 1983, Australia governed the external movement of currency via the Australian banking system, using extensive exchange control measures. With the float of the Australian dollar on 9 December 1983, most exchange controls were removed. As from 1 July 1990, there are no exchange controls in Australia. However, there are several pieces of legislation which may affect foreign currency transactions:

- The *Reserve Bank Act 1959* which establishes the Reserve Bank of Australia and vests it with considerable policy making and regulatory powers. See also other Reserve Bank enabling legislation such as the *Corporations Act 2001*, the *Payment Systems (Regulation) Act 1998* and the *Payments Systems and Netting Act 1988*.

- The *Banking Act 1959*, sec. 39, and the *Banking (Foreign Exchange) Regulations*, which grant companies authority to conduct foreign exchange business.

- The *Foreign Acquisitions and Takeovers Act 1975* which, in conjunction with the Foreign Investment Review Board, covers direct overseas investment by non-residents into Australia. The legislation aims to control interests which may be contrary to the national interest.

- The *Financial Transaction Reports Act 1988* (the FTR Act), which establishes the Australian Transaction Reports and Analysis Centre — Australia's anti-money laundering regulator and specialist financial intelligence unit. The FTR Act requires the reporting of cash transactions (including foreign currency) over minimum levels (AUS$10,000 or more), transfer of currency into and out of Australia (AUS$10,000 or more), all international funds transfer instructions and all suspicious cash transactions of any value, to the Australian Transaction Reports and Analysis Centre (AUSTRAC) (see AUS ¶55-012).

- The *Financial Sector (Collection of Data) Act 2001* (the Act) which repealed the *Financial Corporations Act 1974* on 1 July 2002. The Act transferred responsibility for the registration and categorisation of financial corporations to the Australian Prudential Regulatory Authority (APRA). The Act serves mainly to facilitate the collection of statistical data. It does not serve to alter data collection requirements, and it does not empower APRA to supervise the activities of Registered Financial Corporations. From 1 July 2002, the corporations that were previously registered under the *Financial Corporations Act* are known collectively as Registered Financial Corporations (RFCs).

- The *Income Tax Assessment Act 1936 and 1997*, and related taxation legislation, which covers the taxing of foreign-sourced income, withholding tax, foreign tax credits, tax havens, thin capitalisation, etc.

- Other legislation impacting upon the operation of exchange control in Australia include the *Australian Prudential Regulation Authority Act 1998* and other APRA enabling legislation such as the *Corporate Law Economic Reform Program Act 1999*, as well as other legislation governing authorised deposit-taking institutions in the financial sector including insurance companies and superannuation funds.

AUS ¶55-001

AUS ¶55-002   WHO ADMINISTERS EXCHANGE CONTROL?

The Reserve Bank of Australia

The Reserve Bank of Australia (RBA) is a statutory authority, established by an Act of Parliament, the *Reserve Bank Act 1959*, which gives it specific powers and obligations. The role and functions of the RBA are also underpinned by various other pieces of legislation. The RBA's main function is monetary policy. Policy decisions are made by the Board, with the objective of achieving low and stable inflation over the medium term. Other major roles are maintaining financial system stability and promoting the safety and efficiency of the payments system. The Bank is an active participant in financial markets, manages Australia's foreign reserves, issues Australian currency notes and serves as banker to the Commonwealth Government. The information provided by the Reserve Bank includes statistics — for example, on interest rates, exchanges and money and credit growth — and a range of publications on its operations and research. To access these, visit the RBA website at *www.rba.gov.au*.

The Reserve Bank has two boards with complementary responsibilities. The Bank is accountable to the Commonwealth Parliament, including through the annual report of the Reserve Bank Board. The Reserve Bank Board is responsible for monetary policy and overall financial system stability. The Payments System Board has specific responsibility for the safety and efficiency of the payments system. The Payments System Board also produces an annual report which is tabled in Parliament.

As well as being a policy-making body, the Reserve Bank of Australia (RBA) provides selected banking and registry services to some Federal and State Government customers and some overseas official institutions. Its assets, which include Australia's holdings of gold and foreign exchange, amounted to around AUS$60 billion at 30 June 2002. The Bank is wholly-owned by the Australian Government, to which its profits accrue.

The structure of the RBA is based on groupings of related functions, as follows:

- Economic Group;
- Financial Markets Group;
- Financial System Group;
- Business Services Group;
- Corporate Services Group;
- Information Department;
- Audit Department;
- Personnel Department; and
- Secretary's Department.

For further information, visit the RBA's website at *www.rba.gov.au*.

The Australian Prudential Regulatory Authority

The Australian Prudential Regulatory Authority (APRA) is the prudential regulator of banks, credit unions, building societies, insurance companies, friendly societies and superannuation funds.

APRA is a statutory authority with a considerable degree of autonomy from government. Its Board of nine members, including representatives from the RBA, the Australian Securities and Investments Commission (ASIC) and Treasurer-appointed members, is charged with determining APRA's policy goals, priorities and strategies.

The Financial Sector (Collection of Data) Act 2001

On 1 July 2002, the registration and categorisation of financial corporations became the responsibility of APRA. This transfer of responsibilities is due to the commencement of the *Financial Sector (Collection of Data) Act 2001* (the FSCD Act) which repealed the *Financial Corporations Act 1974* on 1 July 2002.

The FSCD Act as it relates to Registered Financial Corporations (RFCs) requires a wide range of non-bank financial intermediaries to register with, and provide statistics to APRA. It applies to financial corporations with assets over AUS$5 million whose principal business in Australia is the borrowing of money and provision of finance, and which are not already covered by the *Banking Act 1959*. The majority of institutions covered are money market corporations, pastoral finance companies, finance companies and general financiers. Entities excluded from the definition of RFC include life offices, insurance companies and various funds managers such as superannuation funds, trustee companies, unit trusts and friendly societies.

The Act as it relates to RFCs serves mainly to facilitate the collection of statistical data for use in compiling money and credit aggregates. It does not empower APRA to supervise the activities of non-bank financial intermediaries, nor does it confer any particular status on the almost 600 corporations registered under it.

Once registered and categorised, corporations are required to submit the appropriate forms on either a monthly or quarterly basis. These forms are provided to the corporation upon registration. Since 31 December 2002, forms have been required to be submitted to the APRA, rather than to the RBA as was the case before that date.

A corporation may be exempted from the application of the Act. These corporations are required to be registered however APRA may determine that the corporations may be exempted from the provisions of the Act. Penalties apply to any RFC which fails to register within 60 days of becoming eligible for registration.

In order to begin the process of upgrading the data collection forms RFCs, APRA, the Australian Bureau of Statistics and the RBA have proposed new data collection requirements to apply to RFCs from 31 March 2003.

For further information and for details of any changes to data collection requirements visit the APRA's website at *http://www.apra.gov.au/*.

Council of Financial Regulators

The Council of Financial Regulators is a co-ordinating body for Australia's main financial regulatory agencies: the RBA, which chairs the Council; the APRA, and the Australian Securities and Investments Commission (ASIC). The Council's role is to contribute to the efficiency and effectiveness of financial regulation by providing a high level forum for co-operation and collaboration amongst its members.

The Australian Transactions Reports and Analysis Centre

The Australian Transactions Reports and Analysis Centre (AUSTRAC) is Australia's anti-money laundering regulator and specialist financial intelligence unit. In its regulatory role, it oversees compliance with the reporting requirements of the *Financial Transactions Reports Act 1988* (FTR Act) by a wide range of financial services providers, the gambling industry and others. As noted above (see AUS ¶55-001), the FTR Act requires the reporting of financial transaction reports (FTR) information by case dealers and members of the public and account identification requirements. FTR information includes reports of:

- Large cash transactions (AUS$10,000 or more);
- Transfer of currency into or out of Australia (AUS$10,000 or more);
- All international funds transfer instructions; and
- Suspect transactions.

In its intelligence role, AUSTRAC provides financial transaction reports information to Commonwealth, State and Territory law enforcement and revenue agencies.

Established under the FTR Act, AUSTRAC is a prescribed authority within the Commonwealth Attorney General's portfolio. Under the Act, AUSTRAC collects, compiles, analyses and disseminates the information collected, called FTR Information. It provides advice and assistance to the Commissioner of Taxation in relation to FTR Information. It also issues guidelines and circulars to those entities which report to it, called ''cash dealers'', about their obligations under the FTR Act and Financial Transaction Reports Regulations.

AUSTRAC's mission is to make a valued contribution towards a financial environment hostile to money laundering, major crime and tax evasion. It does this, inter alia, by working to ensure that financial service providers and other specified groups (''cash dealers'') identify their customers and so reduce the occurrence of false name bank and other accounts. Through its compilation and analysis functions, it monitors and identifies money laundering related to serious crime and major tax evasion. It provides this financial intelligence to the Australian Taxation Office and Commonwealth, State and Territory law enforcement, security and revenue agencies. Partner agencies that work together with AUSTRAC include:

- Australian Bureau of Criminal Intelligence;
- Australian Customs Service;
- Australian Federal Policy;
- Australian Securities and Investments Commission;

- Australian Taxation Office;
- Crime and Misconduct Commission (Queensland);
- Independent Commission Against Corruption (NSW);
- National Crime Authority;
- NSW Crime Commission;
- NSW Police Integrity Commission;
- State and Territory police forces of Australia;
- State and Territory revenue authorities; and
- Australian Security Intelligence Organisation.

AUSTRAC also watches for money laundering techniques which seek to avoid the formal reporting and identification requirements of the FTR Act. AUSTRAC aims to ensure that the integrity of the system is maintained and that advice is given to the Government where further preventive steps may be warranted. AUSTRAC has powers to take court action for injunction remedies to secure compliance with the requirements of the FTR Act. Criminal sanctions also apply for non-compliance.

The AUSTRAC Service Charter sets out the standards of service which cash dealers and members of the public can expect from AUSTRAC in administering the FTR Act. It includes steps which may be taken if these standards are not met. Where appropriate, and upon request, AUSTRAC will provide a copy of any decision make by it, together with reasons for the decision, to the cash dealer or member of the public concerned. It should be noted that the *Australian Administrative Decisions (Judicial Review) Act 1977* only applies to AUSTRAC decisions taken under sub-section 17(B)(4) or sub-sections 19(2) or 19(3) of the FTR Act.

For further information, visit the AUSTRAC's website at *http:// www.austrac.gov.au/*, or contact the AUSTRAC enquiry help desk on 61 2 9950 0827.

AUS ¶55-003 MAJOR OBJECTIVES OF EXCHANGE CONTROL POLICIES

The mandate or charter of the RBA's Reserve Bank Board with respect to monetary (and exchange control) policies is laid out in sec. 10(2) and 11(1) of the *Reserve Bank Act 1959*:

"...the Reserve Bank Board has power to determine the policy of the Bank in relation to any matter, other than its payments system, and to take such action as is necessary to ensure that effect is given by the Bank to the policy so determined.

"It is the duty of the Reserve Bank Board, within the limits of its powers, to ensure that the monetary and banking policy of the Bank is directed to the greatest advantage of the people of Australia and that the powers of the Bank...are exercised in such a manner as, in the opinion of the Reserve Bank Board, will best contribute to:

- the stability of the currency of Australia;

AUS ¶55-003

- the maintenance of full employment in Australia; and
- the economic prosperity and welfare of the people of Australia.''

Section 11(1) of the Act covers the need to consult with Government:

"the Reserve Bank Board is to inform the Government, from time to time, of the Bank's monetary and banking policy.''

The charter of the RBA's Payments System Board is defined in sec. 10B(3) of the Act as follows:

"It is the duty of the Payments System Board to ensure, within the limits of its powers, that:

- the Bank's payments system policy is directed to the greatest advantage of the people of Australia;
- the powers of the Board under the *Payment Systems (Regulation) Act 1998* and the *Payments Systems and Netting Act 1988* are exercised in a way that, in the Board's opinion, will best contribute to:
  - controlling risk in the financial system;
  - promoting the efficiency of the payments system; and
  - promoting competition in the market for payment services, consistent with the overall stability of the financial system; and
- the powers and functions of the Bank under Part 7.3 of the *Corporations Act 2001* are exercised in a way that, in the Board's opinion, will best contribute to the overall stability of the financial system.''

The Reserve Bank of Australia implements its monetary, banking and exchange control policies through its dealings in the financial markets. Financial transactions between the RBA and the rest of the community affect the amount of funds available for immediate use. Foreign exchange dealers are authorised by the Bank under the *Banking (Foreign Exchange) Regulations.*

The Reserve Bank of Australia buys and sells Australian dollars and foreign currencies in the market for several purposes. In its day-to-day operations, it seeks to enhance the efficiency of the market — by satisfying itself about the strength of pressures or by smoothing the passage of larger transactions through the market. It may trade one currency for another in managing its international reserves.

AUS ¶55-004   APPLICATION OF EXCHANGE CONTROL LAWS TO VARIOUS COUNTRIES

No specific legislative or policy distinctions are made between countries in regard to foreign exchange, but see AUS ¶55-013 and AUS ¶55-042. Note also that the Commonwealth Government has the ability to direct the Reserve Bank of Australia to take any steps considered necessary to block accounts or take other measures with respect to groups or countries identified for any reason as part of Australia's foreign affairs policy.

On 4 June 1992, certain financial transactions concerning the former Republic of Yugoslavia (now Serbia and Montenegro) were prohibited without Reserve Bank approval, as part of wide-ranging sanctions imposed by the UN Security Council. When the sanctions were suspended in December 1995, the requirement for RBA approval was lifted for private transactions. Approval is still required, however, for transactions involving the authorities of the Federal Republic of Yugoslavia (Serbia and Montenegro). Funds and assets of the former Socialist Republic under dispute have also been frozen until the successor states reach agreement on the distribution of assets and liabilities.

In December 1999, the Reserve Bank of Australia was directed by the Commonwealth Government to take steps under the *Banking (Foreign Exchange) Regulations* to give effect to the UN Security Council resolutions imposing sanctions against the Afghan faction known as the Taliban (which also calls itself Islamic Emirate of Afghanistan) and the National Union for the Total Independence of Angola (UNITA).

With effect from 22 December 1999, all transactions involving the transfer of funds or payments to, by the order of, or on behalf of the Taliban, or any undertaking owned or controlled, directly or indirectly, by the Taliban, were specifically prohibited without the specific approval of the Reserve Bank of Australia.

Also with effect from 22 December 1999, transactions involving the transfer of funds or payments to, by the order of, or on behalf of the following are prohibited without the specific approval of the Reserve Bank of Australia:

- UNITA as an organisation;
- Senior officials of UNITA; or
- Adult members of the immediate families of the senior officials of UNITA.

In October 2001, the Reserve Bank of Australia was also directed by the Commonwealth Government to take steps under the *Banking (Foreign Exchange) Regulations* to block any accounts which might be held in Australia by persons or organisations identified by the United Nations and the US as terrorists or their sponsors. This action is part of the Commonwealth Government's response to the UN Resolution on this matter and to President Bush's request to countries to support measures being taken by the United States against terrorists and their sponsors. It builds upon the existing sanctions against the Taliban in place since December 1999.

With effect from 3 October 2001, the Reserve Bank took action to block any accounts that might exist in the names listed below. Since that date, the Bank has prohibited any transactions involving the transfer of funds or payments to, by the order of, or on behalf of the following entities:

- Osama bin Laden;
- The Al-Qaeda organisation; and
- Any other person or entity listed in the Annex (available through the RBA media release website).

The RBA has also written to financial institutions asking them to inform it of the existence of any of the specified accounts.

Prohibited transactions outlined above may only be approved by the Reserve Bank if they are for verified medical or humanitarian purposes.

AUS ¶55-004

AUS ¶55-005   REPATRIATION OF CAPITAL

Apart from distinctions under the taxation laws, no other distinctions are made in the treatment of capital remittances and remittances of any other kind. But note the restrictions imposed on certain types of international transactions outlined in AUS ¶55-004.

AUS ¶55-011   REMITTANCE OF DIVIDENDS, ETC.

The principal considerations affecting the transmission of dividends arise under the taxation laws.

Dividends remitted offshore may be subject to withholding tax. Where a dividend is "unfranked" (i.e. it does not carry any company tax imputation credit), withholding tax is payable. To the extent that a dividend is "franked", and hence carries an imputation credit, it is exempt from withholding tax.

Similarly, remittances of interest by Australian residents to non-residents are subject to withholding tax. A resident person paying certain kinds of royalties to non-residents will also be required to inform the Australian Taxation Office and pay any tax in respect of the royalty on behalf of the non-resident taxpayer.

Apart from the withholding tax provisions, there are no exchange control regulations affecting the transmission of remittances relating to specific kinds of payment such as dividends, interest, royalties, management and other similar fees, machine rentals, guarantee payments and the repatriation of branch profits. However, see AUS ¶55-001; AUS ¶55-002; AUS ¶55-003; AUS ¶55-004; AUS ¶55-012 and AUS ¶55-013 in relation to the reporting of cash transactions generally.

AUS ¶55-012   LIMIT ON AMOUNT OF LOCAL CURRENCY AND FOREIGN CURRENCY TO REMIT OUT OF HOST COUNTRY

There are no value or volume exchange controls on the remittance of Australian currency out of Australia.

However, under the *Financial Transaction Reports Act 1988*, the import or export of Australian or foreign currency in excess of AUS\$10,000 must be reported to the Australian Transaction Reports and Analysis Centre (AUSTRAC). The function of AUSTRAC is to collect data and forward it to various authorities including the Commissioner of Taxation. AUSTRAC does not have the power to restrict the transfer of currency to and from Australia.

AUS ¶55-013   RESTRICTIONS ON REMITTANCE OF CURRENCY

There are no legislative limits or restrictions on the persons to whom, places to which, or purposes for which currency may be remitted.

However, the Australian Transaction Reports and Analysis Centre (AUSTRAC), the body established under the *Financial Transaction Reports Act 1988*, does differentiate on an administrative basis between countries to which currency is forwarded from Australia. Under the *Financial Transaction Reports Act*, where a cash dealer (as defined), has "reasonable grounds to suspect" that a transaction (regardless of whether it is inside or outside Australia) may be relevant to an offence under a Commonwealth law such as the taxation laws, the *Proceeds of Crime Act 1987*, social security or immigration laws, etc., then the cash dealer must report the transaction to AUSTRAC.

AUSTRAC issues guidelines which, although not legally binding on a cash dealer, are indicative of what transactions ought to give rise to "reasonable grounds to suspect" that they are contrary to Commonwealth law.

One guideline lists a number of countries which are "known narcotic source or transit countries", and "regular or unusual transactions" with these countries which do not have an obviously legitimate purpose should be reported. Regular or unusual transactions with countries on another list issued by AUSTRAC should cause cash dealers to suspect "money laundering and/or tax evasion" activities.

Note also the restrictions imposed on certain types of transactions as part of Australia's foreign affairs policy as outlined in AUS ¶55-004. Note also reporting requirements for all transfers of funds out of Australia as outlined in AUS ¶55-001; AUS ¶55-002; and AUS ¶55-003.

AUS ¶55-014   CURRENCY TO BE USED FOR LOANS

Other than international embargoes through the International Monetary Fund (IMF), there are no restrictions, as far as the Australian authorities are concerned, on foreign borrowings. Any currency can be used for loans. Foreign countries may, on the other hand, have policy restrictions on their overseas lending, e.g. for trade purposes only.

However, foreign borrowings in general may be the subject of punitive taxation legislation, for example the thin capitalisation rules (see AUS ¶55-042).

AUS ¶55-015   METHOD OF FIXING EXCHANGE RATE OF HOST COUNTRY'S CURRENCY

Without exchange controls, the value of the Australian dollar is set by the market.

The Reserve Bank of Australia also acts to implement its monetary, banking and exchange control policies through its dealings in the financial markets. Financial transactions between the RBA and the rest of the community affect the amount of funds available for immediate use. The Reserve Bank of Australia also buys and sells Australian dollars and foreign currencies in the market for several purposes. In its day-to-day operations, it seeks to enhance the efficiency of the market — by satisfying itself about the strength of pressures or by smoothing the passage of larger transactions through the market. It may trade one currency for another in managing its international reserves.

AUS ¶55-021 DIFFERING RATES OF EXCHANGE FOR HOST COUNTRY'S CURRENCY

There is no variation in the exchange rate by reference to types of transactions, other than minor differences due to the commercial size of the transaction. Nor is there any difference in the exchange rate by reference to the class of persons involved in the transactions.

AUS ¶55-022 TRANSACTIONS REQUIRING APPROVAL FROM EXCHANGE CONTROL AUTHORITIES

Not applicable, but see AUS ¶55-031. Note also the restrictions imposed on certain types of transactions as part of Australia's foreign affairs policy as outlined in AUS ¶55-004. Note further the existence of reporting requirements for all transfers of funds out of Australia as outlined in AUS ¶55-001; AUS ¶55-002; and AUS ¶55-003.

AUS ¶55-023 TESTS FOR DISTINGUISHING RESIDENTS FROM NON-RESIDENTS

The question of residence is of importance mainly in relation to taxation rather than exchange control. However, under sec. 39 of the *Banking Act*, an individual is resident if he is ordinarily resident in Australia, and a corporation is resident if it is incorporated in Australia.

AUS ¶55-024 DISTINCTIONS BETWEEN FOREIGN-CONTROLLED COMPANIES INCORPORATED INSIDE OR OUT OF THE HOST COUNTRY

There is no distinction for the purposes of exchange control. However, the issue of foreign control may have significant taxation consequences, e.g. in relation to the thin capitalisation rules (see AUS ¶55-042).

AUS ¶55-025 EFFECT OF LOCAL PARTICIPATION ON EXCHANGE CONTROLS

Not applicable.

Without exchange controls, the value of the Australian dollar is set by the market.

The Reserve Bank of Australia also acts to implement its monetary, banking and exchange control policies through its dealings in the financial markets. Financial transactions between the RBA and the rest of the community affect the amount of funds available for immediate use. The Reserve Bank of Australia also buys and sells Australian dollars and foreign currencies in the market for several purposes. In its day-to-day operations, it seeks to enhance the efficiency of the market — by satisfying itself with the strength of pressures or by smoothing the passage of larger transactions through the market. It may trade one currency for another in managing its international reserves.

AUS ¶55-031 EXCHANGE CONTROL EXEMPTIONS

Foreign investment policy in Australia is now controlled by the *Foreign Acquisitions and Takeovers Act*, the *Financial Transaction Reports Act*, the taxation laws and other policy requirements set out by the Australian government. The Federal Treasurer is responsible for the administration of these Acts and is assisted in this by the Foreign Investments Review Board and the Australian Taxation Office.

Generally, if an investment proposal can be shown to be in Australia's national interest, it will be approved. Restrictions are applied in a few areas such as residential real estate and in specific industry sectors, e.g. banking, civil aviation, media (radio, television and newspapers) and minerals (other than oil and gas).

Some Australian State governments also impose laws; for instance, the Tasmanian government imposes certain limits on foreign invested corporations that control casino operations (*Casino Company Control Act 1973*), and the Queensland government controls foreign investment in certain real estate.

AUS ¶55-032 REMITTANCE FROM HOST COUNTRY OF PERSONAL SAVINGS AND PENSION FUND CONTRIBUTIONS BY EXPATRIATE PERSONNEL

There is no limit on local or foreign currency which may be taken into or out of Australia by employees of the enterprise or their families, but see AUS ¶55-001; AUS ¶55-002; AUS ¶55-003; AUS ¶55-004; AUS ¶55-012 and AUS ¶55-013 in relation to the reporting of cash transactions generally, and restrictions imposed on certain types of transactions as a result of United Nations sanctions and Australia's foreign affairs policy. See also AUS ¶55-042.

AUS ¶55-033 EXCHANGE CONTROL FORMALITIES

There are no formalities apart from that dealt with at AUS ¶55-001; AUS ¶55-002; AUS ¶55-003; AUS ¶55-004; AUS ¶55-012 and AUS ¶55-013 in relation to the reporting of cash transactions generally.

AUS ¶55-034 CONSEQUENCES OF BREACH OF EXCHANGE CONTROL LAW

There exists a stringent regime for the monitoring and tracking of the proceeds of serious crime. The *Financial Transactions Reports Act 1988* comprises an important part of that regime. The other major part of this tracking regime is the *Proceeds of Crime Act 1987*, which also imposes record keeping and document retention requirements on financial institutions. Various inconsistencies between the two Acts are currently under review, and the RBA has recommended that the document retention requirements and other aspects of *Proceeds of Crime Act 1987* should be amended to become consistent with the *Financial Transactions Act 1988*. Further information regarding the *Proceeds of Crime Act 1987* is available through the RBA and AUSTRAC webpages.

AUS ¶55-035 FORWARD MARKET FOR FOREIGN EXCHANGE

There is a forward market for foreign exchange; this market has fewer controls than most others in the world. It is the major segment of the 24-hour trading clock for the Australian dollar and an important element in the broader Asia-Pacific market.

AUS ¶55-041 RESTRICTIONS ON REPATRIATION OF CAPITAL DURING CONTINUATION OF INVESTMENT INCENTIVES

Not applicable, as there are no investment incentives exclusively for foreign investments in Australia.

AUS ¶55-042 TAXATION CONSIDERATIONS IN RESPECT OF EXCHANGE CONTROL REGULATIONS

There are a number of taxation laws which have a regulatory effect on currency exchange. The Financial Transaction Reports guidelines of 1988 impose strict reporting requirements, and therefore effectively place a deterrent on investment in tax havens (see AUS ¶55-013).

The "controlled foreign corporations" (CFC) provisions in the *Income Tax Assessment Act 1936 and 2003* ensure attribution of income derived by foreign entities if it accrues to Australian-resident controllers of such entities. This ensures that the income so derived is subject to Australian taxation rules, and provides an effective way to regulate the countries and types of investments made by Australian residents.

According to the Australian Taxation Office, the foreign exchange gains or losses of a CFC can be assessed using the currency in which the CFC generally conducts business. The gain or loss is then converted to Australian dollars.

The various double tax agreements may influence investment in favour of countries with which Australia has an agreement. Withholding tax provisions encourage capital importation into Australia by providing concessionary treatment for repatriated dividends, interest and royalties.

Thin capitalisation rules and the "debt creation" provisions may have an impact on the deductibility of interest on foreign debt investment in related Australian resident companies.

In 2002-2003, the Government enacted legislation to provide the basis for a new regime under which wholly-owned groups of companies (together with eligible trusts and partnerships) can choose to consolidate for tax purposes. This regime may affect the operation of thin capitalisation and/or withholding taxation rules as they apply to the Australian operations of both Australian and foreign multinational investors.

The "thin capitalisation" rules are designed to prevent multinational taxpayers allocating a disproportionate amount of debt to their Australian enterprises in order to exploit the favourable treatment of debt compared to equity. The rules operate by disallowing deductions relating to excessive debt financing.

With effect for income years beginning on or after 1 July 2001, a new thin capitalisation regime applies. Division 820 operates when the amount of debt used to finance the Australian operations exceeds specified limits. It disallows a proportion of the otherwise tax-deductible finance expenses (such as interest) attributable to the Australian operations of both Australian and foreign multinational investors. For further information, see the discussion of Australian taxation law at AUS ¶35-001.

The collection provisions in the income tax law may also affect currency movements by regulating the payment of tax by residents on behalf of non-residents, e.g. resident trustees are required to pay tax on behalf of non-resident beneficiaries. Similarly, where the Australian Taxation Office believes that a non-resident may effectively evade tax on Australian income, the resident payer may be required to withhold the necessary amount of tax.

There are also rules designed to combat tax avoidance by way of transfer pricing, which have an impact on the flow of exchange into and out of Australia. More information is available in relation to Australian taxation at AUS ¶35-001.

Other changes to Taxation Law intended to come into effect during 2003 include:

- The *Taxation Law Amendment Bill (No. 6) 2002* which contains amendments relating to interest withholding tax exemptions, Capital Gains Tax on payments received from the German Forced Labour Compensation Program and friendly society investment products; and

- The *Taxation Laws Amendment Bill (No. 7) 2002* which will give effect to several previously announced measures, including the new foreign income tax exemption for temporary residents.

Changes have been made to Australia's Double Taxation Agreements with numerous other countries. Further changes will occur when a recent protocol to the Australian-United States double taxation treaty comes into effect. The protocol implements changes to the withholding on dividends, interest and royalties in respect of residents of the other country who are beneficially entitled to the income. It also contains provisions to avoid double taxation of visiting employees. Note also the existence of exemptions from Australian taxation for certain US Foreign Investment Fund interests in Australia already subject to US taxation provisions.

For further information see the discussion in relation to Australian taxation at AUS ¶35-001.

Finally, it should be noted that significant changes are currently being planned to Australia's international taxation arrangements and to Australian laws relating to and impacting upon Australian taxation of funds flowing into and/or out of the country, in whatever currency. Most of these are foreshadowed in the Commonwealth Treasury's 2002 consultation paper *Review of International Taxation Arrangements*. For further information, visit the ATO's website at *www.ato.gov.au/*.

LABOUR AND NATIONALITY LAWS

Effect of nationality, citizenship and race on
labour laws .... AUS ¶60-001
Basis of nationality law .... AUS ¶60-002
Nature of relationship between employer
and employee .... AUS ¶60-003
Conditions guaranteed to employees .... AUS ¶60-004
Control of wages and hours .... AUS ¶60-005
Settlement of industrial disputes .... AUS ¶60-011
Parameters of legal system of industrial
dispute settlement .... AUS ¶60-012
Customary method of settling industrial
disputes .... AUS ¶60-013
Status and make-up of trade unions .... AUS ¶60-014
Liabilities and privileges of trade unions ... AUS ¶60-015
Institutional links between government,
trade unions and employer organisations .... AUS ¶60-021
Right to strike or lock out .... AUS ¶60-022
Administration of labour law .... AUS ¶60-023
Legislative control of labour law .... AUS ¶60-024
Obligations of purchaser to employees .... AUS ¶60-025
Additional obligations of employers .... AUS ¶60-031
Special application of labour laws
to foreigners .... AUS ¶60-032
Work permits or visas for foreign workers,
executives and management .... AUS ¶60-033
Required balance of race or nationality ...... AUS ¶60-034
International Labour Organisation Conventions .... AUS ¶60-035

AUS ¶60-001 EFFECT OF NATIONALITY, CITIZENSHIP AND RACE ON LABOUR LAWS

Certain regulations must be followed for a person to legally work in Australia. The Department of Immigration and Ethnic Affairs, requires prospective employers of persons not resident in Australia to justify the hiring of such persons in preference to persons permanently resident in Australia.

It is illegal to employ illegal immigrants. In other words, for a person to work legally in Australia, that person must hold a valid temporary residence or permanent residence visa which must include permission to work.

There are equal opportunity laws and anti-discrimination laws aimed at achieving equal treatment of all persons. Racial discrimination in employment is specifically prohibited by federal and State laws.

Note that Australia is governed under a federal system. In the area of labour law, there are seven jurisdictions operating the federal (central) system and six State systems. If the parties (individual employees and/or their unions on the one hand, and employers on the other) prefer to operate under the federal system in preference to the State system(s), they may do so long as the industrial issue involved extends beyond one State. Mandatory minimum requirements imposed by State regulations on all employers within that State must always be met, regardless of whether the federal system is used as a structure for other aspects of the employment arrangement.

AUS ¶60-002 BASIS OF NATIONALITY LAW

Australian citizenship is regulated by the *Australian Citizenship Act 1948* as amended. An individual can acquire Australian citizenship in the following ways:

- By being born in Australia — provided, in the case of persons born on or after 20 August 1986, at least one parent is an Australian citizen or a permanent resident (i.e. a foreign national who has been granted an entry permit by the Department of Immigration and Ethnic Affairs to reside in Australia without a time limit). Where this is not the case, a person can still acquire Australian citizenship if they remain ordinarily resident in Australia continuously for the first 10 years after the date of birth.

- By being born overseas to an Australian citizen parent. Such a person can be registered (before reaching the age of 18 years) as an Australian citizen by descent.

- By being legally adopted in Australia by an Australian citizen. Australian citizens who adopt a child overseas must apply for the child to be granted citizenship.

- By grant of Australian citizenship (formerly called naturalisation). The grant of citizenship must be applied for. It is not possible to acquire Australian citizenship automatically, simply by having lived in Australia for a certain time or by marriage to an Australian citizen. Any foreign national who is a permanent resident of Australia, who has met the residential requirements of the Australian Citizenship Act, is of good character, has a basic knowledge of English, understands the rights and privileges of citizenship, and is likely to reside permanently in or maintain a close association with Australia, may apply.

Loss of nationality

An adult Australian citizen can lose his or her citizenship by:

- acquiring the nationality or citizenship of another country (except in cases where this occurred due to an act of marriage);

- renouncing Australian citizenship; or

- being deprived of Australian citizenship.

A child (i.e. a person under 18 years of age) can lose Australian citizenship if a responsible parent ceases to be an Australian citizen and the other responsible parent is not an Australian citizen at the time — provided this would not result in the child's having no citizenship.

Australian citizenship can be regained in various ways, depending on how the citizenship was lost and whether the person was an adult or a child at the time (see sections 23A and 23AA of the *Australian Citizenship Act 1948*).

Dual nationality

Generally, adult Australian citizens who apply for and acquire the citizenship of another country lose their Australian citizenship unless the other citizenship was acquired *automatically*, e.g. by marriage.

Citizens of another country who become Australian citizens may retain their former nationality if the citizenship laws of that country allow them to do so. They may also acquire a passport of their other nationality under the laws of that country without any effect on their Australian Citizenship.

Further information on citizenship in Australia can be obtained through the Department of Immigration and Multicultural Affairs website at http://www.immi.gov.au/. The number for the national citizenship telephone inquiry line (CTEL) is 131 880 from anywhere in Australia. Overseas, information can be obtained through the nearest Australian diplomatic office.

AUS ¶60-003 NATURE OF RELATIONSHIP BETWEEN EMPLOYER AND EMPLOYEE

The rights and obligations of employers and employees are derived from a contract between them, from legislation and in some cases from an agreement or award approved by the Australian Industrial Relations Tribunal or a state industrial tribunal. The parties may contract verbally or in writing. Some conditions will be implied by law, e.g. the duty of fidelity owed by an employee to act at all times in the interests of the employer. Whether a particular relationship is an employment relationship depends primarily on the degree of control imposed on the employee by the employer. This is to be contrasted with the position of persons carrying on a business in their own right while working under a contract with another person.

It is important to distinguish between independent contractors and employees. The nature of the relationship between the parties to a contract will determine the parameters of the rights and liabilities of the parties to that contract. In particular, independent contractors do not enjoy the same legal entitlements guaranteed to employees by legislation, awards, workplace agreements and contracts of employment in force throughout Australia. As to these matters, see the following sections.

Some of the tests to determine whether an independent contractual relationship exists include:

- a principal does not have the right of control over performance of work by a contractor;

- contractors are not subject to precise hours of work;
- contractors usually provide materials and/or equipment in addition to their labour;
- contractors are responsible for their own tax, WorkCover, superannuation etc.;
- contractors are usually paid by results or on completion of job — not time based (e.g. hourly) wage rates;
- contractors have the right to employ staff and delegate work;
- contractors take responsibility for risks e.g. loss;
- contractors operate as an independent entity; and
- there is a legal intention to be engaged as a contractor.

These tests are not the only ones that may be applied to a particular relationship. A single test should not be viewed as conclusive in proving the type of relationship — the contract needs to be viewed as a whole.

The powers and responsibilities of the State Industrial Relations Commissions relate primarily to employer and employee relationships, but in some States also extend to cover independent contractors in some circumstances for some purposes. In Queensland, for example, recent amendments to the *Queensland Industrial Relations Act 1999* empower that State's Industrial Relations Commission to declare a group of contractors in an industry to be employees if it is appropriate to do so. The Commission must sit as a full bench to make such a declaration and will take into consideration such matters as the relative bargaining power and economic dependency on the contract by the group of workers and whether the contract is designed to, or does avoid the provisions of an industrial instrument. The Commission may also amend or void an individual contract for services if the contract is unfair. See also the discussion in relation to the NSW Industrial Relations Commission (AUS ¶60-004).

AUS ¶60-004 CONDITIONS GUARANTEED TO EMPLOYEES

As mentioned above, seven different systems regulate employment contracts in Australia — the federal system, together with six state systems, each of which must be considered separately.

The federal system is established by the *Workplace Relations Act 1996* (the "WRA"). There are also State laws which, subject to certain exceptions relating to work-safety etc., are over-ridden by any applicable Commonwealth Award, Australian Workplace Agreement or Certified Agreement. The principle object of the WRA is to give primary responsibility for industrial relations and agreement making to employers and employees at the enterprise workplace levels.

The WRA also establishes a system of industrial Awards to provide a safety-net for most categories of employees in relation to fair minimum wages and employment conditions. Minimum rates awards are made by the Australian Industrial Relations Commission (the "Australian IRC"), which also hears and decides upon industrial disputes between employers and employees. The Commission cannot hear industrial disputes where the employees' wages and conditions are governed by a State award or State employment agreement.

To be bound by the relevant federal award, an employer must be either:

- a respondent to one or more awards made by the Australian IRC;
- a member of a federally-registered employer's organisation which automatically binds the employer to the federal award to which that organisation is named as a party; or
- a company that has taken over the business or party of the business of an employer bound by a federal award.

Employers may be 'roped in' to a federal award after being served with a letter of demand, or a Log of Claims or an order being made by the Australian IRC.

The provisions of federal awards were reduced and simplified following the enactment of the 1996 WRA Act. Awards are now limited to 20 "allowable matters" with other matters to be decided at the enterprise or workplace level. Since July 1998, matters outside the 20 allowable matters (except for those matters deemed by the Australian IRC to be necessary to the operation of the award) have not been enforceable.

Australian Workplace Agreements ("AWAs") can be negotiated by employers with individual employees. Employees may also be represented collectively (e.g. by union representation) in AWA negotiations. AWAs must include at least the minimum rates of employment entitlements spelt out in the WRA. AWAs, once agreed to and signed by the employee, are filed with the Employment Advocate, whose role is to assess and approve AWAs, and to oversee and protect the rights of employers and employees bound by AWAs. Even though AWAs can be made with a group of employees, they only apply to those employees who sign them; unlike Certified Agreements which apply to all employees in a group, provided that a majority of those employees have endorsed it.

To have legal effect under the WRA, one of the following must apply when an AWA is filed:

- the employer is a constitutional corporation (i.e. not a partnership, unincorporated association or sole trade);
- the employer and employee are in Victoria or the employee's primary workplace is in Victoria;
- the employer is the Commonwealth; or
- the employee is a maritime worker or flight crew officer and the employment is in connection with interstate/ overseas trade or commerce.

A Certified Agreement is a collective agreement between an employer and a union representing employees; or an employer and a group of employees. The agreement must be approved by a valid majority of the employees whose employment will be subject to it. Agreements are certified by the Australian IRC, and once certified, will generally prevail over any State award that may be in force. AWAs also generally prevail over laws and regulations, even though they are assessed and approved by the Employment Advocate, and not by the Australian IRC.

The main point to note in relation to both AWAs and Certified Agreements is that both are subject to a 'no disadvantage' test before they can be approved and file by the Employment Advocate or certified by the Commission. The 'no disadvantage' test, in essence, provides that an agreement can only be approved or certified if it does not disadvantage employees in relation to their existing terms and conditions of employment under relevant awards and/or any other laws or regulations of the Commonwealth or a State. The no disadvantage test is subject to a number of exceptions relating to trainees, apprentices and the Supported Wage System that exists to assist long-term unemployed re-enter the workforce.

Under the WRA, employers and employees can choose whether they prefer AWAs, a Certified Agreement with a union, a Certified Agreement with employees or to remain under an award. It is also possible to have a combination of these at the same workplace. For further information on how AWAs, Certified Agreements and/ or awards interact with each other when in force at the same workplace, see the Office of the Employment Advocate website at http://www.oea.gov.au/.

Wage rates set out in awards and agreements will vary according to employees' different classifications and between different awards and agreements. Each award or agreement will describe the way wages may be earned. Some awards and agreements have payment for time worked, others have payment by result (piecework). Everywhere in Australia, wage records concerning payments to employees, times of work and other details must be kept by all employers in accordance with the WRA or the relevant State industrial relations act, whichever applies.

Leave

Part VIA of the *Workplace Relations Act 1986* regulates the minimum entitlements of employees. The minimum terms and conditions of employment guaranteed to employees include:

(1) All employees in Australia are guaranteed the right to equal remuneration for work of equal value in accordance with the following international conventions and ILO Recommendations:

    a.   the Equal Remuneration Convention;

    b.   the Convention on the Elimination of all Forms of Discrimination against Women;

    c.   the Convention concerning Discrimination in respect of Employment and Occupation;

    d.   Articles 3 and 7 of the International Covenant on Economic, Social and Cultural Rights;

    e.   The Equal Remuneration Recommendation, 1951, adopted by the ILO 29 June 1951, also known as ILO Recommendation No. 90; and

    f.   The Discrimination (Employment and Occupation) Recommendation, 1958, adopted by the ILO on 25 June 1958, also known as ILO Recommendation No. 111.

The IR Commission may make orders to protect the rights guaranteed by the above international instruments.

(2) Australia is a signatory to the Workers with Family Responsibilities Convention 1981 and the ILO Workers with Family Responsibilities Recommendation on 2 June 1981 (Recommendation No. 165), which are given effect to by Part VIA and Schedule 14 of the WRA. In particular, Schedule 14 gives effect to the Convention and the Recommendation by enabling either parent of a dependent child to obtain leave of absence (parental leave), without relinquishing employment and with rights resulting from employment being safeguarded.

The child's mother is entitled to maternity leave, and her spouse is entitled to paternity leave, totalling up to 52 weeks following the birth of the child. Except for a period of one week at the time of the birth, maternity and paternity leave cannot overlap.

Regulations exist which establish an analogous system of unpaid adoption leave.

Schedule 14 establishes minimum entitlements and so is intended to supplement, and not to override, entitlements under other Commonwealth, State and Territory legislation and awards.

Additional and supplementary leave entitlements, such as long-service leave etc. are also provided for in most industrial awards, AWAs and Certified Agreements.

Termination of employment

Division 3 of Part VIA of the WRA prohibits unlawful termination of, or unfair dismissal from, employment. It ensures that the Australian IRC may make orders to give effect to Articles 12 or 13 of the Termination of Employment Convention 1982 which Australia has ratified. Part VIA establishes minimum entitlements and so is intended to supplement, and not to override, entitlements under other Commonwealth, State and Territory legislation and awards.

It is unlawful to terminate a person's employment for one of the following reasons:

- temporary absence from work because of illness or injury;
- trade union membership or participation in trade union activities outside working hours or, with the employer's consent, during working hours;
- non-membership of a trade union;
- seeking office as, or acting as, a representative of employees;
- filing a complaint, or participation in proceedings, against an employer involving alleged breaches of laws or regulations;
- race, colour, sex, sexual preference, age, physical or mental disability, marital status, family responsibilities, pregnancy, religion, political opinion, national extraction or social origin. It is not unlawful to terminate an employee for one of the reasons listed here if the reason is based on the inherent requirements of the job;
- refusing to negotiate or sign an Australian Workplace Agreement; or
- being absent from work on maternity leave or other parental leave.

Unfair dismissal occurs when an employee's dismissal is harsh, unjust or unreasonable. The WRA does not define "harsh, unjust or unreasonable" but lists factors which the Australian IRC must take into account in determining if it applies, including:

- Whether there was a valid reason for the termination related to the capacity or conduct of the employee or the operational requirements of the business;

- Whether the employee was notified of that reason;

- Whether the employee was given an opportunity to respond to any reason related to their capacity or conduct;

- If the termination related to unsatisfactory work performance, whether the employee had been warned about that unsatisfactory performance before the termination.

All employees in Australia are covered by the unlawful termination provisions of the WRA. Although not all employees are covered by the unfair dismissal provisions of the WRA, most employees are (including all employees in Victoria, the ACT or the NT, and all employees covered by a federal award, Certified Agreement or AWA and employed by a constitutional corporation in WA, Tasmania, South Australia, Queensland or NSW). The following employees are not covered by the unfair dismissal or unlawful termination provisions of the WRA:

- Employees engaged on contract for a specified period or task;

- Employees on probation where the probationary period is determined in advance and is either no more than three months duration, or, if longer, is otherwise reasonable give the nature of the employment;

- Casuals, unless engaged regularly for at least 12 months, and with reasonable expectation of continuing employment;

- Trainees under National Training Wage awards or approved traineeship agreement where the employment is limited to the duration of the traineeship; and

- Employees not covered by a federal award or agreement and earning more than a specified total remuneration (around AUS$70,000) per year. The amount specified is indexed and varied on 1 July each year.

The WRA sets out requirements for employers to give a minimum period of notice of termination to employees, or pay in lieu. Where employees are employed under a federal award or agreement, longer notice periods than those specified in the WRA may be required by the award or agreement. Summary dismissal, that is, dismissal without notice is a very serious step for an employer to take, and is only justified in cases of misconduct that is so serious that it demonstrates the employee does not intend to fulfil their part of the contract.

In addition to notice or pay in lieu, many awards contain provisions requiring employers to pay severance pay for termination of employment in redundancy situations. Severance pay compensates employees for the loss of their jobs.

An employee may lodge a claim at the Australian IRC in any case of unfair dismissal. A unilateral termination of employment by an employer must not be harsh, unjust or unreasonable. In general, an employer must not terminate an employee's employment without giving the required period of notice or paying the required amount of compensation instead of notice.

For further information, see the Department of Employment, Workplace Relations and Small Business website at http://www.dewrsb.gov.au/ and the government's Wagenet information website at http://www.wagenet.gov.au/. The Australian IRC can provide information on the procedural aspects of lodging or responding to a claim for unfair dismissal, including filing fees and the possibility of cost orders.

Northern Territory and the Australian Capital Territory

In the Northern Territory ("NT") and the Australian Capital Territory ("ACT") employers and employees are covered by the federal workplace relations system. A federal award will apply if the employer is engaged in, or in connection with, the particular industry identified by the NT or ACT federal award.

In the ACT and NT "Common Rule" awards can apply to all employees in a particular industry whether or not their employers are named in the award.

For further information about Public Holidays, Long Service Leave, Annual Leave and Parental Leave in the NT, refer to the applicable federal award first. If the award does not provide for these conditions or one or more employees is not covered by an award, see the NT Wageline website at http://www.wagenet.gov.au/states/NT/ or contact the NT Office of Commissioner for Public Employment on phone (08) 8999 4243.

Victoria

In 1993, the Victorian State Government set aside all State Awards — these were replaced with a set of minimum terms and conditions of employment. Then in 1997, the Victorian government referred most of its powers in relation to employment and industrial relations to the Commonwealth. As a result, the minimum terms and conditions of employment for employees falling within the Victorian industrial relations system are now contained in Schedule 1A of the WRA. These minima must be observed for all employees in Victoria not covered by a federal award or agreement. They are:

- Four weeks paid annual leave for each year worked;
- One week's sick leave for every year of service;
- Minimum wage rates (as contained in the 18 Industry Sectors) are updated annually by the Australian Industrial Relations Commission;
- Maternity, paternity and adoption leave entitlements; and
- Entitlement to a notice period for lawful termination of employment, or compensation instead of notice.

After the referral of powers in 1997, the Victorian Government retained responsibility for a number of employment matters including:

- Workers' compensation and employers' obligation to take out WorkCover Insurance;
- Occupational health and safety;
- Apprenticeship arrangements;
- Long service leave;
- Public holidays;
- Equal employment opportunity; and
- Child employment.

For more information on Industrial Relations in Victoria refer to the government website (http://www.irv.vic.gov.au) and/or contact Industrial Relations Victoria on (03) 9651 5560.

For Awards and Agreements, contact the Department of Employment, Workplace Relations and Small Business on (02) 9240 1010, or Job Watch on (03) 9662 1933 or contact the relevant Trade Union.

For information relating to apprenticeships and traineeships in Victoria, see http://www. pete.vic.gov.au/.

New South Wales

Under the NSW Industrial Relations Act of 1996 (the "IRA"), most employees' minimum entitlements have been set by an independent tribunal called the NSW Industrial Relations Commission (the "NSWIRC"). The NSWIRC approves awards and enterprise agreements dealing with such things as rates of pay, hours of work and minimum leave entitlements.

Recent amendments to the IRA have also ensured that employees covered by federal awards but not able to bring unfair dismissal claims before the Australian IRC due to constitutional constraints can now bring claims before the NSWIRC. A further amendment protects the rights of injured workers by ensuring that they cannot be dismissed during the period that the worker concerned is entitled to accident pay under an applicable federal or State industrial instrument.

When the NSWIRC is called on to approve a non-union enterprise agreement between an employer and a single employee, the employee's union body can also become a party to the enterprise agreement so long as (i) the employee is a union member and has requested the union to lodge a notification with the NSWIRC and (ii) prior to the approval of the proposed agreement, the union notifies the IRC that it wishes to become a party to the agreement.

The parties to a contract of employment cannot agree on or contract outside wage rates or conditions of employment less favourable to those set out in the applicable award or enterprise agreement.

As noted above, it can often be important to distinguish between independent contractors and employees. Independent contractors are not covered by awards or enterprise agreements, and are not guaranteed the entitlements received by employees under NSW law. Similar to the situation in other States, the NSWIRC can review and vary unfair contracts of employment. In NSW, the Industrial Relations Act 1996 also allows the NSWIRC in Court Session to review contracts for services rendered by independent contractors. The Commission may find that a contract for the performance of work by an independent contractor in any industry is an "unfair contract" where:

- it is unfair, harsh or unconscionable;

- unfair tactics or pressure were exerted on the parties to get their agreement;

- it is against the public interest;

- the total remuneration provided is less than that received by an employee performing the work; and

- it avoids, or is designed to avoid, the provisions of an award or enterprise agreement.

See also AUS ¶60-003.

Any principal contractor who engages the services of a sub-contractor in NSW should be aware of section 127 of the IRA. This section ensures that any principal contractor who enters into a contract with a sub-contractor is liable for the remuneration (wages and other payments) of the sub-contractor's employees unless and until the principal contractor receives a written statement from the sub-contractor that all wages for the period have been paid.

As elsewhere in Australia, leave entitlements in NSW depend on whether the employee is employed on a permanent, part time, temporary or casual basis. As a guide, most employees (except some casual employees) are entitled to:

- Under the NSW Annual Holidays Act 1944, four weeks paid annual holidays each year. Most workers are also entitled under awards and agreements to receive an annual leave salary loading when taking annual leave.

- Under the NSW IRA, parental leave, which is usually 12 months unpaid leave available when an employee becomes a parent or adopts a child. Recent amendments to the IRA have intended this entitlement to cover not only full and part-time employees, but also to casual employees who have worked on a systematic and regular basis for an employer for more than two years.

- Under the NSW Long Service Leave Act 1955, full time, part-time and casual workers are entitled to two months paid long service leave after 10 years service with one employer and one month paid leave for each additional five years service.

Usually as a provision of an award or agreement, five days sick leave each year, which can be used when the employee is too ill to work or when it is necessary to look after ill family members.

Personal carers' leave and bereavement leave are available to all employees covered by NSW awards. There are a few exceptions and some awards have slightly different entitlements. Many enterprise agreements also provide for these types of leave.

As in other States, there exists in NSW anti-discrimination legislation (the Anti-Discrimination Act 1977) which prohibits discrimination in employment (including promotion) on the basis of gender, race, religion etc. The Anti-Discrimination Board of NSW has powers to enforce rights protected under the Act and can make orders for payment of compensation and/ or remedial action in cases where those rights are breached.

Occupational Health and Safety standards and their enforcement are dealt with in the Occupational Health and Safety Act 1983 as amended by the Occupational Health and Safety Amendment Act 1997.

For further information, see the NSW Department of Industrial Relations website at http://www.dir.gov.nsw.au/.

Queensland

As elsewhere in Australia, employment relations in Queensland can be covered by either the federal or State workplace relations system. There are two types of awards in the Queensland State system:

- industry awards (covering most employees in a particular industry e.g. The Building and Construction Industry Award);
- awards covering people employed to do a specific type of work (profession or trade award e.g. Dental Assistants award).

The Queensland State Department of Industrial Relations (DIR) is responsible for State awards information. See the DIR website at http://www.wageline.qld.gov.au/.

The *Queensland Industrial Relations Act 1999* (the "Queensland IRA") includes provisions about dismissal that give all employees in Queensland the right to make an application to either the Queensland Industrial Relations Commission or the Australian IRC if they feel they have been unfairly dismissed. A dismissal is unfair if it is harsh, unjust or unreasonable (the procedure was unfair) or occurs for an invalid reason. The Commission may order reinstatement of the employee or compensation in the event of unfair dismissal.

The Queensland IRA does not deal with the issue of redundancy of employees. However almost all awards and agreements make provision for certain redundancy entitlements where the business employs 15 or more people. The Queensland IRA does set down the responsibilities of an employer if they decide to dismiss 15 or more employees for an economic, technological or structural reason when the employees have no redundancy entitlements under an award or agreement. Under these circumstances, the employees or a union, on their behalf, may apply to the Queensland Industrial Relations Commission for an order in relation to severance pay against their employer.

The Queensland IRA has been drafted to protect the entitlements of all employees to the following types of leave:

- Long service leave for all full-time, part-time and casual employees;
- Annual leave but not for casuals or pieceworkers;
- Sick leave but not for casuals or pieceworkers;

AUS ¶60-004   © 2002 CCH Asia Pte Limited

- Parental leave for full-time, part-time and casual employees but not for seasonal employees or pieceworkers;
- Carers leave or special responsibility leave; and
- Bereavement leave but not for casual employees or pieceworkers.

In relation to independent contractors in Queensland, see AUS ¶60-003 above.

South Australia

The principal Act in South Australia is the *Industrial and Employee Relations Act 1994* (the "IER Act"). Part 2 of the IER Act establishes the Industrial Relations Court. The Industrial Relations Court has powers to interpret any award or enterprise agreement, and can also determine monetary claims and/ or provide injunctive relief in relation to any claim arising out of:

(i)   the IER Act, any award, enterprise agreement or contract of employment; or

(ii) the Commonwealth WRA or an award or agreement under the *Commonwealth Act*.

Part 3 of the IER Act establishes the Industrial Relations Commission of South Australia (the "SAIRC"). The SAIRC approves enterprise agreements and makes awards regulating remuneration and other industrial matters. The SAIRC also has jurisdiction to determine industrial matters and to resolve industrial disputes arising in South Australia. The Industrial Registrar is responsible for the smooth running of the operations of the Industrial Relations Court and the SAIRC.

When industrial relations matters are referred to the SAIRC by the Minister responsible, the Commission's advisory powers come into play, enabling it to inquire into and make recommendations on the matter or matters referred. Generally, however, the Minister relies on the Industrial Relations Advisory Committee (established by Part 5 of the IER Act) for assistance in formulating industrial relations policy and legislation.

South Australia also has an Employee Ombudsman (established by Part 6 of the IER Act) to advise and assist employees in relation to their rights under awards and enterprise agreements. The Ombudsman also advises and assists home-based workers not covered by awards or enterprise agreements.

Minimum standards and conditions of employment are set out in Schedules to the IER Act as follows:

- Minimum rates of remuneration must be in accordance with the employee's relevant award and award classification. Where there is no applicable award for a particular class of employees, the Full bench of the SAIRC can and does fix minimum rates for that class. (Schedule 2);
- Minimum standards for sick leave (approx. 10 days accruing for each year of continuous service) are set out in Schedule 3;
- Minimum standards for annual leave are set at four weeks' annual for each completed year of continuous service (Schedule 4);
- Minimum standards for parental leave are in accordance with those established by the Commonwealth WRA and are found in Schedule.

The IER Act also enforces for South Australia the ILO Convention Concerning Equal Remuneration for Men and Women Workers for Work of Equal Value 1951 and the ILO Convention Concerning Termination of Employment at the Initiative of the Employer 1982.

Other important legislation administered by Workplace Services South Australia include the *Long Service Leave Act 1987*; the *Occupational Health Safety and Welfare Act 1986* and the *Employment Agents Registration Act 1993*, each of which must be considered together with their relevant implementing regulations. The South Australian Parliament is currently considering proposed new legislation, the *Industrial and Employee Relations (Workplace Relations) Amendment Bill 1999*, which would repeal the *Long Service Leave Act* and amend the IER Act.

The proposed amendments would establish a system for the negotiation and supervision of Individual and Collective Workplace Agreements. The Employee Ombudsman and the Unions are given powers to represent the interests of employees in negotiating workplace agreements. Workplace Agreements must contain provisions as to conditions of employment that conform with the minimum requirements in force under the Act.

The amended Act would provide for minimum conditions of employment relating to award rates of pay; annual leave; sick leave; bereavement leave where the relevant award provides for bereavement leave; long service leave. Collective workplace agreements must include procedures for preventing and settling industrial disputes between the parties to the agreement. All workplace agreements have to be approved by the Workplace Relations Commission or a newly established Workplace Agreement Authority if the proposed amendments are passed.

For further information relating to industrial relations in SA refer to the Workplace Services Employment Relations Information Website at http://www.eric.sa.gov.au/.

Tasmania

In Tasmania, employees not protected by a federal award or agreement may have their entitlements set out in an award or agreement authorised by the Tasmanian Industrial Commission. Where there is no federal or Tasmania award to cover an employer's industry, or where certain employee classifications do not appear in the businesses award, there will usually still be industrial relations wages and conditions applying to the employees. The *Tasmanian Industrial Relations Act 1984* and the *Industrial Relations Regulations 1993* provide for a number of classifications to have general coverage.

Under virtually all awards, employees in Tasmania, as elsewhere are entitled to the following usual entitlements:

- four weeks paid annual leave for every 12 months continuous employment completed, or less on a pro-rata basis. Some awards specify additional leave for shift-workers. The vast majority of awards also contain annual leave loading provisions.

- long service leave in accordance with the *Tasmanian Long Service Leave Act 1976* (available at http://www.wsa.tas.gov.au/.)

In Tasmania, as elsewhere, Workplace inspectors exist to ensure that the standards and conditions spelt out in federal or State awards and agreements as well as those spelt out in the *Tasmanian Workplace Health and Safety Act 1995* and the regulations issued under that Act. Employees affected by workplace injuries can seek relief under the *Workers Rehabilitation and Compensation Act 1988*.

The *Tasmanian Industrial Relations Act 1984* empowers the Minister responsible to apply for hearings in respect of alleged breaches of awards, registered industrial agreements and/ or enterprise agreements.

For further information contact the Tasmanian Workplace Standards Authority website at http://www.www.wsa.tas.gov.au/.

Western Australia

Wages and conditions of employment in Western Australia are governed by awards, agreements and various pieces of employment legislation.

Employment legislation in Western Australia (WA) includes the *Industrial Relations Act 1979*; the *Minimum Conditions of Employment Act 1993*; the *Equal Opportunity Act 1984*; the *Occupational Safety and Health Act 1984* and the *Long Service Leave Act 1958*.

The negotiation and supervision of workplace agreements is governed by the *Workplace Agreements Act 1993*. The minimum conditions of employment extend to and bind all employees and employers and are taken to be implied in any workplace agreement; in an award or in any contract of employment that is not governed by a workplace agreement or an award. A provision in, or condition of, a workplace agreement, an award or a contract of employment that is less favourable to the employee than a minimum condition of employment has no effect.

The *Minimum Conditions of Employment Act 1993* sets out minimum conditions on issues such as rates of pay, sick leave, annual leave, bereavement leave, public holidays, parental leave and job search leave in the case of redundancy. Employees not covered by the *Minimum Conditions of Employment Act* include apprentices and trainees receiving a wage rate provided for by a relevant award; persons paid wholly by commission or percentage rewards and volunteers.

Other statutory obligations of employers in WA include obligations relating to long service leave under the *Long Service Leave Act 1958*; obligations relating to the keeping of employment records, and obligations relating to Certificates of Separation which are required by the Department of Social Security when an employee finishes work with a company.

For further information relating to employment in WA refer to the Department of Productivity and Labour Relations website at http://www.doplar.wa.gov.au/.

Retirement

The Federal Government's *Superannuation Guarantee Levy Act* requires all employers (including companies) to make superannuation contributions to an approved fund for most employees with gross earnings of more than AUS$450 per month. Employees may also make voluntary contributions to a superannuation fund chosen by the employer.

AUS ¶60-005 CONTROL OF WAGES AND HOURS

Wages

Wage levels are determined by the State and Federal tribunals or negotiated between the parties at the enterprise/workplace level. From time to time, the Australian IRC reviews wage levels and may order a general increase in award minimum rates of pay for workers who have not benefited by a workplace agreement.

Working hours

Maximum ordinary weekly hours (usually 38 or 40) are prescribed by State legislation or Federal rulings. Penalty payments are prescribed for work in excess of the normal hours, but adjustment to the hours usually worked can be negotiated at the workplace or enterprise level. Variations to the standard may be incorporated in an agreement and approved by the State or Federal tribunal.

AUS ¶60-011 SETTLEMENT OF INDUSTRIAL DISPUTES

Most awards have dispute settlement procedures and it is a requirement that agreements have such procedures before they are approved. If these procedures are unsuccessful, the parties are obliged to refer the dispute to an industrial tribunal.

AUS ¶60-012 PARAMETERS OF LEGAL SYSTEM OF INDUSTRIAL DISPUTE SETTLEMENT

The Federal system is dominant and until recent years, the systems have been based on awards made following compulsory conciliation or arbitration. In 1996 Federal reforms gave priority to encouraging and facilitating workplace bargaining and the State systems are undergoing similar reforms. In the Federal system, although the emphasis is on workplace bargaining, awards have been retained to provide a "safety net" and award wages and conditions must be observed by employers where no enterprise agreement has been made. The Australian Industrial Relations Commission ("AIRC") is the Federal tribunal vested with responsibility for award-making and for facilitating enterprise bargaining. When a workplace agreement has been certified or approved, it takes effect as an award and prevails over the terms of any other award.

State and Federal tribunals proceed by way of conciliation, and if necessary, arbitration. The general law courts are rarely involved.

AUS ¶60-013 CUSTOMARY METHOD OF SETTLING INDUSTRIAL DISPUTES

The majority of industrial disputes are settled on site by unions and management. Strikes or other forms of industrial action are sometimes used to bring matters in dispute to a head. Under the Federal reforms of 1996, the AIRC is reluctant to intervene in workplace bargaining, except to insist on "good faith" bargaining practices.

Industrial action can be and is sometimes taken by employees or an employer in the process of negotiating an AWA. If the purpose of the industrial action is to compel or induce the other party to accept particular terms and conditions as part of an AWA, the party taking such action has limited legal immunity. Such immunity from suit is only conferred, however, if three working days' notice of the intention to take AWA industrial action is given to the other party.

Where industrial action (strike, 'go slow' or lock-out) is taken to compel the other party to accept or comply with particular terms or conditions of employment, but is not connected to the making of an AWA, notice to the other party is not required to obtain a degree of legal immunity.

The legal immunity conferred by these provisions of the WRA is very limited — there is no immunity from actions for defamation; and the employer may not dismiss, unfairly withhold wages due to or lockout an employee simply because the employee is proposing to take, is taking, or has taken AWA industrial action.

In the case of lockout by the employer, or strike action by one or more employees, the employer need not, indeed should not, pay the employee(s) for the period of the industrial action.

In the case of industrial disputes relating to a threatened, impending or probable boycott by an employee organisation, either party may notify the AIRC of the dispute. The AIRC is empowered to, and in most cases must, first attempt to settle the dispute by Conciliation.

AUS ¶60-014 STATUS AND MAKE-UP OF TRADE UNIONS

Trade unions (organisations of employees) are recognised by law as having an important role in employer-employee relations. The Australian Council of Trade Unions ("ACTU") is the peak council of unions. Trade unions may be registered with the Australian Industrial Registry, and registered unions are called simply 'organisations' throughout the Act. Organisations must have democratic rules setting out clearly the requirements for membership, procedures for election of officers by secret postal ballot etc.

AUS ¶60-015 LIABILITIES AND PRIVILEGES OF TRADE UNIONS

Employee (and employer) organisations registered under the *Workplace Relations Act 1996* are recognised as having a significant role to play in representing their members in negotiations with employers/employees and before the Australian Industrial Relations Commission and the State industrial tribunals. Unions and officials can be subject to action in the civil law courts, subject to certain immunities.

The WRA contains strong provisions to protect freedom of association, so that employees cannot be required to join a Union, nor can employers discriminate against employees on the basis of union membership. Unions (and employer organisations) registered under the WRA are required to accept a set of rules of association designed to ensure that they are "representative of and accountable to their members".

AUS ¶60-021 INSTITUTIONAL LINKS BETWEEN GOVERNMENT, TRADE UNIONS AND EMPLOYER ORGANISATIONS

One of the principal objects of the WRA is to ensure "that the primary responsibility for determining matters affecting the relationship between employers and employees rests with the employer and employees at the workplace or enterprise level". This is often seen as a downgrading of the previously significant role played by unions in the federal Labour Consultative Council, in negotiations over the federal tripartite accord (reached by the Australian Council of Trade Unions ("ACTU"), employer organisations and the government) and in the reconciliation of industrial relations issues and disputes generally.

The role played by unions under the WRA since 1996 is still significant, but it is also carefully defined and, in many ways, curbed. Employee and employer organisations can be registered by the Australian Industrial Registry. The WRA also establishes an Employment Advocate to, *inter alia*, provide advice to employees and employers about their rights and obligations, to investigate alleged breaches of an AWA or the WRA and, in some circumstances, to represent a party in proceedings under the WRA.

The AIRC is normally only empowered to make minimum rates awards relating to a defined number (around 20) of allowable award matters, and to resolve industrial disputes relating to such award matters, including, in relevant circumstances, exceptional matters ancillary to an award dispute. Industrial disputes can be referred to the AIRC for conciliation by an employer, a registered organisation, the Registrar or the Minister. Conciliation is compulsory before a dispute can proceed to more formal arbitration.

AUS ¶60-022 RIGHT TO STRIKE OR LOCK OUT

The WRA recognises the right to strike by employees and the lock-out by employers. To obtain a defined and limited degree of immunity from civil action, written notices must precede a strike or lock-out relating to an AWA. As with many other features of the WRA, these rights are based on conventions of the International Labour Organisation.

AUS ¶60-023 ADMINISTRATION OF LABOUR LAW

Federal labour law is based on various parts of the Australian constitution and on conventions of the International Labour Organisation. Responsibility for administering the legislation is held by a Federal Minister for Industrial Relations (who heads the Department of Employment, Workplace Relations and Small Business), and responsibility for giving effect to the law lies mainly with the AIRC. Many aspects of Federal labour law are reproduced in State legislation and some States have gone further than the Commonwealth in deregulating the labour market. Each State has a Minister responsible for labour law and each State has an industrial tribunal.

AUS ¶60-024 LEGISLATIVE CONTROL OF LABOUR LAW

A recent High Court decision has confirmed the constitutional validity of the *Workplace Relations Act*. The actual operation of labour law at the federal level is determined to a large degree by AIRC rulings. At the State levels, legislation plays a bigger role, but the State industrial tribunals still have a major say.

AUS ¶60-025 OBLIGATIONS OF PURCHASER TO EMPLOYEES

A purchaser of a business may assume certain liabilities from the vendor in respect of the employees: these can include annual leave, long service leave, maternity leave, redundancy (severance pay) entitlements and superannuation. In some cases, accrued entitlements can be transmitted to the purchaser by virtue of legislation or the provisions of industrial awards.

AUS ¶60-031 ADDITIONAL OBLIGATIONS OF EMPLOYERS

In each of the States, there is legislation providing for compulsory workers' compensation insurance to be taken out by employers. Workplace health and safety is also the primary responsibility of the employer, with State legislation imposing strict obligations on employers.

AUS ¶60-032 SPECIAL APPLICATION OF LABOUR LAWS TO FOREIGNERS

Foreign investors and foreign-based companies employing labour in Australia must comply with Australian law in the same way as Australian companies.

AUS ¶60-033 WORK PERMITS OR VISAS FOR FOREIGN WORKERS, EXECUTIVES AND MANAGEMENT

The Australian Department of Immigration and Multicultural Affairs requires employers in Australia to justify the employment of foreign executives and specialists (see AUS ¶60-001). Australian immigration laws require an Australian employer to sponsor a non-resident employee who it wishes to employ in Australia and to demonstrate that the employee will be of economic benefit to Australia. There are four categories for employer sponsored migration to Australia:

(1) Employer Nomination Scheme (ENS);

(2) Regional Sponsored Migration Scheme (RSMS);

(3) Labour Agreements (LA); and

(4) Regional Headquarters Agreements (RHQ).

These programmes are employer driven. The first three enable Australian employers to recruit highly skilled workers, either from overseas or from people temporarily in Australia, where an employer has been unable to fill their recruitment needs from the Australian labour market or through their own training efforts.

The fourth programme, RHQ, enables employers (who have an approved RHQ), to transfer 'key' employees of their company group who are essential in establishing their Regional Headquarters in Australia.

For all categories except RHQ, the employer must show they have been unable to find an Australian citizen or resident who is suitable for the appointment.

The ENS enables Australian employers to recruit, on a permanent basis, highly skilled staff from overseas or temporary residents currently in Australia, where they have been unable to fill a vacancy from within the Australian labour market or through their own training programmes. The ENS has two distinct stages:

(1) nomination by an employer; and

(2) the nominee's application for a visa.

The RSMS is designed to help employers in regional or low population growth areas of Australia who are unable to fill skilled vacancies from the local labour market.

Any employer can participate in the scheme as long as they are operating their business in an area covered under the RSMS. The RSMS process consists of three distinct stages:

(1) certification of the nominee;

(2) nomination by the employer; and

(3) nominee's application for a visa.

A Labour Agreement is a formal arrangement negotiated between the Australian government and an employer or industrial association. Other interested parties, such as a union, may also be a party to a Labour Agreement. Labour Agreements provide for both permanent and temporary entry to Australia. They are designed to enable employers to recruit a specified number of workers from overseas in response to identified or emerging labour market (or skill) shortages in the Australian labour market. Labour Agreements are aimed at ensuring that overseas recruitment supports the longer term improvement of employment and training opportunities for Australians. Accordingly, employers or industrial associations are required to make commitments to the employment, education, training and career opportunities of Australians as part of the agreement. After the agreement has been negotiated, the process consists of two stages:

(1) nomination by the employer; and

(2) nominee's application for a visa.

Regional Headquarters Agreements provide streamlined immigration arrangements to organisations that the Minister for Industry, Science and Resources has determined as being a company managing functions that support an international operation. RHQs provide for both permanent and temporary entry to Australia. Although RHQ Agreements are defined as 'Labour Agreements', the purpose for which RHQ Agreements are established is different from standard Labour Agreements in that:

•   visas granted under RHQ agreements are to enable the transfer of key expatriate executive and specialist personnel of the company group; and

•   visa applications to which an RHQ agreement applies receive priority over applications made under standard Labour Agreements.

After an RHQ Agreement has been negotiated, the process consists of three stages:

(1) approval of the RHQ for streamlined immigration processing;

(2) lodgment of the endorsement form; and

(3) nominee's application for a visa.

For further information, and to access a copy of the *Employer Sponsored Migration* booklet as well as copies of relevant application forms, see the Department of Immigration and Multicultural Affairs website at http://www.immi.gov.au/.

AUS ¶60-034 REQUIRED BALANCE OF RACE OR NATIONALITY

There are no laws on racial mix, etc. Equal opportunity laws guarantee equal treatment of employees without discrimination based on race, gender, etc. There is federal and some state law on affirmative action designed to ensure that demonstrable systems are in place in business enterprises in an attempt to make certain that women are actually treated equally.

AUS ¶60-035 INTERNATIONAL LABOUR ORGANISATION CONVENTIONS

Australia has been active over the past two decades in ratifying ILO conventions. Labour legislation giving effect to conventions and other international treaties is an important part of the 1994-1996 Federal reforms.

Intellectual Property

International agreements .... AUS ¶65-001

Domestic legislation .... AUS ¶65-002

Copyright .... AUS ¶65-003

Trademarks .... AUS ¶65-004

Patents .... AUS ¶65-005

Industrial designs .... AUS ¶65-011

Trade secrets .... AUS ¶65-012

Circuit layouts .... AUS ¶65-013

Plant varieties .... AUS ¶65-014

Unfair competition .... AUS ¶65-015

Registration procedures .... AUS ¶65-021

Transfers and licensing agreements .... AUS ¶65-022

Compulsory licenses .... AUS ¶65-023

Table of fees .... AUS ¶65-024

Disadvantages for non-residents .... AUS ¶65-025

Enforcement .... AUS ¶65-031

AUS ¶65-001   INTERNATIONAL AGREEMENTS

Australia has signed a number of international treaties relating to intellectual property, including:

Copyright
- The Berne Convention for the Protection of Literary and Artistic Works (1886).
- Universal Copyright Convention (UCC, in force 1955).

Industrial designs
- The Paris Convention for the Protection of Industrial Property (1883). (The latest Act by which Australia is bound is the revision in Stockholm in 1967.)

Integrated circuits
- WIPO Treaty on Protection of Intellectual Property in respect of Integrated Circuits (declared in April 1989).

Patents

- The Paris Convention for the Protection of Industrial Property (1883). (The latest Act by which Australia is bound is the revision in Stockholm in 1967.)
- The Patent Cooperation Treaty (''PCT'').
- The Budapest Treaty on the International Recognition of the Deposit of Microorganisms for the Purposes of Patent Procedure.

Performers' protection

- The International Convention for the Protection of Performers, Producers of Phonograms and Broadcasting Organisations of 1961 (in 1992).

Trademarks

- The Paris Convention for the Protection of Industrial Property of 1883.
- The Nice Agreement Concerning the International Classification of Goods and Services for the Purposes of the Registration of Marks (1961).

Miscellaneous

Australia is a signatory to the Agreement on Trade-Related Aspects of Intellectual Property Rights (''TRIPs''), including Trade in Counterfeit Goods which was signed in 1995 as a part of the conclusion of the Uruguay round of GATT negotiations. TRIPs imposes wide ranging obligations on its members with respect to intellectual property laws.

Domestic legislation

Implementation of these treaty obligations is brought about by various sections of the Australian intellectual property legislation set out at AUS ¶65-002. This is Commonwealth legislation passed by the Australian Commonwealth Parliament mostly under the authority of Constitution sec. 51(xviii) (intellectual property) and 51(xxix) (external affairs) (AUS ¶20-002).

AUS ¶65-002   DOMESTIC LEGISLATION

The law relating to intellectual property is found in the *Copyright Act 1968* (Cth), the *Circuit Layouts Act 1989* (Cth), the *Designs Act 2003* (Cth), the *Patents Act 1990* (Cth), the *Plant Breeder's Rights Act 1994* (Cth) and the *Trade Marks Act 1995* (Cth).

Some intellectual property disputes are dealt with under the *Trade Practices Act 1974* and the *Fair Trading Act* of each Australian State and Territory if they involve misleading or deceptive conduct or false representations.

See generally the resources at IP Australia's homepage at www.ipaustralia.gov.au.

AUS ¶65-003   COPYRIGHT

The *Copyright Act 1968* (Cth) provides automatic protection for original works and other types of subject matter.

AUS ¶65-002

The rights given to a copyright owner depend on the nature of the work or subject matter in question.

The copyright owner of an original literary, dramatic or musical work has exclusive rights to reproduce the work in a material form; to publish the work; to perform the work in public; to communicate the work to the public; to make an adaptation of the work, and to do the above acts to an adaptation of the work (sec. 31(1)(a)).

The copyright owner of an original artistic work has exclusive rights to reproduce the work in a material form; to publish the work and to communicate the work to the public (sec. 31(1)(b)).

The copyright owner of a literary work (other than a computer program) or a musical or dramatic work has the exclusive right to enter into a commercial rental arrangement in respect of the work reproduced in a sound recording (sec. 31(1)(c)).

The copyright owner in a computer program has the exclusive right to enter into a commercial rental arrangement in respect of the program (sec. 31(1)(d)).

The copyright owner in a sound recording has exclusive rights to make a copy of the recording; to cause the recording to be heard in public; to broadcast the recording and to enter a commercial rental arrangement in respect of the recording (sec. 85).

The copyright owner in a cinematograph film has exclusive rights to make a copy of the film; to cause the film, in so far as it consists of visual images, to be seen in public, or, in so far as it consists of sounds, to be heard in public and to communicate the film (sec. 86).

The copyright owner in a television broadcast has exclusive rights, in so far as the broadcast consists of visual images, to make a cinematograph film of the broadcast, or a copy of such a film; in so far as the broadcast consists of sounds, to make a sound recording of the broadcast, or a copy of such a sound recording; and to re-broadcast the broadcast (sec. 87).

The copyright owner in a sound broadcast has exclusive rights to make a sound recording of the broadcast; and to re-broadcast the broadcast (sec. 87).

The copyright owner of a published edition of a literary, dramatic, musical or artistic work has the exclusive right to make a facsimile copy of the edition (sec. 88).

The term of copyright depends on the nature of the work or subject matter in question, and whether it has been published or not.

Duration of copyright

Generally, copyright exists ("subsists") for 50 years after the death of the author. For literary, dramatic or musical work, this is not the case if the work has not been published, publicly performed, broadcast, or had records of it offered or exposed for sale to the public, during the author's lifetime — in this case, the copyright subsists until the end of 50 years after one of those events has happened.

The copyright in a photograph subsists until the end of 50 years after the expiration of the year in which it is first published.

Copyright in a sound recording subsists until the end of 50 years after the expiration of the year in which the recording is first published.

Copyright in an unpublished sound recording subsists indefinitely.

The duration of the copyright in a cinematograph film depends on how the copyright in it arises. If the copyright in the film arises because the maker was a qualified person, or because it was made in Australia, copyright continues to subsist until the film is published, and for a further 50 years after the end of the year of first publication. If the copyright in the film arises only because it was first published in Australia, copyright subsists for 50 years after the end of the year of first publication.

Copyright in a broadcast subsists until the expiration of 50 years after the end of the year in which the broadcast was made. The duration is not extended, however, because of a re-broadcast.

Copyright in a published edition of a work subsists until the expiration of 25 years after the end of the year in which the edition was first published.

Under the current provisions of the *Copyright Act 1968*, the protection period of a performance commences on the day of the performance and continues for 20 calendar years after the performance is given. However, as a result of Australia's obligations under TRIPs, from 1995, the protection period of a performance in relation to unauthorised sound recordings has been extended to 50 years after the calendar year in which the performance was given. The protection period for other unauthorised uses remains at 20 years.

See further the Australian Copyright Council Online Information Centre at www.copyright.org.au.

Character merchandising

There is no single statutory framework for the protection of characters. Protection may be effected by legal action for misleading or deceptive conduct and/or false or misleading representations in breach of the *Trade Practices Act* or State and Territory *Fair Trading Act* equivalents, for passing off and under the *Copyright Act*.

Characters can be protected either by action in passing off, under the *Copyright Act 1968* and under the misleading or deceptive conduct and/or the false representation provisions of the *Trade Practices Act 1974* (sec. 52) or State and Territory *Fair Trading Act* equivalents.

Computer software

The *Copyright Act 1968* provides protection for computer software as computer programs are included in the definition of a "literary work" in the Act.

The period of protection for the copyright in a computer program is the same as that for any other literary work.

The copyright owner in a computer program is given the same rights as a copyright owner in other literary works under the *Copyright Act 1968*.

As a matter of Internet law, linking from one website to another website is likely to be permissable under an implied copyright licence, provided the link does not bypass the front (home) page of the other site.

Performers' protection

The *Copyright Act 1968* provides automatic protection for live performances of a dramatic, musical or literary work or part thereof (including improvisations) and performances of a dance, circus act, variety act or any similar presentation or show. Delivery of news items, performances of a sporting activity, participation in a performance as a member of the audience and certain educational performances are excluded from the performers' protection provisions of the *Copyright Act 1968*.

A performer has the right to bring an action for unauthorised use of his or her performance.

Although the performers' protection provisions are contained in the *Copyright Act 1968*, the performer does not have any proprietary right in the nature of copyright.

AUS ¶65-004   TRADEMARKS

A trademark indicates the origin of goods — to show a connection between the goods and the owner of the trademark. Trademark registration is available to inventors, designers and owners of brand names for use in the course of trade.

The *Trade Marks Act 1995* (Cth) provides a system of registration for trademarks which satisfy requirements of distinctiveness (present or future) or other requirements. The Act expands the definition of a trademark to include the shape, colour, sound, scent and packaging.

The *Trade Marks Act* gives the proprietor of a registered trademark the exclusive right to the exclusive use of the trademark in relation to the goods or services in respect of which the trademark is registered and to obtain relief in respect of infringement of the trademark. Trademark infringement can also be litigated under the *Trade Practices Act 1974* (Cth) as "misleading or deceptive conduct" under sec. 52 with the remedies of the Act available.

At common law, a proprietor can sue for the tort of passing off for trademark infringement where a person has made a misrepresentation to customers calculated to injure the business or goodwill of the proprietor and which causes actual or probable damage to the business or goodwill of the proprietor.

A registered trademark has an initial term of protection of 10 years, extendable continually for further periods of 10 years each.

There is no limited period of protection in relation to claims in passing off. Protection of trademarks through passing off actions is available as long as the conditions for a successful claim are present.

AUS ¶65-005   PATENTS

The *Patents Act 1990* (Cth) provides a system of conferring statutory monopoly for inventions which satisfy the criteria of patentability. To be patented, an invention must

(1) be a new manner of manufacture, (2) which has an inventive step, (3) is novel and (4) is useful. Examples include a new drug, a new process and new business process, such as a patent for dealing with information on a smart card to maintain a loyalty program. Genetic material is patentable, and genes and DNA fragments could meet the requirements of inventiveness and novelty.

The patentee is given the exclusive right by the *Patents Act 1990* to exploit the invention and to authorise another person to exploit the invention during the term of the patent. Patent protection therefore gives security to stimulate research and development during the period of the patent.

Two types of patent are provided for under the *Patents Act 1990*:

- An innovation patent, which provides for eight years protection for inventions which are not sufficiently inventive to qualify for a standard patent. Designed to provide an incentive to small businesses to invest in innovation, they can be obtained inexpensively, quickly and easily from the Australian Patent Office after an initial check and can also be obtained online. They cannot be enforced until examination by the Australian Patent Office. Innovation patents can be opposed by third parties at any time after the patent has been examined and certified.

- A standard patent, which provides protection for 20 years from the date of the patent.

See the IP Australia website at www.ipaustralia.gov.au.

AUS ¶65-011   INDUSTRIAL DESIGNS

Designs law protects the visual form of an articlesuch as the design of a knife, a kitchen container or a dome-shaped tent.

The *Designs Act 1906* (Cth) (in force on 17 June 2004) is designed to encourage innovation by giving designers the exclusive right:

- to exploit their designs for a limited time, and

- to prevent competitors free-riding on design innovations.

The designs protected by the *Designs Act* are defined as: "design, in relation to a product, means the overall appearance of the product resulting from one or more visual features of the product" (sec 5). Section 8 confirms the definition when it requires a design to be a "design in relation to a product".

The *Designs Act* provides a publicly available register of existing designs which helps:

- to make known the creative ideas of designers (community benefit), and

- to stimulate further creative activity

The *Designs Act* protects the appearance of articles, not their function. This means that articles which are innovative because of their visual appearance would qualify for protection under the designs registration system. They would not qualify for a patent which gives patentees exclusive rights relating to items or processes which have a use or function.

The *Designs Act 2003* (Cth) has replaced the original *Designs Act 1906* and involves changes including:

- a higher threshold test for designs, with the new test of "new and distinctive" replacing the former test of "new or original";
- an application for a design can include an application for multiple designs and/or for multiple products;
- a reduced period of registration from the former 16 years to 10 years;
- designs are now registered by the Australian Designs Office without full examination, but the design registration cannot be enforced until it has been examined and certified;
- the new wider test of infringement test of "substantially similar in overall impression" has replaced the earlier narrow test of "fraudulent or obvious imitation", and
- the new "spare parts" defence to infringement proceedings.

Details are available from IP Australia at www.ipaustralia.gov.au.

AUS ¶65-012   TRADE SECRETS

Trade secrets — or, more generally, confidential information — are protected by the common law of passing off, by the equitable doctrine of breach of confidential information and in some circumstances by various express statutory provisions by contractual agreement. Australian case law holds that information is not confidential and is in the public domain if it is available in a newspaper, on television or on the Internet. Everyone may not have access to a computer and modem, but everyone has access to cheap Internet cafes.

There is no single statutory framework or finite period for the protection of trade secrets, and as long as the information remains confidential, information is protected by the courts from unauthorised disclosure and use (and for a limited period after disclosure against certain parties).

Civil remedies such as injunctions, an account of profits, an order for delivery up or destruction and/or an order for seizing evidence (an Anton Piller order) are available to a plaintiff in a successful court action for unauthorised use or disclosure of trade secrets or other confidential information.

AUS ¶65-013   CIRCUIT LAYOUTS

Silicon chips

The *Circuit Layouts Act 1989* provides automatic protection for original circuit layouts.

The period of protection for a circuit layout protected by the *Circuit Layouts Act 1989* depends on the date of the first commercial exploitation of the layout (if any). The maximum possible protection period for a circuit layout is 20 years. Rights in an original layout exist for 10 years from the first commercial exploitation — provided that this occurs within 10 years from the creation of the layout — or for 10 years from the year in which it was made, if not commercially exploited.

The owner of a circuit layout which satisfies certain criteria of protection under the *Circuit Layouts Act 1989* is given "EL rights", i.e. the exclusive rights to copy the layout, directly or indirectly, in a material form; to make an integrated circuit in accordance with the layout or a copy of the layout; and to exploit the layout commercially in Australia.

Further details are available from IP Australia at www.ipaustralia.gov.au.

AUS ¶65-014   PLANT VARIETIES

Plant breeder's rights

The *Plant Breeder's Rights Act 1994* provides a system for granting plant breeder's rights ("PBRs") for plant varieties which satisfy the criteria of registrability. The owner of a plant breeder's right has certain exclusive rights to deal with reproductive material in relation to a new plant variety which the owner has created.

A plant breeder's right gives the breeder of a new plant variety exclusive rights to produce or reproduce, to condition the material for the purpose of propagation, to offer for sale, to sell and to import or export propagating material relating to that new plant variety. The Act also gives the exclusive right to stock propagating material for any of the purposes mentioned in the preceding sentence.

There is also a procedure under the *Plant Breeder's Rights Act 1994* under which a plant breeder's right in a plant variety ("the initial variety") can be extended to a plant variety over which a third party holds a plant breeder's right because the second plant variety is an essentially derived variety from the initial variety. In such circumstances, the grantee of the plant breeder's right over the derived variety also retains its right.

The Act also extends the protection given by a plant breeder's right to other plant varieties ("dependent plant varieties") that are not clearly distinguishable from the variety over which the plant breeder's right is held and that are distinguishable from any plant variety that was a matter of common knowledge at the time the plant breeder's right in question was granted. Dependent plant varieties also exist where the plant variety cannot be reproduced except by repeated use of the variety over which the plant breeder's right is held.

Under the *Plant Breeder's Rights Act 1994*, protection commences when the plant breeder's right in the particular variety is granted. In the case of trees and vines, the exclusive rights provided by the Act last for a period of 25 years. In relation to all other varieties, the protection lasts for a period of 20 years.

Special rules apply in relation to the duration of protection granted to dependent plant varieties and essentially derived varieties.

Further details are available from IP Australia at www.ipaustralia.gov.au.

AUS ¶65-014

AUS ¶65-015   UNFAIR COMPETITION

Unfair competition in Australia is regulated by the *Trade Practices Act 1974*, a Commonwealth statute regulating restrictive trade practices (Part IV) (AUS ¶45-303), unconscionable conduct (Part IVA) (AUS ¶30-015) and providing for consumer protection (Part V) (AUS ¶30-011 and AUS ¶45-301). These Parts include provisions governing contracts, covenants, arrangements, etc. affecting competition in trade, misuse of market power, exclusive dealing, resale price maintenance, misleading, deceptive, false or unconscionable conduct, etc. which may affect the exercise of rights in relation to intellectual property. Because of the constitutional limitations on the federal government's power to pass national trade practices laws operating within State areas (AUS ¶20-002), all Australian States and Territories have passed uniform provisions mirroring the consumer protection provisions of the *Trade Practices Act* and all States have passed uniform provisions mirroring the competition policy provisions of the *Trade Practices Act* as part of the national competition policy package. This legislation may affect the exercise of intellectual property rights.

AUS ¶65-021   REGISTRATION PROCEDURES

The only intellectual property rights discussed above that require registration are under the patents, trademarks, designs and plant breeder's rights legislation. (A business name can be registered under the *Business Names Act* of each State and Territory but this does not confer legal rights).

A trademark, whether registered or not, may be protected by legal action for passing off, but the advantage of trademark registration is to avoid the possible difficulties of proof inherent in a passing off action such as having to prove the necessary reputation in the mark.

Special provisions apply to the overlap between copyright and design protection. If the owner of intellectual property rights in a foreign country is different from, and unrelated to, the registered owner of similar rights in Australia, importation of articles protected by those rights may not be allowed.

Designs

The *Designs Act 2003* (Cth) provides a two-step test for the registration of a design. A design must be:

- new — not identical to another design — to eliminate existing designs, and
- distinctive - not substantially similar in overall impression to another design — from any design published in a document anywhere in the world, or publicly used in Australia. The "world" test of the "prior art base" (the publicly available information that a design is compared with) is very realistic because so many publications are on the Internet. Because a design application is compared against more info, there is more chance that it will be seen to be both new and distinctive.

Multiple design/product applications

An application for design registration can include more than one design in relation to one product, or one or more designs relating to multiple products.

Design examination not required for registration

Design applications can go on to the public record very quickly, as they only undergo a formalities check before registration and publication.

A design owner, the registrar or a third-person (like another designer) can request a full post-registration examination. This may be to provide information that is relevant to the decision whether the design is new and distinctive. Design examiners are required to focus on the similarities rather than the differences between a new design and the "prior art base".

When the Registrar is satisfied that the design is valid, the design registration is certified and the design becomes enforceable. Designs registration is similar to the Australian Innovation Patent system. The design owner can only enforce their rights if a certificate of examination has been issued.

Patents

The steps in getting and maintaining a standard patent are illustrated in the diagram set out in the table accompanying sec 4:

TABLE 1 — GETTING AND MAINTAINING A STANDARD PATENT

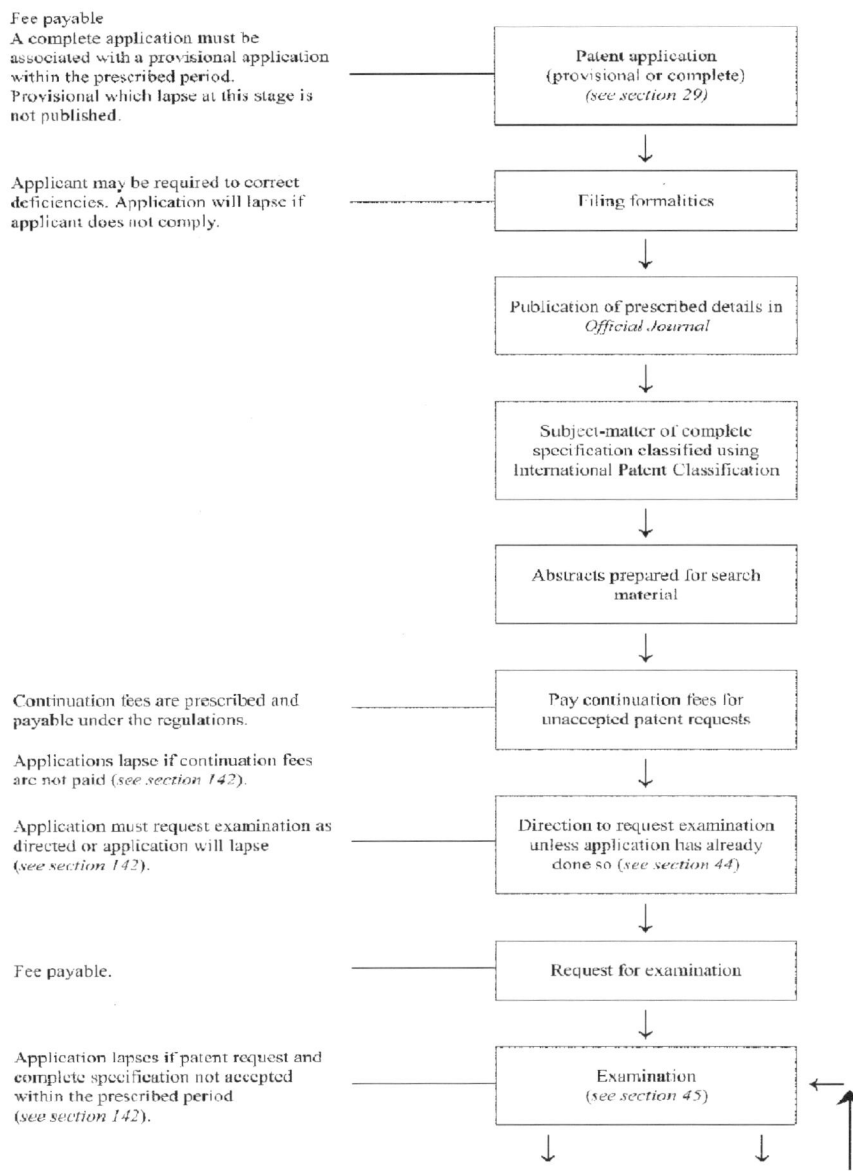

Fee payable
A complete application must be
associated with a provisional application
within the prescribed period.
Provisional which lapse at this stage is
not published.

Applicant may be required to correct
deficiencies. Application will lapse if
applicant does not comply.

Continuation fees are prescribed and
payable under the regulations.

Applications lapse if continuation fees
are not paid (*see section 142*).

Application must request examination as
directed or application will lapse
(*see section 142*).

Fee payable.

Application lapses if patent request and
complete specification not accepted
within the prescribed period
(*see section 142*).

Patent application
(provisional or complete)
(*see section 29*)

Filing formalities

Publication of prescribed details in
Official Journal

Subject-matter of complete
specification classified using
International Patent Classification

Abstracts prepared for search
material

Pay continuation fees for
unaccepted patent requests

Direction to request examination
unless application has already
done so (*see section 44*)

Request for examination

Examination
(*see section 45*)

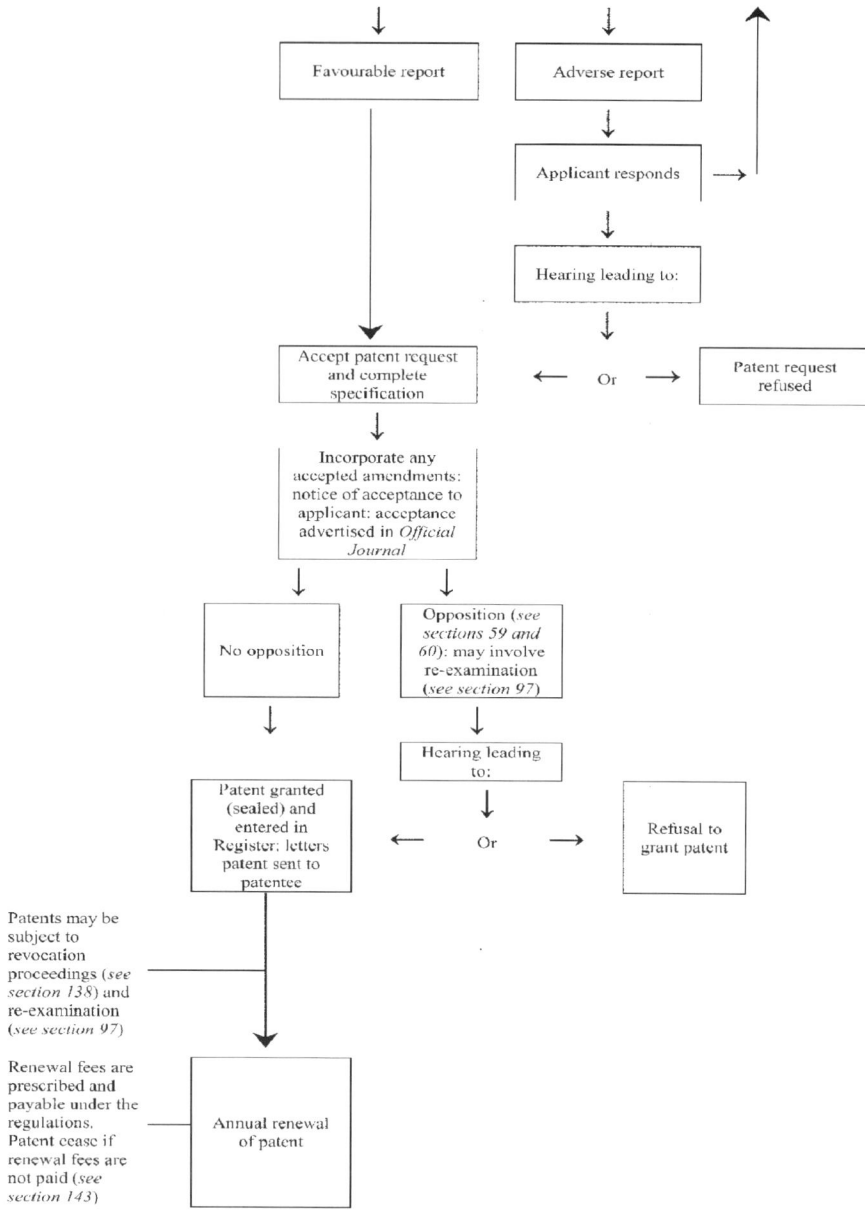

An innovation patent provides for eight years protection for inventions which are not sufficiently inventive to qualify for a standard patent.

Details are available at the IP Australia website at www.ipaustralia.gov.au.

Plant breeder's rights

The *Plant Breeder's Rights Act 1994* provides that an application for registration of a plant variety is made by lodging an application with the Plant Breeder's Rights Australia in the Department of Agriculture, Fisheries and Forestry (AFFA).

An applicant must be able to show that the new variety is distinct, as well as being uniform and stable, and must be able to demonstrate, by a comparative trial, that the variety is clearly distinguishable from any other variety. Objections to the application for a plant breeder's right may be lodged at any time from acceptance of the plant breeder's right until six months after public notice of the detailed description is given.

Trademarks

A person who claims to be the proprietor of a trademark may make an application to the Trade Marks Office for registration. The application will be examined by a trademark examiner, who conducts a search against all similar trademarks and considers its registrability and whether there are objections to its registration. If the examiner's report is not favourable, the applicant can abandon the application or proceed with the application and respond to the report such as by amending the application to overcome the objections. If the objections are maintained, the applicant may request a hearing to consider the application.

If the application is accepted, either because there are no objections or because such objections are removed, the acceptance is advertised. A person would then have three months (unless extended) to make an opposition to the registration. If an opposition has been validly made, exchange of evidence will take place followed by a hearing which decides the matter. The trademark will be registered if no opposition is made, or if the opposition is dismissed.

A trademark can be applied for online at www.ipaustralia.gov.au.

AUS ¶65-022   TRANSFERS AND LICENSING AGREEMENTS

Computer software

Rules governing literary works also apply in relation to computer software.

Copyright

Copyright is capable of being assigned and the assignment can be partial or total. An assignment must be in writing and signed. A copyright owner can also license others to deal with the copyright material so as to avoid copyright infringement.

The *Copyright Act 1968* also contains numerous provisions for compulsory licences. Compulsory licences can arise, on the payment of a fee to the copyright owner, under certain conditions in relation to:

- the making of a sound broadcast of a published literary or dramatic work (or an adaptation thereof) by the holder of a print-handicapped radio licence;
- the making of records of musical works and accompanying literary and dramatic works;

- the public performance and broadcasting of published sound recordings;
- the making of a sound recording or cinematograph film of a literary, dramatic or musical work (or an adaptation thereof) for broadcasting by another person;
- the making of a copy of a sound recording for broadcasting by another person;
- the making of a cinematograph film of an artistic work for a television broadcast by another person; and
- the copying of works and subject matter by educational and other institutions.

There are also provisions for Crown use of copyright material.

Designs

Rights of an owner with respect to a registered design can be assigned, and such assignment should be in writing and signed. There are no governing provisions for licensing but rights in relation to a registered design can be licensed. A person who becomes entitled to a registered design by assignment, agreement, transmission, etc., should apply to the Designs Office to be registered. There are provisions for the use and acquisitions of registered designs by the Crown.

Patents

Rights under a patent are can be assigned. An assignment can be partial or total. An assignment must be in writing and signed. Licences to exploit a patented invention can be granted, although such licences will be void if certain restrictive conditions are included. Assignments and licences should be registered on the Register of Patents.

There are also provisions for the granting of compulsory licences by the courts after a certain period of time if the patentee has failed to satisfy the reasonable requirements of the public with respect to the patented invention, and such a failure is not explained satisfactorily. The *Patents Act 1990* contains provisions concerning the exploitation and acquisition by the Crown of patented inventions.

Performers' protection

The right of a performer to bring an action for unauthorised use of his or her performance is not assignable. Performers' protection rights are not proprietary and so are not able to be licensed as such. Nonetheless, as the right entitles the performer to take action against a use of the performance which has not been authorised by the performer, the performer may give permission for use of the performance on such terms as the performer thinks fits. However, once the performer authorises a recording of the performance, the performer has no right to control later unauthorised uses of the authorised recording except in the case of an unauthorised use of a sound recording in a sound track where the recording was not authorised for use in a sound track.

Plant breeder's rights

A plant breeder's right, subject to any conditions imposed when the plant breeder's right is granted, can be assigned. The assignment must be in writing and signed by the assignee, who must inform Plant Breeder's Rights Australia within seven days of acquiring the plant breeder's right, so that the Register of Plant Breeder's Rights can be updated.

The owner of a plant breeder's right may also license others to do some or all of the exclusive acts which are contained in the right. There is no provision for recording of such licences on the Register of Plant Breeder's Rights.

Silicon chips

Rights in relation to a circuit layout protected by the *Circuit Layouts Act 1989* are capable of being assigned and licensed. An assignment can be partial or total and must be in writing and signed. There are also provisions for Crown use of a protected circuit layout.

Trademarks

A registered trademark is assignable with or without goodwill. However, if the assignment of the trademark is not accompanied by an assignment of the goodwill, the assignment is invalid in certain specific circumstances. An assignee should register its title with the Trade Marks Office. Further, the *Trade Marks Act 1995* permits other interests in a trademark, such as a mortgage, to be registered with the Trade Marks Office.

There is no provision under the *Trade Marks Act 1995* for a person to be registered as registered user of a trademark, approved by the Trade Marks Office. If a trademark owner exercises a specified degree of control over the use of that trademark by another person, the use by that person is taken to be authorised use. An authorised user of a trademark has certain express statutory rights with respect to the mark, set out in the Act.

The *Trade Marks Act* provides for the voluntary recordal of third party interests in a trademark, including licensees and mortgagees.

An unregistered trademark can be assigned but only with an assignment of the goodwill associated with it. An unregistered trademark can be licensed provided that confusion and deception will not arise as a result.

Trade names

As no proprietary rights are conferred by a registration of trade name under the *Business Names Acts* of each State and Territory, there can be no assignment or licensing of rights.

Trade secrets

Confidential information and trade secrets can be licensed although, probably, these rights are not assignable per se.

AUS ¶65-023   COMPULSORY LICENSES

It is not necessary to gain government approval for licensing know-how.

AUS ¶65-024   TABLE OF FEES

Under the trademarks, patents and designs legislation, there are provisions for the payment of fees in relation to various steps in the application for registration, and for the maintaining of the registration. The fees are set out at the relevant websites such as (www.ipaustralia.gov.au).

AUS ¶65-025   DISADVANTAGES FOR NON-RESIDENTS

Protection of intellectual property rights is not restricted to Australian citizens and residents.

The rights of owners or originators of intellectual property in other countries over intellectual rights which are protected by legislation in Australia are discussed below.

For those rights protected in Australia by common law and equity, the availability of protection in Australia to foreign owners depends on the rules of private international law.

Circuit layouts

If the maker of an original circuit layout was, at the time the layout was made, a citizen, national or resident of, or a body incorporated in an ''eligible foreign country'' (listed in the *Circuit Layouts Regulations*), the layout will be protected in Australia by the *Circuit Layouts Act 1989*. Similar protection is available for original layouts first commercially exploited in an eligible foreign country.

Computer software

Refer to the rules for ''copyright'' below.

Copyright

Unpublished works and subject matter authored or made by a person who is a citizen or national of, or a resident of or body incorporated in, a Convention country (listed in the *Copyright (International Protection) Regulations*) are protected in Australia by the *Copyright Act 1968*. If the author or maker falls into one of the above classes when the work or subject matter is first published, or if the work or subject matter is first published in a Convention country, the work or subject matter is similarly protected. Similar protection is also available for sound recordings and cinematograph films made in a Convention country. Special provisions apply to published editions published in or broadcasts made from a Convention country.

Designs

A foreign owner of a design should obtain registration of the design by the Designs Office under the *Designs Act 2003* . As in the case of trademarks and patents, there are provisions for the claiming of earlier priority dates of an application made in a Convention country .

Patents

A person who has been granted a patent for an invention in another country must apply for the grant of an Australian patent under the *Patents Act 1990* if monopoly rights in Australia are desired.

There are provisions allowing for the making of an application in a country which is a member of the Patent Co-operation Treaty which designates Australia as a country in which protection is required, and such an application is treated as an application under the *Patents Act 1990*.

There are also provisions allowing for the taking of the priority date of a patent application made earlier in a Convention country (listed in the *Patents Regulations 1991* from Albania to Zambia).

Persons who want to have patents granted in Australia and another country must be aware of the above provisions, otherwise the publication of a foreign application may result in the invention having been disclosed in the subsequent Australian application.

Performers' protection

Performances given in a Convention country (listed in the *Copyright (International Protection) Regulations 1969*) or by a citizen, national or resident of a Convention country or which are incorporated in a sound recording made in or by a person who is a citizen, national or resident of a Convention country or which are incorporated in a broadcast which is made by a relevant broadcaster from a Convention country are treated in the same manner as other performances protected under the *Copyright Act 1968*.

The United States of America is not a Convention country but special provision has been made in relation to sound recordings, sound broadcasts and sound transmissions of performances which have a relevant connection to the United States of America.

Trademarks

The owner of a trademark in another country — whether registered or not — does not enjoy automatic protection in Australia. The owner of a trademark in a foreign country who wishes to secure trademark protection in Australia must apply for registration under the *Trade Marks Act 1995*. If that person has made an application for registration of a trademark in a "Convention country" (listed in the *Trade Marks Regulations 1995*, that person can claim the priority date of that application in a later Australian application for the same goods or services if made within six months of the overseas application.

Plant breeder's rights

The owner of a plant variety in a country (other than Australia) which is a party to the international convention, the owner may claim the date of the foreign application as a priority date for the purpose of the subsequent Australian application for rights in that variety.

AUS ¶65-031 ENFORCEMENT

The owners of the above intellectual property rights can enforce their rights by commencing actions in the relevant Australian court. The remedies available include injunctions, damages, account of profits, delivery up, and Anton Piller orders (to seize documents). Copyright owners are also given rights in relation to infringing articles as if they were the owners thereof to pursue actions in conversion and detention.

Labelling requirements

Use of another person's registered trademark on a label may constitute trademark infringement (if the trademark is registered) under the *Trade Marks Act* or it may amount to "misleading or deceptive conduct" or the making of a "false or misleading" representation in breach of sec. 52 and 53 of the *Trade Practices Act 1974* and/or the equivalent *Fair Trading Acts* of all the States and Territories.

Further information on this chapter is available on the IP Australia website at http://www.ipaustralia.gov.au.

Settlement of Disputes

Basis of courts' jurisdiction .... AUS ¶70-001

Status of foreign companies .... AUS ¶70-002

Civil procedure for foreign companies .... AUS ¶70-003

Rules of civil procedure and evidence .... AUS ¶70-004

Service and execution of process outside jurisdiction ... AUS ¶70-005

Availability of interlocutory relief .... AUS ¶70-011

Collection of evidence outside the jurisdiction .... AUS ¶70-012

Choice of applicable law .... AUS ¶70-013

Choice of forum .... AUS ¶70-014

Costs and delay associated with litigation .... AUS ¶70-015

Security for costs .... AUS ¶70-021

Language of courts .... AUS ¶70-022

Enforcement and execution of judgments .... AUS ¶70-023

Recognition of foreign judgments .... AUS ¶70-024

Status of foreign lawyers .... AUS ¶70-025

Special procedures for certain disputes .... AUS ¶70-031

Arbitration .... AUS ¶70-101

Conciliation, mediation and alternative dispute
    resolution .... AUS ¶70-201

Framework for dispute resolution .... AUS ¶70-301

Position of government .... AUS ¶70-401

AUS ¶70-001   BASIS OF COURTS' JURISDICTION

The general rules under which Australian courts take jurisdiction are primarily concerned with whether the parties can be served with notice rather than where the cause of action arose. Special rules apply when the litigation involves an overseas defendant.

The general rule is that Australian courts will take jurisdiction in civil matters when:

- an individual defendant is "present" within Australia;
- a corporate defendant carries on business at a fixed location in Australia;

- a defendant submits, usually by making an appearance, to Australian jurisdiction;

- a defendant is domiciled or ordinarily resident in Australia; or

- the property which is the subject matter of the dispute is within Australia.

When the matter involves an overseas defendant, Federal, State and Territory Court Rules provide a number of special circumstances under which proceedings can be served outside Australia. Basically, the *Rules of Court* provide that when the cause of action, the defendant or the subject matter of a dispute is in some way connected with Australia, the courts will take jurisdiction over the matter.

To establish this link with Australia, a party must satisfy a number of particular requirements, which in turn depend on the class of legal issue involved. The basic requirements that need to be satisfied for jurisdiction to be taken over contract and tort matters are:

- if a contract is made within Australia, breached within Australia or governed by Australian law; and

- if the tort was committed within Australia;

- in either contract or tort, if the relevant damage was suffered in Australia no matter where the tort or breach of contract occurred.

To fully determine the meaning of these requirements, reference must be made to the relevant Australian case law.

Australia follows the common law tradition of the doctrine of precedent and the judicial interpretation of common law and statutes through a hierarchy of courts, with the High Court of Australia at the top of the hierarchy.

AUS ¶70-002   STATUS OF FOREIGN COMPANIES

A foreign corporation can sue and be used in Australian courts if the foreign corporation is incorporated according to the laws of its place of incorporation. The position at common law is embodied in the *Foreign Corporations (Application of Laws) Act 1989* (Cth).

AUS ¶70-003   CIVIL PROCEDURE FOR FOREIGN COMPANIES

There are no special rules governing civil procedure in litigation where foreign companies and foreign-owned subsidiaries are involved. Australia's civil procedure is basically an adversarial system where the parties maintain responsibility for the conduct of proceedings in accordance with procedural rules. In commercial matters, the judicial approach is sometimes more interventionist in the interests of efficiency.

The *Corporations Act 2001* (Cth) provides that a company operating in Australia will be administered by the Australian Securities and Investments Commission (ASIC), a Commonwealth government agency operating nationally.

AUS ¶70-004 RULES OF CIVIL PROCEDURE AND EVIDENCE

Rules of civil procedure can be found in the rules relating to the various courts, such as the *Supreme Court Rules*. Although there is increased uniformity in Australian procedural rules of various jurisdictions, specific situations are likely to require specialist advice. Certain rules of procedure may be governed in specific circumstances by other legislation.

AUS ¶70-005 SERVICE AND EXECUTION OF PROCESS OUTSIDE JURISDICTION

Statutory provision is made for the service and execution of process outside the jurisdiction. Because Australia is a federation, this may involve service outside the jurisdiction in another State or Territory but within Australia, or service outside Australia. Regarding the former, the relevant federal, State or Territory court rules, namely the *Supreme Court Rules* of the relevant jurisdiction, will apply. The *Service and Execution of Process Act 1992* (Cth), may apply if Commonwealth law is the relevant law.

For service outside Australia, the source of procedure remains the same, but depending on the jurisdiction there can be variations in the procedural steps. Service may be personal, or by a filing process in an Australian court. Importantly, it may be necessary to obtain leave to obtain service. Criteria are specified in the Rules.

The court will insist upon adherence to the rules of natural justice, particularly, in relation to notification and opportunity to be heard. If the object of service is a foreign State, reference may be made to the *Foreign States Immunities Act 1985* (Cth), although foreign State immunity cannot, except in specific circumstances, be claimed in connection with matters arising from commercial dealings.

AUS ¶70-011 AVAILABILITY OF INTERLOCUTORY RELIEF

The rules of civil procedure provide for interlocutory relief. The *Rules of Court* and the relevant legislation make explicit the jurisdictional basis and procedure for granting interlocutory orders. Usually an injunction will be sought to restrain anticipated breach of contract or other acts which require restraint in order to preserve the existing position pending a full hearing. It is also possible to seek damages. The application will proceed by written notice of motion supported by affidavit evidence.

Two types of interlocutory order commonly sought in the commercial area are:

- the Mareva order — an assets preservation order designed to prevent the defendant dealing with assets where it is shown that there is a real risk that the plaintiff will be left with a hollow victory; and

- the Anton Piller order — a more extreme order, which enables a plaintiff to enter premises to secure property and evidence that is relevant to the hearing.

Since the granting of the interlocutory relief often involves unilateral curtailment of the defendant's rights, the applicant must be prepared to persuade the court that it has a fairly arguable case, that damages would not be an adequate remedy and that the balance of convenience is in favour of making the order. The applicant must give an undertaking to pay damages caused by the granting of the injunction if the defendant suffers loss and yet goes to a full hearing.

AUS ¶70-012 COLLECTION OF EVIDENCE OUTSIDE THE JURISDICTION

The hearing process depends on the availability of witnesses to present evidence and to be subjected to cross-examination. However, there are statutory provisions for the collection of evidence by deposition outside the jurisdiction. The court commissions the taking of evidence, and the powers of the courts under the Commonwealth (federal), State and Territory Evidence Acts and *Rules of Court* are of great breadth and discretion. An authority or regulator outside the jurisdiction may be able to collect evidence for an Australian regulator such as the Australian Securities and Investments Commission (ASIC) if a Memorandum of Understanding (MOU) is in place.

AUS ¶70-013 CHOICE OF APPLICABLE LAW

Australian law seeks to give effect to the intentions of contracting parties, provided that such a result is not in conflict with statute or public policy. A choice of law made by the parties in a contract usually will be applied by the courts in settling a dispute.

In determining the applicable law, an Australian court will choose the proper law by criteria including the place of contracting, where the contract is to be performed, where the parties reside, and the content of the contract. The weight given to these factors will vary depending on particular cases. The aim is to find the system of law to which the agreement has the closest connection.

Specific rules apply to some types of agreement. There are instances where express local statutory provisions have to be enforced and domestic courts may have to decide questions of form and legality. However, Australian courts reflect and respect the need for certainty in commercial and international transactions.

AUS ¶70-014 CHOICE OF FORUM

Parties to a contract are free to submit a dispute arising from the contract to a forum of their choice expressed in the contract. The basic principle is that the choice forms part of the agreement, and it is the fundamental purpose of contract law to give effect to agreements. The parties must not try to oust the jurisdiction of the court or to claim jurisdiction where none exists.

AUS ¶70-015 COSTS AND DELAY ASSOCIATED WITH LITIGATION

Efficiency in court administration has been criticised from time to time, but efficiency is rapidly improving with the application of information technology, electronic courtrooms and so on.

AUS ¶70-012

Courts and the legal profession seek to reduce court delays and to provide a reasonable quality of justice at a price which is affordable by the community. By American standards, the cost of legal services in Australia is moderate.

In recent times, federal, State and Territory Courts throughout Australia have adopted court-connected systems of alternative dispute resolution such as mediation. There is increasing awareness of these techniques in the legal profession and in the commercial sector. Their use is designed to achieve resolution of disputes more speedily, with less expense, and with a high quality result worked out by the parties themselves rather than by a third party umpire. The effect of using these techniques has been to substantially reduce court lists of cases awaiting hearing.

The courts of some jurisdictions are tending to develop divisions specialising in particular types of matters such as specialist commercial divisions. These specialised divisions may apply fast track methods to bring out critical issues at an early stage and ensure that the parties prepare their cases efficiently. It is often necessary to wait from the date when the case is ready for trial until a hearing date is available. Once again, the situation is variable, differing in particular, from jurisdiction to jurisdiction and from matter to matter. Urgent matters receive priority and are usually heard promptly.

In most jurisdictions, there is an independent bar of lawyers practising as barristers. Barristers are specialists in advocacy and are frequently called upon for advice in specialist areas. It is difficult to usefully give a guide as to the cost of litigation because as fees are deregulated, rates charged by practitioners vary substantially.

AUS ¶70-021   SECURITY FOR COSTS

Court rules, and legislation governing companies, make provision for the court to order the party bringing the action to give security for the costs of the proceedings. Where the plaintiff fails to comply with such an order, the court can order the dismissal of the plaintiff's claims for relief. Usually, it is necessary for the other party to have provided evidence raising doubts as to the plaintiff's ability to pay the costs of the defendant if the defence is successful.

AUS ¶70-022   LANGUAGE OF COURTS

Matters in Australian courts are conducted in English. Australia is a multicultural country and interpretation and translation services are available.

AUS ¶70-023   ENFORCEMENT AND EXECUTION OF JUDGMENTS

Enforcement of a judgment depends on the type of judgment. A judgment at common law will often be one for the payment of damages, or an order relating to the possession of land other property. A judgment in equity may involve an injunction or an order for specific performance. It is usually the responsibility of the judgment creditor to enforce the judgment, typically by issuing a writ of execution.

AUS ¶70-024 RECOGNITION OF FOREIGN JUDGMENTS

Statutory authority is required for the recognition and enforcement of a foreign judgment in an Australian jurisdiction. Reciprocal enforcement legislation exists in Australian jurisdictions and streamlines and simplifies enforcement procedures, by making foreign judgments enforceable by registration rather than by an action based on a judgment debt. Most Australian jurisdictions have passed a Foreign Judgments Act (e.g. Commonwealth 1991; NSW 1973; WA 1963)which provides for reciprocal enforcement of foreign judgments. The legislation provides that a foreign judgment may give the basis for an action provided certain criteria are satisfied. The main ones are that the judgment be final, and that the court had appropriate jurisdiction. Where relief other than the payment of money is sought, a common law approach, or one involving relevant legislative estoppel provisions, will be necessary.

AUS ¶70-025 STATUS OF FOREIGN LAWYERS

Generally, a foreign lawyer may not practise law unless admitted as a local lawyer in Australia. Requirements for admission and practice are governed by legislation, the Supreme Courts and the law societies in each State or Territory. There are moves towards a national practising certificate. Restrictions and difficulties regarding the status of foreign lawyers in Australia usually result in the use by foreigners of Australian law firms or international firms with offices in Australia.

AUS ¶70-031 SPECIAL PROCEDURES FOR CERTAIN DISPUTES

Certain types of disputes involve particular procedures.

In Australia, there are specialist courts, tribunals and commissions, and specialist divisions within higher courts of general jurisdiction. For example, Australia has a system of industrial dispute resolution through federal and State legislation involving the Australian Industrial Relations Commission, with appeals to the Industrial Relations Court of Australia. T

Any private commercial investment disputes that arise can be litigated normally. Some Supreme Courts have specialist Commercial Divisions or Lists. Some investment disputes may arise as a result of administrative action, and the avenue of appeal will be a tribunal such as the Administrative Appeals Tribunal.

It may be prudent to determine in advance the view of regulatory bodies such as the Foreign Investment Review Board (FIRB) and the Australian Competition and Consumer Commission (ACCC). To take an example, the *Foreign Acquisitions and Takeovers Act 1975* (Cth) requires proposals to be put to FIRB on a wide range of investment propositions. Usually, a proposal is agreed to without obstruction, unless it has adverse implications for Australia's national development needs. There is an exception to this attitude with regard to investment in Australian urban land, which is under strict control (see AUS ¶25-103).

Particular areas of dispute resolution can be multi-faceted and driven by legislation and regulation.

ARBITRATION

Arbitration system .... AUS ¶70-101

New York Convention on
  Recognition and Enforcement
  of Foreign Arbitral
  Awards .... AUS ¶70-102

Special provisions required for
  arbitration clauses .... AUS ¶70-103

International arbitration
  rules .... AUS ¶70-104

United Nations Model
  Law .... AUS ¶70-105

Distinction between
  international and domestic
  arbitration .... AUS ¶70-111

Tribunals' basis of
  jurisdiction .... AUS ¶70-112

Exceptions .... AUS ¶70-113

Courts' assistance in
  arbitration process .... AUS ¶70-114

Choice of procedural law ... AUS ¶70-115

Choice of applicable law .... AUS ¶70-121

Specification of appointment of
  arbitrators, etc. .... AUS ¶70-122

Rules governing choice of
  arbitrators .... AUS ¶70-123

Expense of arbitration .... AUS ¶70-124

Delays in arbitration .... AUS ¶70-125

Review by court .... AUS ¶70-131

Arbitration by amiable
  composition .... AUS ¶70-132

Participation by foreign
  companies .... AUS ¶70-133

Rules of natural justice ...... AUS ¶70-134

Status of foreign lawyers ... AUS ¶70-135

Assistance from outside
  jurisdiction .... AUS ¶70-141

Language of proceedings ... AUS ¶70-142

Confidentiality of
  proceedings .... AUS ¶70-143

Special procedures for certain
  disputes .... AUS ¶70-144

Arbitration in third
  country .... AUS ¶70-145

AUS ¶70-101   ARBITRATION SYSTEM

Arbitration is a non-judicial settlement of a dispute by means of a hearing before an impartial umpire or tribunal.

Arbitration has become a popular method of settling disputes for companies. Reasons for this include the confidential nature of the proceedings and the ability to enforce judgments overseas.

Each Australian State and Territory has a *Commercial Arbitration Act* which acknowledges the right of parties to agree to resolve their differences through arbitration and aids and regulates the arbitration process by prescribing implied terms which parties may not have not dealt with in their arbitration agreement as well as the procedure for arbitration.

AUS ¶70-102   NEW YORK CONVENTION ON RECOGNITION AND ENFORCEMENT OF FOREIGN ARBITRAL AWARDS

Through the *International Arbitration Act 1974* (Cth), Australia implemented the Convention on the Recognition and Enforcement of Foreign Arbitral Awards (the New York Convention of 1958). This Convention requires contracting parties to recognise and to enforce arbitral awards made in other states where the recognition and enforcement of such awards have been sought. Hence, the Act recognises and enforces foreign awards. The uniform State and Territory Commercial Arbitration Acts also embody the terms of the New York Convention.

AUS ¶70-103   SPECIAL PROVISIONS REQUIRED FOR ARBITRATION CLAUSES

Apart from an agreement to refer a dispute to arbitration, no special provisions are required. International commercial arbitration conducted in Australia will proceed under the UNCITRAL Model Law on International Commercial Arbitration as provided for by the *International Arbitration Act 1974*(Cth), unless specific alternative provision is made in writing.

The Institute of Arbitrators and Mediators Australia has recommended the following clause for those wishing to use its services:

> "Any dispute or difference whatsoever arising out of or in connection with this contract shall be submitted to arbitration in accordance with, and subject to The Institute of Arbitrators Australia Rules for the Conduct of Commercial Arbitrations".

The Rules of the Institute incorporate the UNCITRAL Rules for international arbitration.

Whatever agreement clause is used, it is submitted that it would be prudent to refer to a specific set of rules, to be particularly specific regarding any alteration to an adopted set of procedures, and to ensure that the parties' rights at law are not compromised. Courts are increasingly sensitive to the need for thorough and explicit explanation of the contractual terms which are being agreed to, and a clause acknowledging the parties' understanding of the procedures they are agreeing to could be considered.

AUS ¶70-104   INTERNATIONAL ARBITRATION RULES

Any rules for arbitration are acceptable provided they are not illegal or against public policy, and are expressly and mutually agreed to and ascertainable. The Institute of Arbitrators and Mediators Australia bases its recommended procedure on the UNCITRAL Rules.

AUS ¶70-105   UNITED NATIONS MODEL LAW

The Commonwealth government's *International Arbitration Act 1974* was amended in 1989 to adopt the *UNCITRAL Model Law on International Commercial Arbitration 1985*. This now has the force of law in Australia in the case of international commercial arbitrations where the place of the arbitration is within Australia. To that extent, the application of the *UNCITRAL Model Law* would not be subject to agreement by the parties, provided there was a valid arbitration agreement. The parties would be free to exclude part or all of the *Model Law* on the basis of their free and mutual choice of procedure, but they would be risking the possibility of challenge on the basis of an error of law by the arbitrator if the arbitrator proceeded contrary to the *Model Law*.

AUS ¶70-111   DISTINCTION BETWEEN INTERNATIONAL AND DOMESTIC ARBITRATION

There can be a distinction between international and domestic commercial arbitration. Where there is a dispute between parties belonging to different nations, an arbitration will proceed under the *International Arbitration Act 1974* unless there is written agreement to the contrary. A domestic dispute may be more likely to be litigated in the court system, particularly in relation to the preliminary and the intermediate steps, the court's powers of enforcement and the right of appeal.

At the State and Territory level, each State has enacted uniform Commercial Arbitration Acts which deal with domestic arbitration. Although the Acts distinguish between domestic and non-domestic arbitration, the definition of "arbitration agreement" in the Acts is not limited to domestic arbitration. However, the *International Arbitration Act 1974* would probably apply to an international arbitration to the exclusion of the Commercial Arbitration Acts, unless the parties have elected that the *Model Law* should not apply.

In addition, most Australian States and Territories have legislated to allow the courts the discretion to refer disputes (or parts of a dispute) before them to arbitration for settlement — sometimes without requiring the consent of the parties.

One difference is illustrated in the scope for contracting out of judicial review. In a domestic arbitration, an exclusive agreement of this nature will not be effective unless entered into after arbitration proceedings have commenced. This is prescribed by the uniform Commercial Arbitration Acts of the States and Territories, where a "domestic arbitration agreement" is defined for the particular section (see, for example, the *Commercial Arbitration Act 1984 (NSW)*, sec. 40(7)), as:

> "an arbitration agreement which does not provide, expressly or by implication, for arbitration in a country other than Australia and to which neither —
>
> - an individual who is a national of, or habitually resident in, any country other than Australia; nor
> - a body corporate which is incorporated in, or whose central management and control is exercised in, any country other than Australia —
>
> is a party at the time the arbitration agreement is entered into."

In any event, it is likely that there will be areas of judicial review which cannot be contracted out of in domestic arbitrations, but which may be susceptible to exclusion in certain types of international arbitration.

AUS ¶70-112   TRIBUNALS' BASIS OF JURISDICTION

The jurisdiction of an arbitration tribunal derives from the contractual stipulations of the parties and the relevant legislation, typically the *International Arbitration Act 1974* with regard to international commercial arbitration, and the uniform Commercial Arbitration Acts of the States and Territories in relation to domestic arbitration.

AUS ¶70-113   EXCEPTIONS

Unless the arbitration involved illegality or was contrary to public policy, it is unlikely that a contractual dispute between private parties would not be arbitrable.

AUS ¶70-114   COURTS' ASSISTANCE IN ARBITRATION PROCESS

Both the *UNCITRAL Model Law* (AUS ¶70-103) and the New York Convention of 1958 (AUS ¶70-102), given effect in Australia by the *International Arbitration Act 1974*, provide for a mandatory stay of court proceedings subject to certain criteria having been fulfilled. The *Model Law*, for example, applies only to international arbitrations. Sections 7 and 18 of the *International Arbitration Act 1974* should be consulted, with Art. 6 and 8 of the *Model Law*. Under the uniform Commercial Arbitration legislation of the States and Territories, courts have a discretionary power to stay court proceedings commenced by one party to an arbitration agreement against another party to that agreement. The powers of the courts generally are more extensive and integrated under this regime, as indicated through Part V of that legislation.

AUS ¶70-115   CHOICE OF PROCEDURAL LAW

The parties are free to stipulate the procedural law to be applied by the arbitral tribunal in the settlement of a dispute, provided that the stipulations do not offend the legislative provisions of the governing Act. Arbitral procedure is ascertainable in that federal, State and Territory legislation embodies a suggested scheme, and professional bodies promulgate rules. The UNCITRAL Rules have become the usual foundation.

AUS ¶70-121   CHOICE OF APPLICABLE LAW

The parties are free to stipulate the law to be applied by the arbitral tribunal to the substance of the dispute. In the context of international commercial arbitration, this is provided for by Art. 28(1) of the *Model Law*, which is endorsed by the *International Arbitration Act 1974*. In general terms, provided an agreement is valid, the proper law is the law of the agreement. The validity of the agreement will be determined by the law of the forum in which the arbitration is based.

AUS ¶70-122   SPECIFICATION OF APPOINTMENT OF ARBITRATORS, ETC.

It is not necessary to specify the method of appointment of arbitrators. The *International Arbitration Act*, through its endorsement of the *Model Law*, and the uniform Commercial Arbitration Acts of the States and Territories, specify methods of appointment. Parties may consider it desirable to specify the method of appointment, since the two procedures offer clear alternatives, and to specify the place of arbitration.

AUS ¶70-123   RULES GOVERNING CHOICE OF ARBITRATORS

Unless otherwise agreed, there are special rules governing the choice of arbitrators. The *Model Law* provides for each party to choose an arbitrator, and the two chosen arbitrators then choose a third. The uniform Acts of the States and Territories provide for the joint appointment of a sole arbitrator. There are default and disagreement provisions.

AUS ¶70-124   EXPENSE OF ARBITRATION

Generally, one can say that the cost of arbitration is less than that of litigation. One of the grounds for government and judicial support of arbitration has been its potential for achieving settlement at a lesser cost. For an arbitration of some complexity, a referee's fee might be comparable with senior counsel's fees, which is in addition to the cost of legal advice and representation and room hire.

AUS ¶70-125   DELAYS IN ARBITRATION

Arbitration has the potential for relatively rapid and cost-efficient resolution of disputes, but it may incur the delay that is sometimes comparable to litigation. Generally, if the parties have a strong desire to avoid delay, the contractual nature of arbitration should provide an advantage over a court-oriented resolution.

AUS ¶70-131   REVIEW BY COURT

The *Model Law* and the New York Convention, both of which are endorsed in Australia by the *International Arbitration Act 1974*, require that arbitral awards be enforced. It is clear that courts will become increasingly reluctant to interfere with the arbitration process. The uniform Commercial Arbitration Acts of the States and Territories provide for review in a restricted ambit.

Both systems provide for the setting aside of awards, and the making of interim orders, but proceedings under the *Model Law* are more protected from judicial intervention. Under the uniform Commercial Arbitration Acts of the States and Territories a question of law emerging from the award may give grounds for appeal. The court has the power to vary or set aside the award, or remit the matter to the arbitral tribunal. There is also scope under the uniform legislation for the court to decide preliminary points of law. There is a lack of clarity in the scope of these rights, and there are provisions for their exclusion. Adoption of the *Model Law* should serve to make arbitral hearings virtually autonomous unless the court were to find a matter non-arbitral.

AUS ¶70-132   ARBITRATION BY AMIABLE COMPOSITION

Arbitration by amiable composition is permissible provided it is agreed to in writing by the parties. This condition is contained in the *Model Law* as endorsed in the *International Arbitration Act 1974*, and in the uniform Commercial Arbitration Acts of the States and Territories.

AUS ¶70-133   PARTICIPATION BY FOREIGN COMPANIES

The *International Arbitration Act 1974* assumes the participation of foreign companies and foreign-owned subsidiaries in arbitral proceedings, and contains no special rules for such participation. The uniform Commercial Arbitration Acts of the States and Territories are similarly accessible.

AUS ¶70-134   RULES OF NATURAL JUSTICE

The rules of natural justice — or due process or procedural fairness — would be expected to apply to arbitral proceedings. The rules of natural justice are derived from the principle that hearing procedures must be fair to all parties. Parties must be given adequate notice of proceedings, sufficient detail, the opportunity to be heard, and access to unbiased arbitration, mediation or conciliation. As one moves further from a litigation model, there is the possibility that the forum will have less developed mechanisms for ensuring initial adherence to the rules. However, the various alternative dispute resolution procedures are compatible with the rules and the development of coordinated dispute resolution schemes should further ensure compatibility.

AUS ¶70-135   STATUS OF FOREIGN LAWYERS

The *International Arbitration Act 1974* provides that parties may be represented by foreign lawyers, and parties desiring such representation would be advised to proceed under this regime. The uniform State and Territory Commercial Arbitration Acts favour personal representation generally, unless agreed otherwise in writing, or it can be shown that representation is advantageous for the arbitration. There could be difficulties related to the status of foreign lawyers under the uniform Acts.

AUS ¶70-141   ASSISTANCE FROM OUTSIDE JURISDICTION

Since the Australian government wishes to facilitate international commercial arbitration in Australia, impediments to outside assistance relevant to the arbitration hearing are unlikely.

AUS ¶70-142   LANGUAGE OF PROCEEDINGS

An arbitration would normally be conducted in English. Under the *International Arbitration Act 1974*, the parties are free to agree on the language or languages to be used in proceedings, but documentary evidence and applications for the recognition and enforcement of awards will require the production of English translations. If a language other than English is to be used, it would be desirable to agree upon it in advance.

AUS ¶70-143 CONFIDENTIALITY OF PROCEEDINGS

It would be prudent for the parties to make contractual and material provision for the maintenance of confidentiality. Problems might be anticipated with the practical enforcement of confidentiality. The High Court has said that while privacy is an interest in arbitration, there are restrictions on implied terms of confidentiality agreements such as that of the public interest. The suggestion can be made, with reservations and qualifications, that a court will not be disposed to disturb the confidentiality of documents disclosed without prejudice in attempting to achieve settlement within an arbitration agreement.

AUS ¶70-144 SPECIAL PROCEDURES FOR CERTAIN DISPUTES

Particular procedures for particular types of dispute are not prescribed in general commercial contexts, although statutory and policy considerations will often govern specific disputes. For example, an agreement purporting to exclude the jurisdiction of the court is rendered ineffective by sec. 11 of the *Carriage of Goods by Sea Act 1991* (Cth). Section 11 does not apply to commercial arbitration agreements.

Australia has a specific system of federal and State industrial conciliation and arbitration. As indicated at AUS ¶70-031, the *Workplace Relations Act 1996* (Cth) and the Australian Industrial Relations Commission embody a national legal framework for the regulation of industrial conditions, the aim of which is to prevent and settle industrial disputes through conciliation and arbitration.

AUS ¶70-145 ARBITRATION IN THIRD COUNTRY

Within Australia it is likely that, for international commercial arbitration, the regime offered by the *International Arbitration Act 1974* will remain as the preferred system. If an arbitration is to be heard in a third country, the protection and advantages offered by the *Model Law* could be a determining factor. If, however, parties are familiar with a regime such as is offered by the uniform Commercial Arbitration Acts of the States and Territories, another jurisdiction with similar provisions such as Hong Kong might be preferred.

CONCILIATION, MEDIATION AND ALTERNATIVE DISPUTE RESOLUTION

Alternative methods of dispute
    resolution .... AUS ¶70-201

International conventions .. AUS ¶70-202

Appointment of conciliators
    and mediators .... AUS ¶70-203

Special rules governing
    proceedings .... AUS ¶70-204

Basis of jurisdiction .... AUS ¶70-205

Enforcement of settlement AUS ¶70-211

Right of representation ...... AUS ¶70-212

Choice of applicable law .... AUS ¶70-213

Courts' power of
    intervention .... AUS ¶70-214

Confidentiality of
    proceedings .... AUS ¶70-215

Special rules for foreign
    participation .... AUS ¶70-221

Provisions in contract for forms
    of dispute resolution ...... AUS ¶70-222

Restrictions on types of disputes
    for conciliation, etc. .... AUS ¶70-223

Disadvantages of conciliation,
    etc. .... AUS ¶70-224

Joint methods of dispute
    resolution .... AUS ¶70-225

AUS ¶70-201   ALTERNATIVE METHODS OF DISPUTE RESOLUTION

Alternative dispute resolution has become one means of settling disputes and, in most jurisdictions of Australia, laws have been passed to help the parties resolve their disputes quickly. Courts in many jurisdictions now provide neutral case appraisal and mediation procedures. For example, the *Supreme Court Act* in Victoria provides that unless both parties agree, no evidence of what is said or done at mediation shall be admitted at a hearing of the court.

Mediation involves a mediator assisting both parties to get through their negotiation process and to resolve their dispute. Neutral evaluation may require each party to be accompanied by a solicitor or barrister and for the evaluator to assess the strengths and weaknesses of each party. At the end, the evaluator offers an opinion in case the matter proceed to judgment. If the mediation or neutral evaluation is unsuccessful, both parties share the costs.

Often disputants will select a conciliator or mediator directly on the basis of their own knowledge. Conciliation can be arranged through professional bodies, various dispute resolution bodies, community centres and The Institute of Arbitrators and Mediators Australia. There is debate regarding the extent to which alternative methods of dispute resolution should be formalised. The Australian Commercial Disputes Centre and similar bodies offer a range of dispute resolution services. A number of State and Territory Government entities and courts in some jurisdictions have actively supported

AUS ¶70-201

alternative dispute resolution techniques such as mediation. Some statutes provide recognition of ADR as part of the court processes.

The Federal Court of Australia (under sec. 53A of the *Federal Court of Australia Act 1976* (Cth)) and the Family Court (under sec. 19B and 19D of the *Family Law Act 1975* (Cth)) may refer proceedings, or parts of proceedings, to mediation or arbitration if the parties agree.

AUS ¶70-202   INTERNATIONAL CONVENTIONS

Australia is not a party to any international convention concerning alternative methods of dispute resolution between private parties. Conciliation and mediation are maintained as less formal means of dispute resolution than arbitration or litigation, but the parties would be free to choose or adapt rules to suit their purposes. The Institute of Arbitrators and Mediators Australia has published conciliation rules.

AUS ¶70-203   APPOINTMENT OF CONCILIATORS AND MEDIATORS

In Australia, conciliation and mediation are not subject to regulation, and appointment and choice of conciliators and mediators can be informal. As attempts to reduce congestion in courts increases, judges and court registrars are increasingly suggesting mediation to the parties.

AUS ¶70-204   SPECIAL RULES GOVERNING PROCEEDINGS

There are no special rules governing mediation and conciliation procedures. As mentioned at AUS ¶70-202, The Institute of Arbitrators and Mediators Australia has published conciliation rules, and a number of dispute centres and other bodies have published suggested rules for mediation.

AUS ¶70-205   BASIS OF JURISDICTION

The basis of jurisdiction in mediation and conciliation is the mutual intention of the parties. Court registrars may recommend the use of mediation in the interlocutory stages of litigation.

AUS ¶70-211   ENFORCEMENT OF SETTLEMENT

The basis of enforcement of settlement achieved by conciliation, mediation or other alternative dispute resolution is contractual. It rests on the terms of a settlement agreement.

AUS ¶70-212   RIGHT OF REPRESENTATION

Many proponents of mediation and conciliation would see representation, and particularly legal representation, as contrary to the philosophy and objectives of those processes. However, representation is now common in complex disputes.

AUS ¶70-213   CHOICE OF APPLICABLE LAW

The parties are free to choose the system of substantive and procedural law governing mediation, conciliation or other alternative dispute resolution method.

AUS ¶70-214   COURTS' POWER OF INTERVENTION

Where parties agree to non-litigious forms of dispute resolution, the courts are unlikely to intervene unless a cause of action were to arise out of the process or substance of the dispute resolution.

AUS ¶70-215   CONFIDENTIALITY OF PROCEEDINGS

The extent to which proceedings remain confidential depends on the relevant legislation, the parties and the mediator or conciliator. The mediation or conciliation agreement and procedure should contain confidentiality clauses binding all participants if that is the wish of the participants but there may be restrictions on implied terms of confidentiality such as that of the public interest (see AUS ¶70-143).

AUS ¶70-221   SPECIAL RULES FOR FOREIGN PARTICIPATION

There are no special rules relating to the participation in dispute resolution procedures of foreign companies and foreign-owned subsidiaries.

AUS ¶70-222   PROVISIONS IN CONTRACT FOR FORMS OF DISPUTE RESOLUTION

There is evidence of some corporate support for alternative dispute resolution strategies. A typical contractual provision would express the intention to explore such processes before seeking to enter into arbitration or to litigate. Whether there are advantages in being more specific will depend on the circumstances. On the basis that greater particularity serves efficiency and narrows the ambit of potential dispute, the parties may wish to nominate the use of the services of an established body in formulating procedures and choosing a mediator or conciliator.

AUS ¶70-223   RESTRICTIONS ON TYPES OF DISPUTES FOR CONCILIATION, ETC.

In general, the type of commercial dispute between private parties that can be dealt with by conciliation, mediation, or other form of alternative dispute resolution is not restricted. In this context, no distinction need be made between international and domestic dispute resolution.

AUS ¶70-224   DISADVANTAGES OF CONCILIATION, ETC.

The greatest potential disadvantage in using conciliation, mediation or alternative dispute resolution is the risk of not achieving a conclusive and enforceable result. The success of these forms of dispute resolution depends on the accurate matching of the type of dispute to the process. Disputes involving high levels of antagonism, or more than two parties, for example, may have less chance of successful resolution. Another area of potential disadvantage is the lack of institutional provision of fairness and skill. Great reliance is put on the expertise of the one person such as the mediator.

AUS ¶70-225　JOINT METHODS OF DISPUTE RESOLUTION

Conciliation, mediation and other forms of alternative dispute resolution can be pursued simultaneously with arbitral proceedings, and there is an increasing awareness of the desirability of facilitating the resolution of disputes generally in this manner. The rules of natural justice do apply to arbitral proceedings in Australia, but if the consensual nature of alternative dispute resolution procedures is maintained, there is no necessary impediment to the simultaneous pursuit of alternative methods.

FRAMEWORK FOR DISPUTE RESOLUTION

International conventions .. AUS ¶70-301

Recognised arbitration
　centres .... AUS ¶70-302

Internationally acceptable
　arbitrators .... AUS ¶70-303

Availability of local
　advisers .... AUS ¶70-304

AUS ¶70-301　INTERNATIONAL CONVENTIONS

International conventions applicable in Australia include the New York Convention on the Recognition and Enforcement of Foreign Arbitral Awards (see AUS ¶70-102) and the UNCITRAL Model Law on International Commercial Arbitration (see AUS ¶70-103)
.

AUS ¶70-302　RECOGNISED ARBITRATION CENTRES

The Australian Centre for International Commercial Arbitration (ACICA), affiliated with The Institute of Arbitrators and Mediators Australia, was established in Melbourne in 1985. The Australian Commercial Disputes Centre (ACDC), supported by the New South Wales government, commenced in Sydney in 1986. It offers a range of services, including less formal processes of alternative dispute resolution including mediation and the training of mediators. The Australasian Disputes Centre (ADC), based in Brisbane, is an umbrella organisation covering a number of groups offering specialist dispute resolution services in arbitration, mediation, conciliation and expert appraisal.

AUS ¶70-303   INTERNATIONALLY ACCEPTABLE ARBITRATORS

The Australian Centre for International Commercial Arbitration includes arbitrators of high international repute on its panel of arbitrators. Expertise is readily available in traditional areas such as construction and engineering matters through to newer areas such as leading edge technology and e-commerce. More specific advice can be sought from the Centres mentioned above, the State and Territory Law Societies, relevant professional bodies and the Institute of Arbitrators Australia.

AUS ¶70-304   AVAILABILITY OF LOCAL ADVISERS

A number of Australian law firms have extensive experience in advising on arbitration. Some are members of international networks. Advice on arbitration, conciliation and other forms of dispute resolution is available from bodies mentioned at AUS ¶70-303.

POSITION OF GOVERNMENT

Status of government .... AUS ¶70-401   Enforcement of orders .... AUS ¶70-403

Choice of forum .... AUS ¶70-402   International conventions .. AUS ¶70-404

AUS ¶70-401   STATUS OF GOVERNMENT

According to specific legislation, any person may bring civil proceedings against the government, and the matter will proceed as if it were being conducted between private parties. Further to this assertion, two apparently contradictory propositions may be advanced:

- Australia has adopted a theory of immunity which maintains government immunity in acts or transactions that are governmental in nature; and

- the common law of contract applies to the government and the individual party equally.

The theory of government protection from legal action relies on the essentially public and accountable nature of government, which can never risk compromise by private dealings, nor be held to representations concerning the future. Further, the legislative sovereignty of Parliament can be argued as rendering it immune from statute-based action. On these bases, it could be argued that holding the government to a purported agreement might prove difficult.

Against this, it can be argued that, provided the threshold question of the capacity of a government to enter into a contract is satisfied and the specific action is not statute-barred, there is ample provision and precedent for a government to be sued. Crown proceedings legislation, or its equivalent, in the States and Territories makes provision for legal action against government. For example, sec. 5 of the *Crown Proceedings Act 1988* (NSW) empowers any person to sue the Crown as if the Crown were a private party. The *Judiciary Act 1903* (Cth) contains the jurisdictional empowering provisions on which a claim against the Commonwealth government would be brought. Further, sec. 64 of the *Judiciary Act* provides that the rights of the parties are to be upheld as closely as possible to the rights that would be enjoyed by private parties to a legal action.

Following this reasoning, commercial activities of government attract liability. The government may claim a defence of "executive necessity", but the denial of liability on that basis would be arguable. It may be difficult to distinguish between the governmental and commercial nature of government action, and clarity of definition may be important. For example, it might not always be obvious that a commercial transaction encompasses a guarantee in respect of a financial obligation.

It will be necessary to establish a case according to the principles of the law of contract and associated principles. Hence, for example, whether a government agency is acting outside its authority will be determined according to the law of agency. Specialist advice must be obtained in any contemplated action against the government.

AUS ¶70-402   CHOICE OF FORUM

In an action against the Commonwealth government, the High Court has original jurisdiction by virtue of sec. 75 of the Commonwealth Constitution. Section 56 of the *Judiciary Act 1903* provides that an action may be brought in either the High Court or another competent court. In effect, this means that the Commonwealth government can be sued in a State court. An action against a State or Territory government would proceed in a court exercising the jurisdiction of that jurisdiction.

AUS ¶70-403   ENFORCEMENT OF ORDERS

Orders arising out of a successful contractual claim against the government are not limited in terms of remedy or enforcement.

AUS ¶70-404   INTERNATIONAL CONVENTIONS

The Commonwealth is a party to the Convention on the Settlement of Investment Disputes between States and Nationals of Other States (ICSID).

Australia is not a party to the Convention establishing the Multilateral Investment Guarantee Agency (MIGA).

For further information, refer to the Institute of Arbitrators and Mediators Australia homepage at www.instarb.com.au.

Regulation of Local Finance

Identification of sources .... AUS ¶75-001

Control of financing .... AUS ¶75-101

Terms of financing .... AUS ¶75-201

Legal securities for finance .... AUS ¶75-301

IDENTIFICATION OF SOURCES

Types of local financial
institutions .... AUS ¶75-001

How do financial institutions
raise and supply
finance? .... AUS ¶75-002

Methods used to access
international capital
markets .... AUS ¶75-003

Specialised institutions for
investment and
development .... AUS ¶75-004

Specialised institutions for
financing exports .... AUS ¶75-005

Local and foreign equity-loan
ratios .... AUS ¶75-011

AUS ¶75-001   TYPES OF LOCAL FINANCIAL INSTITUTIONS

The following are the types of local financial institutions in Australia operating in the Australian money market:

- Government and semi-government financing agencies. These include:
  - Commonwealth Bank Group, which includes the Commonwealth Bank, ASB Bank, Colonial, Colonial First State Investments, Commonwealth Financial Services Ltd., Commonwealth Life Ltd., Commonwealth Securities Ltd. (Comsec), Commonwealth Bank Finance Corporation (CBFC), and Commonwealth Insurance Ltd. (www.commbank.com.au); and
  - State and Territory Government financial institutions promoting small business and special development projects.
- Local publicly-owned banks:
  - Australia and New Zealand Banking Group (ANZ);
  - National Australia Bank (NAB); and
  - Westpac Banking Corporation (Westpac).

In addition, there are a number of State government and smaller banks.

- Branches of foreign banks. Only three foreign banks are permitted to set up branches in Australia:
  - Bank of China;
  - Bank of New Zealand; and
  - Banque Nationale de Paris.
- Subsidiaries of foreign banks.

Sixteen subsidiaries were licensed to operate in Australia in 1985 including the Bank of America, Bank of Singapore, Bank of Tokyo, Bankers Trust, Barclays, Chase AMP, Citibank, Citibank Savings, Deutsche Bank, Hong Kong Bank, IBT, Lloyds, Mitsubishi, Natwest and Standard Chartered.

Other foreign banks are active in Australia but are restricted to merchant banking.

- Merchant banks — active in the wholesale money market.
- Finance companies (including pastoral finance companies) — consumer credit and commercial finance.
- Insurance companies.
- "Managed investment schemes" and managed funds — collective investments, mutual funds, unit trusts, superannuation funds.
- Trustee companies — these are growing rapidly with the growth of compulsory superannuation.
- Management and investment companies.
- Venture capital or "risk capital" companies — equity capital invested in high risk projects, with tax advantages.
- Building societies — non-profit, non-bank financial institutions applying members' funds generally for housing finance.
- Credit unions — incorporated co-operative associations lending member's money at interest.
- Friendly societies.
- Registered money market dealers.
- Australian Stock Exchange (ASX) and several other "licensed financial markets" for equities.
- Sydney Futures Exchange (SFE) and several other "licensed financial markets" for derivatives.
- The Reserve Bank of Australia which operates as a banker for the Commonwealth government.

In addition, there are also Superannuation and Pension Funds and Approved Deposit Funds providing finance in Australia.

In 1992, Australia liberalised the regulation of foreign banks by allowing branches to be opened in Australia to conduct wholesale banking rather than requiring the incorporation of an Australian subsidiary.

Foreign banks wishing to operate a branch in Australia must satisfy the requisite authorities that the applicant is prepared to comply with relevant prudential requirements and has the appropriate standing in the banking community.

The Reserve Bank of Australia has issued requirements for foreign bank branches operating in Australia. These requirements deal with situations where a foreign bank operates both a branch and a subsidiary in Australia.

Refer to its website at: www.rba.gov.au.

AUS ¶75-002   HOW DO FINANCIAL INSTITUTIONS RAISE AND SUPPLY FINANCE?

The financial market in Australia has five main components:

- the inter-bank market — short-term lending and borrowing between banks;
- the official market — the short-term money market established by the Reserve Bank making available lender of last resort facilities through its authorised dealers;
- the unofficial market — the market for the making available of surplus funds in addition to that provided by the authorised dealers in the short-term money market;
- the inter-company market — the movement of funds between companies with offsetting financial needs; and
- the government securities market.

The unofficial market is the biggest source of funds and consists mainly of general deposits, bank bills and promissory notes. Funds are raised on term or call, with term funding usually up to five years. Apart from deposits, funds are raised by the issue of bonds, stocks and notes, which in the Australian context means unsecured notes.

The funds of commercial banks are distributed for the purposes of lending in the form of fixed loans, overdrafts commercial bills and leasing.

Loans are usually for fixed terms of three to 10 years, while overdrafts are reviewed on an agreed basis — usually annually. Normally, bills are 90- or 180-day but bill facilities may be established for a longer period such as three years. Leasing, where the bank acts as lessor, usually applies for terms of three to five years, with some periods extending to seven years. Leveraged leasing is used to finance larger capital transactions.

Interest rates for fixed loans are linked to an appropriate indication rate such as the overdraft rate, which banks publish regularly. The interest for fixed loans is usually more than the overdraft rate to reflect the longer term commitment of the bank. Interest rates on fixed loans are rarely set for the duration of the loan, but are open to change according to prevailing conditions in the market. As noted previously, overdraft rates are published regularly but often banks require a slightly higher margin depending upon risk. The interest rate for commercial bills is set according to market conditions.

Refer to the Reserve Bank website at: www.rba.gov.au.

AUS ¶75-003   METHODS USED TO ACCESS INTERNATIONAL CAPITAL MARKETS

The Eurodollar or Euro currency markets — USD held outside the US — are a major source of overseas funding which is available to Australian companies. This funding may take the form of short-term advances, term loans or backup facilities. Dealers are readily available to arrange these funds.

Australia also has access to the US commercial paper which is available through appointed dealers some of which have offices in Australia, including Bankers Trust and Citicorp.

Australian borrowers can access other overseas funds such as transferable loan certificates available through Hong Kong. The currency is usually the US dollar.

AUS ¶75-004   SPECIALISED INSTITUTIONS FOR INVESTMENT AND DEVELOPMENT

There are a number of financial institutions in Australia which provide financial assistance to specific types of investment or development.

In addition, there are a number of specific State and Territory government bodies including small business development corporations which provide small assistance grants and specialised development authorities which commonly provide assistance to encourage policies such as decentralisation or rural development.

The Export Finance and Insurance Corporation provides assistance to exporters (see AUS ¶75-005).

AUS ¶75-005   SPECIALISED INSTITUTIONS FOR FINANCING EXPORTS

The Export Finance and Insurance Corporation (EFIC), a subsidiary of the Australian Trade Commission, was established primarily to encourage Australian exports by insuring exporters against non-payment for goods. EFIC also provides loans to overseas buyers to assist with the export of Australian capital goods and associated services. In addition, EFIC guarantees banks and insurance companies against export bond losses.

For more information, see EFIC homepage at www.efic.gov.au.

Confirming houses provide some financial assistance but this is a role which is increasingly being taken by the commercial banks.

AUS ¶75-011   LOCAL AND FOREIGN EQUITY-LOAN RATIOS

There are no regulatory requirements covering local debt to equity ratios. Financial institutions have their own guidelines which vary according to risk and the type of loan. If a borrower seeks a loan which is above the usual debt to equity ratio, the lender may require mortgage insurance.

So far as foreign investment is concerned, there are no formal equity/debt requirements. However, the tax law ''thin capitalisation'' rules (revised as from 2001) affect Australian resident entities investing overseas, their associate entities, foreign controlled Australian entities and foreign entities investing directly into Australia.

A thinly capitalised entity is one whose assets are funded by a high level of debt with little equity. For example, a highly geared entity may have AUS$3 of debt to AUS$1 of equity.

The thin capitalisation rules seek to limit the amount of debt used to fund those Australian operations or investments by disallowing the debt deductions an entity can claim against Australian assessable income when the entity's debt used to fund Australian assets exceeds certain limits.

If there is an excess of the adjusted average debt of the Australian entity over the following maximum allowable debt, there is a reduction in the amount of interest that can be claimed as a deduction against Australian assessable income:

- 75% of the average value of the Australian entity's assets;

- the arm's length maximum amount of debt which the entity could have borrowed from third parties, and

- the worldwide gearing debt based on 120% of thw worldwide gearing of the group.

CONTROL OF FINANCING

Criteria for regulation of
     sources of loan finance .. AUS ¶75-101

Manner in which sources of
     loan finance controlled .. AUS ¶75-102

Regulations covering raising of
     local equity capital .... AUS ¶75-103

Manner of regulating raising of
     local equity capital .... AUS ¶75-104

Self-regulation by credit and
     financial institutions ...... AUS ¶75-105

Methods used for raising
     capital .... AUS ¶75-111

Taxation of dividends or
     interest to non-
     residents .... AUS ¶75-112

AUS ¶75-101   CRITERIA FOR REGULATION OF SOURCES OF LOAN FINANCE

The regulation and control of sources of loan finance is related principally to the institution which acts as lender but there is also control by reference to the type of borrower or the type of transaction. Greater control has been exercised on banks as institutions; less control is exercised over other financial institutions.

AUS ¶75-102   MANNER IN WHICH SOURCES OF LOAN FINANCE CONTROLLED

Banks in Australia are regulated by the *Banking Act 1959* (Cth). This Act deals with those companies entitled to carry on banking business, the supervision of banks by the Reserve Bank and the influence of the Reserve Bank on foreign investment. The Reserve Bank is set up under the *Reserve Bank Act 1959* (Cth) which provides for its role as the central bank of Australia and as banker for the federal government. The Reserve Bank issues currency, determines monetary and banking policies and sets interest rates. The Reserve Bank of Australia, headquartered in Sydney, has responsibility for the monetary policy, regulation of the payments system and the overall stability of the financial system in Australia.

The Commonwealth Bank, which operates principally as a commercial bank was originally established by the Commonwealth government in 1911 to carry on ordinary banking business. It was privatised in 1997. The Commonwealth Bank does not exercise control over sources of loan finance and it now offers a fully integrated financial services business, including retail, business and investment banking; stockbroking services; insurance; finance company activities and funds management.

The Commonwealth government also controls life insurance companies through the *Life Insurance Act 1995* (Cth). This Act deals with the registration of life insurance companies and is primarily concerned with the protection of policyholders.

All States and Territories have legislation dealing with other non-bank financial institutions such as building societies and credit unions.

The Australian Prudential Regulation Authority (APRA), located in Sydney, is responsible for the prudential supervision of deposit-taking institutions, life and general insurance companies and superannuation funds.

See the APRA homepage at www.apra.gov.au.

The Australian Securities and Investments Commission (ASIC), headquartered in Sydney, regulates the market operations of superannuation funds; life and general companies and deposit-taking by banks, credit unions, building societies and friendly societies. Those carrying on a ''financial services business'' must have an Australian financial services licence issued by ASIC under sec. 911A of the *Corporations Act 2001* (Cth). ASIC sets standards about disclosure to customers, monitors their sales practices and compliance with codes of practice, checks customer complaints systems, co-operates with APRA and investigates and takes action against misconduct.

See the ASIC homepage at www.asic.gov.au.

Control of transactions

In Australia, there is a range of general regulatory legislation which provides consumer protection for borrowers. Operating nationally is the *Trade Practices Act 1974* (Cth) (AUS ¶30-011), while at the State or Territory level, there are parallels in the Fair Trading Acts and legislation covering such matters as moneylenders, pawnbrokers and consumer credit transactions generally.

The *Code of Banking Practice*, released by the Commonwealth government and the banking industry in 1993, came into effect in 1996. The code has been revised and the "new generation" code commences in August 2003.

Banks that adopt the Code are obliged to ensure that they adhere to certain standards of good practice and conduct when dealing with their retail customers.

The Code is intended to:

- prescribe standards of good practice and service;
- require banks to have available, on request, general information regarding their obligations to their customers;
- underscore the banks' obligations to protect customers' privacy;
- promote informed and effective relationships between banks and their customers;
- ensure that liability incurred by a guarantor under a third party guarantee is limited and clearly specified and that guarantors are informed of their right to review all relevant information regarding their prospective liability prior to entering into the guarantee; and
- oblige banks to provide effective procedures for the resolution of customer disputes.

The *Code of Banking Practice* is available at www.bankers.asn.au.

The *Code of Banking Practice* does not apply to non-consumers: the relations of small business with their banks is regulated by the "Small Business Principles" designed to foster good working relations.

Similar codes of practice have been released for credit unions and building societies, resulting in industry codes of practice now covering the majority of customers using retail banking services.

AUS ¶75-103 REGULATIONS COVERING RAISING OF LOCAL EQUITY CAPITAL

The principal means of raising local equity is through floatation on the Australian Stock Exchange (ASX). The equity forms most commonly used are:

- *Ordinary shares in limited liability companies.* Here, the risk capital is represented by the ordinary shares which entitle the holder to dividends and to a division of the company's assets on liquidation. The holder of ordinary shares is only liable for the unpaid amount (if any) on the nominal value of the shares.
- *Ordinary shares in no liability companies.* This type of shareholding is only available for companies involved in mining or exploration. A shareholder in this instance is not liable for calls made on the shares but can forfeit the shares to the company.
- *"Managed investment schemes" including unit trusts.* Here, the investor purchases an interest or unit from a professional manager representing a direct beneficial interest in the assets of the business enterprise. Examples include property, equities

and cash management trusts, where management of the fund seeks to produce a return.

Major amendments came into force in March 2000 regarding fund-raising.

A standard full-disclosure prospectus must still be lodged with the Austrian Securities and Investments Commission (ASIC) where there is an offer of shares or interests in managed investment schemes, subject to the exceptions below. It must contain all relevant information vital to potential investors in deciding on the state and prospects of the company (sec. 710 and 711).

A short form prospectus may be used if it refers to material already lodged with ASIC (sec. 712).

A brief profile statement may be used instead of a prospectus to simplify and reduce the amount of disclosure material (sec. 721).

An offer information statement may be used instead of a prospectus if the amount raised is AUS$5 million or less (sec. 709(4)).

Exemptions from the disclosure requirements of the *Corporations Act 2001* (Cth) now apply to:

- an offer of securities to 20 investors not exceeding AUS$2 million;
- an offer of securities to "sophisticated investors" where the minimum amount payable is AUS$500,000; and
- an offer of securities to "professional investors" such as securities dealers, life and superannuation companies (sec. 708).

The Australian Stock Exchange (ASX) also exercises control over floats by ensuring that the stock market listing rules are complied with. These rules stipulate the minimum size and capital requirements for the various entities making the float.

The ASX had a strong history of self-regulation, but it is no longer entirely independent as it now operates as the front-line regulator within the general framework of ASIC control (the second-line regulator), comprising a system of "co-regulation" with ASIC.

Once a foreign company is registered in Australia, it would be entitled to raise equity subject to the same rules as resident companies.

For more details, refer to the ASX homepage at www.asx.com.au.

AUS ¶75-104   MANNER OF REGULATING RAISING OF LOCAL EQUITY CAPITAL

As noted at AUS ¶75-103, the principal regulatory body concerned with the raising of equity is ASIC. It does this through its requirements concerning regulation of fund-raising including prospectuses. If a company proposes to list its securities then the listing rules of the ASX become relevant.

ASIC is set up under the *Australian Securities and Investments Commission Act 2001* (Cth) and administers the *Corporations Act 2001*. This statute is of general application to all companies. It lays down specific rules governing the issue of a prospectus and other disclosure documents, their content, registration, the need for the application for securities to be attached, the control of publicity and the effect of statements that are false or misleading. ASIC can also issue orders (a "stop" order) to prevent the circulation or issue of a non-complying prospectus or other disclosure document and prosecutes offenders under the law.

AUS ¶75-105 SELF-REGULATION BY CREDIT AND FINANCIAL INSTITUTIONS

The Australian Securities and Investments Commission (ASIC) regulates the market activities of superannuation funds, life and general insurance companies, deposit taking by banks, credit unions, building societies and friendly societies. These market activities include setting standards about disclosure to customers, sales practices and dealing with customer complaints. ASIC monitors compliance with the relevant industry codes of conduct (which provide or some self-regulation by banks including electronic banking [EFTS], building societies and credit unions). It can investigate and it can take action for misconduct.

AUS ¶75-111 METHODS USED FOR RAISING CAPITAL

Traditionally, capital has been raised in Australia in both debt and equity forms. Australia is now a country of shareholders, with some 53% of the adult population in year 2004 holding Australian shares directly or indirectly through managed investments.

AUS ¶75-112 TAXATION OF DIVIDENDS OR INTEREST TO NON-RESIDENTS

Interest and dividends paid to non-residents is subject to withholding tax.

TERMS OF FINANCING

Customary terms for lending or
investing money .... AUS ¶75-201

Flexibility of customary terms
for lending or investing
money .... AUS ¶75-202

Interest rates .... AUS ¶75-203

Covenants, financial ratios and
security interests .... AUS ¶75-204

Local arrangements concerning
currency exchange and
rates .... AUS ¶75-205

Which law governs
financing? .... AUS ¶75-211

AUS ¶75-201   CUSTOMARY TERMS FOR LENDING OR INVESTING MONEY

The usual terms on which money is lent are clear but as in any competitive market, variations will exist in interest charged or on securities required. Variations will be found in the lender/customer relationship and in investment contracts.

AUS ¶75-202   FLEXIBILITY OF CUSTOMARY TERMS FOR LENDING OR INVESTING MONEY

The adoption of customary terms does not arise from any government policy directives or statutory rules. However, governmental control is exercised in the setting of interest rates which is discussed at AUS ¶75-203. Otherwise, the terms upon which money is lent and invested is the subject of internal policy decisions and market forces. This is particularly so since the deregulation of the financial system in the mid-1980s.

AUS ¶75-203   INTEREST RATES

Interest rates are led by the Board of the Reserve Bank of Australia. In implementing government monetary policy, the Reserve Bank exercises its influence over interest rates by its actions in buying or selling treasury bills and treasury notes. Factors which bear upon interest rates are overseas rates, balance of payments and external debt, foreign investment in Australia, inflation and the overall manipulation of the economy through monetary policy.

As at May 2004, the interest rate in Australia was about 5.25% with an inflation rate of about 2%. The rates are both fixed and variable depending upon the type and length of the loan. There is a very strong tendency for the banks to use variable rates for long-term loans as there has been considerable fluctuation in interest rates in recent times. Short-term finance such as that provided by commercial bills is provided at fixed rates.

See further details at www.rba.gov.au.

AUS ¶75-201

AUS ¶75-204 COVENANTS, FINANCIAL RATIOS AND SECURITY INTERESTS

The ratio of debt to equity varies with the type and extent of security and the relationship between the borrower and the lending institution. Traditionally, banks are more conservative than other lenders and require an equity contribution of between one-third to one-quarter of the value of the assets over which security is being taken. Finance companies, credit unions and building societies may lend on a higher loan to value ratio but will often require mortgage insurance. Where companies are concerned, a lender is likely to take security over all assets of the company by means of a floating charge. In addition, mortgages or charges will be taken over specific assets such as land. Directors of the company will be required to personally guarantee the loan. For companies in a group, cross guarantees from other members of the group are common.

Loans to individuals will usually be secured over the asset for which the loan monies are intended.

A common covenant to be found in loan documents is the negative pledge. Here, the borrower undertakes not to provide any new security to another lender; in some cases, additional securities may be allowed but the clause contains a dollar or percentage limit. The use of the negative pledge during the ''excesses of the '80s'' — the Australian property and investment boom of the 1980s — led to an increasing number of companies financing their operations by means of unsecured borrowings extended by lenders upon the strength of the negative pledge. Banks have now reverted to secured lending.

AUS ¶75-205 LOCAL ARRANGEMENTS CONCERNING CURRENCY EXCHANGE AND RATES

A number of options are available for a company in Australia wishing to manage its foreign exchange risk. It may:

- purchase an option contract;
- borrow in a basket of currencies;
- enter into a forward exchange contract for a specified currency; or
- enter into a hedge contract.

Where money is borrowed in a foreign currency, the bank is likely to include a covenant requiring the borrower to top up the security or make partial repayment so that agreed security levels are maintained. Alternatively, the lender may require the borrower to hedge all or part of the exposure by using any of the methods referred to above.

AUS ¶75-211 WHICH LAW GOVERNS FINANCING?

In keeping with general principles of private international law, the parties are free to make their own choice as to the applicable law. Since the lender is likely to have the strongest bargaining power, it is likely to be the domicile of the lender.

An Australian court will ordinarily uphold the parties' choice of law, whether that choice points to a foreign or domestic jurisdiction. On occasions, the laws of New York or England may be chosen even by parties who are not domiciled there, because of the countries' strong establishment as financial centres.

LEGAL SECURITIES FOR FINANCE

Security interests in
   property .... AUS ¶75-301

Recognised forms of security
   rights .... AUS ¶75-401

Security rights .... AUS ¶75-501

AUS ¶75-301   SECURITY INTERESTS IN PROPERTY

Security interests may be taken over all kinds of property including:

- immovables (e.g. land);
- tangible movables (e.g. chattels, vehicles, goods); and
- intangible movables (e.g. intellectual property rights).

A security interest cannot be taken over a contract for personal services.

AUS ¶75-401   RECOGNISED FORMS OF SECURITY RIGHTS

In Australia, security rights or interests arise by transfer, mortgage, charge, lien or pledge. These rights vary according to the asset over which the security is taken and the circumstances in which the security arises. The only security interest which is peculiar to a type of lender is the banker's lien.

For the different types of property, the following security interests are the most common:

- immovables: legal mortgage (arising by transfer of title); equitable mortgage (arising by agreement);
- tangible movables: equitable mortgage and equitable charge, pledge and lien; and
- intangible movables: assignment, charge.

Security Rights

Can subject property be readily
    identified? .... AUS ¶75-501

Can borrower's interest be readily
    identified? .... AUS ¶75-502

Formalities for creation of
    security .... AUS ¶75-503

Priority of security interests . AUS ¶75-504

Number of security interests
    against one property .... AUS ¶75-505

Floating securities over classes of
    assets .... AUS ¶75-511

Securities for further
    advances .... AUS ¶75-512

Is the continuing interest of the
    borrower recognised and
    protected? .... AUS ¶75-513

Retention of possession by
    borrower .... AUS ¶75-514

Realisation of security by
    lender .... AUS ¶75-515

Transferability of lender's
    security .... AUS ¶75-521

Forms of personal security ... AUS ¶75-522

Acceptable securities .... AUS ¶75-523

Charges for registration of
    securities .... AUS ¶75-524

Tax implications and choice of
    security .... AUS ¶75-525

AUS ¶75-501   CAN SUBJECT PROPERTY BE READILY IDENTIFIED?

In general, most forms of property can be identified through registration. The rationale for the different systems of registration applying in Australia is essentially to make for easy identification of property. At the same time, registration protects third parties from taking the secured property without notice of a prior security interest as all securities need to be registered. The following registration regimes are likely to cover most forms of security interest:

- land titles office (AUS ¶25-112);
- company charges;
- security interests over ships;
- security interests over goods;
- security interests over motor vehicles;
- security interests over patents; and
- security interests over mining tenements.

AUS ¶75-502   CAN BORROWER'S INTEREST BE READILY IDENTIFIED?

If the security interest is registered through one of the systems referred to at AUS ¶75-501, then the borrower's interest is easily identifiable.

- *Land titles registration.* In each State and Territory in Australia, there is a system for the registration of title to land where transfers of title and mortgage interests are noted (AUS ¶25-112).

- *Company charges.* There is a national system for the registration of charges given by companies with ASIC which are not security interests over land. The register is kept in the name of the company showing details of the charges.

- *Ships.* Under the *Shipping Registration Act 1981* (Cth), certain ships, principally Australian-owned commercial vessels, are required to be registered. Mortgages over ships can be registered but only in respect of ships which themselves are registered.

- *Security interests over goods.* In each State or Territory, there is a *Bills of Sale Act* or equivalent which requires security documents relating to chattels to be registered. The registration shows the name of the owner of the chattels and the security interest.

- *Motor vehicles.* In all States and Territories of Australia, there is a vehicles securities register where security interests over motor vehicles can be registered (e.g. in NSW, "REVS" (the Register of Encumbered Vehicles), discussed below. Details are entered against the motor vehicle which is identified by reference to an engine or chassis number and/or registered number of the vehicle.

- *Patents and trademarks.* A mortgage interest can be registered under the *Patents Act* and the *Trade Marks Act* or at common law.

- *Mining tenements.* In all States and Territories, there is a system for the registration of title to mining leases or licences. Mortgage interests and other security interests are noted in the registers.

AUS ¶75-503   FORMALITIES FOR CREATION OF SECURITY

The actual creation of a security is not generally accompanied by any particular formality. However, to perfect the security, registration is required in those jurisdictions where registration is possible. Accordingly, it is usual to provide for the creation of the security interest by a document to enable registration. In certain cases, however, the security is constituted by possession, such as a lien and in this case, no document is required and registration is not provided for.

The position concerning the creation and registration of securities (apart from company charges and patent rights) is a State or Territory matter, as discussed below in general terms.

Securities over land

In the case of land, two types of security interests are possible: legal mortgages and equitable mortgages:

- *Legal mortgages.* A written mortgage document in the correct form is drawn up, signed and lodged for registration at the land titles office, located in the capital city in each State or Territory. Registration time varies but is likely to take several weeks. It is the mortgage document which is registered. This enables any search to

AUS ¶75-503

be made by a member of the public. There are no time limits for registration but failure to register may give third parties a priority interest if they become registered first. Prior to registration, a security interest may be protected by a caveat.

There are no special problems associated with the taking of security over land, so long as registration is accomplished. In each State or Territory in Australia, the system of land registration is the Torrens Title which gives registrants an indefeasible (absolute) title to the land.

- *Equitable mortgages.* Equitable mortgages arise when a mortgage document is never registered or where title deeds are deposited with the lender as security for the loan. The holder of an equitable mortgage will take subject to any registered mortgage over the same property. Hence, equitable mortgages are inferior to legal mortgages and will rank second after legal mortgages where mortgagees compete for the same land.

Refer to the Land Titles Office (NSW) at www.lpi.nsw.gov.au for case examples.

Company charges

Under the *Corporations Act 2001*, certain charges by companies have to be registered with the Australian Securities and Investments Commission (ASIC) under *Corporations Act* sec. 262. Failure to register creates an offence but more importantly it also means that third parties may gain priority if they become registered. The charge has to be registered within 45 days of creation, although that period can be extended by order of the court. The charge may be a fixed charge but more commonly it is a floating charge, which enables the company to carry on its normal business including buying and selling assets. This means that the security over which the charge extends can be depleted and theoretically the company can give a fixed charge over the same asset which will have priority over the floating charge. This eventuality can be eliminated by providing in the floating charge itself that such fixed charges cannot be created.

Registration of company charges with ASIC is effected centrally but with increasing sophistication in technology, this can be accomplished electronically. Once lodged, registration of the charge is effected more or less immediately in that a notice of charge is placed on the register which serves to protect the lodging party.

Failure to register a charge means that a liquidator of the company can treat the lender as unsecured. Also, later charges will ordinarily take priority if registered first.

Refer to the ASIC homepage at www.asic.gov.au for more details.

Security interests over ships

The *Shipping Registration Act 1981* (Cth) provides certain statutory requirements for a mortgage of a ship although no particular form is stipulated. Upon lodgment, registration of the mortgage is required "as soon as practicable". The effect of registration is to create a priority in favour of the party registered. If the owner of the ship is a company, registration under the *Shipping Registration Act* does not relieve it from registering the charge with ASIC under the *Corporations Act*.

Security over goods

If the security interest taken over the goods is regarded as a bill of sale, then it can be registered. In some States and Territories and for some types of bills of sale, a failure to register renders the bill of sale invalid. The expression "bill of sale" is usually widely defined to include assignments, transfers, declarations of trust without transfer and licences to take possession but it does not cover every transaction where a security interest is taken over goods. Because bills of sale law is State and Territory based, there is no consolidated national registry where all securities over goods can be inspected.

Upon lodgment of the documents, registration is usually effected within several weeks. There is no system of registering caveats. Ordinarily, registration has to be renewed every five to seven years. This is not the case with the other forms of registration previously discussed.

Motor vehicles

The Australian States and Territories have moved to a system of providing for registration of security interests over motor vehicles on a government vehicles securities register. For example, in New South Wales the register is the Register of Encumbered Vehicles ("REVS"). These schemes operate separately from the bills of sale legislation. Under the system, an intending purchaser of a motor vehicle can search the register by means of the registration details of the vehicle. Upon obtaining a certificate as to the result of the search, the intending purchaser is protected against security interests not shown. Registration of a security interest is effected very promptly.

Mining tenements

Under the various legislative schemes in the States and Territories governing mining, there are systems allowing for the registration of mortgages over mining leases and licences. In some jurisdictions, for instance Western Australia where due to the large volume of mining activity mortgages are common, a mortgage of a mining tenement will not be effective until it is registered.

Further details are available on the website of Mining Australia.

General

Where no system of registration is available, the security interest usually arises by the lender obtaining possession of either the goods or title deeds to land. The value of the security lies in the lender holding custody or possession of the item in question.

AUS ¶75-504   PRIORITY OF SECURITY INTERESTS

The main factor affecting priorities of competing creditors is registration, as noted at AUS ¶75-503. However, where registration is not available or where two competing securities are both unregistered, more detailed and complex rules have to be considered. The operation of these rules usually depends upon the nature of the interest, time of creation and notice by other parties of its creation. As a general rule, the following principles apply:

AUS ¶75-504

- if the nature of the interest is the same (e.g. legal or equitable), then the first in time prevails.
- legal interests have priority over equitable interests even if the legal interest was created later unless the holder of the legal interest had notice of the prior equitable interest.

With the exception of company charges (where an unregistered charge is void against a liquidator), an unregistered security interest will still prevail over ordinary general creditors of the company.

Under bankruptcy or liquidation, priority is determined by the liquidator or trustee in bankruptcy upon receipt of proof of debt documentation which is forwarded to each known creditor.

The liquidator's or trustee's decisions on priority contests can be challenged in court.

The priority for payment of debts is set out in the *Bankruptcy Act 1966* (Cth). The rules for priority of payment of debts are:

- certain costs of the petitioning creditor and costs of the administration;
- funeral expenses;
- payment of wages to a prescribed amount;
- workers' compensation; and
- certain workers' entitlement, such as annual and long service leave.

Certain taxation liabilities of the bankrupt or company in liquidation also have priority.

AUS ¶75-505   NUMBER OF SECURITY INTERESTS AGAINST ONE PROPERTY

There is no particular limit to the number of security interests that can be created over one property. The limitations that will arise in practice are the presence of a ''negative pledge'' in the security document or the need to obtain the approval of a prior registered creditor who holds the title deeds.

AUS ¶75-511   FLOATING SECURITIES OVER CLASSES OF ASSETS

Only companies can create floating charges over their assets (see AUS ¶75-503). A floating charge cannot be created over land; otherwise all items of movable tangibles of a company can be included. After-acquired property is included, assuming that this is not excluded by the terms of the charge. Future property is not usually covered by the security in the case of a bill of sale.

Where two floating charges are registered over the same asset, the first registered will prevail unless it was created second and the holder of the first registered charge knew of the existence of the earlier charge when it (the first registered charge) was created.

AUS ¶75-512   SECURITIES FOR FURTHER ADVANCES

The securities referred to at AUS ¶75-301 can be used to secure further advances unless a negative pledge covenant exists in the security documentation (AUS ¶75-204).

In relation to the priority of future advances, the position under the *Corporations Act* is that a creditor who has contracted to allow future advances is able to retain priority unless that person has agreed not to exercise that right.

AUS ¶75-513   IS THE CONTINUING INTEREST OF THE BORROWER RECOGNISED AND PROTECTED?

The borrower's rights are recognised either by statute or by the equity of redemption. This means the borrower is entitled to discharge the debt and to have the title transferred back free of any prior interest. This right cannot be taken away.

The extent to which a borrower can create further securities depends upon the terms of the security document, but normally the borrower cannot do this without the consent of the lender.

If the borrower disposes of the property, the lender is entitled to the net proceeds arising from the sale. The secured party is entitled to the discharge of any principal, interest and other agreed charges. The lender cannot assign or charge the property free of the borrower's interest unless the borrower is in default.

AUS ¶75-514   RETENTION OF POSSESSION BY BORROWER

In general, a borrower who is not in default will retain possession of the property, unless the lender's security interest is based on possession, such as a possessory lien, pawn or pledge.

AUS ¶75-515   REALISATION OF SECURITY BY LENDER

The ability of the lender to realise the security depends on the type of security interest held.

Where the lender holds a legal mortgage over land under general law, the power of sale resides in the lender by reason of the transfer of legal title. In the case of land under Torrens title, the power of sale is provided for under statute.

However, if the lender only has an equitable mortgage, it may be necessary to obtain a court order as there is no inherent right to sell the property secured. Where the equitable mortgage is contained in a document, the terms of the document usually give a power of sale without the need to seek a court order. However, where the lender simply relies upon the actions of the borrower in depositing the title deed with the lender to secure the indebtedness, a judicial sale is required.

With floating charges, the security documents usually set out the events which will crystallise the charge, thereby freezing the secured property. The document will also enable the lender to appoint a receiver and manager who can realise the assets.

For some securities, such as possessory liens and pledges, there is no power of sale at common law. Statutes in this case provide the basis for realisation of the security, such as the *Pawnbrokers Act* in all States and Territories or statutes in the various States and Territories dealing with uncollected goods.

Where statutes provide the power to lenders to realise securities, they set out the procedures to be followed, such as the giving of notices, auction sales and the disbursement of proceeds.

Secured creditors have priority over unsecured creditors. A secured creditor can in fact elect not to participate at all in the bankruptcy. A lender who has realised a security must account to the borrower for the surplus after payment of the principal, interest and the reasonable costs of realisation. The lender, in realising the security, must protect the interest of the borrower by taking reasonable steps to ensure that an appropriate price is obtained. If there is a deficit, it can be recovered from the borrower.

The most likely situation where a business is the subject of a security is where the assets of a company are secured by a floating charge. Here, it is permissible under the terms of the charge to sell the business as a going concern. Alternatively, as in all cases of security realisation, the Supreme Court may order the sale and may make necessary ancillary orders.

AUS ¶75-521   TRANSFERABILITY OF LENDER'S SECURITY

The lender's interest is usually freely transferable so long as the transfer is registered to ensure the security is perfected and, where relevant, so long as the law dealing with assignment of debts is followed. This will require notice of the assignment to be given to the borrower.

AUS ¶75-522   FORMS OF PERSONAL SECURITY

Personal guarantees are frequently required by financial institutions and may be given as additional security. They are particularly common where the borrower is a small to medium-sized company. In this case, directors are called upon to personally guarantee the indebtedness of the company. Guarantees signed by a wife at the request of her husband over family property such as the family home may be categorised as unconscionable and may become unenforceable if not entered into with full understanding and with free consent.

AUS ¶75-523   ACCEPTABLE SECURITIES

A registered first mortgage over land is the most desirable security. Registered second mortgages over land are also acceptable so long as there is sufficient equity in the property.

Securities over goods are also acceptable although they may not be used as the only security. A fixed charge provides more security to the lender than a floating charge, but in some cases a floating charge is the only possibility where, for example, security is taken over stock. Pledges and liens are not likely to be relied on to any great extent.

Loans to individuals are likely to be secured over the item of property being financed, such as a car. In contrast, where a company is the borrower, a lender usually seeks a wider range of securities. These will usually include a mortgage or charge over fixed assets (including land), a floating charge over movables and personal guarantees from the directors of the company.

AUS ¶75-524   CHARGES FOR REGISTRATION OF SECURITIES

The charges payable for the registration of securities vary depending on the type of security concerned and the State or Territory in which registration is sought.

AUS ¶75-525   TAX IMPLICATIONS AND CHOICE OF SECURITY

The choice of security is not affected by taxation laws but may affect those who have to pay tax on the interest earned.

MOVEMENT OF GOODS
(TRANSPORT AND SHIPPING)

Laws relating to inward and outward transport .... AUS ¶80-001
Laws relating to movement and storage of
    goods .... AUS ¶80-002
International conventions .... AUS ¶80-003
Laws relating to movement of dangerous
    substances .... AUS ¶80-004
Arrest of vessels, etc. .... AUS ¶80-005
Regulation of shipbuilding industry .... AUS ¶80-011
Laws relating to shipping register .... AUS ¶80-012

AUS ¶80-001   LAWS RELATING TO INWARD AND OUTWARD TRANSPORT

In Australia there are a variety of laws which regulate international movement of ships, aircraft and goods.

International shipping

The principal Act is the *Navigation Act* (Cth). This statute regulates the following:

- the limits of the Act itself (i.e. it does not generally apply to vessels trading only between States, fishing vessels, pleasure craft, naval vessels or inland waterways vessels);
- exclusion of liability for certain claims;
- crew wages/discharges;
- trading vessels;
- tonnage requirements;
- seaman's medical expenses;
- salvage awards/rights to compensation;
- seaworthiness;
- carriage of dangerous goods;
- collision regulations;
- wrecks;
- accidents/loss of life in ships;
- damage to property in/by ships;
- Marine Courts of Inquiry;
- pilots/pilotage.

Another Act of importance is the Commonwealth's *Seafarers Rehabilitation and Compensation Act 1992* which relates to compensation for seafarers injured in the course of their employment. The Act serves a similar purpose to the various States' *Workers Compensation Acts*, but applies to categories of persons who would not otherwise qualify for such protection. It applies to seafarers engaged on trade or commerce-related voyages:

(a) between Australia and places outside Australia;

(b) among the states of Australia; or

(c) within a Territory, between a State and a Territory or between two Territories.

The Act creates the Seafarers Rehabilitation and Compensation Authority for the purposes of administering and assessing claims made by seafarers for compensation and rehabilitation under the Act. The Authority administers a fund into which certain employers of seafarers must contribute and from which compensation and rehabilitation claims are paid.

Seafarers making claims must elect either to pursue a claim under the Act, or to pursue an independent tort action against an employer, fellow employee or third party. Compensation can in appropriate circumstances, be paid to family members or other beneficiaries of the injured or deceased. The Act requires that claimants whose injuries are of a certain type and degree undertake approved rehabilitation programs in order to hasten their return to productive work.

The other and most recent Act of importance to inward and outward shipping regulation is the *Admiralty Act 1988* (Cth). This was the product of many years' research and discussion aimed at removing the many confusing provisions and ambiguities which had evolved as a result of Australian maritime jurisdiction being a mixture of colonial, English and States' legislation.

It vests Admiralty jurisdiction over maritime claims in the Federal Court of Australia, with concurrent jurisdiction in the Supreme Courts of the States.

The Act governs all categories of maritime claims and liens created in respect of ships and cargo. It provides for rights in rem, including provisions for the arrest of ships (including "surrogate" ships and vessels owned or chartered by the same owner or demise charterer). The Act does, however, place restrictions on the circumstances in which claims will be enforced by the use of arrest powers and casts a strict onus on the arresting party to prove its rights in rem, at the risk of substantial costs for false arrest or unsubstantiated claims.

Coastal and interstate shipping

The various Australian States retain power to govern in matters which do not have a federal or interstate implication. In some circumstances where uniform legislation is desirable, States will simultaneously enact laws which effectively create a uniform code throughout Australia, or which complement federal laws enacted to bring international treaties into domestic law.

Overseas carriers, shippers and traders may frequently be confronted with further regulation by State governments. In relation to shipping and transport, they should be aware that there is often concurrent State legislation, such as:

- Harbour Acts;
- State Navigation Acts;
- Seamen's Acts;
- Marine Acts;
- Commercial Arbitration Acts;
- Port Authority Acts;
- Pilotage and associated Acts;
- State Pollution Acts.

Air transportation

Air navigation and aviation generally are regulated by three Commonwealth Acts, the *Air Navigation Act 1920,* the *Air Services Act 1995* and the *Civil Aviation Act 1988.*

In addition, each State government has enacted its own *Air Navigation Act,* in concert with the federal government so that all air navigation and civil aviation, either internationally or internally, is governed by entirely uniform legislation.

These State Acts make the Commonwealth *Air Navigation Regulations* applicable in each jurisdiction as if separately passed in each respective State.

The *Civil Aviation Regulations* and *Air Services Regulations* similarly apply uniformly throughout the Commonwealth. The matters principally covered by these regulations are:

- registration and marking of aircraft;
- airworthiness;
- maintenance;
- qualifications of flight crew (including student, private and commercial pilots);
- medical examinations;
- navigation logs;
- radio facilities;
- air routes and airways;
- aerodromes and air traffic services;
- conditions of flight;
- rules of the air;
- signals for the control of air traffic;
- air service operations;
- dangerous goods;

- fares and timetables;
- aviation security;
- suspension and cancellation of licences;
- accident inquiries;
- penalties for breaches of regulations.

In addition to the regulations, there are also numerous other instruments which govern air navigation and civil aviation such as Air Navigation Orders, Civil Aviation Orders, Notices to Airmen, and Aeronautical Information Publications. These are all issued pursuant to statutes or regulations.

Damage by aircraft Acts

Damage by aircraft and third party liability for damages for death, bodily injury or damage caused by an aircraft in flight, or by a person or thing falling from an aircraft is governed by the *Civil Aviation (Damage by Aircraft) Act 1958*, which embodies the text of the Rome Convention of 1952.

Additionally, some of the States have also enacted forms of legislation which complement the federal statute.

Regulation of carriage of goods and passengers

Most international air carriage, whether of cargo, passengers or baggage, is governed by the *Civil Aviation (Carriers' Liability) Act 1959*. In essence, the purpose of this Act is to give effect in Australia to the Warsaw Convention of 1929, as amended by the Hague Protocol of 1955. Since it was enacted, the Act has been amended on a number of occasions, most notably by the introduction in 1962 of Part 111A to give effect to the 1961 Guadalajara Convention and by amendments (Parts IIIB and IIIC), enacted in 1991 but not yet operative, to give effect to the Montreal No. 3 Convention and the Montreal No. 4 Convention. These two Conventions were made on 25 September 1975, but are not yet in force for Australia.

Part IV of the Act extends the principles of the amended Warsaw Convention to domestic carriage between states in Australia, but with modifications. Unlike other parts of the Act, Part IV does not carry any international convention directly into domestic law. Subsequent amendments to Part IV have broadened the scope of carriers' liability beyond the corresponding liability of international carrier under the Conventions and Part II, III and IIIA; but it remains true that Part IV extends the basic principles of international law into domestic law.

The exact regime which applies in any particular case is governed, broadly speaking, by the place of origin and the destination of the contract of carriage, as explained below at AUS 80-002. The Act itself governs the following broad areas of responsibility:

- matters covered by the conventions;
- domestic civil aviation matters such as:
- liability for death, injury, damage or loss of baggage;

AUS ¶80-001

- limitation of liability;
- contracting out;
- servants and agents of the carrier;
- limitation of actions;
- liability in respect of death and injury;
- contributory negligence;
- regulations relating to tickets and baggage checks;
- stowaways.

A further convention to which Australia is a party is the Chicago Convention of 1944. This is found as a Schedule to the *Air Navigation Act 1920* (Cwth). It exists for the purpose of regularising air travel between States. Its preamble says that its object is to agree on "certain principles and arrangements in order that international civil aviation may be developed in a safe and orderly manner and that international air transport services may be established on the basis of equality of opportunity and operated soundly and economically..."

Domestic air regulation

As mentioned earlier, regulation of domestic carriage is found in Part V of the *Civil Aviation (Carrier's Liability) Act 1959*. In relation to intrastate air regulation, each State has enacted its own *Civil Aviation (Carrier's Liability) Act*.

AUS ¶80-002 LAWS RELATING TO MOVEMENT AND STORAGE OF GOODS

Shipping

Leaving aside questions of coastal and intrastate shipping, international carriage of goods by sea is regulated by the *Carriage of Goods by Sea Act 1991* (Cwth), as in force after significant amendments in 1997 and 1998. In essence, the Act was passed in 1991 to provide for the adoption of the international convention known as the *Hague-Visby Rules* (or "*Amended Hague Rules*"), a regime which regulates (and balances) the competing interests of sea carriers and cargo shippers. Schedule 1 to the Act (the text of the international convention) sets out the respective rights and obligations of both carrier and shipper and provides for the issue of sea carriage documents. It also ensures that the monetary liability of carriers when goods are lost or damaged is limited.

For shipments occurring between 1 November 1991, and 1 July 1998, the *Hague-Visby Rules* applied only to Goods carried under a Bill of Lading issued in Australia or any other state member of the *Hague-Visby rules*. The *Hague-Visby Rules* are called the *amended Hague Rules* in the *Carriage of Goods by Sea Act*, and the term 'amended Hague Rules' refers to the International Convention for the Unification of Certain Rules of Law relating to Bills of Lading, done at Brussels on 25 August 1924, as amended by the Visby Protocol (the Protocol amending the Brussels Convention, done at Brussels on 23 February 1968) and the SDR Protocol (the Protocol amending the Brussels

Convention as amended by the Visby Protocol, done at Brussels on 21 December 1979). The amended Hague Rules can be found in Schedule 1 of the *Carriage of Goods by Sea Act*.

In 1998, a new Schedule 1A was inserted into the Act by *the Carriage of Goods by Sea Regulations 1998* which came into force on 1 July 1998. Claims in respect of loss of, or damage to, goods carried under a sea carriage document from a port in Australia to a port outside Australia are subject to the new, modified version of the Hague-Rules set out in Schedule 1A (the modified Rules). Sea carriage document is defined broadly to include any negotiable or non-negotiable document that contains or evidences a contract of carriage by sea. Charterparties (which are contracts of hire rather than of carriage) are not covered, but sea carriage documents issued under a charterparty are.

In respect of carriage of goods into Australia from a foreign country, the modified Rules will apply only if none of the other Conventions which govern carriage of goods by sea applies. In other words, if the sea carriage document, or the country in which that document was issued, requires that one of the other relevant treaties should apply, then the Australian courts will respect that requirement.

The other relevant treaties are the original Brussels Convention, the amended Brussels Convention and the Hamburg Convention (the UN Convention on the Carriage of Goods by Sea, being Annex 1 of the Final Act of the UN Conference on the Carriage of Goods by Sea done at Hamburg on 31 March 1978), which Australia has not yet ratified.

As well as determining which version of which set of rules will apply in a particular case, the Carriage of Goods by Sea Act also regulates the ability of Australian courts to exercise jurisdiction in respect of claims arising under the Act. In essence, section 11 ensures that all sea carriage documents relating to carriage of goods outward from Australia are governed by Australian law, and that any clause in a contract of carriage which attempts to limit or oust the jurisdiction of the Australian courts in respect of such documents shall be deemed void. Thus, "foreign" arbitration clauses can be disregarded by Australian courts once an action is commenced in Australia. Agreements for resolution of disputes by arbitration within Australia are permitted, however, as an exception to the otherwise compulsory jurisdiction of the courts.

If the parties to the contract of carriage wish to avoid litigation, therefore, a clause should be inserted into the sea carriage document to provide for arbitration in Australia, using the well-established body of arbitrators existing in Australia. An Australian court will enforce such agreements before allowing the dispute to proceed to litigation.

General scheme of the Hague-Visby Rules

The modified Hague-Visby Rules provide a basic framework for the carriage of goods by sea. Where they are applicable, either by force of law or incorporation into contracts of carriage, they are compulsory. The Rules apply to the carriage contracted for in the sea carriage document and the Rules thus relate to the existence of the contract. The parties are, however, free to negotiate any other terms outside the rules, provided that the carrier does not seek to avoid or lessen its liabilities under the rules. Carriage of live animals is excluded from the operation of the rules, due to the special circumstances that exist in such cases.

Duration of coverage

The *Hague-Visby Rules* were modified for Australia in 1998 to broaden the extent of their coverage. The Rules now ensure that the 'Carriage of Goods' covered by the Rules begins when the goods are delivered to the carrier (or its agent) within the limits of a port or wharf, and lasts until the goods are delivered to, or placed at the disposal of, the consignee within the limits of the port or wharf that is the intended destination of the goods. This may turn out to be a somewhat misleading definition since modern trading customs are such that carriers can and do take charge of goods under more complicated conditions than simple port to port transit arrangements.

For instance, where one carrier contracts for an entire journey 'from warehouse to warehouse', and multi-modal forms of transport are used, the contract itself may ensure that the carrier's responsibilities begin before the goods arrive at the port of shipment, and continue after they leave the port of destination. If the contract does not do this, the shipper may find itself without any contractual remedy against the carrier in some circumstances.

Responsibilities and Immunities of the Carrier

The rules impose two general categories of responsibilities upon sea carriers. First, there are the minimum requirements of seaworthiness imposed on the carrier for the proper reception, storage, care and delivery of the cargo. Article 3 of the rules stipulates that the carrier must "exercise due diligence to—

(a) Make the ship seaworthy.

(b) Properly man, equip and supply the ship.

(c) Make the holds, refrigerating and cool chambers, and all other parts of the ship in which goods are carried, fit and safe for their reception, carriage and preservation."

The obligation is therefore to provide a ship in good physical condition, an efficient crew and equipment and a cargo-worthy vessel. The obligation commences at least at the beginning of loading and continues to the time the vessel sails. Defects which arise after the vessel sails will thus usually be outside the scope of the carrier's responsibility, even if damage to cargo is thereby caused.

Second, article 3 makes the carrier responsible for ensuring that the goods are "properly and carefully" loaded, stowed, carried, kept, cared for and discharged. This second category of responsibilities, however, is expressly made subject to the exemptions from liability specified in Art. 4. Article 4 provides that:

"Neither the carrier nor the ship shall be responsible for loss or damage arising or resulting from—

(a) Act, neglect, or default of the master, mariner, pilot or the servants of the carrier in the navigation or in the management of the ship.

(b) Fire, unless caused by the actual fault or privity of the carrier.

(c) Perils, dangers and accidents of the sea or other navigable waters.

(d) Act of God.

(e) Act of war.

(f) Act of public enemies.

(g) Arrest or restraint of princes, rulers or people, or seizure under legal process.

(h) Quarantine restrictions.

(i) Act or omission of the shipper or owner of the goods, his agent or representative.

(j) Strikes or lock-outs or stoppage or restraint of labour from whatever cause, whether partial or general.

(k) Riots and civil commotions.

(l) Saving or attempting to save life or property at sea.

(m) Wastage in bulk or weight or any other loss or damage arising from inherent defect, quality or vice of the goods.

(n) Insufficiency of packing.

(o) Insufficiency or inadequacy of marks.

(p) Latent defects not discoverable by due diligence.

(q) Any other cause arising without the actual fault or privity of the carrier, or without the fault or neglect of the agents or servants of the carrier, but the burden of proof shall be on the person claiming the benefit of this exception to show that neither the actual fault or privity of the carrier nor the fault or neglect of the agents or servants of the carrier contributed to the loss or damage."

Burden of proof

It is first the responsibility of the shipper or owner of the goods which have been lost or damaged to prove the loss or damage, and to assert that the cause was due to a breach of the carrier's responsibilities as set out in Art. 3. Whenever loss or damage has resulted from unseaworthiness the burden of proving the exercise of due diligence shall be on the carrier or other person claiming exemption under Art. 4.

To what extent is the carrier liable if goods are lost or damaged due a combination of causes – one involving a breach of duty by the carrier, and another involving a cause beyond the carrier's control, such as those outlined in article 4? Unlike the *Hamburg rules*, the *Amended Hague Rules*, even in their modified form, do not provide for proportionate liability according to the extent to which the carrier is responsible for loss, damage or delay of goods.

It seems that under the *Amended Hague rules*, the carrier must be either fully liable, or not liable at all. This conclusion is supported by the cases. In *The Shipping Corporation of India Ltd v Gamlen Chemical Co (A/Asia) Pty Ltd (1980) CLR 142*, the high court further held that if fault or neglect on the part of the carrier combines with another cause to produce loss or damage, the carrier is nonetheless fully liable for the loss or damage, even if another cause of the loss, damage or delay cannot be attributed to the carrier.

Time limits

Unless suit is brought within one year of the delivery of the goods or of the date when they should have been delivered, the carrier and the ship are discharged from all liability whatsoever in respect of the goods (Art. 3 rule 6). This period may, however, be extended if the parties so agree after the cause of action has arisen. These provisions apply both to formal court proceedings or to arbitration.

Limitation of liability

The Hague-Visby Rules enable the carrier, once liability is proved, to limit its liability by calculation of an amount equal to the number of the "packages" lost or damaged, or the weight of the lost or damaged cargo, whichever is the higher (Art. 4, rule 5).

The monetary limits of liability are set by reference to a mechanism known as a Special Drawing Right (SDR). This is a form of daily exchange rate, computed by the International Monetary Fund against a "basket" of currencies of IMF members. It provides that the carrier, under bills of lading, may seek to limit liability by applying a formula based on multiplying the prevailing SDR rate by either the number of packages lost or damaged or by their weight, whichever is greater.

Liability for delay

In 1998, a new article 4A was inserted into the *Hague-Visby rules* as applicable in Australia. Article 4A provides that notwithstanding the fact that article 4 and other provisions of the rules seem only to impose liability on carrier's for loss or damage to goods, "a carrier is liable to a shipper for loss (including but not limited to, pure economic loss, loss of markets or deterioration) caused to the shipper by the shipper's goods being delayed while the carrier is in charge of the goods." If the carrier wishes to avoid liability, it bears the burden of proof to show that the delay was excusable and that all measures were taken to avoid it.

Air carriage

As noted above at AUS ¶80-001, the main conventions which establish the law governing international carriage of goods by air in Australia are:

- The Warsaw Convention of 1929;
- The Hague Protocol of 1955, which amended the Warsaw Convention in a number of respects; and
- The Guadalajara Convention which further modifies and elaborates the rules and principles established in the Warsaw Convention, as amended by the Hague Protocol.

Australia is a party to these three instruments, and they have been adopted by the Commonwealth *Civil Aviation (Carriers' Liability) Act 1959*.

The first step in considering an air cargo claim is to work out what law applies, and that depends on what conventions, if any, the countries of departure and destination are both parties to. The relevant law is that which is common to both the country of origin and the country of destination. In other words, before any of the above three conventions can apply, both the country of departure and the country of destination must be party to that convention.

Liability

There is a presumption of liability against the air carrier (Art. 18). The air carrier can only avoid liability if it can prove that it took all necessary measures to avoid the damage or that it was impossible for the carrier to take such measures (Art. 20). Contributory negligence on the part of the consignor can be taken into account to reduce the air carrier's liability (Art. 21). If the carrier cannot avoid liability under Art. 20, its liability may be limited on a weight basis: Art. 22.

The carrier cannot limit its liability on a weight basis if it has been guilty of what is called "wilful misconduct" in the Warsaw Convention and what is referred to as "intent to cause damage or recklessly and with knowledge that damage would probably result" in the Warsaw Convention as amended by the Hague Protocol: Art. 25.

Articles 22 and 25 have recently been the subject of litigation in Australia. The practical effect has been to establish very high limitation amounts, while also making it harder for carriers to limit their liability to less than the established amounts. Amounts recoverable are generally likely to exceed the $US20 per kg offered by some airlines. Legal advice should be obtained in all cases prior to accepting any sum in settlement of cargo, passenger or baggage claims.

Time bars

In the case of damage to cargo, the importer/exporter or its customs agent should send a written letter of complaint to the air carrier within the seven days' time limit where the Warsaw Convention applies, or within 14 days under Warsaw/Hague (14 days or 21 days respectively in the case of delay to cargo). Court proceedings must be brought within two years of the aircraft's arrival.

Freight forwarders

Air carriage of goods is increasingly being placed through air freight forwarders. Depending on their role and the documentation they use, they may be mere agents of the consignor, or they may be principals. If they are merely agents arranging the carriage on behalf of the consignor of goods, they will not themselves be liable for any negligent handling by the airline. If, however, they issue a house airway bill of their own, and if, depending on its terms, they have contracted to undertake the carriage themselves and then have subcontracted the air stage to an airline, they will be vicariously liable as principals for any airline negligence. Accordingly, a claim may coexist against both the freight forwarder and the airline.

AUS ¶80-003   INTERNATIONAL CONVENTIONS

Australia has acceded to and/or signed a number of conventions which have not been ratified by Parliament, and so have not been adopted into law. International conventions which Australia has acceded to, accepted or ratified include:

Air transportation

- Chicago Convention 1944, including:
  - the "Two Freedoms" Agreement 1944
  - the "Five Freedoms" Agreement 1944

  Effective for Australia 4 April 1947
- 1968 Buenos Aires Protocol on the Authentic Trilingual Text of the Convention on International Civil Aviation of 1944. Effective for Australia 12 February 1969.
- Montreal Protocol 1977
- Warsaw Convention 1929
- Hague Protocol 1955
- Guadalajara Convention 1961 (supplementary to Warsaw)
- Geneva Convention 1948 (signature only)
- Rome Convention 1952 (Damage by Foreign Aircraft) (entered into force for Australia 8 February 1958)
- Tokyo Convention 1963 (Crimes on board Aircraft) (entered into force for Australia 20 September 1970)
- Hague Convention 1970 (Unlawful Seizure of Aircraft) (entered into force for Australia 9 December 1972)
- Montreal Convention 1971 (Unlawful Acts against Civil Aviation) (entered into force for Australia 11 Australia 1973)
- Montreal Protocol 1988 (Unlawful Acts of Violence at Airports) (entered into force for Australia 22 November 1990)

The Montreal Convention and the Montreal Protocol are enacted into Australian law by the *Crimes (Aviation) Act* 1991.

Shipping

- United Nations Convention for the Unification of Certain Rules relating to Bills of Lading, signed at Brussels (1924), supplemented by the Visby Protocol and the SDR Protocol (the Hague-Visby Rules).
- United Nations Convention on the Carriage of Goods by Sea, including Annex 1 and Annex 2 of the Final Act of the United Nations Conference on the Carriage of Goods by Sea done at Hamburg on 31 March 1978 (the Hamburg Convention and the Hamburg Rules) (signed only).

- 1976 Convention on Limitation of Liability of Owners for Maritime Claims (entered into force for Australia 1 June 1991).

- International Convention on Tonnage Measurements 1969 (entered into force for Australia 21 August 1982).

- International Convention on Safe Containers 1976 (entered into force for Australia 22 February 1981) .

- International Convention for the Safety of Life at Sea 1974 (entered into force for Australia 17 November 1983).

- International Convention on Load Lines 1966 – Australia has also accepted Amendments to this Convention finalised on 23 March 1995.

International Rules for the Prevention of Collisions at Sea. 1960. The 1982 UN Convention on the Law of the Sea, which entered into force generally and for Australia 16 November 1994, imposes an obligation on all member states to enforce within its own territory a number of standards and regulations relating to travel on the high seas, including the rules for prevention of collisions at sea.

AUS ¶80-004 LAWS RELATING TO MOVEMENT OF DANGEROUS SUBSTANCES

Surface transportation

It should be remembered that Australia is a federation of States and that not all legislative power is vested in the central (federal) government. Some matters, including transport and storage of dangerous substances, are the responsibility of the States and Territory governments.

To ensure uniformity of laws in this most important area, a common code has been brought into existence whose object is to form the basis of uniform legislation throughout Australia. It is known as the Australian Code for the Transportation of Dangerous Goods by Road and Rail (the "ADG Code") and is found in Australian Government Gazette No. P15 of 7 April 1987.

The Code is expressed to be subject to the laws in the various States and Territories concerning transport and handling of dangerous substances, but it can safely be assumed by non-Australian exporters to Australia that these rules will have a high degree of uniformity throughout the country. In any event, freight handlers, customs brokers and transport operators in Australia will be familiar with all the relevant requirements in their respective ports.

The ADG Code applies to all surface land transport in Australia. It is intended that adherence to the Code will also ensure near compliance with the requirements for transport by sea from Australian ports. However, it must be noted that there are some differences between the ADG Code and certain international carriage of goods rules.

The Code allows for the situation when goods arriving from overseas enter with substandard packaging and enables the imposition of extra requirements for outward rail or road transport.

In relation to the transport of radioactive materials, the federal government has drafted the Code of Practice for the Safe Transport of Radioactive Substances and Guidelines to that Code. This Code is drafted pursuant to the *Environment Protection (Nuclear Codes) Act 1978*. Both codes must be read together when transporting radioactive materials.

The ADG Code, known commonly as "the P15", comprises 10 main sections:

1. Definitions;

2. Classification of dangerous goods;

3. Marking of packaging, vehicles and transport containers;

4. Documentation;

5. Packaging for dangerous goods;

6. Transport in bulk;

7. Stowage and compatibilities;

8. Requirements and procedures for the transport of dangerous goods;

9. Index of dangerous goods: provides an alphabetical listing of correct shipping names for dangerous goods together with relevant information on UN Number, classification, labelling emergency guide, packing and properties, and observations. In section 9 is also included a numerical listing on UN Numbers and their designation, and a list of substances too dangerous to be transported. The *Hazchem Emergency Code* is also explained; and

10. Index of dangerous goods of Class I (explosives), including details on packing methods.

An important feature of the Code is the requirement for packaging and proper marking with approved symbols and codes.

Air carriage

In relation to the carriage of dangerous goods on Australian aircraft, the *Air Navigation Orders* (Parts 33.1 and 33.2) issued pursuant to the Commonwealth *Air Navigation Act 1920* are relevant. They apply equally to foreign civil aircraft operating over Australian territory.

Also relevant is the *Crimes (Aviation) Act 1991*, which enacts into Australian law the *Montreal Convention of 1971 (Unlawful Acts against Civil Aviation)* and the *Montreal Protocol of 1988 (Acts of Violence at Airports)*.

Pollution

It is important to consider the laws relating to pollution in any discussion of carriage of dangerous substances into Australia.

There is a statutory liability Code established in respect of ship owners and carriers bringing bulk liquids into and out of Australia. Statutory liability rules have been established in accordance with a growing number of international conventions and other international instruments signed and, in most cases, ratified by Australia. Conventions which Australia has accepted include:

- International Convention for the Prevention of Pollution of the Sea by Oil 1954, effective for Australia 29 November 1962. Amendments made in 1962 entered into force for Australia May-June 1967. Amendments made in 1969 entered into force for Australia in January 1978.

- International Convention for the Prevention of Pollution from Ships [MARPOL 1973], and Protocols I and II, signed for Australia, with declaration and subject to ratification, 24 December 1974. The Convention did not enter into force, but see:

  Protocol of 17 February 1978 relating to the Convention for the Prevention of Pollution from Ships, November 1973, as amended (Text incorporates the text of MARPOL 1973), effective for Australia from 14 January 1988; except Annex III to the Protocol, as amended 1992, which entered into force for Australia 10 January 1995.

- Protocol Relating to the Intervention on the High Seas in Cases of Pollution by Substances other than Oil, 1973, entered into force for Australia from 5 February 1984.

- International Convention on Civil Liability for Oil Pollution Damage as amended by the Protocol of 1992. The *Protection of the Sea (Civil Liability) Act* 1981 enacts into force for Australia Articles 1 to IV (inclusive), paragraphs 1, 8 and 9 of Article VII, Article VIII, paragraphs 1 and 3 of Article IX, Article XII bis (other than paragraph (b)), paragraph 1 of Article XI of the Convention. Both the Convention and the 1992 Protocol are annexed to the Act.

- International Convention on Oil Pollution Preparedness, Response and Cooperation 1990 (entered into Australia for Australia 13 May 1995).

In addition to the *Protection of the Sea (Civil Liability) Act* 1981, the *Environment Protection (Sea Dumping) Act 1981* (Cwth) governs dumping or burning of waste at sea. All States have enacted concurrent (equivalent) legislation.

Additionally, the Protection of the *Sea (Prevention of Pollution from Ships) Act 1983* governs prevention of pollution by oil, noxious substances, packaged harmful substances, sewage and garbage. Again, this is a federal statute enacted pursuant to relevant international conventions, such as the 1989 Basel Convention on the Control of Transboundary Movements of Hazardous Wastes and their Disposal, which entered into force for Australia and generally in May 1992.

In relation to radioactive wastes, Australia has recently enacted into law the 1995 Waigani Convention to Ban the Importation into Forum Island Countries of Hazardous and Radioactive Wastes and to Control the Transboundary Movement and Management of Hazardous Wastes Within the South Pacific Region. The rules and standards established by this Convention are given force of law in Australia, *inter alia*, by the *Hazardous Waste (Regulation of Exports and Imports) (Waigani Convention) Regulations* of 1999.

Shipping

The Commonwealth *Navigation Act* at Part IV, Div. 12 and 12A (sec. 266-267Y) governs ships carrying or using oil and ships carrying noxious liquid substances in bulk. It specifies the requirements, in regard to both Australian and foreign registered ships for matters such as periodic surveys, carrying of relevant International Oil Pollution Prevention Certificates, Chemical Tanker Construction Certificates, International Pollution Prevention Certificates for the Carriage of Noxious Liquid Substances in Bulk, and requirements in relation to alteration of vessels, and cancellation of certificates. Sec. 267ZA-267ZC (Division 12B) relates to Ships Carrying Packaged Harmful Substances, while sec. 267ZD-267ZS (Divisions 12C) relates to Sewage and prevention of sewage pollution prevention.

AUS ¶80-005 ARREST OF VESSELS, ETC.

The *Admiralty Act 1988* is the statute which regulates the powers to arrest seagoing vessels.

All superior courts, i.e. the Federal Court and the Supreme Courts of each State, have concurrent original jurisdiction in respect of all proceedings commenced as actions in *rem*. None of the inferior courts has a specific in *rem* jurisdiction though provision is made in the Act for courts to be proclaimed, as necessary, as having in *rem* jurisdiction under the Act.

The Act confers jurisdiction to proceed in *rem* on:

(a) maritime liens (e.g. salvage, damage to ships, wages, disbursements);

(b) proprietary maritime claims (e.g. claims involving disputes over title to, or possession of, ships, mortgages, co-ownership disputes, etc.);

(c) general maritime claims;

(d) owners' liabilities;

(e) demise charterers' liabilities.

The Act also confers jurisdiction against "surrogate" ships in much the same way as the internationally accepted "sister ship" concept.

The Act prevents arrest of more than one ship under any one claim, though it does not prevent subsequent service of process on another ship if service on the first ship has been struck out or discontinued, even if the first ship was wrongly served, or where the first ship has broken arrest and custody has not been regained.

Ships, subject to the jurisdiction of the Act, may be arrested anywhere in Australia, including the territorial sea (currently 12nm).

The Act confers power on the courts to retain custody of, and enforce judgements against, ships in cases where proceedings may be pending in other courts, whether in Australia or overseas. The courts may also stay or dismiss proceedings if alternative securities are provided.

The Act also creates a very extensive regime of liability for damages for unjustified arrest or unjustified refusal to release a ship from arrest. Damages can be awarded where the plaintiff (i.e. party seeking to arrest) acts "unreasonably and without good cause".

Recovery is limited in those circumstances to the loss directly resulting to the innocent party.

It should be noted that the Act does not allow for arrest of bunkers or cargo within the Admiralty jurisdiction.

Mareva injunctions

A further remedy exists in parallel to those provisions of the *Admiralty Act* which relate to arrest. At common law there is a procedure for obtaining an injunction in respect of property within the jurisdiction when that property is the only asset held by a person or corporation and there is a possibility that it will be removed from the jurisdiction.

In practical terms this could mean, for example, that a cargo could be detained or restrained from sailing, even though there may be no legal right under Admiralty legislation to arrest or detain the vessel. (This can, of course, also apply in the aviation context.) Very stringent conditions must be satisfied before the courts will grant such remedies, but they are available. They can also be granted in aid of a foreign court's judgement or arbitration award.

AUS ¶80-011 REGULATION OF SHIPBUILDING INDUSTRY

The shipbuilding industry in Australia is generally a fragmented industry, in which the principal activity is concentrated in small tonnage, such as high-speed ferries, catamarans, coastal vessels and pleasure craft. Little large tonnage activity has occurred in recent years, though the federal government has been active in placing contracts for major naval vessels.

Regulatory bodies

Control of shipbuilding standards is generally vested in two separate areas, viz. Classification Societies and government authorities.

In general, the Classification Societies comprise representatives of the shipbuilding industry, underwriters and owners. They effectively set the acceptable standards for ship construction. They are non-profit organisations.

The governmental responsibilities are primarily concerned with safety aspects. In some cases, the Commonwealth government vests in the Classification Societies authority to administer its regulations. Broadly speaking, the Classification Societies are mainly concerned with seaworthiness and structural integrity, while the Commonwealth government, through its agency, the Australian Maritime Safety Authority (AMSA), is concerned with regulating and safety oversight of Australia's shipping fleet and management of Australia's international maritime obligations relating to safety and navigation as well as protection of the marine environment. .

The Australian Maritime Safety Authority

This Authority came into being on 1 January 1991. It undertakes functions formerly discharged by the (former) Maritime Safety Division of the Department of Transport and Communications. It now often works cooperatively with the Cross-Modal and Maritime Transport section of the Department of Transport and Regional Services with on policy and legislative review matter.

The AMSA provides services to stakeholders in the shipping industry in two ways. Firstly, on a cost recovery basis through fees and levies paid by the shipping industry, and through funds provided by the Commonwealth Government as a community service obligation. The latter relates specifically to search and rescue operations, marine communications and boating safety education.

The Authority is required, under the *Navigation Act 1912*, to take responsibility for the safety certification of Australian flag trading ships operating on interstate and international voyages and imported foreign flag ships engaged in similar operations. These responsibilities are discharged through a combination of surveys by the Authority's marine surveyors and functions delegated to those international Classification Societies which are accredited under the Act. Vessels which are excluded from the application of the Act, such as trading ships operating on intrastate voyages, come under the jurisdiction of State and Territory marine authorities.

The safety requirements applying to Australian shipping are generally contained in the various Parts of Marine Orders.

For further information, or to contact the AMSA, visit the AMSA website at http://www.amsa.gov.au.

Structure of the industry

In terms of the skills and processes involved, the products of the Australian industry encompass three main elements, namely:

(1) conventional steel ships, including cargo ships, tugs, offshore supply vessels, fishing trawlers, naval vessels, Antarctic, surveying, scientific research ships and some ferries;

(2) high speed craft built in aluminium alloy, including most tourist craft and some ferries and special purpose vessels such as Customs launches; and

(3) boats, mostly constructed in fibre reinforced plastics, including leisure craft, some fishing vessels and other small service and commercial vessels.

Impact of existing safety-related regulations on the industry

The AMSA's policy, following that of the Department of Transport and Regional Services, is to implement internationally agreed safety requirements as far as they may be appropriately applied to Australian ships.

Australian legislation gives effect to the principal safety conventions of the International Maritime Organisation (IMO), relating to ships' construction, to which Australia is a signatory, including the International Convention for the Safety of Life at

Sea of 1974 (SOLAS 74), the International Convention on Load Lines of 1966 and the International Convention on Tonnage Measurement of Ships of 1969. In addition, a number of other international instruments relating to maritime safety have been implemented including the Code of Safety for Special Purpose Ships (IMO Resolution A.534(13)) and the Code of Safety for Dynamically Supported Craft (IMO Resolution A.373(X)). The legislation also implements the International Convention for the Prevention of Pollution from Ships of 1973 (MARPOL).

The effect of this codification of requirements is that shipowners and shipbuilders are able to have full knowledge of the regulatory requirements applying to a ship during all stages of tendering, design development and construction.

In relation to standards applying to the construction of small commercial vessels, the Authority plays an active role in the development of the *Uniform Shipping Laws Code* (USL). The Code has been adopted by the Commonwealth, the States and Territories, meeting as the Australian Transport Advisory Council (ATAC), as a basis for uniform legislation relating to the survey, manning and operation of commercial vessels in Australia. The Code is given effect either by reference or by repetition of its provisions in the laws of the various jurisdictions. Where appropriate, the Code calls up the relevant Australian or international standards.

Internationally agreed standards of safety are rigidly adhered to so that Australian registered ships are able to ply trade with foreign countries without the risk of the delay caused when port nations question the validity of a vessel's certification. In a similar manner, design and construction of ships in accordance with agreed standards is also well controlled. Conversely, AMSA has also been instrumental in recent times in detaining foreign-registered ships trading to Australian ports which are considered unsafe or unseaworthy to leave Australia. This is an uncompromising policy designed to ensure that Australia plays its part in the international community in preventing maritime disasters.

As mentioned above, the laws and regulations specifically dealing with the shipbuilding industry are almost uniformly concerned with vessel and personnel safety. The common law and general legislation govern most other aspects of the industry, such as export licensing, financing guarantees, suppliers' credits, performance bonds, guarantee insurance and the shipbuilding contract.

Specific Laws

- The *Ships (Capital Grants) Act 1987*, as amended, deals with grants to the shipbuilding industry. The policy and administration of any subsidy or grant that may be available are under the jurisdiction of the Cross-Modal and Maritime Transport Team of the Department of Transport and Regional Services. Further information can be obtained by referring to the Department's website at http://www.dot.gov.au/xmt/index.htm.

- The registration of rights in and mortgages on ships under construction is dealt with by the *Shipping Registration Act 1981* (Cwth).

On 13 August 1996 the (then) Minister for Transport and Regional Development established the Shipping Reform Group (the SRG) to look at ways of increasing the competitiveness of Australian shipping, *inter alia*, through the introduction, if appropriate, of a second register-type structure; and the windback of cabotage restrictions.

Cabotage

Cabotage is the practice of limiting access to a country's coastal trade to national ship operators or national flag vessels with national crews. In Australia, all vessels engaging in coastal trade do so under a system of licenses or permits available under certain conditions and applicable to both Australian and international operators. The *Navigation Act* 1912 applies Australian wage standards to vessels operating with a licence in domestic trades, regardless of the nationality of the ship or the crew.

Cabotage in Australia is achieved by the interaction of the Navigation Act 1912, Customs requirements and Immigration provisions. About 90% of the Australian coastal trade is undertaken by Australian manned ships despite a significant cost disadvantage.

The SRG reported in March 1997 and while the Government has made no formal response to the SRG recommendations it has taken several measures to liberalise the licence/permit system and enable greater participation by foreign flag vessels in the coastal trade. These measures include:

Halving the average cost of applying for permits;

- Exempting cruise line shipping, as well as the Christmas Island trade, from the requirement to have a licence or permit;

- Dropping the requirement that continuing voyage permits only be issued in circumstances that provided long term benefit to the shipping industry; and

- Significantly streamlining the administration of the permit system, with new ministerial guidelines issues in June 1998.

The Government has also established a system of company employment and ended the engagement system.

The Shipping Reform Working Group

In December 1998, the Minister for Transport and Regional Services established the Shipping Reform Working Group to build on the work of the SRG and advise the Government on how to create an internationally competitive shipping industry taking into account the economic and defence values of the industry. The Working Group has now reported to the Minister, and a response from the Government is expected later in 2000.

AUS ¶80-012 LAWS RELATING TO SHIPPING REGISTER

Australian Shipping Registration Office

The Australian Shipping Registration Office was established in 1982 under the provisions of the Shipping Registration Act 1981. Since the formation of the Australian Maritime Safety Authority in 1991, the office has been a part of the Authority.

The main purpose of the Act is to fix the conditions for the registration of ships in Australia and to grant ships Australian nationality. It also provides for Australian ships to fly the Australian National Flag or the Australian Red Ensign in accordance with

Australia's obligations under the Geneva Convention on the High Seas 1958, to which Australia is a party.

The business of the office includes the establishment of the ownership of ships, the registration of mortgages and caveats, the granting of certificates and providing public access to the information held in the Australian Register of Ships.

It should be noted that the Australian States also keep records of ships and small craft that are subject to their jurisdiction. The State records, however, are not registers of ownership or nationality.

For further information, or to contact the Australian Shipping Registration Office, visit the ARO website at http://www.amsa.gov.au/sro/srohome.htm.

Regulatory Requirements

Registration of ships in Australia is governed by the provisions of the *Shipping Registration Act* and its associated Regulations. This statute contains a broad definition of the term "ship" for registration purposes, and its principal object is to compel the registration in Australia of virtually all Australian-owned commercial ships. In addition, it facilitates registration of other ships if the owners wish to avail themselves of the facility.

An Australian ship is, in essence, one which is more than 50% owned by Australian nationals, including Australian corporations.

Small vessels (less than 24 metres tonnage length), government ships, fishing vessels, pleasure craft and vessels demise chartered by foreign residents are "exempt" from compulsory registration.

The Act sets out, in detail, the formalities for registration and its consequences. It defines how property is vested in ships, the mode of transfer, mortgage and priorities. It also guarantees the rights to travel, to claim Australian nationality, Australian naval protection and the benefits of Australian law.

Broadly, all Australian-owned ships must be registered on the Australian Register, though Australian-owned ships under demise charter to foreign nationals may obtain written exemption from the Minister responsible.

Failure to register is an offence under the Act and the ship may be detained until registration is completed.

Applications for registration of ships less than 24 metres in tonnage length, government ships, fishing vessels and pleasure craft can all still be made, even though these ships are exempt from compulsory registration. A certificate of tonnage measurement is required to register a ship, and should also be obtained in cases of doubt for unregistered ships that may not in fact come under one of the exempt categories. Where registration is desired, there is no minimum size of ship which may be registered.

Prior to registration the ship must be marked in accordance with the Regulations with the marks directed by the Registrar. It is an offence not to maintain those markings. There is no property in the registered name of a ship, with the result that two different ships can be registered with the same name (though they will still be distinguished by other compulsory marks and numbers).

The Act further prescribes provisions relating to transfers and transmissions of vessels, mortgages and disposal of vessels. Legal title is transferred by bill of sale followed by a registered transmission under the Act. The Act does not recognise notice of any trust, whether express, implied or constructive, though beneficial interests may be enforced by or against an owner or mortgagee in the same way as for other personal property.

Persons claiming interests in a ship or a share of a ship (of which there can be 64 shares) may lodge caveats in respect of those interests.

The Act stipulates that any ship which is required to be registered and which is not so registered will not be recognised as an Australian ship and will not enjoy the benefits, privileges, advantages or protection enjoyed by a registered ship, though it will remain liable for all fees, charges, fines, forfeitures and penalties, as though it were a registered ship. The Act sets out a detailed list of other provisions and prohibitions relating to unregistered ships.

The administrative requirements to be fulfilled prior to registration are contained in the Shipping Registration Regulations, and, as previously mentioned, the provisions of the Act relating to tonnage measurement and marking.

Application to register is made by the owner lodging a written application in the form of an "Application for Registration of an Australian Ship" (Form A), annexed to which are specified documents, as set out in the Regulations. These are lodged with the Registrar of Ships. Those documents will establish the description, ownership, nationality of the ship and identity of the ship's agent, together with details of any charterparty where the registration depends on the ship being on demise charter to an Australian operator.

Once the formalities are complete, the entry is made in the Register and the Registrar is then required to grant a Registration Certificate, the purpose of which is then strictly limited by the Act for the purposes only of lawful navigation of the ship. It cannot be used for any other reason such as detention of the ship, security for any money, loan, pledge, or compliance with any promise or undertaking. Improper use of a certificate is an offence under the Act.

Insurance

Use of state-owned or resident brokers .... AUS ¶85-001

Classes of insurance underwriters .... AUS ¶85-002

Available range of insurance .... AUS ¶85-003

Insurance required for financing arrangements .... AUS ¶85-004

Compulsory insurance .... AUS ¶85-011

Insurance of local employees .... AUS ¶85-012

Legislation affecting choice of insurance company .... AUS ¶85-013

Application for insurance payments .... AUS ¶85-014

Product liability insurance .... AUS ¶85-021

AUS ¶85-001   USE OF STATE-OWNED OR RESIDENT BROKERS

The insurance industry in Australia is regulated by the Australian Prudential Regulatory Authority (APRA) in the interests of industry integrity and prudential standards: www.apra.gov.au. The market aspects of insurance including consumer protection, customer relations, sales practices and insurance intermediaries are regulated by the Australian Securities and Investments Commission (ASIC): www.asic.gov.au.

To carry on general (non-life) insurance business, an insurer must be authorised under the *Insurance Act 1973* (Cth). Companies which are not incorporated in Australia may be authorised to carry on insurance business under the *Insurance Act* but they must have a principal office in Australia. The *Insurance Act*, administered by APRA, requires insurers to have a certain level of solvency.

Most types of insurance contracts are regulated by the *Insurance Contracts Act 1984* (Cth). Regulations made under the Act provide standard cover (cover of a minimum level) to the insured in respect of certain contracts of consumer or household insurance.

Where the insured and the subject matter of the insurance are within Australia, the provisions of the *Insurance Contracts Act* will apply. In these circumstances, an underwriter based outside Australia will need to comply with the Australian Act.

The certain limited classes of insurance to which this Act does not apply include contracts of:

- reinsurance;
- insurance by a registered medical or hospital benefits organisation under the *National Health Act 1953* (Cth);
- marine insurance to which the *Marine Insurance Act 1909* (Cth) applies;

- workers compensation and statutory third party motor vehicle insurance (these are covered by State and Territory legislation — see below); and
- insurance in respect of commercial aircraft.

To carry on life insurance business, the underwriter must be registered under the *Life Insurance Act 1995* (Cth), administered by APRA. Foreign companies may be registered under the *Life Insurance Act*, but they must appoint a person resident in Australia as their principal officer. The *Life Insurance Act* provides for solvency and capital adequacy standards.

In addition, insurers, like any other entity carrying on a "financial services business", must have an Australian financial services licence under sec. 911A of the *Corporations Act 2001* (Cth), administered by ASIC.

Representatives of insurance companies, insurance brokers and insurance agents do not need to be registered with ASIC but they must have a written authorisation of an Australian financial services licensee.

The scheme in respect of workers compensation insurance in Australia varies from jurisdiction to jurisdiction. Each State and Territory has its own principal authority authorising either statutory or private insurers to handle workers compensation insurance. Some jurisdictions allow larger employers to self-insure. Refer, for example, to the New South Wales' WorkCover's homepage at www.workcover.nsw.gov.au.

Similarly, schemes requiring motor vehicle compulsory third party insurance, providing cover for death or bodily injury, also vary from jurisdiction to jurisdiction. Again, depending on the jurisdiction, insurance must be effected with either a statutory body or private insurer authorised under the relevant legislation such as the Motor Accident Authority (in New South Wales) or the Motor Accident Insurance Commission (in Queensland): see further AUS ¶85-011.

There are no government-owned insurance brokers in Australia, and it is not compulsory to use any particular resident insurer, broker or agent for any other class of insurance.

AUS ¶85-002   CLASSES OF INSURANCE UNDERWRITERS

Australia has both private insurers and government insurers.

Some State government insurers are not subject to the standards of the *Insurance Act 1973* and the *Life Insurance Act 1995* (although in general they do endeavour to meet these standards).

With the exception of insurers authorised to handle workers compensation insurance or motor vehicle compulsory third party insurance (see AUS ¶85-001), insurers in Australia do not enjoy any particular advantage or disadvantage under the law of Australia.

AUS ¶85-003   AVAILABLE RANGE OF INSURANCE

Insurance is readily available in Australia to cover most risks. Examples of classes of insurance which are available in Australia are as follows:

- Aviation insurance;
- Burglary insurance;
- Business interruption or consequential loss insurance;
- Contract works insurance;
- Export and import insurances;
- Farm produce (or crop) and livestock insurance;
- Fidelity guarantee insurance;
- Fire insurance;
- Householders'/houseowners' insurance;
- Industrial special risks (or combined material damage and consequential loss) insurance;
- Legal expenses insurance;
- Life insurance;
- Machinery breakdown and/or boiler explosion insurance;
- Marine hull insurance;
- Marine transit insurance;
- Money insurance;
- Motor vehicle — compulsory third party insurance;
- Motor vehicle — comprehensive insurance;
- Personal liability insurance;
- Product liability insurance;
- Public liability insurance;
- Professional indemnity insurance;
- Travel insurance; and
- Workers compensation insurance.

AUS ¶85-004   INSURANCE REQUIRED FOR FINANCING ARRANGEMENTS

Under Australian law, there is no compulsion upon parties involved in financing transactions to insure against financing risks although there are many insurance products available to lenders and businesses to cover such risks.

For example, there are specialist insurers who provide mortgage guarantee insurance. Mortgage guarantee insurance covers the mortgagee if the mortgagor breaches his or her obligations under the mortgage. Insurance concerning other forms of consumer credit is also available. Performance bond insurance can be taken out to cover the performance of bonds. Trade credit insurance will cover the policy holder against the risks connected with the performance and solvency of debtors.

The availability of such insurance would depend on the particular exposures involved.

Australian exporters who trade on credit terms can insure themselves against the risk of non-payment by overseas buyers. This "export payments insurance" is issued by the Export Finance and Insurance Corporation (EFIC), a Commonwealth statutory body, and covers exporters against non-payments which are caused by a range of commercial, economic and political reasons. EFIC also insures Australian overseas investments against the risks of loss from expropriation, war damage or exchange delays.

It would be prudent, depending on the risk and the availability of insurance, to take out a policy to cover the risks associated with financing arrangements.

Refer to EFIC at www.efic.gov.au.

AUS ¶85-011   COMPULSORY INSURANCE

All workers in Australia must be covered by workers compensation insurance at Commonwealth, State or Territory level. This must be effected by the employer, and covers the employer's liability to provide compensation to employees suffering injury, disease or death arising out of or in the course of their employment. However, in some jurisdictions it is possible for larger employers to self-insure. See AUS ¶85-001.

In Australia, the owners of motor vehicles must insure against liability incurred in respect of the death of or bodily injury to third parties caused by or arising out of the use of the vehicle. Compulsory third party schemes vary from jurisdiction to jurisdiction. For example, in New South Wales compulsory third party insurance is governed by the *Motor Accidents Act 1988* which authorises a number of insurers to issue compulsory third party policies.

AUS ¶85-012   INSURANCE OF LOCAL EMPLOYEES

Workers compensation cover must be provided to all employees in Australia to insure them against injury, disease or death arising out of or in the course of their employment (see AUS ¶85-011 above).

Superannuation

An industrial award-based superannuation system and a Superannuation Contribution Guarantee (SG) scheme apply to provide superannuation coverage for all employees in Australia. The SG scheme operates independently of, but in conjunction with, Australia's industrial award system. An employer who is liable under both arrangements must comply with the requirements of both arrangements, although superannuation contributions under the award system may be counted as superannuation support under the SG scheme.

The award system arises from an industrial agreement (or award) under which an employer is required to pay a specified percentage of each employee's wages as superannuation contributions into an industry superannuation fund or other approved fund in accordance with the agreement or award. Superannuation benefits under the award system must fully vest in, and be preserved for, the employee. This means that the benefits belong to the employee immediately but are only payable in certain circumstances. For example, the benefits must be paid on genuine retirement at or after

AUS ¶85-011

age 55, when the employee attains age 65, in the event of death or permanent incapacity for work. Employer contributions are tax deductible.

The Superannuation Guarantee scheme was introduced in 1992 to provide universal superannuation coverage for all employees, with limited exceptions (discussed below). Under the SG scheme, employers must provide a minimum level of superannuation support for each of their eligible employees. An employer who does not make superannuation contributions to a superannuation fund must pay a tax called the Superannuation Guarantee Charge equivalent to the amount of the shortfall plus interest and an administrative charge to the Australian Taxation Office, which distributes it to a superannuation fund for the benefit of the employees in respect of whom the charge was paid.

The level of employer support required under the Superannuation Guarantee Scheme has increased since its introduction in 1992 (originally it was 7% of an employee's ordinary earnings) and is now 9% of each employee's earnings base as from 2002/2003. There is, however, a ceiling on the maximum amount of contributions that has to be made for any individual employee. Employer contributions under the scheme are generally tax deductible, but the Superannuation Guarantee Charge is not deductible. All benefits under the scheme must be fully preserved from 1994.

Employers do not have to provide Superannuation Guarantee support for the following employees (whose salaries and wages are excluded from the scheme):

- employees who are 70 years of age and over;
- non-resident employees who are paid solely for work undertaken outside Australia;
- resident employees employed by non-resident employers who are paid solely for work undertaken outside Australia;
- certain foreign executives who are in Australia on a temporary entry permit;
- employees who earn less than AUS$450 a month;
- employees under 18 years of age who are employed part-time (i.e. 30 hours per week or less); and
- a person paid to do part-time employment wholly or principally of a domestic or private nature: *Superannuation Guarantee (Administration) Act 1992* (Cth) sec. 27.

The Superannuation Guarantee scheme requires employers to offer employees a choice of superannuation funds where the contributions for the employees are to be made.

Further information on the SG scheme is available from the ATO at www.ato.gov.au.

AUS ¶85-013 LEGISLATION AFFECTING CHOICE OF INSURANCE COMPANY

The laws regulating insurance in Australia are discussed at AUS ¶85-001.

In Australia, there is a free market for insurers. The free market is promoted by the *Trade Practices Act 1974* (Cth), of which Part IV prohibits restrictive trade practices such as misuse of market power and price fixing among competitors (see AUS ¶45-303) and Part V (sec. 52ff) promotes consumer protection (AUS ¶31-011).

However, workers compensation cover and motor vehicle compulsory third party cover for death or bodily injury are regulated by legislation in each jurisdiction. Accordingly, in these two areas there are laws which affect the ability of an enterprise to insure with the insurer of its choice (see AUS ¶85-001).

AUS ¶85-014   APPLICATION FOR INSURANCE PAYMENTS

As mentioned at AUS ¶85-001, most contracts of insurance are governed by the *Insurance Contracts Act 1984*. The financial services legislation in the *Corporations Act 2001* (Cth) and the *Insurance Contracts Act* governs the relationship between the insurer and the insured, including the making of claims and the ability of an insurer to refuse to pay any particular claim. The *Insurance Contracts Act* also allows for the payment of interest on outstanding insurance moneys if an insurer unreasonably withholds payment.

The proceeds of insurance claims can be freely paid to an insured. However, the payment of insurance moneys both to overseas insureds and to insureds within Australia, may be subject to reporting requirements under the *Financial Transaction Reports Act 1988* (Cth) (see also AUS ¶55-001).

AUS ¶85-021   PRODUCT LIABILITY INSURANCE

Product liability insurance is generally available in Australia. Specially tailored product liability policies with extensive coverage are available at higher premiums. So-called ''standard'' product liability policies, with substantially less coverage than tailored policies, are available at lower premiums. Product liability insurance policies generally limit the amount recoverable, and provide that all claims arising from a single source make up a single claim. Policies usually have both an annual aggregate limiting the amount of cover, and an aggregate with respect to any one event. The size of an insured's business, and the nature of the products it sells as well as the nature of the risks posed by those products, determine the type of policy acquired.

As discussed at AUS ¶30-012, there are different product liability laws in Australia arising out of the common law (mainly contract and negligence) and statute (the *Trade Practices Act 1974* (Cth)).

CHINA

Table of Contents

An overview (the system of law and
    government) ....CHN ¶20-001
Land tenure — the site of the investment ....CHN ¶25-001
The structure of the investment ....CHN ¶30-001
Taxation ....CHN ¶35-001
Regulation of business ....CHN ¶45-001
Import and export controls ....CHN ¶50-001
Exchange control — the movement of money ....CHN ¶55-001
Labour and nationality laws ....CHN ¶60-001
Intellectual property ....CHN ¶65-001
Settlement of disputes ....CHN ¶70-001
Regulation of local finance ....CHN ¶75-001
Movement of goods (transport and shipping) ....CHN ¶80-001
Insurance ....CHN ¶85-000

GUANXI ZHENG (Partner in Charge) DAVID HUANG

Dorsey & Whitney

Suite 3008, One Pacific Place

88 Queensway

Hong Kong

Tel: (852) 2526 5000

Fax: (852) 2524 3000

Dorsey & Whitney

Dorsey & Whitney

1701-05 One Corporate Avenue

No. 222 Hubin Road

Shanghai 200040

China

Tel: (86) 21 6288 2323

Fax: (86) 21 6288 3222

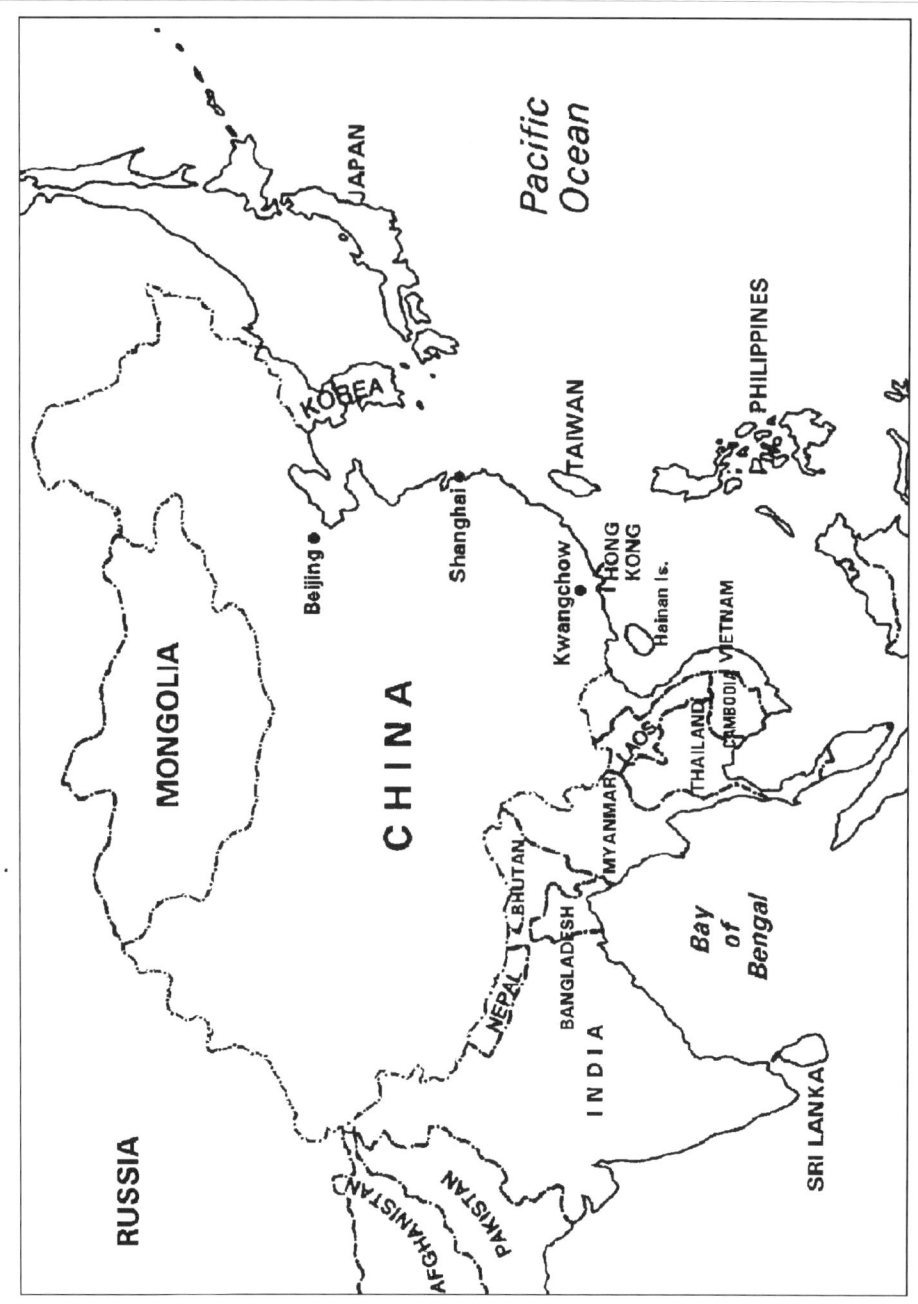

STATISTICAL SUMMARY

CHINA	
People	
Population:	299 billion (Jul 2004 est)
Ethnic groups:	Han Chinese 91.59%, Zhuang, Uygur, Mongol, Korean, Manchu, Hua, Yi, Tibetan
Languages:	Mandarin (official), Yue, Wu, Hakka, Xiang, Gan, Minnan, Minbei
Geography	
Land area:	9.6 million sq km
Climate:	Extremely diverse, tropical in south, subarctic in north
Average temperature:	South 20°C to 25°C; North -5°C to 0°C
Government	
Government type:	Communist party-led state
Head of State:	President Hu Jintao
Head of government:	Premier Wen Jiabao
Exchange rate:	RMB8.28 = US$1 (September 2003)
Economy (2003)	
GDP (US$)	1.41 trillion
Growth rate (%)	9.1%
Employment by sector (%)	
Agriculture	50
Industry	22
Services	28
Trade (2003)	
Total exports (US$ billion):	436.1.1
Total imports (US$ billion):	397.4
Leading three export items: 1. Machinery 2. Textiles & textile articles 3. Footwear, headgear etc.	Leading three export markets: 1. US 2. Hong Kong 3. Japan
Leading three import items: 1. Machinery 2. Mineral fuel 3. Plastics	Leading three import markets: 1. Japan 2. Taiwan 3. South Korea

INTRODUCTION

China's population is the largest of any country in the world. In an effort to curb population growth, the Chinese government has instituted policies designed to encourage late marriages, contraception and abortion, and the creation of "one-child" families.

The record of Chinese history dates back more than 3,000 years. Until the Republican revolution at the beginning of last century, China was ruled by successive dynasties or periods of centralised rule by different royal families which rose and fell over time. This pattern was characterised by the emperor system, the creation of a state bureaucracy and the emergence of Confucianism which provided a state ethic supported by imperial power.

The Tang Dynasty (618 A.D. to 907 A.D.) and the Song Dynasty (960 to 1279) are remembered as the most illustrious periods of traditional Chinese history. During their rule, the Tang established an empire which became one of the most powerful and developed in the world. The Tang reunited the empire and strengthened China's trade links to central Asia along the Silk Road. Both Confucianism and Buddhism flourished during this period. Significant advances were made in the cultural arts — painting, music, theatre — and in the Sciences.

At the beginning of the 19th century, however, a threat began to appear from the West. The main commodities sought by the West were tea and silk for which they were required to pay in silver. By the early 1800s, the imbalance in trade had become severe. The British found a solution to the problem with the sale of opium to China. Within a very short time, the flow of silver into China's coffers declined dramatically and sales of opium soared. The ruling Qing court attempted to ban the trade with little success. This led to the Opium Wars (1839 to 1842).

China's humiliating defeat in these struggles led ultimately to the forced cession of Hong Kong to the British and the opening up of four ports to traders, missionaries and other foreigners who enjoyed rights extra-territorially and other privileges.

Japan declared war on China in 1894. Upon China's defeat, Korea, Taiwan and the Pescadores Islands were ceded to the Japanese. The continuing encroachment of Western powers fanned both anti-foreign and anti-Qing sentiment among the Chinese. This encouraged revolutionary movements and in 1911, one movement led by Dr. Sun Yatsen ultimately succeeded in overthrowing Qing Rule. Influenced by Western ideas, Sun's success led to the creation of a republic.

The Republican Era

The first government of the Republic of China was proclaimed on 1 January 1912. In 1921, the Communist Party was formed in Shanghai. Beginning in the 1930s, the Japanese began to move openly against China, taking Manchuria in 1931. At the end of World War II in 1945, the Japanese surrendered to the Nationalist forces. Civil war ensued between the Nationalists and Communists and by 1949, the Communists, under the leadership of Mao Zedong, emerged victorious, declaring the People's Republic of China on 1 October of that year. The Nationalists, with their leader Chiang Kaishek, withdrew and fled to Taiwan.

1949 to 1976

A large-scale land reform was undertaken during which plots owned by landlords and other "capitalists" were confiscated for redistribution to the peasants. Later, in 1953, the nation's first Five-Year Plan was unveiled which called for the collectivisation of agriculture and a thorough reconstruction of the Chinese economy along Soviet lines.

China's second Five-Year Plan was announced in 1958. The plan called for radical changes in Chinese Society and in the economy with the aim to speed up the pace of socialist transformation. Under the "Great Leap Forward" program, farms and factories were ordered to comply with unrealistic production targets. These policies, coupled with several seasons of bad weather, brought about a significant drop in grain production and caused widespread food shortages.

In 1966, Mao launched the Great Proletarian Cultural Revolution. Designed to move China back onto the path of true communism and to enable Mao to regain complete control over the Party, the Cultural Revolution evolved into a mass movement on an unprecedented scale.

Workers and manual labour were glorified and intellectuals persecuted. Schools were closed, factories were shut and the government became paralysed as the entire country degenerated into chaos. In 1971, with the worst excesses of the Cultural Revolution ended, China turned her attention to re-establishing relations with the outside world which had all been cut off in the preceding eight years of strife. After Mao passed away in 1976, Deng Xiaoping was reinstated and the post-Mao era had begun.

1976 to 2000

China announced a new program of political and economic reform aimed at the modernisation of industry, agriculture, the military and science and technology which would propel China into the ranks of the developed countries by the year 2000. Foreign investment was encouraged but by the late 1980s, China's reform policies were threatened by economic stagnation and high inflation. Conservative Party economist led by Premier Li Peng called for a slow-down in the reforms and a return to central planning in some economic sectors.

At the same time, students and intellectuals began to press the Chinese government for political reforms. After several months of mass demonstrations in Tiananmen Square in central Beijing, martial law was declared in May 1989 and the Communist Party Chairman replaced. On 4 June 1989, thousands of the People's Liberation Army troops were sent into central Beijing to put an end to pro-democracy demonstrations, resulting in hundreds of deaths and thousands of arrests.

Despite the events of 4 June, China pledged to continue the "open door" policy on reforms while strictly adhering to the socialist path.

2000 onwards

In the new millennium, China's macroeconomic conditions will remain stable and remain a bright spot in the developing world for both FDI and portfolio investors. China's aggressive privatisation plan, including but not limited to the planned overseas IPOs of an increasing number of large companies, will open a wider door for foreign investors to participate in China's economic growth.

China's accession to the WTO in end 2001 will provide a host of new business opportunities for foreign companies in the vast China market. However, such economic benefits will not come easily and quickly. Since China's WTO commitments are unprecedented and will involve sweeping changes across all sectors of Chinese economy, its WTO implementations will be a long and difficult process. Before foreign companies can enjoy the full benefits of China's WTO accession, China needs to develop and enhance its legal and regulatory systems to be in full compliance with WTO requirements.

ABBREVIATIONS — CHINA

Art	Article
CAA	China Arbitration Association
CCPIT	China Council for the Promotion of International Trade
CHC	Chinese holding company
CIETAC	China International Economic and Trade Arbitration Commission
CIRC	China Insurance Regulatory Commission
CITIC	China International Trust and Investment Corporation
CMAC	China Maritime Arbitration Commission
CPA	Certified Public Accountant
CPC	Communist Party of China
CSRC	China Securities RegulatoryCommission
CSSC	China Securities Supervisory Commission
ECL	Economic Contract Law
EIL	Enterprise Insolvency Law
ETDZ	Economic technological development zone
FEC	Foreign exchange certificate
FECL	Foreign Economic Contract Law
FFI	Foreign financial institution
FIE	Foreign investment enterprises
FTZ	Free trade zone
IBC	Investment Bank of China
ICBC	Industrial and Commercial Bank of China
ICC	International Chamber of Commerce
ICCT/CICT	Industrial and commercial consolidated tax
ILO	International Labour Organisation
LIBOR	London Inter-Bank Offered Rate
M&A	Mergers and acquisitions
MIGA	Multilateral Investment guarantee Agency
MOC	Ministry of Construction
MOFCOM	Ministry of Commerce
MOFTEC	Ministry of Foreign Trade and Economic Cooperation
NPC	National People's Congress

OECD	Organisation for Economic Cooperation and Development
PBOC	People's Bank of China
PCT	Patent Co-operation Treaty
PICC	People's Insurance Company of China
QFII	Qualified foreign institutional investor
RMB	Renminbi (the Chinese unit of currency)
SAFE	State Administration of Foreign Exchange
SAIC	State Administration for Industry and Commerce
Sec	Section
SEPA	State Environmental Protection Agency
SETC	State Economic and Trade Commission
SEZ	Special economic zone
SOE	State-owned enterprise
SPDC	State Planning and Development Commission
TRIPs	Trade-Related Aspects of Intellectual Property Rights
UNICITRAL	United Nation Committee on International Trade Law
VAT	Value -added tax
WFOE	Wholly foreign-owned enterprise
WIPO	World Intellectual Property Organisation
WTO	World Trade Organisation

LATEST ADDITIONS TO INDEX

CHINA

As additional information is added to the "China" tab, relevant index entries may appear in the first instance on this page until such time as they can be incorporated into the principal index. These "Latest Additions" should always be consulted together with the principal index.

Paragraph

E

Exchange control
Administration of Verification and
Reconciliation of Foreign Exchange
Received from Exports Procedures .... CHN 55-002

F

Free trade zones .... CHN 50-021
bonded warehouses .... CHN 50-021
goods stored therein .... CHN 50-021

G

Geographical indications .... CHN 65-018

Paragraph

I

Intellectual property
circuit layouts .... CHN 65-013
compulsory licenses .... CHN 65-023
copyright .... CHN 65-003
disadvantages for non-residents .... CHN 65-025
domestic legislation .... CHN 65-002
enforcement .... CHN 65-031
industrial designs .... CHN 65-011
international agreements .... CHN 65-001
patents .... CHN 65-005
plant varieties .... CHN 65-014
registration procedures .... CHN 65-021
table of fees .... CHN 65-024
trademarks .... CHN 65-004
trade secrets .... CHN 65-012
transfers and licensing agreements ...... CHN 65-022
unfair competition .... CHN 65-015

INDEX

CHINA

Paragraph

A

Accelerated depreciation
foreign-invested enterprises .... CHN 35-501

Accounts
certification .... CHN 35-103
statutory — see Statutory accounts

Accounting requirements
companies .... CHN 35-103
foreign-invested enterprises .... CHN 35-103

Accounting system
foreign joint ventures .... CHN 35-103

Acquired land
compensation .... CHN 25-123

Acquisition
rights in land
– restrictions .... CHN 25-103

Advanced technological industries
incentives .... CHN 55-021

Advertising and promotion
laws governing .... CHN 45-306

Advisory fees
remittance .... CHN 55-011

Agreements
bilateral
– investment protection .... CHN 70-403
land use, restriction on .... CHN 25-115

Agriculture
tax incentives .... CHN 35-501

All-China Federation of Trade Unions
trade union activity, coordination .... CHN 60-014

Amiable composition
arbitration .... CHN 70-132

Animal husbandry
tax incentives .... CHN 35-501

Annual leave .... CHN 60-004

Anti-dumping duties .... CHN 50-025

Anti-trust laws
contracts, regulation of .... CHN 45-303

Appeals
dismissal from employment .... CHN 60-004

Applicable law
arbitration .... CHN 70-121

Paragraph

conciliation .... CHN 70-213
dispute resolution .... CHN 70-213
mediation .... CHN 70-213

Appointment
arbitrators .... CHN 70-122
conciliators .... CHN 70-203
mediators .... CHN 70-203

Approval seal
imports .... CHN 50-001

Arbitral awards
enforcement
– application, venue .... CHN 70-102
– procedure .... CHN 70-102

Arbitral proceedings
confidentiality .... CHN 70-143
language .... CHN 70-142

Arbitral tribunals
jurisdiction .... CHN 70-112

Arbitration
amiable composition .... CHN 70-132
applicable law, choice of .... CHN 70-121
arbitrators
– appointment .... CHN 70-122
– choice .... CHN 70-123
centres .... CHN 70-302
conciliation in conjunction .... CHN 70-134
confidentiality of proceedings .... CHN 70-143
convention .... CHN 70-102
cost .... CHN 70-103
courts' assistance .... CHN 70-114
delays .... CHN 70-125
domestic .... CHN 70-111
exceptions .... CHN 70-113
expense .... CHN 70-124
foreign companies' participation .... CHN 70-133
foreign lawyers' status .... CHN 70-135
foreign-related
– forum .... CHN 20-014
– method .... CHN 20-014
international .... CHN 70-111
international rules .... CHN 70-104
jurisdiction
– external assistance .... CHN 70-141
natural justice .... CHN 70-134
procedural law, choice of .... CHN 70-115
review by court .... CHN 70-131
special provisions re clauses .... CHN 70-103
special procedure re disputes .... CHN 70-144

Arbitration — continued   **Paragraph**

system .... CHN 70-101
third country .... CHN 70-145
tribunals' basis of jurisdiction .... CHN 70-112
United Nations Model Law .... CHN 70-105
venue .... CHN 70-122

Arbitration clauses
effectiveness .... CHN 70-103

Arbitrators
appointment .... CHN 70-122
choice, rules governing .... CHN 70-123
internationally acceptable .... CHN 70-303

Arrests
vessels .... CHN 80-005

Articles of Association
equity joint ventures .... CHN 30-113

Artistes
tax exemption .... CHN 35-105

Asian Development Bank
membership .... CHN 20-101

Assembly projects
tax incentives .... CHN 35-501

Assessment to tax
reconsideration .... CHN 35-003

Assets
acquisition
– repatriation, guarantees against .... CHN 20-204
– expropriation, guarantees against ... CHN 20-204;
                                          CHN 45-114
floating securities .... CHN 75-511
payment for shares .... CHN 30-104

Athletes
tax exemption .... CHN 35-105

Auditors
accounts, certification of .... CHN 35-103

B

Bank of China
foreign investment enterprises
– bank account .... CHN 45-102

Bankruptcy law .... CHN 30-114

Bearer shares
subsidiaries .... CHN 30-104

Beijing Conciliation Centre
conciliation rules .... CHN 70-202

Board of directors
powers .... CHN 30-112

Bonding
declared economic regions .... CHN 50-032
special economic zones .... CHN 50-032

Borrower   **Paragraph**
security
– retention of possession .... CHN 75-514
– recognised and protected .... CHN 75-513

Borrowings
foreign enterprises .... CHN 75-102
source outside China
– restrictions .... CHN 55-022

Branches
subsidiaries .... CHN 30-104

Branch profits
remittance .... CHN 55-011

Breach of contract
commercial law .... CHN 30-016
contract law .... CHN 30-016
damages .... CHN 30-016
– amount .... CHN 30-016
– apportionment .... CHN 30-016
– computation .... CHN 30-016
– time for payment .... CHN 30-016
deposits .... CHN 30-016
exemption from liability .... CHN 30-015
liability for compensation .... CHN 30-016
remedies .... CHN 30-016

Brokers — see **Insurance brokers**

Buildings
depreciation .... CHN 35-103

Businesses
existing
– obligations of purchaser .... CHN 60-025;
                                          CHN 60-031
foreign companies .... CHN 30-102
registration
– beyond tax registration area .... CHN 35-103
– cancellation .... CHN 35-103
– change .... CHN 35-103
– closing and re-opening .... CHN 35-103
– opening .... CHN 35-103
– penalties .... CHN 35-103

Business activities
disincentives .... CHN 45-004
enterprises conducting .... CHN 45-001
licensing .... CHN 45-001
non-residents, special provisions .... CHN 45-305
registration .... CHN 45-001
regulations .... CHN 45-001
taxation .... CHN 35-102

Business licence
approval .... CHN 45-002
issue .... CHN 45-002

Business profits
taxation .... CHN 35-101

Paragraph

Business undertakings
taxation .... CHN 35-102

C

Capital
repatriation .... CHN 55-005
repatriation during continuation of
investment incentives .... CHN 55-041
remittance .... CHN 55-005

Capital gains
taxation .... CHN 35-401– CHN 35-404

Chambers of commerce
import-export .... CHN 50-002

China International Economic and Trade Arbitration Commission (CIETAC) .... CHN 70-101
rules .... CHN 70-103

China International Maritime Arbitration Commission (CIMAC)
rules .... CHN 70-103

Chinese holding companies .... CHN 30-101

Choice of forum
dispute settlement .... CHN 70-014

Circuit layouts
exclusive right .... CHN 65-013
industrial property .... CHN 65-013
protection .... CHN 65-013
Regulation for Protection of Integrated Circuit Layout Designs .... CHN 65-013

Citizenship
labour law, effect on .... CHN 60-001

City districts
tax incentives .... CHN 35-512

Civil disputes
special procedures .... CHN 70-031

Civil procedure
arbitration
– courts' assistance .... CHN 70-114
– procedural law .... CHN 70-115
– representation, right of .... CHN 70-212
conciliation
– applicable law, choice of .... CHN 70-213
– courts' power of intervention .... CHN 70-214
– jurisdiction, basis of .... CHN 70-205
convention re arbitral awards .... CHN 70-102
costs, security for .... CHN 70-021
courts' jurisdiction re dispute
settlement .... CHN 70-001
courts, language of .... CHN 70-022
disputes
– special procedures .... CHN 70-031

Paragraph

dispute resolution
– government's status .... CHN 70-401
foreign companies .... CHN 70-003
foreign lawyers' status .... CHN 70-025
forum, choice of .... CHN 70-014
judgments
– enforcement .... CHN 70-023
– execution .... CHN 70-023
– foreign judgment, recognition of ..... CHN 70-024
jurisdiction .... CHN 70-014
rules .... CHN 70-004
– interlocutory relief .... CHN 70-011
settlement re arbitration,
enforcement of .... CHN 70-211

Coastal development zone
incentives .... CHN 45-105

Codification of law .... CHN 30-002
contract law .... CHN 30-002
economic law .... CHN 30-002
international treaties .... CHN 30-002

Commerce
cost of sales .... CHN 35-103
net sales .... CHN 35-103
profit on sales .... CHN 35-103
taxable income .... CHN 35-103

Commercial contracts
governing provisions .... CHN 30-013
settlement outside courts .... CHN 30-013

Commercial disputes
conciliation .... CHN 70-202

Commercial law
breach of contract .... CHN 30-016
contract law distinguished .... CHN 30-003
historical source .... CHN 30-001
institutions, special rules .... CHN 30-014
remedies .... CHN 30-016

Commercial organisations
forms .... CHN 30-101
legal persons .... CHN 30-101

Commercial profits
taxation .... CHN 35-101

Commercial secrets
industrial property .... CHN 65-012

Companies
accounting requirements .... CHN 35-103
foreign ownership, percentage of .... CHN 30-111
investment companies,
establishment of .... CHN 30-101
local — see Local companies
managing structures .... CHN 30-112

Companies limited by shares
definition .... CHN 30-101

Paragraph

Company law ....CHN 30-101– CHN 30-113

Compensation
acquired land......................................CHN 25-123
injury at work.....................................CHN 60-004
insurance...CHN 85-014

Compensation trade projects
tax incentives ....CHN 35-501

Compulsory acquisition
compensation.....................................CHN 20-205

Compulsory insurance ....CHN 85-011

Compulsory licenses
copyright...CHN 65-023
patents...CHN 65-023
trademarks...CHN 65-023

Computer software
registration ....CHN 65-021

Concessions
entry of goods ....CHN 50-015
foreign investment enterprises ....CHN 55-012

Conciliation ....CHN 70-134
applicable law, choice of ....CHN 70-213
commercial disputes ....CHN 70-202
conciliators, appointment of ....CHN 70-203
courts' power of intervention..............CHN 70-214
disadvantages.....................................CHN 70-224
dispute resolution...............................CHN 70-201
foreign participation, rules of ....CHN 70-221
forms, provisions in contract ....CHN 70-222
industrial disputes, settlement of ....CHN 60-011
joint methods ....CHN 70-225
jurisdiction, basis of...........................CHN 70-205
maritime disputes ....CHN 70-202
proceedings, confidentiality of ....CHN 70-215
restriction ....CHN 70-223
rules governing proceedings ....CHN 70-204
settlement, enforcement of.................CHN 70-211

Conciliators
appointment ....CHN 70-203
internationally acceptable ....CHN 70-303

Constitution
fundamental law.................................CHN 20-003

Construction project
environmental impact
report......................... CHN 25-203; CHN 25-205

Constructive ownership ....CHN 35-103

Consumer contracts
treatment ....CHN 30-011

Consumer protection
injuries, principles governing ....CHN 45-302
legislation ....CHN 45-301

Paragraph

Contracts
basis..CHN 30-014
breach — see Breach of contract
cancellation..CHN 30-017
conciliation, forms of.........................CHN 70-222
consumer contracts ....CHN 30-011
court's power to review ....CHN 30-017
dispute resolution, forms of...............CHN 70-222
exclusion clauses ....CHN 30-015
foreign exchange related provisions
– approval of......................................CHN 55-022
general consideration..........................CHN 30-015
foreign entities...................................CHN 30-005
government contracts — see
Government contracts
mediation, forms of............................CHN 70-222
modification..CHN 30-017
non-performance due to
force majeure ....CHN 30-015
performance under changed
circumstances ....CHN 30-017
requirements ....CHN 30-017
standardised ....CHN 30-015
termination...CHN 30-017
unfair contracts, review of.................CHN 45-307

Contract law
commercial law distinguished ....CHN 30-003
codification...CHN 30-002
historical sources ....CHN 30-001
institutions, special rules ....CHN 30-014
remedies..CHN 30-016

Contract of employment
when effective ....CHN 60-005

Contract processing projects
tax incentives.....................................CHN 35-501

Contractual interest
land...CHN 25-101

Contractual joint ventures — see also
Cooperative joint ventures
establishment.............CHN 30-113; CHN 45-104
foreign exchange profits,
remission of ....CHN 45-114
foreign-related direct
investment ....CHN 30-101; CHN 30-102

Conventions
Berne Convention...............................CHN 65-001
dispute resolution ....CHN 70-301; CHN 70-404
foreign arbitral awards.......................CHN 70-102
international..CHN 70-202
MIGA Convention.............................CHN 20-102
New York Convention on the Recognition
and Enforcement of Foreign Arbitral
Awards..CHN 20-102

Com

Paragraph

Paris Convention for Protection of Industrial
Property .... CHN 65-001
United Nations Convention on Contracts
for the International Sale
of Goods .... CHN 20-102
Universal Copyright Convention .... CHN 65-001
WIPO .... CHN 65-001

Cooperative joint ventures — see also
Contractual joint ventures
legislation applicable .... CHN 45-101
supervision by SAIC .... CHN 45-102
taxation .... CHN 45-112

Copyright .... CHN 65-003
compulsory licenses .... CHN 65-023
Copyright Law .... CHN 65-003
duration .... CHN 65-003
fees .... CHN 65-024
licensing agreements .... CHN 65-021
protection .... CHN 65-003
registration .... CHN 65-021
transfers .... CHN 65-022

Costs
land, transfer of .... CHN 25-102
litigation .... CHN 70-015
security re dispute settlement .... CHN 70-021

Costs of goods manufactured
industry .... CHN 35-103

Costs of goods sold
industry .... CHN 35-103

Cost of sales
commerce .... CHN 35-103

Countervailing duties .... CHN 50-025

Court
arbitral awards, review of .... CHN 70-131
arbitral proceedings, review of .... CHN 70-131
arbitral tribunals, review of .... CHN 70-131
arbitration, assistance in .... CHN 70-114
contracts, unfair
– review .... CHN 45-307
intervention
– conciliation .... CHN 70-214
– mediation .... CHN 70-214
language .... CHN 70-022
powers to review contract .... CHN 30-017

Cultural innovation
awards tax exempt .... CHN 35-501

Currency
remittance, restrictions on .... CHN 55-013
used in loans .... CHN 55-014

Currency swap centres .... CHN 55-015
exchange rate
– market forces determining .... CHN 55-021

Paragraph

Customs duties
rates .... CHN 50-012
technological imports exempted .... CHN 50-012

Customary rights
land .... CHN 25-011

D

Damages
amount .... CHN 30-016
apportionment .... CHN 30-016
breach of contract .... CHN 30-016
computation .... CHN 30-016
remedies .... CHN 30-016
time for payment .... CHN 30-016

Dangerous substances
movement
– laws regulating .... CHN 80-004

Declared economic regions
bonding .... CHN 50-032

Definitions
Chinese holding companies .... CHN 30-101
grant of a leasehold .... CHN 25-001
judicial assistance .... CHN 70-012
legal persons .... CHN 30-101
limited liability companies .... CHN 30-101
plant varieties .... CHN 65-014
urban state-owned land .... CHN 25-001

Defective products
liability for injury .... CHN 30-012

Defunct ventures
foreign exchange deposit account
– remittance of capital .... CHN 55-005

Deposits
breach of contract .... CHN 30-016
foreign currency
– law governing .... CHN 55-001
remedies for breach of contract .... CHN 30-016

Depreciation
buildings .... CHN 35-103
plant and equipment .... CHN 35-103

Depreciation allowances .... CHN 35-103

Depreciation periods
fixed assets of foreign-invested
enterprises .... CHN 35-501

Development zones
tax incentives .... CHN 35-512

Direct foreign trade
liberalisation .... CHN 50-011

Directors
nationality requirement .... CHN 30-104
shareholding qualification .... CHN 30-104

Paragraph

Disposal of shares
subsidiaries .... CHN 30-104

Disputes
arbitration
– exception .... CHN 70-113
intellectual property .... CHN 70-031
maritime .... CHN 70-143
special procedures .... CHN 70-031
– arbitration .... CHN 70-144
technology .... CHN 70-143
types restricted for conciliation .... CHN 70-223
types restricted for mediation .... CHN 70-223

Dispute resolution
alternative methods .... CHN 70-201
applicable law, choice of .... CHN 70-213
arbitration centres .... CHN 70-302
conciliators, appointment of .... CHN 70-203
courts' power of intervention .... CHN 70-214
disadvantages .... CHN 70-224
domestic .... CHN 70-223
foreign participation of rules .... CHN 70-221
forms, provisions in contract .... CHN 70-222
forum, choice of .... CHN 70-402
framework .... CHN 70-301– CHN 70-304
government's status .... CHN 70-401
international .... CHN 70-223
international conventions .... CHN 70-202;
                                     CHN 70-301
internationally acceptable
   arbitrators .... CHN 70-303
joint methods .... CHN 70-225
jurisdiction, basis of .... CHN 70-205
local advisers .... CHN 70-304
mediators, appointment of .... CHN 70-203
orders, enforcement of .... CHN 70-403
proceedings, confidentiality of .... CHN 70-215
representation, right of .... CHN 70-212
rules governing proceedings .... CHN 70-204
settlement, enforcement of .... CHN 70-211

Dispute settlement
applicable law, choice of .... CHN 70-013
arbitration .... CHN 70-101– CHN 70-145
basis of courts' jurisdiction .... CHN 70-001
civil procedure, rules of .... CHN 70-004
conciliation .... CHN 70-134
costs re litigation .... CHN 70-015
costs, security for .... CHN 70-021
evidence outside jurisdiction .... CHN 70-012
evidence, rules of .... CHN 70-004
foreign companies' status .... CHN 70-002
foreign judgments .... CHN 70-024
foreign lawyers' status .... CHN 70-025
forum, choice of .... CHN 70-014
interlocutory relief .... CHN 70-011

Paragraph

judgments
– enforcement .... CHN 70-023
– execution .... CHN 70-023
judicial assistance defined .... CHN 70-012
outside courts .... CHN 30-013
People's Courts .... CHN 70-002
service of process outside
   jurisdiction .... CHN 70-005
special procedures .... CHN 70-031
time limit re litigation .... CHN 70-015

Dispute settlement mechanism
applicable law .... CHN 20-013
forum .... CHN 20-014
method .... CHN 20-014

Dividends
remittance .... CHN 55-011
tax exempt .... CHN 35-501
taxation .... CHN 35-104
– non-residents .... CHN 75-112

Domestic arbitration .... CHN 70-111

Domestic business organisation .... CHN 30-101

Domestic economy
targeted sectors
– incentives .... CHN 45-003

Domestic enterprises
disincentives
– administration .... CHN 45-004
incentives .... CHN 45-003
– administration .... CHN 45-004
laws regulating operation .... CHN 45-003

Domestic legislation
industrial property .... CHN 65-002

Double taxation agreements .... CHN 35-001

E

Economy
centrally planned, command
   economy .... CHN 20-005

Economic law
government contracts,
   requirements .... CHN 30-004
codification .... CHN 30-002

Economic and technological development zones —
see also **Development zones** .... CHN 20-205
land use
– regulations .... CHN 25-005

Economic priorities
preferred investments .... CHN 45-004

Employees
annual leave .... CHN 60-004

Paragraph

dismissal .... CHN 60-004
injury at work
– compensation .... CHN 60-004
insurance.. CHN 60-004
legal guarantees .... CHN 60-004
legal relationship with employer .... CHN 60-003
lock-out.. CHN 60-022
minimum wage .... CHN 60-004
obligations of purchaser.................... CHN 60-025;
CHN 60-031
severance pay.................................... CHN 60-004
sick leavve .... CHN 60-004
strike .... CHN 60-022

Employers
existing business, purchaser of
– obligations to employees .... CHN 60-025;
CHN 60-031
legal relationship with employee .... CHN 60-003
lock out employees, right to .... CHN 60-022

Employer-employee relationship .... CHN 60-003

Employer organisations .... CHN 60-014
government, institutional link............ CHN 60-021
trade unions, institutional link .... CHN 60-021

Employment
labour-contract system...................... CHN 60-003
long-term .... CHN 60-003
protection for women......................... CHN 60-004
short-term... CHN 60-003

Employment contract
termination... CHN 60-004

Enforcement
intellectual property.......................... CHN 65-031

Enterprise income tax
exemptions
– representative offices of foreign
enterprises....................................... CHN 35-501

Entry of goods
concession... CHN 50-015

Environment
detriment.. CHN 25-212

Environmental assessment
governmental requirements................ CHN 25-203

Environmental controls
nature .... CHN 25-211
regulations .... CHN 25-202

Environmental impact report
construction project .... CHN 25-203;
CHN 25-205

Environmental protection
controls, nature of............................. CHN 25-211

Paragraph

non-polluting plants
– incentives....................................... CHN 25-205
pollution standards .... CHN 25-204

**Environmental Protection Administrative
Department**.................................... CHN 25-202

Environmental restrictions................ CHN 25-201

Equity
raising of capital .... CHN 75-103
– regulations ....CHN 75-103; CHN 75-104

Equity joint ventures
Articles of Association .... CHN 30-113
establishment.................................... CHN 30-113
– laws regulating............................... CHN 45-104
foreign exchange profits,
remission of .... CHN 45-114
foreign-related direct
investment ....CHN 30-101; CHN 30-102
legislation applicable........................ CHN 45-101
supervision by SAIC.......................... CHN 45-102
taxation .... CHN 45-112

Equity loan ratios .... CHN 75-011

Evidence
jurisdiction
– dispute settlement........................... CHN 70-012
rules .... CHN 70-004

Exchange control
administering body .... CHN 55-002
exemptions... CHN 55-031
formalities.. CHN 55-033
laws.. CHN 55-001
– application to various countries....... CHN 55-004
– breach .... CHN 55-034
local participation, effect of.............. CHN 55-025
policy objectives................................ CHN 55-003
regulations
– taxation considerations................... CHN 55-042

Exchange rate
fixing, method of............................... CHN 55-015
local arrangements............................. CHN 75-205
market forces determining................. CHN 55-021

Exclusion clauses .... CHN 30-015

Executives
taxation .... CHN 35-105

Exemptions
enterprise income tax........................ CHN 35-501
individual income tax .... CHN 35-501

Expatriate personnel
pension fund contributions,
remittance of..................................... CHN 55-032
personal savings, remittance of .... CHN 55-032

Paragraph

Expenses
arbitration .... CHN 70-123

Exports
financing .... CHN 75-005
labelling requirements .... CHN 50-022
licence .... CHN 50-003
– regulation .... CHN 50-004
packaging requirements .... CHN 50-022
restrictions .... CHN 50-003
special tariff treatment .... CHN 50-014
taxes on freight .... CHN 50-013

Export allowances
determination .... CHN 35-511
eligibility
– non-resident companies .... CHN 35-505

Export business
foreign-controlled
– registration .... CHN 50-005

Export duty
exemption
– value-added products .... CHN 35-501

Export enterprises
incentives, eligibility for .... CHN 45-003
special incentives .... CHN 45-111; CHN 45-113

Export incentives .... CHN 35-504
foreign-invested enterprises .... CHN 55-001

Export-producing industries
incentives .... CHN 55-021

Expropriation
provisions against .... CHN 20-205
investments
– protection .... CHN 70-403

F

Farmers
insurance .... CHN 85-012

Fees
copyright .... CHN 65-024
industrial property .... CHN 65-024
patents .... CHN 65-024
trademarks .... CHN 65-024

Finance
exports .... CHN 75-005
legal securities .... CHN 75-301– CHN 75-501
raising and supplying
– financial institutions .... CHN 75-002

Financial institutions
foreign .... CHN 75-001
non-bank .... CHN 75-001
raising finance .... CHN 75-002

Paragraph

self regulation .... CHN 75-105
specialised
– exports .... CHN 75-005
– investment and development .... CHN 75-004
supplying finance .... CHN 75-002
types of .... CHN 75-001

Financing
insurance .... CHN 85-004
law governing .... CHN 75-211

Fiscal year .... CHN 35-004

Floating security
classes of assets .... CHN 75-511

Force majeure
non-performance of contracts .... CHN 30-015

Foreign banks
loans to Chinese entities,
approval of .... CHN 55-014

Foreign businesses
earning foreign exchange .... CHN 55-001

Foreign businessman
determination .... CHN 45-103

Foreign companies
accounting system .... CHN 35-103
carrying on business .... CHN 30-102
civil procedure
– litigation .... CHN 70-003
investment .... CHN 30-102
local participation
– effect on exchange control .... CHN 55-025
participation
– arbitral proceedings .... CHN 70-133
registration .... CHN 30-103
representative offices .... CHN 30-103
shares .... CHN 75-104
status in dispute settlement .... CHN 70-002

Foreign company representative offices
import-export businesses .... CHN 50-005

Foreign contractors
engaging in engineering projects
– tax incentives .... CHN 35-501
providing labour services
– tax incentives .... CHN 35-501

Foreign-controlled businesses
import-export
– registration .... CHN 50-005
incorporation outside China
– foreign exchange control
regulations .... CHN 55-024
locally incorporated
– foreign exchange control
regulations .... CHN 55-024

Paragraph

Foreign corporations
incorporation outside China............... CHN 45-103

Foreign currency
criteria when used as payment........... CHN 55-001
deposits
– law governing .... CHN 55-001
remittance, limit on........................... CHN 55-012
repatriation, guarantees against .... CHN 20-204

Foreign enterprises
accounts certified by auditors............. CHN 35-103
bankruptcy law .... CHN 30-114
borrowings.. CHN 75-102
incentives... CHN 45-003
– administration of scheme................ CHN 45-003
– eligibility...................................... CHN 45-003
labour insurance............................... CHN 85-012
lending .... CHN 75-101
losses, how treated .... CHN 35-103
low-profit
– exemption from tax........................ CHN 35-501
permanent representative offices
– tax incentives............................... CHN 35-501
registration requirements .... CHN 35-103
small-scale
– exemption from tax........................ CHN 35-501
tax
– base... CHN 35-103
– legislation .... CHN 35-101
tax liability
– time for payment........................... CHN 35-103
– payment, method of .... CHN 35-005
tax returns
– time for filing................................ CHN 35-103
with establishment in China
– how treated .... CHN 35-104
withholding tax................................. CHN 35-103
without establishment in China
– how treated .... CHN 35-104

Foreign enterprise association............. CHN 60-014

Foreign entities
dispute resolution
– forum .... CHN 20-014
– method .... CHN 20-014
requirements re contracts .... CHN 30-005

Foreign equity-loan ratios................... CHN 75-011

Foreign exchange............................... CHN 45-102
availability .... CHN 45-003
foreign business .... CHN 55-001

Foreign exchange control
foreign-controlled companies
– locally incorporated .... CHN 55-024
remittance abroad
– approval .... CHN 55-005

Paragraph

Foreign exchange deposit account
defunct venture
– remittance of capital .... CHN 55-005
foreign ventures
– approval to open account................. CHN 55-001
– requirement to maintain.................. CHN 55-012
forward market .... CHN 55-035
receipts and expenditures, report........ CHN 55-001
topping up.. CHN 55-012

Foreign exchange transactions
exchange control authorities'
approval.. CHN 55-022

Foreign-funded enterprises
land, rent of...................................... CHN 25-001

Foreign-invested enterprises
accelerated depreciation .... CHN 35-501
accounting requirements.................... CHN 35-103
Beijing
– tax exemption .... CHN 35-501
contracts, unfair
– review .... CHN 45-307
export incentives............................... CHN 55-001
fixed assets
– depreciation periods....................... CHN 35-501
foreign exchange
– receipts and expenditures .... CHN 55-001
– receipts and expenditures,
balance... CHN 55-001
foreign exchange from exports
– remittance .... CHN 55-001
taxation .... CHN 35-103

Foreign investment
categories... CHN 30-102
disincentives .... CHN 45-004
– administration ....CHN 45-004; CHN 45-113
encouragement.................................. CHN 20-205
– legislative changes.......................... CHN 45-113
incentives... CHN 45-103
– administration ....CHN 45-004; CHN 45-113
preferences....................................... CHN 45-003
preferential terms.............................. CHN 35-102
regulation... CHN 45-101
targeted areas .... CHN 20-205

Foreign investment enterprises
books of account............................... CHN 45-102
concessions .... CHN 55-012
control.. CHN 45-102
foreign exchange, control of.............. CHN 45-102
import and export, control of............. CHN 45-102
incentives, eligibility for.................... CHN 45-113
industrial dispute settlement
– legal parameters............................. CHN 60-012
labour laws, special application.......... CHN 60-032
legislation regulating activities........... CHN 45-112

Foreign investment enterprises   Paragraph
— continued

legislative restrictions .... CHN 45-204
management
– racial requirement .... CHN 60-034
– nationality requirement.................... CHN 60-034
nationality, required balance.............. CHN 60-034
non-management level employment
– nationality requirement.................... CHN 60-034
priorities for investment.................... CHN 45-111;
    CHN 45-113
remuneration of employees................ CHN 60-005
shares .... CHN 30-104
trade unions, role of .... CHN 60-014
training schemes required .... CHN 60-024

Foreign investors
activities, approval of .... CHN 45-102
determination .... CHN 45-103
government guarantees .... CHN 20-204
investment companies,
  establishment of.............................. CHN 30-101
local consultant, retention of .... CHN 45-115
protection .... CHN 20-205
remittance of capital on
  liquidation...................................... CHN 55-005

Foreign joint ventures
accounting system.............................. CHN 35-103
tax legislation..................................... CHN 35-101

Foreign judgments
enforcement and recognition
– pre-conditions .... CHN 70-024

Foreign law firms
consultation services, provision of ..... CHN 20-012

Foreign lawyers
local court, appearance before .... CHN 20-012
practice, right of................................ CHN 20-012
status .... CHN 70-025
status in arbitration .... CHN 70-135

Foreign management
nationality .... CHN 30-104

Foreign-owned enterprises
directors, nationality requirement....... CHN 30-104
establishment requirements................ CHN 30-104
statutory accounts .... CHN 30-104

Foreign ownership
percentage.. CHN 30-111

Foreign participation
conciliation .... CHN 70-221
dispute resolution.............................. CHN 70-221

Foreign personnel
income tax reduction .... CHN 35-501

Foreign-related business
organisation .... CHN 30-101

Foreign-related direct investment
forms...........................CHN 30-101; CHN 30-102

Foreign trade
direct
– liberalisation .... CHN 50-011
operators
– code of conduct .... CHN 45-303
policy objectives................................ CHN 50-011
regulation.. CHN 45-101
restrictions .... CHN 50-011

Foreign ventures
foreign exchange deposit account
– permission for establishment .... CHN 55-001

Foreigners
income tax .... CHN 35-105
registration with tax authorities .... CHN 35-105
tax, time for payment......................... CHN 35-105
taxation declaration .... CHN 35-105

Forestry
tax incentives..................................... CHN 35-501

Forms
joint venture....................................... CHN 30-113

Forum
dispute resolution .... CHN 70-402
dispute settlement.............................. CHN 70-014

Forward market
foreign exchange .... CHN 55-035

Franking rebates .... CHN 35-202

Free trade zones................................ CHN 50-021

Fringe benefits
taxation.. CHN 35-103

Futures trading
registration.. CHN 45-001

G

General Agreement on Tariffs Trade
membership .... CHN 50-023

General processing projects
tax incentives..................................... CHN 35-501

Geographical areas
priority areas/regions
– investment incentives .... CHN 45-003

Geographical restrictions
local companies, investment in........... CHN 30-105

Goods
detention by State Administration of
  Commodity Inspection .... CHN 50-031
invoice value, regulation of............... CHN 35-104

For

Paragraph

Governing structures
companies .... CHN 30-112
types .... CHN 30-112

Government
employer organisations,
institutional links .... CHN 60-021
MIGA Convention, accession to .... CHN 70-404
organisation .... CHN 20-005
participation in profits .... CHN 45-205
requirements re environmental
assessment .... CHN 25-203
status in dispute resolution .... CHN 70-401
trade unions, institutional
links .... CHN 60-021

Government agencies
contracts, unfair
– review .... CHN 45-307

Government contracts
requirements .... CHN 30-004

Government guarantees
foreign investors .... CHN 20-204

Government participation
local companies, investment in .... CHN 30-105
profits .... CHN 45-205

Grant of leasehold
definition .... CHN 25-001

Guarantees
amounts payable under guarantee
– remittance .... CHN 55-011

H

Hainan Island
tax incentives .... CHN 35-512

Hamburg Conciliation Centre
conciliation rules .... CHN 70-202

High technology industries
exchange control exemptions .... CHN 55-031
import tax exemption .... CHN 35-501

Holiday zones
state-designated
– tax reductions .... CHN 35-501

Host country
foreign trade policy, objective of .... CHN 50-011

Hours of work
control .... CHN 60-005
maximum .... CHN 60-005

House rentals
tax .... CHN 35-301

Paragraph

I

Imports
approval seal .... CHN 50-001
approved .... CHN 50-001
concessional entry .... CHN 50-015
inspection .... CHN 50-001
labelling requirements .... CHN 50-022
licence, regulation of .... CHN 50-004
packaging requirements .... CHN 50-022
preferences .... CHN 50-012
prohibited .... CHN 50-001
restrictions .... CHN 50-001
taxes on freight .... CHN 50-013

Import business
foreign-controlled
– registration .... CHN 50-005

Import duty
exemption
– hi-tech enterprise .... CHN 35-501

Import-export
chambers of commerce .... CHN 50-002
international treaties .... CHN 50-023
penalties for non-compliance .... CHN 50-024
policy objectives .... CHN 50-011

Import-export business
foreign company representative
offices .... CHN 50-005

Imported goods
taxation .... CHN 35-104

Importers
special requirements .... CHN 50-002

Incentives
advanced technological industries ...... CHN 55-021
export-producing industries .... CHN 55-021
non-polluting plants .... CHN 25-205

Incentive legislation .... CHN 45-003

Income tax
non-residents .... CHN 35-105
rates .... CHN 35-105
residents .... CHN 35-105

Individual owned enterprises .... CHN 45-001

Individuals
income tax .... CHN 35-501
– exemption .... CHN 35-501
– reduction .... CHN 35-501
taxable income .... CHN 35-105
taxation
– system of withholding .... CHN 35-005

Industrial designs .... CHN 65-011
exterior designs .... CHN 65-011
patent .... CHN 65-011

Paragraph

Industrial disputes
settlement .... CHN 60-011
– customary method .... CHN 60-013
– legal system, parameters of .... CHN 60-012

Industrial property
circuit layouts .... CHN 65-013
commercial secrets .... CHN 65-012
compulsory licenses .... CHN 65-023
copyright .... CHN 65-003
disadvantages for non-residents .... CHN 65-025
disputes .... CHN 70-031
domestic legislation .... CHN 65-002
enforcement .... CHN 65-031
fees .... CHN 65-024
industrial designs .... CHN 65-011
international agreements .... CHN 65-001
licensing agreements .... CHN 65-021
patents .... CHN 65-005
plant varieties .... CHN 65-014
registration .... CHN 65-021
trademarks .... CHN 65-004
trade secrets .... CHN 65-012
transfers .... CHN 65-022
unfair competition .... CHN 65-015

Industry
costs of goods manufactured .... CHN 35-103
costs of goods sold .... CHN 35-103
manufacturing costs .... CHN 35-103
net sales .... CHN 35-103
profit on sales .... CHN 35-103
taxable income .... CHN 35-103

Infringement
commercial secrets .... CHN 65-012
intellectual property rights
– penalties .... CHN 65-015
patent .... CHN 65-005
trademark .... CHN 65-004

Injuries
consumer protection .... CHN 45-302
cause
– defective products .... CHN 30-012

Inspection
imports .... CHN 50-001

Insurance
available range .... CHN 85-003
compulsory .... CHN 85-011
employees .... CHN 85-012
farmers .... CHN 85-012
financing arrangements .... CHN 85-004
law regulating .... CHN 85-000
payments .... CHN 85-014
product liability .... CHN 85-021
unemployment .... CHN 85-012

Paragraph

Insurance brokers
state-owned, use of .... CHN 85-001

Insurance company
legislation affecting .... CHN 85-013

Insurance underwriters
classes of .... CHN 85-002

Intellectual property — see **Industrial property**

Inter-company accounts
with non-resident parent .... CHN 55-022

Interest
remittance .... CHN 55-011
tax exempt .... CHN 35-501
taxation .... CHN 35-104
– non-residents .... CHN 75-112

Interest on loans
tax incentives .... CHN 35-501

Interest rates .... CHN 75-203

Interlocutory relief
dispute settlement .... CHN 70-011

International agreements .... CHN 20-102
industrial property .... CHN 65-001

International arbitration .... CHN 70-111
rules .... CHN 70-104

International banks
membership .... CHN 20-101

International capital market
access .... CHN 75-003

International Chamber of Commerce
rules .... CHN 70-104

International conventions .... CHN 80-003
dispute resolution .... CHN 70-202; CHN 70-301;
           CHN 70-404
intellectual property .... CHN 65-001

International Labour Organisation
Conventions .... CHN 60-035

International Monetary Fund (IMF)
membership .... CHN 20-101

International tax treaties .... CHN 35-001

International treaties
codification .... CHN 30-002
import-export .... CHN 50-023
taking effect .... CHN 20-003

Investing money
customary terms .... CHN 75-201
– flexibility .... CHN 75-202

Investment
encouragement .... CHN 20-201
foreign companies .... CHN 30-102

Paragraph

insurance agreements.......................... CHN 20-201
local companies .... CHN 30-105
production of goods for import substitution
– exchange control exemption .... CHN 55-031
protection .... CHN 20-201
– agreements .... CHN 70-403
– bilateral agreements .... CHN 20-201
– multilateral treaties .... CHN 20-203
specialised institutions....................... CHN 75-004

Investment companies
establishment of................................. CHN 30-101

Investment in local companies
geographical restrictions.................... CHN 30-105
government participation .... CHN 30-105
local employees .... CHN 30-105
restrictions .... CHN 30-105

Investment profits
deduction for tax................................ CHN 35-212

Investment protection
treaties... CHN 20-201

J

Joint methods
conciliation .... CHN 70-225
dispute resolution.............................. CHN 70-225

Joint trade agreements........................ CHN 20-202

Joint ventures.................................... CHN 20-205
accounting requirement .... CHN 35-103
arbitral proceedings .... CHN 70-133
contractual joint ventures — see Contractual
joint ventures
cooperative joint ventures — see Cooperative
joint ventures
contract, approval of........................... CHN 45-102
equity joint ventures — see Equity joint ventures
foreign joint ventures — see Foreign joint
ventures
form .... CHN 30-113
incentives... CHN 45-003
law .... CHN 70-002
local consultant, retention of .... CHN 45-115
main provisions.................................. CHN 30-113
powers.. CHN 30-113
reinvesting profits
– tax refund .... CHN 35- 501
restrictions .... CHN 30-113
structure .... CHN 30-113
tax
– exemption .... CHN 35-501
– reduction .... CHN 35-501
– time for payment............................. CHN 35-103
tax return
– time for filing.................................. CHN 35-103
taxable income................................... CHN 35-103

Paragraph

Joint venture contract
approval .... CHN 45-003
examination .... CHN 45-003

Judgments
enforcement .... CHN 70-023
execution .... CHN 70-023
foreign judgment, recognition of........ CHN 70-024

Judicial Court.................................... CHN 20-005

Jurisdiction
arbitral tribunals................................. CHN 70-112
arbitration
– external assistance .... CHN 70-141
conciliation .... CHN 70-205
dispute resolution .... CHN 70-205
dispute settlement.............................. CHN 70-001
evidence
– dispute settlement........................... CHN 70-012
execution, external.............................. CHN 70-005
mediation .... CHN 70-205
service, external.................................. CHN 70-005

K

Know-how fees
tax incentives..................................... CHN 35-501

L

Labelling requirements
exports .... CHN 50-022
imports.. CHN 50-022
industrial property .... CHN 65-024

Labour insurance .... CHN 85-012

Labour law
administration..................................... CHN 60-023
citizenship, effect of .... CHN 60-001
foreigners, special application .... CHN 60-032
legislative control .... CHN 60-024
nationality, effect of........................... CHN 60-001
race, effect of .... CHN 60-001

Land
acquired land
– compensation................................... CHN 25-123
acquisition
– power of Land Bureau .... CHN 25-122
acquisition by state .... CHN 25-001
contract interest .... CHN 25-101
customary rights .... CHN 25-011
development zones
– facilities, provision of...................... CHN 25-101
economic technological development
zones.. CHN 25-005
local regulations .... CHN 25-004
ownership
– absolute.. CHN 25-101

Land — continued   **Paragraph**
- definition... CHN 25-001
- private .... CHN 25-002
- registration .... CHN 25-111
registration
- system .... CHN 25-112
rights — see Rights in land
right to use
- approval by state .... CHN 25-001
- consignment.................................... CHN 25-001
- contractual .... CHN 25-001; CHN 25-101
- registration .... CHN 25-111
- transfer .... CHN 25-003
security
- creation of .... CHN 75-503
- registration .... CHN 25-105
seizure.. CHN 25-125
special areas...................................... CHN 25-005
special economic zones..................... CHN 25-005
specific rights.................................... CHN 25-113
structures as collateral...................... CHN 25-101
survey... CHN 25-104
tenure
- forms .... CHN 25-001
transfer — see Transfer of land
use
- agreements restricting .... CHN 25-115
- environmental impact report........... CHN 25-211
- environmental restrictions .... CHN 25-201
- existing restrictions......................... CHN 25-121
- restrictions .... CHN 25-001

Land Bureau
compensation for acquired land
- determination .... CHN 25-123
land
- transfer, approval of........................ CHN 25-102
land use rights
- revocation of .... CHN 25-101; CHN 25-122
power re acquisition of land .... CHN 25-122
seizure of land................................... CHN 25-125

Land tenure
forms.. CHN 25-001

Land value added tax .... CHN 35-301

Language
arbitral proceedings .... CHN 70-142
courts .... CHN 70-022
lawyers... CHN 20-011
litigation.. CHN 70-022

Laws
Anti-Unfair Competition Law .... CHN 65-002
applicable law, determination of........ CHN 20-013
choice re dispute settlement............... CHN 70-013
codification .... CHN 20-003; CHN 30-002
commercial law — see Commercial law

     Paragraph
contract law — see Contract law
contract and commercial law
distinguished.................................. CHN 30-003
Copyright Law .... CHN 65-002
exchange control..........CHN 55-001; CHN 55-004
financing.. CHN 75-211
foreign currency deposits................... CHN 55-001
industrial property .... CHN 65-002
- enforcement..................................... CHN 65-031
insurance activities .... CHN 85-000
inward and outward transport............. CHN 80-001
language... CHN 20-011
movement of dangerous substances.... CHN 80-004
movement of goods .... CHN 80-002
Patent Law... CHN 65-002
shipping register .... CHN 80-012
sources .... CHN 20-003
storage of goods................................. CHN 80-002
system, characteristics of................... CHN 20-001
Trademark Law................................... CHN 65-002

Law-making bodies
power .... CHN 20-004

Lawyers
admittance to practice........................ CHN 20-012
language... CHN 20-011
regulations .... CHN 20-012

Leasehold
grant, definition .... CHN 25-001

Leasing
tax incentives.................................... CHN 35-501

Legal database .... CHN 20-011

Legal persons
definition .... CHN 30-101
determination..................................... CHN 30-101
status, conditions for obtaining.......... CHN 45-001

Legal profession — see also **Lawyers**
organisation .... CHN 20-012
professional standards,
enforcement of............................... CHN 20-012
structure .... CHN 20-012

Legal system
origin .... CHN 20-002
socialist law .... CHN 20-001

Legislation
English translations .... CHN 20-011
foreign investment,
encouragement of .... CHN 20-205
industrial property .... CHN 65-002
labour law .... CHN 60-024

Legislative authority
where found .... CHN 20-004

Paragraph

Lender
security, realisation of......................... CHN 75-515
security, transferability .... CHN 75-521

Lending
foreign enterprises .... CHN 75-102
money
– customary loans .... CHN 75-201
– flexibility .... CHN 75-201

Liability
injury caused by defective products ... CHN 30-012

Licences
business activities .... CHN 45-001
compulsory
– industrial property........................... CHN 65-023
exports .... CHN 50-003; CHN 50-004
imports... CHN 50-004
statutory monopolies.......................... CHN 45-304

Licence fees
remittance .... CHN 55-011
withholding tax................................... CHN 35-104

Licensing agreements
industrial property.............................. CHN 65-022

Limited liability companies
definition.. CHN 30-101

Liquidation
provisions... CHN 30-104
security interests, priority of.............. CHN 75-504
subsidiaries .... CHN 30-104

Litigation
costs .... CHN 70-015
foreign companies
– civil procedure .... CHN 70-003
language.. CHN 70-022
prior payment
– circumstances.................................. CHN 70-021
security for costs .... CHN 70-021
time limits .... CHN 70-015

Loans
currency to use................................... CHN 55-014
foreign banks providing
– approval .... CHN 55-014
interest rates...................................... CHN 75-203
security... CHN 75-204

Loan finance
sources of — see Sources of loan finance

Local advisers
dispute resolution............................... CHN 70-304

Local agents
non-resident companies .... CHN 30-103

Local companies
government participation..................... CHN 30-105

Paragraph

investment .... CHN 30-105
– geographical restrictions................. CHN 30-105
local employees, employment of........ CHN 30-105

Local consultant
local customs and practices .... CHN 45-115

Local currency
exchange rate
– method of fixing .... CHN 55-015
remittance, limit on............................ CHN 55-012

Local customs and practices
local consultant.................................. CHN 45-115

Local Dispute Arbitration Committee
dismissal from employment
– appeals.. CHN 60-004

Local employees
employment in local companies .... CHN 30-105

Local equity capital
raising of.. CHN 75-103

Local participation
exchange control, effect on................ CHN 55-025

Local regulations
land.. CHN 25-004

Lock-outs
restriction on right .... CHN 60-022

London Court of International Arbitration
rules .... CHN 70-104

Losses
carry forward .... CHN 35-103
treatment.. CHN 35-103

M

Machine rental
remittance .... CHN 55-011

Management
foreign investment enterprises
– nationality requirement................... CHN 60-034
– racial requirement............................ CHN 60-034
nationality requirement....................... CHN 30-104

Management fees
remittance .... CHN 55-011

Managing structures
companies.. CHN 30-112
types.. CHN 30-112

Manufacturing costs
industry... CHN 35-103

Maritime Arbitration Commission ..... CHN 70-101

Maritime disputes............................... CHN 70-143
conciliation .... CHN 70-202

Paragraph

Maritime matters
arbitration
– special procedures .... CHN 70-144

Mediation
applicable law, choice of .... CHN 70-213
disadvantages .... CHN 70-224
dispute resolution .... CHN 70-201
forms, provisions in contract .... CHN 70-222
jurisdiction, basis of .... CHN 70-205
mediators, appointment of .... CHN 70-203
proceedings, confidentiality of .... CHN 70-215
restrictions .... CHN 70-223
rules governing proceedings .... CHN 70-204
settlement, enforcement of .... CHN 70-211

Mediators
appointment .... CHN 70-203

MIGA Convention .... CHN 70-404
investment protection .... CHN 20-203
ratification .... CHN 20-102; CHN 20-203

Minimum wage .... CHN 60-004; CHN 60-005
regulation .... CHN 60-004

Ministry of Finance
taxation rules, interpretation of .... CHN 35-003

**Ministry of Foreign Trade and Economic
Cooperation (MOFTEC)**
foreign investor
– approval of activities .... CHN 45-102
joint venture contract
– approval .... CHN 45-003; CHN 45-102
– examination .... CHN 45-003
import and export licences,
   regulation of .... CHN 50-004
imports, approved and prohibited
– publication of lists .... CHN 50-001

Ministry of Labour
minimum pay, regulation .... CHN 60-004
occupational safety, regulation of .... CHN 60-004

Ministry of Personnel
minimum pay, regulation of .... CHN 60-004
occupational safety, regulation of ...... CHN 60-004

Miscellaneous taxes
property tax .... CHN 35-301
real estate tax .... CHN 35-301

Movement of goods
laws regulating .... CHN 80-002

N

Nationals
racial description .... CHN 60-002

National People's Congress (NPC)
functions .... CHN 20-005

Paragraph

legislative authority .... CHN 20-004
powers .... CHN 20-005
Standing Committee .... CHN 20-005
State Plan, passing of .... CHN 45-202

Nationalisation
investments, protection of .... CHN 70-403

Nationality
determination .... CHN 45-103
directors of subsidiaries .... CHN 30-104
dual .... CHN 60-002
labour laws, effect on .... CHN 60-001
loss .... CHN 60-002
management of subsidiaries .... CHN 30-104
required balance in employment .... CHN 60-034

Nationality laws
basis .... CHN 60-002

Natural justice
arbitration .... CHN 70-134

Net business income
service trades .... CHN 35-103

Net sales
commerce .... CHN 35-103
industry .... CHN 35-103

New industries
tax incentives .... CHN 35-501
New York Convention .... CHN 70-102;
                                          CHN 70-301
ratification .... CHN 20-102

Nominal capital
subsidiaries .... CHN 30-104

Non-agricultural individual enterprises
governing provisions .... CHN 45-001

Non-joint venture foreign enterprises
taxation .... CHN 35-103

Non-polluting plants
incentives .... CHN 25-205

Non-residents
bank accounts
– debiting and crediting, control of .... CHN 55-022
business activities
– special provisions .... CHN 45-305
industrial property
– disadvantages .... CHN 65-025
rate of tax .... CHN 35-105
residents distinguished .... CHN 55-023
subsidiaries
– share capital, percentage of .... CHN 30-104
taxation of dividends .... CHN 75-112
taxation of interest .... CHN 75-112

Non-resident companies
bodies exercising jurisdiction .... CHN 30-103

Paragraph

export allowances, eligibility for .... CHN 35-505
local agents .... CHN 30-103
registration .... CHN 30-103
– fees.. CHN 30-103
– procedures... CHN 30-103
statutory accounts .... CHN 30-103
taxation .... CHN 35-103

O

OECD
membership... CHN 20-103

Occupational safety
regulation.. CHN 60-004
violation of provisions .... CHN 60-004

Offshore oil exploration
exchange control exemptions .... CHN 55-031

Offshore petroleum
exploitation
– incentive .... CHN 35-501
– special regulations .... CHN 45-112

Open coastal cities .... CHN 20-205; CHN 45-003
incentives.. CHN 45-105

Orders
enforcement
– dispute resolution............................ CHN 70-403

P

Packaging requirements
exports .... CHN 50-022
imports.. CHN 50-022

Patents .... CHN 65-005
compulsory licenses............................ CHN 65-023
exterior designs................................... CHN 65-011
fees.. CHN 65-024
infringement.. CHN 65-005
licensing agreements........................... CHN 65-022
Patent Law .... CHN 65-005
– exceptions .... CHN 65-005
registration .... CHN 65-021
transfers... CHN 65-022

Payment of tax
foreign enterprises .... CHN 35-103
joint venture.. CHN 35-103

People's Courts
dispute settlement .... CHN 70-002
judicial organ .... CHN 20-005

People's Procuratorates
legal supervision .... CHN 20-005

Penalties
breach of import-export provisions..... CHN 50-024
infringement
– intellectual property rights.............. CHN 65-015

Paragraph

registration .... CHN 35-103
– violation... CHN 30-103

Pensioners
tax exemption .... CHN 35-105

Pension fund contributions
remittance by expatriates.................... CHN 55-032

Personal savings
remittance by expatriates.................... CHN 55-032

Personal security .... CHN 75-522

Plant and equipment
depreciation .... CHN 35-103

Plant varieties
exclusive right .... CHN 65-014
industrial property .... CHN 65-014

Pollution
controls, non-compliance .... CHN 25-211
standards.. CHN 25-204

Power
separation of .... CHN 20-005

Price control
commodities subject to control........... CHN 45-201
criteria for application .... CHN 45-206
exemptions.. CHN 45-203

Private enterprises
legislation regulating activities........... CHN 45-001

Private ownership
land.. CHN 25-002

Procedural law
arbitration .... CHN 70-115

Procedure for arbitration
whether ascertainable .... CHN 70-115
whether variable .... CHN 70-115

Proceedings
arbitration
– confidentiality.................................. CHN 70-143
– language... CHN 70-142
special rules .... CHN 70-204

Products
advertising .... CHN 45-306
information standards .... CHN 45-301
promotion .... CHN 45-306
safety standards .... CHN 45-301
sub-standard quality............................ CHN 30-012

Product liability insurance .... CHN 85-021

Professors
tax exemption .... CHN 35-105

Profit on sales
commerce .... CHN 35-103
industry.. CHN 35-103

Paragraph

Profit sharing
government authority..........................CHN 45-205

Promotion of products
laws..CHN 45-306

Properties
security, creation of ....CHN 75-503
security interests ....CHN 75-301
– identification..................................CHN 75-501
security rights ....CHN 75-401

Property tax ....CHN 35-301

Proprietary technology
provision
– tax incentives for know-how fees ....CHN 35-501

Protection
circuit layouts ....CHN 65-013
copyright..CHN 65-003
trademark ....CHN 65-004

R

Race
labour laws, effect on ....CHN 60-001
required balance in employment ....CHN 60-034

Raising capital
equity.......................... CHN 75-103; CHN 75-104
methods used ....CHN 75-111

Real estate tax ....CHN 35-301

Rebates
franking ....CHN 35-202

Receipts and expenditures
foreign exchange deposit account of
foreign venture ....CHN 55-001

Refund
turnover tax.......................................CHN 35-202

Registration
business
– beyond tax registration area............CHN 35-103
– closing and re-opening....................CHN 35-103
business activities ....CHN 45-001
business in Shenzhen ....CHN 45-001
cancelling...CHN 35-103
change..CHN 35-103
computer software..............................CHN 65-021
copyright..CHN 65-021
examination ....CHN 35-103
extraordinary taxpayers treatment ......CHN 35-103
foreign companies ....CHN 30-103
foreign-controlled export or import
businesses ....CHN 50-005
foreign enterprise representative
office...CHN 30-103

Paragraph

futures trading....................................CHN 45-001
land ....CHN 25-112
– ownership, rights of ....CHN 25-111
– security in ....CHN 25-105
– use, rights of ....CHN 25-111
non-resident companies ....CHN 30-103
opening business.................................CHN 35-103
patents..CHN 65-021
penalties...CHN 35-103
trademarks ....CHN 65-021

Registration fees
non-resident companies ....CHN 30-103
securities..CHN 75-524
subsidiaries ....CHN 30-104

Remedies
breach of contract ....CHN 30-016
commercial law ....CHN 30-016
contract law ....CHN 30-016
damages ....CHN 30-016
deposits ....CHN 30-016

Remittance
advisory fees ....CHN 55-011
amounts payable under guarantee ......CHN 55-011
branch profits ....CHN 55-011
currency ....CHN 55-013
dividends ....CHN 55-011
foreign currency, limit on amount .....CHN 55-012
interest ....CHN 55-011
licence fees ....CHN 55-011
local currency, limit on amount ....CHN 55-012
machine rental ....CHN 55-011
management fees ....CHN 55-011
pension fund contributions of
expatriates ....CHN 55-032
personal savings of expatriates ....CHN 55-032
royalties ....CHN 55-011

Rent
land
– foreign-funded enterprise ....CHN 25-001
– joint venture...................................CHN 25-001

Repatriation of capital ....CHN 55-005
when investment incentives
continuing ....CHN 55-041

Representation
rights
– dispute resolution ....CHN 70-212

Representative offices
foreign ....CHN 30-103

Residents
foreign-sourced income
– tax returns, submission of ....CHN 35-005
non-residents distinguished ....CHN 55-023
rate of tax ....CHN 35-105

Paragraph

Resident companies
taxation .... CHN 35-103

Restraint of trade
foreign trade law .... CHN 45-303

Rights in land
acquisition, restrictions on .... CHN 25-103
assignment as mortgage .... CHN 25-101
dispute re transfer, settlement of .... CHN 25-101
duration, determination of .... CHN 25-101
extent .... CHN 25-114
fees .... CHN 25-124
granting contract
– change .... CHN 25-101; CHN 25-102
– expiration .... CHN 25-101
inheritance .... CHN 25-102
nature .... CHN 25-101
registration .... CHN 25-111
revocation .... CHN 25-101; CHN 25-122
transfer .... CHN 25-101
– approval .... CHN 25-102
– costs .... CHN 25-102
– form of .... CHN 25-102
– venue of proceeding .... CHN 25-102
use as collateral .... CHN 25-101

Royalties
remittance .... CHN 55-011
withholding tax .... CHN 35-104

S

Scientific innovation
awards tax exempt .... CHN 35-501

Securities
acceptable .... CHN 75-523
allotment to non-residents
outside China .... CHN 55-022
borrower
– retention of possession .... CHN 75-514
borrower's interest
– identification .... CHN 75-502
– whether recognised and protected.... CHN 75-513
choice
– tax implication .... CHN 75-525
creation of, formalities .... CHN 75-503
floating, classes of assets .... CHN 75-511
further advances .... CHN 75-512
lender, transferability .... CHN 75-521
personal .... CHN 75-522
property
– identification .... CHN 75-501
realisation by lender .... CHN 75-515
registration charges .... CHN 75-524
with foreign exchange value
– issue of .... CHN 55-022

Security interests .... CHN 75-204

Paragraph

number of security against one
property .... CHN 75-505
priority .... CHN 75-504
property .... CHN 75-301

Security in land
registration .... CHN 25-105

Security rights
forms .... CHN 75-401

Severance pay .... CHN 60-004

Service
process outside jurisdiction .... CHN 70-005

Service trades
net business trade .... CHN 35-103
taxable income .... CHN 35-103

**Settlement of disputes — see Dispute resolution;
Dispute settlement**

Shanghai Real Estate Registry
land use rights, transfer of .... CHN 25-121

Shares
asset as payment .... CHN 30-104
disposal by subsidiaries .... CHN 30-104
foreign companies .... CHN 75-104
foreign investment enterprises .... CHN 30-104
subsidiaries .... CHN 30-104

Share capital
subsidiaries
– non-residents .... CHN 30-104

Shareholding qualification
directors of subsidiaris .... CHN 30-104

Shenzhen
registration of business .... CHN 45-001

Shipbuilding industry
regulation .... CHN 80-011

Shipping
laws regulating .... CHN 80-001
registration .... CHN 80-012

Sick leave .... CHN 60-004

Sino-foreign joint ventures
port and harbour construction
– tax incentives .... CHN 35-501

Sources of loan finance
control .... CHN 75-102
foreign investment enterprises .... CHN 75-101
law regulating .... CHN 75-101

Special accounts
goods traded through
– tax exemption .... CHN 35-501

Special areas
land .... CHN 25-005

Paragraph

Special economic zones .... CHN 20-205;
                           CHN 45-003; CHN 55-021
bonding .... CHN 50-032
incentives .... CHN 45-105
land, right to use .... CHN 25-005
land use
 – regulation .... CHN 25-005
tax incentives .... CHN 35-512

Special jurisdiction
dispute settlement .... CHN 70-001

Special tariff treatment
exports .... CHN 50-014

Stamp tax .... CHN 35-301

Standard purchase price
rate of tax .... CHN 35-301

Standardised contracts
use of .... CHN 30-015

State Administration of Commodity Inspection
power to detain goods .... CHN 50-031

State Administration of Exchange Control
powers .... CHN 55-002

State Administration of Foreign Exchange Control
foreign exchange .... CHN 45-003
foreign investment enterprises .... CHN 45-102
remittance of foreign exchange .... CHN 55-005

State Administration of Industry and Commerce
joint venture activities,
  supervision of .... CHN 45-102
licensing authority .... CHN 45-002
wholly-owned foreign enterprise,
  control of .... CHN 45-102

State Council
executive body .... CHN 20-005
functions .... CHN 20-005
powers .... CHN 20-005

State monopolies .... CHN 20-005

State Plan
passed as legislation .... CHN 45-202

Statutory accounts
foreign-owned enterprises .... CHN 30-104
non-residents companies .... CHN 30-103
subsidiaries .... CHN 30-104

Statutory approvals
non-resident companies .... CHN 30-103

Statutory monopolies
licence .... CHN 45-304

Stock exchange .... CHN 75-001

Paragraph

Storage of goods
laws regulating .... CHN 80-002

Strikes
restriction on right .... CHN 60-002

Structures
joint ventures .... CHN 30-113

Students
tax exemption .... CHN 35-105

Subsidiaries
bearer shares .... CHN 30-104
branches .... CHN 30-104
directors .... CHN 30-104
establishment .... CHN 30-104
liquidation .... CHN 30-104
management .... CHN 30-104
nominal capital .... CHN 30-104
registration fees .... CHN 30-104
shares .... CHN 30-104
share capital .... CHN 30-104
statutory accounts .... CHN 30-104

Supreme People's Court
judicial organ .... CHN 20-005

Survey
land .... CHN 25-104

System of law .... CHN 20-001

T

Tax
collection .... CHN 45-003
deduction from investment profits ..... CHN 35-212
freight of export goods .... CHN 50-013
freight of import goods .... CHN 50-013
house rental .... CHN 35-301
rates .... CHN 35-101
unitary .... CHN 35-302
vehicle licence plates .... CHN 35-301

Tax base
foreign enterprise .... CHN 35-103

Tax credits .... CHN 35-002

Tax disputes
resolution .... CHN 35-003

Tax exemption
artistes .... CHN 35-105
athletes .... CHN 35-105
foreign investment enterprise
 – Beijing .... CHN 35-501
goods traded through special
  accounts .... CHN 35-501
joint ventures .... CHN 35-501

	Paragraph			Paragraph
pensioners	CHN 35-105		individuals	CHN 35-105
professors	CHN 35-105		industry	CHN 35-103
state-designated tourist and holiday			joint venture	CHN 35-103
zones	CHN 35-501		service trade	CHN 35-103
students	CHN 35-105		**Taxation**	
teachers	CHN 35-105		business activities	CHN 35-102
trainees	CHN 35-105		business profits	CHN 35-101
Tax differentials			business undertakings	CHN 35-102
resident and non-resident			capital gains	CHN 35-401– CHN 35-404
companies	CHN 35-103		commercial profits	CHN 35-101
Tax incentives	CHN 20-205		dividends	CHN 35-104
agriculture	CHN 35-501		– non-residents	CHN 75-112
animal husbandry	CHN 35-501		executives	CHN 35-105
assembly projects	CHN 35-501		foreign-invested enterprises	CHN 35-103
compensation trade projects	CHN 35-501		fringe benefits	CHN 35-103
contract processing projects	CHN 35-501		imported goods	CHN 35-104
development zones	CHN 35-512		individuals	CHN 35-005
export enterprises	CHN 35-504		interest	CHN 35-104
foreign contractors			– non-residents	CHN 75-112
– engaging in engineering projects	CHN 35-501		non-joint venture foreign	
– providing labour services	CHN 35-501		enterprises	CHN 35-103
foreign enterprises			non-resident companies	CHN 35-103
– permanent representative offices	CHN 35-501		resident companies	CHN 35-103
forestry	CHN 35-501		rules, interpretation of	CHN 35-003
general processing projects	CHN 35-501		**Taxation Bureau**	
Hainan Island	CHN 35-512		taxes, collection of	CHN 45-003
know-how fees	CHN 35-501		**Teachers**	
interest on loans	CHN 35-501		tax exemption	CHN 35-105
leasing	CHN 35-501		**Technological development zones**	
new industries	CHN 35-501		incentives	CHN 45-105
offshore petroleum, exploitation of	CHN 35-501		**Technological imports**	
old city districts	CHN 35-512		exemptions from duty	CHN 50-012
sino-foreign joint ventures			**Technological innovation**	
– port and harbour construction	CHN 35-501		awards tax exempt	CHN 35-501
special economic zones	CHN 35-512		**Technologically advanced enterprise**	
technologically advanced			incentives, eligibility for	CHN 45-003
enterprises	CHN 35-504		special incentives	CHN 45-111; CHN 45-113
Tax liabilities			tax incentives	CHN 35-504
payment, method of	CHN 35-005		**Technology**	
Tax relief			dispute	CHN 70-143
criteria	CHN 35-503		**Thin capitalisation**	CHN 35-103
period	CHN 35-502		**Third country**	
Tax returns			arbitration	CHN 70-145
time for filing			**Time limits**	
– foreign enterprises	CHN 35-103		litigation	CHN 70-015
– joint ventures	CHN 35-103		**Tourist zones**	
when to submit	CHN 35-005		state-designated	
Tax treaties			– tax reductions	CHN 35-501
international	CHN 35-001		**Trade**	
Taxable income			prohibition	CHN 50-001
commerce	CHN 35-103			
computation	CHN 35-101			

Paragraph

Trade contracts
anti-trust laws .... CHN 45-303
prohibition .... CHN 45-303

Trade marks................................... CHN 65-004
compulsory licenses.......................... CHN 65-023
exclusive right.................................. CHN 65-004
fees... CHN 65-024
infringement..................................... CHN 65-004
licensing agreements......................... CHN 65-022
period of validity .... CHN 65-004
protection.. CHN 65-004
registration...................................... CHN 65-021
Trademark Law............................... CHN 65-004
transfers.. CHN 65-022
well-known trademarks...................... CHN 65-004

Trade names

Trade secrets................................. CHN 65-012
Anti-Unfair Competition Law .... CHN 65-012
commercial secrets............................ CHN 65-012
infringement..................................... CHN 65-012

Trade unions
employer organisations, institutional
links .... CHN 60-021
government, institutional links .... CHN 60-021
liabilities .... CHN 60-015
powers .... CHN 60-014
privileges .... CHN 60-015
representatives .... CHN 60-014
rights .... CHN 60-014
role in foreign investment
enterprises .... CHN 60-014
supervisory role .... CHN 60-014
status .... CHN 60-014

Trainees
tax exemption .... CHN 35-105

Transfer of land
regulations .... CHN 25-004
restrictions .... CHN 25-003

Transfers
copyright.. CHN 65-022
patents... CHN 65-022
trade marks...................................... CHN 65-022

Transportation
inward and outward .... CHN 80-001

Treaties
bilateral
– investment protection .... CHN 20-201
investment protection . CHN 20-201; CHN 20-203

Treaty obligations ....CHN 20-101– CHN 20-103

Turnover tax
refund.. CHN 35-202

Paragraph

U

Underwriters — see **Insurance underwriters**

Undistributed profits .... CHN 35-103

Unemployment insurance .... CHN 85-012

Unfair competition
Anti-Unfair Competition Law .... CHN 65-015
industrial property
– laws .... CHN 65-015

Unified foreign tax........................... CHN 35-301

Unified tax law............................... CHN 35-101

Unitary tax .... CHN 35-302

**United Nations Committee on International
Trade Law**
rules .... CHN 70-104

**United Nations Convention on Contracts for
International Sale of Goods**
ratification .... CHN 20-102

United Nations Modern Law
arbitration .... CHN 70-105

Urban state-owned land
definition .... CHN 25-001

V

Value-added product
export duty exemption....................... CHN 35-501

Value-added tax............................... CHN 35-301

Vehicle and vessel license tax .... CHN 35-301

Vehicle licence plates
tax .... CHN 35-301

Vessels
arrests... CHN 80-005

W

Wages
control .... CHN 60-005

"Well-known trademarks"................. CHN 65-004

Wholly-owned foreign enterprise
approval .... CHN 45-102
assets, expropriation of .... CHN 45-114
control by SAIC................................ CHN 45-102
establishment ....CHN 30-113; CHN 45-102
foreign-related direct
investment ....CHN 30-101; CHN 30-102
legislation applicable .... CHN 45-101
local consultant, retention of .... CHN 45-115

Withholding tax .... CHN 35-103
foreign enterprises .... CHN 35-103

Tra

	Paragraph
royalties	CHN 35-104
licence fees	CHN 35-104

Work hours — see **Hours of work**

Workers' Congress
role	CHN 60-012

Workers' Counsel
functions	CHN 60-011
powers	CHN 60-011

	Paragraph
World Bank	
membership	CHN 20-101

Women
protection in employment	CHN 60-004

INTRODUCTION

China's population is the largest of any country in the world. In an effort to curb population growth, the Chinese government has instituted policies designed to encourage late marriages, contraception and abortion, and the creation of "one-child" families.

The record of Chinese history dates back more than 3,000 years. Until the Republican revolution at the beginning of last century, China was ruled by successive dynasties or periods of centralised rule by different royal families which rose and fell over time. This pattern was characterised by the emperor system, the creation of a state bureaucracy and the emergence of Confucianism which provided a state ethic supported by imperial power.

The Tang Dynasty (618 A.D. to 907 A.D.) and the Song Dynasty (960 to 1279) are remembered as the most illustrious periods of traditional Chinese history. During their rule, the Tang established an empire which became one of the most powerful and developed in the world. The Tang reunited the empire and strengthened China's trade links to central Asia along the Silk Road. Both Confucianism and Buddhism flourished during this period. Significant advances were made in the cultural arts — painting, music, theatre — and in the Sciences.

At the beginning of the 19th century, however, a threat began to appear from the West. The main commodities sought by the West were tea and silk for which they were required to pay in silver. By the early 1800s, the imbalance in trade had become severe. The British found a solution to the problem with the sale of opium to China. Within a very short time, the flow of silver into China's coffers declined dramatically and sales of opium soared. The ruling Qing court attempted to ban the trade with little success. This led to the Opium Wars (1839 to 1842).

China's humiliating defeat in these struggles led ultimately to the forced cession of Hong Kong to the British and the opening up of four ports to traders, missionaries and other foreigners who enjoyed rights extraterritorially and other privileges.

Japan declared war on China in 1894. Upon China's defeat, Korea, Taiwan and the Pescadores Islands were ceded to the Japanese. The continuing encroachment of Western powers fanned both anti-foreign and anti-Qing sentiment among the Chinese. This encouraged revolutionary movements and in 1911, one movement led by Dr. Sun Yatsen ultimately succeeded in overthrowing Qing Rule. Influenced by Western ideas, Sun's success led to the creation of a republic.

The Republican Era

The first government of the Republic of China was proclaimed on 1 January 1912. In 1921, the Communist Party was formed in Shanghai. Beginning in the 1930s, the Japanese began to move openly against China, taking Manchuria in 1931. At the end of World War II in 1945, the Japanese surrendered to the Nationalist forces. Civil war ensued between the Nationalists and Communists and by 1949, the Communists, under the leadership of Mao Zedong, emerged victorious, declaring the People's Republic of China on 1 October of that year. The Nationalists, with their leader Chiang Kaishek, withdrew and fled to Taiwan.

1949 to 1976

A large-scale land reform was undertaken during which plots owned by landlords and other "capitalists" were confiscated for redistribution to the peasants. Later, in 1953, the nation's first Five-Year Plan was unveiled which called for the collectivisation of agriculture and a thorough reconstruction of the Chinese economy along Soviet lines.

China's second Five-Year Plan was announced in 1958. The plan called for radical changes in Chinese Society and in the economy with the aim to speed up the pace of socialist transformation. Under the "Great Leap Forward" program, farms and factories were ordered to comply with unrealistic production targets. These policies, coupled with several seasons of bad weather, brought about a significant drop in grain production and caused widespread food shortages.

In 1966, Mao launched the Great Proletarian Cultural Revolution. Designed to move China back onto the path of true communism and to enable Mao to regain complete control over the Party, the Cultural Revolution evolved into a mass movement on an unprecedented scale.

Workers and manual labor were glorified and intellectuals persecuted. Schools were closed, factories were shut and the government became paralysed as the entire country degenerated into chaos. In 1971, with the worst excesses of the Cultural Revolution ended, China turned her attention to re-establishing relations with the outside world which had all been cut off in the preceding eight years of strife. After Mao passed away in 1976, Deng Xiaoping was reinstated and the post-Mao era had begun.

1976 to 2000

China announced a new program of political and economic reform aimed at the modernisation of industry, agriculture, the military and science and technology which would propel China into the ranks of the developed countries by the year 2000. Foreign investment was encouraged but by the late 1980s, China's reform policies were threatened by economic stagnations and high inflation. Conservative Party economist led by Premier Li Peng called for a slow-down in the reforms and a return to central planning in some economic sectors.

At the same time, students and intellectuals began to press the Chinese government for political reforms. After several months of mass demonstrations in Tiananmen Square in central Beijing, martial law was declared in May 1989 and the Communist Party Chairman replaced. On 4 June 1989, thousands of the People's Liberation Army troops were sent into central Beijing to put an end to pro-democracy demonstrations, resulting in hundreds of deaths and thousands of arrests.

Despite the events of 4 June, China pledged to continue the "open door" policy on reforms while strictly adhering to the socialist path.

2000 onwards

In the new millennium, China's macroeconomic conditions will remain stable and remain a bright spot in the developing world for both FDI and portfolio investors. China's aggressive privatisation plan, including but not limited to the planned overseas IPOs of an increasing number of large companies, will open a wider door for foreign investors to participate in China's economic growth.

China's accession to the WTO in end 2001 will provide a host of new business opportunities for foreign companies in the vast China market. However, such economic benefits will not come easily and quickly. Since China's WTO commitments are unprecedented and will involve sweeping changes across all sectors of Chinese economy, its WTO implementations will be a long and difficult process. Before foreign companies can enjoy the full benefits of China's WTO accession, China needs to develop and enhance its legal and regulatory systems to be in full compliance with WTO requirements.

An Overview (The System of Law and Government)

System of law .... CHN ¶20-001

Origin of legal system .... CHN ¶20-002

Sources of law .... CHN ¶20-003

Law-making bodies .... CHN ¶20-004

Organisation of government .... CHN ¶20-005

Language of the law .... CHN ¶20-011

Structure of legal profession .... CHN ¶20-012

Determination of applicable law .... CHN ¶20-013

Choice of method and forum .... CHN ¶20-014

Treaty obligations .... CHN ¶20-101

Guarantees and incentives .... CHN ¶20-201

CHN ¶20-001 SYSTEM OF LAW

China has a system of socialist law. The legal structures and organs are based upon the civil law model. Law and policy are both socialist in nature with Chinese characteristics.

CHN ¶20-002 ORIGIN OF LEGAL SYSTEM

The present Chinese system of law is not derived from any one particular system or country, but is the result of the combined influence of several systems of law and political thought. The main influences shaping the present Chinese legal system are:

- Marxist, Leninist legal writings and Mao Ze Dong thought;

- the legal experience based upon the revolution carried out since 1949 under the democratic leadership of the Communist Party of China (CPC);

- the Chinese legal tradition;

- Soviet legal theory and the Soviet legal system; and

- some areas of Western legislation and legal system — particularly in areas of foreign-related legislation and legislation specifically aimed at implementing the open-door policy.

CHN ¶20-003   SOURCES OF LAW

Law is principally found in statutory sources. The work of codification is progressing at a great rate. As with the governmental structure, Chinese legislative authority and legislation is organised on a unitary and hierarchical basis, with the Constitution being the fundamental law with which all other laws must comply. In areas where there is no legislation or the relevant laws are incomplete, basic principles will be established through policy directives issued by the CPC and through normative documents issued by various organs of government and by the CPC. International treaties acceded to by the Standing Committee of the National People's Congress (NPC) and the State Council take effect without the need for implementing legislation and will override contrary provisions of domestic legislation where the domestic legislation so provides.

CHN ¶20-004   LAW-MAKING BODIES

Legislative authority rests in the People's Congresses which are organised on a unitary and hierarchical basis.

The supreme legislative authority is the National People's Congress which also has final authority to interpret legislation. Much power has been delegated to the Standing Committee of the NPC, whose powers are set out in Art. 67 of the Constitution. At the central level, the chief executive organ of government is the State Council, the head of which is the Premier. The local organs of state power with legislative authority are the local people's congresses at different levels. The levels are arranged on a geographic basis, the next level being congresses of the provinces, municipalities directly under the central government and autonomous regions and under that congresses at the levels of city, county, municipal district, township, nationality township and towns. The legislative authority of the people's congresses and their Standing Committees is set out in the Constitution and comprises the making of regulations and administrative rules in their administrative areas which do not contravene the Constitution, statutes and administrative rules passed at higher levels.

CHN ¶20-005   ORGANISATION OF GOVERNMENT

The People's Republic of China is a socialist state under the People's Democratic Dictatorship led by the working class and based on the alliance of workers and peasants (Constitution, Art. 1). All power in the People's Republic of China belongs to the people, who exercise power through the National People's Congress (NPC) and the local people's congresses at different levels (Constitution, Art. 2).

Article 3 of the Constitution provides that all administrative, judicial and procuratorial organs of the state are created by the people's congresses to which they are responsible and under whose supervision they operate.

Each of these organs is also responsible to its own higher level organ.

There is no separation of power between the people's congress, government, judicial and procuratory organs at each level, as the people's congresses create and supervise the operation of these organs. Technically, there is a division of function between the legislative, judicial, executive and administrative organs of state.

The structure of the state is set out in Chapter 3 of the Constitution.

National People's Congress (NPC)

The National People's Congress of the People's Republic of China is the highest organ of state power. Its permanent body is the Standing Committee of the NPC (Standing Committee) (Constitution, Art. 57).

The NPC and its Standing Committee exercise the legislative power of the state (Constitution, Art. 58).

Article 62 of the Constitution sets out the functions and powers exercised by the NPC which include the following:

- to amend and supervise the enforcement of the Constitution;
- to enact and amend basic statutes;
- to elect the President and Vice President of the People's Republic of China;
- to decide on the choice of Premier of the State Council in the prescribed manner;
- to elect the Chairman of the Central Military Commission;
- to elect the President of the Supreme People's Court;
- to elect the Procurator General of the Supreme People's Procuratorate; and
- to examine and approve the plan for the national economic and social development.

The Standing Committee is a permanent body of the NPC and exercises the functions and powers set out in Art. 67 of the Constitution.

The State Council

The State Council, that is, the Central People's Government of the People's Republic of China, is the executive body of the highest organ of state power; it is the highest organ of state administration (Constitution, Art. 85). Its functions and powers are set out at Art. 89 and include the following:

- to adopt administrative measures, enact administrative rules and regulations and issue decisions and orders in accordance with the Constitution and the statutes;
- to submit proposals to the NPC or its Standing Committee;
- to lay down the tasks and responsibilities of the Ministries and Commissions of the State Council, to exercise unified leadership over the work of the Ministries and Commissions and to direct all other administrative work of a national character that does not fall within the jurisdiction of the Ministries and Commissions;
- to exercise unified leadership over the work of local organs of state administration at different levels throughout the country and to lay down the detailed division of functions and powers between the central government and the organs of state administration of the provinces, autonomous regions and municipalities directly under the central government;
- to draw up and implement the plan for national, economic and social development and the state budget;
- to direct and administer economic affairs and urban and rural development;

[Next page is 13,331]

- to direct and administer civil affairs, public security, judicial administration, supervision and other related matters;
- to conduct foreign affairs and conclude treaties and agreements with foreign states.

The People's Courts

The People's Courts in the People's Republic of China are the judicial organs of the state. The Constitution at Art. 126 provides that the People's Courts shall, in accordance with the law, exercise judicial power independently and are not subject to interference by administrative organs, public organisations or individuals.

The Supreme People's Court is the highest judicial organ which supervises the administration of justice by the local People's Courts at different levels and by the Special People's Courts; People's Courts at higher levels supervise the administration of justice by those at lower levels (Constitution, Art. 127).

The Supreme People's Court is responsible to the NPC and its Standing Committee. Local People's Courts at different levels are responsible to the organs of state power which created them (Constitution, Art. 128).

People's Procuratorates

The Constitution also establishes the system of People's Procuratorates. The procuratorates are the state organs for legal supervision. Their organisational structure is the same as the system of People's Courts.

The detailed structure and functions and powers of the People's Courts and the People's Procuratorates are set out in the *Organic Law of the People's Courts of the People's Republic of China* and the *Organic Law of the People's Procuratorates of the People's Republic of China* respectively. The duties, rights, obligations, qualifications and other employment aspects of judges and procurators are set out in the *Judges Law* and the *Procurators Law*, both adopted on 28 February 1995 and amended on 30 June 2001.

CHN ¶20-011   LANGUAGE OF THE LAW

Chinese is the language of both the law and the lawyers. Texts of legislation passed by the Standing Committee of the NPC are contained in the Bulletin of the Standing Committee of the NPC, in Chinese, and texts of the regulations passed by the State Council can be found in the Bulletin of the State Council of the PRC, also in Chinese. Authoritative statements concerning the interpretation and application of laws made by the Supreme People's Court are contained in the Bulletin of the Supreme People's Court of the PRC.

There are also a large number of journals and other publications, which provide commentary and discussion upon various issues of Chinese law which are also in Chinese.

The Chinese government has produced books of Chinese laws translated into English on an *ad hoc* basis. Peking University has produced a legal database, in both English and Chinese, of national and selected regional legislation, regulations and authoritative interpretations of those laws and regulations. CCH produces a loose-leaf service, *China Laws for Foreign Business — Business Regulation and China Laws for Foreign Business — Taxation and Customs* which contains English translations of legislation in areas relevant to business.

CHN ¶20-012   STRUCTURE OF LEGAL PROFESSION

The organisation, division and function of lawyers in China is set out in the *Lawyers Tentative Regulations*, which were promulgated in 1980. Those regulations provide that lawyers are legal workers of the state. The *PRC Lawyers Law* which comes into effect on 1 January 1997 repeals the earlier *PRC Lawyers Tentative Regulations* (1980) and sets out the basic requirements for establishing a domestic law firm in the PRC.

Since the re-establishment of law schools and legal education around 1978, the Chinese government has emphasised legal education in an effort to improve the standards of its lawyers, judges and other legal personnel. As a result, there are an increasing number of lawyers and judges with formal legal qualifications. In 1986, a National Bar Exam for lawyers was introduced. From 1992, this examination is held annually and must be passed by those not previously admitted to practise as a lawyer. In 2001, in order to ultimately unify the qualification systems for lawyers, judges and procurators, a National Judicial Exam was introduced to replace the National Bar Exam, and it is compulsory for all those wishing to embark on these legal professions to pass this exam.

The *PRC Lawyers Law* state that in order to practise as a lawyer in the PRC, a person must have obtained a lawyers' practising licence. To obtain a license, an individual must pass the national judicial examination before being eligible. Applications for a practising licence are to be made to the Ministry of Justice at the State Council level. Lawyers who have obtained their practising licence are entitled to work and practise in any province or city in China. However, lawyers are prohibited from practising in two or more law firms concurrently. Further, employees in government institutions are prohibited from practising law.

Foreign lawyers

Foreign lawyers are not permitted to practise law in China and do not have the right to appear before any Chinese court. Some limited exceptions exist, for example the rules of the China International Economic and Trade Arbitration Commission (CIETAC) and the China International Maritime Arbitration Commission (CIMAC) permit parties to arbitration and conciliation before those bodies to be represented by foreign lawyers.

Operation of foreign law firms

With effect from 1 February 2002, the operation of foreign law firms is governed by the *Regulations for Administration of Foreign Law Firms' Representative Offices in China*. Foreign law firms may set up offices in China if they are approved by the Ministry of Justice and must register with the State General Administration for Industry and Commerce. As of August 2000, there were approximately 103 foreign law firms. Approved foreign firms are permitted to provide legal advice to clients on the law of their own country, international conventions, trade law, world trade and customs law. They are not permitted to handle Chinese legal affairs or hire Chinese lawyers. A foreign firm must have a sponsoring Chinese office for use of lawyers to represent foreign clients in Chinese courts. They may also instruct a Chinese law firm to handle legal affairs in China on behalf of their clients from overseas.

CHN ¶20-013   DETERMINATION OF APPLICABLE LAW

In civil matters, Chapter 8 of the *General Principles of the Civil Law* provides for application of law to foreign civil relationships. That chapter provides conflicts of law rules for activities such as contract, tort, marriage, ownership of immovable property and succession. In relation to a foreign contract, Art. 145 provides that the parties may choose the law applicable to the settlement of disputes arising from a contract unless the law otherwise provides.

Where the parties to a foreign contract have not made a choice of applicable law, the law of the country which has the closest connection with the contract applies. The *PRC Contract Law* (Contract Law), which came into effect on 1 October 1999, requires three types of contract to have Chinese law as the applicable law; those for cooperative exploration and development of natural resources which are performed within the territory of the People's Republic of China, those for the establishment of an equity joint venture and those for the establishment of a contractual joint venture.

Except for these three situations, the principle of freedom to choose the applicable law is affirmed.

CHN ¶20-014   CHOICE OF METHOD AND FORUM

The *Contract Law* applies to civil contracts, excluding those involving personal relations such as marriage, adoption and guardianship, between civil parties of equal status. It allows the parties to choose either arbitration or litigation. However, if the contract contains a clause agreeing to submit any dispute arising out of the contract to arbitration, then the Chinese courts will be incompetent to hear and resolve such a dispute.

In foreign-related arbitration, the parties are free to choose arbitration in the country of either of the parties or in a third country. The *Contract Law* permits the parties to make an express agreement on the choice of law, which may be either Chinese, Hong Kong, Macao or foreign law. The People's Court will apply such a law to any dispute brought before it. Parties to a contract governed by the *Contract Law* are permitted to choose the law to be applied to a dispute any time before the hearing of the case or by the court after it has accepted such a case. If the parties have failed to choose the applicable law, the People's Court shall apply the law of the country with the "closest connection" to the dispute. In matters before the People's Court, Chinese procedural rules and conflict of laws principles will be applied. The *General Principles of the Civil Law* makes provision for the appropriate jurisdiction of the People's Courts. If the *General Principles of the Civil Law* provides that a particular People's Court had jurisdiction to hear a matter, a question would exist as to whether the Supreme People's Court would agree to enforce a judgement made in that matter by a foreign court (see "Dispute Resolution" at CHN ¶70-001).

TREATY OBLIGATIONS

Membership of international
  organisations .... CHN ¶20-101
International agreements   CHN ¶20-102

OECD declaration ...... CHN ¶20-103

CHN ¶20-101 MEMBERSHIP OF INTERNATIONAL ORGANISATIONS

The Chinese government is a member of the World Bank, the Asian Development Bank, the International Monetary Fund, and as of 11 December 2001, the World Trade Organisation.

CHN ¶20-102 INTERNATIONAL AGREEMENTS

China has ratified and put into effect a number of international agreements including the New York Convention on the Recognition and Enforcement of Foreign Arbitral Awards, the UN Convention on Contracts for the International Sale of Goods (Vienna Convention), and the MIGA Convention. China has entered into a large number of international maritime conventions.

CHN ¶20-103 OECD DECLARATION

China is not a member of the OECD.

GUARANTEES AND INCENTIVES

Investment protection
  treaties .... CHN ¶20-201
Joint trade agreements .. CHN ¶20-202
Multilateral investment
  protection treaties .... CHN ¶20-203

Government guarantees for
  foreign investors ..... CHN ¶20-204
Protection for foreign
  investors .... CHN ¶20-205

CHN ¶20-201 INVESTMENT PROTECTION TREATIES

China has entered into bilateral agreements with over 20 countries for the encouragement and reciprocal protection of interest. These countries include: Australia, Austria, Belgium-Luxembourg Economic Union, Denmark, Finland, France, Italy, Japan, Kuwait, Mongolia, The Netherlands, Norway, Romania, Singapore, Sri Lanka, Sweden, Switzerland, Thailand, The Federal Republic of Germany and the United Kingdom.

CHN ¶20-202   JOINT TRADE AGREEMENTS

China has trade agreements with the United States and other trading nations including Australia, South Korea and Kazakhstan. Each trade agreement differs so it is necessary to refer to the trade agreement itself for actual details.

CHN ¶20-203   MULTILATERAL INVESTMENT PROTECTION TREATIES

China ratified the convention establishing the MIGA on 30 April 1988. This offers nationals a guarantee against non-commercial risks affecting foreign investment.

CHN ¶20-204   GOVERNMENT GUARANTEES FOR FOREIGN INVESTORS

Government guarantees against expropriation of assets, repatriation of foreign currency and the proceeds of compulsory acquisition of assets of a foreign interest in China are assured under the terms of bilateral investment protection agreements.

CHN ¶20-205   PROTECTION FOR FOREIGN INVESTORS

Provisions protecting against expropriation, and providing for compensation for compulsory acquisition are contained in bilateral investment protection agreements.

China has put in place a comprehensive set of legislation aimed at encouraging foreign investment in the country. This legislation covers such areas as the establishment of joint ventures, taxation incentives and other provisions intended to facilitate the repatriation of profits such as those contained in the *Provisions of the State Council of the People's Republic of China for the Encouragement of Foreign Investment*, of 11 October 1986.

China has also established special economic zones, economic technological developments zones, open coastal cities and has designated the eastern coastal region and more recently, the western inland region, as areas where special legislative and economic benefits will be given to encourage foreign investment in these specific targeted areas.

Land Tenure — The Site of the Investment

Land tenure ....CHN ¶25-001

Rights in land ....CHN ¶25-101

LAND TENURE

Forms of land tenure .... CHN ¶25-001   Local regulations .... CHN ¶25-004

Private ownership of land CHN ¶25-002
                               Special areas .... CHN ¶25-005

Restrictions on transfer of
   land .... CHN ¶25-003   Customary land rights .. CHN ¶25-011

CHN ¶25-001   FORMS OF LAND TENURE

Definition of ownership

The Constitution provides that land is owned either by the state (the whole people) or by collectives (see Art 9 and 10).

Article 10 further provides that the state may in the public interest take over land for its use in accordance with the law. No organisation or individual may appropriate, buy, sell or lease land, or unlawfully transfer land in other ways.

Article 71 of the *General Principles of the Civil Law* defines "ownership" as:

"The owner's right in accordance with law to possess, use, benefit from and dispose of his own property."

The right of individuals to own personal property and the type of property which that includes are set out in Art 75 of the *General Principles of the Civil Law*.

Articles 73 and 74 add to the provisions made in Art 9 and 10 of the Constitution which distinguish between ownership by the whole people (by the state) and ownership by collectives.

It is possible to own buildings and other structures on the land, but not the land they stand on. Land use rights can be acquired.

Leaseholds

After the amendment of Art 10 to the Constitution in 1988, several pieces of legislation were passed to implement the granting and assignment of leaseholds in the land. These include amendments to the following:

- The *Law of Land Administration*. The amended *Land Administration Law* takes effect from 1 January 1999. The amended *Land Law* establishes a new system for controlling land use and protecting cultivated land to ensure the balanced development of total cultivated land, reforms the compensation method for requisition of land, enhances the standard of compensation for land requisition, and elaborates on the implementation and default provisions;

- The *Rules for the Implementation of the Law of Land Administration*. The amended Rules also take effect from 1 January 1999, and contain detailed rules for the implementation of the *Land Administration Law*;

- The PRC *Granting and Assigning Leaseholds in State-owned Urban Land Tentative Regulations*, 24 May 1990;

- The *Land Administration Regulations of Hainan Special Economic Zone*, 18 July 1994; and

- The *Several Provisions on the Administration of Real Estate in the Shenzhen Special Economic Zone Tentative Provisions*, 9 November 1993.

Despite being called leaseholds, it cannot be assumed that a proprietary interest is created in the land. In fact, the PRC *Granting and Assigning Leaseholds in State-owned Urban Land Tentative Regulations*, whilst at the same time creating "leasehold interests", indicates the contractual nature of these interests. For example, Art 8 provides:

"(a) The term 'grant of a leasehold' refers to the act by which the State, in its capacity as landowner, grants the right to use land for a fixed term in years to a user of land and the user of land pays to the State a sum for the grant of the leasehold.

(b) When a leasehold is granted, the parties shall enter into a grant contract."

And further at Art 2:

"(a) In accordance with the principles of separating the ownership of land and the right to use land, the State shall implement a system for the granting and assignment of leaseholds in urban state-owned land. Underground resources, concealed objects and public utilities shall not be included [in leaseholds].

(b) The term 'urban state-owned land', as used in the preceding paragraph, refers to land owned by the whole people within municipalities, county seats, officially established towns and industrial and mining areas. . ."

Acquiring land use rights

A foreign investment enterprise which has acquired land use rights will be permitted to use the land only in the manner approved. A 1988 amendment to the Constitution permits individuals and entities to acquire and transfer land use rights for value. In order to facilitate acquisition of such rights by foreign investment enterprises, specific regulations have been made in Shanghai, Shenzhen and Hainan which complement this amendment, for example the *Measures of the Shanghai Municipality on Compensated*

Transfer of Land Use Rights. These Measures are very liberal and, though limited in geographical scope and to which parties they are applicable, represent the attempt to encourage foreign investment by creating a system of greater flexibility and certainty than those existing previously.

From 1991, foreign joint ventures and solely foreign-funded enterprises must pay rent on land which they occupy.

Compensatory transfer of the right to use land falls into two broad categories discussed below.

Use by approval

Where a project is approved by the state which requires land for its implementation, the approval carries with it an agreement to allow use of land necessary to implement the project. An amount of money is required to be paid to the state for use of this land.

Approval can only be granted by the People's Government above county level. This type of approval applies not only to foreign investment enterprises, but also to Chinese entities and individuals. The maximum period for this type of land use right is 70 years. For foreign investment enterprises, the term of the land use right corresponds with the duration of the project as well as the type of use, which is restricted to that required to implement the approved project.

Consignment of the right to use land

This form of transfer is in its trial stage and exists only in Tianjin, Shanghai, Shenzhen and Guangdong. The right to use the land is obtained through competitive bidding or auction and the period in which the land use right is granted is negotiated and contained in the contract for the transfer of the right to use this land. However, the maximum period is fixed by regulation. Only city governments specifically empowered by the State Council have the capacity to enter into this type of contract. The price for obtaining the right to use land is payable as a lump sum at the conclusion of the contract. This type of consignment contract usually relates to specific parcels of land in special economic development zones or technological development zones. The consignor can use the land for any lawful purpose, with the restriction that the land must be developed before any dealing is permitted with the land use right. Lease, sale or transfer of the right to use land also carries with it the right to use the structure or structures on the land. After development of the land, the entity with the right to use the land can deal with the right in any lawful way, which includes mortgage of the right, transfer and gift. The right is also inheritable. Any dealing with structures on the land and the right to use land must be registered with the responsible government agency and the required fee paid.

The rights created in the land are contractual and no proprietary right over the land itself exists. After dealing with the land, the entity or individual acquiring the contractual right will step into the shoes of the original holder and take on the same contractual responsibilities including the duty to return the land to the government at the expiry of the term of the right, which the original contracting party took.

CHN ¶25-002   PRIVATE OWNERSHIP OF LAND

Both forms of land use rights permit the private ownership of the contractual rights granted. No proprietary interest is created, nor can it be acquired. Natural resources, minerals and other buried or hidden objects under the land are not within the scope of the transfer of land use rights.

CHN ¶25-003   RESTRICTIONS ON TRANSFER OF LAND

All land in China is owned either by the state (the whole people) or, mainly in rural areas, collectively. Rights to use the land are personal. Transfer, lease and inheritance of land use rights and the right to profit from the deal with appurtenances to the land are restricted in accordance with the provisions of the *Law of Land Administration*. However, land itself and any interest in land is not transferable.

CHN ¶25-004   LOCAL REGULATIONS

The system of compensatory transfer of land use rights exists only in the cities to which this power has been delegated by the State Council (see CHN ¶25-001 above) and is governed by special measures promulgated by the municipal government of those cities. In rural areas, procedures exist whereby the right to use collectively-owned land may be allocated to members of the collective or households in the collective for their use.

CHN ¶25-005   SPECIAL AREAS

In the special economic zones and designated municipalities, foreign investors may acquire the right to use land in accordance with the procedures described at CHN ¶25-001 above and the terms of the right to use the land are contained in locally promulgated measures described at CHN ¶25-004 above.

There are numerous local regulations relating to land use in the special economic zones and economic technological development zones; for example Shanghai has promulgated the *Measures of the Shanghai Municipality on the Transfer of Real Estate*, the *Shanghai Provisional Regulations on RMB Loans Secured by Mortgages* and the *Measures of the Shanghai Municipality for the Administration of the Use of Land in Foreign Invested Enterprises*. Reference should also be made to national legislation such as the *Law of the People's Republic of China on Land Management* and to other laws and regulations for the encouragement of foreign investment which contain provisions granting preferential treatment to eligible foreign investors in many areas, including areas such as the payment of all forms of tax, land use fees, access to infrastructure and communication facilities.

Prior to China's accession to the WTO, real estate was categorised in the then-current version of the *Foreign Investment Industrial Guidance Catalogue* (Catalogue) as a "restricted" industry and foreign investors were prohibited from establishing wholly foreign-owned enterprises (WFOEs) in the real estate sector. As a result of revisions to

CHN ¶25-002   © 2003 CCH Asia Pte Limited the Catalogue in 2002 that reflects China's commitments set forth in its Protocol of Accession to the WTO (Protocol), development and construction projects of ordinary residential housing are now all under the "encouraged" category and foreign investors may freely participate in such projects in the form of WFOEs or joint ventures (JVs). However, the new Catalogue does not provide any guidance on the distinction between ordinary residential housing projects and other residential housing projects.

China did not make any commitment in the Protocol in respect of tract land development. Under the new Catalogue, tract land development is categorised as "restricted" and foreign investors are only permitted to participate in such projects in the form of equity or cooperative JVs. Although there is no PRC law or regulation that explicitly limits foreign equity participation in tract land development JVs, in practice, officials of the Ministry of Commerce (MOFCOM, formerly the Ministry of Foreign Trade and Economic Cooperation, or MOFTEC) have stated that they generally discourage foreign investors from holding equity interests of more than 75% in tract land development JVs. In respect of companies engaging in real estate services on a fee or contract basis (such as real estate brokerage services), the Protocol provides that foreign companies are permitted to participate in this sector only in the form of equity JVs, with foreign companies allowed to hold majority shareholding percentage in such enterprises. Nevertheless, there is no such restriction under the new Catalogue and it is well known in the industry that there are a number of real estate agencies or brokers already operating in China in the form of WFOEs.

On 13 June 2003, China's central bank issued the *Circular on Further Tightening of Real Estate Loan Management* (the "Circular"). The Circular restricts loans to developers, construction firms and home buyers with a view to discourage speculation activities. The Circular ordered commercial banks to be strict when issuing loans under the category of "real estate development credit". The real estate developer's own capital should not be less than 30% of the total amount of project investment when it applies for loan from the banks. The Circular also requires construction companies to stop developers using their working-capital bank loans, a widespread practice which the bank believed had increased construction firms' financial burden.

CHN ¶25-011   CUSTOMARY LAND RIGHTS

The sole basis for ownership of land or ownership of rights or interests association with land are found in the Constitution. Article 10 of the Constitution provides that:

> "Land in the cities is owned by the State. Land in the rural and suburban areas is owned by collectives except for those portions which belong to the State in accordance with the law. House sites and privately funded plots of crop land and hilly land are also owned by collectives. The State may in the public interest take over land for its use in accordance with the law. No organisation or individual may appropriate, buy, sell or lease land, or unlawfully transfer land in other ways."

All organisations and individuals who use land must make rational use of the land.

Amendments were made to the Constitution in 1988, including an amendment to Art 10 of the Constitution which added a sentence to the fourth paragraph of Art 10 to include:

"The right to the use of land may be transferred according to law".

This amendment is the constitutional basis for permitting the creation and transfer of land use rights (see CHN ¶25-001).

No other rights to the ownership of land, be they customary or unwritten, are acknowledged.

RIGHTS IN LAND

Nature of rights in land .. CHN ¶25-101

Transfer of rights in land   CHN ¶25-102

Restrictions on acquisition of rights in land .... CHN ¶25-103

Land surveying .... CHN ¶25-104

Registration of security in land .... CHN ¶25-105

Registration of rights of land use and ownership .... CHN ¶25-111

System of land registration .... CHN ¶25-112

Specific rights .... CHN ¶25-113

Extent of rights in land .. CHN ¶25-114

Agreements restricting land use .... CHN ¶25-115

Ascertainment of existing restrictions .... CHN ¶25-121

Powers of acquisition of land .... CHN ¶25-122

Compensation for acquired land .... CHN ¶25-123

Taxes and rates .... CHN ¶25-124

Seizure of land in execution of judgment .... CHN ¶25-125

Environmental restrictions .... CHN ¶25-201

Regulation of environmental controls .... CHN ¶25-202

Governmental requirements for environmental assessment .... CHN ¶25-203

Pollution standards ..... CHN ¶25-204

Incentives for non-polluting plants .... CHN ¶25-205

Nature of controls .... CHN ¶25-211

Detriment to the environment .... CHN ¶25-212

CHN ¶25-101   NATURE OF RIGHTS IN LAND

The greatest interest that a foreign entity or individual may acquire in land (as opposed to buildings or other fixtures on land) is a contractual interest.

The contractual interest may be obtained either as a consequence of approval or by the system of compensated transfer (see CHN ¶25-001).

CHN ¶25-101

The contractual rights granted by the first of these methods are very limited. They are restricted to use of the land in the manner, for the purpose and for the period of the project for which the land use rights are approved.

It is not possible to deal with these rights except as permitted in the approved project, or as otherwise approved by the government body responsible for approval of the original project.

More rights attached to a contractual interest are obtained by means of compensated transfer of land use rights (see CHN ¶25-001). However, it is only possible to obtain these rights with respect to certain specially designated and offered land within specially authorised cities, special economic zones and provinces (see CHN ¶25-001).

The creation of compensated transfer of land use rights, which creates the ability to possess and deal with land use rights, are the first rules of this type. They go some way towards separating, in theory, the land from the conglomerate of rights and duties which form part of the approval and implementation of a foreign investment enterprise.

General regulations, forming part of the legislative scheme for the encouragement of foreign investment, also contain provisions giving foreign investment enterprises which fulfil set criteria, priority in relation to access to and preferential treatment as to cost of utilities and other fees which are associated with land use.

Land use rights

Land use rights acquired along with the approval of a specific project can only be used for the approved purpose for the term of the project. Thereafter, the land use rights revert to the state.

Land use rights acquired by means of compensated transfer will be governed in accordance with the measures promulgated by each of the cities authorised by the State Council to conduct such a transfer. The *Measures of the Shanghai Municipality on the Grant of Land Use Rights*, promulgated in 1996 and amended in 2001, will be used to discuss the nature and content of land use rights in the narrow context of compensated transfer of land use rights. They provide:

- No absolute ownership is available. The ownership of land remains with the People's Republic of China.

- Land use rights are contractual in nature and the contract does not create any proprietary rights in the land.

- The framework for the maximum term of years for granting land use rights will be determined within the following framework:

— land use for residence	70 years
— land use for industry	50 years
— land use for education, science, technology, culture, health and sports	50 years

— land use for commerce, tourism and entertainment	40 years
— land use for comprehensive or other purposes	50 years

- An application for extending the period may be made one year before its expiry. Unless social public interests require withdrawal of the land use rights, the application will be approved and then a new granting fee shall be determined and a new contract shall be entered into (Art 28).

- Land use rights may be assigned in accordance with the Measures (Art 8). Land use rights owned by natural persons can be inherited (Art 10).

- A grantee wishing to change the nature of the land use and planning requirement specified under the granting contract must obtain the approval of the Land Bureau and a granting fee must be paid (Art 26).

- Land use rights can be granted by way of agreement, tender, auction or another way approved by the municipal government (Art 14).

Information concerning location, planned use of land, the term for completion of the construction project, minimum investment amount required for the construction project, planning requirements, environmental protection, present condition of the land, a copy of the Standing Granting Contract and other matters shall be provided by the Land Bureau to any prospective land use rights grantee (Art 16).

At the expiration of the granting contract, the land use rights for the land shall revert to the Land Bureau without compensation, if no application for extension is made and approved. The buildings and structures, etc shall be dealt with in accordance with the granting contract (Art 29).

If the term of the granting contract has not expired, the land use rights shall not be taken back until the termination of the period of grant. The Land Bureau has the right to revoke land use rights following legal procedures, on the basis of social and public interest (Art 30).

Urban real estate management law

China passed its first urban real estate management law in July 1994, laying down tough regulations for real estate transactions to curb speculation. The law became effective from 1 January 1995 and provides that developers who fail to start construction within a year of the launch date, as agreed to in their leasing contract, would face a fine of as much as 20% of the leasing fee. The amount of land that city governments can sell or lease will be specified in annual official plans.

If after two years no development has taken place, land use rights can be withdrawn. The law also provides that land cannot be leased again until a developer has committed 25% of the capital he pledged to invest in his leasing contract.

Where an economic dispute arises from the compensated transfer of land use rights, parties can submit the dispute to a Chinese arbitration institution or other arbitration institutions for settlement in accordance with an arbitration clause in the contract or a written arbitration agreement reached after the arising of the dispute.

If there is no arbitration clause in the contract, or the parties cannot reach an arbitration agreement independently, either party is entitled to file a suit in the People's Court for settlement of disputes.

The State Council promulgated the *Regulations on the Development and Management of Urban Real Estates* on 21 July 1998. The Regulations stipulate the conditions and procedures for establishing a real estate development of real estate (including transfer of a real estate project, pre-sale of a commodity house and sale of a built-up commodity house); condition, necessary documents and procedure for the management of real estate; and legal liabilities for violating the Regulations.

As of 1 September 1998, the *Administrative Provisions on Registration of Real Estate Appraiser* became effective. It defines the Real Estate Appraiser and stipulates the administrative authorities of registration; the conditions, procedure and materials required for initial registration, changing registration, extending registration and cancelling registration; working requirements for real estate appraiser; rights and obligations of real estate appraiser; and penalties for violating the Provisions.

Also effective as of 1 September 1998, the *Provisions on Establishing the System of House Quality Guaranty and House Use Specification for House Sold in the Market* requires the real estate companies to provide with House Quality Guaranty and House Use Specifications when they deliver the brand new house to the user. The Provisions stipulate the content of the said two Certificates; the manner for providing the Certificates; the calculation of period of guarantee; and the inspection procedure for delivering the House, etc.

CHN ¶25-102   TRANSFER OF RIGHTS IN LAND

The transfer of land use rights can be conducted in or outside China. If the transfer is conducted outside China, acknowledgment by the notary public of the local country or region, attestation by the diplomatic institution of the local country or region and attestation by the Chinese embassy or consulate or commercial representative office in that country are needed. If the transfer is conducted within China, it shall be notarised by the Shanghai Notary Public Office or by another notary public office with jurisdiction.

The inheritance of land use rights must be notarised by the Shanghai Notary Public Office, except if it has been mediated or decided by a court.

Procedure

Chapter 2 of the Measures contains detailed provisions for the transfer of land use rights and the procedures which must be followed in order to transfer those rights.

The transferee of the land use rights and buildings shall be responsible for complying with transfer procedures of the Land Bureau and the Real Estate Bureau respectively. The transferee shall pay the transfer fee and all taxes. Any transfer undertaken without compliance with the transfer procedure will be void.

Article 25 of the Measures further provides that the grantee shall pay, in addition to the granting fee, a land use fee annually at the rate of RMB1 per square metre.

For any business activities undertaken on designated land by virtue of land use rights, the project sponsor shall be responsible for fulfilling all procedural requirements including, but not limited to, filing applications, obtaining approvals, making industrial and commercial registration, and registration and payment of taxes in the relevant departments in Shanghai.

The granting fee will be determined by negotiation and included as a term of the contract for land use rights, or shall be included in the tendered bid of the successful tenderer, or shall be determined by auction.

When land use rights are transferred or inherited, the transferees or inheritors shall continue to perform the granting contract (Art 8).

If the grantee wishes to change the nature of the land use specified in the granting contract, approval must be obtained from the Land Bureau and the grantee shall pay in full the granting fee in accordance with the Land Bureau's requirements (Art 26).

Form of transfer

The Measures provide for procedures such as notarisation of the transfer, control and registration in the Municipal Registry for transfer, mortgage, sale and inheritance of land use rights.

Necessary approvals

The Land Bureau is vested with the responsibility for handling the registration of all transfers of land use rights. On 17 February 1998, the State Bureau of Land Administration issued *Decree No. 8* regarding the *Interim Provisions on the Management of Transferring the Land Use Right in the Reform of State-owned Enterprises*. The Decree states that state-owned enterprises shall pay for their land (allocated land) use right according to the law. Based on the different situations in the reforms, these enterprises may take the forms of transfer, lease, purchase of shares by valuation of the land use right or retaining the allocated land use right.

CHN ¶25-103   RESTRICTIONS ON ACQUISITION OF RIGHTS IN LAND

The *People's Republic of China Urban Real Estate Management Law* which came into effect on 1 January 1995 provides that the amount of land city governments can sell or lease will be restricted and specified in annual official plans.

CHN ¶25-104   LAND SURVEYING

The Shanghai Land Administration Bureau is responsible for providing information including planning and environmental requirements and the location, boundary, dimension and topographic map of the land to any prospective land use rights grantee (Art 16).

CHN ¶25-105   REGISTRATION OF SECURITY IN LAND

Land use rights and any dealing therewith must be registered with the (Shanghai) Municipal Registry. Priority will be determined by date of registration of any such interest in the land use rights and buildings thereon.

CHN ¶25-111   REGISTRATION OF RIGHTS OF LAND USE AND OWNERSHIP

The *Land Registration Provisions* went into effect on 1 February 1996. The Provisions provide a uniform set of procedures and standards for the registration of land rights which are to be implemented nationwide, subject to the administrative authority of the State Land Administration Bureau. The Provisions call for local governments to oversee proper registration of initial land rights within their respective jurisdictions, including notice and recording of the following details: boundaries and location, effective duration and land rights, location of registration and evidence of the rights of applicants for registration of land rights.

CHN ¶25-112   SYSTEM OF LAND REGISTRATION

It appears from the Measures that all rights to land use must be registered and interests not registered will be void.

CHN ¶25-113   SPECIFIC RIGHTS

Natural resources, minerals and other buried or hidden objects under the land are not within the scope of a transfer of land use rights (Art 4). However, to explore for mineral resources, it is necessary to register and obtain an exploration license according to the *Mineral Resources Law* promulgated in March 1986. The law specifically extends investment in the mining sector to foreign companies.

CHN ¶25-114   EXTENT OF RIGHTS IN LAND

Land use rights include buildings attached to the land. The grant of land use rights is conditional upon undertaking the obligation to build as contracted. Land cannot be transferred until such conditions are fulfilled. Buildings and other structures not contracted for must be demolished at the expiry of the term of the grant of land use rights, or a fee paid for the demolition and removal.

CHN ¶25-115   AGREEMENTS RESTRICTING LAND USE

Land use rights granted under these Measures will be restricted. Only certain lots of land in certain areas will be made available.

The location of land and the terms and conditions of the granting shall be collectively determined by the Land and Real Estate Bureau and the Shanghai City Planning and Construction and Administrative Bureau and shall be implemented after being approved by the municipal government.

The Land Bureau may grant land use rights by means of a bilateral agreement, tendered bids or auction, or in a manner otherwise approved by the municipal government (Art 14).

CHN ¶25-121   ASCERTAINMENT OF EXISTING RESTRICTIONS

The Shanghai Real Estate Registry is vested with the responsibility for handling the registration of all transfers of land use rights. Registration records shall be available to the public for examination.

CHN ¶25-122   POWERS OF ACQUISITION OF LAND

Land use rights shall revert to the Land Bureau at the expiration of the term of the granting contract without compensation, if no application for extension is made and approved. The buildings and other attachments on the land shall be dealt with in accordance with the terms of the granting contract (Art 29).

The Land Bureau has the right to revoke land use rights following legal procedures, on the basis of social and public interest. The grantee shall be compensated correspondingly (Art 32). The Measures do not specify the legal procedures to be followed, the scope of the term ''social and public interest'', or the basis for assessment of reasonable compensation.

CHN ¶25-123   COMPENSATION FOR ACQUIRED LAND

Article 32 of the Measures provides that the grantee shall be compensated correspondingly for the loss of land use rights.

Assessment of compensation

The Measures, at Art 32, provide that the compensation for return of land use rights before the expiration of the contract shall be decided by the Land Bureau and the grantee through consultation, based on the remaining years under the contract, the nature of the land use, the value of the buildings constructed on the land, the value of other improvements, the granting fee, etc.

Resolution of dispute

If the amount of compensation cannot be resolved in consultation, either party can bring a suit in the People's Court for final determination. The return of the land use rights on the date specified in the public notice shall not affect the final determination on the amount of compensation.

Reference should also be made to any international agreements for the protection of investments. For example, the *Bilateral Agreement between the Australian and the Chinese Governments on the Reciprocal Encouragement and Protection of Investments* provides that expropriation, or nationalisation or other measures having a similar effect relating to any investment shall not be taken unless they are in the public interest, non-discriminatory and in accordance with the law of the contracting party which has admitted the investment and against reasonable compensation.

Compensation should be calculated on the basis of the market value of the investment or in accordance with generally recognised principles of valuations and equitable principles taking into account the capital invested, depreciation, capital already repatriated, replacement value and other relevant factors. It further provides that the compensation shall include interest at a reasonable rate from the date the Measures were taken, to the date of payment. The compensation should be freely convertible and transferable.

CHN ¶25-124   TAXES AND RATES

The new *Tax Regulations for Land Development and the Compensatory Transfer of Land Use Rights by Foreign Investment Enterprise* set out the tax obligations of foreign investors in land development as well as the procedures for compensatory transfer of land use rights.

Land use tax applies to all units and individuals who use land in cities, county towns, towns operated under an organisational system and industrial and mining districts.

Land value-added tax arises whenever income is derived from the sale of land use rights, buildings and other structures on the land. Tax rates vary from 30% to 60% depending upon the percentage gain, the value of non-luxury residential property is tax-exempt provided the percentage gain on the sale of the property is not more than 20%. The rights are generally sold for a 70-year period. China plans to expand its housing reforms and it is hoped that the land use tax would help regulate real estate prices.

The Ministry of Finance recently issued the *Implementing Rules on Provisional Regulations on Deed Tax of the PRC* (as of 1 October 1997). It interprets the *Provisional Regulations on Deed Tax of the PRC* (the "Provisional Regulations") and concerns the following issues:

- the interpretation of the following terms in the Provisional Regulations;
- right related to land, buildings and their commitment;
- units and individuals;
- transfer of State-owned land use right;
- transfer, sale, donation and exchange of land use right;
- donational and exchange of buildings;
- transaction price;
- used for working, educational, medical and military purpose;

- employees in cities and towns who purchase the public-owned house according to relevant rules for the first time;
- force majeure;
- other evidence with nature of contract on transferring the rights related to land and/ or buildings;
- collection and exemption of deed tax;
- further implementation provisions will be set up by authorities at provincial level; and
- regulations and rules by the Ministry of Finance before the issuance of the Implementation Rules are declared to be annulled.

Non-payment

The grant of land use rights under the Measures is effected by way of contract. Therefore, the grantee will have a contractual duty to fulfil all obligations contained within the contract.

CHN ¶25-125   SEIZURE OF LAND IN EXECUTION OF JUDGMENT

The Measures grant rights to the Land Bureau to grant land use rights within the scope of the Measures and to approve and register transfers, mortgages and other dealings with the land as well as revoking the land use rights on certain grounds and following legal procedures. When the period of grant of land use has expired, the land use rights, buildings and other improvements on the land shall be dealt with in accordance with the terms of the granting contract.

No other judicial, government or administrative body is empowered to seize and sell the land use rights, subject to Art 10 of the Constitution which provides that the state may, in the public interest, take over land for its own use in accordance with the law.

CHN ¶25-201   ENVIRONMENTAL RESTRICTIONS

China has established an extensive administrative structure for environmental control which exists at all levels of government under the NPC. The main organ of responsibility is the Environmental Protection Administrative Department of the State Council.

The legislative regime derives authority from various articles of the Constitution including Art 26 which states that:

"The State protects and improves the living environment and the ecological environment, and prevents and remedies pollution and other public hazards. The state organises and encourages afforestation and the protection of forests."

Article 22 provides that:

"The State protects places of scenic and historical interest, valuable cultural monuments, treasures and other important items of China's historical and cultural heritage."

Article 9 provides that:

"The State ensures the rational use of natural resources and protects rare animals and plants. The appropriation or damage of natural resources by any organisation or individual by whatever means is prohibited."

The *Environmental Protection Law* (for trial implementation) of 1979 was repealed by the *Environmental Protection Law*, adopted by the Standing Committee of the NPC on 26 December 1989. Under the umbrella of this basic law are a series of specialised laws, which are implemented by specific administrative decrees, orders and regulations. The state has also published a series of both ambient and emission standards.

The *Provisional Regulations for Prevention of Water Pollution in the Hai River Basin* was issued by the State Council and came into effect on 8 August 1995. The Regulations cover the prevention of water pollution in all rivers, lakes, reservoirs and canals in the Hai River Basin.

On 30 October 1995, the PRC *Preventing Solid Waste from Polluting the Environment Law* was promulgated and came into effect from 1 April 1996. The law provides detailed measures for the prevention of pollution caused by solid waste disposed by enterprises, individuals and other users, garbage in urban areas and dangerous waste disposed by work units. This includes encouragement of the use of degradable and recyclable packaging materials, charging of a sewage fee and setting up sites for the collection and disposal of solid waste.

The *Administration of Environmental Protection Against Imported Waste Tentative Provisions* was promulgated on 1 March 1996 and came into effect on 1 April 1996. The Provisions ban dumping, storing and disposing inside China of waste imported from abroad. This is effected by the introduction of a classification system for imported waste and imposing penalties for acts in violation of the Provisions.

CHN ¶25-202   REGULATION OF ENVIRONMENTAL CONTROLS

Part 2 of the *Environmental Protection Law* makes provisions in relation to supervision and administration of the environment. At the central government level, the Environmental Protection Administrative Department of the State Council is responsible for formulating national environment quality standards (Art 9), and monitoring and arranging to monitor the environment (Art 11). Under this central authority, the Environmental Protection Administrative Department of the People's Government has responsibility for formulating environmental protection plans, formulating local environment quality standards where the national standards do not apply, and monitoring and enforcing compliance with the plan and the standards.

The *Environmental Protection Law* places responsibility on the Local People's Government at all levels for the quality of the environment in their jurisdictions (Art 16).

CHN ¶25-203   GOVERNMENTAL REQUIREMENTS FOR ENVIRONMENTAL ASSESSMENT

The Environmental Protection Administrative Departments of the People's Government at and above county level and other departments authorised to supervise compliance with the Environmental Protection Plans and Pollution Standards have the right to make spot inspections of polluting units (Art 14).

The *Environmental Protection Law* requires an environmental impact report be prepared in relation to any construction project before it can be approved (Art 13). The Law also places an obligation on work units which generate environmental pollution to establish a responsibility system for environmental protection (Art 24). All new projects are required to implement pollution control measures and devices concurrently with the establishment of the project. It is prohibited to dismantle or not use facilities designed for the prevention and treatment of pollution without authorisation (Art 26). A general responsibility is placed upon all individuals and units to protect the environment and to report polluters (Art 6).

The PRC *Environmental Impact Assessment Law* was promulgated on 28 October 2002 and comes into effect on 1 September 2003. This Law is intended to implement a sustainable development strategy, to prevent adverse impact on the environment after the implementation of plans and construction projects, and to promote harmonious development of the economy, society and environment. The environmental impact assessment referred to in this Law means a method and system for analysing, forecasting and assessing the potential impact on the environment after implementation of plans and construction projects, putting forward strategies and measures to prevent or alleviate adverse impacts on the environment, and for carrying out follow-up and monitoring.

Article 7 provides that relevant departments of the State Council, people's governments at or above the municipal level and their relevant departments that organise the drafting of plans on land use, exploration, utilisation and development in river basin and sea areas, shall in the course of drafting organise and conduct environmental impact assessments and provide writings or explanations on the environmental impact of these plans. The environmental impact writings or explanations of the plans shall provide analysis, forecasts and assessment on potential environmental impact after plan implementation, and set forth counter measures and steps that prevent or alleviate adverse environmental impacts. These writings or explanations shall be part of the draft plans and be submitted to the plan examination and approval authority. The examination and approval authority will not examine and approve any draft plans without environmental impact writings or explanations.

Environmental impact reports for Special Plans shall include the following contents:

(i) analysis, forecast and assessment on the potential environmental impact after implementation of the plans;

(ii) measures and counter-measures to prevent or alleviate adverse environmental impacts; and

(iii) an environmental impact assessment conclusion.

On 10 September 2002, the State Planning and Development Commission (SPDC), the Ministry of Construction (MOC) and the State Environmental Protection Agency (SEPA) jointly issued the *Promoting Development of Industrialisation of Urban Sewage and Waste Treatment Sectors Opinion* (the Opinion) in an effort to improve the quality of the urban environment and achieve sustainable socio-economic development. The Opinion has mainly tackled reforms in the pricing and management systems in these two sectors and is aimed at generating a real market economy for these sectors. The Opinion requires those cities that have built treatment facilities to immediately introduce sewage and waste treatment fee charges. All other cities shall introduce such charges by the end of 2003. In both cases, charges are to be approved by municipal governments after price hearings are properly conducted.

The government has signalled its support for projects operated and managed in accordance with the Opinion. Preferential and supportive policies for favourable projects will include the following:

(i) electricity consumption for the projects will be charged at a discounted price;

(ii) concessionaires of Greenfield projects may be allocated the necessary land use rights for the entire concession term;

(iii) municipal governments may pledge sewage or waste treatment fees as a security for financing, and raise funds to develop urban drainage pipelines, and waste collection and transportation facilities;

(iv) the government may earmark a certain percentage of funds, sourced from municipal maintenance and construction taxes, urban infrastructure connection fees and state-owned land grant premiums, for the purposes of the construction of sewage collection systems, and waste collection and transportation facilities, as well as to contribute towards operational costs for sewage and waste treatment facilities, in case treatment fees have not been fully collected;

(v) the government will help project companies to have access to overseas financing; and

(vi) appropriate subsidies will be provided to projects in the central and western parts of China.

The government has changed its role in these sectors from direct management to macro-supervision. As a consequence, the government is now also in the process of enacting ancillary legislation on such diverse topics as mergers and acquisitions, construction, auctioning, the provision of security, asset restructuring and fee collection management, in preparation for the full opening of the urban sewage and waste treatment sectors to private investment and participation.

CHN ¶25-204   POLLUTION STANDARDS

The Environmental Protection Administrative Department of the State Council has responsibility for formulation of national environment quality standards. Local environment quality standards which are not covered by the national standards may be set by the People's Government of that area. These standards must be filed with the Environmental Protection Administrative Department of the State Council (Art 9).

The *Environmental Protection Law* places an obligation on the People's Government and State Council to formulate standards in relation to pollution discharge in the same manner as their obligation to formulate environmental quality standards. The People's Government of the provinces, autonomous regions and centrally governed municipalities are authorised to formulate local pollution discharge standards where none exist at the state level and may make stricter standards than already existing national standards (Art 10).

The revised *Law of the PRC on the Prevention and Control of Air Pollution* came into effect on 1 September 1995. The amendments affecting foreign investors are as follows:

- Enterprises must give priority to adopting efficient use of energy sources, clean production technology that emits the least amount of pollution and reducing the production of air pollution (Art 15).

- The State shall carry out a system to eliminate backward production technology that produces serious air pollution (Art 15).

- Pursuant to Art 15, the manufacture, sale, importation and use of such items shall be prohibited as well as the transfer of such items to others for use.

- Pursuant to Art 40, parties who violate the requirements of Art 15 shall be ordered to take corrective action and in serious circumstances the operations of the relevant factory or business may be suspended or closed down.

- Enterprises using coal require the use of low sulphur coal and coal cleaning technology (Art 24 to 27).

- Enterprises must progressively adopt equipment which controls nitrogen gas produced by coal production (Art 27).

CHN ¶25-205   INCENTIVES FOR NON-POLLUTING PLANTS

Article 8 makes provision for the rewarding by the People's Government of those with outstanding achievements in protecting and improving the environment. The *Environmental Protection Law* imposes controls in relation to developing and implementing plans for environmental protection and setting and enforcing standards for pollution discharge. Legislation has been passed at the central level which deals with specific aspects of the environment; for example, the *Forestry Law of the PRC*, the *Grasslands Law of the PRC*, the *Water Pollution Control Law of the PRC*, the *Marine Environment Protection Law of the PRC* and so on (see CHN ¶25-211).

CHN ¶25-211   NATURE OF CONTROLS

Article 6 of the *Environmental Protection Law* provides that in selecting construction sites, making designs, carrying out construction projects and embarking on production, all enterprises and other undertakings shall pay adequate attention to preventing environmental pollution and damage. While carrying out new construction or renovation projects, an environmental impact report shall be submitted first, and design work can be started only after such a report has been reviewed and approved by the department concerned. Facilities for preventing pollution and other hazards to the public must be designed, built and put into operation simultaneously with the principal project. The discharge of all harmful materials shall be carried out in accordance with the standards described by the state. Those units that have already caused environmental pollution or other hazards to the public shall work out plans and bring them under effective control in accordance with the principle that whoever has caused the pollution must bring it under control, or they shall obtain necessary approval from the competent authorities for a change in the type of operation, or seek relocation. The provisions of the *Environmental Protection Law* apply equally to foreign nationals, residents in vessels, vehicles, materials and aircraft entering or transmitting the territorial land, water or air space of China (Art 9).

The State Council's decision on strengthening environmental protection work in the period of national economic re-adjustment requires that an environmental impact report must be prepared before the start of any newly planned large and medium scale construction project and be approved by the Environmental Protection Department. Approval may not be given for construction projects, unless the environmental impact report required to be produced for that project has been approved (Art 13).

There are a number of pieces of legislation which contain provisions aimed at preventing and controlling pollution. These laws contain preventative measures and measures for punishing those who violate the laws. Punishments include warnings, fines and requirements to eliminate the pollution — they may be ordered to suspend operations or close down and compensate units or individuals which directly suffer loss. In serious matters, criminal sanctions may be applied to the persons responsible.

Polluters must apply for registration and pay fees for pollutant discharge in excess of the applicable standards. Articles 27 and 28 provide that enterprises and institutions discharging pollutants must register in accordance with the State Council Regulations, for example, under the terms of the *Prevention of Atmospheric Pollution Law of the PRC*.

Article 28 provides that, where the provisions of the *Water Pollution Control Law* differ from those of the *Environmental Protection Law* in relation to fees payable for excess discharge of pollutants, the provisions of the *Water Pollution Control Law* will prevail.

The *Environmental Protection Law* makes provision for enforcement of environmental protection and pollution control in the following ways:

• exacting a fee for excess pollutant discharge;

- giving warnings or charging fines where the *Environmental Protection Law* is violated in the ways specified in Art 35;
- suspending production or use and imposition of a fine for construction projects failing to satisfy state standards;
- making an order for reinstallation and a fine where facilities for prevention and treatment of pollution are dismantled or idle;
- providing that fines shall be levied in accordance with the severity of the pollution;
- providing that in relatively serious cases, administrative sanctions may be imposed upon responsible persons (Art 38);
- providing that in some circumstances, enterprises or institutions may be ordered to suspend business or close down (Art 39);
- providing that polluters will be responsible for cleaning up and paying compensation to those suffering loss as a direct result of the pollution (Art 41);
- providing that violations of the *Environmental Protection Law* with serious consequences may result in a criminal prosecution against the persons directly responsible (Art 43);
- providing that liability shall be borne under the specific relevant legislation where there is destruction of such resources as land, forests, grasslands, water and so on (Art 44); and
- providing that administrative sanctions shall be imposed upon environmental protection supervisory and administrative personnel for misfeasance and non-feasance. A criminal prosecution may be instituted where these acts constitute a criminal offence (Art 45).

CHN ¶25-212   DETRIMENT TO THE ENVIRONMENT

The objective of the *Environmental Protection Law*, as expressed in Art 1, is:

"to protect and improve the living and ecological environment, to prevent and treat pollution and other public hazards, to protect human health and to promote socialist modernisation".

The formulation of standards under the law and environmental protection plans have, as their specific objective, protection of and prevention of detriment to the environment.

The system of land use occupies a focal position in the political system. Domestically, land use rights and housing are allocated by either the local government through the work unit, or by the collective.

Rights to possess, transfer, lease and inherit attach only to the rights acquired to use the property and structures affixed to it. These rights may be exercised in accordance with the provisions of the *Law on Land Administration*.

The Structure of the Investment

Historical sources of contract and commercial law .... CHN ¶30-001

Codification of law .... CHN ¶30-002

Distinction between contract and commercial law .... CHN ¶30-003

Requirements for government contracts .... CHN ¶30-004

Requirements for contracts with foreign entities .... CHN ¶30-005

Treatment of consumer contracts .... CHN ¶30-011

Liability for injury caused by defective products .... CHN ¶30-012

Methods of settlement outside court system .... CHN ¶30-013

Special rules for institutions .... CHN ¶30-014

Use of standardised contracts .... CHN ¶30-015

Remedies under the commercial law .... CHN ¶30-016

Performance of contracts under changed
    circumstances .... CHN ¶30-017

Company law .... CHN ¶30-101

CHN ¶30-001   HISTORICAL SOURCES OF CONTRACT AND COMMERCIAL LAW

China's commercial and contractual law and legislative regime have developed at a remarkable rate. The Chinese government has concentrated on legislating in the area of commercial law in an attempt to establish a comprehensive legal system. Its express aim has been the speeding up and facilitating of the process of economic development. Specifically, foreign-related economic legislation has had as one of its primary aims the encouragement of the development of China's foreign economic relations in the areas of investment, technology transfer and trade.

There has been a strong emphasis in foreign-related economic legislation upon the reception of international law and practice. China has participated in a large number of bilateral and multilateral treaties and conventions.

In drafting legislation, for example the copyright law, the departments charged with drafting that law have conducted extensive research into the copyright systems of many western and socialist countries. Concepts and issues embodied in foreign legislation have assisted in the drafting of Chinese legislation. Of course, Chinese legislation reflects China's specific situation and needs, and serves to implement current policy.

The fundamental importance of socialist principles as enunciated in Marxism, Leninism and Mao Zedong Thought, by socialist jurisprudence (especially Soviet jurisprudence) and the influence of China's legal tradition in shaping the commercial and contract regime cannot be underestimated.

CHN ¶30-002   CODIFICATION OF LAW

In China, there are two major pieces of legislation dealing with contract: the *General Principles of the Civil Law* and the *Contract Law*.

The General Principles of the Civil Law

This is a basic level law passed by the National People's Congress (NPC) and took effect on 1 January 1987. The principles set out in it serve as a foundation for civil relationships and capacities and include principles relevant to contract. It covers contractual relations between individuals and between entities and individuals.

Contract Law

The *Contract Law* was adopted by the Second Session of the 9th NPC on 15 March 1999, and became effective on 1 October 1999. The *Economic Contract Law* (ECL), the *Foreign Economic Contract Law* (FECL), and the *Technology Contract Law* were all abolished simultaneously. The *Contract Law* stipulates on general principles on conclusion, effectiveness, performance, amendment, transfer and termination of contracts as well as responsibilities for breach of contracts. The *Contract Law* details comprehensively 15 types of named contracts.

International treaties

When authorised government bodies enter into an international treaty, the terms of the treaty become effective from the date of accession to the treaty without the need for specific implementing legislation. Specific domestic legislation often contains a provision, which in the case of conflict between the provision of the international treaty and the domestic legislation, specifies that the treaty is to prevail. This type of provision exists in the *General Principles of the Civil Law* (Art 142).

Applicable provisions of legislation are mandatory in effect.

CHN ¶30-003   DISTINCTION BETWEEN CONTRACT AND COMMERCIAL LAW

Contract and commercial law are both subsumed within the general category of economic law. Within that category, there is a distinction drawn between domestic economic legislation and foreign-related economic legislation. For example, before the entry into force of the *Contract Law*, there was no overlapping between the applicability of the ECL and the FECL in economic contracts; the former applied to domestic economic contracts and the latter related purely to economic contracts that have a ''foreign'' element. Despite the promulgation of the uniform *Contract Law*, the said distinction widely exists elsewhere.

CHN ¶30-002

The other main categorisation is that of the *Civil Law*, the scope of which overlaps with economic law. There has been a great deal of scholarly debate about the scope of these two categories. There is also an area of overlap with the category of *Administrative Law*.

CHN ¶30-004   REQUIREMENTS FOR GOVERNMENT CONTRACTS

There is no separate legal regime per se for government contracts or contracts involving government or government agencies. Many economic laws relate particularly to government contracts or government activities because of the transitional nature of the Chinese economy from a command economy to a market economy. All areas of economic activities, be they in the state-owned, collective or private sectors, are heavily regulated by government, either because of their ownership of, or other interest in the economic consequences of enterprise activities although the private sectors are dramatically increasing in Chinese economy. Objectives established in the state plans are implemented by means of policy directives, legal regulation and administrative control.

CHN ¶30-005   REQUIREMENTS FOR CONTRACTS WITH FOREIGN ENTITIES

In the sphere of economic contracts, prior to the uniform *Contract Law*, foreign-related economic contracts were regulated separately in accordance with the provisions of the FECL which was adopted by the Standing Committee of the NPC on 27 March 1985. Meanwhile, the ECL which was adopted by the NPC on 13 December 1981 applied to agreements between Chinese legal persons (Art 2) but not to agreements involving a foreign party.

Since 1 October 1999, both foreign-related economic contracts and domestic economic contracts have been governed by the same uniform *Contract Law*.

Note that, unlike the ECL and FECL, the uniform *Contract Law* includes in its scope of applicability the contracts to which a Chinese individual is a party.

Points of difference

The uniform *Contract Law* contains in Art 126, 128 and 129 certain provisions that are applicable to foreign-related economic contracts only:

- Parties to a foreign-related contract may select the law to govern the settlement of contractual disputes, unless the law provides otherwise. Where the parties to a foreign-related contract fails to make such selection, the law of the country with the closest connection with the contract shall apply. This provision better upholds the principle of freedom of contract. However, equity and cooperative joint venture contracts and contracts for the cooperative exploitation and development of natural resources to be performed in the PRC shall be governed by the laws of the PRC.

- Parties to a foreign-related contract may, in accordance with an arbitration agreement, apply for arbitration to a Chinese arbitration body or some other arbitration body. It is unclear whether this provision is suggesting that parties to a domestic contract are precluded from applying for arbitration to a foreign arbitration body.

- There is a limitation period of four years to take a legal action or apply for arbitration to an arbitration institution in relation to a dispute arising from a contract for international sale of goods or a contract for import and export of technology, as calculated from the date on which the party knows or ought to know that there has been an infringement of its rights. The prescribed period for lodging a law suit or submitting to arbitration any disputes arising over other kinds of contracts are stipulated separately by law.

The *General Principles of the Civil Law* provides at Art 136 that the period of limitation for the following law suits is one year:

- law suits seeking compensation for bodily injuries;
- a law suit based on sale without notice of products of sub-standard quality;
- a law suit based on delay or default of payment of rent; and
- a law suit based on loss of or damage to bailed property.

Apart from these situations, the general period of limitation under the *General Principles of the Civil Law* within which a civil suit must be brought is two years, unless otherwise provided (Art 135).

CHN ¶30-011 TREATMENT OF CONSUMER CONTRACTS

Contracts entered into between individuals can now be governed by the uniform *Contract Law*.

The principles governing capacity of natural persons to have civil rights and their competence to perform civil acts are set out in Chapter 2 of the *General Principles of the Civil Law*. The *General Principles of the Civil Law* also set out provisions relating to civil liability for breach of contract and for tort. Damage suffered as a result of the sub-standard quality of goods is compensable under Art 122, which is contained in the section on Civil Liability for Torts. This article, together with the product quality regulations, serves as the basis for liability for damage resulting from defective products.

On 29 October 2002, the Shanghai Municipality issued the *Protection of the Rights and Interests of Consumers Provisions* which became effective on 1 January 2003. Consumers have the right to demand products that comply with state, industrial and local standards regarding safety to individuals and property (Art 7) and the right to establish social organisations that protect their rights and interests (Art 13). Article 16 stipulates that price, quality and after-sale liability must comply with the promises made by the business operator; the business operator shall not use a form contract format to apply conditions that are unfair or unreasonable, that free the retailer from liability, that increase the consumer's liability or that void a consumer's rights. Sales agents for imported products must affix their name and address to the product (Art 20). Unless otherwise required by law, a business operator may not in any form or manner disclose a consumer's personal information to a third party without the consumer's permission (Art 29). Business operators shall be responsible for repairing durable goods they sell for a period of not less than six months (Art 31). Government authorities may conduct inspection at the production or retail premises of enterprises that may be in violation of consumers' lawful rights and interests (Art 38). To resolve consumer disputes, the consumer may opt for arbitration or litigation (Art 51).

CHN ¶30-012 LIABILITY FOR INJURY CAUSED BY DEFECTIVE PRODUCTS

Article 122 of the *General Principles of the Civil Law* provides that where, because of the sub-standard quality of goods, damage is caused to the property or person of another, the manufacturer or seller of the goods must bear civil liability according to the law.

The "sub-standard quality" of the product or products is assessed in relation to administrative regulations promulgated by various arms of government which also give administrative organs power to handle disputes concerning product quality. The regulations include:

- the *Industrial Product Quality Liability Regulations*, State Council, 5 April 1986;
- the *Guide to Administering Rural and Township Enterprise Industrial Product Quality*, State Economic Commission, 30 June 1987;
- the *Standardisation Law of the People's Republic of China*, Standing Committee of the NPC, 29 December 1988;
- the *Implementing Rules for the Standardisation Law*, State Council, 6 April 1990; and
- the *Product Quality Law of the People's Republic of China*, Standing Committee of the 7th NPC, 22 February 1993.

Article 153 of the *Opinion (for trial use) of the Supreme People's Court on Questions Concerning the Implementation of the General Principles of the Civil Law of the People's Republic of China* further elaborates on this Article: "where the use of goods of sub-standard quality causes personal injury or property loss to a consumer, user or other person, the injured party suffering the loss may demand compensation from the manufacturer or seller". This explanation indicates that the injured party may seek compensation from either the manufacturer or seller of the defective products and that ability to claim damages is not restricted to the consumer or user of those goods, but can be asserted by anybody whose person or property has suffered damage as a result of the use of the sub-standard quality goods.

Article 122 further provides that where transporters and bailors are responsible for damage, the manufacturers and sellers have the right to demand compensation for loss. In such a case, the transporter or bailor may be joined by the manufacturer or retailer as a defendant in the proceedings.

In order to ensure that the right of redress against the manufacturer is not an empty one, regulations have been passed which require that products be labelled with the name and address of the manufacturer before being permitted to be sold in any shop. In any case, the seller of the goods is also primarily liable for damage caused as a result of the use of sub-standard products. The level of science or technology available at the time the product was manufactured, however, can be used as a defence. If it can be proved that the manufacturer would have been unable to detect the defect using available science or technology, the manufacturer will escape liability (Art 29 of the *Product Quality Law*).

China's *Product Quality Law of the People's Republic of China* took effect on 1 September 1993 and was amended on 8 July 2000. While the law mainly emphasises compliance with explicit written control standards, it also creates a general duty on manufacturers and retailers not to manufacture or sell defective goods.

Producers are liable to pay compensation if a defective product causes physical injury or damage to property. Penalties for non-compliance with state or industry standards include fines, directives to cease production of the non-complying products as well as confiscation of both the products and the illegal income. Enterprises may also have their business licence revoked and be subject to criminal prosecution.

CHN ¶30-013   METHODS OF SETTLEMENT OUTSIDE COURT SYSTEM

Commercial contracts are primarily governed by the provisions of relevant laws. Where there is a gap or ambiguity in the law, then policy directives will be referred to. In any case, the contents of commercial contracts will not be permitted to diverge from policy guidelines and government and administrative bodies charged with the task of examination and approval of commercial contracts will have regard to policy and administrative regulation when examining the contract.

China has an extensive system of alternative dispute resolution which includes conciliation/mediation and friendly negotiations. Litigation and arbitration are last resort measures. Between litigation and arbitration, parties are encouraged to resolve contract disputes through arbitration. If the parties are unwilling (or unable) to resolve the dispute, then they may apply for arbitration in accordance with the arbitration clauses in the contract. When arbitration is to be used for dispute resolution and the parties submit to arbitration to resolve the dispute, the decision of the arbitration tribunal is final and binding under the *Arbitration Law* which came into effect on 1 September 1995. Previously, PRC domestic arbitration tribunal decisions could be appealed in a People's Court.

Apart from these structures, there are also a number of government departments and bodies which are willing to act on an informal basis as intermediaries between disputing parties. It is also an accepted principle of *Contract Law* that performance is a priority, and should the situation change, the parties to the contract are encouraged to re-negotiate or alter the contract in light of the changed circumstances, rather than rigidly relying on the rights and duties set out in the terms of the original contract.

CHN ¶30-014   SPECIAL RULES FOR INSTITUTIONS

The basic principles of contract set out in the *Contract Law* and the *General Principles of the Civil Law* form the basis for contracts in China. Specific administrative regulations and reference contracts exist in relation to various specialised areas. They act as specific application of promulgated legal principles and policy (see CHN ¶30-002, CHN ¶30-004 and CHN ¶30-005).

CHN ¶30-015   USE OF STANDARDISED CONTRACTS

Government departments and state-owned enterprises have for a long time relied on model or reference contracts in many areas. The use of the model contract was in existence before the promulgation of foreign-related or domestic contract or commercial legislation. For example, international trade contracts were used in the 1960s. They were developed by the Ministry of Foreign Trade and Economic Cooperation (MOFTEC) and other ministries involved in international trade. These model contracts were based on the principles of international law.

Model contracts are used as the basis for negotiation where such a contract exists. Although the use of a model contract is not compulsory, it will often be difficult, as a matter of practice, to deviate significantly from its provisions.

Exclusion clauses, limitation of liability

The *Contract Law* makes provision for exclusion and limitation of liability. In relation to standard clauses, Art 39 requires that the party proposing the standard clauses takes reasonable steps to draw the other party's attention to those clauses which eliminate or limit the said party's liabilities and, upon request by the other party, explains the effect of the said clauses; Art 40 provides that where the party proposing the standard clauses excludes its liability, increases the other party's liability or excludes the other party's major rights, such clause shall be without effect.

Article 53 provides that the following exclusion clauses shall have no effect: clauses relating to personal injuries caused to the other party; and clauses relating to property losses caused to the other party because of the first party's deliberate acts or its gross negligence.

Article 127 provides that in accordance with the circumstances, a party may be partly or completely excused from liability for breach of contract where it cannot perform due to *force majeure*. A certificate must be obtained acknowledging the event of *force majeure*.

General considerations

The general considerations which must be taken into account when concluding a contract under the *Contract Law* are that the law protects the lawful rights and interests of parties, maintains social and economic order and promotes the development of China's socialist modernisation. Contracts should be made in conformity with the principles of equality, voluntariness, fairness, and being honest and trustworthy, and should not disturb the social and economic order or harm social and public interests (Art 3 to 7).

Article 13 provides that the parties shall adopt the method of offer and acceptance in concluding a contract. The contents of a contract may be agreed upon by the parties, but in general should include the provisions concerning the names and addresses of the parties, the subject matter, quantity, quality, price or remuneration, time period, place and methods for performance, liability for breach of contract and methods for settlement of dispute (Art 12).

Chapters 2 to 7 of the *Contract Law* contain detailed provisions on the conclusion, validity and performance of contracts, and their amendment, assignment, termination and the liability for breach of contract.

The specific provisions of the *Contract Law* address a total of 15 types of named contracts, including purchase and sales contracts; contracts for the supply and consumption of electricity, water, gas and heating; gift contracts; loan contracts; leasing contracts; financial leasing contracts; work contracts; contracts for construction projects; transport contracts; technology contracts; storage contracts; warehousing contracts; mandate contracts; commission contracts; and contracts for intermediary services.

The *General Principles of the Civil Law* provides at Art 5 that a civil legal act must satisfy the following conditions:

- the person performing the act has the appropriate competence;
- the real intent is expressed in the contract; and
- there is no violation of law or the public interest.

Parties concluding contracts under the provisions of the *General Principles of the Civil Law* thus have freedom within the parameters of Art 55 to negotiate the terms of the contract. There is also an obligation to comply with the other provisions of the *General Principles of the Civil Law* which include provisions on liability for tortious actions. Articles 121 to 125 are strict liability offences and Art 126 and 127 impose liability unless it can be proven that the party upon whom the obligation is placed was not at fault. Therefore, a clause attempting to limit liability in the areas specified in these articles would be invalid. There is at least one example where an attempt by an employer to exclude liability for work-related injuries in a contract for hire was declared an invalid civil act and the exclusion clause was not able to be relied upon to limit or exclude the liability of the employer.

CHN ¶30-016   REMEDIES UNDER THE COMMERCIAL LAW

The primary remedy granted under Chinese *Contract Law* for breach of contract is specific performance.

The *General Principles of the Civil Law* provides that where one party fails to perform his or her contractual duty, or performance of his or her contractual duty is not in accordance with the agreed terms, the other party has the right to demand performance, or to take measures to correct the defective performance, and has the right to demand compensation for loss (Art 111).

The *Contract Law* provides at Art 8 that once established in accordance with law, a contract is legally binding. The parties should fulfil all obligations stipulated in the contract. No party should arbitrarily alter or terminate the contract. This provision places an emphasis upon performance of the obligations in the contract, though it does not place any legal or procedural barrier in the way of claiming liquidated or other damages as set out in the contract.

Article 110 further provides that where a party does not perform a non-monetary obligation or does not perform a non-monetary obligation as agreed, the other party may demand performance of the obligation, except in one of the following three circumstances:

- it is legally or practically impossible to perform the obligation;
- compelling performance is inappropriate given the subject matter of the obligation or the expenses associated with the performance are too high; and
- the obligee has not demanded performance within a reasonable period of time.

Articles 111 and 112 of the *General Principles of the Civil Law* set out four types of remedies available for breach of contract. These are:

- performance of the contractual duty;
- correction of the defective performance;
- payment of the sum contracted for as breach of contract monies (*wei yue jin*); and
- compensation for the actual loss suffered.

These remedies are cumulative.

Damages

The *General Principles of the Civil Law* provides that where a party fails to perform a contract or to take measures to correct defective performance of the contract, the other party has the right to demand compensation for loss (Art 111). The liability for compensation of a party who breaches a contract must be equal to the loss the other party incurred as a result of the breach.

Parties may provide in a contract that when there is a breach of contract, the party in breach pays to the other side a certain specified sum; (this is an amount of money which is provided for in the contract and used as a penalty for failure to perform: *wei yue jin*). The parties may also provide in the contract for a method to calculate damages caused by breach (liquidated damages) (Art 112).

Deposits

One party may pay a deposit to the other party. After the contract is performed, the deposit shall be returned or offset against the price. If the party that pays the deposit does not perform the contract, it will have no right to claim return of the deposit. If the party that receives the deposit does not perform the contract, it must return twice the amount of the deposit (*Contract Law*, Art 115).

Breach of contract

If a party breaches a contract, it must pay damages for breach of contract to the other party. If the breach of contract has already caused the other party to suffer losses that exceed the amount of the damages for breach of contract, the party in breach should pay compensation and supplement the breach of contract damages by the insufficient amount (*Contract Law*, Art 114).

Amount of damages

The *Contract Law* provides at Art 113 that in case of breach of contract, the amount of the compensation for the loss shall be equal to the loss suffered by the other party as a consequence of the breach. Such loss as incurred by the other party includes the benefits that the other party would have been able to obtain upon the performance of the contract. However, the amount of compensation for such loss shall not exceed the total losses resulting from breach of contract that the breaching party, at the time of concluding the contract, foresaw or should have foreseen.

The parties may agree in the contract that a certain amount of the liquidated damages shall be paid to the other party if one party violates its contractual obligations, and may also agree upon a method for calculating the damages arising out of such a breach of contract.

Liquidated damages shall be regarded as damages caused by breach of contract. However, if the fixed amount of the liquidated damages is substantially more or less than the actual loss, the parties may request a court or arbitration agency to have the amount appropriately lowered or increased (*Contract Law*, Art 114).

Apportionment and mitigation of damages

The *General Principles of the Civil Law* and the *Contract Law* also make provision for apportionment of damages and liability to compensate for damage where both parties are in breach of the contract. There is a duty on the aggrieved party to mitigate its loss and so there may be no recovery of loss suffered as a consequence of failure to mitigate.

Where it is no longer economically desirable or feasible to insist upon performance of the contract, the aggrieved party may require damages to be paid to compensate for its actual loss.

Computation of damages

There is provision in the *Contract Law* for the payment of breach of contract monies (*wei yue jin*) upon failure to perform a contract, whether or not there is damage suffered. However, the calculation for damages payable as a consequence of a breach of contract is otherwise calculable in accordance with the actual loss suffered. Where the amount of loss exceeds the amount specified as breach of contract monies, the aggrieved party may claim the difference. The *Contract Law* provides that where an amount of liquidated damages is less than, or substantially exceeds the actual amount of damages, an application may be made to either an arbitration agency or a court to adjust the amount of damages payable.

CHN ¶30-017   PERFORMANCE OF CONTRACTS UNDER CHANGED CIRCUMSTANCES

The *Contract Law* provides that a contract may be modified after agreement has been reached through consultation by the parties concerned (Art 77).

Where laws and regulations provide that approval, registration or other procedures must be completed when a contract is modified, such provisions shall be adhered to (Art 77). Failure to comply may result in the modification being invalid or ineligible to rely upon to oppose third parties.

However, modification, cancellation or termination of a contract does not affect the rights of a party to the contract to claim damages, and does not affect any provision for the settlement of disputes or for the settlement of accounts or winding up of operations stipulated in that contract.

Article 38 requires that where the State assigns mandatory tasks or tasks relating to state orders for goods, relevant legal persons and other entities shall conclude contracts between themselves in accordance with the rights and obligations stipulated in the relevant laws and regulations.

Modification, cancellation and termination

Principles for modification, cancellation and termination of contracts are specifically provided in the *General Principles of the Civil Law* and the *Contract Law*. Parties are free to re-negotiate contractual terms, but approval, registration and/or other procedures required under laws and regulations should be complied with.

The powers of the People's Courts to make judgments and rulings are set out in Art 120 to 123 of the *Civil Procedure Law*. This power is to, *inter alia*, determine the facts of the case and apply the relevant substantive law to the facts to determine the rights and duties of the parties. On its face, the law makes no provision for the People's Court to amend the terms of a contract. However, the *Civil Procedure Law* requires that the People's Court invites the parties to participate in court-directed mediation in all cases. In practice, the People's Court conducts mediation or conciliation in the course of proceedings in most cases, but the *Civil Procedure Law* itself provides that mediation or conciliation must only be conducted by the People's Court with the agreement of the parties concerned. Any agreement reached between the parties concerning the resolution of their dispute will be embodied in a *Bill of Mediation* which, when signed and sealed, becomes legally effective.

COMPANY LAW

Forms of commercial organisations .... CHN ¶30-101

Foreign companies .... CHN ¶30-102

Registration of non-resident companies .... CHN ¶30-103

Requirements for establishment of subsidiaries .... CHN ¶30-104

Investment in local companies .... CHN ¶30-105

Percentage of foreign ownership .... CHN ¶30-111

Types of governing and managing structures .... CHN ¶30-112

Structure and powers of joint venture .... CHN ¶30-113

Bankruptcy Law .... CHN ¶30-114

CHN ¶30-101   FORMS OF COMMERCIAL ORGANISATIONS

National company law

The *Company Law* of the People's Republic of China became effective on 1 July 1994.

The law regulates two types of companies: limited liability companies and companies limited by shares. Further, it spells out the process for transforming state corporations into the two forms of corporate entities.

Both limited liability companies and companies limited by shares enjoy limited liability, they have shareholders who must hold meetings as well as boards of directors. Decision-making power and the right to appoint a general manager of the company rest with the board of directors.

Companies are required to consider the opinions of their trade unions or employee representatives on decisions concerning such matters as workers' salaries, benefits and safety. They must also consult trade unions and employees on major issues such as production and operations and in formulating important internal rules.

On 25 December 1999, the 9th Standing Committee of the NPC adopted the following amendments to the *Company Law*:

- Article 67, following the amendment, states: the Board of Supervisors of the wholly state-owned company mainly comprises personnel appointed by the State Council or the institutions and departments authorised by the State Council. The representative of the company's staff shall join in the Board of Supervisors and the members thereof shall not be less than three. The authority of the Board of Supervisors is provided by Art 54(1)(i) and (ii) of the *Company Law* and the others granted by the State Council. The supervisors shall participate in the meeting of the Board of Directors. Any director, manager or financial director shall not concurrently be a supervisor; and

CHN ¶30-101

- An additional clause to Art 229 states: if the company is verified as a company limited by shares with high and new technology, conditions for the company's issuance of new stocks and its application for listing, and issues such as the percentage between the initiator's contribution by intellectual property and the registered capital, will be stipulated by the State Council.

Limited liability companies

A limited liability company is defined as an enterprise with legal person status under which the liability of each shareholder is limited to the amount of its respective capital contribution. Limited liability companies must have between two and 50 shareholders.

The minimum equity requirements for limited liability companies depends upon the type of business venture. Manufacturing companies must have a minimum capital contribution of RMB500,000. For companies engaged primarily in the retail business, the minimum capital required is RMB300,000. Companies engaging in the development of technology, consultancy or other service industries must have a capital amount of at least RMB100,000.

There is no residency requirement for the shareholders in contrast to the rules relating to companies limited by shares which require that at least 50% of the promoters must be Chinese residents.

Transfer of interests in a limited liability company from a shareholder to a non-shareholder requires the consent of a majority of the shareholders. If the shareholders who do not consent, however, do not purchase the interest which is proposed to be transferred, their refusal to purchase will be regarded as approval of the transfer.

Directors, supervisors and managers have an obligation to maintain confidentiality of company secrets.

Companies limited by shares

A company limited by shares is a corporate entity with legal person status whose shareholders are liable only to the extent of their share subscription. All shares must be of equal value. The minimum amount of registered or paid-up capital for a company limited by shares is RMB10 million. Companies that wish to have their shares traded on a stock exchange must have a minimum capital of RMB50 million and at least 1,000 shareholders each holding more than RMB1,000 in shares. Further, the public shareholders must hold at least 25% of the shares.

A supervisory committee must be established by a company limited by shares. This committee is to comprise at least three members who represent the shareholders and the company's employees. The functions of the supervisory committee include the following:

- inspecting the company's financial plans;
- supervising the acts of the directors and the general manager; and
- proposing interim shareholders' general meetings.

There must be a minimum of five promoters, at least half of whom must be resident in China. In the case of a company established by its promoters, all shares are bought by them whereas if it was established by share offer, the law provides that the promoters must subscribe for at least 35% of the shares.

The transfer of an interest by a shareholder in a company limited by shares is less onerous than in a case of a limited liability company. Promoters, however, may not assign their shares in the company for a period of three years from the establishment of the company. In addition, directors, supervisors and managers of the company may not transfer their shares during their term of office. Lastly, the transfer of shares in the company must be conducted at a legally established stock exchange.

The *Notice Regarding the Conditions for Issuance of New Shares by Listed Companies*was issued on 24 July 2002 by the China Securities Supervisory Commission (CSSC). According to the Notice, the weighted average return on net assets for the last three consecutive years of an eligible company for issuance shall not be less than 10%. Moreover, the weighted average return on net assets for the latest financial year shall be no less than 10%. CSSC promulgated the *Content and Form of the Prospectus for Issuance of New Shares by Listed Companies*(promulgated on 10 April 2001) as the eleventh Rules on *Content and Form of Information Disclosure of Public Listing Companies*. The *Administrative Measures on the Issuance of New Shares by Listed Companies*issued on 28 March 2001 also regulates such matters including those related to B shares.

Foreign investment companies limited by shares

The *Provisional Regulations on Certain Issues Concerning Establishing Foreign Invested Companies Limited by Shares*was issued and made effective on 10 January 1995. The Regulations set out the procedures and requirements for foreign-invested enterprises and maintain the standard requirement that one or more foreign shareholders must own and hold a total of at least 25% of the total registered capital of the company in order for the company to maintain "foreign investment enterprise" status.

The minimum amount of registered capital for a foreign-invested enterprise which is to issue shares is RMB30 million. Existing enterprises must reflect at least three consecutive years of profitability in order to convert into companies limited by shares. Different document submissions exist for conversion of status to a company limited by shares depending on certain factors of the company, ie current company status, type of shares to be issued (eg H shares) etc.

Domestic/foreign-related

Regulation of business entities in China falls into two overlapping groups:

- domestic; and
- foreign-related.

Domestic

Chinese law recognises a variety of domestic business organisations. The number of such organisations has grown rapidly since the 1982 constitutional ratification of private business as a "necessary supplement" to the socialist foundation of rural/urban collectives and state-owned enterprises.

Enterprises are classified according to their ownership as either state-owned, collectively-owned or privately-owned and according to whether they are business enterprises or non-business enterprises. For example, a university would be a non-business enterprise. Joint operations exist which can take the form of either a legal person

CHN ¶30-101

or a non-legal person. Joint operations may exist only between Chinese enterprises or individuals.

Foreign-related

Foreign-related direct investment in China has taken on three main forms:

- the equity joint venture;
- the cooperative joint venture; and
- wholly-owned foreign enterprise.

Establishment of a Chinese-foreign equity joint venture necessitates a direct equity pledge from its investors but limits the liability of each party to its subscribed capital contribution. Cooperative joint ventures may or may not enjoy limited liability, depending on the degree of cooperation. Cooperative joint ventures are generally flexible in their management structure.

The *Provisional Regulations on Investment-oriented Companies established by Foreign Investors*was promulgated and went into effect on 4 April 1995. The regulations permit the establishment of both solely foreign-funded and joint Chinese and foreign-funded companies for the purpose of making direct investment in China. Such companies are referred to as ''investment companies''.

Investment companies

A foreign investor seeking to establish an investment company must satisfy one of the following two criteria:

- The foreign investor has adequate financial capacity to operate an investment company and its total assets must be at least US$400 million, at least one year before the date of application, and the foreign investor has already established at least one foreign investment enterprise in China with paid-up registered capital of over US$10 million, in addition to having already obtained approval for over three investment projects in China.
- The foreign investor has adequate financial capacity to operate an investment company and has already established over 10 foreign investment enterprises in China for purposes of engaging in manufacturing or infrastructure development activities having total paid-up registered capital exceeding US$30 million.

Application for the establishment of investment companies is made with MOFTEC (now known as MOFCOM).

The investments nature companies with foreign investors shall be governed by the following laws and regulations:

- Establishment of Companies with an Investment Nature by Foreign Investors Tentative Provisions;
- Problems Concerning the ''Establishment of Companies with an Investment Nature by Foreign Investors Tentative Provisions'';
- ''Establishment of Companies with an Investment Nature by Foreign Investors Tentative Provisions'' Supplementary Provisions (1) and (2);
- Amending the ''Establishment of Companies with an Investment Nature by Foreign Investors Tentative Provisions'' and Its Supplementary Provisions Decision; and

- The Establishment of Companies with an Investment Nature by Foreign Investors Provisions.

Legal persons

The test to determine whether the organisation has limited liability is to determine whether that organisation is a "legal person".

The definition of legal person is contained in Art 6 of the *General Principles of the Civil Law*as follows:

> "legal persons are organisations that have civil capacity, are competent to perform civil acts, and according to law independently enjoy civil rights and civil duties".

The civil capacity of a legal person and its competence to perform civil acts arise when the legal person is established and ceases when a legal person is terminated.

Article 37 provides the conditions which must be satisfied in order to be a legal person:

- It must be established in accordance with the law.
- It must possess the necessary property or funds.
- It must possess its own name, organisational structure and premises.
- It must be able to assume civil obligations independently.

Article 41 envisages that state-owned and collective enterprises, upon fulfilling the requirements set out in that article and in Art 37 may attain the status of a legal person upon approval and registration by the responsible agency. Equity joint ventures, contractual joint ventures and wholly foreign-owned enterprises established in the territory of the People's Republic of China may acquire the status of a Chinese legal person upon meeting the requirements and upon approval and registration in accordance with law by the State Administration for Industry and Commerce (SAIC).

SAIC promulgated the *Provisions on Administration of Legal Representatives of Enterprise Legal Persons*on 7 April 1998, stipulating the required qualification of a legal representative, procedure for appointing and/or removing a legal representative, as well as his registration and change of registration. A list of persons who cannot be appointed or approved as a legal representative is provided. Further, if a person is registered as a legal representative by deceit, or an enterprise fails to change legal representative registration when required, penalties are provided eg the enterprise may be fined up to RMB100,000 or its registration may be cancelled.

The Provisions replace the *Temporary Provisions on Conditions for Examining and Approving Legal Representatives of Enterprise Legal Persons and their Registration Administration*(promulgated on 20 November 1990).

CHN ¶30-102   Foreign companies

China encourages both business and investment in China which can take many forms.

Direct foreign investment generally falls into three major categories:

- The sino-foreign equity joint venture, which results in the formation of a Chinese legal person. The formation and other details concerning the equity joint venture are governed by the *Law of the People's Republic of China on Sino-foreign Equity Joint Ventures*("Equity Joint Venture Law") and their Implementing Regulations.

- The contractual or cooperative joint venture, which can either result in the formation of a Chinese legal entity or not as the joint venture partners choose. Cooperative joint ventures are regulated by the *Sino-foreign Contractual Joint Venture Law of the People's Republic of China and its Implementing Regulations*.

- The wholly foreign-owned enterprise, which is operated in China exclusively with foreign capital but is registered in China as a Chinese legal person. This form of investment is governed by the *Law of the People's Republic of China on Foreign Capital Enterprises and its Implementing Regulations*.

Other forms of corporate representation in China which do not take the form of a Chinese legal person are representative offices or liaison offices. These offices must be registered and if they fall within the definition of "permanent establishment" will be liable to be taxed in China under the foreign enterprise investment tax.

CHN ¶30-103   Registration of non-resident companies

The principal method by which foreign companies have a presence in China is through the resident representative office.

Regulations covering the establishment and operation of representative offices include:

- the *Provisional Regulations of the State Council of the People's Republic of China Concerning the Control of Resident Representative Offices of Foreign Enterprises*, 1980; and

- the *Implementing Rules of the Ministry of Foreign Trade and Economic Cooperation for Approval and Administration of Resident Representative Offices of Foreign Enterprises*, 1995.

Regulations have also been issued by the People's Bank of China in relation to representative offices established by foreign banks and insurance companies.

Under the implementing rules, representative offices within the PRC may be set up by a broad range of foreign enterprises, including trade companies, manufacturers, freight agencies, contractors, consulting companies, advertising companies, investment companies, leasing companies and other economic and trade organisations.

Resident representative offices which do not register under these regulations may have their business activities terminated and may incur a fine.

On 22 April 1999, the *Administrative Provisions on Representative Offices of Foreign Securities Companies* was promulgated by the China Securities Supervisory Commission (CSSC) and took effect on the same day. The Provisions stipulate the application and revocation procedures as well as supervision of these representative offices by CSSC. In comparison with the previous similar administrative provisions, the Provisions first set up rules for the establishment of a general representative office; the Provisions also require the representative office to submit annually the report to local office of CSSC and emphasise the obligation of the chief representative to stay in China and monitor the overall management of the representative office.

Fees

A registration fee is payable to the local branch of SAIC and must be submitted with an application for establishment (or extension) of representative offices of foreign enterprises within 30 days of the issue of approval documents. A renewal must be made each year though foreign staff of the representative office may obtain long-term visas if it can be established that they are reasonably required. A fee is incurred for an application for extension.

Statutory accounts

Resident offices falling within the scope of the regulations must submit an annual report on a SAIC registration form which must be completed in Chinese and the chief resident representative will be responsible for the accuracy of the contents of that form. The form requires, *inter alia*, disclosure of signed contracts, service revenues and Chinese taxes paid.

Offices which are not registered under the regulations, apart from risking the termination of their business activities and incurring a fine will not be able to enter into long-term office leases, obtain multiple entry visas, import office equipment and supplies, open a bank account, hire Chinese employees, rent telecommunication lines and equipment or display their sign or use business cards identifying their presence in China.

Foreign trade and industrial trade enterprises which conduct import-export operations must submit monthly accounting statements to the relevant trade and finance authorities. This is just one of a range of mandatory reporting requirements set out in the Regulations issued by the Ministry of Finance and MOFTEC.

Other information required by the authorities include the following:

- monthly statements regarding financial targets;
- funds statements;
- profit/loss statements;
- profit distribution schedules; and
- special use loan and capital construction loan statements.

On 28 February 1995, the NPC *Penalties for Crimes of Violating the Company Law Decision*took effect. The similar provisions in the PRC *Criminal Law*effective on 1 October 1997 replaced it. It stipulates that where a company provides false information in its financial or accounting report or withheld certain facts in the report, thereby damaging the interests of other persons, the person(s)-in-charge will be subject to imprisonment or criminal detention of up to three years and may additionally be fined approximately RMB200,000 or lower.

On 23 August 1999, SAFE promulgated the *Notice Regarding the Adjustment of Relevant Provisions on Management of Settlement Accounts of Foreign Invested Enterprises*(the ''Adjustment Notice'') according to which funds in foreign exchange settlement accounts (the ''Settlement Accounts''), subject to amount ceilings of the same, can be transferred into time deposits. When funds in the Settlement Accounts are transferred to any other bank as foreign exchange pledge for applying Renminbi loans, the bank with which the Settlement Accounts are opened shall accordingly lower the amount ceiling till the pledged foreign exchange return to the Settlement Accounts.

Local agents

In order to obtain registration of a resident representative office, a formal approval document must be obtained from a Chinese sponsor. Article 4 of the *Provisional Regulations of the State Council of the People's Republic of China Concerning the Control of Resident Representative Offices of Foreign Enterprises*lists the Chinese organisations which may provide sponsorship. In general, the relevant ministry in charge of the type of activities to be conducted by the representative office is the appropriate sponsorship organ. For example, traders, manufacturers and shipping agents must apply to MOFTEC, ocean shipping companies and ocean shipping agents must apply to the Ministry of Communications, and air transport companies must apply to the Civil Aviation Administration of China.

Registration procedures

The specific requirements for registration of a foreign enterprise representative office include submission of the following:

- an application letter signed by the Chairman of the Board;
- a certified copy of evidence that the foreign enterprise is legally in existence;
- a letter of creditworthiness from a bank which has business relations with the foreign enterprise;
- a letter of entrustment, signed by either the Chairman or General Manager/President/CEO of the foreign enterprise authorising the chief representative of the company;
- a completed "application form for registration of foreign enterprise representative entity" and "application report on employees of foreign enterprise long term representative entity"; and
- other application materials as required from the approving organisations.

The registration procedures are as follows:

- Obtain the approval of the appropriate Chinese sponsor. To obtain an approval document, the relevant Chinese organisation must assess whether it has a "genuine need" for the applicant representative office.
- An application letter, signed by the Chairman or President of the company requesting registration which gives information about the company and a copy of the applicant's official licence to conduct business in its own jurisdiction, a letter of creditworthiness from the applicant's bank, notarised authorisation for each person appointed to the representative office and completed application forms in relation to personnel proposed to be appointed as representative staff must be submitted.
- After obtaining the approval document, registration must be completed with the Beijing branch of SAIC. However, SAIC has authorised the branches in the place of the proposed representative office to complete the registration procedures.
- The registration fee must be submitted with the application for establishment of representative offices of foreign enterprises.

The application requires the name and location of the representative office, the number of representatives and foreign staff, scope of business and total value of the company's exports and imports to and from China for the three preceding years to be included in the application form. A foreign enterprise is normally granted registration with effect for a period of three years, commencing from the date the approval of registration is formally issued. Applications for extension of a foreign enterprise representative office must be submitted 60 days before the registration has expired.

On 7 May 1998, the *Implementation Provisions on the Regulations on Several Issues Related to Investment by High and/or New Technologies*(effective from 4 July 1998) was issued by the Ministry of Science and Technology and SAIC. The Implementation Provisions provide that if high and/or new technology is invested towards the registered capital of a company with limited liability or a science-technology development enterprise and is valued as more than 20% of the registered capital, relevant documents and materials must be submitted (the ''Application Documents'') to the science and technology administration authority at different levels (the ''Examination and Ratification Authority'') for examination and ratification. The decision shall be made by the Examination and Ratification Authority within two months after the complete set of Application Documents has been received. For applications satisfying the conditions required for high and/or new technology, a Ratification Certificate for Investing by High and/or New Technology (the ''Ratification Certificate'') will be issued by the Examination and Ratification Authority. Otherwise, an examination opinion in writing will be sent to the applicant. The investor must register with the proper administration for industry and commerce within three months after receipt of the Ratification Certificate. The Implementation Provisions also set out the penalties in cases where the Ratification Certificate is obtained by deceit.

Bodies exercising jurisdiction

Apart from obtaining approval from the relevant Chinese Ministry which acts as the sponsorship organisation, control over foreign representative offices is exercised by SAIC through its local authorised branches.

Penalties for violation

The PRC *Criminal Law*provides that an applicant for company registration who falsely declares registered capital, by fraudulent means, to deceive the company registrar and thus obtain registration will be subject to imprisonment or criminal detention of up to three years and may additionally be fined from 1% to 5% of the falsely declared registered capital in serious cases.

CHN ¶30-104   Requirements for establishment of subsidiaries

Wholly foreign-owned enterprises wishing to be registered as a Chinese legal person will fall within the scope of the *Law of the People's Republic of China on Foreign Capital Enterprises*. If the foreign entity wishes to have Chinese participation in the new entity, it can choose either the equity joint venture vehicle, in which case it will be governed by the *Law of the People's Republic of China on Sino-foreign Equity Joint Ventures*or choose whether it wishes to become a Chinese person under the *Law on Cooperative Joint Ventures*. The main purpose for these laws is to provide a legal framework to encourage investment in projects in specifically targeted areas and not to register a legal person with a broad capacity to act.

Application procedures for registration of a company in China are governed by the individual laws and regulations relating to the establishment of each equity joint venture, contractual joint venture and wholly foreign-owned enterprise. In each case, registration will result in the formation of a Chinese legal entity.

Fees

The relevant time for paying fees is upon registration of the entity with SAIC and the issuing of a business licence. The amount of fee payable is determined by the amount of registered capital of the business and is governed by the *Regulations on Standards for the Payment of Registration Fees by Enterprise Legal Persons*. Joint ventures with a registered capital of up to RMB10 million must pay a registration fee of 0.1% of the registered capital; joint ventures having a registered capital of more than RMB10 million will need to pay an additional fee of 0.05% of the amount in excess of RMB10 million.

Nationality of directors

In the case of the equity joint venture, the board of directors must contain at least three members and seats will be held by the Chinese and foreign parties in proportion to the amount of capital contribution of each party. The Chairman may be either from the Chinese or foreign party and the Vice-Chairman shall be selected from the party not selecting the Chairman. This requirement also applies to contractual joint ventures which form an entity. Contractual joint ventures which do not form an entity are managed by each party to the venture separately and so there will be no board of directors. However, this type of contractual joint venture will have a joint management committee which consists of representatives of each party to the venture. The law governing wholly foreign-owned enterprises provides that the entity shall have autonomy in its operational and management activities.

Nationality of management

Generally, the only foreign personnel employed by a joint venture will be management and technical personnel.

Percentage of share capital for non-residents

The *Equity Joint Venture Law* at Art 4 stipulates that the foreign party generally should hold at least 25% of the registered capital of the joint venture. There is no maximum amount prescribed. This minimum requirement also applies to contractual joint ventures which take the form of a legal entity.

Bearer shares

The concept of ''share'' in a foreign investment enterprise refers to the proportion of registered capital contributed by each party, which cannot be altered without specific approval by the department or ministry responsible for granting the original approval for the project.

Nominal capital

Each party to a joint venture is required to contribute its proportion of the registered capital in order for the entity to obtain registration. The *Provisional Regulations of the State Administration of Industry and Commerce Concerning the Ratio between the Registered Capital and the Total Amount of Investment of Joint Ventures Using Chinese and Foreign Investment* governs the amount of external borrowing permitted to be made by the venture in proportion to the amount of registered capital. Total investment means the amount of registered capital plus the borrowings of the venture. For example, joint ventures with a total investment of up to US$3 million must have registered capital of 70% of the total investment. For projects with a total investment of between US$3 million and US$10 million, registered capital must be at least 50% of the total investment. In those ventures with total investment between US$10 million and US$30 million, the registered capital must be at least 40% and where the total investment exceeds US$30 million the registered capital must be at least one-third of the total investment.

Directors' shareholding qualification

There is no minimum shareholder's requirement for directors.

Time taken for establishment

The time taken to complete all the preliminary matters required to gain approval for the establishment of a joint venture varies dramatically depending on the proposed location of the joint venture, the nature of the joint venture and the extent to which it accords with the priorities set by the state. After obtaining approval, the joint venture must register with the local branch of SAIC within one month.

Branches

The establishment of a branch is a matter for approval, either at the stage of establishing the joint venture or, after the establishment of a joint venture, as a separate matter.

On 22 April 1999, the *Administrative Provisions on Representative Offices of Foreign Securities Companies*was promulgated by the China Securities Supervisory Commission (CSSC) and took effect on the same day. The Provisions stipulate the application and revocation procedures as well as supervision of these representative offices by CSSC. In comparison with the previous similar administrative provisions, the Provisions first set up rules for the establishment of a general representative office; the Provisions also require the representative office to submit annually the report to local office of CSSC and emphasise the obligation of the chief representative to stay in China and monitor the overall management of the representative office.

Statutory accounts

The accounting procedures to be followed by an equity joint venture are set out in the *Income Tax Law on Foreign Invested Enterprises and Foreign Enterprise*, the *Implementing Regulations of the Joint Venture Law*and the *Accounting Regulations of the People's Republic of China for Joint Ventures Using Chinese and Foreign*

Investment. Accounts must be audited by a Chinese-registered accountant in order to be valid (Implementing Regulations, Art 90). Wholly foreign-owned enterprises must keep their accounts in China and submit an audited financial statement to the local finance and tax departments and are subject to their supervision.

Information as to shareholdings

Not applicable.

Payment for shares

The *Equity Joint Venture Law* allows parties to the proposed joint venture to introduce assets other than cash, although these contributions must be reduced to a monetary figure. The cooperative joint venture has more flexible provisions which do not require that contributions in kind be reduced to a monetary figure as the parties may agree to share profits on a basis other than according to their proportional contribution to the registered capital.

Liquidations

Amendments have been made to the *Equity Joint Venture Law* which include an amendment to Art 13: The joint venture contract may be terminated upon agreement by the parties to the joint venture upon approval by the approval authority and registration with SAIC. Another basis upon which the joint venture contract may be terminated include the occurrence of heavy losses; breach of contract and *force majeure*. The *Implementing Regulations for the Law of the People's Republic of China on Joint Ventures Using Chinese and Foreign Investment* makes provision at Art 90 for early dissolution of the joint venture. Article 91 requires that a liquidation committee be established to value the assets and liabilities of the joint venture and formulate the plan for liquidation. This plan must be ratified by the board and implemented under the supervision of the approval authorities. The *Wholly Foreign-Owned Enterprise Law* contains only a very general provision that upon termination, they are required to liquidate ''in accordance with legal procedures'' and go through procedures for cancellation of their business licence (Art 21).

The effect of liquidation is that a Chinese legal person is lost and so legal capacity, by Art 36 of the *General Principles of the Civil Law*, is lost also. Loss of civil capacity results in loss of competence to perform civil acts which may have serious consequences in relation to obligations to perform existing contractual obligations.

Disposal of shares

A party to a joint venture may not transfer its share in the joint venture without the approval of the other party to the joint venture and the relevant approval authorities.

CHN ¶30-105　INVESTMENT IN LOCAL COMPANIES

Chinese companies or entities do not take the form of companies limited by shares, and so it would not be possible to acquire an interest in a Chinese company without going through the procedures enumerated for the establishment of the selected form of joint venture. Recently, the government has been willing to permit an increased diversity in forms of investment, one of which is a foreign party taking over the management of a Chinese enterprise.

Government participation

It is possible that the Chinese party to the joint venture may be a state-owned enterprise, in which case there is indirect involvement of the government. The establishment, operation and all other activities of a joint venture will be overseen by relevant government departments, for example, the Taxation Department, SAIC and other local and central organisations.

Geographical restrictions

The feasibility study prepared as a prerequisite to obtaining approval for a proposed joint venture must clearly state, amongst other things, the scope of business and the geographical area of operation of the enterprise. Once approved, this will form the basis for the legitimate activities of the joint venture unless otherwise provided by the relevant laws and regulations. There are no geographical restrictions in the majority of foreign investments in China.

Local employees

There is normally a requirement to use local staff, contractors or sub-contractors.

CHN ¶30-111   PERCENTAGE OF FOREIGN OWNERSHIP

The *Equity Joint Venture Law* set out a minimum contribution to the registered capital of the foreign party which is set at 25% of the registered capital. The status of the company is determined at the time of approval of the joint venture (see also CHN ¶30-104).

CHN ¶30-112   TYPES OF GOVERNING AND MANAGING STRUCTURES

The *Implementing Regulations of the Joint Venture Law* provides that the board of directors is the "highest organ of authority" and "decides all major questions". The other level of management is the managerial staff who are responsible for daily operational managerial work (Implementing Regulations, Art 33 and 38).

CHN ¶30-113   STRUCTURE AND POWERS OF JOINT VENTURE

Contractual joint venture

In order to conduct business in China, a cooperative joint venture whether it becomes a legal entity or not, must obtain registration. The establishment of an entry is made with reference to the requirements of the *Equity Joint Venture Law*, where applicable. Otherwise, the contents of the contract which have been negotiated between the parties to the contractual joint venture and approved by the relevant authority will define its structure and the parameters within which it operates.

Form of an equity joint venture

The documents required for establishment of the joint venture as an entity include the agreement, contract and Articles of Association and the documents required under Art 7 of the Implementing Regulations. The *Regulations for the Implementation of the Law of the People's Republic of China on Joint Ventures Using Chinese and Foreign Investment* at Art 10 states that the joint venture "agreement" is a document agreed upon by the parties to the joint venture setting out some main points and principles governing the establishment of a proposed joint venture. The "joint venture contract" refers to a document agreed upon and concluded by the parties to the joint venture on their rights and obligations. "Articles of Association" refers to a document agreed upon by the parties to the joint venture indicating the purpose, organisational principles and method of management of a joint venture in compliance with the principles of the joint venture contract.

If the joint venture agreement conflicts with the contract, the contract shall prevail.

Main provisions

Article 11 makes provision for the main items to be included in a joint venture contract:

- details concerning the names, addresses and registrations of the parties to the joint venture and their legal representatives;
- name and address of the joint venture, purpose and scope and scale of business;
- total amount of business and registered capital of the joint venture, details concerning the proportion of each party's investment, its forms, time limits, provisions concerning incomplete contributions and assignment of investment;
- the ratio of profit and loss distribution;
- the composition of the board of directors, distribution of number of directors, responsibilities, powers and means of employment of the general manager, deputy general manager and high ranking management personnel; and
- other detailed provisions concerning the use of technology, source of supply and sale of finished products, detailed financial and accounting arrangements, labour provisions, the duration of the venture, dissolution and liquidation procedures, liabilities for breach of contract, and dispute resolution procedures.

Article 13 includes detailed provisions about the matters which are to be included in the Articles of Association of the joint venture company which should reflect the matters contained in the contract and act as the code by which the joint venture will be governed.

These regulations relate specifically to equity joint ventures, though in the absence of any detailed regulations to the contrary, contractual joint ventures taking the form of a legal entity would be treated in an analogous fashion.

Wholly foreign-owned enterprise

The *Law of the People's Republic of China on Enterprises Operated Exclusively with Foreign Capital* contains only general provisions concerning application to the relevant Department for approval to establish the enterprise. Article 11 provides that the enterprise shall be free from interference in its operations and management so long as these are conducted in accordance with the approved Articles of Association.

Restrictions

In all forms of joint ventures in China, the joint venture contract and additionally in relation to legal entities, the Articles of Association are required to make provisions for the management of the joint venture enterprise. In order to alter any of the provisions in these constituent documents, it is necessary to first obtain the approval from the original approval authority. Foreign investors and foreign parties to equity/contractual joint ventures should note that without the approval from the competent authorities, the agreements reached between the parties during the cooperation period are invalid and have no legal effect. Therefore, in many cases, when dispute arises, the parties, both foreign and Chinese, find they cannot rely on the agreements in arbitration or litigation.

CHN ¶30-114 BANKRUPTCY LAW

A bankruptcy law has been drafted and submitted to NPC for approval. The law is expected to cover all enterprise legal persons including some cooperative organisations which are not enterprise legal persons. It also establishes a liquidation system whereby the representative of the creditor is charged with the supervision of the bankruptcy clearing procedure. It also allows for a temporary manager to take care of the property. For cases involving less than RMB500,000, a simplified procedure can be used to settle dispute between the creditor and debtor.

The draft law will cover every types of enterprise and reduce the role of the government in the bankruptcy hearings. The revised legislation will be more compatible with international standards and punishments for abuse of bankruptcy will be set out. The government will be relieved from the responsibility of dealing with the aftermath of bankruptcies such as providing employment for redundant employers. There will also be bankruptcy insurance provisions.

Current provisions are too narrow and apply mainly to state-owned enterprises. There is also an absence of explicit regulations on how to file for bankruptcy.

State-owned enterprises

The *Enterprise Bankruptcy Law of the People's Republic of China* (the "Bankruptcy Law") applies only to Chinese state-owned enterprises. Moreover, the law is stated to apply only to state enterprises that have suffered serious losses and are unable to clear their debts within a fixed period of time because of poor management. Certain state-owned enterprises such as public utilities and enterprises which are important to the national economy will not be declared bankrupt if the government is providing them with financial assistance.

Under this law, a debtor state-owned enterprises or any creditor of a state-owned enterprise may file a bankruptcy petition in the People's Court where the enterprise is located. Provided that the applicant is able to demonstrate that the debtor is unable to repay its debts "on time" (a term that is left undefined), the bankruptcy application will be accepted by court officials. Thereafter, those creditors who are known to the court will be notified of the proceedings and of a date for holding the first creditors' meeting. A corresponding public announcement will also be made.

Foreign enterprises

Under Chapter 19 of the PRC *Civil Procedure Code*, an application may be made to a People's Court to have a FIE declared bankrupt. After ruling to declare a party subject to bankruptcy repayment procedure, a People's Court shall notify the debtor and known creditors within 10 days, as well as make a public announcement. Notified creditors have 30 days from the notice to declare their claims and other creditors shall do so within three months of the public announcement.

After deduction of bankruptcy expenses from bankrupt property, repayments shall be made in the following order:

- wages owed to employees of the bankrupt enterprise and labour insurance premiums;
- outstanding tax payments; and
- bankruptcy claims.

If the property is insufficient to settle claim repayments within the same category, a proportionate method of distribution shall be adopted. The *Foreign Investment Enterprise Liquidation Procedures* was promulgated in July 1996 and provides the process of ordinary liquidation. During liquidation, a liquidation committee of at least three persons must be set up. After which, the liquidation committee should notify the creditors to declare their claims. If the liquidated property is not enough to settle all the debts, the liquidation committee should apply to a People's Court for enterprise bankruptcy.

Guangdong

The Guangdong province has put into place a bankruptcy law which came into effect on 1 August 1993. The regulations apply to all companies in the Province, including the Shenzhen SEZ. The Guangdong bankruptcy law supersedes the Shenzhen bankruptcy law which was enacted in 1987. The People's Court can declare a company bankrupt if it is unable to pay its debts in full, have its business registration cancelled and distribute property owned by the company to pay social insurance, tax liability, staff members and creditors.

If a company has obtained security and discharged its liabilities within six months from the date on which the bankruptcy application was lodged, the company will not be declared bankrupt.

Shanghai

The liquidation of foreign investment enterprises in Shanghai is governed by the *Regulations of the Shanghai Municipality Concerning the Liquidation of Foreign Investment Enterprises*. This covers the liquidation of Chinese-foreign equity joint ventures, Chinese-foreign cooperative joint ventures and wholly foreign-owned enterprises but does not govern the liquidation of wholly foreign-owned financial institutions or Chinese-foreign joint venture financial institutions.

On 18 July 2002, the Judicial Committee of the Supreme People's Court issued the *Several Issues on Trial of Enterprise Bankruptcy Cases Provisions* (the "Provisions"), which became effective on 1 September 2002. The Provisions stipulate (at Art 6 for a debtor's application and Art 7 for a creditor's application) the facts and materials that are to be submitted to the People's Court in support of a bankruptcy application. The Provisions grant the debtor an opportunity to contest the creditor's application (Art 8 and 9). Under Art 8, the People's Court to which the creditor's application has been submitted may call upon the debtor to verify the debt claimed to be outstanding. Further, under Art 9, upon a successful challenge by the debtor, the creditor's application will be rejected and the creditor notified to commence civil proceedings with respect to the debt purportedly owed.

Article 12(1) of the Provisions confers upon the People's Court the power to reject a debtor's application where it is discovered that the debtor has concealed or disposed of its assets and has applied for bankruptcy in an attempt to avoid liability. Similarly, a creditor's application can be rejected (Art 12(2)) if it is intended to damage the debtor's business reputation (although it remains to be seen how this rule would operate in the face of a valid claim that the debtor is unable to pay its debts when due). Article 20 of the Provisions echoes the Supreme People's Court's opinion on the *State Enterprise Insolvency Law (Trial Implementation) of 1986* (the "EIL") in providing that, after the People's Court has accepted a bankruptcy application, trials over financial disputes that have not been concluded against the debtor shall be discontinued. Similarly, if the trial has concluded but execution proceedings have not been completed, the latter will also be discontinued. It is now clear that this will apply to both state-owned enterprise (SOE) and non-SOE bankruptcies, and that the plaintiff would only be permitted to file its claim to the People's Court having jurisdiction over the bankruptcy matter.

Article 18 introduces a provision allowing the People's Court to appoint an "enterprise management committee" — a body akin to an interim manager — for the period of time after the acceptance of the bankruptcy case. Article 50(1) of the Provisions suggests that the enterprise management committee is only to relinquish its responsibilities to a liquidation committee established after the formal declaration of bankruptcy. Under Art 47 to 49 of the Provisions, the People's Court must establish a liquidation committee within 15 days of declaring an enterprise bankrupt. The liquidation committee may comprise representatives from various governmental bodies including the State Administration of Industry and Commerce, the State Administration of Taxation, the Labour Department and the bankrupt enterprise's supervisory body.

Parts 9 and 10 of the Provisions seek to detail assets that would fall within the pool of bankruptcy assets for distribution to creditors. It reiterates the general rule (at Art 71) that goods subject to mortgage, lien and pledges are not bankruptcy assets (although secured creditors of an enterprise must generally obtain the approval of the People's Court before they may enforce their security rights against the bankrupt enterprise) save where the security holder waives its right to be paid in priority. The Provisions also stipulate that, if an employment contract is terminated as a result of the bankruptcy, the compensation to be paid with respect to the termination shall also be ranked first (Art 56 and 57). The Provisions also state that funds provided by employees to the bankrupt enterprise shall be paid in priority. Finally, during the period when the bankrupt enterprise is being liquidated, the employees' daily and medical expenses can be paid in priority out of the bankruptcy assets. The Provisions state that upon the People's Court's acceptance of a bankruptcy case, it shall inform the bankrupt enterprise's bankers that no setting-off of liabilities owed to the bank is permitted (Art 15(4)). However, the People's Court is given the discretion to decide otherwise.

Taxation

General taxation ....CHN ¶35-001

Commercial and business profits ....CHN ¶35-101

Investment profits ....CHN ¶35-201

Miscellaneous taxes ....CHN ¶35-301

Capital gains tax ....CHN ¶35-401

Tax incentives ....CHN ¶35-501

GENERAL TAXATION

International tax treaties .. CHN ¶35-001

Existence of tax credits ..... CHN ¶35-002

Procedures for resolving tax
   disputes .... CHN ¶35-003

Fiscal year .... CHN ¶35-004

Method of payment of tax
   liabilities .... CHN ¶35-005

CHN ¶35-001   INTERNATIONAL TAX TREATIES

China has signed double taxation agreements with a number of countries, including without limitation:

- Australia
- Belgium
- Brazil
- Bulgaria
- Canada
- Cyprus
- Czechoslovakia
- Denmark
- Finland
- France
- Germany (Federal Republic)
- Hungary
- Iceland
- Italy
- Japan
- Korea
- Kuwait
- Luxembourg
- Malaysia
- Malta
- Mongolia
- The Netherlands
- New Zealand
- Norway
- Pakistan
- Poland
- Romania
- Singapore

- Spain
- Sweden
- Switzerland
- Thailand
- Turkey

- United Arab Emirates
- United Kingdom
- United States
- USSR
- Yugoslavia

Most of the tax treaties follow closely the Model Treaty of 1977 prepared by the Organisation of Economic Cooperation and Development (OECD). However, different treaties do provide different treatment in certain respects. Therefore, specific treaty provisions should be consulted depending on the nationality of the parties involved.

CHN ¶35-002   EXISTENCE OF TAX CREDITS

Under the tax treaties which China has signed, relevant rules allow credit to residents for tax imposed by the other country on income, including credit for underlying tax on profits from which dividends are paid. Participation in a tax exemption project or designated tax exemption area in China will alter the allowance of tax credits whereby the remittance of income would otherwise be incorporated in assessable income for tax purposes where tax has been paid in China and a tax credit becomes allowable.

The *Individual Income Tax Law* provides for a tax credit for individuals residing in China for one year or more whose non-China source income is subject to tax in China. Where individuals have already paid income tax on their income gained outside China to the relevant authority abroad, they may by presentation of their foreign tax payment receipt apply for a credit against the amount of Chinese income tax due.

CHN ¶35-003   PROCEDURES FOR RESOLVING TAX DISPUTES

The resolution of taxation disputes does not fall for consideration until after the tax has been paid. After payment, an appeal may be made to the tax authorities such as the State Taxation Bureau for reconsideration. Where reconsideration of taxation assessment is applied for, tax authorities are required to make a determination within two months of receipt of the application. Excess payments are refunded by tax authorities or deficiencies made good by the taxpayer. If a taxpayer disagrees with the disposition of the case after appeal, he may lodge a suit in the local People's Court. The interpretation of taxation rules is the responsibility of the Ministry of Finance and the State Taxation Bureau.

CHN ¶35-004   FISCAL YEAR

China's fiscal year for foreign enterprises starts on 1 January and ends on 31 December.

CHN ¶35-005   METHOD OF PAYMENT OF TAX LIABILITIES

Income tax is paid to the local authority in which the enterprise is situated. The Regulations require that tax returns be filed and taxes paid monthly for all income from Chinese sources within the first seven days of the month following that in which the income is earned. Individual returns are to be filed by each taxpayer. Refunds for over-payments or supplemental payments for deficiency are paid on determination and final settlement.

Provisional income tax returns and accounting statements must be filed with the tax authority within 15 days from the end of each month or quarter. Within 45 days from the end of the fiscal year, the final accounting statements and income tax returns must be filed.

COMMERCIAL AND BUSINESS PROFITS

Taxation of commercial and
  business profits .... CHN ¶35-101

Taxable activities and
  undertakings .... CHN ¶35-102

Details of tax on
  companies .... CHN ¶35-103

Details of business profits
  tax .... CHN ¶35-104

Taxation of executives .... CHN ¶35-105

CHN ¶35-101   TAXATION OF COMMERCIAL AND BUSINESS PROFITS

The *Provisional Rules of the People's Republic of China on Enterprise Income Tax* took effect on 1 January 1994. The legislation does not apply to foreign enterprises. Domestic enterprises are now required to pay a reduced enterprise income tax of 33% compared to 55% previously. The income tax is levied annually and prepaid by monthly or quarterly instalments. Taxpayers may claim deductions for such items as wages and salaries, donations and employee welfare expenses.

According to the Notice issued by the State Council, since 1 January 2000, individual-invested and wholly-owned enterprises and enterprises in partnership will not be levied the enterprise income tax any longer. The investors of such enterprises will be levied individual income tax like the individual industrial and commercial runner.

The *Income Tax Law for Enterprises with Foreign Investment and Foreign Enterprises* (the "Unified Tax Law") applies to all foreign investment enterprises (equity joint ventures, cooperative joint ventures and wholly foreign-owned enterprises) as well as foreign companies. The unified foreign tax came into effect on 1 July 1991 and replaced the joint venture income tax and the foreign enterprise income tax.

Any foreign enterprise shall pay its income tax on its income derived from sources within China (Art 3). The taxable income of an enterprise with foreign investment shall be the amount remaining from its gross income in a tax year after the cost, expenses and losses have been deducted (Art 4). There has been talk about unifying corporate income tax rates for domestic and foreign-funded enterprises to provide equal treatment to all businesses as required under the World Trade Organisation.

Key features of the Unified Tax Law

- A flat 30% national tax and a flat 3% local tax will apply to all foreign investment enterprises and establishments of foreign companies in China, subject to any available tax incentives.

- All foreign investment enterprises having a term of more than 10 years and engaged in production will obtain a two-year tax exemption, followed by a three-year 50% reduction as from the first profitable year (except for those engaged in petroleum, natural gas, rare metal and precious metal explosion for which separate provisions will be formulated by the State Council).

- Equity joint ventures in service industries are no longer entitled to a tax holiday.

- Potential tax exposure for foreign companies selling into China through agents and for foreign companies deriving service income in China.

- Basic withholding tax rate of 20% for interest, royalties, rentals and certain other PRC-sourced income, including capital gains.

- Foreign investment enterprises may continue to enjoy tax rates and tax holiday treatment under prior law if they are more favourable.

    Consolidation of incentives available in China's special investment areas:

- 15% tax rate in SEZs for both foreign investment enterprises and the establishment of foreign companies;

- 15% tax rate for production enterprises in the ETDZs; and

- 24% tax rate in old urban districts of cities with ETDZs and SEZs, and in coastal open economic zones, with a lower 15% rate applicable to infrastructure projects.

Tax rates

(1) Equity joint ventures

Under the Unified Tax Law, equity joint ventures are subject to tax at a flat rate of 33% of net income, which includes a national tax of 30% of net income and a local income tax at a flat rate of 3%.

Prior to this law, the local income tax was levied by the *Joint Venture Income Tax Law* as a percentage of the national tax payable, rather than a flat rate. This rate structure means that local governments now have the discretion to maintain the full 3% local tax even when the national tax is exempt or reduced.

The Unified Tax Law provides a blanket withholding tax exemption in respect of the profits of joint ventures remitted from China by foreign parties. Previously, a 10% withholding tax was imposed under the *Joint Venture Income Tax Law* on the profits of equity joint ventures remitted abroad by a foreign party. Some relief, however, was provided by incentive legislation which exempted the withholding tax for foreign parties in many export-oriented and technological advanced joint ventures.

(2) Wholly foreign-owned enterprises, cooperative joint ventures and PRC establishments of foreign companies

Under the Unified Tax Law, wholly foreign-owned enterprises, cooperative joint ventures and PRC establishments of foreign companies are all subject to tax at the same flat rate of 33%, comprising a national tax of 30% and a local tax of 3%.

Previously, under the *Foreign Enterprise Income Tax Law*, wholly foreign-owned enterprises, foreign parties to cooperative joint ventures and PRC establishments of foreign companies were subject to national income tax at progressive rates ranging from 20% (on annual net income of less than RMB250,000) to 40% (on annual net income in excess of RMB1 million). The local income tax rate was set at a flat rate of 10%.

With the passage of the Unified Tax Law, a foreign investor may now base its choice of investment vehicle on factors other than taxation as tax is levied at the same flat rate on all types of enterprises. In the past, foreign investors considering establishing a joint venture or a wholly foreign-owned enterprise in China were required to weigh carefully the different tax structures applicable to each of these entities.

A foreign company may be deemed to have an establishment in China for taxation purposes by the presence of a ''business agent'' (Art 3). A ''business agent'' refers to an establishment which:

- regularly negotiates purchasing matters, signs purchasing contracts and buys goods on behalf of the foreign company;
- has entered into an agency agreement or contract with the foreign company, regularly stores commodities or products owned by the foreign company, and delivers products or commodities to other parties on behalf of the foreign company; and
- has the authority to regularly represent the foreign company in signing sales contracts and accepting orders.

If strictly enforced, this provision could mean foreign companies selling into China could be regarded as having a taxable establishment in the PRC and liable to taxation at the flat rate of 33%.

(3) Withholding tax

The Unified Tax Law provides for a withholding tax for certain PRC-sourced income derived by foreign companies, unconnected with any PRC establishment of such foreign companies. The withholding tax is levied under the new legislation at a flat rate of 20%, which maintains the tax rate which existed under the *Foreign Enterprise Income Tax Law*.

On 12 March 2003, the State Administration of Taxation issued the *Tax Administration Issues Relevant to Resident Representative Offices of Foreign Enterprises Circular*, which became effective on 1 July 2003. The Circular clarifies some issues arising from the implementation of the State Administration of Taxation, *Strengthening the Administration and Payment of Taxes of Resident Representative Offices of Foreign Enterprises Relevant Issues Circular* (the ''1996 Circular''). It concerns:

(1) the tax registration and filing of tax returns of representatives offices that are not taxed or are exempt from tax;

(2) methods for levy of tax on different types of representative offices;

(3) tax exemption of foreign governments, non-profit organisations and others; and

(4) administration and spot checking of representative offices.

Section II(2) of the Circular stipulates that revenue of representative offices engaged in agency or trading services (Items one, four and five of the first paragraph of Art 1 of the 1996 Circular) should be converted from their expenses as long as the representative offices do not directly conclude a contract with the service receiver and service charges are collected by the parent company. Representative offices engaged in commercial, legal, tax, audit and accounting services (Item two of the first paragraph of Art 1 of the 1996 Circular) shall keep complete accounts books and correctly calculate their revenue and taxable income.

On 28 March 2003, the State Administration of Taxation issued the *Supplementary Notice of State Administration of Taxation on Issues Relating to Tax Incentives for Additional Investments by Foreign Investment Enterprises*. The Circular clarifies that foreign-invested projects whose additional investments are approved before 1 April 2002 shall belong to the Encouraged Category or type B of the Restricted Category of the *Foreign Investment Industrial Guidance Catalogue* promulgated in 1997 while those projects whose additional investments are approved on or after 1 April 2002 shall belong to the Encouraged Category of the *Foreign Investment Industrial Guidance Catalogue* promulgated in 2002 (Item one). The Circular also clarifies that additional investments that have created production or business projects and that have not enjoyed regular tax reduction or exemption preferential treatment may be put together for the calculation of registered capital increase and enjoy tax reduction or exemption thereon (Item two). The preferential period should start from the profit year of the production or business project created by the first additional investment (Item four).

CHN ¶35-102   TAXABLE ACTIVITIES AND UNDERTAKINGS

Income taxes are levied on production and business operations income from dividends and interest, income from the release or transfer of tangible property, trademark rights, copyright and other property and income of those who have invested but have set up no establishment in China, including dividend, interest, income from leases and royalties.

CHN ¶35-103   DETAILS OF TAX ON COMPANIES

China's corporate income tax rate is at 33%. The *Provisional Regulations on Enterprise Income Tax* governs domestic enterprises whereas the *Income Tax Law for Enterprises with Foreign Investment and Foreign Enterprises* (''Unified Tax Law'') applies to all foreign investment enterprises and foreign companies.

Firms operating in Special Economic Zones pay a lower corporate income tax rate (see CHN ¶35-501).

CHN ¶35-102

The *Provisional Rules of the People's Republic of China on Business Tax* has imposed business tax on a range of services. The tax is imposed on all individuals and entities which provide taxable labour services, assign intangible assets or sell immovable property within China. Services affected include transportation, construction, finance, insurance, postal and telecommunication services and entertainment.

The tax rate varies from 3% to 20% depending on the type of service. The highest rate applies in the entertainment area. Transportation, construction and postal telecommunications businesses will be taxed at 3%. Finance and insurance companies, service enterprises and those involved in the sale of fixed assets and intellectual property rights will be taxed at 5%.

If the turnover of a taxpayer does not reach the taxable threshold specified by the Ministry of Finance, tax will not be payable. Additionally, the following services are tax exempt: educational and nursing services; medical services; services rendered by students to pay for their education; various agricultural services, income from the sale of tickets for cultural activities staged, art galleries and other cultural centres.

The State Administration of Taxation's *Decree on Taxation of Enterprise Income Tax for Foreign Investment Enterprises* was issued on 14 April 1999, clarifying the taxation on the failure in making timely capital injection by foreign investors of foreign investment enterprises. The Decree defines the capital commitment of foreign investors, failure in making timely capital injection and stipulates that the State Administration of Taxation shall, with reference to each particular case of such failure, determine the applicable taxation policy and taxation criteria.

On 28 September 2002, the State Administration of Taxation issued the *Notice of State Administration of Taxation on Issues Relating to Taxation Treatment for Services Provided by Foreign Investment Companies to their Subsidiaries*. It provides that the charges and fees for services that a foreign investment company with an investment nature provides to its subsidiaries shall conform to an amount normally charged for arm's length transactions (Item one). The foreign investment company and its subsidiary shall execute a detailed service contract and income the investment company gains in providing the service shall be reported as taxable income (Item two). A foreign investment company with an investment nature cannot claim office expenses, management salaries and other investment costs that it incurs when it invests in its subsidiary as tax deductions for operational expenses or losses (Item four). When the foreign investment company executes a contract for the provision of services to itself and the subsidiary by another independent company, costs collected from the subsidiary that were covered by the foreign investment company shall not be counted as taxable income for business (Item five). A foreign investment company with an investment nature shall not collect management costs from its subsidiaries or share management costs in any form (Item six).

On 30 December 2002, the Ministry of Foreign Trade and Economic Cooperation (MOFTEC), the State Administration of Taxation, the State Administration for Industry and Commerce (SAIC) and the State Administration of Foreign Exchange (SAFE) jointly issued the *Notice on Issues Relevant to Strengthening the Administration of the Examination, Approval, Registration, Foreign Exchange Issues and Taxation of Foreign Investment Enterprises* which became effective on 1 January 2003. The Notice clarifies issues concerning the examination and approval, taxation policies and capital payment of foreign-invested enterprises where the ratio of the foreign investor's capital contribution accounts for less than 25%. The Notice also covers issues concerning acquisition of equity interests in domestic enterprises by foreign investors.

On April 18 2003, the State Administration of Taxation issued the Enterprise Tax Treatment Issues Concerning Foreign-Invested Enterprises in which the Proportion of Foreign Investor Contribution is Less Than 25% Circular. The Circular clarifies that unless the State Council provided otherwise the applicable taxation system and tax registration of enterprises with less than 25% foreign contribution shall follow those of domestic enterprises and such enterprises shall not enjoy tax treatment as foreign invested enterprises.

On 7 January 2003, the State Administration of Taxation issued the *Notice on Tax Issues Relating to Engagement in the Business of Financial Asset Disposal by Foreign Investment Enterprises and Foreign Enterprises*. The Notice defines ''business of disposing of financial assets'' as an enterprise's acquisition of equity, claims, physical assets or the entire assets (comprising a combination of the aforementioned assets) of another enterprise in China (Replacement Assets) from a financial asset management company in China (such acquisition being achieved by means of purchase of such assets; by means of receiving an injection of such assets in exchange for equity; or by other means), followed by the disposal of such Replacement Assets by way of assignment, recovery, replacement or sale, etc and the obtaining of corresponding remuneration thereof.

When an enterprise obtains Replacement Assets, the price actually paid at the time of purchase thereof, or the value appraised at the time of injection thereof in exchange for equity, shall be the original value. The classification of Replacement Assets shall depend on the subject matter of evaluation at the time the assets were obtained. The said subject matter may be a single asset in the form of an individually evaluated equity holding in, claim against or physical asset of an enterprise, or be a bundle of several assets evaluated collectively.

If an enterprise reclassifies or rebundles some or all of the Replacement Assets it has acquired, it may determine the original value of a single Replacement Asset or a bundle of Replacement Assets on the basis of the reclassification or rebundling, provided that the original value of the reclassified or rebundled Replacement Asset(s) does/do not exceed the original value of the Replacement Asset(s) at the time they were acquired by the enterprise.

Business tax and value-added tax on Replacement Assets disposed of by an enterprise shall be levied or exempted in accordance with the following provisions:

(1) business tax shall not be levied on the disposal of Replacement Assets that were in the form of claims;

(2) revenue derived from the disposal of Replacement Assets that were in the form of equity (including disposals by way of debt for equity swaps) shall not be subject to business tax; and

(3) revenue derived from the disposal of physical Replacement Assets owned by the enterprise shall be subject to business tax if such assets are immovables; if such

assets are goods, the revenue shall be subject to value-added tax in accordance with the *Value-added Tax Regulations* and the relevant provisions.

On 28 May 2003, State Administration of Taxation issued Tax Issues Relevant to Acquisition of Equity Interest in Domestic Enterprises by Foreign Investors Circular to clarify several transition issues concerning enterprise income tax preferential treatment for foreign-invested enterprises established after acquisition of equity interests in domestic enterprises by foreign investors. The operation period of such foreign-invested enterprises shall start from the date of the business license issuance of the restructured foreign-invested enterprise and end at the date prescribed in the industrial and commerce registration for the restructured foreign-invested enterprise. The profit-making year of the restructured foreign-invested enterprise shall be the year that it is being restructured and remains profitable after the deduction of the losses of previous years allowed to be made up. The enterprise may decide which year to start tax reduction and exemption in case the actual production and operation period of the profit-making year is less than six months.

The enterprise income tax shall be calculated and paid on the net gain derived by an enterprise from the disposal of Replacement Assets, the net gain being the revenue derived less the original value of, expenses related to, and loss in respect of the assets. If an enterprise disposes of Replacement Assets in stages or in batches, once the revenue it derives from the disposal of the assets exceeds the original value of the relevant single Replacement Asset or the bundled Replacement Assets, it shall enter that portion exceeding the original value as taxable income for that period and calculate and pay enterprise income tax thereon. A loss incurred by an enterprise in disposing of a single Replacement Asset or a bundle of Replacement Assets may be deducted from the enterprise's taxable income for the relevant period. A loss on bundled assets may only be calculated after the entire bundle has been completely disposed of.

A foreign enterprise with no establishment or site in China shall file returns and pay its taxes itself or cause them to be filed and paid by an agent in China appointed by it. It may opt to pay its payable enterprise income tax in the place where the enterprise to which a Replacement Asset belongs is located. The place of payment of its payable business tax or value-added tax shall be determined in accordance with relevant provisions.

On 23 January 2003, the State Administration of Taxation issued the *Income Tax Treatment of Enterprise Debt Restructuring Procedures* which became effective on 1 March 2003. Debt restructuring may include discharge of a debt with an amount of cash that is less than the amount of the taxable cost of debt, with a non-cash asset, through conversion of the debt into capital, other modification of the terms of the debt or any combination of the above methods (Art 3). Generally, the difference between the taxable cost of the debt being restructured and the amount of cash paid or the fair value of the non-cash asset transferred in discharging the debt shall be credited to the taxable income of the debtor as a current debt restructuring gain and debited against the taxable income of the creditor as a current debt restructuring loss (Art 6).

Where a debt restructuring is between two affiliated parties and involves a transfer of profits, such transfer may also be treated as provided in Art 4 to 8 of the Procedures if it is agreed in a court judgment or among all creditors or is part of an approved debt-equity swap of a state-owned enterprise (Art 9). Otherwise, the concessions made by one affiliate to another in a debt restructuring shall be treated as donation and shall not be recognised by the creditor as a debt restructuring loss (Art 10). The Procedures also provide that if the debt restructuring gain so determined is large and results in an amount of income tax difficult to pay in a lump sum, the income tax may be amortised over no more than five years subject to approval of the competent tax authority (Art 8).

Accounting requirements

Prescribed requirements for keeping books, accounts and supporting documents are general in nature although currently subject to review by relevant authorities. Regulations governing foreign-invested enterprises encompass aspects of fiscal affairs including the employment of a treasurer, the fiscal year to be adopted, the need to appoint an auditor and the use of both the accruals basis and double entry accounting. There is a general requirement to keep accounting books and to file statements with the fiscal and taxation authorities. Failure to comply results in the imposition of fines.

On 6 May 1999, the People's Bank of China (PBOC) promulgated the *Guiding Opinion on External Audit of Foreign Capitalised Banks* (the ''Guiding Opinion'') under which the following items are covered:

- principles for foreign capitalised banks to retain certified public accountants (CPA);
- qualifications of a firm of CPA engaged in the external audit of a foreign capitalised bank;
- the control on CPA's work and the appraisal on the quality thereof;
- content and scope of the audit (including assets, liabilities, loss and profits as well as asset quality of a foreign capitalised bank, financial statements submitted by a foreign capitalised bank to PBOC, internal control system as well as computer and information administration system of a foreign capitalised bank, etc);
- training of CPA; and
- audit report and suggestion on administration.

Accounts to be submitted

The accounts required to be submitted to revenue authorities will vary according to the type of investment. However, China's law for joint venture accounting systems may be employed as a model for other foreign-invested projects. The underlying principles of reporting remain the same although the stipulation in the accounting system of joint ventures can be contrasted with those for cooperative enterprises and other foreign business structures.

The principles prescribed in the accounting system for Chinese foreign joint ventures are as follows:

- Legality.
- Authenticity, correctness, completeness and timeliness.
- Consistency in methods adopted for accounting in various periods, changes having to be registered with local tax authorities for reference along with explanatory memoranda.

- Income received and expenses incurred in a period must be entered into records for that period.
- Valuations must be made in accordance with actual cost such that book value should not be adjusted irrespective of whether there is a change in the market price.
- Income and expenses must be coordinated so that income and related costs and expenses in a given period are entered into account books in the same period.
- Capital expenditure and profit expenditure must be distinguished.
- The accounting year begins on 1 January and ends on 31 December.
- Double entry records must be maintained for the borrowing or lending of money.
- All certificates, account books and report forms must be prepared in Chinese.
- The Chinese currency RMB is the standard currency for keeping accounts although this may be varied by negotiation.

Certification by auditors

Accounting statements submitted must enclose audit certificates of chartered public accountants registered in the People's Republic of China.

Registration requirements

Foreign enterprises are required to present relevant certificates to local tax authorities for tax registration when they go into operation.

The *Administrative Provisions on Tax Registration* became effective as of 1 July 1998. The Provisions are formulated in accordance with the *Administrative Provisions on Tax Collection of the PRC* and its implementation rules. According to the Provisions, all kinds of taxpayers and withholding agents shall declare and register with the proper taxation authority. The procedures that either taxpayers and withholding agents or the taxation authorities shall observe are as follows:

Opening business registration

Within 30 days after the taxpayers' business licence or for those without business licence upon becoming taxpayers in the light of tax laws and regulations, taxpayers shall apply to the proper taxation authority for tax registration with documents demanded and complete the registration forms. The result of the examination will be released within 30 days after the tax authority accepts the demanded documents and forms.

Registration of change

Within 30 days after a business licence has been changed or the change of tax registration has been approved or declared by relevant authorities, the taxpayer shall apply to the original tax registration authority for change of tax registration with demanded documents and complete the Tax Change Registration Form.

Closing temporarily and re-opening business registration

In the case that taxpayers need to temporarily stop doing business, the closing business registration is required. Before re-opening business, taxpayers shall apply to taxation authorities for re-opening business registration.

Cancelling registration

In the event of dissolution, bankruptcy, cancellation and other events, or in the event of changing business place which causes the change of tax registration authority, taxpayers shall apply to original tax authority to cancel its tax registration before the cancellation of business licence. In the event that the cancellation of business licence is not required by relevant rules, or in the case that the business licence is revoked, taxpayers shall apply to cancel its tax registration within 15 days after its termination is approved or declared by relevant authorities or after revoking of its business license.

Registration for doing business beyond the area where tax registration authority is located

When they need to do business beyond the area where the tax registration authority is located, taxpayers shall apply for the Certificate of Tax Administration on Doing Business Outside whose term is 30 days for sales of goods or one year for construction project. After the transaction is completed, taxpayers shall complete Declaration Form for Doing Business Outside and be levied relevant taxes by the taxation authority locating in the area where the taxpayers do business. Within 10 days after the expiration of the Certificate of Tax Administration on Doing Business Outside, taxpayers shall hand it to the original taxation authority.

Registration examination

Taxation authorities examine the tax registration annually. Tax registration certificates have to be changed every three years.

Extraordinary taxpayers treatment

If a registered taxpayer does not declare tax to the taxation authority for three months in succession and does not make correction before the deadline announced by the taxation authorities, he may be treated as an extraordinary taxpayer and his tax registration may be cancelled one year later.

Penalties

The *Administration Provisions on Tax Collection of the PRC* applies.

On 1 January 1999, the *Provisions on Appraisal and Decision on Tax Declaration of Foreign-funded Enterprises, Foreign Enterprises and Aliens* (the ''Provisions'') became effective.

The Provisions are made in accordance with the *Administrative Law on Tax Collection of the PRC*, its Implementing Rules and *Supplementary Opinion on Promoting the Reform of Collection of Foreign-related Taxes* to strengthen the supervision of taxation on foreign-funded enterprises, foreign entities and aliens.

The Provisions cover principles on the scope, items, deadline and procedure of the appraisal and decision on tax declaration of foreign-funded enterprises, foreign entities and aliens. The implementation rules and detailed tax items are to be formulated by local taxation authorities according to the Provisions.

On December 17 2003, the State Administration of Taxation promulgated the Administration of Tax Registration Procedures. The Procedures exclude state authorities, individuals and mobile small rural merchants from requirements for tax registration as specified in Article 2. The Procedures also clarifies the use of unified tax registration code for each taxpayer, temporary tax registration and dispute resolution among tax authorities.

Tax base

The taxable income of the foreign enterprise is the net income in a tax year after deduction of costs, expenses and losses in that year.

Depreciation allowances

Depreciation allowances are allowed in respect of existing stock, fixed assets and intangibles.

Plant and equipment whose service is above one year and whose per unit value is above RMB500 may be depreciated with regard to the service life of the asset with the shorter service life of machinery, equipment and other production equipment being 10 years. Scrap value is at 10% of the value of the asset. The speeding up of the depreciation process and changes to calculation of depreciation methods must be reported to tax authorities for examination and approval.

Buildings with a service life of more than one year have, for the purposes of depreciation, a shortest service life of 20 years.

Treatment of losses

Foreign enterprises and joint venture participants may carry over to the next year a loss incurred in a tax year so that it is made up with a matching amount drawn from that year's income. Should the income in the subsequent tax year be insufficient to make up for the said loss, the balance may be made up with further deductions from income year by year over a period not exceeding five years.

Currently, there is no provision for carry back of losses and credits.

Time for payment

Joint venture enterprises have tax levied on an annual basis and must pay the tax in quarterly instalments within 15 days after the end of each quarter. Final settlement is made within five months after the end of a tax year. Provisional income tax returns must be filed with local tax authorities within the period prescribed for provisional payments and a final annual income tax return and final accounts must be filed within four months after the end of the tax year. Failure to pay within the prescribed time will result in a surcharge for overdue payments at 0.5% of the overdue tax for every day in arrears beginning from the first day of default.

Foreign enterprises, similarly, make quarterly instalments of provisional payments within 15 days of the end of each quarter. Final settlement is made within five months after the end of the tax year. Enterprise taxpayers must file final annual income tax returns and final accounts within four months after the end of the tax year. Although the tax year for foreign enterprises begins on 1 January and ends on 31 December, where foreign enterprises find it difficult to compute income on that basis, they may apply to local tax authorities for approval to use their own 12-month fiscal year for tax computation and payment.

Withholding tax and fringe benefits

For individual income tax, the paying unit may be the withholding agent, or where taxpayers are not covered by withholding, they must personally file declarations as to their income and pay tax themselves. All entities or natural persons who pay individuals taxable income are withholding agents, and are obligated to withhold and pay to the tax authority the individual income tax. The monthly remuneration of Chinese employees are to be withheld for individual income tax chargeable on remuneration in excess of RMB800 at graduated rates which vary from 5% to 45%. A commission fee of 3% of the tax withheld will be paid to the foreign representative office. Fringe benefits are not taxed as such. However, enterprises are subject to a reasonable ceiling figure for allowable deductions.

Withholding agents and individual taxpayers must lodge returns within seven days after the end of each month. A fine of up to RMB5,000 may be imposed for non-compliance of the withholding tax requirements.

Constructive ownership

The relevant taxes do not specifically provide for constructive ownership.

Undistributed profits

A participant in a joint venture which reinvests its share of profit in China for a period of not less than five years may, on approval of the tax authorities, obtain a refund of 40% of the income tax and paid on the reinvested amount.

Thin capitalisation

Although a maximum foreign debt to foreign equity ratio is not specified under the relevant tax laws and interest deductions will, in theory, not be denied on excess in-house debt, the funding of the foreign investment that is excessively geared up with in-house interest bearing foreign loans instead of being provided with appropriate equity funding in the form of capital will be unlikely to gain the requisite authority for registration. It should be noted that legitimate deductions for interest will only be allowed on those loans deemed to be ''normal loans''.

CHN ¶35-104   DETAILS OF BUSINESS PROFITS TAX

For business enterprises, different rules will apply according to whether the enterprise has an establishment in China or whether it merely derives income of various kinds from Chinese sources.

Dividends paid from or representing profits shared with enterprises in China are treated as derived from a Chinese source. Different considerations will be applied on dividends paid by joint venture corporations and dividends paid by non-Chinese corporations having China-sourced income. Tax is paid on interest on deposits, loans and securities and the like.

Exemptions are available to foreign banks lending to certain Chinese enterprises. Royalties or licence fees for the use of patents and other intellectual property are subject to withholding tax. Moreover, fees for technical training, technical services and documentation provided by a foreign company to an enterprise in China may fall within this category of income.

Rules applying to foreign enterprises with an establishment in China, including business organisations, business agents engaged in production or business operations, management organisations, branches and representative offices as well as factories and construction sites pay varying range of tax. The calendar year is the basis of the accounting period. A double entry accrual system in the official currency must be used.

Also see CHN ¶35-101 and CHN ¶35-103.

CHN ¶35-105   TAXATION OF EXECUTIVES

The taxation of executives is governed by the *Individual Income Tax Law 1980*, revised with effect from 1 January 1994. The *Individual Income Tax Law* is supplemented by the *Detailed Rules for the Implementation of the Individual Income Tax Law of the People's Republic of China*. These rules are also supplemented by various other administrative rulings of the Ministry of Finance and practices of local tax bureaus which, although not codified, do have the force of law. The *Temporary Provisions on Administration of Taxation of Individual Incomes Obtained outside China* (the "Temporary Provisions") has been issued on 12 August 1998 by the General Administration of Taxation and took effect from 1 July 1998. The Temporary Provisions applies to individual taxpayers who reside in China and derive incomes outside China. It stipulates the taxable incomes in cash, in kind and negotiable securities obtained outside China through five channels as well as taxation procedure and calculation method.

Different tax treatment

The principal criteria for determining when an individual is subject to tax in China are residence and source.

The law provides for different tax treatment depending on whether an individual is a resident or a non-resident. Residents of countries which have concluded with China an effective treaty for the avoidance of double taxation are subject to different rules regarding residence and source than residents of countries which have not concluded a treaty.

Residents for less than one year

Once an individual is registered with the PRC authorities as a resident, they will be taxed as a resident from the time they are deemed to have commenced their residency. Individuals who are residents of China for less than a year are subject to tax on income "gained within China". Tax treatment for individuals under this category depend on whether they reside in a country which has a double taxation treaty with China.

Residents for one year or more

Individuals who reside in China for "one year or more" are subject to tax on all of their income, whether such income is gained within or outside China. There are two exceptions to this rule.

First, if an individual resides in China for one year or more, but not more than five years, income gained outside China will be subject to tax in China only if it is remitted to China. All income earned by an individual residing in China for more than five years is subject to tax, regardless of whether such income is gained within or outside China and regardless of whether non-China source income is remitted to China.

The second exception is contained in a 1983 document issued by the Ministry of Finance which amends the statutory rule and exception with regard to the treatment of non-China source income earned by residents of China for one year or more. The document provides that such income will not be subject to tax in China, even if it is remitted to China and if the individual's presence in China is attributable to his employment by a joint venture and it is not his general intention to take up a long-term residency in China.

In calculating the taxable income of an individual, a monthly deduction of RMB800 is allowed. The rates of income tax are based upon a progressive scale ranging from 5% for income within the range RMB501 to RMB2,000 to 45% on income above RMB100,000.

Foreigners who are liable to individual income tax must register with local tax authorities and submit a taxation declaration form and pay tax within seven days after the end of each calendar month.

INVESTMENT PROFITS

Taxes on investment
   profits .... CHN ¶35-201

Tax credits .... CHN ¶35-202

Treatment of residents and non-
   residents .... CHN ¶35-203

Approval of outward
   remittances .... CHN ¶35-204

Form of outward
   remittances .... CHN ¶35-205

Meaning of "royalty" .... CHN ¶35-211

Must tax be deducted from
   investment profits? .... CHN ¶35-212

CHN ¶35-201   TAXES ON INVESTMENT PROFITS

See CHN ¶35-102 and following.

CHN ¶35-202   TAX CREDITS

The tax refunds available to foreign investors for funds reinvested in other foreign investment enterprises have been clarified in a couple of notices issued by the State Bureau of Taxation. The notices stipulate that to be eligible for a tax refund, a foreign investor which reinvests its profits in an existing enterprise must invest in an enterprise which has at least five years of its period of operations remaining. It has been clear that the reinvestment does not necessarily have to be made to a new FIE, it may also be reinvested in another existing FIE. The phrase "operate for a period of not less than five years" in Art 10 of the *Income Tax Law* refers to a period from the time the profits are reinvested. Tax refund is also available in the case of capital increase by using the FIE's enterprise expansion fund or reserve fund which have been allocated from profits after enterprise income tax in accordance with relevant regulations.

It is also stated that tax refunds are not available when a foreign investor reinvests income gained from the liquidation of a foreign investment enterprise.

In some circumstances, a foreign investor may have to repay 60% of the tax refunded. Repayment of the refund is required if:

- an enterprise fails to meet the standards for an export enterprise within three years from the time the reinvested profits are contributed; or

- the enterprise has its status as a technologically advanced enterprise cancelled within three years from the time the reinvested profits are contributed.

Franking rebates are not applicable in the PRC.

Refund for turnover taxes

On 1 January 1994, three turnover taxes came into effect — the value-added tax (VAT), business tax and consumption tax. The NPC issued a provision as part of the NPC Standing Committee, *Applicability of the VAT, Consumption Tax and Business Tax Tentative Regulations to Foreign Investment Enterprises Decision* of 29 December 1993.

This deals with foreign investment enterprises previously paying consolidated industrial and commercial tax (CICT) and now paying VAT, business tax and consumption tax.

The provision states that where the tax burden of the FIEs established before 31 December 1993 would increase due to the introduction of VAT, business tax and consumption tax, such enterprises may, upon application to and with the approval of the tax authorities, obtain a refund on the excess taxes paid. The deadline of this provision is five years, ie 31 December 1998.

CHN ¶35-203 TREATMENT OF RESIDENTS AND NON-RESIDENTS

Significant tax differentials exist between companies controlled or owned by non-residents and companies controlled or owned by residents. While legal person registration in the People's Republic of China in theory entitles one to equal treatment under the law, in practice foreign-invested enterprises are subject to a much stricter code of accountability than their state enterprise counterparts. The nature of the mandatory plan for state enterprises has meant in the past that those organisations have not had to concern themselves with taxation in the commonly accepted sense. Being subject to arbitrary direction from the central government and being instructed to engage in production according to the plan, profit and loss is not of fundamental importance. While the introduction of bankruptcy legislation pertaining to state enterprises has stimulated a re-evaluation of methods of accounting, state budgets consistently provide subsidisation under the plan for uneconomical productive units. Foreign investment enterprises operate in an environment distinct from the plan, although subject to it. The growth of taxation regulation and control in the People's Republic of China as it impacts on business operations is directly attributable to the emergence of foreign finance. It is, therefore, fair to say that while resident business groups under the immediate umbrella of the state enjoy a perpetual tax holiday except where they engage in offshore activity, foreign interests are subject to the close attention of taxation authorities and cannot expect to operate in the tax-free vacuum arising as a consequence of the centrally planned economy.

See also CHN ¶35-105.

CHN ¶35-204 APPROVAL OF OUTWARD REMITTANCES

See CHN ¶35-103.

CHN ¶35-205 FORM OF OUTWARD REMITTANCES

See CHN ¶35-103.

CHN ¶35-211 MEANING OF "ROYALTY"

Royalty income is received from licensing and assigning such rights as patents, copyrights, rights to proprietary technology and other similar rights.

On 26 August 2002, the State Administration of Taxation issued the *Circular on Questions Pertaining to Consumption Tax Policies on Liquor Products*. The Circular

CHN ¶35-203

stipulates that the tax authority may re-assess the taxable income for consumption tax of a liquor producer if the liquor producer is found to have transactions with its affiliates that were not conducted at arm's length in terms of price. The re-assessment may be based on the price of the same or a similar transaction conducted on an arm's length basis (sec 1). The Circular also states that the tax rate applicable to cereal-based white spirits applies to white spirits for which the ingredients cannot be determined clearly (sec 2). "Brand royalty" received by liquor producers from purchasers shall be deemed part of the sales revenue and subject to consumption tax (sec 3).

CHN ¶35-212 MUST TAX BE DEDUCTED FROM INVESTMENT PROFITS?

No.

MISCELLANEOUS TAXES

Miscellaneous taxes .... CHN ¶35-301   Unitary tax .... CHN ¶35-302

CHN ¶35-301 MISCELLANEOUS TAXES

Value-added tax (VAT)

VAT applies to all enterprises (both foreign and domestic) operating in the PRC. The VAT replaces the CICT and other indirect taxes, including the product tax.

VAT must be paid whenever goods and "taxable services" are sold or imported. The tax must be paid on the value added to goods and taxable services at the various stages of the production process — from importation to retail. A flat VAT rate of 17% applies to most goods and services, although a lower rate of 13% applies to items such as cereals, air-conditioning, heaters, books, farm machinery and other goods specified by the State Council. Small enterprises are only liable for 6%.

A range of goods exempt from VAT include contraceptive drugs, second-hand goods, agricultural products produced and sold, products imported for the handicapped, products imported as free economic aid from foreign governments and equipment used for scientific research and teaching.

In addition, a new policy effective from 1 January 1998 exempts payment of VAT on the import of capital goods for encouraged foreign investment enterprises, except where other prohibitions or restrictions apply (see CHN ¶45-102 for list of "encouraged" enterprises). Foreign investment enterprises approved to be established before 31 March 1996 will continue to enjoy exemption from VAT until the import of their capital goods is completed, up to the level of their originally approved total investment. Projects approved from 1 April 1996 to 31 December 1997 involving the import of equipment pursuant to foreign government loans and international financial institution loans will also enjoy VAT exemptions, subject to prohibitions by law. VAT is collected by tax authorities, except for VAT on imports which is collected by Customs. Payment periods are determined by the local tax authorities based on the amount payable and can range from one day to one month whereas VAT on imported goods must be paid within seven days from the date of the statement.

In contrast to the VAT systems of most developed countries, the input tax on exported goods in China was not fully refunded. To boost exports, with effect from 1 July 1999, the rate of input tax refund has been increased from 13% to 17% for exported goods.

The input tax credit may be claimed by completing a declaration form for the goods exported. The date when the declaration form is issued determines whether the new rate applies.

The State Administration of Taxation's *Decree Regarding the Taxation on the Sale of Exhibits by Foreign Entities* was issued on 26 April 1999, stating that the sales of exhibits by foreign entities are subject to value-added tax and foreign enterprise income tax. The State Administration of Taxation explained in this Decree particularly the tax rate and determination of taxable income for value-added tax and foreign enterprise income tax on such sales.

Consumption tax

This tax is levied on the manufacturers, importers and subcontractors of the following items (mostly luxury items):

- tobacco and liquor;
- hair conditioners and cosmetics;
- expensive ornaments, pearls, jewels and jade;
- fireworks;
- petrol and diesel oil;
- motor vehicles, motor cycles and tyres.

Tax rates vary from 3% to 45% depending upon the type of product. Exports are generally exempt from this tax.

Prior to 1 July 1998, consumption tax on all tobacco products was 40%. With effect from 1 July 1998, consumption tax on cigarettes has been adjusted according to the quality of the product as follows:

- 50% on first class and imported cigarettes;
- 40% on second and third class cigarettes; and
- 25% on fourth and fifth class cigarettes and cigars.

The classification was subsequently modified by a supplementary notice issued on 6 July 1998, which divides cigarettes into the following classes instead of the above:

- Class A cigarettes (taxed at 50%) are those with a price exceeding RMB6,410 per 50,000 cigarettes;
- Class B cigarettes (taxed at 40%) are those priced between RMB2,137 and RMB6,410 per 50,000 cigarettes; and

CHN ¶35-301

- Class C cigarettes (taxed at 25%) are those priced under RMB2,137 per 50,000 cigarettes.

For existing brands of cigarettes, the prices before 30 June 1998 determine the class. For new price, the class is determined by the actual sales price. If prices fluctuate frequently, the average price will be used for tax purposes. Cigarettes without packaging and handmade cigarettes which are produced without the approval of the State Council are taxed at 50%.

The tax authorities are authorised to adjust prices for tobacco tax purposes.

On September 2002, the Ministry of Finance, the State Development Planning Commission, the State Economic and Trade Commission, MOFTEC, the General Administration of Customs and the State Administration of Taxation jointly issued the *Circular on Adjustment of Certain Preferential Import Tax Policies* which became effective on 1 October 2002. The relevant adjustment matters are as follows:

(1) Adjustment in respect of taxation policies applicable to relevant investment projects approved before 1 April 1996: Technology transformation projects, capital construction projects (including major construction projects) and foreign investment projects approved prior to 1 April 1996, including commodities imported within the remaining quota by projects that enjoy foreign investment policies and are funded with loans from foreign governments and international financial institutions, shall invariably be governed by the State Council's *Adjustment of Tax Policies on Imported Equipment Circular* (Guofa (1997) No. 37), ie equipment imported within the project quota or total investment for the project's own use shall be exempt from import customs duty and import-stage value-added tax, with the exception of commodities listed in the *Imported Commodities Not Exempt from Duty and Tax for Domestic Investment Projects Catalogue* and the *Imported Commodities Not Exempt from Duty and Tax for Foreign Investment Projects Catalogue*.

(2) Implementation procedures for the adjustment of policies applicable to the "Permitted Category of Foreign Investment Projects that Directly Export all its Products" (hereafter, the All-For-Export Project) as defined in the Foreign Investment Industrial Guidance Catalogue:

    (i) All equipment imported under an All-for-Export Project that is approved as of the implementation date of the policy adjustment shall invariably be subject to the levy of import duty and import-related value-added tax in accordance with the regulations. As of the date when the project is put into production, a joint verification team shall be formed by MOFTEC in conjunction with relevant departments to verify the direct export of products. The verification term shall be five years. Specific verification procedures shall be formulated by MOFTEC in conjunction with relevant departments. If exports are proven to be true after the verification, 20% of paid taxes shall be refunded each year, ie all paid taxes shall be refunded within five years; and, if exports are proven to be untrue, the taxes paid in the relevant year shall not be refunded and tax payments already refunded for the project shall be recovered together with legally prescribed penalties.

(ii) The tax-exemption policy shall still be applicable to an All-for-Export Project that is already approved before the implementation date of the policy adjustment and still needs to import equipment under such project, provided that the relevant department conducts an investigation in respect of the direct export of products within the five-year verification period commencing from the date when the project is put into production. For an All-for-Export Project that is approved before the implementation date of the policy adjustment and has completed its import of equipment, no verification shall be made of product exports prior to the implementation date of the policy adjustment and, in the remaining verification period after the implementation date of the policy adjustment, selective investigation will be conducted of product exports. Problems discovered in the investigation mentioned above shall be handled in accordance with the laws. Specific procedures shall be formulated by MOFTEC in conjunction with the relevant departments.

(iii) The procedures for refund of tax payments within five years in connection with equipment imported by newly approved All-for-Export Projects shall be in accordance with the *Tax Refund for Certain Imported Commodities Circular* (Caiyuzi (1994) No. 42) jointly issued by the Ministry of Finance, the State Economic and Trade Commission, the State Administration of Taxation and the General Administration of Customs.

On 17 December 2002, the State Administration of Taxation issued the *Circular on Tax Refund Issues Relating to Exported Goods Being Deemed to be Self-Produced Goods*. The Circular allows certain goods of a production enterprise that are:

(1) purchased from external sources;

(2) purchased from external sources and are to be exported as accessories of the enterprise's self-produced products to foreign investors that import the enterprise's self-produced products;

(3) purchased by its parent company; or

(4) entrusted to another enterprise for processing to be deemed to be self-produced products and enjoy tax refund or exemption if the stipulated conditions are simultaneously satisfied.

Land value-added tax

Land value-added tax arises whenever income is derived from the sale of land use rights, buildings and other structures on the land. Tax rates vary from 30% to 60%, depending upon the percentage gain on the value of the property. The sale of a non-luxury residential property is tax exempt provided the percentage gain on the sale of the property is not more than 20%.

Real estate tax

The real estate tax is imposed on owners of land and buildings in urban areas.

Vehicle and vessel license tax

The tax is a local tax levied on vehicles and vessels owned by individuals and enterprises in China. The tax is a kind of license fee which is imposed at the discretion of local authorities.

Stamp tax

The stamp tax is levied on certain types of documents — contracts, account books and other materials — executed and "used" in China. Tax rates vary depending on the nature of the document.

Unified foreign tax

The *Income Tax Law for Enterprises with Foreign Investment and Foreign Enterprises* applies to all foreign investment enterprises (equity joint ventures, cooperative joint ventures and wholly foreign-owned enterprises), as well as foreign companies. The unified foreign tax came into effect on 1 July 1991 and replaced the joint venture income tax and the foreign enterprise income tax.

On 22 January 2003, the Ministry of Finance issued the *Circular of State Administration of Taxation and General Administration of Customs on Issues Relating to the 29th Olympics Taxation Policy*, which became effective on the same day. Section 1 of the Circular relates to preferential tax policies applicable to the Organising Committee of the 29th Olympics. Part Two contains preferential tax policies enjoyed by the International Olympic Committee and other participants in the Olympics. Enterprises and social organisations can deduct the full amount of the funds or expenses on materials they donate or sponsor to the Olympics from taxable income (sec 2(4)). The International Olympic Committee and the Chinese Olympic Committee shall also be exempt from paying the stamp tax on any Olympics-related contracts they sign (sec 2(5)).

CHN ¶35-302   UNITARY TAX

Unitary taxes exist in the form of fixed amounts payable to local taxation authorities by reference to total taxation liability.

CAPITAL GAINS TAX

Method of taxing capital
   gains .... CHN ¶35-401

Roll-overs .... CHN ¶35-402

Offset of capital losses against
   revenue gains .... CHN ¶35-403

Offset of revenue losses against
   capital gains .... CHN ¶35-404

CHN ¶35-401   METHOD OF TAXING CAPITAL GAINS

Under the revisions to the *Individual Income Tax Law* which came into effect on 1 January 1994, all gains from the sale of exchange property is subject to a flat rate capital gains of 20%.

Land value appreciation tax

In 1995, China launched a capital gains tax on real estate investment to curb real estate speculation. Real estate agreements signed before 1 January 1994 are exempt from the tax regardless of when the actual transfer took place. New projects will be eligible for tax breaks. Projects approved by the government involving a large scale land development with longer construction terms can enjoy a tax exemption period longer than five years.

CHN ¶35-402   ROLL-OVERS

Not applicable.

CHN ¶35-403   OFFSET OF CAPITAL LOSSES AGAINST REVENUE GAINS

Not applicable.

CHN ¶35-404   OFFSET OF REVENUE LOSSES AGAINST CAPITAL GAINS

Not applicable.

TAX INCENTIVES

Tax relief for new
  industries .... CHN ¶35-501
Period of tax relief .... CHN ¶35-502
Criteria affecting relief ..... CHN ¶35-503
Existence and nature of export
  incentives .... CHN ¶35-504
Applicability of export
  allowances .... CHN ¶35-505
Industries excluded from export
  allowances .... CHN ¶35-511

Export processing zones ... CHN ¶35-512
Accelerated depreciation
  allowance .... CHN ¶35-513
Applicability of accelerated
  depreciation allowance   CHN ¶35-514
Deductibility of expenses
  incurred exploring export
  opportunities .... CHN ¶35-515

CHN ¶35-501   TAX RELIEF FOR NEW INDUSTRIES

The Chinese government has established a complex scheme of tax incentives for new industries. The incentives are as follows:

- Tax incentives available under the enterprise income tax laws.

- Tax incentives for know-how fees.

- Tax incentives for interest on loans.

- Tax incentives for leasing.

- Tax incentives for sino-foreign joint ventures engaging in port and harbour construction.

- Tax incentives for exploitation of offshore petroleum.

- Individual income tax reduction and exemption.

- Tax incentives for export enterprises and technologically advanced enterprises (see CHN ¶35-504).

- Tax incentives in the special economic zones (see CHN ¶45-112).

- Tax incentives in Hainan Island (see CHN ¶45-112).

- Tax incentives in the economic and technological development zones (see CHN ¶45-112).

- Tax incentives in the old city districts of the 14 coastal port cities and the delta regions (see CHN ¶45-112).

- Tax incentives for hi-tech industries.

- Tax exemptions and reductions in Beijing.

- Tax reductions in State-designated tourist and holiday zones.

These exemptions will now be discussed in detail except for measures dealing with export incentives which are discussed under CHN ¶35-504 and export processing zones which are discussed under CHN ¶35-512. However, on 29 November 1997, State Science and Technology Commission and seven other Departments issued a circular on the *Provisions Governing the Plan for State Major New Products*. New products mainly refer to hi-tech products and those products that are manufactured by using imported technology with the domestic production rate over 80%. New products do not include food, cosmetics, products manufactured with imported parts, products manufactured by using imported technology but with a below-60% domestic production rate, products only for military use, traditional art crafts, energy-consuming products that will affect environmental protection.

It should be noted that the PRC *Value-Added Tax Tentative Regulations* in conjunction with the PRC *Business Tax Tentative Regulations* replaced the CICT as the main turnover taxes affecting enterprises, including foreign investment enterprises in the PRC from 1 January 1994.

Tax incentives available under the enterprise income tax laws

A joint venture scheduled to operate for a period of 10 years or more may be exempted from income tax in the first and second profit-making years and allowed a 50% reduction in the third to fifth year.

Joint ventures engaged in low-profit operations such as agriculture and forestry or located in economically underdeveloped remote areas may be allowed a 15% to 30% reduction in income tax for a period of 10 years following the expiration of the term for exemption and reduction.

A participant in the joint venture which reinvests its share of profit for a period of not less than five years may obtain a refund of 40% of the income tax paid on the amount of reinvestment.

Reduction or exemption of the local income tax on account of special circumstances may be determined by the people's government of the province, municipality or autonomous region in which the joint venture is located.

Cooperative ventures and enterprises with foreign investment scheduled to operate for a period of 10 years or more in agriculture, forestry, animal husbandry or other low-profit industries (including deep well exploitation of coal resources) may submit application and obtain approval to exempt the enterprise from income tax in the first profit-making year and allow a 50% reduction in the second and third year.

With the approval of the Ministry of Finance, a 15% to 30% reduction in income tax may be granted to foreign enterprises for a period of 10 years following the expiration of the term for exemption and reduction in the preceding paragraph.

The depreciation periods for fixed assets of enterprises with foreign investment are classified into three categories and range from five to 20 years. In special circumstances, enterprises with foreign investment may apply for accelerated depreciation. Depreciation of various kinds of fixed assets resulting from the investment of enterprises engaging in exploitation of offshore petroleum resources, during and after the period of development, may be calculated by using the composite life method of a period of not less than six years. Exploration expenses incurred by foreign enterprises which are engaged in exploitation of offshore petroleum resources may be amortised against the revenues derived from any hydrocarbon fuel that has gone into commercial production over a period of not less than one year.

Reduction in or exemption from local income tax of small scale and low-profit foreign enterprises may be determined by the people's government of the province, municipality or autonomous region.

Issues Relevant to Preferential Tax Policy Enjoyed by "Two Intensive" Projects of Foreign-invested Enterprises Circular, which was issued on 7 November 2003 provides that if the main product of the "two intensive" project of a foreign-invested enterprise is listed under the High and New Technology Products State Catalogue and the sales revenue of the current year of such product exceeds 50% of the sales revenue of all the products of the enterprise in that year, the preferential tax policy stated in Article 73 of the *PRC Foreign-invested Enterprise* and Foreign Enterprise Income Tax Law Implementing Rules shall be applicable.

Tax holiday for follow-up foreign investment

The *Notice of the Ministry of Finance and the State Administration of Taxation on the Eligibility of Follow-Up Foreign-Invested Enterprise Investment for Preferential Enterprise Income Tax Policies* was issued on 1 June 2002. The Notice provides that if the investor of an existing FIE makes follow-up investment in the same FIE, the enterprise income derived from the follow-up investment projects that are not covered by the original contract will be eligible for independent fixed-period tax exemptions and reductions (typically the two-year exemption and three-year 50% reduction) if the foreign-invested enterprise is engaged in an Encouraged Category project and if one of the following conditions is met:

- the additional registered capital formed by the follow-up investment reaches or exceeds US$60 million; or
- the additional registered capital formed by the follow-up investment reaches or exceeds US$15 million, and it reaches or exceeds 50% of the enterprise's original registered capital.

Tax incentives for know-how fees

Foreign companies, enterprises and other economic organisations which do not have an establishment in China shall pay income tax at the reduced rate of 10% on know-how fees obtained from the provision of the following proprietary technology for use in China. Income tax may be exempted where the technologies are advanced or the terms are preferential:

- Fees received for providing proprietary technology in the development of agricultural, forestry, fishery and animal husbandry industries, including proprietary technology provided for the improvement of soil or green pasture; development of barren hills and for the full utilisation of natural conditions; proprietary technology provided for new breeds of animals and plants and for the production of highly effective, low toxic agricultural chemicals; and proprietary technology provided in such areas as the conduct of scientific management of agricultural, forestry, fishery and animal husbandry production, the maintenance of ecological balance and the enhancement of the ability to defend against natural disasters.

- Know-how fees received for proprietary technology for the conduct of scientific research or scientific experiments provided to China's academies of science, institutes of higher education and other scientific research units, or working in cooperation with China's scientific research units in the conduct of scientific research.

- Know-how fees received for proprietary technology provided to China's key construction projects and the development of energy and transportation.

- Know-how fees received for a proprietary technology provided in the areas of energy conservation, and the prevention and control of environmental pollution.

- Know-how fees for the following proprietary technology provided for the development of China's important technological spheres:

  — Technology for production of major advanced mechanical and electrical equipment.

  — Nuclear energy technology.

  — Technology for the production of large scale integrated circuits.

  — Technology for the production of optical integration, microwave semi-conductors, and microwave integrated circuits as well as technology for the manufacture of microwave electronic tubes.

  — Technology for the production of super-speed computers and microprocessors.

  — Technology for photoconductive communication.

  — Technology for long distance super-high pressure direct current transmission.

  — Technology for liquefication, gasification and comprehensive utilisation of coal.

Tax incentives for interest on loans

Interest income from loans provided to the Chinese government or to China's state banks by international financing organisations shall be exempted from income tax. Interest income from loans provided at a preferential interest rate by foreign banks to China's state banks shall also be exempted from income tax.

Interest income derived by foreign banks from deposits with China's state banks and from loans provided to China's state banks at normal interest rates shall be subject to income tax. However, reciprocal exemption from income tax shall be granted to those foreign banks which are from countries which exempt China's state banks from income tax on interest income from deposits and loans.

Income tax on interest derived from loans, advances and deferred payments provided under credit contracts or trade contracts signed before the end of 1995 by foreign companies, enterprises and other economic organisations with China's companies or enterprises may, during the effective period of the contract, be taxed at the reduced rate of 10%.

The Issues Concerning the Implementation Approach, etc. of Relevant Provisions on Income Tax Preferential Policies for Software Enterprses and High and New Technology

Enterprises Circular, issued by State Administration of Taxation on 29 May 2003, defines that newly run software production enterprises means to software production enterprises newly run after 1 July 2000; the first profit-making year of such enterprise refers to the first year the enterprise has taxable income after starting operation.

The following items of interest income may be exempted from income tax:

- Interest income from loans provided to China's state banks by foreign banks at international inter-bank offer rates. The stipulations in the preceding clause may also be applied to trust and investment companies which are authorised by the State Council to engage in foreign exchange business.

- Interest from loans to the China National Offshore Oil Corporation by foreign banks at interest rates not higher than the inter-bank offer rates.

- In the case of seller's credits provided by the foreign party's state bank for the import of technology, equipment and commodities by China's companies, enterprises or institutions, interest on deferred payments paid by the Chinese party to be received in turn by the seller at an interest rate not higher than that on the Chinese party's buyer credit.

- Interest received by foreign banks and individuals from deposits with China's state banks when the interest rate on such deposits is lower than the interest rate on deposits in the home country or the depositing bank of the depositor.

- In cases where equipment and technology are provided to China's companies or enterprises and in consideration, and the Chinese side uses such methods as buy-back or the delivery of products to repay the principal and interest, or uses the processing fees or assembly fees to offset the principal and interest.

Tax incentives for leasing

Income tax on leasing fees, after deducting the equipment price, obtained by foreign leasing companies from the supply of equipment and related articles to China's companies or enterprises through leasing arrangements entered into before the end of 1990 may, during the effective period of the contract, be paid at a reduced tax rate of 10%.

Where interest is included in leasing fees, if the loan agreement or contract and the documents and vouchers for the interest payment are sufficient to prove that the interest rate conforms to the seller's or buyer's credit interest rate, income tax shall be levied at the rate of 10% on the amount remaining after deduction of the interest.

Leasing fees obtained by foreign leasing companies through such methods as buy-back or the delivery of products may be exempt from income tax.

Tax incentives for sino-foreign joint ventures engaging in port and harbour construction

Income tax shall be levied on sino-foreign joint ventures engaged in port and harbour construction at a reduced rate of 15%. Where the joint venture is for a period of 15 years or more, the enterprise shall be exempt from income tax for the first five profit-making years and allowed a 50% reduction during the sixth to tenth years.

After the expiration of the tax reduction and exemption period which is provided for in the preceding paragraph, if the joint venture engaging in port and harbour construction still encounters difficulties in making tax payments, such tax exemption and reduction period may be appropriately extended with the approval of the Ministry of Finance.

Reduction or exemption from the local income tax of joint ventures engaging in port and harbour construction is subject to the approval of the people's government of the province, autonomous region or municipality where the joint venture is located.

When the foreign partners of the joint venture engaging in harbour construction remits abroad its share of profits obtained from the joint venture, such profits shall be exempt from income tax.

Tax incentives for exploitation of offshore petroleum

If a foreign enterprise engaged in the cooperative exploitation of offshore petroleum resources holds two contract areas, the loss incurred in one contract area, owing to the termination of operation or other causes, shall be allowed to be offset from the proceeds of the other contract area. The taxable income shall be computed by combining the results of the two contract areas.

In order to encourage sino-foreign cooperative exploration of offshore petroleum, the following imported goods for offshore operation shall be exempt from VAT:

• Machinery, equipment, spare parts and materials to be directly used in exploration or development.

• Parts, components and materials that are required to be imported for manufacturing machinery and equipment in China for the exploitation of offshore petroleum (including prospecting, well drilling, well cementing, well logging, oil extracting, work-over, etc).

• Machinery and other engineering equipment, temporarily imported for the exploitation of offshore petroleum and guaranteed to be re-exported by foreign contractors.

Local surtax shall be exempted when VAT is levied on the crude oil income derived from the sino-foreign cooperative exploitation of offshore petroleum.

Reasonable exploration expenses incurred by a foreign enterprise in a contract case, regardless of tangible or intangible costs, shall be capitalised and then amortised from the revenues derived from any oil (or gas) field within the same contract area that has gone into commercial production, but the time limit of such amortisation shall not be less than one year. Any subsequent exploration expenses incurred after the commencement of commercial production shall be accumulated on a yearly basis and amortised in a chronological order against the income of the following year, but the time limit of such amortisation of annual exploration expenses shall not be less than one year.

For enterprises which are engaged in the exploitation of offshore petroleum resources, all investments at the development period shall be counted as capital expenditure with an oil (or gas) field as a unit, and depreciation shall be calculated from the month when the oil (or gas) field begins commercial production. But the time limit of such depreciation shall not be less than six years.

Tax incentives for the software and integrated circuit industries

The *Certain Policies on the Encouragement of Development of the Software and Integrated Circuit Industries*, issued by the State Council in 2000, provides for various tax incentives for the development of these industries. Enterprises are now entitled to a VAT refund for the VAT paid on the sale of self-developed or localised software products in excess of 3% until the year 2009. Newly established software enterprises are also entitled to the two-year exemption and three-year 50% reduction of their enterprise income tax as from their first profitable year, which previously was available to certain foreign-invested enterprises only. Further, if identified as a "key software industry" by the competent government authorities, a software enterprise may be levied the enterprise income tax at a reduced rate of 10%.

Tax incentives for the development of western areas of China

Inspired by political as well as economic considerations, Chinese government officially launched the significant, ambitious project of Great Development of Western Areas (of China) in early 2000. Tax incentives were introduced in the *State Council Notice Concerning Several Policies and Measures for the Implementation of the Development of Western Areas* effective 1 January 2001. Among them are:

- domestic and foreign-funded enterprises in those industries encouraged by the State will be entitled to a reduced enterprise income tax rate of 15%;

- enterprises in minority groups autonomous areas will be granted tax reduction or exemption subject to approval by the government at the provincial level;

- enterprises engaged in transportation, power, water control and conservancy, post, radio and television sectors will be entitled to the two-year exemption and three-year 50% reduction of their enterprise income tax; and

- imports of advanced technologies and equipment to be used in the encouraged domestic or foreign funded projects or in the "advantageous projects in the western areas" will generally be exempt from customs duties and import VAT.

Individual income tax reduction and exemption

For wage and salary income derived by foreign personnel working in sino-foreign joint ventures, sino-foreign cooperative ventures and foreign investment enterprises in China, foreign personnel working in the resident offices of foreign companies, enterprises and other economic organisations in China, and other foreign personnel working in China, the amount of individual income tax payable in accordance with the *Individual Income Tax Law* shall be reduced by 50%.

Non-China source investment income such as dividends, interests, etc received from outside China by foreign employees working in sino-foreign joint ventures or cooperative ventures, and foreign employees of foreign companies, enterprises, and other economic organisations working in China shall, regardless of whether the income is remitted into China, be exempted from individual income tax, provided that the employee has no intention of residing permanently in China and that the purpose of his/her being stationed in China for more than one year or over five years is merely to execute his/her duties and to fulfil his/her business assignments.

Interest received by individuals on savings deposits with state banks and credit cooperatives of the PRC including interest on renminbi (RMB) and foreign currency deposits shall be exempted from individual income tax.

On 30 September 1999, the *Implementation Rule for Collecting Individual Income Tax on Interest of Deposit* (the "Implementation Rule") was promulgated by the State Council and implemented since 1 November 1999. According to the Implementation Rule, individual income tax on the interest of deposit will be paid at the rate of 20%. The entity paying the deposit interest is withholder of such individual income tax and will be paid consequently service fee at the rate of 2%. The exceptions of the Implementation Rule are:

- deposit in designated bank for the purpose of education;
- particular deposit approved by the Financial Department of the State Council; and
- particular funds in the form of deposit.

Dividends received by individuals from investment in local Chinese construction (investment) companies which do not pay bonuses shall be exempted from individual income tax provided that the dividends are not higher than the interest on savings deposits with the state banks and credit cooperatives.

Prizes and awards given to individuals by the Chinese government or Chinese or foreign scientific, technological or cultural organisations for inventions or innovations in the fields of science, technology and culture shall be exempted from individual income tax.

For individuals from countries which do not have double tax agreements with China residing in China for a period of not more than 90 days in a calendar year or individuals from countries which have double tax agreements with China residing in China for a period of not more than 183 days in a calendar year, their wage and salary income received from employers outside China shall be exempted from individual income tax.

Hi-tech enterprises

Enterprises operating in any of China's hi-tech industry development zones may now be eligible for exemptions from import duty and product tax.

Import tax exemptions

Equipment which is necessary for a hi-tech industry project is now exempt from import duty and VAT. An import license may still be required, however, if the goods are already subject to import license control. Unauthorised transport of this equipment outside the development zone and the sale or lease of the goods are prohibited. Hi-tech enterprises may also import samples or prototypes for "dissections, investigations and experimentation" without attracting any import duty. The sale or assignment of these goods is similarly prohibited.

The State Council issued the *Notice Concerning Adjustment of the Tax Policies on the Import of Equipment* stating that, as from 1 January 1998, import of equipment for self-use for Encouraged or Restricted B foreign-funded projects involving transfer of technologies will be exempt from customs duties and import VAT, and import of equipment for self-use for those domestic funded projects that are particularly encouraged will also be exempt from customs duties and import VAT. Such exemption also extends to the technologies, accessory parts and components that are to be imported in association with the said equipment. Restrictions yet exist: such imports shall not go beyond the total amount of investment of the underlying project, and the equipment shall not fall on the lists of equipment that is not eligible for tax exemption.

Export duty exemptions on value-added products

Products manufactured within a development zone are exempt from customs export duty. However, products purchased from outside the development zone, which have not undergone "substantial processing", will attract export duty. Goods will be deemed to have undergone "substantial processing" if the value of the goods is increased by a minimum of 20%.

Exempt goods traded through special accounts

Special accounts must be established by enterprises receiving preferential tax treatment. All goods eligible for tax exemptions must be traded through these accounts. Customs authorities have the right to inspect these accounts and any other relevant information in their enforcement of these regulations.

Enterprises operating within a hi-tech industry development zone which is, in turn, located within an open port city, a special economic zone or an economic and technological development zone are not excluded from taking advantage of various preferential tax policies which may be in force in these areas.

The General Administration of Customs is responsible for interpreting these Measures. Violations are dealt with under the relevant provisions of the *Customs Law* of the People's Republic of China.

Tax exemptions and reductions in Beijing

"Product exporting" and "technologically advanced" foreign investment enterprises are exempt from paying local income tax, under provisional regulations issued by the Beijing Taxation Bureau (Art 2) (*Interim Regulations of Beijing Tax Bureau on the Reduction and Exemption of Local Income Tax for Foreign-Funded and Foreign Enterprises*). Enterprises which are verified as "high-technology enterprises" (and set up in specified areas) will also be exempt from local income tax.

Production type enterprises with operating terms of 10 or more years will enjoy this exemption for the first five profit-making years, and then pay half the prevailing rate for the next five years (Art 4). Exemptions from tax, under prescribed conditions, also apply to non-production type enterprises (Art 5).

Enterprises need to apply to the relevant taxation organs to enjoy a reduction or exemption from tax (Art 8).

Tax reductions in State-designated tourist and holiday zones

China has a number of preferential tax policies in place to promote tourism. These preferential policies, which include tax reductions and tax holidays, apply to foreign investment enterprises which are set up in State-designated tourist and holiday zones.

Foreign investment enterprises set up in a State tourist zone will have income tax levied at the reduced rate of 24%. A "production-type" foreign investment enterprise with an operational period of 10 years or more will be exempt from income tax for two years from its profit-making year. Additionally, income tax need only be paid at half the prevailing rate from the third to the fifth years.

CHN ¶35-502   PERIOD OF TAX RELIEF

The expiry date for tax concessions available to foreign companies on rental and interest income is at the end of 1995. Income tax is payable at a reduced rate of 10% on:

- interest derived from loans, advances and deferred payments provided under credit contracts or trade contracts signed before the end of 1995; and

- leasing fees, after deduction of the equipment price, obtained from foreign leasing companies from the supply of equipment and related articles to China's companies or enterprises through leasing arrangements entered into before the end of 1995.

It should be noted that the PRC *Value-Added Tax Tentative Regulations* in conjunction with the PRC *Business Tax Tentative Regulations* replaced the CICT as the main turnover taxes affecting enterprises, including foreign investment enterprises in the PRC from 1 January 1994.

CHN ¶35-503   CRITERIA AFFECTING RELIEF

Tax relief is usually given to certain industry types in a bid to attract investment into these industries and also to certain areas. For example, enterprises operating in any of China's hi-tech industry development zones may now be eligible for exemptions from import duty and product tax.

See also CHN ¶35-501.

CHN ¶35-504   EXISTENCE AND NATURE OF EXPORT INCENTIVES

After the period allowed for the reduction or exemption of enterprise income tax in accordance with the provisions of the state expires, export enterprises exporting 70% or more of their products, in value terms, in any particular year may pay their enterprise income tax at half of the existing tax rate for that year. If the resultant tax rate after the 50% reduction of enterprise income tax payable is below 10%, income tax shall be levied at the rate of 10%.

After the period allowed for reduction or exemption of enterprise income tax in accordance with the provisions of the state expires, technologically advanced enterprises may enjoy a three-year tax reduction period during which enterprise income tax shall be paid at half of the existing rate. Technologically advanced enterprises which do not qualify for such tax reduction or exemption may pay enterprise income tax at half of the existing rate in the first three profit-making years. If the resultant tax rate after the 50% reduction of enterprise income tax is below 10%, enterprise income tax shall be levied at the rate of 10%.

Profits remitted abroad by foreign investors of export enterprises and technologically advanced enterprises with Chinese and foreign investment shall be exempt from income tax.

Foreign investors who reinvest the profits distributed by the enterprise to establish or expand an export enterprise or a technologically advanced enterprise for a period of not less than five years shall receive a full refund of enterprise income tax already paid on the amount of reinvestment.

The payments are not made by way of allowance but by way of reduction in tax payable. The tax allowance is computed by reference to increases in exports, and qualifying export enterprises must export more than 70% of their products, in value terms.

CHN ¶35-505   APPLICABILITY OF EXPORT ALLOWANCES

Non-resident companies are eligible for these export allowances and specific provision is made for them as set out in CHN ¶35-504 above.

CHN ¶35-511   INDUSTRIES EXCLUDED FROM EXPORT ALLOWANCES

No exporting industries are excluded from the export allowances. The allowance is related to the volume of export.

CHN ¶35-512   EXPORT PROCESSING ZONES

One of the key elements in Chinese economic development has been the development of a variety of special economic zones for export processing purposes. The tax incentives available under these zones are as follows:

- Tax incentives in the special zones.
- Tax incentives in Hainan Island.
- Tax incentives in the economic and technological development zones.
- Tax incentives in the old port city districts of the 14 coastal port cities and the delta regions.

See CHN ¶45-112 for further details.

An international trade centre and export processing zone may soon be set up in China's northern province of Heilongjiang.

CHN ¶35-513   ACCELERATED DEPRECIATION ALLOWANCE

See CHN ¶35-103.

CHN ¶35-514　APPLICABILITY OF ACCELERATED DEPRECIATION ALLOWANCE

See CHN ¶35-103.

CHN ¶35-515　DEDUCTIBILITY OF EXPENSES INCURRED EXPLORING EXPORT OPPORTUNITIES

See CHN ¶35-501 and following.

Regulation of Business

Licensing and registration of business activities .... CHN ¶45-001

Granting and nature of licence or registration .... CHN ¶45-002

Incentive legislation .... CHN ¶45-003

Disincentives or restrictions on certain business
activities .... CHN ¶45-004

Special regulation of foreign investment .... CHN ¶45-101

Price and profit controls .... CHN ¶45-201

Unfair trading practices and consumer protection .... CHN ¶45-301

CHN ¶45-001 LICENSING AND REGISTRATION OF BUSINESS ACTIVITIES

All forms of business activities in China are regulated. There are a variety of categories of domestic entities which conduct business activities in China. These include:

- state-owned enterprises, most of which are those established prior to the adoption of the PRC *Company Law*, effective as of 1 July 1994;
- collectively-owned enterprises, most of which are village and township enterprises;
- privately-owned enterprises, organised under the PRC *Interim Regulations on Administration of Privately-Owned Enterprises*;
- individual-owned enterprises, organised under the PRC *Law on Individual-Owned Enterprises*;
- partnership enterprises, organised under the PRC *Partnership Enterprise Law*, effective as of 1 August 1997;
- joint-operation enterprises, organised pursuant to the *General Principles of the Civil Law of the PRC*, effective as of 1 January 1987;
- limited liability companies, organised under the PRC *Company Law*; and
- companies limited by shares, also organised under the PRC *Company Law*.

The conditions for a business to obtain the status of legal person are set out in the *General Principles of the Civil Law* at Chapter 3. Article 37 provides:

A legal person must satisfy the following conditions:
- be established in accordance with law;
- possess the necessary property or funds;
- possess its own name, organisation or structure and premises; and

- be able to bear civil liability independently.

The PRC *Law on Individual-Owned Enterprises* (the "IOE Law") was promulgated on 30 August 1999 and became effective on 1 January 2000. The IOE Law defines the individual-owned enterprise (IOE) as an operation entity established in the PRC with investment of a natural individual person and owned by the investor. The investor's liability is unlimited. In addition, the IOE Law provides:

- the conditions that an IOE should satisfy;
- the procedure for applying and registering an IOE;
- the conditions that the investor of an IOE should satisfy;
- the administration of an IOE;
- the dissolution and liquidation of an IOE; and
- the penalties on breach of the IOE Law.

Further, the IOE Law is not applicable to foreign wholly-owned enterprises.

The *Provisions on Administration of Registration of Individual-Owned Enterprises* (the "Provisions") was drafted pursuant to the PRC *Law on Individual-Owned Enterprises*. The Provisions were promulgated on 13 January 2000 and stipulate on the following issues:

- the State Administration of Industry and Commerce (SAIC) is the authority for the registration of individual capitalised enterprises;
- limitation on name of an individual-invested enterprise;
- procedure for the establishment, change and cancellation of an individual-invested enterprise;
- registration of branches of an individual-invested enterprise;
- administration of annual inspection and certificates renewal; and
- penalties on activities violating the Provisions.

Regulation of registration

SAIC at national, provincial and local levels is responsible for the administration of registration of various business activities.

Major legislation governing registration of business activities includes the following:

- the *Regulations of the PRC on Administration of Registration of Enterprise Legal Persons*, which governs registration of various enterprises with legal person status;
- the *Detailed Rules for the Implementation of the Regulations of the PRC on Administration of Registration of Enterprise Legal Persons*;
- the *Regulations of the PRC on Administration of Registration of Companies*, which governs registration of limited liability companies and companies limited by shares;
- the *Provisions on Several Issues Concerning Administration of Company Registration*; and

- the *Provisions on Administration of Registration of Enterprise Names*, which governs the registration of various enterprise names.

Companies applying to be established as a limited liability company are required to supply certain documents to the registration authority, which include the following:

- articles of association;

- a capital verification certificate; and

- a notice for advance approval and certification of the enterprise name.

For companies limited by shares, the documents required include the minutes of the founding meeting and a financial audit report. A company which intends to set up a branch office is required to register with the municipal or county registration authority in the place where the branch is located. It also needs to submit the following documents:

- an application to register the establishment of the branch office, signed by the legal representative of the company;

- the articles of association and a copy of the company's corporate business licence affixed with the seal of the company registration authority;

- a certificate for use of business premises; and

- other documents required by the company registration authority.

As of 25 October 1998, the *Temporary Regulation on Administration of Registration of Entities without Enterprise Characteristics and Run by the Local People* became effective. It defines entity without enterprise characteristics and run by the local people (Entity) and stipulates the registration authority and supervising unit, conditions for establishing an Entity and procedure for application for examination, approval and registration, procedure for changing and cancelling an Entity's registration, the supervision and administration conducted by the registration administration authority and supervising unit and penalties. The Entity established before the implementation of the Temporary Regulation shall apply for registration again in accordance with the new Regulation within one year after its effectiveness.

As of 25 October 1998, the *Regulation on Administration of Social Entities Registration* became effective. It defines social entity and stipulates social entity's registration administration authority and supervising unit, conditions for establishing a social entity and procedure for application for examination, approval and registration, procedure for changing and cancelling a social entity's registration, the supervision and administration conducted by the registration and administration authority and supervising unit and penalties. The social entities established before the implementation of the Regulation shall apply for registration again within one year in accordance with the Regulation after its effectiveness. In addition, the *Regulation on Administration of Social Entities Registration* promulgated on 25 October 1998 by the State Council was abolished.

Registration in Shenzhen

New rules issued by the Shenzhen Administration of Industry and Commerce (the Shenzhen AIC) require certain enterprises to register their businesses with this body. Enterprises which must register include foreign investment enterprises and their branch offices in China, foreign contractual operations and representative offices of foreign companies in Shenzhen.

Enterprises must satisfy the following registration requirements:

- business and products must conform with the regulations set out in the Shenzhen Investment Directives Index;
- the enterprise must have a company name, articles of association and other documentation required by law;
- the business site must be compatible with the enterprise's scale of operations and comply with relevant Planning Authority regulations; and
- the enterprise must meet minimum statutory capital adequacy requirements.

In addition, the enterprises in Shenzhen must apply for a business licence. Similar prerequisites to those listed above exist for these applications.

If a foreign enterprise wishes to establish a branch office in Shenzhen, it must first get approval from the Trade Development Council of Shenzhen Municipality.

Note that the Shenzhen *Registration Rules* allow the registration of certain types of foreign investment enterprises, even though they may not have received approval from relevant examination and approval authorities. This conflicts with State policy and a number of State laws and regulations.

Registration of futures market players

New registration procedures apply to companies dealing in futures trading. These companies must apply to SAIC for registration. In order to obtain approval to engage in futures trading, companies need to satisfy certain pre-conditions, including the following:

- have a company name that complies with regulations;
- have articles of association;
- have fixed premises and certified communications equipment;
- have a registered capital of at least RMB10,000,000; and
- have appropriate operational personnel with not less than 20 full-time futures dealers.

Companies dealing in futures trading are required to observe the following rules:

- provide objective, accurate, prompt and efficient services;
- maintain a specific amount of ''client guarantee funds'' with a financial institution (designated by the authority in charge of registration) which must be deposited separately from the futures company's own funds;
- correctly record client orders and execute those orders promptly;
- keep daily trading records, accounting documents and other important information for at least five years;
- maintain business confidentiality with clients;
- make available to clients an open letter setting out the risks associated with futures trading; and

- within 60 days of registration, deposit the required business guarantee funds, of not less than 25% of the total registered capital, with a financial institution designated by the competent registration organ.

Companies dealing in futures are also specifically prohibited from performing certain activities which include:

- private collaboration and market monopolisation;
- promising to clients of investment profits;
- creating and circulating false or misleading information; and
- agreeing to share benefits or bear risk in association with clients.

Companies found violating the prescribed rules or engaging in prohibited activities may incur a warning, fine or confiscation of related income. An order for suspension of business operations until the matter is rectified or for revocation of the business licence may also be made, as determined by SAIC.

Permit for foreign economic cooperation

On 26 December 2000, MOFTEC promulgated the *Administrative Provisions* relating to foreign economic cooperation, including contracting projects, labour cooperation, surveying, designing, consultancy and supervision abroad. To conduct any of such foreign economic cooperation, an enterprise must obtain a PRC Foreign Economic Cooperation Operation Qualifications Certificate. Prior to these Provisions, a Permit for Contracting Projects or a Permit for Labour Cooperation was required, as the case might be. The Provisions also set out the certificate application procedure, period of validity and change on the expiration; and penalties for violating the Provisions.

CHN ¶45-002   Granting and nature of licence or registration

SAIC is the registration authority for all enterprises, both public and private. SAIC at city and county levels is responsible for the examination and approval of applications for the issue of business licences.

Discretionary nature

Applications for the issue of a business licence will be assessed by SAIC to determine whether the procedural and substantive measures required to be complied with by the applicant have been done in accordance with the laws and regulations applicable to that type of enterprise.

Approval procedure in Hainan

Foreigners engaging in certain types of investment are permitted to set up their enterprise through a special investment centre. The centre provides a "one-stop" approval procedure through which foreign investors can obtain all the necessary government approvals, as well as an investment advisory service. Foreigners involved in aviation, transport, port development or finance operations can take advantage of this streamlined investment approval process.

CHN ¶45-003 Incentive legislation

Since 1978, the government of the People's Republic of China has introduced a series of economic reforms, which include the encouragement of private enterprise within the scope set out by regulation and in certain areas of investment by foreign enterprises and individuals in the Chinese economy.

Foreign enterprises or foreign-related enterprises which fall within the scope of national priorities for development receive incentives in the form of favourable tax treatment and tax rebates in some circumstances and priority allocation of energy, communication and land resources. General incentives have been put in place to encourage development of targeted sectors of the domestic economy.

Since 1978, the reform of the economic system has resulted in a great range of reforms which cover a broad range of areas. In order to increase productivity and efficiency in the public sector, a management responsibility system has been implemented, aimed at placing more autonomy and responsibility for management of the enterprise in the hands of the management of the enterprise itself.

Special regulations have also been issued in relation to the exploitation of offshore petroleum resources, specifically the *Regulations of the People's Republic of China on the Exploitation of Offshore Petroleum Resources in Cooperation with Foreign Enterprises*, promulgated on 30 January 1982.

Domestic enterprises

Domestic enterprises are generally not regulated by the same laws and regulations as foreign investment enterprises (with the exception of equity joint ventures, wholly foreign-owned enterprises and contractual joint venture legal persons) and as such do not receive the obvious incentives contained in them. However, the development of economic reform has indirectly led to incentives being given to enterprises engaged in those priority industries for development or in those undeveloped inland areas. Domestic enterprises falling outside the parameters of economic modernisation as specified in the State Plan and in law will be subject to disincentives. They will either be unable to gain or renew their business licence with SAIC under the relevant regulations, or will be unable to obtain the resources from the state, eg energy and raw materials, needed to successfully run their business.

Administration of scheme

There is only one scheme for incentives in existence, in so far as state policy can be said to be a scheme. Administration of the incentives offered to eligible foreign investment enterprises is conducted through the relevant government departments in charge. For instance, MOFTEC, (now the MOFCOM) at the appropriate level, is responsible for examination and approval of the joint venture contract which establishes the enterprise, the Taxation Bureau is responsible for the collection of taxes, and the State Administration on Foreign Exchange Control controls the availability of foreign exchange. Utilities costs are paid at the local level in accordance with relevant laws, regulations and policy guidelines. Similarly, domestic enterprises are subject to the control of SAIC for licensing and will be responsible for utilities and other costs in accordance with relevant laws and regulations of the place of their business. New regulations for annual enterprise inspections, the *Measures for Annual Enterprise*

*Inspection*came into effect on 1 January 1997. Under these regulations, all enterprises are required to make annual reports to SAIC. SAIC has the power to revoke the business licences of enterprises which fail to report or meet standards. It may classify an enterprise as Grade B for committing minor breaches of the regulations. Grade B enterprises will not be permitted to expand operations, invest abroad or open new branches. SAIC issued the *Provision on Authentication of Contracts*on 3 November 1997, regulating the contents to be authenticated. The contents to be authenticated mainly refer to the validity of the contract and whether the contract relates to any restricted business stipulated by the Government. In terms of taxation, the State Council issued the *Circular on Tightening Up the Administration of Taxation According to Law and Rigorously Enforcing the Division of Authority Over Tax Administration*on 12 March 1998. This shows a sign of the central Government's intention to strengthen taxation administration across the country.

Discretionary nature

Foreign investment enterprises will become eligible for incentives on the basis of the existence of certain objective criteria; for example, they are established in an area, such as a special economic zone or open coastal city, where the law provides for enterprises of that type to receive tax holidays or reduced taxation, or they are a category of enterprise which falls within the scope of the definition of an "export enterprise" or a "technologically advanced enterprise" as defined in the *Provisions of the State Council of the People's Republic of China for the Encouragement of Foreign Investment*, and other related legislation.

CHN ¶45-004   Disincentives or restrictions on certain business activities

The economic priorities of the nation are listed in the State Plan. In accordance with the plan and specific policy directives based on implementation of the plan, the relevant examination and approval authorities at the national, provincial and local levels compile lists of types of projects which are encouraged, permitted but not encouraged, discouraged and not permitted. Foreign investment enterprises find that the ease of obtaining approval for their proposed project will relate directly to its categorisation as a priority in accordance with the State Plan.

Types of disincentives

Foreign investment projects which are not encouraged will have difficulty obtaining approval from the relevant approval authority. Existing businesses also require approval for expansion from the relevant approval authority. Foreign investment enterprises can be discouraged through various means during the course of their operation if the priority accorded to that type of investment is reassessed and one method is not to grant the relevant import or export licences to enterprise, especially where the project requires certain products or materials to be imported for the operation of the project.

Administration

Incentives or disincentives to both foreign investment enterprises and domestic enterprises are administered through relevant government departments at various levels in accordance with the policies embodied in the State Plan, specific policy directives, relevant laws and regulations.

Special Regulation of Foreign Investment

Special controls for foreign
    businesses or investors . CHN ¶45-101
Control of foreign
    investor .... CHN ¶45-102
Definition of foreign businessman
    or investor .... CHN ¶45-103
Special regulations covering joint
    ventures .... CHN ¶45-104
Incentives and disincentives for
    geographical areas .... CHN ¶45-105
Incentives and disincentives for
    particular industries .... CHN ¶45-111

Types of incentives, disincentives
    and controls .... CHN ¶45-112
Nature of incentives,
    disincentives and
    controls .... CHN ¶45-113
Guarantees against expropriation
    of assets .... CHN ¶45-114
Retention of local
    consultant .... CHN ¶45-115

CHN ¶45-101   Special controls for foreign businesses or investors

Beginning with the promulgation in 1979 of the *Law of the People's Republic of China on Sino-foreign Equity Joint Ventures*, the Chinese government has promulgated an extensive set of foreign-related legislation. The overriding aim of this type of legislation is to create a legal framework for the encouragement of foreign trade and investment in China. The primary investment vehicles are:

- The equity joint venture. Relevant legislation includes the *Law of the People's Republic of China on Sino-foreign Equity Joint Ventures*, and their Implementing Regulations;

- The cooperative joint venture (sometimes called the contractual joint venture). The primary law regulating this investment vehicle is the *Law of the People's Republic of China on Sino-foreign Contractual Joint Ventures* , and the Detailed Rules for their Implementation;

- The wholly-owned foreign enterprise. Relevant legislation includes the *Law of the People's Republic of China on Foreign Capital Enterprises*, and the Detailed Rules for their Implementation.

There have been a large number of laws and regulations promulgated at various levels to deal with all aspects of foreign-related economic activities including contracts, insurance, import and export, foreign exchange regulation, taxation, loans, resident representative offices and labour.

CHN ¶45-102   Control of foreign investor

Supervision by the relevant Chinese government departments over a foreign investment enterprise commences with the initial proposal for the investment. Regulations in relation to the approval of foreign investment projects came into effect on 27 June 1995. The *Interim Provisions on Guiding the Direction of Foreign Investment*was jointly issued by the State Planning Commission, the State Economic and Trade Commission and MOFCOM. At the same time, a *Guidance Catalogue for Foreign Investment Industries*was published. The Interim Provisions have classified foreignfunded projects into prohibited, encouraged, permitted and restricted activities and mainly apply to foreign investments in the form of sino-foreign equity joint ventures, wholly foreign-owned enterprises and sino-foreign shareholding companies etc.

The Catalogue was amended in 1997 and 2002. The 2002 amendment was primarily intended to bring the Catalogue in line with China's commitments relating to its WTO accession as well as to reflect the structural changes of China's national economy. It makes some changes to the list of prohibited, encouraged, permitted and restricted activities for foreign investment. The amended list includes the following:

Prohibited

- Agriculture, forestry, animal husbandry, fishery industries:
  - Breeding and planting of precious and rare species found in China (including good genetics from the plantation industry, animal husbandry industry and aquatic product industry);
  - Production and development of seeds of genetically changed plants; and
  - Fishing of aquatic products in sea areas and inland waters of China.
- Excavation industry:
  - Exploration, mining and screening of radioactive minerals; and
  - Exploration, mining and screening of rare-earths.
- Manufacturing industries:
  - Processing of traditional green tea and special kinds of tea (famous tea, black tea, etc) of China;
  - Processing of Chinese medicinal herbs classified as the protected resources of the State (musk, licorice root, jute, etc);
  - Application of the traditional techniques for the preparation of Chinese medicinal soluble tablets and production of Chinese patent medicines products using secret formulae;
  - Refining and processing of radioactive minerals;
  - Weapons and ammunition manufacturing industry;
  - Ivory carving;
  - Tiger bone processing;
  - Production of bodiless lacquerware;
  - Production of products made of enamel;
  - Production of Xuan paper and ingot-shaped ink tablets; and
  - Production of products causing cancer, deformity and mutation and products of sustaining organic pollutants.
- Production and supply industries of electricity, gas and water — Construction and operation of power grids.
- Transportation, warehousing and post and telecommunications:
  - Air traffic control companies; and
  - Postal service companies.

- Finance and insurance industries — Futures companies.
- Social service industry:
  - Development of resources of wild animals and plants protected by the State;
  - Construction and operation of natural protection zones for animals and plants;
  - Lottery industry (including horse-racing courses for gambling); and
  - Pornographic industry.
- Education, cultural arts, and radio, film and television industries:
  - Foundation education (mandatory education) institutions;
  - Publication, main distribution and import business of books, newspapers and periodicals;
  - Publication, production, main distribution and import business of audio and video products and electronic publications;
  - News institutions;
  - Radio stations (bases) and television stations (bases) at all levels and radio and television transmission coverage networks (transmission stations, relay stations, radio television satellites, satellite uplink stations, satellite receiving and transmitting stations, microwave stations, monitoring stations, cable television broadcasting transmission coverage networks);
  - Production, publication, distribution and broadcasting companies of radio and television programs;
  - Film production and distribution companies; and
  - Broadcasting companies for videos.
- Other industries — Projects endangering the safety and usefulness of military facilities.
- Other industries prohibited by the State or by international treaties signed or acceded to by China.

Encouraged
- Agricultural new technology;
- Power and transportation;
- Raw materials;
- High technology projects;
- New equipment projects which utilise natural resources without harming the environment;
- Environment protection (in relation to agriculture, forestry, animal husbandry and fishery);
- Transport and telecommunications industries;
- Coal industry;
- Power industry;
- Petroleum, petrochemical and chemical industries;

- Mechanical industry;
- Electronic industry;
- Medical and pharmaceutical industries;
- Medical apparatus and equipment;
- Newly emerged industries (emphasising environment protection);
- Service industries (emphasising high technology and development of new products); and
- Other projects.

Permitted

Permitted foreign investment projects are those not falling under the encouraged, restricted and prohibited categories.

Restricted

- Projects developed in China;
- Trial projects for attracting foreign investment;
- Projects in industries which enjoy monopolies;
- Projects in the exploration and exploitation of rare and precious mineral resources; and
- Other projects restricted by law.

Penalties for contravention of the Interim Provisions authorise the approval authorities to rescind approvals, not issue business licences, not handle relevant import/export procedures and make joint venture contracts void.

Implementing Provisions on Regulation on Several Issues Related to Investing in High and/or New Technology

On 7 May 1998, the *Implementation Provisions on Regulation on Several Issues Related to Investing in High and/or New Technology*(interpreted by the Ministry of Science and Technology and the State Administration for Industry and Commerce) became effective. Under the Implementation Provisions, if high or new technology is invested as part of the registered capital of a company with limited liability or a science and technology development enterprise, and accounts for more than 20% of the registered capital, the details and valuation of the high or new technology must be submitted together with relevant documents and materials (the Application Documents) to the science and technology administration authority at different levels (the Examination and Ratification Authority) for examination and ratification. The decision shall be made by the Examination and Ratification Authority within two months after the receipt of a complete set of Application Documents.

A Ratification Certificate will be issued by the Examination and Ratification Authority for applications which satisfy the conditions required for high and/or new technology. Otherwise, an examination opinion in writing must be sent to the applicant.

The applicant must register with the proper administration for industry and commerce within three months after receipt of the Ratification Certificate. The

Implementation Provisions also set out penalties in cases where Ratification Certificates are obtained by deceit.

The *Conditions and Methods for Identifying the High-new Technical Enterprises in the State High-new Technical Development Zone*(the "Methods"), which was implemented on 23 July 2000, stipulates mainly on the following items:

- the authority responsible for the identification and administration of the high-new technical enterprises: the Science and Technology Ministry and its local branches;

- the list of the high-new technique: including 11 kinds of techniques such as electronics and information technique, biological engineering and new medical technique, new materials and its application, etc;

- the requirements that a high-new technical enterprise should meet; and

- application procedure for identification as a high-new technical enterprise.

According to the Methods, a re-examination on the high-new technical enterprise is required every two years.

The High and New Technology Products Encouraged for Foreign Investment Catalogue, issued by Ministry of Science and Technology and Ministry of Commerce on 18 July 2003, includes 917 items of products in 11 categories, such as electronics and information; software; aviation and aerospace; biomedicine and medical instrument; new energy and energy efficiency etc.

Wholly foreign owned enterprises

Article 6 of the *Law of the People's Republic of China on Foreign Capital Enterprises* provides:

> "The application to establish an enterprise exclusively with foreign capital shall be submitted for examination and approval by the department under the State Council which is in charge of foreign economic relations and trade or by other authorities entrusted with such powers by the State Council. The department or said authorities shall, within 90 days from the date when such application is received, make a decision on whether or not to grant approval."

After obtaining approval, the foreign investor must apply to SAIC for registration and obtain a business licence from the relevant level of SAIC.

The scope of business that is permitted to be undertaken by the foreign investor must be set out on prior approval from the appropriate level of MOFCOM and will be set out in the business licence issued by SAIC. Failure to operate the business in conformity with the business licence will result in its revocation. SAIC is responsible for inspecting and monitoring the investment situation of the wholly-owned foreign enterprise or foreign investment enterprise (Art 9). Joint annual inspections by SAIC's various departments will be carried out between 1 January and 30 April. The *Circular on Carrying on Joint Annual Inspection of Foreign Investment Enterprises*came into effect on 1 January 1997, and sets out documents required for submission to the inspecting departments. After inspection, various departments may conduct random inspections. Those enterprises which make false statements or withhold information will have to pay a penalty as will accountants, auditors and other intermediaries on their behalf.

Equity and contractual joint ventures

The scope and permitted activities of the equity joint venture and the cooperative joint venture are similarly set out in the laws relating to each of those investment vehicles. The scope of the business permitted to be undertaken by joint ventures is set out in the joint venture contract which must be approved by the relevant level of MOFCOM before an application for a business licence can be made to SAIC. The scope of the business licence will reflect the scope of the approved joint venture contract. Supervision of the activities of the joint venture is the responsibility of the relevant level of SAIC.

There are also a wide range of controls placed upon the conduct of foreign investment enterprises in specific areas. For example, books of account are required to be kept in China and the enterprise is subject to relevant Chinese taxation laws. The import and export of products is controlled in accordance with the State Plan and specific legal regulation through the issue of import and export licences, the obtaining of foreign exchange is controlled through the State Administration of Foreign Exchange Control and enterprises are required to open a bank account with the Bank of China, through which banking activities and the remission of foreign exchange is conducted.

Asset evaluation procedures for foreign firms

All non-cash contributions of assets (contributions of "assets in kind") made by foreign parties investing into China must undergo detailed evaluation procedures. As of 1 May 1994, assets in kind which contributed by foreign investors are subject to evaluation by the PRC Import and Export Commodities Inspection Bureau.

Asset valuation is particularly significant in the context of foreign investment enterprises because the value given to asset contributions may affect procedures for the registration and approval of foreign investments in China.

Parties applying for asset evaluation must provide invoices, customs reports, insurance policy information and copies of their contracts, and must also provide the reason for requesting the evaluation. Once evaluation procedures have been completed, the Bureau will issue an Evaluation Certificate. This certificate must be referred to by Chinese certified accountants when verifying contributions of assets in kind made by foreign investment enterprises.

China has cancelled the compulsory customs evaluation requirement for wholly foreign-owned enterprises. The scope of compulsory customs evaluation for other types of foreign investment enterprises will be narrowed gradually. The Chinese government is shifting the customs evaluation to intermediary agencies. The compulsory evaluation will become discretionary. However, if the foreign investors voluntarily appraise the assets of an FIE, Chinese law does not prohibit such an evaluation.

CHN ¶45-103 Definition of foreign businessman or investor

There are no definitive guidelines by which to determine conclusively in which situations a businessman or investor will be categorised as "foreign".

The nationality law provides that nationality is the basis for determining foreign or other status in China. As a result, Hong Kong, Macao and Taiwan "compatriots" are considered to be of Chinese nationality and so receive different treatment from "foreigners" under the Chinese law. However, in principle, all those investment from foreign countries, Hong Kong, Macao and Taiwan are regarded as foreign investment though Hong Kong, Macao and Taiwan have been regarded as a part of China by the Chinese government. Investors from these areas receive the same treatment as those from foreign countries. Companies incorporated outside China will be considered to be foreign corporations whilst legal persons registered within China will be considered Chinese entities. For example, the legal person formed pursuant to an equity joint venture is a Chinese entity. Recently, the question of the nationality status of a wholly-owned subsidiary of a Chinese corporation incorporated overseas was considered by MOFCOM. MOFCOM decided that despite the fact that the capital of the corporation came from China, because its place of incorporation was not within China, it would be considered to be a foreign entity. However, there have been accounts of recent situations where wholly-owned subsidiaries of Chinese corporations incorporated overseas have not been granted ''foreign'' status.

CHN ¶45-104   Special regulations covering joint ventures

The establishment of both forms of joint ventures, ie equity and contractual, are governed by individual laws and implementing regulations.

The basic laws regulating the establishment of an equity joint venture are as follows:

- the *Law of the People's Republic of China on Sino-Foreign Equity Joint Ventures*;

- the *Regulations of the People's Republic of China for Implementing the Equity Joint Venture Law*; and

- the *Interim Provisions on Guiding the Direction of Foreign Investment.* (See CHN ¶45-102).

On 4 September 1995, MOFTEC (now the MOFCOM) announced the *Detailed Implementing Regulations for Sino-Foreign Cooperative Joint Ventures*to take effect the same day. The regulations are the first comprehensive legislation to be issued specifically to supplement the *Law on Sino-Foreign Cooperative Joint Ventures*(13 April 1988). Both of them were amended on 31 October 2000.

The new regulations address the following subject areas:

- establishment of cooperative enterprises;

- organisational structure;

- purchase of goods and sale of products;

- distribution of revenues and return of investment;

- term and termination; and

- special provisions for cooperative enterprises that do not have legal person status.

The new regulations require that the following documents be submitted in an application for approval to establish a sino-foreign cooperative joint venture:

- Project proposal document regarding the cooperative joint venture to be established and related approval documents from the relevant authorities;

- Feasibility study report prepared by investing parties in the venture and related approval documents from the relevant authorities;

- Agreement, contract and Articles of Association for the venture signed by the authorised representative of each investing party or their authorised delegate;

- Evidence of the incorporation of each investing party in the venture, evidence of their credit-worthiness and proof of the authority of their authorised legal representatives (where the foreign party is a natural person, the relevant identification documents, background information and evidence of credit worthiness should be provided);

- Names of the individuals selected through the investing parties' mutual agreement to serves as chairman of the Board, directors or management committee members (such as director, vice director, members); and

- Such other documents as required by the approving authority.

MOFTEC (now the MOFCOM) published the *Provisional Rule on Establishment of Equity Joint-Venture Foreign Trading Companies*as MOFTEC(now known as MOFCOM)Order [2003] No. 1 on 18 February 2003. The rule will take effect 30 days from its 31 January approval, presumably on 1 March 2003. The rule replaces the 1996 *Provisional Trial Rule on Establishment of Chinese-Foreign Joint-Venture Foreign Trade Companies*, under which a handful of foreign companies had invested in foreign trading companies. The new rule maintains provisions in the earlier rule that requires foreign equity participation to be between 25% and 49%, though the new rule stipulates that this restriction will be lifted 11 December 2003, at which time foreign majority equity participation will be allowed.

In addition to that, the foreign party is no longer required to have been established in China nor is the Chinese party required to have invested in companies outside China (Art 4). The foreign party is still required to have an average trade volume with China of at least US$30 million over the previous three years but the average annual import and export volume over the previous three years of the Chinese party is now lowered to be at least US$30 million instead of US$200 million with no minimum requirement on the export volume (Art 4). The minimum registered capital of a foreign trading equity joint venture is now lowered from RMB100 million to RMB50 million. The requirement is lower if the joint venture is established in the central and western areas (Art 4). The foreign party can now use money capital, material goods and intangible assets as its capital contribution (Art 7).

CHN ¶45-105   Incentives and disincentives for geographical areas

A distinct set of incentives is given to foreign enterprises and sino-foreign joint ventures to encourage investment in priority areas and the priority regions in China, such as Key Industries for Foreign Investment in Shanghai Municipality Catalogue. Special incentives exist in geographical areas, in particular the special economic zones, the 14 open coastal cities, the coastal development zone, the province of Hainan Island, various designated technological development zones located along the eastern coast of China, and, more recently, the inland western areas. All have a higher degree of autonomy to approve projects and pass regulations and tax provisions, without the need for central government approval, than do other areas of China.

The notable incentives available in these areas are tax holidays and reduced taxation for designated types of enterprises. Special economic zones and open coastal cities, including Hainan Island, have increased autonomy to make local regulations implement the open-door policy. These laws and regulations often establish a more liberal regime by which to regulate activities of foreign investors as their aim is to encourage foreign investment in that area. In particular, the Shenzhen special economic zone has been responsible for the trial of many new laws implementing economic modernisation. After trial in that special economic zone, the laws are reassessed in light of experience and often promulgated at a national level.

CHN ¶45-111   Incentives and disincentives for particular industries

The State Council promulgated the *Provisions for the Encouragement of Foreign Investment* on 11 October 1986. The Provisions stipulate that the specified preferences referred to therein shall apply to enterprises with foreign investment of the following types:

- production enterprises whose products are mainly for export and which have a foreign exchange surplus; and

- production enterprises possessing advanced technology supplied by the foreign investor which either results in the development of new products, the upgrading and replacing of products in order to increase foreign exchange generated by exports or for import substitution.

There are two categories of foreign investment enterprises which are identified as priorities for investment and as such receive special incentives. These are enterprises which are defined as "export enterprises" and "technologically advanced enterprises".

On 22 August 1995, the Ministry of Finance issued amendments to the rules governing royalties for production in sino-foreign cooperative developed oil and gas fields in onshore areas within China and the shallow water continental shelf. The amendments aim to attract foreign investment in areas where the investment risks are high. The amendments include royalty exemptions for an oil field where the annual production is below one million tons and gas fields with production of less than two billion standard cubic metres if they are located in Qinghai, Tibet, Xinhang and shallow water on the continental shelf. On a frontier oil field, where annual production is more than four million tons, the maximum royalty is 12.5% of production.

CHN ¶45-112   Types of incentives, disincentives and controls

Tax incentives in the special economic zones

Foreign-invested enterprises operating in Shenzhen, Zhuhai, Shantou, Xiamen and Hainan (hereinafter referred to as "special zone enterprises") pay a reduced corporate income tax rate of 15% on the income derived from production, business and other sources by joint ventures, cooperative ventures or enterprises with foreign investment.

For special zone enterprises engaged in industry, communication and transportation, agriculture, forestry and animal husbandry, which have a contract life of 10 years or longer, a two-year tax holiday commencing from the first profit-making year shall be allowed followed by a 50% reduction in the third to fifth year.

Special zone enterprises engaged in the service industry, with an overseas investment exceeding US$5 million and a contract life of 10 years or longer, shall be exempt from income tax in the first profit-making year followed by a 50% reduction in the second and third year.

Foreign investors of joint ventures in the special economic zones shall be exempt from enterprise income tax when repatriating profits distributed from the enterprise.

After the expiration of the reduction or exemption period of enterprise income tax in accordance with the relevant provisions of the state, export enterprises within the special economic zones exporting 70% or more of their products, in value terms, in any one year, may pay enterprise income tax at the reduced rate of 10% for that year.

After the expiration of the reduction or exemption period of enterprise income tax in accordance with the relevant provisions of the state, technologically advanced enterprises may pay enterprise income tax at a reduced rate of 10% for another three years.

Dividends, interests, rentals, royalties and other kinds of income which are sourced in special economic zones and derived by foreign investors which have no establishments in China shall be subject to income tax at the reduced rate of 10% except in cases where tax exemption is provided under the law. Where the terms and conditions for the provision of capital and equipment are preferential or the technology transferred is advanced such that it is necessary to grant additional reduction or exemption, the matter shall be decided by the people's government of the special economic zones.

Reduction or exemption of local income tax for special zone enterprises shall be decided by the people's government of the special economic zones.

VAT shall be exempt on all goods (excluding oil, cigarettes and alcohol produced/imported/sold in the zones).

The business income of the branches of Hong Kong, Macao and foreign banks established in the special economic zones are eligible for a tax exemption for a certain period (currently five years).

Interest income received by a foreign, Hong Kong or Macao bank for loans made to the branch office of a foreign bank in the special economic zones at inter-bank offer rates shall be exempt from withholding tax.

Interest income received by a Hong Kong, Macao or overseas depositor from the branch office of a foreign bank in the special economic zones shall be exempt from withholding tax or individual income tax.

Withholding tax shall be exempt for interest paid by the branch office of a foreign bank to its head office on the working capital borrowed provided that the interest rate is not higher than the international inter-bank offer rates.

Tax incentives in the economic and technological development zones

A 15% preferential enterprise income tax shall be allowed for income derived from production, business operation and other sources by joint ventures of a productive nature, cooperative enterprises or foreign enterprises operating in the economic and technological development zones of the 14 coastal port cities of Dalian, Qinhuangdao, Tianjin, Yantai, Qingdao, Lianyungang, Nantong, Shanghai, Ningbo, Wenzhou, Fuzhou, Guangzhou, Zhanjiang and Beihai. Those with a contract life of 10 years or longer shall enjoy a two-year tax holiday commencing from the first profit-making year followed by a 50% reduction in the third to fifth year.

Foreign investors of a joint venture in the development zones are exempt from enterprise income tax when repatriating their share of profits from the enterprise.

After the expiration of the reduction of exemption period of enterprise income tax in accordance with the relevant provisions of the state, export enterprises in the development zones exporting 70% or more of their production, in value terms, in any one year, may pay enterprise income tax at the reduced rate of 10% for that year.

After the expiration of the reduction or exemption period of enterprise income tax in accordance with the relevant provisions of the state, technologically advanced enterprises in the development zones may pay enterprise income tax at the reduced tax of 10% for another three years.

A 10% preferential income tax shall be levied on dividends, interests, rentals, royalties and other income sourced in development zones by overseas investors who do not have an establishment in China, except in cases where tax exemption is provided under the law. Where the terms and conditions for the provision of funds or equipment are preferential, or the technology transferred is advanced, such that it is necessary to grant additional tax reduction or exemption, the matter shall be decided by the people's governments of the municipalities where the development zones are located.

The reduction and exemption of local income tax for development zone enterprises shall be decided by the people's governments of the municipalities where the development zones are located. Plans to phase out some of the preferential tax rates have been suggested. Domestic enterprises operating in the zones will also lose preferential treatment, including access to half-rate import tariffs by the end of 1995. Currently, local enterprises pay 33% tax on profits, while foreign companies pay 26.4% in coastal cities and only 15% in the special zones.

VAT shall be exempt on building materials, production equipment, raw materials, spare parts and accessories, components, means of transport and office supplies imported by development zone enterprises for their own use.

Tax incentives in the old city districts of the 14 coastal port cities and the delta regions

For manufacturing enterprises with foreign investment which are established in the old city districts of the 14 coastal port cities, or in the municipalities or towns within the three delta regions (hereinafter referred to as "the old city and open economic zone enterprises"), if the enterprise is engaged in technology-intensive or know-how intensive projects, or in projects in which the foreign investors invest US$30 million or more and have a long pay-back period, or in energy, transportation and harbour construction projects, upon approval by the Ministry of Finance, enterprise income tax shall be levied at the reduced rate of 15%.

Subject to the approval of the Ministry of Finance, tax shall be paid at 80% of the enterprise income tax rate as prescribed in the tax law for those enterprises which are not entitled to tax reduction as prescribed in the preceding paragraph but are engaged in the following industries:

- Machine building, electronic, industry;
- Metallurgy, chemicals, building materials;
- Light industry, textiles and packaging;

- Medical apparatus, pharmaceuticals;

- Agriculture, forestry, animal husbandry, aquaculture and their related processing industries; and

- Building and construction.

The reduction and exemption of local income tax for old city and open economic zone enterprises shall be decided by the provincial or municipal people's government.

A 10% preferential income tax shall be levied on dividends, interests, rentals, royalties and other income sourced in the old city districts and the open economic zones by overseas investors who do not have an establishment in China, except in cases where tax exemption is provided under the law. Where the terms and conditions for the provision of funds or equipment are preferential, or the technology transferred is advanced, such that it is necessary to grant additional tax reduction or exemption, the matter shall be decided by the provincial or municipal people's government.

VAT shall be exempt for production equipment, office or business equipment and building materials imported as part of the investment or additional investment of the old city and open economic zone enterprises, as well as for vehicles and office supplies imported for the enterprise's own use.

VAT shall be exempt for raw materials, spare parts and accessories, components and packaging materials imported by old city and open economic zone enterprises for the manufacturing of export products.

VAT shall be exempt for products manufactured and exported by old city and open economic zone enterprises, with the exception of crude oil, processed oil and other goods for which the state has separate provisions.

Pudong New Area

An application can be made for exemption from income tax in the first five profit-making years for foreign-invested ventures launching airports, ports, railroad, highways or power stations for a period of 15 years or more. After five years, a firm may also apply for a 50% reduction upon approval by the Shanghai taxation administration.

Tax incentives for the development of western areas of China

Inspired by political as well as economic considerations, the Chinese government officially launched the significant, ambitious project of Great Development of Western Areas (of China) in early 2000. Tax incentives were introduced in the *State Council Notice Concerning Several Policies and Measures for the Implementation of the Development of Western Areas* effective 1 January 2001. Among them are:

- domestic and foreign-funded enterprises in those industries encouraged by the State will be entitled to a reduced enterprise income tax rate of 15%;

- enterprises in minority groups autonomous areas will be granted tax reduction or exemption subject to approval by the government at the provincial level;

- enterprises engaged in transportation, power, water control and conservancy, post, radio and television sectors will be entitled to the two-year exemption and three-year 50% reduction of their enterprise income tax; and

- imports of advanced technologies and equipment to be used in the encouraged domestic or foreign-funded projects or in the "advantageous projects in the western areas" will generally be exempt from customs duties and import VAT.

Reinvestment

Foreign investors who reinvest profits received from a foreign-invested venture (to establish another foreign-invested venture for an operation of at least five years or to increase its registered capital) may receive a refund of 40% of the tax paid on the reinvested amount. However, approval for the refund is required by the taxation administration.

CHN ¶45-113 Nature of incentives, disincentives and controls

Administration

All incentives are administered by the Ministries or departments at the relevant level which are responsible for implementing the relevant legislation.

Discretionary or mandatory

Incentives and controls are administered according to the provisions of the relevant laws or regulations.

Potential tax liability

The basis for determining whether and what incentives, disincentives or other controls are to be imposed on a foreign investment enterprise are determined in accordance with state policy and relevant legislation. Incentives and disincentives are administered in order to encourage the types of enterprises upon which the Chinese government has placed a high priority and to discourage enterprises which are either outside the priority areas or are considered to be positively detrimental to the national interest. Consequently, incentives are granted to foreign investment enterprises falling within the priority areas and especially those which are "export enterprises" or "technologically advanced enterprises" within the meaning of the *Provisions of the State Council of the People's Republic of China for the Encouragement of Foreign Investment*.

Legislative changes

Legislation and regulation for the encouragement of foreign investment in China can be changed in the same manner as ordinary legislation or regulations in the manner provided by the organ promulgating that law or regulation. The initiative for making such regulations and legislation is derived from state policy, which is embodied in the State Plan and other policy and government leadership given at the central NPC level or the central levels of the Communist Party of China (CPC).

Laws and regulations passed at the provincial or local levels have force within the jurisdiction or competence of the government or government department promulgating them. However, all such regulation and legislation is sent for reference to the Standing Committee of the NPC, which has the power to annul any local regulations or decisions which are inconsistent with the Constitution, the statutes, or the administrative rules and regulations.

Retroactive changes

Legislation and regulations may be changed with retroactive effect. However, one of the fundamental policy objectives in creating foreign-related legislation is to create a stable and comprehensive legal system upon which potential foreign investors would feel confident to rely. So it is less likely, for this reason, that legislation or regulations, will be passed which have retrospective effect.

Economic policy

All incentives, disincentives or controls are linked to the implementation of the State Plan and the general economic policy objectives revealed therein.

CHN ¶45-114　Guarantees against expropriation of assets

Government protection against expropriation is contained in specific legislation relating to the particular foreign investment vehicle involved. For instance, the *Law of the People's Republic of China on Foreign Capital Enterprises* provides:

> "Except under special circumstances, the State shall not nationalise or expropriate wholly-owned foreign enterprises. Should it prove necessary to do so in the public interest, legal procedures will be followed and reasonable compensation will be made."

The *Law of the People's Republic of China on Sino-foreign Equity Joint Ventures* was amended on 15 March 2001 and the same provision was added. Similarly, the *Sino-Foreign Contractual Joint Venture Law*, asserts *inter alia* that:

> "The State shall protect the lawful rights and interests of joint ventures and Chinese and foreign partners."

Despite the lack of specific protection against expropriation or nationalisation in the case of contractual joint ventures and the failure to specify what the "legal procedures" specified in the *Law of the People's Republic of China on Foreign Capital Enterprises* and the *Law of the People's Republic of China on Sino-foreign Equity Joint Ventures* might be, foreign enterprises will be dealt with in accordance with the terms of any treaty concluded between their country and China on the Reciprocal Encouragement and Protection of Investments which makes provision for expropriation or nationalisation of investment projects in each other's territories.

Article 8 provides:

> "(1)　A contracting party shall not take measures of expropriation or nationalisation or other measures having a similar effect relating to any investment unless the measures are in the public interest, non-discriminatory, in accordance with the law of the contracting party which has admitted the investment and against reasonable compensation.
>
> (2)　The compensation referred to in paragraph (1) of this article shall be computed on the basis of the market value of the investment immediately before the measures became public knowledge. Where the market value cannot be readily ascertained, the compensation shall be determined in accordance with generally recognised principles of valuation and equitable principles taking into account the capital invested, depreciation, capital

already repatriated, replacement value and other relevant factors. The compensation shall include interest at a reasonable rate from the date the measures were taken to the date of payment, shall be paid without undue delay, shall be freely convertible and shall be freely transferable between the territories of the contracting parties at the average of the daily exchange rates, determined on each of those days in accordance with the law of the contracting party which has admitted the investment, over the six months immediately prior to the taking of the measures.''

CHN ¶45-115 RETENTION OF LOCAL CONSULTANT

In the case of joint ventures, the intention of the Chinese party is that a local consultant is not required because the Chinese party will be able to provide advice about the local situation and guide the foreign party through any administrative matters which need to be handled. In the case of the wholly-owned foreign enterprise, the foreign investor is intended to have a close relationship with a local agent in making application for approval of the proposed project. The retention of a local consultant is a matter for the discretion of the foreign investor and should be assessed in light of his or her needs and particular situation.

PRICE AND PROFIT CONTROLS

Commodities subject to price
   control .... CHN ¶45-201

Price control body .... CHN ¶45-202

Exemptions from price
   control .... CHN ¶45-203

Special restrictions for certain
   companies .... CHN ¶45-204

Right of government authority
   to share in profits .... CHN ¶45-205

Criteria for application of
   controls .... CHN ¶45-206

CHN ¶45-201 COMMODITIES SUBJECT TO PRICE CONTROL

The prices of commodities and services are in theory subject to strict control in the People's Republic of China. In practice, however, due in large part to underdeveloped regulation of the relationship between various government bodies and authorities and the private economy, price control mechanisms have come under severe pressure. This process has led to a rapid deterioration of the control sectors of the economy which have been unable to compete in the market for scarce resources. Attempts to peg the price of necessary industrial supplies have met with limited success. Legislation does not provide for limiting controls on the profits or dividends of any enterprise. However, the governing philosophy permitting foreign investment is prefaced on the mutual benefit of Chinese organisations and their foreign counterparts. On 29 December 1997, the NPC passed the *Price Law* which became effective as from 1 May 1998. The Law covers the following parts:

- General Rules;
- Individual's pricing activities;
- Government's pricing activities;
- General price control;
- Price supervision;
- Legal responsibilities; and
- Supplements.

On 18 June 2003, The National Development and Reform Commission promulgated the *Suppression of Acts of Price Monopoly Tentative Provisions*. ''Price monopoly acts'' is defined in the Provisions as acts of business operators that manipulate market-oriented price, disrupt normal production and business principles, prejudice the lawful rights and interests of other businesses or consumers, of jeopardise public interest through mutual collusion or abuse of their leading roles in the market. The Provisions specify the acts of collusion among business that are prohibited.

CHN ¶45-202 PRICE CONTROL BODY

The State Planning Commission is the principal body which exercises control over the command economy. The State Planning Commission is the pre-eminent ministry under the State Council. The State Plan for each year is passed into legislation by the NPC. Invariably, subsequent legislative amendment to the plan is required.

CHN ¶45-203 EXEMPTIONS FROM PRICE CONTROL

In a move to make state-owned enterprises more market-oriented, state control of prices for some basic industrial goods will eventually be phased out. Prices of these goods will be determined by free market forces. In a further step towards market reform, a wide variety of agricultural products will no longer be centrally controlled. The following will still remain under government control: grain, cotton, tobacco, tea, timber, sugar and oil. Wool and herbs used for medicinal purposes will be subject to state-set ''guide prices'' to limit fluctuations.

CHN ¶45-204 SPECIAL RESTRICTIONS FOR CERTAIN COMPANIES

Legislative restrictions in economic law have largely developed owing to the impact of foreign investment ventures in China. By and large, until such legislative restrictions began to be applied to domestic industry, the local economic entities conducted operations in accordance with the state mandatory plan and by reference to received policy. Broad areas of the law governing foreign investment enterprises apply to particular enterprises, namely, domestic enterprises enjoying government largesse.

CHN ¶45-205 RIGHT OF GOVERNMENT AUTHORITY TO SHARE IN PROFITS

Various government authorities having dealings with foreign investment organisations will participate in profits at a number of levels.

CHN ¶45-206 CRITERIA FOR APPLICATION OF CONTROLS

The lack of criteria used for application of existing price and profit controls is reflected in the absence of penalties for infringement of existing regulatory structures.

UNFAIR TRADING PRACTICES AND CONSUMER PROTECTION

Consumer protection
  laws .... CHN ¶45-301

General principles governing
  injuries .... CHN ¶45-302

Prohibition or regulation of
  restraint of trade
  contracts .... CHN ¶45-303

Licences under statutory
  monopolies .... CHN ¶45-304

Special provisions relating to
  business activities of non-
  residents .... CHN ¶45-305

Laws governing advertising and
  promotion of products . CHN ¶45-306

Review of "unfair"
  contracts .... CHN ¶45-307

CHN ¶45-301 CONSUMER PROTECTIONS LAWS

Consumer protection legislation is in its infancy in the People's Republic of China. However, consumer interests are now better protected than before.

China has promulgated a detailed *Product Liability Law*, which became effective from 1 September 1993 and was amended in 2000. While the law mainly emphasises compliance with explicit, written control standards, it also creates a general duty on manufacturers and retailers not to manufacture or sell defective goods.

Scope

The law applies to the production and/or sale of goods in the PRC. The law does not, however, apply to construction projects.

Hazardous industrial products

Industrial products which may be hazardous to personal health or to property must conform to national and industry standards. If there are no such standards, the products must conform to the requirements for protecting health, personal safety and property.

Obligations of producers

Producers are, generally, to be held responsible for the quality of their products. Goods must not constitute an ''unreasonable danger'' to personal safety or to property. They must possess the properties that should be possessed by that type of product. In addition, goods must match the product description on packaging, and conform to samples.

Retailer liable to pay compensation to consumers

Retailers are required to repair, replace or give refunds for faulty products in certain circumstances. Retailers are also liable to pay compensation for losses that are incurred by the user or consumer through use of the faulty product. If appropriate, the retailer will then have the right of recovery against either the manufacturer or the supplier.

Producer's liability

Producers are liable to pay compensation if a defective product causes physical injury or damage to property. The level of science or technology available at the time the product was manufactured, however, can be used as a defence. If it can be proved that the manufacturer would have been unable to detect the defect using available science or technology, the manufacturer will escape liability.

Time limitations

A party must make a claim within two years from the time that the party knew, or ought to have known that his or her rights had been infringed. The right to claim compensation also expires 10 years from the date the defective product is first delivered to a user or consumer.

Penalties

Penalties for non-compliance with state or industry standards include fines, directives to cease production of the non-complying products, as well as confiscation of both the products and the illegal income. Enterprises may also have their business licence revoked and be subject to criminal prosecution.

More sophisticated questions regarding exclusion of warranties and like implication have not as yet come before the courts except in rare instances. In the past decade, the China Consumer Association and its branches handled two million consumer complaints and recovered about RMB800 million. The number of consumer associations has reached approximately 2,580.

CHN ¶45-302   GENERAL PRINCIPLES GOVERNING INJURIES

The general principles governing products or other injury to persons or property and the standards of care required are set out in general fashion in the *General Principles of the Civil Law*. On 8 March 2001, the Supreme People's Court interpreted certain issues related to establishing liability for emotional injury in civil tort cases and the interpretation became effective on 10 March 2001. The Interpretation clarifies the circumstances under which the People's Court will hear claims for compensation for emotional injury. Article 1 lists the individual rights that, when illegally infringed upon, can constitute the basis for a claim by a natural person. These include the rights to life, health, personal safety, name, personal image, reputation, honour and personal freedom. Article 2 states that the court will hear a claim for compensation for emotional injury by a guardian where the person under his or her custody is illegally caused to leave that custody, with the result that the parent-offspring or kinship relationship is seriously compromised. The court will not hear claims for emotional injury by legal persons or organisations (Art 5). Compensation for emotional injury cannot be sought in a case that has previously gone before the court when no claim for compensation for emotional injury was made in that instance (Art 6). Spouses, parents or offspring become plaintiffs when they seek compensation where a natural person has died as the result of tort, or where the deceased person's character or physical remains suffer damage after death (Art 7). The People's Court may reject a claim for compensation for emotional injury when significant injury has not occurred. In such cases, the People's Court may order the defendant to cease the injurious action.

CHN ¶45-303   Prohibition or regulation of restraint of trade contracts

China has not yet enacted a formal anti-trust law. So far, there are only some rules and regulations concerning restriction of competition in specific fields, such as the *Restriction of Competition of Utility Enterprises Provisions*and the PRC *Pricing Law*. In the latter, monopoly pricing determined through negotiations between enterprises or trade associations is regarded as a violation of law. Currently, the regulations governing mergers and acquisitions (M&A) by foreign investors in China mainly consist of the *Transfer of State Shares and Legal Person Shares in Listed Companies to Foreign Investors Circular*, the *Use of Foreign Investment to Restructure State-owned Enterprises Tentative Procedures*and the *Acquisition of Domestic Enterprises by Foreign Investors Tentative Provisions*(the "Tentative Provisions"). The first two only offer some details regarding anti-trust, while the Tentative Provisions regulate anti-trust activities in more detail. They include stipulations that a foreign investor must make a report to MOFCOM and SAIC if:

(a) the foreign investor involved in the acquisition has a turnover in the Chinese market during the current year that exceeds RMB1.5 billion;

(b) the foreign investor has acquired 10 or more enterprises in related industries in China within one year;

(c) the foreign investor in the acquisition already has a market share of 20% in China; or

(d) the acquisition will cause the foreign investor to have a market share of 25% in China.

Further, if MOFCOM and SAIC, at the request of competing domestic enterprises, relevant functional authorities or trade associations, are of the opinion that the acquisition by the foreign investor would involve capture of significant market share or would affect market competition, people's livelihood or national economic security, they will still require the foreign investor to file a report, even though the circumstances described in the proceeding paragraph have not occurred. MOFCOM and SAIC will not approve the relevant acquisition after hearings if such acquisition results in over-concentration in a particular market.

The Tentative Provisions also state that MOFCOM and SAIC will examine the acquisition scheme submitted by the foreign investor to see if it results in over-concentration, thereby prejudicing fair competition and damaging the interests of consumers, and will then make a decision on whether to grant approval if:

(a) the foreign investor in the acquisition owns assets in China valued at RMB3 billion or above;

(b) the foreign investor has a turnover of RMB1.5 billion or above in the Chinese market during the current year;

(c) the foreign investor together with its affiliates already has a market share of 20% in China;

(d) the acquisition will cause the foreign investor together with its affiliates to have a market share of 25% in China; or

(e) the acquisition will cause the number of FIEs directly or indirectly owned by such foreign investor in related industries in China to exceed 15.

Anti-trust laws prohibiting or regulating contracts, arrangements, understandings and combinations in restraint of trade or commerce have not to date been considered to require enactment.

Controls and regulations over contracts relating to exclusive dealing, monopolisation, mergers, franchises, price discrimination and resale price maintenance have not been provided for. However, faking registered trademarks, revealing commercial secrets, collusive bidding and using misleading packaging have been made illegal by the law.

Foreign Trade Law

The *Revised Foreign Trade Law* which came into effect as of 1 July 2004 has liberalised the availability of the right to import and export goods. The right to engage in foreign trade in the PRC can now be obtained by a Chinese individual or Chinese enterprise through a filing for the record. This type of filing is in principle a mere clerical procedure, as is required by WTO obligations. According to China's WTO commitments, within three years after China's accession into the WTO, all enterprises would have the right to import and export all goods (except for products otherwise specified in Annex 2A to the Protocol) throughout the territory of China.

CHN ¶45-304   Licences under statutory monopolies

Refer to ''Intellectual Property'' at CHN ¶65-001.

CHN ¶45-305   Special provisions relating to business activities of non-residents

In 2000, China adopted the PRC *Regulations on Anti-dumping* and the PRC *Regulations on Countervailing* dealing with unfair trading practices of non-residents. MOFTEC and the State Economic and Trade Commission are the two responsible ministries handling the anti-dumping and countervailing cases brought by Chinese domestic industries against foreign business operators.

CHN ¶45-306   Laws governing advertising and promotion of products

Advertising and promotional statements about products are regulated by the terms of:

- the *Regulations for the Control of Advertising*, promulgated by the State Council on 26 October 1987;

- the *Detailed Implementing Rules Governing the Regulations for the Control of Advertising*, promulgated on 9 January 1988 by SAIC; and

- the PRC *Advertising Law*, adopted on 27 October 1994.

Registration of eligible organisations or enterprises is obtained through and supervised by SAIC at various levels. Regulations and Detailed Implementing Rules make provision in relation to the permissible content and form of advertisements. Penalties are provided for breach of the Regulations and Detailed Implementing Rules and involvement in any prescribed activities.

Article 3 of the Regulations provides the general guidelines concerning promotional statements about products (amongst other things) to which advertisements must comply.

Articles 11 and 12 of the Regulations require certification that an advertised commodity meets the quality standards set by the state, that commodities advertised as prize or honour winners, or under the title of a high grade product, have the certification to such effect checked and approved by the advertising operator prior to publication, broadcast, display or posting of an advertisement. Penalties are imposed for failure to comply with these articles. The Detailed Implementing Rules provide for the certification which must be produced in specific instances and detailed enforcement and penalty provisions for failure to comply with these Regulations.

False advertising is just one of a range of business practices that has been banned under the law to promote fair competition. Faking registered trademarks, revealing commercial secrets, collusive bidding and using misleading packaging have also been made illegal by the law.

CHN ¶45-307   Review of "unfair" contracts

Broad ranging and general laws allowing courts and/or government agencies to review contracts or arrangements deemed unfair or unconscionable are implied in the legislative scheme governing foreign-invested enterprises. Articles 58 and 59 of the *General Principles of the Civil Law* set out the circumstances under which contracts may be held void or voidable.

IMPORT AND EXPORT CONTROLS

Restrictions on import of goods ....CHN ¶50-001
Special requirements for importers ....CHN ¶50-002
Restrictions on export of goods ....CHN ¶50-003
Regulation of export and import licences ....CHN ¶50-004
Special restrictions relating to foreign control of
      business ....CHN ¶50-005
Major objectives of host country ....CHN ¶50-011
Rates of customs duties ....CHN ¶50-012

Taxes ....CHN ¶50-013

Tariff agreements ....CHN ¶50-014

Concessional entry of goods ....CHN ¶50-015

Free trade zones ....CHN ¶50-021

Labelling and packaging requirements ....CHN ¶50-022

International treaties ....CHN ¶50-023

Penalties and additional taxes ....CHN ¶50-024

Anti-dumping and countervailing duties ....CHN ¶50-025

Power to detain goods ....CHN ¶50-031

When is duty or tax payable? ....CHN ¶50-032

CHN ¶50-001   Restrictions on import of goods

The Government of the People's Republic of China has a stated policy of promoting free trade.

The Revised *PRC Foreign Trade Law* which came into effect on 1 July 2004 and the 2001 *Regulations of the People's Republic of China on Administration of the Import and Export of Goods*set forth China's legal regime for the import and export of goods. Under the import and export regime, China applies the import licence and import quota system in a range of merchandise, including luxury consumer products, outside the category of raw materials and key technological equipment, and China is reducing the range gradually. Concessions in respect of otherwise prohibited imports are, however, from time to time extended to foreign investment enterprises.

Under China's import regime, there are four basic categories of goods: (i) goods the import of which is prohibited; (ii) goods the import of which is restricted; (iii) goods that may be freely imported; and (iv) goods subject to tariff rate quotas.

In addition to the above restrictions, a number of import items are subject to inspection pursuant to the provisions of the *Import and Export Commodity Inspection Law*. The list of items published by the State Administration of Commodity Inspection from time to time are subject to quality, quantity, weight, packaging, safety and sanitation/hygiene standards and are cross-referenced to individual foreign trade contracts. An appropriate fee scale applies. Import commodities subject to inspection require an approval seal of the State Administration of Commodity Inspection on customs declarations prior to release. Fines apply for violation of the law and falsification of documentation is a criminal offence. Foreign-invested enterprises which must import commodities for which importation into China is generally restricted shall be exempt from the requirement to obtain an import quota certificate where the importation is part of a party's capital investment in the enterprise. Where such commodities are to be imported for production activities of the enterprise, a fiscal plan for import quotas and import licences should be prepared and application for a quota certificate should be submitted.

The Ministry of Commerce ("MOFCOM") publishes lists of approved and prohibited imports on a regular basis.

On 20 December 2002, MOFTEC ("Ministry of Foreign Trade and Economic Cooperation", now the MOFCOM) and the State Intellectual Property Office issued the *Strengthening Patent Administration in Foreign Trade Opinions*, which provides that

CHN ¶50-001

where the goods to be imported or the materials or parts to be used in processing trade involve patents, the foreign trade operator shall request the relevant exporter and the relevant processing trade entrusting party to provide the relevant evidence of its legal interests in the patent concerned. The contract for the imports or the processing trade may specifically require the exporter or the processing trade entrusting party to bear the legal liability concerning infringement claims or other patent disputes arising from the performance of the contract (Item 5). Where technological equipment to be imported involves transfer of patents or patent application rights, or patent licences, the transferor or licensor shall be required to provide evidence of its legal interests in the patent (Item 6). Where the exports involve new technology, new invention or technological equipment, the foreign trade operator shall conduct a patent search in the importing country or region to avoid patent infringement (Items 7 and 8). Foreign trade operators shall make customs filings for their patents and, upon discovery in imported or exported goods of any infringement of their patents, request protective measures from customs or patent administrative departments (Item 11).

On 30 May 2003, the General Administration of Customs promulgated the *Valuation of Royalties of Imported Goods Procedures*, which set forth the conditions where royalties shall be included in the calculation of the customs value of imported goods and explain how the calculation shall be dealt with. Royalties herein is defined as the payment made by the buyer of imported goods in order to obtain a license for using a patent, trademark, proprietary technology, copyrighted works and other rights, including the royalties of patent, trademark, copyright, proprietary technology, right to distribute or re-sell and other similar charges. Royalty payment obligations related to and as condition of sale of goods shall be included in the goods' customs value, unless they are payable by the same PRC buyer and to the same foreign seller as were parties to the goods' sale into the PRC.

CHN ¶50-002   Special requirements for importers

Limited recourse to foreign exchange reserves has confined China's import market to the major state-sanctioned trading houses which can gain foreign currency expenditure approval from state-controlled banking and finance authorities. Chambers of commerce for import and export have been established. Enterprises engaged in import and export business are obliged to join one or other of the chambers which will exercise discipline over members through sanctions. However, with the increase of China's foreign currency reserve and the convertibility of RMB under current account, China is on its way to gradually lifting its long-established control over import of foreign goods, and the *Revised Foreign Trade Law* has liberalised the availability of the right to import and export goods. The right to engage in foreign trade in the PRC can now be obtained by a Chinese individual or Chinese enterprise through a filing for the record This type of filing is in principle a mere clerical procedure, as is required by WTO obligations. According to China's WTO commitments, within three years after China's accession into WTO, all enterprises would have the right to import and export all goods (except for products otherwise specified in Annex 2A to the Protocol) throughout the territory of China.

CHN ¶50-003 Restrictions on export of goods

China also performs the export licence and export quota system in a number of categories of merchandise, and will gradually reduce the list. The export licence may be exempt in the trades of material processing and spares assembling for products to be re-exported.

MOFTEC (now known as MOFCOM) publishes regular lists of prohibited exports. These goods are in the main those designated as essential to the fulfilment of the state mandatory plan.

In recent times, export goods have become subject to stricter controls and approval procedures under the *Commodity Import and Export Inspection Law*. At present, 54 categories of commodities are subject to the export licence list.

Other export restrictions include a ban on the export of goods manufactured in prisons.

CHN ¶50-004 Regulation of export and import licences

Export and import licences, permits and approvals are coordinated by MOFTEC (now known as MOFTEC (now known as MOFCOM)). The procedures for obtaining an export licence, as well as the necessary documentation, have been detailed under the *Administrative Measures on Import Licence of Goods*issued by MOFTEC (now known as MOFCOM) on 20 December 2001. The MOFTEC (now known as MOFTEC's (now known as MOFCOM)*Administrative Rules on Export Licence*on January 2002 also outlines export control procedures for restricted exports, and set out the penalties for breaches of the Rules.

Licensing procedures

When applying for a licence, exporters must provide relevant approval documents and a copy of the export contract. They must also complete an export licence application form. Each licence may only be used for a single dispatch of goods (the ''one batch, one licence'' rule) and is valid for a six-month period from the date of issue.

Commodities exported by foreign investment enterprises or under compensation trade agreements, however, are not subject to the ''one batch, one licence'' rule. Licences issued to these enterprises are valid for six months and may be used for numerous export consignments. This separate licensing system has also been extended to enterprises exporting any of a number of commodities, including crude oil, processed oil products, coal, tea, livestock exports and various types of perishable agricultural produce.

Whether or not any goods are actually exported under an export licence, the licence must be returned to the original licensing authority within 30 days of its expiry.

Penalties

Exporters must provide accurate information when applying for an export licence. Approved export quotas may not be exceeded, and the assignment of export licences to other enterprises is prohibited.

Penalties for breaches include the circulation of a notice of criticism, the confiscation of foreign exchange earnings or even the temporary suspension or cancellation of the enterprise's right to conduct export operations. The severity of the penalty depends upon the seriousness of the breach. If a failure to comply with the Notice results in the State incurring substantial losses, or if the criminal law has been violated, the matter will be referred to the relevant judicial organs for investigation.

CHN ¶50-005   Special restrictions relating to foreign control of business

Foreign-controlled export or import businesses based in China must be registered with commercial authorities and restricted by objectives approved at the time of registration. Foreign company representative offices may be established to conduct promotional and liaison work but may not conduct business. The *General Principles of the Civil Law*deals in some details with the obligations of agents in their relationships with principles, although, like other areas of Chinese civil law, the law relating to liability for tortious acts is underdeveloped.

On 31 January 2003, MOFTEC (now known as MOFCOM) issued the *Establishment of Sino-Foreign Trading Equity Joint Ventures Tentative Procedures*(the "Tentative Procedures"), aiming to accelerate the development of the country's foreign trade sector by introducing greater foreign competition. The new Provisions are effective from 2 March 2003, and replace the *Establishment of Pilot Sino-Foreign Foreign Trading Equity Joint Ventures*which was issued in 1996 (the "1996 Regulations"). Under the Tentative Procedures, a foreign investor is allowed to form a sino-foreign joint venture foreign trading company (foreign trading JV) with a Chinese partner to conduct a foreign trading business. A foreign trading business includes the import and export of goods and technologies and the provision of associated services. Foreign investors are not yet allowed to establish a wholly foreign-owned enterprise (WFOE) to conduct foreign trade business. Despite the impossibility of forming a WFOE at this stage, these new regulations demonstrate the PRC's commitment to free up the business environment in this key sector of the economy, and demonstrate their commitment to implement the WTO protocols to which the PRC agreed in December 2001.

The Tentative Procedures have lifted or lessened some of the restrictions on the establishment of a foreign trading JV that were contained in the 1996 Regulations, including geographic restrictions, high qualification requirements of the proposed investors and capital requirements for forming a foreign trading JV. Although a number of restrictions have been removed, the restriction on maximum shareholding held by the foreign partner in a foreign trading JV still remains. The new regulations provide that the Chinese shareholdings in the foreign trading JV must be not less than 51%. Therefore, the foreign partner in the foreign trading JV is only allowed to have minority ownership of the JV company, while majority shareholding and board control of the JV company will still be held by the Chinese partner. According to the new regulations, this limitation on foreign shareholding will not be removed until 11 December 2003. This stipulation follows China's commitments in the Working Party Report, which provided for majority ownership by foreign investors in joint venture trading companies two years after WTO accession.

In addition to the limit on foreign shareholding, and the high capital investment and qualification requirements, the establishment of the foreign trading JV is also subject to government approval. The investors must apply to a Chinese approval authority to establish the foreign trading JV. They must also complete registration formalities with a number of PRC authorities after they have obtained the government approval in order to legally establish the JV company. The whole process would take several months.

CHN ¶50-011   Major objectives of host country

From about 1978, the government of the People's Republic of China has gradually liberalised restrictions on foreign trade relationships as part of its policy of opening up to the outside world. During the decade until 1988, this policy resulted in a proliferation of both domestic and foreign trade organisations and entities along China's eastern seaboard. Whereas previously China's trade with the western hemisphere since 1949 had been conducted almost exclusively through Hong Kong, from 1978, private and governmental trade delegations began arriving in China on an increasingly frequent basis. This activity was matched by Chinese trade delegations visiting western countries, such as delegations coordinated by MOFTEC (now known as the MOFCOM) and the State Economic Commission Foreign Trade Bureau. As foreign capital became increasingly freely available in China from 1978, the trade deficit widened and the government of the People's Republic of China took steps to clamp down on the import of foreign goods not deemed essential for economic development. Since 1988, the government further restricted an import demand in response to soaring inflation. Currently, in an attempt to meet its WTO commitments, China is in the process of gradually lifting its long-established control over import and export to realise the goal of free trade under WTO system.

Direct foreign trade liberalised

As from March 1997, China has officially relaxed conditions for domestic enterprises to conduct direct foreign trade. These measures are aimed at bringing Chinese practices in line with WTO rules on trading rights, and also to rejuvenate China's state enterprises.

Under the revised rules, enterprises turning out machinery and electronics products are allowed to trade directly if they can certify that they have, on average, exported US$1 million worth of products a year in the preceding two years. (The previous requirement was US$2 million.) For technology-intensive products, the requirement has been lowered from US$1 million to US$500,000. In the case of large state-owned or majority-controlled enterprises, the restriction has been completely removed.

The new rules are contained in a March 1997 circular issued jointly by the State Economic and Trade Commission (SETC) and MOFTEC(now known as MOFCOM).

The circular also expands the scope of businesses that productive enterprises are allowed to conduct in the future. Large enterprises that export more than US$10 million a year will be permitted to set up their own limited liability trading companies. Those capable of designing and manufacturing complete plants for export will be allowed to independently sign contracts for project construction, labour supply and other support services.

MOFTEC (now known as MOFCOM) promulgated the *Provisional Rules on Authorising Private Manufacturing Enterprises and Science Research Institute to Be Engaged in Import and Export*(the "Provisional Rules") on 1 October 1998. It authorised for the first time the private manufacturing enterprises and science research institute (the Private Entities) to be engaged in import and export. The Provisional Rules stipulate the qualification of the Private Entities who can apply for being engaged in import and export; the application document; the application procedure and examining and approval authority; and the rights and obligations of the Private Entities having been authorised to be engaged in import and export.

Now an individual is also entitled to engage in foreign trade business activities according to the *Revised Foreign Trade Law*. However the state may exercise state-operated trading management for import and export of certain goods. The business of import and export of goods subject to state-operated trading management can only be operated by delegated enterprises, except where the state permits the business of importing and exporting of a certain number of goods subject to state-operated trading management to be operated by non-delegated enterprises.

In July 2001, MOFTEC (now known as MOFCOM) issued the *Notice concerning Issues related to Expanding the Import and Export Rights of Foreign Investment Enterprises*. The Notice allows foreign-funded production enterprises to engage in export of purchased goods that are not subject to quota or licensing control and that are not their main line of products. The Notice also allows foreign-funded investment companies, whose parent companies are production conglomerates, to import ancillary system integration products or products for trial sale. R&D centres with foreign investment are also allowed to import a small amount of hi-tech products produced by their parent company for trial sale.

CHN ¶50-012   Rates of customs duties

The power to impose special rates of customs duty on imports into China has been granted to the State Council Customs Tariff Commission. Under amendments to import and export duty regulations, this power may be exercised when products of the PRC are subject to discriminatory import duty rates or other discriminatory treatment by another country. Preferences exist in respect of imports from certain countries including a number of middle-eastern countries and African countries. However, such preferences are in the process of being either revoked or disguised as China seeks to gain admission to multilateral trade agreements.

Exemptions from duty are available in respect of key technological imports, as a means of concession to foreign investment enterprises, and to a limited extent in respect of some goods imported to special economic zones and declared coastal trade regions. Goods imported for processing and destined for export are exempt from duty. A policy effective from 1 January 1998 allows customs duty exemption on the import of capital goods for encouraged foreign investment enterprises, except where other prohibitions or restrictions apply (see CHN ¶45-102for list of "encouraged" enterprises). The policy will apply only to that scope of duty-free capital imports which have been approved for duty-free treatment by the original review and approval authority, as well as by the Customs Bureau, in accordance with the new policy parameters. Foreign investment enterprises approved to be established before 31 March 1996 will continue to enjoy exemption from customs duty until the import of their capital goods is completed, up to the level of their originally approved total investment. Projects approved from 1 April 1996 to 31 December 1997 involving the import of equipment pursuant to foreign government loans and international financial institution loans will also enjoy customs duty exemptions, except where these capital goods fall within the category of commercial goods for which duty-free treatment is prohibited.

As of Year 2003, under its WTO commitments, China further cuts import tariffs for more than 4,000 categories from the Year 2002 average of 12.7% to a new average rate of 11.5%. The tariff rate for 111 commodities has been reduced to zero as of 1 January 2003. The publication of China's new import tariff list is being published in *International Business*, the newspaper of MOFTEC.

On 8 July 2000, the *Customs Law* was amended by the 16th conference held by the Standing Committee of the National People's Congress, and the Amendments have been implemented since 1 January 2001. Many issues such as the following are covered in the Amendments:

- Documents and certificates for declaration are not permitted to be amended or withdrawn without consent of the Customs once they are presented.

- With the consent of the Customs, the consignee of imported goods may examine goods or keep samples before declaration.

- The Customs protect intellectual property rights related to the imported and exported goods according to relevant laws and regulations. Consignors, consignees and their agents shall present legal documents certifying their intellectual property rights claimed.

- Guarantee for the Customs Affairs is stipulated in a separate chapter of the *Customs Law*.

On 23 November 2003, the State Council promulgated *PRC Import and Export Customs Duty Regulations*, which came into effect on 1 January 2004 to repeal 1992's *PRC Import and Export Customs Duty Regulations*. Compared with the 1992 Regulations, Article 18 of the 2003 Regulations set forth the criteria that transaction prices of imported goods shall be fulfilled. There shall be no restrictions on the buyer's disposal and use of the goods except for the restrictions set by laws and administrative regulations, geographical restrictions on re-sale and other restrictions that do not have substantial influence on the prices of the goods. Article 19 lists fees that shall be counted in the dutiable value of imported goods, including commissions and broker's fees apart from the commissions borne by the buyer on purchase of the goods, expenses on materials and labour used for packaging borne by the buyer as well as proceeds derived from the re-sale, disposal or use of the goods after import obtained by the seller directly or indirectly from the buyer. Article 20 lists the taxes and fees, such as customs duties and domestic taxes, which shall not be counted in the dutiable value of imported goods. Article 21 stipulates new guidelines for assessment, in consultation with the taxpayer, of the dutiable value of imported goods where the transaction price does not comply with relevant provisions or cannot be ascertained. The dutiable value shall first be assessed according to the transaction price of identical goods sold at the same time or about the same time to the PRC. Article 26 provides that the dutiable value of exported goods shall be examined and determined by customs based on the transaction price, and the transportation fees, transportation-related fees and insurance premiums before loading of the goods when they are transported to the place of shipment within the territory of the PRC.

The 2003 Regulations also provided how unpaid tax payments are handled in the case of merger, division, closure, dissolution and bankruptcy. It is stated that imported goods subject to customs duties and quotas shall follow tax rates on customs duty and quota administration in Article 12. For imported goods on which anti-dumping, anti-subsidy or safeguard measures are applied, the tax rates shall be in compliance with the relevant provisions of the *PRC Anti-dumping Regulations*, PRC Anti-subsidy Regulations and PRC Safeguard Measures Regulations.

CHN ¶50-013   Taxes

The restrictive nature of China's laws governing imports and the generally prohibitive rates of customs duties leave little room for other taxes. However, a number of hidden charges may be encountered on a region-by-region basis including special taxes on the freight of import and export goods.

CHN ¶50-014   Tariff agreements

China became a member of the World Trade Organisation (WTO) effective as of 11 November 2001. Under the non-discrimination principle of this multilateral trading system, China is expected to accord the most-favoured-nation treatment to all WTO members. However, export from China can still enjoy special tariff treatment in a number of non-WTO-member countries under relevant tariff agreements.

CHN ¶50-015   Concessional entry of goods

Certain concessions allowing entry of goods are available including goods imported to regions targeted for economic development.

CHN ¶50-021   FREE TRADE ZONES

China's first free trade zone (FTZ), located in the north-eastern city of Tianjin, has been officially launched. Foreign enterprises located in the FTZ will enjoy more fiscal incentives than those available in special economic zones (SEZs).

China has a number of partially free trade zones, in particular, the special economic zones of Shenzhen and Zhuhai in close proximity to Hong Kong. In addition to special trade incentives available in SEZs and declared regions, detailed incentives directed primarily at foreign investment in export-producing and advanced technological industries are available. These incentives are coordinated by MOFTEC and eligibility criteria are strict including significant restrictions affecting rights to free trade and the protection of intellectual property. Incentives are normally granted for short periods subject to annual review.

Unofficial zones

Of greatest concern to the foreign investor is the crackdown on China's unofficial zones. Only zones which have been approved by a provincial government or by the State Council may continue to offer preferential investment policies to foreigners. In response to this, various provincial governments are independently rectifying their special investment areas.

This crackdown on unofficial development zones has made the officially approved areas even more important features on the PRC investment landscape. Unlike the current situation with the unofficial zones, foreign investors operating in the State Council approved zones are not in danger of losing their special incentives. What follows is an outline of the major special investment areas in China, including details of recent developments. All of the zones mentioned below have retained their official status.

China's ETDZs

China has 30 officially approved economic and technological development zones (ETDZs). All of these zones have been approved by the State Council, and their status is not threatened by the current development zone purge. Eleven of these zones were approved in 1993.

China's ETDZs are:

- Changchun ETDZ (approved 1993);
- Chongqing ETDZ (approved 1993);
- Dalian ETDZ;
- Dongshan (approved 1993; note that according to the State Council notice approving this zone, the only ETDZ policy it can offer is the 15% income tax levy);
- Fuzhou ETDZ (expanded from 4.4km square to 10km square in 1993);
- Guangzhou ETDZ;
- Hangzhou ETDZ (approved 1993);
- Harbin ETDZ (approved 1993);
- Huizhou Daya Bay ETDZ (approved 1993);

- Kunshan ETDZ;
- Lianyungang ETDZ;
- Nantong ETDZ;
- Ningbo ETDZ;
- Panyu Nansha ETDZ (approved 1993);
- Qingdao ETDZ;
- Qinhuangdao ETDZ;
- Rongqiao ETDZ;
- Shanghai Caohejing (''Hi-tech park'') ETDZ;
- Shanghai Hongqiao ETDZ;
- Shanghai Minhang ETDZ;
- Shenyang ETDZ (approved 1993);
- Tianjin ETDZ;
- Weihai ETDZ;
- Wenzhou ETDZ;
- Wuhan ETDZ (approved 1993);
- Wuhu ETDZ (approved 1993);
- Xiaoshan ETDZ (approved 1993);
- Yantai ETDZ;
- Yingkou ETDZ; and
- Zhanjiang ETDZ.

''Fourteen Coastal Cities''

The investment incentives and other preferential policies available in China's Fourteen Coastal Cities, often referred to as open port cities, remain intact.

Special economic zones

China's five SEZs have not been affected by the development zone purge. All of the SEZs were originally set up with State Council approval.

Eighteen provincial capitals and the five ''Yangtze River Cities''

In 1992, the State Administration of Taxation issued regulations which gave ''open coastal city'' status to 18 border, coastal and inland provincial capitals in China, and also to five designated ''Yangtze River Cities''. The general taxation and other preferential policies parallel those for the original 14 coastal cities.

The 18 provincial capitals are as follows:

- Changchun;
- Changsha;
- Chengdu;
- Guiyang;
- Harbin;
- Hefei;

- Hohhot;
- Kunming;
- Lanzhou;
- Nanchang;
- Nanning;
- Shijiazhuang;

- Taiyuan;
- Urumchi;
- Xi'an;
- Xining;
- Yinchuan; and
- Zhengzhou.

      The five Yangtze River Cities are:

- Chongqing;
- Jiujiang;
- Wuhan;

- Wuhu; and

- Yueyang.

High and new technology zones

    There are currently 52 high and new technology zones which have received approval from the State Council. Of these zones, 25 were approved at the beginning of 1993. These new zones are located in the following cities:

- Anshan;
- Baoding;
- Baoji;
- Baotou;
- Changzhou;
- Daqing;
- Foshan;
- Guiyang;
- Huizhou;
- Jilin;
- Kunming;
- Luoyang;
- Mianyang;

- Nanchang;
- Nanning;
- Qingdao;
- Suzhou;
- Taiyuan;
- Urumchi;
- Weifang;
- Wuxi;
- Xiangfan;
- Zhuhai;
- Zhuzhou; and
- Zibo.

Municipalities with separately listed economic plans

    Press reports have suggested that some cities have lost their status as "municipalities with separately listed economic plans". These cities are Guangzhou, Shenyang, Xi'an, Wuhan and Nanjing.

    This loss of status results from Zhu Rongji's economic rectification program and will reduce the financial independence of these cities in planning infrastructure developments. It does not, however, impact upon open port city status or affect any State Council approved ETDZs operating within these municipalities.

Bonded warehouses and goods stored therein

    On 5 December 2003, the General Administration of Customs promulgated the (LEGREF) Administration of Bonded Warehouses and the Goods Stored Therein

Provisions. "Bonded warehouses" is defined as warehouses established with the approval of customs specially for the storage of bonded goods and other goods whose customs formalities have not been completed as specified in Article 2.

Article 5 stipulates that, with the approval of customs, certain goods such as imported goods for processing trade, transit goods and goods of foreign investors for temporary storage may be stored in bonded warehouses. To establish a bonded warehouse, an enterprise shall havea registered capital of at least RMB 3 million. The bonded warehouse shall satisfy the criteria provided in Article 9, such as compliance with customs' requirements on the design and reaching the minimum size or capacity. Bonded warehouses cannot be rented or lent to others to manage. Branch warehouses are prohibited. Bonded warehouses are subject to customs inspection and annual review. Goods stored in bonded warehouses may undergo simple processing such as packaging, dissembling and assembling, but not substantial processing. Such goods shall not be sold, assigned, mortgaged or disposed of in other ways without the approval of customs. Goods stored in bonded warehouses shall only be stored for one year and shall be transported abroad, transferred to bonded zones, export processing zones or other bonded warehouses, changed to be imports for processing trade, or sold to the domestic market as specified as Articles 24 and 25. Bonded warehouses shall pay taxes to customs and bear corresponding legal liability for goods that are damaged or destroyed during their storage in bonded warehouses.

CHN ¶50-022   LABELLING AND PACKAGING REQUIREMENTS

Special requirements concerning labelling, packaging and other standards are governed by the *Commodity Import and Export Inspection Law*. That Law has regard to other enacted requirements and standards. The State Bureau also issued a law on food labelling, *General Standards for Food Labelling*, which came into force on 1 October 1995. Food producers, including foreign companies, who fail to properly label containers may face severe consequences. This includes having their goods confiscated, fines and administrative punishments.

Violations of the law include:

* labels without the quality standards or product standard codes;

* ambiguous or misleading illustrations; and

* foreign words which are bigger in size than the Chinese characters on the label.

There is a maximum fine of RMB3,000 (or 15% of the value of the goods) which will be imposed on those who do not provide such information as the weight, name of producer, date of production and date of expiry on the labels. Foreign producers who fail to provide food labels in Chinese will be fined up to RMB5,000 or 20% of the value of the seized goods. Importers and retailers of imported food have until 1 May 1996 before imported food labels are inspected.

On 4 September 1997, MOFTEC issued the *Rules on the Administration of Codes for Import and Export Companies of the PRC*, stipulating the issuance and administration of codes for import and export companies (the ''companies'') including the following issues:

- the administration of codes shall be borne by MOFTEC, while those of local companies shall be done by authorities at provincial level;
- MOFTEC is responsible for drafting the Norms of Codes for Import and Export Companies of the PRC as well as printing registration forms and establishing electronic databases;
- the application and issuance of codes are subject to the principle of ''registrant where it be'';
- the authorities of code administration shall issue codes for the companies within three working days upon receiving the stipulated materials;
- the companies shall ascertain the completion and accuracy of their application forms and any change in the contents of the form shall initiate the modification of registration with proper authorities; and
- the codes will be used by the companies in going through the formalities for their foreign trade business.

CHN ¶50-023   International treaties

China obtained full member status in the World Trade Organisation (previously known as GATT) on November 2001. In addition to multilateral agreements, China is a party to numerous bilateral trade agreements.

CHN ¶50-024   Penalties and additional taxes

Sanctions imposed for breaches of the code governing import and export include fines and in severe cases may lead to criminal charges and imprisonment.

According to the *Revised Foreign Trade Law*, where goods subject to state-operated trading management are imported or exported without authorisation, the State Council department in charge of foreign trade or other relevant departments may impose a fine of less than RMB50,000 (Art. 60) Import or export of goods whose import and export are prohibited, or import or export of goods whose import and export are restricted without authorisation, shall be handled and penalised by customs in accordance with laws and administrative regulations. If a crime is committed, criminal liability shall be pursued according to law (Art. 61).

CHN ¶50-025   Anti-dumping and countervailing duties

China has enacted anti-dumping legislation. The *Regulations of the People's Republic of China on Anti-dumping and Anti-subsidies* was promulgated and came into effect on 25 March 1997. The regulations are designed to regulate foreign trade, promote fair competition and protect China's manufacturing industry. They allow the Chinese government to take action against foreign companies which export products at lower than the normal price to China. The regulations empower MOFTEC and the General Administration of Customs to investigate cases of dumping. SETC is empowered to investigate jointly with the relevant State Council departments cases of damage caused by dumping. MOFTEC, SETC and the relevant State Council departments are also empowered to jointly formulate measures for dealing with dumping and subsidised imports.

Anti-dumping disputes soar in the entire year of 2002 as detailed procedures and rules in this respect have also been introduced and developed during the same period by MOFTEC, including the following:

- *Provisional Rules of Anti-dumping Site Investigation*;
- *Provisional Rules of Anti-dumping New Exporter Review*;
- *Provisional Rules of Mid-term Review of Anti-dumping and Dumping Margin*; and
- *Provisional Rules of Anti-dumping Questionnaire Survey*.

CHN ¶50-031 Power to detain goods

The State Administration of Commodity Inspection has a general power of detention of goods in addition to powers of custom authorities. Limited appeal rights are provided for.

CHN ¶50-032 When is duty or tax payable?

Provision for bonding is available in the special economic zones and declared economic regions.

Exchange Control — The Movement of Money

Which laws apply to exchange control? ....CHN ¶55-001

Who administers exchange control? ....CHN ¶55-002

Major objectives of exchange control policies ....CHN ¶55-003

Application of exchange control laws to various
    countries ....CHN ¶55-004

Repatriation of capital ....CHN ¶55-005

Remittance of dividends, etc. ....CHN ¶55-011

Limit on amount of local currency and foreign
    currency to remit out of host country ....CHN ¶55-012

Restrictions on remittance of currency ....CHN ¶55-013

Currency to be used for loans ....CHN ¶55-014

Method of fixing exchange rate of host country's
    currency ....CHN ¶55-015

Differing rates of exchange for host country's
    currency ....CHN ¶55-021

Transactions requiring approval from exchange
    control authorities ....CHN ¶55-022

Tests for distinguishing residents from non-residents ...CHN ¶55-023

Distinctions between foreign-controlled companies
    incorporated inside or out of the host country ....CHN ¶55-024

Effect of local participation on exchange controls ....CHN ¶55-025

Exchange control exemptions ....CHN ¶55-031

Remittance from host country of personal savings and
    pension fund contributions by expatriate personnel ..CHN ¶55-032

Exchange control formalities ....CHN ¶55-033

Consequences of breach of exchange control law ....CHN ¶55-034

Forward market for foreign exchange ....CHN ¶55-035

Restrictions on repatriation of capital during
    continuation of investment incentives ....CHN ¶55-041

Taxation considerations in respect of exchange control
    regulations ....CHN ¶55-042

CHN ¶55-001   WHICH LAWS APPLY TO EXCHANGE CONTROL?

China exercises centralised management over foreign exchange, this function being performed by the State Administration of Foreign Exchange (SAFE).

In 1994, reforms were carried out in the administration of foreign currencies. A combination of exchange rates (from the simultaneous existence of several exchange rates to a single market exchange rate) was adopted together with unified settlement and sale of foreign exchange, and a unified inter-bank foreign exchange market was established. This had an important impact on China's economic development and reform, opening the country to the outside world. From 1 October 2003, the China Foreign Exchange Trade Centre allows members to carry out purchases and sales at the same time through the trading system of the inter-bank foreign exchange market. Since 1996, foreign currency business of foreign-invested enterprises has been directed into the banking system of settlement and sale. On 1 December 1996, China formally accepted Art 8 of the Agreement on International Currencies and Funds, realising the convertibility of the RMB under the current account ahead of schedule. This was a major breakthrough in reforming the country's foreign exchange control system. The following regulations currently apply to foreign exchange control:

- the *Regulations of the People's Republic of China on Foreign Exchange Control* amended on 14 January 1997 (replaces the *Provisional Regulations for Foreign Exchange Control of the People's Republic of China* of 18 December 1980);
- the *Administrative Measures on Foreign Exchange Control in Bonded Area* on 14 August 2002;
- the *Administrative Regulations on Domestic Foreign Exchange Accounts* on 7 October 1997;
- the *Provisional Administrative Regulations on Domestic Allocation and Transfer of Foreign Exchange* on 25 September 1997;
- the *Announcement of the People's Bank of China concerning Further Reform of Foreign Exchange Control System* on 28 December 1993;
- the *Administrative Regulations on Foreign Exchange Settlements, Sales and Payments* on 20 June 1996; and
- the *Provisional Measures of Foreign Debt Administration*, effective as of 1 March 2003.

Regulations on Foreign Exchange Control

The *Regulations on Foreign Exchange Control* came into effect on 1 April 1996 and was amended on 14 January 1997. The Regulations mark a further move towards full convertibility of the renminbi. Foreign-invested enterprises with foreign currency accounts are permitted under the Regulations to exchange renminbi for foreign currency at the local branches of authorised local PRC banks, rather than handling such transactions through the swap centres. This is seen as a step towards the elimination of swap centres.

On 28 December 1993, the *Announcement of the People's Bank of China concerning the Further Reform of the Foreign Exchange Control System* was issued stipulating that the renminbi exchange rate will be subject to a single rate based on market supply and demand. The Regulations support this 1993 policy and further emphasise the prohibition against circulation of foreign currency within the PRC and the pricing of goods in foreign currency. The law governs the foreign exchange business of financial institutions, the setting of currency exchange rates, the administration of foreign exchange revenue relating to current and capital account items, as well as the handling of foreign exchange violations.

The purpose of the above Regulations is to exert uniform control over all foreign exchange issue and expenditure, the issuance of all foreign currency payment instruments, the transportation into and out of China of foreign exchange, and precious metals. The principle features of those laws and regulations are as follows:

- Foreign exchange is defined to include:
    - foreign currencies, including bank notes, coins, etc;
    - securities in foreign currency, including government bonds, treasury bills, corporate bonds and debentures, shares, interest and dividend coupons, etc;
    - instruments payable in foreign currency, including bills, drafts, cheques, bank deposit certificates, postal savings certificates, etc; and
    - other foreign exchange funds.

- Foreign exchange revenue must be sold to a designated foreign exchange bank or deposited in a foreign exchange account (upon approval) with a designated foreign exchange bank. Approval is necessary before foreign exchange is deposited outside the PRC.

- Foreign exchange held by individuals may be deposited in a bank or sold to a designated foreign exchange bank. Expatriate experts recruited by organisations inside the PRC may remit their after-tax wages out of the PRC. If they are paid in renminbi, they can remit their after-tax wages in foreign currencies purchased from a designated foreign exchange bank.

- Organisations within the PRC who wish to invest outside the country must first obtain approval from the foreign exchange control authorities concerning the source of foreign exchange funds.

- A foreign venture shall apply for and obtain permission from SAFE before it can establish a foreign exchange deposit account with an overseas bank. Those enterprises with approval to open such accounts must report receipts and expenditures of that account to the administration within 30 days at the end of each quarter. Offshore oil resource exploration organisations enjoy certain special exemptions from this rule.

- Excepting foreign exchange approvals by the administration, foreign-invested enterprises are required to remit to China foreign exchange earned by export products and deposit it in foreign exchange accounts and generally go through procedures of accounting and verification. Export and foreign exchange sold by a foreign investment enterprise to the Bank of China is calculated in accordance with the exchange rate issued by SAFE.

- Financial institutions, which operate foreign exchange business, require approval from the foreign exchange control authorities. These bodies are also required to submit foreign exchange balance sheets, profit and loss statements and accounting statements and information to the foreign exchange authorities.

- Following liquidation of a foreign investment enterprise, the renminbi belonging to the foreign investor may be remitted out of the PRC in foreign exchange and that belonging to the Chinese investor may be sold to a designated foreign exchange bank.

- Where foreign-invested enterprises are unable to balance foreign exchange receipts and expenditure, foreign exchange control regulations provide that accounts may be settled and paid in foreign exchange for products sold domestically where the following criteria are met:

  — On approval by foreign trade departments of the government, accounts may be settled in foreign currency for products needed by China which are sold to Chinese institutions engaged in foreign trade so as to replace imports with these products.

  — Accounts for commodities in short supply on China's domestic market that are sold to Chinese purchasing institutions may be settled in foreign currency.

  — Products sold to Chinese institutions which are manufactured by foreign-invested enterprises with advanced technology and equipment may be settled in foreign currency.

  — Products of foreign-invested enterprises sold in special economic zones and those products purchased by one foreign investment enterprise from another foreign investment enterprise may be settled in foreign currency.

Foreign currency deposits

Two laws designed to control foreign currency deposits have been issued by the Bank of China: the *Regulations of the Bank of China on Foreign Currency Deposits* (Category A) and the *Regulations of the Bank of China on Foreign Currency Deposits* (Category B). The regulations, which came into effect on 1 March 1993, allow Chinese citizens and foreigners to open foreign currency accounts with the Bank of China.

There are two main types of deposit accounts — Category A and Category B deposits. Generally, Category A deposits may be made by enterprises (including state-owned and foreign investment enterprises), various non-governmental institutions, and other approved organisations with independent legal status. Category B deposit accounts, on the other hand, can only be opened by individuals in their own name. Foreigners, Chinese with foreign nationality, overseas Chinese, and persons from Hong Kong, Macao and Taiwan who are resident abroad or in China, are permitted to open Category B deposit accounts.

Category A deposits

Application

Category A foreign currency deposit accounts may be opened by the following bodies (Art 2):

- foreign diplomatic and commercial entities, offices of non-governmental organisations and organs of international bodies in China;
- Chinese and foreign enterprises and organisations having independent legal person status set up in foreign countries or in Hong Kong, Macao and Taiwan;
- Chinese and foreign enterprises set up within the bonded zones in China;
- foreign investment enterprises and units set up within Chinese territory;
- bodies which are allowed to hold foreign exchange in accordance with the State Foreign Exchange Control Regulations; and
- financial institutions which may conduct foreign exchange transactions with the approval of the People's Bank of China.

Types of deposits

There are four types of foreign exchange deposits: fixed, agreed, notified and demand deposits (Art 4). These are restricted to six kinds of currencies: US dollar, pound sterling, Deutschemark, French franc, Japanese yen and Hong Kong dollar. Accounts in other currencies may be opened in special circumstances with bank approval (Art 5).

Use of funds

Deposited funds may be remitted to places inside and outside China, converted into renminbi, or transferred to another foreign currency account kept at the bank. With approval, a specified amount may also be withdrawn and taken out of the PRC (Art 7).

Interest

Interest on deposits will be calculated and paid at the foreign currency deposit rate issued by the State (Art 9).

Category B deposits

Funds

Foreign exchange in convertible currency remitted, carried or sent into China from abroad or from Hong Kong, Macao and Taiwan may be deposited in Category B accounts. Additionally, other foreign exchange which the Bank of China has agreed to accept for deposit may be deposited in these accounts.

Types of deposits

Funds may be deposited in foreign exchange accounts or foreign currency cash accounts (Art 4). They may be either fixed deposits or on-call deposits (Art 5).

Currency restrictions

As with Category A deposits, Category B deposits are restricted to six major currencies: US dollar, pound sterling, Deutschemark, French franc, Japanese yen and Hong Kong dollar (Art 66).

Use of funds

Deposit funds may be remitted to places within or outside China. They may also be converted to renminbi. If a depositor leaves China, funds in a foreign cash account may be directly withdrawn as cash or may be remitted abroad (Art 8).

On 15 October 2002, SAFE issued the *Issues Relevant to Further Adjusting the Policies on Foreign Exchange Accounts for Current Account Items Circular*. The Circular unifies the conditions for wholly Chinese-owned enterprises and foreign-invested enterprises opening foreign exchange accounts for current account items. Wholly Chinese-owned enterprises shall face less stringent requirements when applying to open foreign exchange accounts for current account items. Any domestic enterprise (Chinese or foreign-invested) authorised to engage in foreign business or that has foreign exchange income under current items may apply to SAFE to open a foreign exchange account for current account items (Item 1). Existing foreign exchange settlement accounts for current account items and designated foreign exchange accounts shall be consolidated to form foreign exchange accounts for current account items (Item 2). The balance of a foreign exchange account for current account items of domestic organisations shall be limited to 20% of the foreign exchange income under current account items of the previous year. The balance of new foreign exchange accounts for current account items opened by domestic organisations that has no foreign exchange income under current account items in the previous year shall not exceed US$100,000 (Item 3). The scope and limit on payments and receipts applied to current account foreign exchange settlement accounts and foreign exchange accounts opened before the implementation of this Circular shall remain in effect (Item 4).

Attached to the Circular is the *Administration of Foreign Exchange Accounts for Current Account Items of Domestic Organisations Implementing Rules*, which details the opening, using and closing of foreign exchange accounts for current account items. On 3 March 2003, SAFE issued the *Issues Relevant to Improving Foreign Exchange Control on Foreign Direct Investment Circular* (the "Circular"), which became effective as of 1 April 2003. The Circular mainly provides administration rules regarding:

- administration of the accounts opened and the capital contributed by foreign investors;

- confirmation request in connection with investment verification and foreign exchange registration for foreign capital of foreign-invested enterprises; and

- administration of reduction in capital by foreign-invested enterprises and adjustment of some administrative business.

On 6 March 2003, SAFE issued the *Relevant to the Sale and Payment of Foreign Exchange for Non-trade Items that are not Expressly Specified in Prevailing Laws and Regulations Circular* (the "Circular"), which became effective as of 1 April 2003. This

Circular sets out the procedures for the sale and payment of foreign exchange for non-trade items that are not expressly specified in prevailing laws and regulations:

- For those with an amount of US$50,000 or below, a domestic organisation may directly complete verification, and sale and payment of foreign exchange with a designated foreign exchange bank.
- For those with an amount more than US$50,000 but less than or equal to US$500,000, the domestic organisation shall obtain verification from a SAFE branch before it can proceed with a designated bank for sale and payment of foreign exchange.
- For those with an amount over US$500,000, it shall apply to a SAFE branch at the locality, which will forward relevant documents to SAFE for verification. Then, it can handle sale and payment of foreign exchange with a designated foreign exchange bank on the strength of the approval of the SAFE branch at the locality (Item 1).

Certain enterprises or work units can be exempt from the above requirements after permitted by a SAFE branch at the locality and may proceed with the bank directly. The local SAFE branches may formulate their own permission conditions. In case of a violation by an approved organisation, the local SAFE branch shall notify the bank to immediately disqualify it (Item 2). Designated foreign exchange banks shall register and report each foreign exchange sale and payment transaction to the SAFE branch at the locality (Item 6).

CHN ¶55-002   WHO ADMINISTERS EXCHANGE CONTROL?

The authority administering foreign exchange control in China is SAFE. The administration has broad discretionary powers but nevertheless works within a system where the free conversion of foreign exchange is not possible. The discretion available to the administration comes about by way of necessity as the rules governing foreign exchange, when interpreted strictly, state that Chinese currency received by foreign-invested enterprises can only be used in China for such purposes as purchasing Chinese material and paying salaries and other similar expenses. Issues of tax avoidance or minimisation, while not directly relevant to the exercise of discretion, may have a bearing.

The approval trial branches of the SAFE may directly issue examination opinions on the source of foreign exchange for overseas investment projects in which the Chinese party's foreign exchange investment is below US$3 million. Authorised sub-branches may also directly issue such opinions for those below US$1 million.

SAFE has issued several provisions and notices since 2000 regarding foreign exchange control.

The Notice on Adjustment of Approving Authority on Open Special Foreign Exchange Accounts and Sale of Foreign Exchange Income Concerning the Issue of Domestic B Shares and Overseas Listing

On 13 December 1999, the *Notice on Adjustment of Approving Authority on Open Special Foreign Exchange Accounts and Sale of Foreign Exchange Income Concerning the Issue of Domestic B Shares and Overseas Listing* was promulgated. According to the Notice, enterprises issuing domestic B shares who wish to open special accounts for the shares, as well as foreign-listed enterprises who wish to open special accounts for foreign exchange stock, must apply to and get approval by local SAFE branch offices.

Foreign-listed enterprises wishing to open foreign exchange accounts shall apply to local SAFE branch offices. Approval by SAFE will be based on preliminary examination by its branch office.

The Notice on Authorising Local SAFE Branches to Deal with Foreign Exchange Matters Concerning Share Transfer and Liquidation of Foreign-Invested Enterprises

On 22 December 1999, SAFE issued the *Notice on Authorising Local SAFE Branches to Deal with Foreign Exchange Matters Concerning Share Transfer and Liquidation of Foreign-Invested Enterprises*. According to the Notice, local branch offices of SAFE are authorised to examine and approve foreign currency purchases resulting from the share transfer and liquidation of foreign-invested enterprises. In addition, the Notice stipulates respectively the documents required to be submitted for examination and approval in case of share transfer and liquidation.

Trial Provisions on Rewards to Informers of Illegal Foreign Exchange Activities

On 3 January 2000, the *Trial Provisions on Rewards to Informers of Illegal Activities in the Field of Foreign Exchange* was promulgated. According to the Provisions, the informer of an activity violating the laws and regulations on the foreign exchange administration will be granted honour and/or money award. The money award is within 10% of the total fine made by SAFE in each case, and will not exceed RMB100,000.

The Notice on Sale and Payment of Foreign Currency and Verification Administration by Classifying Evidence Sheet of Imported Goods on Customs Declaration Form

On 2 February 2000, SAFE and the General Administration of Customs jointly issued the *Notice on Sale and Payment of Foreign Currency and Verification Administration by Classifying Evidence Sheet of Imported Goods on Customs Declaration Form*. According to the Notice, the Declaration Form is classified by means of trade:

- trade permitted for the sale (payment) of foreign currency;
- trade permitted under conditions for the sale (payment) of foreign currency; and
- trade prohibited for the sale (payment) of foreign currency.

The designated foreign exchange banks and SAFE will sell and pay foreign exchange or administer their verification of the aforementioned based on the classification on the Customs Form.

The Notice Concerning Adjustment of Policies for Reconciliation of Foreign Exchange Received from Exports and Administration of Foreign Exchange Accounts

On 12 November 2001, SAFE issued the *Notice Concerning Adjustment of Policies for Reconciliation of Foreign Exchange Received from Exports and Administration of Foreign Exchange Accounts*. The adjustments delineated in the Notice are made to help domestic enterprises adapt to the new export environment following China's entry into the WTO. These adjustments include relaxation of the requirements for Chinese-funded enterprises to open foreign exchange settlement accounts, submission of documents to the foreign exchange authority through the port-of-entry system, and relaxation of the conditions for approving differences between receivable and actually received foreign exchange.

The Notice on Strengthening Administration of the Sale and Payment of Foreign Exchange in Connection with Technology Import Contracts

On 20 February 2002, MOFTEC and SAFE jointly issued the *Notice on Strengthening Administration of the Sale and Payment of Foreign Exchange in Connection with Technology Import Contracts*. The Notice specifies the documents that must be presented to a designated foreign exchange bank in order to complete foreign exchange sale and payment procedures for the import of technology. The Notice lists the types of technology import contracts and sets forth rules on how to handle changes, the types of forms to use, an online verification system and tampering with certificates and forms.

The Notice Concerning Trial Operation on a Nationwide Basis of the "Port Electronic Law Implementation System" for Foreign Exchange Received for Exports

On 29 May 2001, SAFE and the General Administration of Customs jointly issued this Notice introducing the new "verification and cancellation" system for foreign exchange received for exports. Under the new system, electronic Verification and Cancellation Statement record books are to be established at "Shared Data Centres" under China's public telecommunications networks. This will enable Customs and tax authorities to achieve network data checking of Verification and Cancellation Statements in the Customs export declaration stage and the export rebate stage. This will also enable enterprises—

- to make online applications to the foreign exchange authorities for the number of Verification and Cancellation Statements required;
- to make online Verification and Cancellation Statement filings with the local Customs authorities before carrying out Customs declaration procedures; and
- to submit the Verification and Cancellation Statements online after export.

The Notice Concerning Issues Related to Making Further Adjustments to the Policies for Administration of Current Account Foreign Exchange Accounts

Effective as of 15 October 2002, the Notice introduces a unified legal regime for the current account foreign exchange accounts which applies to both wholly Chinese-owned enterprises and foreign-invested enterprises. Under the new regime, generally, the cap for an enterprise's current account foreign exchange account shall be 20% of the enterprise's current account foreign exchange income for the proceeding year, which replaces the cap rules that previously applied to foreign-invested enterprises. The Notice also provides for the consolidation of current account foreign exchange settlement accounts and special-purpose foreign exchange accounts.

The Administration of Verification and Reconciliation of Foreign Exchange Received from Exports Procedures

Effective as of 1 October 2003, the Procedures set forth the procedures an export work unit shall follow once it has acquired the right to export. The Procedures provides on protocol if an export work unit ceases business, has its qualification to conduct foreign trade revoked, or where there are splits or mergers etc. The Procedures also set forth protocol for customs and deal with the submission of unused verification and reconciliation certificates to the SAFE.

CHN ¶55-003   MAJOR OBJECTIVES OF EXCHANGE CONTROL POLICIES

On 28 December 1993, the *Announcement of the People's Bank of China Concerning the Further Reform of the Foreign Exchange Control System* was issued, stipulating that the renminbi exchange rate will be subject to a single rate based on market supply and demand. This has been China's main foreign exchange control policy as well as the curbing of an increasingly high inflation rate. In order to attain this goal, the government issued the *Regulations on Management of Foreign Exchange* on 1 April 1996 and the *Notice of the State Council Concerning Strengthening Control Over Taking Out and Use of International Commercial Loans* on 12 January 1989. Pursuant to the notice, there are only 10 organisations within the People's Republic of China which have the capacity to engage relatively freely in foreign exchange dealings. Other organisations are restricted by rules applied by the People's Bank of China on a loan-by-loan basis. Implementation rules issued by SAFE further enforced strict control over foreign exchange.

CHN ¶55-004   APPLICATION OF EXCHANGE CONTROL LAWS TO VARIOUS COUNTRIES

China's foreign exchange control laws are, in theory, applied uniformly in relation to all countries recognised outside the host country.

CHN ¶55-003

CHN ¶55-005   REPATRIATION OF CAPITAL

If a foreign exchange investor wishes to transfer its capital in foreign exchange outside China, it should apply to SAFE for permission and state the source of foreign exchange funds and reasons for the transfer. Extensive documentary materials in support of the application will be required. On obtaining permission, capital may be drawn from the foreign exchange deposit of the investor and remitted abroad.

Upon completion of the liquidation of a foreign-invested enterprise, the renminbi belonging to the foreign investor may be remitted out of the PRC in foreign exchange and that belonging to the Chinese investor may be sold to a designated foreign exchange bank. Such capital is to be drawn and remitted from the foreign exchange deposit account of the defunct venture.

CHN ¶55-011   REMITTANCE OF DIVIDENDS, ETC

The remittance of dividends, branch profits, interest, royalties, advisory fees, licence fees, management fees, and machine rental and amounts payable under guarantee, etc is allowed.

On 15 October 2003, SAFE issued the Relevant to Further Intensifying the Reform of Foreign Exchange Control on Overseas Investment Circular, which became effective on 1 November 2003. The Circular provides that upon approval by the trial branches, investors may remit the preliminary capital out of China before the overseas investee enterprise is established. After the overseas investee enterprise has been registered, the remaining preliminary capital may be directly deposited in the overseas enterprise's account. If the establishment of the overseas enterprise fails, the remaining preliminary capital must be fully remitted back to China within severn days of the resolution to terminate the investment.

On 29 March 2003, SAFE issued the *Foreign Exchange Control Issues Relevant to Fund Management Companies with Foreign Equity Participation Circular*, which became effective on 1 May 2003. The Circular lists the documents required for opening of foreign exchange capital fund accounts, foreign exchange settlement as well as purchase of foreign exchange for profit payment to foreign shareholders, share transfer and foreign capital reduction (withdrawal). The receipt of foreign exchange capital fund accounts of fund management companies with foreign equity participation shall be limited to remittance of capital contributions of foreign shareholders while the expenditure of such foreign exchange capital account shall be limited to external expenditure under current account items or other foreign exchange expenditure approved by SAFE (Item 4). Item 10 prohibits fund management companies with foreign equity participation from engaging in external borrowing or security.

CHN ¶55-012   LIMIT ON AMOUNT OF LOCAL CURRENCY AND FOREIGN CURRENCY TO REMIT OUT OF HOST COUNTRY

While the availability of currency of the host country does not present a problem in the People's Republic of China, an enterprise's ability to obtain foreign currency to remit out of China is a serious problem, especially under the capital account. The venture must itself maintain a foreign exchange account sufficient to meet its foreign obligations. Contracts with Chinese parties should incorporate contingency arrangements to enable topping up of such foreign exchange earnings for the purpose of remitting the profits.

CHN ¶55-013 RESTRICTIONS ON REMITTANCE OF CURRENCY

Foreign exchange settlements, sales and payments are subject to the *Administrative Regulations on Foreign Exchange Settlements, Sales and Payments* which came into force on July 1996. The provisions provide that profits and bonuses of foreign parties in foreign investment enterprises, after taxes are paid, can be remitted out of China by making withdrawals from their foreign exchange accounts or at designated foreign exchange banks.

Foreign exchange used for some non-trade and non-operational purposes by individuals must be converted and paid at designated foreign exchange banks. This includes renminbi wages and living expenses received by foreign experts who have been employed by domestic organisations and which require conversion into foreign exchange.

Renminbi which has not been used when leaving the country by foreigners, overseas Chinese and Hong Kong, Macao and Taiwanese compatriots who came to China for a temporary stay may be converted into foreign exchange for taking out of China on the strength of their passports and the original conversion receipts (whose term of validity is six months). Non-residents must make a declaration to Customs if they are carrying more than US$5,000 into or out of China. If a non-resident carries more than US$5,000 out of China and there is no record that he or she declared that foreign exchange on entering China, he or she must present Customs with a permit signed and issued by a designated foreign exchange bank. A bank will issue a permit only if it is presented with verification documents issued by SAFE. This is a requirement of the *Measures on the Control of the Entrance and Departure from China Carrying Foreign Exchange* which came into effect on 10 February 1997. The measures apply to all non-residents including foreigners, overseas Chinese and residents of Hong Kong and Macao.

Currency remitted in foreign exchange should be used to pay, principally, for imported materials, the repayment of principal and interest on loans in foreign exchange, the payment of profits due to foreign investors, salary and wages of staff and workers of foreign nationality and other like expenses.

Expenditure geared to the upgrading of technology, the raising of the quality of products, the lowering of costs and the improvement of management is also acceptable.

On 14 September 1999, SAFE promulgated the *Notice Regarding the Amendment to Remittance Abroad of Profits, Dividends and Bonus by the Bank Designated to Engage in Foreign Exchange Business* (the ''Amendment Notice'').

According to the Amendment Notice, only with the approval of competent authorities can foreign-invested enterprises remit abroad profits and bonuses in foreign currencies before they fully perform their obligation of contributing the registered capital in compliance with relevant contracts.

When a Chinese enterprise having issued stock abroad fails to draw funds collected thereby back to China according to the *Regulation of Foreign Exchange Control*, it will be fined by SAFE or its local branches, although dividends and bonus can be remitted abroad through banks.

Regulation on Administration of Renminbi

The *Regulation on Administration of Renminbi* was promulgated on 3 February 2000 and came into effect on 1 May 2000. The Administration Regulation stipulates the design, print, issue, circulation and retrieval of the renminbi and the penalties for violation of the Administration Regulation.

CHN ¶55-014   CURRENCY TO BE USED FOR LOANS

The foreign exchange regulations state that loans to Chinese entities from foreign banks and companies must be approved under the State Mandatory Plan and submitted for examination by SAFE and MOFTEC. Foreign approval may need to be sought at the State Council level. Joint ventures may seek working capital loans, loans for the settlement of accounts and fixed asset loans in renminbi or foreign exchange from the Bank of China. Such borrowings must be reported to SAFE for recording.

On 22 June 1998, SAFE issued the *Notice on Strengthening Administration of Approval of the Payment of Foreign Debts including Principal and Interests*, stipulating mainly the policy for dealing with the examination and approval of the payment of foreign debts in the event that loan contract terms on payment are modified either by the creditor or by the debtor.

On 20 August 1998, to address the problem of purchasing foreign exchange to prepay loans, the People's Bank of China (PBOC) and SAFE jointly issued the *Notice on Issues Related to Prohibition on Purchasing Foreign Exchange to Prepay Loans* (the Notice) to reaffirm the policy relating to the administration of foreign debts. The Notice provides, *inter alia*, as follows:

- SAFE shall strengthen the administration of registration and payment of foreign debts, registration of foreign debts and the examination of the payment, including prepayment of loans.

- Commercial banks shall control the purpose of loans in RMB and prevent the purchase of foreign exchange to prepay loans.

On 31 August 1998, in order to prohibit the purchase of foreign exchange to prepay loans, PBOC and SAFE jointly issued the *Urgent Notice on Prohibition on Purchasing Foreign Exchange to Prepay Loans* (the ''Urgent Notice'') in which the following issues are emphasised:

- Commercial banks shall strengthen their administration of loans;

- SAFE shall strengthen the work on examination and approval of the expenditure of foreign exchange under the capital item;

- Banks appointed officially to be engaged in the foreign exchange business shall strengthen their supervision on the sales and purchases of foreign exchange under the capital item;

- The risk administration of financial entities in the foreign exchange business under the capital item shall be strengthened; and

- A complete examination on purchasing foreign exchange to prepay loans is required and violators discovered by such examination are at risk of penalty.

CHN ¶55-015   METHOD OF FIXING EXCHANGE RATE OF HOST COUNTRY'S CURRENCY

Prior to 1 January 1994, China's rate of exchange in relation to other currencies was set at a fixed rate against the principal trading currencies. Currency swap centres for foreign-invested enterprises existed to provide a market for surplus foreign exchange.

From 1 April 1994, China reformed its foreign currency market with the "floating" of the renminbi. The rate will be determined by market forces and closely managed as the exchange rate will be determined from day to day by PBOC.

The Chinese Government has announced that it is aiming to make the renminbi fully convertible in the near future.

CHN ¶55-021   DIFFERING RATES OF EXCHANGE FOR HOST COUNTRY'S CURRENCY

China has adopted a combination of exchange rates (from the simultaneous existence of several exchange rates to a single market exchange rate). The dual exchange rate system as well as the nation's swap centres have been phased out.

CHN ¶55-022   TRANSACTIONS REQUIRING APPROVAL FROM EXCHANGE CONTROL AUTHORITIES

All foreign exchange transactions in the People's Republic of China require approval by the exchange control authorities or else are monitored by the process of requiring the reporting of foreign exchange transactions.

In particular, the allotment of securities to non-residents out of the host country must be approved. No Chinese domestic organisation may issue securities with a foreign exchange value inside or outside China without the approval of the State Council.

Exchange control authorities through PBOC closely control the debiting and crediting of bank accounts of non-residents.

Restrictions on foreign bank participation limit the availability of inter-company accounts with non-resident parent or associated companies.

China has realised the convertibility of RMB under current account; contracts (as coordinated by MOFTEC) falling within the current account category do not require advance approval by the relevant authorities.

Restrictions on borrowing or otherwise raising capital inside or from outside the host country are designed to enable close monitoring of foreign currency flow in the economy.

CHN ¶55-015

CHN ¶55-023 TESTS FOR DISTINGUISHING RESIDENTS FROM NON-RESIDENTS

In 1980, the foreign exchange certificate (FEC) was introduced. Foreigners entering China exchange their foreign currency for FECs which are then spent on consumption of goods and services. FECs are denominated in yuan and are stated to be of equal value with RMB yuan.

However, the introduction of FEC has resulted in two separate currencies. A black market has also arisen in FECs among Chinese residents which has reached serious proportions. As a result, from 1 January 1994, the Chinese government unified its dual-track foreign exchange system. FECs which have already been issued and are in circulation may continue to be used but will be progressively phased out.

CHN ¶55-024 DISTINCTIONS BETWEEN FOREIGN-CONTROLLED COMPANIES INCORPORATED INSIDE OR OUT OF THE HOST COUNTRY

Regulations governing foreign exchange control are equally onerous for foreign-controlled companies incorporated outside the PRC as for those companies incorporated inside the PRC, although the latter may be eligible for various exemptions and incentives.

CHN ¶55-025 EFFECT OF LOCAL PARTICIPATION ON EXCHANGE CONTROLS

Foreign exchange controls do not vary according to the extent of local participation in the enterprise.

CHN ¶55-031 EXCHANGE CONTROL EXEMPTIONS

A number of foreign exchange control exemptions and incentives are available for particular types of investments, in particular, for offshore oil exploration, for high technology industries and for those investments capable of producing goods for import substitution.

CHN ¶55-032 REMITTANCE FROM HOST COUNTRY OF PERSONAL SAVINGS AND PENSION FUND CONTRIBUTIONS BY EXPATRIATE PERSONNEL

Remittance out of the host country of personal savings and other contributions by expatriate personnel of enterprises is allowed, providing that such foreign exchange sums come from an enterprise's foreign exchange deposit. Subject to such restriction, there is no limit on the amount of foreign currency which may be taken into or out of the host country.

CHN ¶55-033   EXCHANGE CONTROL FORMALITIES

The single most important formality for compliance with foreign exchange regulations is that all foreign exchange deposits and disbursements must flow through a venture's bank account with the Bank of China or other bank approved by the Bank of China.

CHN ¶55-034   CONSEQUENCES OF BREACH OF EXCHANGE CONTROL LAW

The breach of foreign exchange control laws may involve criminal sanctions. Contracts which fail to provide for the obtaining of foreign exchange control approval will be unenforceable.

CHN ¶55-035   FORWARD MARKET FOR FOREIGN EXCHANGE

China's underdeveloped economy does not provide for a forward market for foreign exchange.

CHN ¶55-041   RESTRICTIONS ON REPATRIATION OF CAPITAL DURING CONTINUATION OF INVESTMENT INCENTIVES

Restrictions on the ability to repatriate capital or remit profits during the continuation of investment incentives will fall to be determined by pre-incorporation agreement. However, taxation considerations may have a significant bearing on this.

CHN ¶55-042   TAXATION CONSIDERATIONS IN RESPECT OF EXCHANGE CONTROL REGULATIONS

While taxation considerations are not directly relevant to the administration of exchange control regulations beyond the obvious on the repatriation of profits, etc before tax is paid, various taxation incentives will govern a venture's attitude to the repatriation of foreign exchange.

Labour and Nationality Laws

Effect of nationality, citizenship and race on labour
laws ....CHN ¶60-001

Basis of nationality law ....CHN ¶60-002

Nature of relationship between employer and
employee ....CHN ¶60-003

Conditions guaranteed to employees ....CHN ¶60-004

Control of wages and hours ....CHN ¶60-005

Settlement of industrial disputes ....CHN ¶60-011

Parameters of legal system of industrial dispute
settlement ....CHN ¶60-012

Customary method of settling industrial disputes ....CHN ¶60-013

Status and make-up of trade unions ....CHN ¶60-014

Liabilities and privileges of trade unions ....CHN ¶60-015

Institutional links between government, trade unions
and employer organisations ....CHN ¶60-021

Right to strike or lock out ....CHN ¶60-022

Administration of labour law ....CHN ¶60-023

Legislative control of labour law ....CHN ¶60-024

Transmission of business ....CHN ¶60-025

Additional obligations of employers ....CHN ¶60-031

Special application of labour laws to foreigners ....CHN ¶60-032

Work permits or visas for foreign workers, executives
and management ....CHN ¶60-033

Required balance of race or nationality ....CHN ¶60-034

International Labour Organisation conventions ....CHN ¶60-035

CHN ¶60-001   EFFECT OF NATIONALITY, CITIZENSHIP AND RACE ON LABOUR LAWS

Laws relating to nationality, citizenship, and to a lesser extent race, of both natural but more particularly juristic persons, are directly relevant to carrying on business in China. Status under those laws will directly impact on the application of general labour laws.

While China remains a comparatively closed society because of a deliberate policy to expunge a past history of exploitation during the period of Foreign Concessions until 1949, non-nationals will be subject to a number of business employment-related prohibitions under the *Labour Law* regime. Despite prohibitions being less restrictive in declared coastal cities and provinces, the application of specially tailored labour laws for non-nationals is a disincentive to the attraction of investment to China.

However, a new *Labour Law* was promulgated on 5 July 1994 to take effect on 1 January 1995 which prohibits discrimination because of nationality, race, gender or religious belief.

CHN ¶60-002   BASIS OF NATIONALITY LAW

The general basis of nationality laws is blood, although there are celebrated instances of foreigners being accorded full nationality rights. In addition to the Han Chinese majority, the remaining 5% of Chinese mainly comprise Mongols, Tibetans, Uighurs, Chuangs and Huis, who reside in the five autonomous regions established for the largest of the minority groups.

Generally, nationality cannot be lost and dual nationality is impossible.

On 26 March 2003, the Ministry of Public Security, Ministry of Foreign Affairs, Ministry of Education, Ministry of Science and Technology, Ministry of Personnel, Ministry of Labour and Social Security, Ministry of Foreign Trade and Economic Cooperation, Overseas Chinese Office of State Council and State Administration of Foreign Expert Affairs issued the *Providing Entry and Residential Conveniences to High Level Experts and Investors of Foreign Nationalities Provisions*. Under the Provisions, entry and residential conveniences shall be provided to foreigners falling into any of the following categories:

(1) senior advisors invited or appointed by ministry level government authorities and high technology and high level managerial personnel performing State, provincial or ministerial level key project agreements or talent exchange projects;

(2) persons who have significant or outstanding contributions to Chinese society or who perform inter-government assistance gratis agreements;

(3) academic or research leaders employed by State or provincial scientific research institutions or key universities;

(4) senior managerial personnel and key technical personnel of deputy general manager ranking in enterprises or institutions;

CHN ¶60-001

(5) managerial and technical personnel of foreign enterprises that invested over US$1 million in the western or central regions of China or US$3 million in other regions of China; and

(6) Chinese of foreign nationalities who are major international science award winners or who have outstanding or important status (sec 1).

Entry conveniences include multiple entry visas and residence permits valid for two to five years (sec 2).

The Ministry of Labour and Social Security, Ministry of Public Security and State Administration for Industry and Commerce issued the *Overseas-Employment Agency Provisions*, which became effective on 1 July 2002. The Provisions apply to agencies acting as intermediaries between foreign employers and Chinese nationals seeking overseas employment (Art 2). The Provisions do not apply to agency services for employment in Hong Kong, Macao or Taiwan for Chinese citizens (Art 42).

Part Two of the Provision deals with the establishment of an overseas-employment agency. Article 5 requires that agencies have personnel possessing the requisite legal, language, finance and accounting qualifications, and possess a contingency fund of not less than RMB500,000. Article 6 stipulates that a permit (valid for three years) can be applied for at the provincial level labour and social security administrative department, and forbids foreign organisations, foreign individuals and foreign resident organisations from engaging in overseas-employment agency activities.

Part Three contains provisions related to agency operation and administration. Article 9 lists different types of overseas-employment agency activities such as: providing consultation services to Chinese citizens; being entrusted by foreign employers to recommend sought-after personnel; assisting in the processing of certification, passports and visas; and helping the expatriate employee protect his/her legal rights through intermediation, arbitration and litigation. Article 10 makes it the legal obligation of the agency to verify that a foreign employer is operating legally and has the right to hire foreign labour, and assist the employee in the signing of the employment contract. Article 12 requires that a detailed service agreement (between the agency and the client) and the labour contract (between the client and the foreign employer) should be submitted to the provincial level labour and social security administrative department for approval. Article 14 outlaws contracting or subcontracting overseas-employment agency activities to an unauthorised organisation. Article 39 states that agencies that obtained permission before the implementation of the Provisions must re-apply for permission within 90 days.

CHN ¶60-003   NATURE OF RELATIONSHIP BETWEEN EMPLOYER AND EMPLOYEE

The nature of the legal relationship between employer and employee was previously premised on a number of principles set out in the Constitution. The Constitution stated that all citizens have the right as well as the duty to work, work being the glorious duty of every able-bodied citizen. The Constitution also explicitly demands the observance of labour discipline. Such injunctions proceed from the basis that the state is led by the working classes whose public ownership of the means of production is the basis of the economic system.

On 1 January 1995, China's first *Labour Law* came into effect. It introduced the labour contract system, which has been implemented nationwide. The labour contract system is defined as agreements between workers and enterprises that establish a labour relationship and set out the various rights and obligations of the parties. Labour contracts which contravene laws or regulations, or which are concluded by means of fraud or coercion are invalid.

The Ministry of Labour issued the *Procedures for Compensation of Violations of the Provisions of the Labour Law Concerning Labour Contracts* on 10 May 1995 to govern matters related to payment of compensation for breach of contract by either the employer or employee. Where the employer intentionally delays signing or renewing a labour contract after employing an employee or where the employer infringes the rights of women or minors or breaches contractual stipulations in a labour contract, then he must pay compensation to the employee. The same applies to an employee who breaches the labour contract thus causing losses to the employer.

CHN ¶60-004   CONDITIONS GUARANTEED TO EMPLOYEES

Legal guarantees afforded to employees, including minimum wage, compensation for injury at work, sick leave, annual leave and severance pay, derive from the Constitution and also from the *Labour Law* which took effect on 1 January 1995.

The Constitution provides that workers in the People's Republic of China have the right to rest and that the state expands facilities for rest and recuperation of working people and prescribes working hours and vacations for workers and staff. It further provides that the state prescribes by law the system of retirement for workers and staff in enterprises and undertakings and that the livelihood of retired personnel is ensured by the state and society. Moreover, under the Constitution, women in the People's Republic of China enjoy equal rights with men in all spheres of life and the state protects the rights and interests of women and applies the principle of equal pay for equal work for men and women alike.

The *Labour Law* reinforces these rights. The principle of equal rights for all workers is now guaranteed in the law. If workers are required to work overtime, they are to be paid 150% of their regular wage. If workers work on rest days and are not provided with the same days for rest later on, they are to be paid 200% of their regular wage. Workers who must work on statutory rest days are to be paid 300% of their regular wage. Statutory rest days under the *Labour Law* are: New Year's Day, the Spring Festival, International Labour Day, National Day and any other holidays set out in relevant laws or regulations.

Employers must implement a health and safety program for workers. Regular physical examinations must also be conducted for workers in hazardous occupations.

The Ministries have sole competence to interpret the *Labour Law* regulations which provide that an enterprise may not dismiss a worker suffering from an occupational disease or work injury or otherwise during a period of medical treatment of up to 12 months. Enterprises may not terminate a contract of employment in the case of a woman worker during pregnancy, maternity or maternity leave. Women employees, moreover, are protected by extensive health and safety provisions governing heavy work and work with dangerous substances as well as provisions as to facilities, rostering, overtime, rest breaks and leave.

Enterprises in the PRC shall purchase insurance for their workers. The Work-Related Injury Insurance Regulations promulgated by the State Council on 27 April 2003 lays out in detail the kind of treatment and compensation that the workers shall receive for their work-related injury, including medical equipment and living expenses under certain circumstances.

When dismissing an employee, an enterprise must consult with the enterprise's trade union and record the dismissal with the local labour administration. If there is a disagreement regarding the decision to dismiss, an appeal may be made to the Local Dispute Arbitration Committee. Further appeal as of right to the local court is provided for. Liability for economic loss borne by either party in the event of contract breach gives rise to a right to compensation.

Violations of occupational safety provisions are pursued by the enterprise's trade union who will institute proceedings before organs of the public prosecutor and the law courts if necessary.

The PRC *Law on Prevention and Handling of Occupational Diseases* was adopted on 27 October 2001 and became effective on 1 May 2002. The law specifies the responsibilities, rights and obligations of the government, employers, employees and trade unions in relation to prevention and handling of occupational diseases, including without limitation methods for prevention during the working process, diagnosing and treating of patients suffering from occupational diseases, and remedies available to the patients.

CHN ¶60-005   CONTROL OF WAGES AND HOURS

Maximum working week

Under the *Decision on Amending the State Council Regulations on Staff Working Hours* and the Labour Department's *Implementing Regulations for the State Council Regulations on Staff Working Hours*, a 40-hour work week policy for employees was formalised. The weekly working hours of employees in state organisations, business units and enterprises within China has been reduced from 44 hours to 40 hours beginning 1 May 1995.

Minimum wage

The *Labour Law* requires that minimum wages be set. Currently, all provinces and municipalities directly under the central government and autonomous regions other than Tibet have published their levels of minimum wages. Minimum wage levels must not be less than one-half the local average wage.

State enterprises

In state enterprises, the objective of labour regulations is that all employees enjoy similar benefits. Contract employees must be remunerated at the same level as workers with lifetime employment. Generally, wage levels are set according to performance criteria applied on recruitment.

Foreign investment enterprises (FIEs)

Under the *Labour Law*, foreign investment enterprises and domestic enterprises are given the right to autonomously determine the wage and salary levels for their employees. Internal regulations circulated in 1990 put a cap on the wages and salaries that FIEs were allowed to pay, the new *Labour Law* effectively repeals these regulations.

CHN ¶60-011   SETTLEMENT OF INDUSTRIAL DISPUTES

Labour dispute settlement mechanisms in China are underdeveloped. Institutional arrangements including reconciliation by the courts are secondary to quasi-legal arbitration bodies within the labour administration, although the court hierarchy does provide a formal means of dealing with intractable disputes. Policy advocates that dispute settlement should ideally be confined to consultation and conciliation within the enterprise. Labour reform regulations promulgated in 1987 made it mandatory for every enterprise to establish a Workers' Council or Staff and Workers' Representative Assembly to represent workers' interest. Workers' Councils have significant powers with respect to the right to review and adjust plans on wages, incentives and labour discipline.

The containment of labour disputes within state enterprises will depend on compromise mechanisms previously established under the provisions of the 1988 *Enterprise Law*. In enterprises with foreign investment, trade unions play an enhanced role in the resolution of disputes through consultation. Failing resolution by consultation, a labour dispute is deemed to be constituted. If further consultation does not resolve areas of disagreement, either party to the dispute may request arbitration by the labour management department of the people's government. A party dissenting from an arbitration award may file suit in the courts.

China's *Labour Law* which took effect on 1 January 1995 repeals most of the PRC *Handling of Enterprise Labour Disputes Regulations* — 1 August 1993 and shortens the period for a worker to submit a complaint from 120 days to 60 days from the time when the dispute arose. Appeals must be filed within 15 days of receipt of the written award. It further extends the arbitrability of disputes from individual to collective labour contracts.

CHN ¶60-012   PARAMETERS OF LEGAL SYSTEM OF INDUSTRIAL DISPUTE SETTLEMENT

The parameters of the legal system of industrial dispute settlement as provided by conciliation and arbitration and collective bargaining as established by the contract relationship are, in the main, restricted to the framework of Workers' Congresses in the state enterprise system. Created in principle to permit workers a role in enterprise management, the Workers' Congresses are largely concerned with workers' welfare issues. The distribution of housing and other benefits immediately concerning the well-being of workers is the primary role of Workers' Congresses. Thus, while the administrative systems of state enterprises are headed by factory directors who take a central position and assume overall responsibility for an enterprise, enterprises must establish management committees or other forms of organisation involving workers' participation in decision-making, especially where major issues of importance to the enterprise are concerned. As a result, management bodies vary from enterprise to enterprise. Some enterprises have introduced the system of the board of directors, some maintain the Workers' Congress System as the highest power organ and others have established joint enterprise management committees.

In enterprises with foreign investment, where management and administrative structures are more clearly defined, the legal parameters of industrial dispute settlement by resort to conciliation and arbitration and collective bargaining are, as a consequence, more stark. In enterprises with foreign investment, the employment relationship is, as a rule, determined more precisely by labour contract terms. Labour contract provisions in agreements between labour and enterprises with foreign investment are focused moreover by the process of application, review and approval prior to allowing equity registration. Under the general principles of China's foreign investment laws and regulations, matters regarding the recruitment and dismissal of employees, including the size of the entire staff, their remuneration, welfare benefits, labour protection and labour insurance must be stipulated in contracts subscribing capital to the venture.

CHN ¶60-013 CUSTOMARY METHOD OF SETTLING INDUSTRIAL DISPUTES

The formal legal rules for the settlement of industrial disputes incorporate the customarily preferred system of conciliation through negotiation. Prior to a relatively recent evolution of labour regulation, labour force management was characterised by government planning which determined compulsory resolution. This practice, naturally, blocked the legal and judicial avenue for the development of labour practice and theory. Nationwide reform of *Labour Law* since the advent of foreign investment resulted in essential conversion to a labour contract system.

CHN ¶60-014 STATUS AND MAKE-UP OF TRADE UNIONS

Trade unions in China are developed upon industry lines. The legal status of trade unions is provided for under the *Trade Union Law of the People's Republic of China* which was adopted on 3 April 1992 at the 5th Session of the 7th National People's Congress and amended on 27 October 2001. The *Trade Union Law* gives all workers in the PRC the right to form trade unions regardless of nationality, race, sex, occupation, religious belief or level of education. No such right was reserved for workers under the *Trade Union Law 1950* which was one of the first legislative laws of the People's Republic.

The trade union umbrella group, the All-China Federation of Trade Unions, coordinates trade union activity. Employer organisations, such as foreign investment enterprises associations, have also been established in some coastal areas.

Rights of trade unions

Trade unions have the following rights:

- To actively participate in the occupational health and safety issues concerning their workers.

- Request that the administrative authority of an enterprise or public institution rectify violations of any laws safeguarding the "special rights and interests" of women.

- Trade unions have the right to take part in production management and to sign collective contracts with the administrations of enterprises on behalf of workers.

- To ask the administrations of enterprises to report on their work to general workers' membership meetings or worker representative assemblies.

- To attend meetings of the management committees or administrations of the enterprises on behalf of workers.

- To be notified by state-owned and collectively-owned enterprises before an employee is dismissed and to put forward their views if that dismissal is believed to be inappropriate.

- Whenever an employer plans to employ workers, it is required to notify its primary trade union committee. If the trade union committee concludes that the plan is in contravention of the spirit of the established collective contracts, it has the right to lodge a protest. Pending dismissals of workers also require notification.

- To attend meetings of the board of directors of foreign-invested enterprises in a non-voting capacity.

- To put forward suggestions on matters involving the personal rights and interests of their workers and must "negotiate and resolve" these matters in conjunction with the enterprise. Sino-foreign equity joint ventures and sino-foreign cooperative enterprises are required to "heed the views" of their trade unions when making decisions on matters involving the personal rights and interests of their workers.

- Representatives of trade unions will assert rights to inspect the living quarters of enterprise employees.

Responsibilities

Primary trade union committees are required to be established in all production units where the number of workers and employees exceeds 25 persons.

Trade unions in foreign investment enterprises play a significant role in labour protection. Foreign-financed project contracts must contain provisions on safety and health standards. These ventures must also implement government rules and regulations to ensure safe production. Government labour management departments reserve the right to carry out supervision and inspection, and production processes with a high risk factor must be approved by that administration. Moreover, it is the trade union representative who is responsible in most instances for labour protection. As foreign investment enterprises are required to appoint personnel for this purpose, it is sensible to coordinate the task with its trade union.

They are, in theory, entitled to involve themselves in discussions relating to development plans and production and operation in addition to those relating to wage and benefit-related systems and labour protection. In practice, trade unions generally take over the duty of protecting the interests of the workers and employees by supervising the implementation by the administration of the employer of labour protection, labour insurance, standards of wage payments, rules on sanitation and technical security. Trade unions play a watch-dog role in relation to relevant legislation and ordinances. Matters in relation to the material and cultural life of workers and employees will naturally fall to the attention of the trade union. Death and injuries in the workplace must be reported to the trade union as well as the labour administration.

Requirement of enterprises

According to the All-China Federation of Trade Unions, 30% of foreign-invested enterprises have established their own enterprise labour unions. Such unions are expected to affiliate with the federation. Foreign-invested enterprises are required under the law to actively support the work of trade unions. The People's Courts shall recognise the legal status of labour union organisations established in accordance with the labour union law when trying cases involving labour union organisations. Moreover, they must provide facilities and finance to the trade union in the form of an allocation of 2% of total real wages, including wages in currency and in kind. Employer enterprises must also provide releases from production work to trade union committee members to allow them to take up their trade union duties. Where a foreign investment enterprise employs more than 100 workers, it will be required to supply offices for the trade union committee free-of-charge.

CHN ¶60-015 LIABILITIES AND PRIVILEGES OF TRADE UNIONS

The liabilities of trade unions have not to date been tested in China. They do, however, have legal personality within the civil system of law and there are no exemptions or privileges such as immunity from legal action in industrial disputes.

CHN ¶60-021 INSTITUTIONAL LINKS BETWEEN GOVERNMENT, TRADE UNIONS AND EMPLOYER ORGANISATIONS

The organisational principles of trade unions are stipulated by the All-China Federation of Trade Unions which meets in a national conference of the individual industrial trade unions. Trade union committees at all levels obey the resolutions and directives of trade unions at a higher level. At the highest level, the All-China Federation of Trade Unions' primary function is to serve the state's interest by promoting labour discipline, enhancing labour productivity, conducting political and ideological indoctrination, and improving workers' educational and technical skills. The rigidity of this labour discipline system explains, in part, the absence of significant instances of disputes requiring resolution outside the work environment and the consequent under-developed state of formal institutions catering for labour dispute resolution. China's trade unions are closely controlled by the CPC and serious conflicts between the principles guiding workers' wages and conditions and national economic objectives are resolved at the political level. The All-China Federation of Trade Unions executive has, however, brought to the attention of the government the fact that undue stress on communist party principles in the past had made trade unions virtually government organisations and that a re-definition of the role of trade unions would be welcomed. The 2001 amendment of the *Trade Union Law* has made progress in this respect. Among others, the amended law highlights the trade union's responsibility for "lawfully safeguarding legitimate rights and interests of workers", stating that this responsibility is a basic responsibility of the trade union. It also requires the trade union to "safeguard the overall interests of the people nationwide".

CHN ¶60-022   RIGHT TO STRIKE OR LOCK-OUT

While collective bargaining is permitted, trade unions have a positive duty under the law to oppose acts that violate law or interrupt production. Chinese workers are, therefore, restricted in their right to strike and lock-out of employees does not become a relevant question. Included in the 1978 Constitution, the workers' assured right to strike was omitted in the 1982 Constitution revision. The omission, however, does not necessarily mean that strikes are illegal. A narrow range of circumstances, including risks to workers' safety, might justify industrial action for a brief time. Where there is a danger, serious accident or an occupational hazard likely to endanger the lives of workers, a trade union occupational safety inspector may support or organise the cessation of work where management ignores his recommendation. Examples of spontaneous industrial action over opposition to wage reform by workers protesting the linking of wages to productivity, while uncommon, have been documented.

CHN ¶60-023   ADMINISTRATION OF LABOUR LAW

The supervision and administration of China's labour laws is the responsibility of the relevant provincial, municipal and special economic zone labour and social security departments. The departments responsible for particular enterprises and industries are also involved in employment matters including recruitment and redundancy. Labour and social security departments at the local level are ultimately responsible to the Ministry of Labour and Social Security, which is responsible to the State Council and then to the NPC and its Standing Committee.

CHN ¶60-024   LEGISLATIVE CONTROL OF LABOUR LAW

Established ideological values regarding labour have resulted in a broad administrative control in workplace regulation. However, significant reforms have taken place in recent years with the introduction of the PRC *Labour Law* which came into effect on 1 January 1995. In the context of China's drive to modernise and industrialise, the need for a *Labour Law* became essential in such a populous nation. However, urbanisation is at a low level and the vast majority of the working population is engaged in rural or village industry. To this extent, the sophistication of the *Labour Law* regime is of most particular relevance only to the eastern coastal urban agglomerations. Immediate benefits have flowed to those regions since the first tentative steps were made in the contracting of assembly work with foreign business. The Ministry of Labour plays an important part in scrutinising the labour situation in China and in May 1995 issued the *Procedures for Compensation of Violations of the Provisions of the Labour Law Concerning Labour Contracts* to govern matters related to payment of compensation for breach of contract by either the employer or employee.

CHN ¶60-025 TRANSMISSION OF BUSINESS

While the obligation of a purchaser of a business to the existing employees in that business who are offered or not offered new employment by the purchaser is not a cause for concern in relation to state enterprises, it raises particularly acute matters for contract negotiation in respect of foreign-invested enterprises. An average 40% to 45% of an enterprise's staff will have to be made redundant on the merger of a Chinese enterprise with a foreign-invested venture. While staff appointed to a new venture are entitled to higher rates of pay and other benefits, those made redundant by foreign management are a hindrance to transformation. Current labour regulations provide that Chinese enterprise should make provisions for redundant staff before the joint venture begins operation. In practice, however, a major problem arises as to who will pay insurance and welfare for workers who are made to retire. In some regions, these costs are drawn from the welfare and insurance fund of the new venture, thereby diluting the retirement and age pension reserve of the newly established group.

CHN ¶60-031 ADDITIONAL OBLIGATIONS OF EMPLOYERS

Employer obligations to employees are extensive because of the work-unit-based organisation of social life in China. It is normal for the responsibility to extend from cradle-to-grave and this system of welfare has been enjoyed by employees since 1949. The "iron rice-bowl" mentality which promises employment in China has its origins in the culture and, until recently, has been supported by official policy. For the foreign investor, these responsibilities are reflected in the various subsidies that have to be paid in respect of housing, community welfare, education and food. Subsidisation is so extensive as to, in some cases, effectively double base rates of pay. Recent developments have changed this system and reform programs have already been implemented by the government to phase out the old welfare-oriented system. The system of providing housing at negligible rents has created a massive burden on money-losing enterprises and so the government intends to phase out this cradle-to-grave welfare package by the year 2000. The Beijing Municipal Government has also amended the *Labour Protection and Supervision Rules* with a view to improving the safety of workers. The new rule has been drafted in accordance with the requirements of China's *Labour Law*. It stipulates that violators of the law will be reprimanded and could face fines and criminal charges.

The *People's Republic of China Labour Law* which took effect on 1 January 1995 contains a list of penalties that may be imposed on employers or their agents for violations of the provisions of the *Labour Law*. The penalties include fines, damages, revocation of business license and criminal liability. The *Labour Law* prohibits the recruitment of a worker whose labour contract has not yet been rescinded and established an obligation on the new employer to pay damages to the previous employer.

CHN ¶60-032 SPECIAL APPLICATION OF LABOUR LAWS TO FOREIGNERS

The State Bureau of Foreign Experts requires job agencies in China or abroad to be registered and to carry the Bureau's licence to recruit foreigners. This rule commenced in October 1993. Other rules require expatriates to be registered with a licensed local agency after they complete a contract before they can be offered new employment by a local employer. The Bureau must also be informed of overseas experts coming to work in China through government agreements and exchange programs.

MOFTEC has issued a notice outlawing foreigners from concurrently holding the posts of general manager of an overseas enterprise and general manager of a sino-foreign joint equity enterprise. MOFTEC has stated that this is in violation of Chinese laws and will not be accepted. The notice also provides that any amendment to the main contents of a contract concerning a sino-foreign joint equity enterprise must be approved by the original approving authority.

As regards to the *Labour Law*, China has created a labour system for foreign investment enterprises which more closely resembles a western model in order to attract foreign capital. To this extent, such enterprises are given greater flexibility in recruitment, discipline and dismissal. This system of labour relations has resulted in special tensions where management often represents the interests of foreign investors while the labour force is mainly Chinese.

Such complications naturally arising from a two-systems approach are heightened in the special economic zones where authorities have more autonomy in the enactment of law and discrepancies of national labour laws are more pronounced.

Generally, foreign investment enterprises must give priority in recruitment to Chinese applicants except those personnel representing foreign investors.

On 1 May 1996, regulations relating to the administration of foreign workers came into effect. The provisions lay down requirements and responsibilities of work units for hiring foreigners. All foreigners must be at least 18 years old, in good health, possess professional skills and relevant working experience, no criminal record and a valid travel document amongst other things. The regulations do not apply to foreigners who enjoy diplomatic immunity in the embassies and consulates, representative offices of the United Nations in China or other international organisations.

CHN ¶60-033 WORK PERMITS OR VISAS FOR FOREIGN WORKERS, EXECUTIVES AND MANAGEMENT

Foreign nationals in foreign investment enterprises will be issued with work permits. However, these work permits cannot be used as a substitute for a passport, residence permit or travel document. The availability of work permits to private foreign nationals is restricted. Three-month visas are generally available on request at diplomatic offices where the foreign national has an invitation from a business or institution. Work permits and visas for longer periods are generally only available after negotiation with the appropriate authorities within China.

Regulations on foreign workers were published in January 1996 to establish a comprehensive work permit system and to ban foreign unskilled labour. The rules took effect from 1 May 1996 and are designed to protect employment for Chinese citizens. Local companies will only be able to hire foreign workers in cases of special needs or to make up for temporary shortages. The rules were jointly published by the foreign, public security, labour and trade ministries. A three-step process will be in place requiring foreigners who wish to work in China to get a work permit prior to being granted a work visa. Representatives of foreign firms require work visas but are exempt from the work permit procedures.

CHN ¶60-034   REQUIRED BALANCE OF RACE OR NATIONALITY

The conditions imposed on foreign investors in relation to the maintenance of a balance of race at various levels of employment will not be significant because the greater majority of foreign investment is concentrated in the coastal regions where there is little or no ethnic diversity. The problem may arise, however, in the more remote geographical areas where difficulties may be faced attracting competent personnel and where inter-regional recruitment may be required to supplement the skills base of the local labour force. Ethnic unrest has featured prominently in recent times in China's western autonomous regions. Foreign investment enterprises operating in those areas should be aware not to exacerbate existing racial strife and endeavour to accommodate policies intended to reduce the potentialities of conflict.

The maintenance of a balance of nationality in employment at foreign-invested enterprises will generally be non-negotiable at the non-management level. Priority in recruitment must go to Chinese applicants. At the management level, the question will fall to be determined according to the nature of the foreign investment. Since foreign employees' wages are substantially higher than Chinese employees, the recruitment of foreign employees is generally stated in the joint venture or joint cooperative venture contract. Therefore, it is more likely a matter of finance rather than the balance of race or nationality. In joint venture enterprises, the Chinese management will be represented at the highest level of the venture, including, subject to exceptions, at the position of chairman of the board. Questions of managerial control will ultimately be determined by the strength of the foreign investor's bargaining position. Legislation governing incentives to foreign enterprises have dealt with the question of management control in detail in recent years and it is now less of a problem than during the early stages following the announcement of the open-door policy. Where investment is wholly foreign in nature, this fact will be reflected in the control at the board level.

CHN ¶60-035   INTERNATIONAL LABOUR ORGANISATION CONVENTIONS

China first attended as a delegate to the International Labour Organisation (ILO) at its 96th session in 1983. Since that time, China has had increasing closer cooperation with the ILO and a major statement of China's supporting role on the international stage of organised labour was given at an ILO conference held in Southern China in 1988.

Since 1985, China has worked closely with ILO in the development of its *Labour Law* program, including legislation for trade union occupational safety inspectors, employment contracts in state-run enterprises, unemployment insurance for workers and employees in state-run enterprises, and on recruitment in state-run enterprises.

Intellectual Property

International agreements .... CHN ¶65-001

Domestic legislation .... CHN ¶65-002

Copyright .... CHN ¶65-003

Trademarks .... CHN ¶65-004

Patents .... CHN ¶65-005

Industrial designs .... CHN ¶65-011

Trade secrets .... CHN ¶65-012

Circuit layouts .... CHN ¶65-013

Plant varieties .... CHN ¶65-014

Unfair competition .... CHN ¶65-015

Geographical indications .... CHN ¶65-018

Registration procedures .... CHN ¶65-021

Transfers and licensing agreements .... CHN ¶65-022

Compulsory licenses .... CHN ¶65-023

Table of fees .... CHN ¶65-024

Disadvantages for non-residents .... CHN ¶65-025

Enforcement .... CHN ¶65-031

CHN ¶65-001   INTERNATIONAL AGREEMENTS

China has entered into the following agreements:

- The Convention Establishing the World Intellectual Property Organisation (WIPO) in 1980.

- The Paris Convention for the Protection of Industrial Property (as amended at Stockholm in 1967) in 1985. The *Patent Law* (Art 29 and 30) recognises priority for foreign applicants pursuant to the Paris Convention.

- The Madrid Agreement Concerning the International Registration of Marks (as amended at Stockholm in 1967 and 1979) in 1989. This permits owners of so-called ''international registrations'' to obtain trademark registrations in over 30 other Madrid Union countries.

- The Treaty on Intellectual Property in Respect of Integrated Circuits in 1990.

- The Berne Convention for the Protection of Literary and Artistic Works in 1992.
- The Universal Copyright Convention (as revised at Paris in 1971) in 1992.
- The Convention for the Protection of Producers of Phonograms against Unauthorised Duplication of Their Phonograms in 1993. This ensures the rights of recorded music producers registered in the other 44 signatory countries to the convention to be protected in China.
- The Patent Cooperation Agreement (as revised in 1984) in 1994.
- The Nice Agreement Concerning the International Classification of Goods and Services for the Purpose of the Registration of Marks in 1994.
- The Protocol Relating to the Madrid Agreement Concerning the International Registration of Marks in 1995.
- The Agreement on Trade-Related Aspects of Intellectual Property Rights (TRIPs).

CHN ¶65-002   DOMESTIC LEGISLATION

Since the implementation of its open-door policy in late 1970s, China has been making great efforts in its intellectual property legislation. At present, relevant domestic legislation includes the following:

- The *General Principle of the Civil Law*, effective as of 9 April 1991;
- The *Copyright Law*, effective as of 1 June 1991 (as amended in 2001);
- The *Implementing Rules to the Copyright Law*, effective as of 15 September 2002, which repeal those effective as of 1 June 1991;
- The *Regulations on the Implementation of International Copyright Treaties*, effective as of 30 September 1992;
- The *Computer Software Protection Regulations*, effective as of 1 January 2002, which repeal those effective as of 1 October 1991;
- The *Measures on the Registration of Copyright to Computer Software*, effective as of 4 June 1992 (as amended on 20 February 2002);
- The *Trademark Law*, effective as of 1 March 1983 (as amended in 1993 and 2001);
- The *Implementing Rules to the Trademark Law*, effective as of 15 September 2002, repeal those effective as of 10 March 1983;
- The *Interim Regulations Governing Applications for Priority Registration of Trademarks*, effective as of 15 March 1985;
- The *Patent Law*, effective as of 1 April 1985 (as amended in 1992 and 2000);
- The *Implementing Regulations to the Patent Law*, effective as of 1 April 1985 (as amended in 1992 and 2001);
- The *Regulations on Patent Agencies*, effective as of 1 April 1991; and
- The *Anti-Unfair Competition Law*, effective as of 1 December 1993.

CHN ¶65-002

CHN ¶65-003 COPYRIGHT

China joined the WIPO in 1980 and established the State Copyright Bureau to develop a *Copyright Law* in 1985. Regulations have been passed which provide for remuneration to be given to authors of books and provide limited protection against copying. Thereafter, the *Copyright Law* of the PRC came into effect on 1 June 1991.

The *Copyright Law* protects the works (as defined) of Chinese citizens, legal persons and non-legal person work units regardless of whether they are published.

Works of foreign persons (the term is not defined) will be protected under the law where they are first published (not defined) in China, or in accordance with bilateral or multilateral agreements (Art 2).

An author's right to attribution, to revise and protect the integrity of the work has no time restriction (Art 20).

The duration of the right to publish, use and receive remuneration for the work is the author's lifetime plus 50 years, ending on 31 December of the 50th year after the author's death.

The duration of the right to publish, use and receive remuneration by a legal person or non-legal person work unit is 50 years from the date of its first publication.

The same period of protection applies in relation to cinematographic, television, video or photographic work (Art 21).

China for the first time amended its *Copyright Law* in 2001 with a view to (i) bringing its copyright protection more in line with the WTO requirements and applicable international conventions; (ii) enhancing law enforcement against infringements upon copyrights; and (iii) adjusting to the upcoming information age and digital world. Major amendments include the following:

- *National treatment available to eligible foreigners or persons without nationality.* Those whose works are initially published in China, or whose nationality or residence country has signed bilateral copyright protection agreements with China or has acceded to a related international convention to which China is a member country, or whose works are initially published in a member country to such convention or initially published both in a member country and a non-member country simultaneously are eligible for Chinese copyright protection.

- *Expanded scope of protected works.* Software works, engineering works, model works and acrobatic works are now expressly covered. Databases will also be protected.

- *Expanded rights of copyright owners.* In addition to those rights provided for in the old law, new rights such as the right of rental, the right of broadcast, and the right of dissemination via information network are now included.

- *New collective copyright management mechanism.* The collective copyright management organisation may now in its own name exercise the copyrights and related rights as authorised by the copyright owners.

- *Compensation for broadcast.* Radio and TV stations must compensate copyright owners for use of their published works, whether the use is for commercial purposes or otherwise.

- *Permission and remuneration for performance.* A performer who wishes to use another's works for a performance must obtain permission from and pay remuneration to the copyright owner.

- *Injunctions available.* An injunction order, a property preservation order and an evidence preservation order are now available from the People's Court.

- *Penalties on copyright infringement.* Copyright administrative departments now have powers to order that an infringing activity be stopped, to confiscate illegal income, to confiscate the materials, tools and equipment used for infringement purposes, and to impose a fine. Damages comprise actual loss to the copyright owner, and the statutory maximum damages of RMB500,000 can apply where the amount cannot be ascertained. A timely appeal can be filed with a People's Court if a decision from the copyright administrative departments is not satisfied.

CHN ¶65-004   TRADEMARKS

The *Trademark Law* makes trademark protection available for both goods and services. The registrant enjoys an exclusive right to use the registered trademark. The law provides that users of trademarks are responsible for the quality of the goods/services in respect of which the trademark is used. Article 37 of the *Implementation Rules of Trade Mark Law* provides that if a registered trademark is used, the Chinese characters for "Registered Trademark" or the symbol for registration or ® shall be marked. If it is unsuitable to mark a product itself, the registered trademark shall be noted on its packaging, in its instruction booklet or on other attachments.

As with the trademark systems of other countries, the Chinese law provides that registration will not be granted for certain words or designs, eg those identical with or similar to state names, generic words or designs and those detrimental to socialist morals or customs, or having other unhealthy influences.

Specifically, Art 8 of the *Trademark Law* provides as follows:

"In trademarks, the following words or designs shall not be used:

- Those identical with or similar to the state name, national flag, national emblem, military flag or medals of the People's Republic of China, and those identical with the specific names of the places where central state authorities are located or the names or images of their landmark buildings;

- Those identical with or similar to state names, national flags, national emblems or military flags of foreign countries, unless otherwise approved by the governments of the foreign countries;

- Those identical with or similar to the names, flags or emblems of international inter-governmental organisations, unless with their consent or unless this would not be likely to confuse the public;

- Generic name or graphic of the product in question;

- Those identical with or similar to the symbols, or names of the Red Cross or the Red Crescent;
- Those having the nature of discrimination against any nationality;
- Those having the nature of exaggeration and deceit in advertising goods or services;
- Those indicate the quality, major raw material, function, use, weight, quantity and other features of the product; and
- Those detrimental to socialist morals or customs, or having other unhealthy influences.

Place names of Chinese administrative regions at county level or commonly-known foreign place names may not be used as trademarks, except where such names have other meanings or are an integral part of a collective mark or certification mark. Trademarks using place names that have already been registered shall remain valid.''

Under the *Trademark Law*, infringement is defined to include using an identical or similar trademark in respect of the same or similar goods or services without the proprietor's permission; selling goods or services that infringe upon the exclusive right to use a registered trademark; representations of the registered trademark of another person or selling representation so forged or manufactured without authorisation; substituting the trademark of a trademark registrant without his consent and putting back on the market goods bearing such substituted trademark; or causing other harm to another's exclusive right to use a registered trademark.

In the case of infringement, the registered proprietor may request the local administrative authority for industry and commerce to handle the matter. The authority has power to issue an injunction, or to order the infringer to pay damages or compensation. An appeal lies to the People's Court from a decision of the authority. Where the exclusive right to use the trademark is infringed, the registered proprietor may institute proceedings directly with the People's Court.

The period of validity of a registered trademark shall be 10 years counted from the date of the approval of the registration. The registration may be renewed for a further 10 years by an application filed within six months before the current registration expires. A grace period of six months may be allowed. If no application has been filed at the expiration of the grace period, the registered trademark will be cancelled.

The latest amendment of the *Trademark Law* was adopted on 27 October 2001, the same day as the amended *Copyright Law* was adopted. Likely, the main purpose of the amendment is also to bring China more in line with WTO requirements and international conventions. Major amendments include:

- *All symbols eligible for trademark registration.* All visible symbols that can distinguish products and/or services between different providers, including characters, graphs, letters, numbers, three-dimensional signs and colour combinations as well as combination of these elements, may now be registered as trademarks.

- *Collective trademarks and certification trademarks.* These types of trademarks have been covered under the amendment.

- *Well-known trademarks.* The amendment affords protection to well-known trademarks, which in the past were governed by certain provisions promulgated by the State Administration for Industry and Commerce (SAIC), such as *Recognition and Protection of Well-known Trademarks Provisions* which came into effect on June 2003.

- *Owners and ownership.* Now domestic as well as foreign individuals are permitted to own trademarks. The amendment also allows joint ownership of a trademark by two or more individuals, legal persons and other organisations.

- *Priority rights.* An applicant will be entitled to priority rights as required by the Paris Convention in relation to a trademark which has been registered in a foreign country or has been used in international exhibitions.

- *Existing rights.* The amendment requires that trademarks for which registration is applied for shall not conflict with existing lawful rights obtained by any third party.

- *Reverse counterfeiting.* Reverse counterfeiting of trademarks is now expressly prohibited.

- *Administrative and judicial remedies for violation.* Additional administrative remedies, including an injunction order, confiscation and destruction of infringing products and equipment used for sole purposes of manufacturing infringing products or forging registered trademarks, and confiscation of materials, tools and equipment used mainly for the infringement purposes, are now available. The People's Court may also take tentative measures, including issuance of injunction orders or preservation of the property or evidence, to avoid irrevocable losses caused by any delay in action.

- *Damages.* The amendment makes it clear that damages for trademark infringement may include any of the following: the illegal gains of the infringers; or the actual losses of the trademark owner, including the reasonable expenses incurred by the trademark owner in stopping the infringement; or an amount not exceeding RMB500,000, if neither of the aforesaid can be ascertained.

Again, the amendment of the trademark rules is now awaited.

CHN ¶65-005   PATENTS

The *Patent Law* provides for three types of patentable invention-creations: inventions, utility models and designs (Art 2). These are defined by the Implementing Rules. No patent rights will be granted for any of the following (Art 25):

- scientific discoveries;

- rules and methods for intellectual activities;

- methods for the diagnosis or for the treatment of disease;

- animal and plant varieties (however, process patents may be granted); and

- substances obtained by means of nuclear transformation.

Article 5 provides that no patent rights shall be granted for any invention-creation that is contrary to the laws of the state or social morality or that is detrimental to public interest.

As part of the endeavours to comply with the WTO requirements, China amended for the second time the *Patent Law* in August 2000 and the *Implementing Regulations to the Patent Law* in June 2001, both effective as of 1 July 2001. Major amendments include the following:

- *Abolishment of the revocation procedure.* The procedure for "revocation" of patents, whereby a third party could apply to the patent authorities for revocation of a patent within six months after the date of the announcement of the grant of such patent, has now been abolished and incorporated into the procedure as amended for "invalidation" of patents, whereby a third party could apply for invalidation of a patent at any time after its grant.

- *Increased rewards and remuneration for work-related inventions.* Chapter VI of the new Regulations specifies the minimum rewards and remuneration to be given to the investor or designer of a work-related invention, reflecting an increase over the previous rewards and remuneration levels. Such rewards and remuneration requirements, however, apply to state-owned entities only.

- *Transfer of rights to foreigners.* Transfer to a foreigner of the right to apply for a patent or of the rights to a patent must be approved by the foreign economic and trade administration department, together with the science and technology administration department of the State Council (Art 14 of the new Regulations).

- *Clarification of fees.* Chapter IX of the new Regulations specifies various categories of fees and addresses the payment issues, such as time limit and requirements. Applicants are now required to pay the application maintenance fee only if a patent right is granted.

- *Searching a utility model.* The new Law provides that a court of law or the patent administrative authorities may request the patent holder of a utility model to submit a utility model search report from the patent administrative authorities for purposes of handling a patent infringement (Art 57), and the new Regulations set forth the relevant procedures (Art 55 and 56).

- *Handling and punishing infringements on or counterfeiting of patents.* The new Regulations set forth the scope of patent disputes that may be mediated by the patent authorities (Art 79), and the concepts such as "counterfeiting patents" and "passing off as patents" were further defined and clarified (Art 84 and 85). The new Regulations also make it clear that authorities in charge of patent affairs should be established under each province, autonomous region and centrally-administered municipal government.

- *Attention to the judicial procedures.* The patent authorities are now required to suspend relevant administrative procedures to assist judicial procedures if so required by the court of law (Art 87 of the new Regulation).

- *Damages for patent infringement.* The 2001 amendment makes it clear that patent administrative authorities can order injunction, confiscation and destruction of infringing products, and that the patent administrative authorities can no longer award damages for patent infringement. Damages including loss profits, reasonable loyalties, treble damages, etc are awarded by a People's Court.

- *Conforming with the TRIPs.* Article 5 of the new Law provides that no patent shall be granted for any invention against the laws of the State. To avoid conflicting with relevant requirements of the TRIPs, the new Regulations further provide that an invention that the laws of the States merely prohibit its implementation does not constitute an invention against the laws of the State for purposes of Art 5 of the new Law (Art 9). For the same reason, the new Regulations require that a compulsory licence relating to semi-conductor technology be for public and non-commercial purposes, or for purposes of rending remedies for anti-unfair competitions as determined through judicial or administrative proceedings (Art 72 of the new Regulations).

- *Conforming with the Patent Cooperation Agreement.* For purposes of consistency, the new Regulations revise the previous requirements for the description, the claims and the abstract of the description in the application (Art 18, 24 and 25); the time period designated by the Patent Re-examination Committee in respect of examination of application for invalidation should not be extended (Art 70 of the new Regulations). The new law provides that Chinese individuals and entities may apply for an international patent in accordance with relevant international agreements to which China is a party (Art 20) and the new Regulations in Chapter X set forth the procedures for such an application; the new Regulations also address the applications relating to biological materials (Art 25 and 26).

- *Revisions regarding patent registration and gazette.* Revisions have also been made to the previous provisions concerning patent registration and patent gazette (Chapter VIII of the new Regulations).

- *Power to formulate examination guidelines.* The patent administrative authorities have the right to formulate the patent examination guidelines (Art 121 of the new Regulations).

Exceptions

Article 63 of the *Patent Law* deems the following acts not to be infringements:

- Where, after the sale of a patented product that was made or imported by the patentee or with the authorisation of the patentee, or of a product derived directly from a patented process, any other person uses, offers for sale or sells that product.

- Where, before the date of the application for a patent, any identical product has been manufactured, any identical process has been used, or any necessary preparation for the manufacture or the use has been made, the product or process will continue to be manufactured or used within the original scope only.

- Where any foreign means of transport, which temporarily passes through Chinese sovereign territory, territorial waters or territorial airspace, uses the patent concerned, in accordance with any agreement concluded between China and the home country of the foreign means of transport, or in accordance with any international treaty to which both countries are parties, or on the basis of the principle of reciprocity, for its own needs in its devices and equipment.

- Where any person uses the patent concerned solely for the purpose of scientific research and experimentation.

CHN ¶65-011 INDUSTRIAL DESIGNS

Exterior designs

Patents for exterior designs (any new design of the shape and/or the pattern and/or the colour of a product which has aesthetic appeal and is capable of industrial application), like patents for practical and new models, are granted 10 years from the date of filing.

Design patent applications may only be altered so long as the amendments do not exceed the scope contained in the original drawings.

CHN ¶65-012 TRADE SECRETS

Commercial secrets

China's *Anti-Unfair Competition Law* which came into effect on 1 December 1993, for the first time, provides intellectual property protection for commercial secrets, which are defined as technical and operational information that are not known to the public, that can produce economic benefits to their proprietors, that has practical use, and that their proprietors have taken measures to keep confidential (Art 10).

Article 10 provides that each of the following acts constitute an infringement of another party's commercial secrets:

- using improper means, including theft, inducement and coercion, to obtain commercial secrets;
- revealing, using or allowing others to use commercial secrets obtained by improper means; and
- revealing, using or allowing others to use commercial secrets of the proprietors of those secrets, in violation of agreements or requests by the proprietors to maintain secrecy.

The above infringements also apply to third parties who knew or should have known that the secrets were obtained by improper means or revealed or used in violation of agreements or requests by the proprietors to maintain secrecy.

The *Certain Provisions Concerning Prohibition of Infringements of Commercial Secrets*, promulgated by SAIC on 23 November 1995 and amended on 3 December 1998, serves as the detailed implementing rules of the *Anti-Unfair Competition Law* with respect to commercial secrets. Article 2 clarifies the concept of commercial secrets by providing that, among others, (i) "not known to the public" means it is not obtainable directly from a public source; (ii) having "economic benefits" and "practical use" means having specific practical applicability and capabilities to bring actual or potential economic benefits or competitive advantage; (iii) entering into a secrecy agreement and formulating secrecy rules shall be deemed as measures to maintain secrecy; and (iv) "technical and operational information" shall include information such as designs, programs, product formulas, production techniques and methods, managerial know-how, customer list, suppliers' information, production and sales strategies, and base amount and contents of a tender.

Article 3 of the *Certain Provisions Concerning Prohibition of Infringements of Commercial Secrets* makes it clear that "agreements or requests by the proprietors to maintain secrecy" shall include not only those arising from business relations but also those resulting from employment relationship. The PRC *Labour Law* also provides that employment contracts can include provisions on protection of employers' commercial secrets. According to a notice issued by the Labour Ministry in October 1996, in order to better protect their commercial secrets, employers may require employees knowing such commercial secrets not to be employed by their competitors or engage in competitive production or operations with a maximum of three years after termination of their employment. However, employees shall be entitled to certain compensation.

CHN ¶65-013   CIRCUIT LAYOUTS

On 4 April 2001, the State Council promulgated the *Regulations for Protection of Integrated Circuit Layout Designs*, which came into effect on 1 October 2001. Article 2 defines an integrated circuit layout design as a three-dimensional configuration comprising two components at least one of which is an active component in a partially or fully connected circuit, or such three-dimensional configuration for the manufacturing of integrated circuits.

According to Art 7, a holder of the rights of layout designs has the exclusive right to duplicate his layout design as protected in whole or in part or to put it or the integrated circuit or thing incorporating it into commercial use. However, registration in accordance with the Regulations of layout designs with the State Council department in charge of intellectual property is a prerequisite for protection of such exclusive right, and application for such registration must be filed within two years after its first commercial use (Art 8 and 17). The exclusive right can be protected for a period of 15 years from the date of its registration or its first commercial use, whichever is longer, but no longer than 15 years from the date of its completion of creation, and can be assigned or licensed to other parties (Art 12 and 22).

Generally, the exclusive right vests in the creator of the layout design, or where the layout design is created by collaborators or based on commission, the concerned parties shall agree upon the ownership of such exclusive right, failing which all collaborators or the commissioned party shall be deemed as the holder (Art 9, 10 and 11). Foreigners or foreign parties can obtain the exclusive right of their layout designs within China if such layout designs are first put into commercial use in China or their country and China has signed a layout design protection agreement or are both parties to an international treaty on protection of layout design (Art 3).

CHN ¶65-014   PLANT VARIETIES

On 20 March 1997, the State Council promulgated the *Regulations for the Protection of New Varieties of Plants*, which became effective as of 1 October 1997. The term "new varieties of plants" is defined as varieties of plants that are artificially-bred or developed from known wild plants, possess the characteristics of novelty, distinctiveness, consistency and stability, and have been properly named (Art 2). The State Council departments in charge of agriculture and forestry (the ''Approval Authority'') shall be jointly responsible for acceptance and examination of applications for the rights to new varieties of plants (Art 3). Such application requires the submission of a request, a description and photographs of the plant variety (Art 21). A foreigner may file such application in accordance with the agreements entered into between China and the applicant's country or international treaties to which both countries are parties or based on the principle of reciprocity, and may also claim priority (Art 20 and 23).

The owner of the rights to an approved plant variety shall have an exclusive right to it, which can be assigned or licensed. Unless otherwise provided in the Regulations, without the licence of the owner, no entity or individual shall produce or sell the breeding material of such plant variety or repeatedly employ such material in order to produce breeding material of another variety for commercial purposes (Art 6). The said licence is unnecessary, nor shall royalty be paid, in the circumstances where the approved plant variety is utilised for breeding or for scientific research activities or where farmers breed and use the breeding materials of the approved plant variety by themselves (Art 10).

The rights to an approved plant variety shall be valid for a term of 20 years for lianas, forest trees, fruit trees and ornamental trees, and 15 years for other plants.

CHN ¶65-015   UNFAIR COMPETITION

The *Anti-Unfair Competition Law* prohibits other types of infringements of intellectual property rights, including:

- passing off another party's registered trademark;
- unauthorised use of another party's name or similar name;
- unauthorised use of imitation of well-known brand name goods or services;
- forging or counterfeiting identification marks and other quality marks; and
- falsifying the place of origin or using other false indicators to mislead people.

Other practices harmful to competitors that have been prohibited include:

- selling commodities at prices below cost to defeat competitors;
- fabricating or spreading false facts to harm competitors' commercial credit or the reputation of their commodities; and
- colluding with other tenderers to harm competitors.

Supervision and examination authorities at county level and above are responsible for monitoring acts of unfair competition. The authorities are empowered to:

- compel parties to supply them with evidence of unfair competition;
- copy agreements, account books, bills and invoices, documents, recordings, business letters or telegrams and other material associated with the conduct of unfair competition;
- check money or objects associated with the conduct of unfair competition;
- order those business operators who are being examined to disclose the source and quantity of commodities concerned; and

- temporarily suspend sales and order operators not to transfer, conceal or destroy the money and materials which await examination.

Penalties for infringements of intellectual property rights include fines, confiscation of proceeds from the illegal act and revocation of business licences. Business operators may seek compensation by bringing an action in the People's Court. If damages cannot be calculated, the injured party may claim the amount of profits obtained by the infringing party together with reasonable fees arising from the investigation of the illegal conduct.

The *Regulations on the Prohibition of Unfair Competitive Behaviour* regarding the imitation of specific brand names, packaging and decoration of well-known goods or services supplement the *Anti-Unfair Competition Law*. The regulations clarify what constitutes infringement in these prescribed areas and famous goods or services are defined as those enjoying certain market celebrity and which are well-known to the public. SAIC has been assigned the responsibility of determining exactly what is a famous product. They are also responsible for giving clear guidelines for the implementation of special names, packaging and decoration of certain goods or services. The regulations also set out penalties for those who sell imitation goods or services.

CHN ¶65-018   Geographical indications

A number of treaties administered by WIPO provide for the protection of geographical indications, most notably the Paris Convention for the Protection of Industrial Property of 1883, and the Lisbon Agreement for the Protection of Appellations of Origin and Their International Registration. In addition, Article 22 to 24 of TRIPs deal with the international protection of geographical indications within the framework of WTO. TRIPs, of which China is a member country, came into effect in 1995.

CHN ¶65-021   REGISTRATION PROCEDURES

Trademarks

All applicants for trademark registration must file an application with the Trademark Office which is the administrative authority for the registration and administration of trademarks (Art 2 of the *Trademark Law*). The application must indicate the class of goods or services and the designation of the goods or services in different classes and where the trademark is intended to be used in respect of other goods or services of the same class (Art 11 and 12).

Where a trademark is examined by the Trademark Office and found to be in conformity with the Law, which in practice may be as long as one year and a half, it receives preliminary approval and is published (Art 16). After the publication, there is a three-month period in which opposition may be filed (Art 19).

In the case of two or more applicants applying for the registration of identical or similar trademarks for same or similar goods or services, preliminary approval is given to the trademark which was first applied for or, if applied for on the same date, first used (Art 18).

Trademark registration by foreigners and foreign enterprises (and, under the new *Trademark Law*, perhaps persons without nationality) must be handled through a Chinese trademark agent so licensed (Art 10). The *Trade Mark Rules* provide that the registration forms must be in Chinese and accompanied by power of attorney (Art 14).

Patents

In order to be granted as a patent, patents for inventions and utility models must possess novelty, inventiveness and utility. However, patents for designs need only possess novelty and inventiveness (Art 22 and 23).

Patent applications for inventions or utility models require the submission of a request, a description of the invention or utility model and its abstract and claims (Art 26). Patent applications for design require a request, drawings or photographs, an indication of the product incorporating the design plus the class to which the product belongs (Art 27). A non-Chinese applicant must commission a patent agent to handle its application with a power of attorney. The *Patent Law* requires that patent applications be filed in Chinese (except that an application entered into China claiming Patent Cooperation Treaty (PCT) priority has a grace period for translating a non-Chinese PCT application into Chinese).

The *Patent Law* adopts the system of early publication and deferred examination. For a patent invention, there is a preliminary examination to determine whether the application is in conformity with the Law (Art 34) and, if so, the Chinese Patent Office shall publish the application within 18 months from the date of filing (Art 34). The Chinese Patent Office will then examine the application as to the substance, upon the request of the applicant, at any time within three years from the date of filing (Art 35). Where there is no cause for rejection of the application, the department in charge of patent administration shall make a decision on the grant of patent, announce it and notify the applicant (Art 39).

With respect to a patent for utility model or design, if the Chinese Patent Office determines upon preliminary examination that the application is in conformity with the Law, it shall immediately make an announcement for grant and notify the applicant (Art 40). There is no substantive examination for a patent for utility model or design.

If the Chinese Patent Office rejects the application, the applicant may within three months from the date of receipt of the notification, request a patent re-examination (Art 41). The applicant may also bring an action before the Patent Re-examination Board of the Chinese Patent Office for review. A decision made by the Board with respect to patents for utility model or design is final. Any party or individual may, at any time after a patent is granted to a third party, request that the Patent Re-examination Board invalidates such patent, and, similarly, a court action may also be brought with respect to the outcome of such request of invalidation (Art 46).

With respect to patents for invention, an applicant whose application has been rejected by the Patent Office may request for re-examination and subsequently appeal to the Patent Re-examination Board and further appeal to a People's Court (Art 43).

Copyright

Registration of copyrightable materials is optional. However, registration is required in case of seeking damages of copyright infringement. Chinese Copyright Office is the administrative body for copyright registrations and administrative enforcement.

Registration of computer software

Registration of computer software for copyright purposes is subject to procedures and to a formal administrative review process. The China Software Registration Centre has been established to administer all aspects of computer software registration, including examining applications for software registration and maintaining software registration files. Under the current *Computer Software Protection Regulations*, the registration of software for copyright purpose is optional, not compulsory.

Trademarks

The *Trademark Law* provides that where the state prescribes that certain kinds of goods or services must bear a registered trademark, registration must be applied for in respect of such goods. In the absence of registration, such goods or services shall not be sold in the market (Art 5). This provision is in accordance with the purposes of the Law which, *inter alia*, are to encourage producers to guarantee the quality of their goods or services and maintain the reputation of their trademarks (Art 1).

Pharmaceuticals for human use and tobacco products listed by the state and publicly announced by SAIC shall be required to use a registered trademark.

CHN ¶65-022 TRANSFERS AND LICENSING AGREEMENTS

Trademarks

A registered trademark may be assigned by an application filed jointly by an assignee and an assignor, and the assignee is required to guarantee the quality of goods/ services in respect of which the registered trademark is used (Art 25). The registered proprietor may also license the others to use its registered trademark. Article 26 provides that the licensor shall supervise the quality of the goods or services in respect of which the licensee uses its registered trademark, and the licensee shall guarantee the quality of the goods or services in respect of which the registered trademark is used. Trademark licence agreements are required to be recorded with the Trademark Office for record (Art 26).

Patents

Patent rights and the right to apply for a patent may be assigned (Art 10). Any assignment to a foreigner by a Chinese entity or individual must be approved by the appropriate department of the State Council. In the case of an assignment, the parties must conclude a written contract which will come into effect after it is duly registered with the department in charge of patent administration (Art 10).

Patent rights may be licensed to third parties. The entity or individual exploiting the patent of another must pay the patentee a fee and conclude with him or her, a written licence contract for exploitation (Art 12). The licensee cannot authorise a third party to exploit the patent. With the approval of the State Council, a patent right to an invention of great significance to the interests of the state or public interest that is owned by a state-owned entity may be distributed to allow other entities designated by the relevant ministries or provincial governments to exploit the right (Art 14). Patents of a Chinese individual or entity under collective ownership, which are of great significance to the interests of the state or public interest, may be treated likewise (Art 14).

Copyright

Article 23 requires that a licence be obtained if the works of another person are to be used, except where the law provides that licensing is not necessary. No rights over a work may be exercised by a licensee which have not been explicitly licensed (Art 25).

The contents required to be contained in a licensing contract are set out in Art 24.

The term of a licensing contract is limited to 10 years but may be renewed on the expiration of that term (Art 26).

Rates of remuneration are set by the copyright administrative departments of the State Council, though the parties may be able to agree to a fee among themselves (Art 27).

Article 28 protects the moral rights of another to licensed materials, to be attributed, to revision of their works, to protection of the integrity of their works and to receiving remuneration.

According to *Questions Concerning the Trading and Licensing of Copyrights Opinion* issued by the National Copyright Administration on 4 June 2003, the sale and purchase of copyrights do not require approval, whereas agency services for assignment or licensing of foreign related copyrights require the approval of the National Copyright Administration.

Foreign technology licensing

The *Regulations of the PRC on the Administration of Technology Import and Export* promulgated on 10 December 2001 went into effect as of 1 January 2002. By asserting to cover all kinds of cross-border technology transfer activities, the Regulations have a broader scope of application as it applies to both technology import and technology export.

Under the new regulation and other related implementation rules introduced thereafter, for both import and export of technology, technology is classified into three categories, ie technology prohibited from import or export ("prohibited technology"), technology restrictive for import or export ("restrictive technology") and technology for import or export freely ("non-restrictive technology"). The import/export of non-restrictive technology is subject to registration, while the import/export of restrictive technology, will be subject to approval of foreign trade administration authorities.

CHN ¶65-023   COMPULSORY LICENSES

Trademarks

No compulsory licensing is provided for in the *Trademark Law* and its implementing rules.

Patents

According to Chapter 6 of the *Patent Law*, a compulsory licence may be granted in the following circumstances:

- Where an entity has requested from a patentee of invention or practical and new model on reasonable terms and conditions to exploit such patent but has not obtained the licence within a reasonable period of time, the State Council department in charge of patent administration may, upon an application of the said entity, grant a compulsory licence to exploit the said patent.

- Where a national emergency or any other extraordinary situation or if necessitated by public interest, the State Council department in charge of patent administration may grant a compulsory licence to exploit an invention or a practical and new model patent.

- Where a patented invention or practical and new model has undergone great technological advancement of more notable economic significance than the invention or practical and new model for which the patent was previously granted, and the exploitation of the later invention or practical and new model relies on the exploitation of the earlier invention or practical and new model, the State Council department in charge of patent administration may, upon the request of the later patentee, grant a compulsory licence to exploit the earlier invention or practical and new model, and, thereafter, upon the request of the earlier patentee, grant a compulsory licence to exploit the later invention or practical and new model.

The scope and duration of exploitation under the compulsory licence shall be prescribed by the State Council department in charge of patent administration. A reasonable exploitation fee shall be agreed upon by the parties, and, if no agreement can be reached, be determined by the State Council department in charge of patent administration. The compulsory licensing shall not entitle the licensee an exclusive right to exploit. If a party is not satisfied with relevant decisions of the State Council department in charge of patent administration in this respect, a court action may be initiated within three months from the receipt of the notice thereof.

Copyright

Article 22 of the *Copyright Law* enumerates various circumstances where no licence shall be required and no remuneration shall be paid for the use of a work, including, for example, using another person's published work for personal study, research or appreciation, or using in one's own work appropriate quotations from another person's published work to introduce or comment on a certain work or to explain a certain issue. The author's name and the name of the work shall be shown clearly and other rights prescribed under the *Copyright Law* shall not be infringed upon.

CHN ¶65-024   TABLE OF FEES

Trademarks

Applications for trademark registration and other proceedings in trademark matters are subject to the payment of fees, the rates of which are formulated and announced by SAIC (Art 47 of the Rules).

Patents

Article 90 of the *Implementing Rules to the Patent Law* specifies the categories of fees that shall be paid to the State Council department in charge of patent administration in connection with patent applications and other patent-related matters. Such fees include the following:

- filing fee, supplementary filing fee, and publication and printing fee;
- substantive examination fee with respect to patents for invention, and re-examination fee;
- patent registration fee, fee for publication of announcement, application maintenance fee, and annual fee;
- fee for a change in the bibliographic data, fee for claiming priority, fee for a request for restoration of rights, fee for a request for extension of time period, and fee for a new and practical model patent search report;
- fee for a request for invalidation, fee for a request for suspension of relevant procedures, fee for a request for compulsory licence, and fee for a request for a ruling concerning exploitation fee of compulsory licence.

The rates of the fees shall be prescribed by the State Council department in charge of pricing administration in conjunction with the State Council department in charge of patent administration.

Copyright

Article 27 of the *Copyright Law* provides that fee standards for the use of works may be set forth by the parties of the contract, or, if there is no contract provision on this or such provision is unclear, be in accordance with those determined by the State Council department in charge of copyright administration in conjunction with other relevant departments.

CHN ¶65-025   DISADVANTAGES FOR NON-RESIDENTS

Under Art 19 of the *Patent Law*, a foreigner or foreign entity must appoint a "patent agency" for the purpose of an application unless it has a habitual residence or business office in China.

Under Art 20, Chinese entities or individuals are entitled to file their patent applications directly with the State Council department in charge of patent administration.

Similarly, although Chinese entities may file their trademark applications directly with the Trademark Office, foreign applicants must commission a "trademark agency" to handle their trademark application procedures with the Trademark Office.

CHN ¶65-031   ENFORCEMENT

As mentioned above, in anticipation of the WTO accession, China has revised its *Patent Law, Implementing Rules to the Patent Law, Copyright Law* and *Trademark Law*. Domestic and overseas experts agree that the development of intellectual property law in China has kept in pace with international standards but challenges lie in enforcement. It is widely believed that with its WTO accession, China will enforce the protection of intellectual property in a more serious and stricter manner.

Settlement of Disputes

Basis of courts' jurisdiction .... CHN ¶70-001

Status of foreign companies .... CHN ¶70-002

Civil procedure for foreign companies .... CHN ¶70-003

Rules of civil procedure and evidence .... CHN ¶70-004

Service and execution of process outside jurisdiction .. CHN ¶70-005

Availability of interlocutory relief .... CHN ¶70-011

Collection of evidence outside the jurisdiction .... CHN ¶70-012

Choice of applicable law .... CHN ¶70-013

Choice of forum .... CHN ¶70-014

Costs and delay associated with litigation .... CHN ¶70-015

Security for costs .... CHN ¶70-021

Language of courts .... CHN ¶70-022

Enforcement and execution of judgments .... CHN ¶70-023

Recognition of foreign judgments .... CHN ¶70-024

Status of foreign lawyers .... CHN ¶70-025

Special procedures for certain disputes .... CHN ¶70-031

Arbitration .... CHN ¶70-101

Conciliation, mediation and alternative dispute
   resolution .... CHN ¶70-201

Framework for dispute resolution .... CHN ¶70-301

Position of government .... CHN ¶70-401

CHN ¶70-001   BASIS OF COURTS' JURISDICTION

The civil jurisdiction of the People's Courts is exercised in accordance with the provisions of the *Code of Civil Procedure* of the People's Republic of China (1991).

Chapter II, sec. 1 of the *Code of Civil Procedure* sets out the differentiated jurisdiction of the People's Courts at various levels to hear matters at first instance.

Article 22 provides that, in a civil action, the People's Court which has jurisdiction is the one in the location of the defendant's domicile. If a defendant's domicile is different from the place of residence, then the People's Court at the place of residence will have jurisdiction to hear the matter. Where there are several defendants whose places of residence are within the jurisdiction of more than one People's Court, all the People's Courts concerned will be competent to hear the matter.

Article 23 provides certain circumstances under which the jurisdiction of the People's Court will be at the place of domicile of the plaintiff, or where the domicile of the plaintiff is different from the residence, then the People's Court at the place of residence will be the court which has jurisdiction. Circumstances under which place of domicile of the plaintiff shall exercise jurisdiction are:

- actions concerning the status of persons whose whereabouts are unknown or who have been declared missing;
- actions concerning the identity of persons who do not reside within the territory of the People's Republic of China;
- actions against persons undergoing rehabilitation through labour;
- actions against persons in prison.

The *Code of Civil Procedure* also makes specific provision in relation to civil suits which will fall within the area of particular jurisdiction. They are:

- actions arising from disputes over contracts come under the jurisdiction of the People's Court at the place of implementation of the contract (Art. 24);
- actions arising from disputes over insurance contracts come under the jurisdiction of the People's Court at the place where the insured object is located (Art. 26);
- actions arising from disputes over bill come under the jurisdiction of the People's Court at the place where the bills are paid (Art. 27);
- actions arising from disputes over transport contracts involving rail, road, sea or air come under the jurisdiction of the People's Court at the place where the means of transport started or its place of destination (Art. 28);
- actions arising from tortious acts come under the jurisdiction of the People's Court at the place where the acts were committed (Art. 29);
- action claiming compensation for damages as a result of a rail, road, water or aviation accident come under the jurisdiction of the People's Court at the place where the accident occurred or the place of primary arrival of the vehicle, ship or aircraft concerned (Art. 30); and
- actions claiming compensation for damages as a result of collisions of ships or other maritime accidents come under the jurisdiction of the People's Court at the place where the collisions occurred or at the place of primary arrival of the damaged ship or the place of detention of the ship responsible for the collision (Art. 31). In addition, Art. 32 provides that actions claiming salvage money come under the jurisdiction of the People's Court at the place of the salvage or the place of the primary arrival of the salvage ship.

Where it is difficult to implement the provisions in relation to a particular jurisdiction, then the provisions contained in Art. 22 and 23 for general jurisdiction should be applied.

Special jurisdiction

Exclusive or special jurisdiction of the People's Court is provided for in Art. 34 in relation to:

- actions concerning real estate which come under the jurisdiction of the People's Court at the place where the real estate is situated;

- actions arising from harbour operations, which come under the jurisdiction of the People's Court at the place of the harbour; and

- actions for inheriting property, which come under the jurisdiction of the People's Court at the place of domicile of the deceased before his or her death, or the place where the principal property is located.

Section 3 of Chapter II of the *Code of Civil Procedure* (Art. 36 to 39) makes provision for transferring jurisdiction from one court to another and for determining which of the People's Courts should properly exercise jurisdiction.

CHN ¶70-002 STATUS OF FOREIGN COMPANIES

The Supreme People's Court has issued an *Opinion on Several Problems in the Application of the Civil Procedure Law*. Chapter 18 of this document clarifies several points on arbitration and litigation involving foreigners.

Scope. Chapter 18 applies to all civil cases "involving a foreign element". This means:

(i) cases in which one or both parties are foreigners, stateless persons, foreign enterprises or foreign organisations;

(ii) cases in which the establishment, modification or termination of the civil legal relationship between the parties legally occurred in a foreign country; or

(iii) cases in which the object of the civil action is located in a foreign country.

Jurisdiction. If a civil action is subject to the exclusive jurisdiction of the People's Courts, parties may not use a written agreement to have a matter heard by the courts in another country. This prohibition does not apply, however, to parties which agree to select arbitration.

Enforcement procedure when defendant is absent. If a judgment in a civil action is made in the absence of the defendant, the court is required to serve its judgment by public announcement in accordance with Art. 247 of the *Civil Procedure Law*. Under Art. 247, the judgment is deemed to have been served six months from the date of publication of the announcement. If the party does not appeal within 30 days from the expiry of this six-month period, the judgment of the People's Court will take effect.

Mediation. If the parties to a civil action reach an agreement following mediation, a mediation statement is to be issued. A party may also request a written judgment to be prepared according to the contents of the agreement.

Time limit for appeals. Parties residing outside the PRC have 30 days to appeal a judgment or ruling of the People's Court. A party which resides within the PRC, however, only has 15 days to appeal a decision. If an appeal is not lodged within the relevant time limit, the decision of the court will become legally effective.

Enforcement of arbitration awards. Applications for the enforcement of an arbitral award must be made in Chinese, and must include the original version of the award. In certain circumstances, if an objection is made to the enforcement of an award, the People's Court may stay the enforcement after security (in the form of property) is provided. The People's Court will then examine the objection and decide whether or not to enforce the award.

Termination of economic contracts containing arbitration agreements. The annulment or termination of an economic contract will not affect the validity of the arbitration clause of the contract. Parties which have annulled or terminated a contract with an arbitration clause may not begin an action in the People's Courts.

CHN ¶70-003   CIVIL PROCEDURES FOR FOREIGN COMPANIES

Part IV of the *Code of Civil Procedure* makes special provisions in relation to civil actions involving foreigner. General principles are set out in Chapter XXIV (Art. 237 to 242).

Article 237 provides that the *Code of Civil Procedure* will apply to any foreign parties (individuals, enterprises or organisations) and stateless persons within Chinese territory.

Article 238 provides that where provisions of international treaties to which China is a member are at variance with the *Code of Civil Procedure*, then the provision of the international treaty is to apply, except where China has declared a reservation in that treaty.

Article 241 provides that where a foreign national, stateless person, foreign enterprise or organisation suing or being sued before a People's Court wishes to appoint a lawyer to act as an agent *ad litem*, a lawyer of the PRC must be appointed.

CHN ¶70-004   RULES OF CIVIL PROCEDURE AND EVIDENCE

The rules of civil procedure and evidence are contained within the *Code of Civil Procedure* of the People's Republic of China, 1991. Chapter VI deals specifically with the rules of evidence.

The *Several Provisions Concerning Evidence in Civil Actions*, published by the Supreme People's Court on 21 December 2001 and effective as of 1 April 2002, sets forth detailed rules of evidence in relation to parties' burden of evidence, court's collection of evidence, time limits for producing evidence, exchange and cross-examination of evidence, examination of the effect of evidence, etc.

CHN ¶70-005   SERVICE AND EXECUTION OF PROCESS OUTSIDE JURISDICTION

Article 247 of the *Code of Civil Procedure* provides for six means by which litigation documents may be served upon litigants not residing within the territory of the People's Republic of China. They are:

- through diplomatic channels;

- where the litigants are of Chinese nationality, the documents may be entrusted to the service of the embassy or consulate of the People's Republic of China in the country where they reside;

- service by mail where the law of the country of residence of the litigant permits;

- through a method specified in international treaties entered into or acceded to by both the People's Republic of China and the country of domicile of the litigant;

- through the attorney *ad litem* of the litigant if the attorney is authorised to receive service of process;

- through the representative office of the litigant stationed within the People's Republic of China or a branch organisation or business agent authorised to receive a service of process; and

- through public notice if delivery cannot be made by any of the above methods.

The defendant has 30 days after receipt of the initiating process to respond. An extension of this term may be requested and shall be decided by the People's Court.

Chapter XXIX of the *Code of Civil Procedure* provides for enforcement of foreign judgments in China on the basis of international treaties signed (for example, judicial assistance agreements) or otherwise on the principle of mutual reciprocity.

CHN ¶70-011   AVAILABILITY OF INTERLOCUTORY RELIEF

Articles 92 to 99 make specific provision for "security in litigation" measures to be taken. They include sealing up, confiscation, the freezing of assets or other methods prescribed by law (Art. 94).

Articles 92 and 93 empower the People's Court to order the applicant seeking security to provide a guarantee.

The People's Court may order prior payment under the provisions of Art. 97 in the following circumstances:

- cases claiming alimony costs, costs of support or upbringing, compensation for the disabled or for the family of the deceased;

- cases claiming labour remuneration; or

- other matters that require prior payment.

Special provisions are made in relation to foreign litigants in Chapter XXVII (Art. 251 to 256). The specific measures provided are:

- the People's Court may make a ruling for security in litigation upon the application of either the plaintiff or the defendant;

- upon making the ruling, the People's Court will notify the relevant party to provide a guarantee or security (usually bank credit). If the party refuses, then the People's Court will rule to grant property preservation;

- the applicant shall bear any costs or losses resulting from any error in the application; and

- the People's Court will make a ruling to cancel a property preservation order when it finds that it is no longer necessary. This order will be carried out by an execution officer.

See also CHN ¶70-021.

CHN ¶70-012   COLLECTION OF EVIDENCE OUTSIDE THE JURISDICTION

Chapter XXIX of the *Code of Civil Procedure* provides for judicial assistance between the People's Courts and the courts of a foreign country on the basis of international treaties or the principle of mutual reciprocity. The activities comprehended within the term "judicial assistance" are:

- service of process or delivery of documents;

- investigation and collection of evidence; and

- recognition and enforcement of judicial or arbitral awards.

CHN ¶70-013   CHOICE OF APPLICABLE LAW

Article 126 of the *Contract Law* of the People's Republic of China, adopted on 15 March 1999, provides that parties to a foreign-related contract may choose the law applicable to the settlement of disputes arising out of the contract. There are three exceptions to this principle of freedom to choose the applicable law. They are:

- the joint venture contract of the equity joint venture;

- the joint venture contract of a contractual joint venture; and

- contracts for cooperative exploitation and development of natural resources, which are performed within the territory of the People's Republic of China.

In these three situations, the governing law must be the law of the People's Republic of China.

In the absence of a choice of law, the law of the country which has the closest connection with the contract will apply.

CHN ¶70-014   CHOICE OF FORUM

Article 244 of the *Code of Civil Procedure* provides that parties to a dispute over a foreign-related contract or over foreign-related property rights and interests may through a written agreement select as the jurisdictional court a court at a place with actual connections with the dispute. However, if a People's Court is so selected, the principles of exclusive jurisdiction and hierarchical jurisdiction (the Intermediate People's Court is competent to hear foreign related civil cases at first instance) set forth in the *Code of Civil Procedure* should not be contravened.

In an effort to ensure quality of foreign-related judgments and rulings, the Supreme People's Court published the *Provisions Concerning Several Issues of Jurisdiction over Foreign Related Civil and Commercial Litigations* on 25 February 2002. Under these Provisions, People's Courts that are competent to hear foreign-related cases at first instance are restricted to the following ones (while in the past all the Intermediate People's Courts are competent):

- People's Courts established in the economic and technological development zones approved by the State Council;
- Intermediate People's Courts established in the capital cities of provinces and autonomous regions and in the municipalities directly under the Central Government;
- Intermediate People's Courts established in the special economic zones and the municipalities with separate planning;
- Other Intermediate People's Courts designated by the Supreme People's Court; and
- Higher People's Courts.

CHN ¶70-015 COSTS AND DELAY ASSOCIATED WITH LITIGATION

Article 107 of the *Code of Civil Procedure* provides that a fee shall be payable for acceptance of the case in accordance with regulations. There are separate regulations setting out the scale of fees payable by parties to litigation.

Time limits for accepting a case, conducting the pre-trial preparation, mediation and hearings are set out in the *Code of Civil Procedure*.

Costs and fees payable to the People's Court in respect of litigation are set out in the *People's Courts Costs Procedures*, effective from 1 September 1989. Provision is made for specified charges in addition to the case acceptance fee, case acceptance fees for different matters, enforcement application fees and the like.

A party facing genuine difficulty in paying court costs may apply for deferment, reduction or exemption from payment (Art. 107).

These procedures apply to foreign parties involved in litigation in China, with the exception being where differential treatment is accorded to foreign nationals in the courts of the country of the foreign party, in which case, the principle of reciprocity will be applied (Art. 5).

CHN ¶70-021 SECURITY FOR COSTS

Provisions for security for costs and prior payment are made in Chapter IX of the *Code of Civil Procedure*.

Article 94 provides that security in litigation in the form of property preservation shall be limited to the scope of the claim or to property relevant to the case.

Any party may apply to the People's Court to take measures for security in litigation. The People's Court shall require the applicant to provide security (Art. 93).

A recent ruling provides that prior payment may be made and executed by the People's Court in the following circumstances:

- in cases claiming alimony, costs of support or upbringing, compensation for the disabled or for the family of the deceased;
- cases claiming labour remuneration; and
- other matters that require prior payment (Art. 97).

The party against whom a ruling for granting property preservation or preliminary execution is made may apply for reconsideration of that decision. However, execution of the decision will not be suspended during the course of reconsideration (Art. 99).

CHN ¶70-022   LANGUAGE OF COURTS

Court proceedings may be conducted in any of the native spoken and written languages of all ethnic groups. In an area densely inhabited by a minority ethnic group or by several ethnic groups, hearings shall be conducted by the People's Courts in the spoken language in common use in the area (Art. 11). In cases involving foreigners, the People's Courts shall use the spoken and written language in common use in the People's Republic of China. Upon request by the litigant, an interpreter may be provided and the costs shall be borne by the litigant concerned.

CHN ¶70-023   ENFORCEMENT AND EXECUTION OF JUDGMENTS

The process for the execution of judgments in China is set out in Chapters XX to XXIII of the *Code of Civil Procedure*. The litigant must first make a request for execution under Chapter XXI to the People's Court in charge of the matter. The request must be made within six months where both parties are enterprises, institutions, organs or organisations. The time limit is computed from the last day of the period for performance set out in the original judgment. Execution officers are responsible for pursuing the property of the defendant by means of the processes set out in Chapter XXII.

CHN ¶70-024   RECOGNITION OF FOREIGN JUDGMENTS

In order to recognise and enforce a foreign judgment, the *Code of Civil Procedure* provides that three pre-conditions must be met:

- there must be reciprocity between the two countries;
- the judgment or award must be final and the request for assistance must be specific and certain; and
- the request for judicial assistance must be made by a foreign court.

The *Code of Civil Procedure* also makes provision in relation to certain types of cases which will not be enforced by a Chinese court. These cases are:

- cases incompatible with the sovereignty and security of the People's Republic of China. For example, where the case or evidence involves China's national defence secrets or relates to a case to which China has reserved exclusive jurisdiction to its own courts;
- if the case is outside the jurisdiction of the People's Court; or
- if the judgment or ruling is incompatible with the national and social interests of the People's Republic of China.

(See Art. 268.)

With effect from 22 May 1998, the Supreme People's Court issued the *Provisions on Recognition by the People's Courts of Civil Judgment made by the Courts of Taiwan Area.*

According to the Provisions, in case the residence, actual residence or the property to be enforced of the party to the civil judgment made by the courts of Taiwan area is located on the mainland, the parties can apply or retain an attorney to apply to the People's Court for recognition of the Taiwanese judgment within one year. A judgment includes civil holdings and awards made by any court or arbitration organisation in Taiwan.

After the People's Court recognises the judgment made by the Taiwanese court, action cannot be commenced for the same matter in the mainland.

Before a civil judgment is made by the People's Court, if a party applies for the recognition of the judgment made by the court in Taiwan in the same case, the litigation shall be suspended and the application shall be examined.

CHN ¶70-025   STATUS OF FOREIGN LAWYERS

The *Code of Civil Procedure* provides in Art. 241 that any foreign or stateless parties to an action in China must entrust their cases to lawyers of the People's Republic of China. Powers of attorney entrusting the case to such a lawyer must be notarised in the country where that party resides and authenticated by the Chinese Embassy or Consulate in that country. At present, foreign lawyers are not permitted to practise Chinese law at all in China.

CHN ¶70-031   SPECIAL PROCEDURES FOR CERTAIN DISPUTES

Civil disputes

The procedure for the hearing of all civil disputes before the People's Courts is contained within the *Code of Civil Procedure*. See CHN ¶70-001 and CHN ¶70-002.

Intellectual property

In Beijing (and some other more developed areas), specialised tribunals known as the Beijing Municipal Higher and Intermediate Intellectual Property Adjudication Division have been set up to deal with various intellectual property disputes involving foreigners. The following types of cases may be accepted by the Adjudication Division:

- patent disputes;
- trademark disputes;
- copyright disputes, including disputes over computer software rights;
- disputes over invention rights, discovery rights and rights in other scientific and technological achievements;
- technology contract disputes; and
- all intellectual property disputes involving foreigners, including those from Hong Kong, Macao and Taiwan.

ARBITRATION

Arbitration system ...... CHN ¶70-101

New York Convention on Recognition and Enforcement of Foreign Arbitral Awards .... CHN ¶70-102

Special provisions required for arbitration clauses .... CHN ¶70-103

International arbitration rules .... CHN ¶70-104

United Nations Model Law .... CHN ¶70-105

Distinction between international and domestic arbitration .... CHN ¶70-111

Tribunal's basis of jurisdiction .... CHN ¶70-112

Exceptions .... CHN ¶70-113

Courts' assistance in arbitration process ... CHN ¶70-114

Choice of procedural law CHN ¶70-115

Choice of applicable law . CHN ¶70-121

Specification of appointment of arbitrators, etc. ...... CHN ¶70-122

Rules governing choice of arbitrators .... CHN ¶70-123

Expense of arbitration ... CHN ¶70-124

Delays in arbitration .... CHN ¶70-125

Review by court .... CHN ¶70-131

Arbitration by amiable composition .... CHN ¶70-132

Participation by foreign companies .... CHN ¶70-133

Rules of natural justice .. CHN ¶70-134

Status of foreign lawyers CHN ¶70-135

Assistance from outside jurisdictions .... CHN ¶70-141

Language of proceedings CHN ¶70-142

Confidentiality of proceedings .... CHN ¶70-143

Special procedures for certain disputes .... CHN ¶70-144

Arbitration in third country .... CHN ¶70-145

CHN ¶70-031

CHN ¶70-101   ARBITRATION SYSTEM

China has a well-developed system of arbitration. In addition to the various municipal arbitration commissions which accept foreign-related cases as well as Chinese domestic ones, there are two arbitration commissions established under the auspices of the China Council for the Promotion of International Trade (CCPIT) which focus particularly on foreign-related and international cases:

- the China International Economic and Trade Arbitration Commission (CIETAC); and
- the China Maritime Arbitration Commission (CMAC).

The *Code of Civil Procedure* at Chapter XXVIII deals with arbitration, the application for interlocutory measures and the enforcement of arbitral awards in arbitrations involving foreigners in China.

The PRC *Arbitration Law* was promulgated on 31 August 1994 and came into effect on 1 September 1995. It deals with the establishment of arbitration committees, the appointment of arbitrators and the issuance and enforcement of awards. The law applies to disputes between citizens, legal persons and disputes involving a foreign element. It also introduces a new national arbitration organ, the China Arbitration Association (CAA) to supervise all the arbitration commissions.

On 6 May 1998, CIETAC revised and adopted the *Arbitration Rules* which became effective as from 10 May 1998. This is a significant step taken by CIETAC to resolve disputes between the enterprises with foreign investment and disputes between an enterprise with foreign investment and another Chinese legal person, physical person and/or economic organisation. The disputes also cover those that arise from project financing, invitation for tender, bidding, construction and other activities conducted by Chinese legal persons, physical persons and/or other economic organisations through utilising the capital, technology or service from foreign countries, international organisations or from the Hong Kong SAR, Macao and Taiwan regions (Art 2).

On 5 September 2000, CIETAC further revised and adopted the *Arbitration Rules* which became effective as of 1 October 2001. The scope of disputes that can be resolved before CIETAC is expanded to cover all domestic disputes referred by the parties through agreements for arbitration by CIETAC.

On 4 April 2003, CIETAC issued the *Financial Disputes Arbitration Rules*, which became effective on 8 May 2003. The Rules apply when the parties concerned agree to apply the Rules to their financial disputes handled by CIETAC (Art 3). When there is a discrepancy between the Rules and the CIETAC *Arbitration Rules*, the Rules shall prevail. In the case of matters not covered in the Rules, the CIETAC *Arbitration Rules* shall apply (Art 26). The Rules deal with disputes in the monetary, capital, foreign exchange, gold and insurance markets over transactions concerning loans, security, letters of guarantee, negotiable instruments, funds, bonds, etc. The Rules contain provisions on arbitration procedures and judgment. Article 21 stipulates that the tribunal should take into consideration the contract clauses and the relevant industrial practices and standards under any circumstances.

CHN ¶70-102   NEW YORK CONVENTION ON RECOGNITION AND ENFORCEMENT OF FOREIGN ARBITRAL AWARDS

China is a party to the New York Convention on the Recognition and Enforcement of Foreign Arbitral Awards ("Convention"). The Convention was ratified by the Standing Committee of the NPC on 2 December 1986. The adoption of the Convention was subject to two reservations:

- pursuant to Art 1(3) of the Convention, China will apply the Convention in respect of the recognition and enforcement of an arbitral award which was made in the territory of another contracting state subject to the reservation of reciprocity; and

- China will only apply the Convention in respect of differences arising out of legal relationships, whether contractual or not which are considered commercial under Chinese law. Enforcement will not include disputes between foreign investors and the government of their host countries.

Where provisions of the Convention differ from the *Code of Civil Procedure*, matters shall be dealt with in accordance with the Convention (see Art 238 of the *Code of Civil Procedure*).

Where an arbitral award is made within the territory of a country which is not a party to the Convention, the question of recognition and enforcement by Chinese courts shall be dealt with in accordance with Art 269 of the *Code of Civil Procedure*.

Place of application

Applications by parties for enforcement of an arbitral award under the Convention shall be made to the People's Courts set forth in the above-mentioned *Provisions of the Supreme People's Court Concerning Several Issues of Jurisdiction over Foreign Related Civil and Commercial Litigations* published on 25 February 2002.

Procedures for enforcement

Procedures for enforcement of the arbitral award will be conducted by the relevant People's Court as follows:

- an examination will be undertaken to determine whether the application falls within the conditions of Art 5(1) and (2) of the Convention, which makes provision for the refusal in certain enumerated circumstances by the court to enforce such an arbitral award;

- if the court finds that the application does not fall within the conditions of Art 5(1) and (2), it shall make an order recognising the validity of the award and enforce it in accordance with the provisions of the *Code of Civil Procedure*; and

- if the conditions of Art 5(1) or (2) are fulfilled, an order will be made rejecting the application and enforcement and recognition will be refused.

Other rules governing the recognition and enforcement of foreign arbitral awards are found in the *Code of Civil Procedure* at Chapter XXIX.

CHN ¶70-103   SPECIAL PROVISIONS REQUIRED FOR ARBITRATION CLAUSES

If the parties to an agreement wish to include an arbitration clause in it, they should specify the country in which arbitration is to take place and the rules to be applied. Arbitration in China involving a foreign party will be conducted in accordance with the arbitration rules of the CIETAC or the arbitration rules of the CMAC (also referred to as the Arbitration Commission and the *Arbitration Rules* where convenient). Arbitration involving a foreign party can also be referred to any of the local Arbitration Commissions established under the *Arbitration Law* where the parties agree.

Parties wishing to refer any disputes to arbitration may either include an arbitration clause in the contract, or include a reference in the contract to a separate arbitration agreement to be concluded between the parties. Both these matters will provide the necessary evidence to show that the parties voluntarily agreed to submit any dispute arising between them to arbitration.

In order to ensure certainty of the arbitration clause or arbitration agreement, the following matters should be dealt with:

- the place of arbitration;
- the arbitration body;
- the arbitration procedure; and
- the binding force of the arbitration award.

CHN ¶70-104   INTERNATIONAL ARBITRATION RULES

The law does not specifically state whether the Chinese Arbitration Commission will apply the International Chamber of Commerce (ICC) rules, the UNCITRAL rules or the rules of the London Court of International Arbitration. Article 7 of the *Arbitration Rules* of CIETAC as revised in 2000 provides that if the parties concerned agree to refer their dispute to the Arbitration Commission for arbitration, it shall be deemed that they have agreed that the arbitration will be conducted in accordance with these arbitration rules. However, if the parties have agreed otherwise, and subject to agreement by the Arbitration Commission, the parties' agreement shall prevail.

China has become the world's largest centre for arbitrating international commercial disputes in terms of caseload with CIETAC dealing with 842 cases in 1995. New rules for foreign arbitration took effect on 1 June 1994 allowing international disputes to be settled in languages other than Chinese and also widening the scope of CIETAC's jurisdiction to international or external transactions. In doing so, companies would be less inclined to go to courts in other countries.

CHN ¶70-105   UNITED NATIONS MODEL LAW

The parties are free to select arbitration in China on the basis stated at CHN ¶70-104 above. If the defendant is Chinese, arbitration conducted in China by either CIETAC or CMAC will be conducted in accordance with their own arbitration rules, unless the parties have otherwise agreed and the Arbitration Commission has also consented to the parties' agreement. If arbitration is selected to be conducted in a third country, then the parties may, if permitted by the arbitration rules of that place, select the arbitration rules to be applied.

CHN ¶70-111   DISTINCTION BETWEEN INTERNATIONAL AND DOMESTIC ARBITRATION

In China, international and domestic commercial arbitration were for a long time governed by different bodies and different sets of rules. Foreign-related commercial arbitration was dealt with solely by CIETAC or CMAC under their own arbitration rules. Domestic arbitration for economic contracts was governed by the *Regulations on Arbitration for Economic Contracts of the People's Republic of China*. However, since the promulgation of the *Arbitration Law*, there has been a convergence between international and domestic arbitration. Currently, CIETAC and the various municipal arbitration commission can both resolve foreign-related disputes, and likewise, they can both resolve domestic disputes. The jurisdiction of CIETAC is set out in the CIETAC's *Arbitration Rules*.

See CHN ¶70-112.

CHN ¶70-112   TRIBUNALS' BASIS OF JURISDICTION

The jurisdictional basis of CIETAC and CMAC are set out in the current *Arbitration Rules*.

The Year 2000 amended rules provide that CIETAC's jurisdiction will extend to domestic disputes that have no foreign-related element at all.

CHN ¶70-113   EXCEPTIONS

As CIETAC and CMAC have power to decide on the validity of arbitration agreements and jurisdiction over arbitration cases, the arbitrability or otherwise of a dispute is within their scope of authority to decide in accordance with their Rules. But Art 20 of the *Arbitration Law* provides that if one party applies to the Chinese Courts for a ruling, the Chinese Courts' ruling on the above-mentioned matter shall prevail.

CHN ¶70-114 COURTS' ASSISTANCE IN ARBITRATION PROCESS

The *Code of Civil Procedure* makes specific provision in Chapter XXVIII concerning the relationship between the courts and arbitration bodies in relation to the resolution of disputes involving foreigners. That chapter provides *inter alia* that:

- where a written agreement to submit to arbitration exists between the parties, disputes may not be brought to the People's Court. However, where there is no such agreement, the People's Court may accept such a case (Art 257);

- the People's Courts may not accept cases which have already been resolved by a foreign affairs arbitration organisation of the People's Republic of China (Art 259);

- the foreign affairs arbitration organisation of the People's Republic of China may bring a matter to the intermediate People's Court at the request of one of the parties to the arbitration, seeking an order to adopt security measures in accordance with the provisions of the *Code of Civil Procedure* (Art 258); and

- where one party to an arbitration does not carry out the arbitral award made by either CIETAC or CMAC, the aggrieved party may apply for execution of the award under the provisions of the *Code of Civil Procedure* to the intermediate People's Court at the place of the arbitration organisation or the place of the property (Art 259).

CHN ¶70-115 CHOICE OF PROCEDURAL LAW

It is a principle of Chinese law that any matter brought before a Chinese court will be dealt with in accordance with the *Code of Civil Procedure* of the People's Republic of China. Should the parties or the arbitration tribunal have recourse to the People's Courts, then procedural matters will be dealt with in accordance with the Chinese *Code of Civil Procedure*. However, it is not clear whether the parties to arbitration must submit to the rules of civil procedure in the *Arbitration Rules*.

CIETAC and CMAC adhere to the following three principles in the handling of cases:

- independence and initiative (ie to abide by the Chinese law);

- equality and mutual benefit (to apply the conditions of the contract and laws other than Chinese laws where appropriate); and

- reference to international practice.

In sales contracts, the applicable substantive law can be chosen by the parties. In the absence of a choice of law by the parties, the arbitral tribunal shall decide what law is to be applied. However, Chinese law must be applied in equity and contractual joint ventures and in contracts for cooperative exploitation and development of natural resources which are performed within the territory of the People's Republic of China (see CHN ¶70-013).

The procedure for arbitration is set out in the *Arbitration Rules* of CIETAC and CMAC.

CHN ¶70-121 CHOICE OF APPLICABLE LAW

The parties are free to select the law of the contract with certain exceptions set out in accordance with Art 126 of the *Contract Law* of the People's Republic of China (see CHN ¶70-013). The law of the contract will be applied by the arbitral tribunal to the substance of the dispute in accordance with the three basic principles of independence and initiative, equality and mutual benefit, and reference to international practice (see CHN ¶70-115).

CHN ¶70-122 SPECIFICATION OF APPOINTMENT OF ARBITRATORS, ETC

The *Arbitration Rules* of CIETAC and CMAC provide that the Arbitration Commissions are located in Beijing. However, they are also authorised to establish sub-commissions in other places within Chinese territory. CIETAC established Shenzhen Sub-Commission in 1984 and Shanghai Sub-Commission in 1990. It is therefore wise to specify the place of arbitration, if arbitration is to be conducted in China.

The selection of arbitrators is included within the *Arbitration Rules* as part of the arbitration proceedings and so it is not necessary to stipulate the method of appointment of arbitrators if the arbitration is to be submitted to CIETAC or CMAC.

CHN ¶70-123 RULES GOVERNING CHOICE Of ARBITRATORS

The rules contain a provision in Art 28 which requires an arbitrator having a personal interest in a case to voluntarily disclose the circumstances of its interest and to withdraw from office. The current panel includes a total of 492 members, out of which 158 are from Hong Kong and foreign countries and regions. Many of the foreign members of the panel are practitioners in international arbitration from Europe, United States, Russia, Japan, Singapore and other countries.

CHN ¶70-124 EXPENSE OF ARBITRATION

Different costs between litigation and arbitration have not been an issue in relation to the settlement of international commercial disputes in China, as virtually all contracts concluded contain some forms of arbitration clause.

The costs of arbitration are set out in the Arbitration Fees Schedule which is a schedule to the *Arbitration Rules* of CIETAC and CMAC. The schedule provides a fee which is a set fee plus a proportion of the amount claimed on a scale of five separate categories. In addition, the *Arbitration Rules* provides that the Arbitration Commission may collect, in addition to the amount set out in the Schedule other actual expenses, which include the arbitrators' remuneration and their travel and boarding expenses for dealing with the case and the fees and expenses for experts, appraisers and interpreters appointed by the Arbitration Tribunal, etc. Certain fees and actual expenses may be collected by the Arbitration Commission where a case is withdrawn after the parties have reached an agreement.

CHN ¶70-125   DELAYS IN ARBITRATION

The times within which certain procedures must be completed are set out in the *Arbitration Rules.*

The Rules require the tribunal to render its award within nine months after the date the arbitration tribunal has been formed. It also permits the arbitrators to make corrections to arbitral awards which have already been rendered, or to render additional awards supplementing an earlier decision. Corrections may be made within stipulated time limits upon the request of the parties or by the tribunal on its own initiative.

CHN ¶70-131   REVIEW BY COURT

The relationship between the arbitral tribunal, the proceedings and awards and the People's Courts is set out at CHN ¶70-114.

CHN ¶70-132   ARBITRATION BY AMIABLE COMPOSITION

China has been very concerned to ensure that the substantive law applied in arbitration disputes is Chinese law. But in CIETAC and CMAC arbitration, foreign law (substantive law) can also be applied in accordance with the parties' authority or the principles of conflict law. The choice of law issue is often hard fought. There is no express statement in the laws but the award must accord with Chinese public policy.

CHN ¶70-133   PARTICIPATION BY FOREIGN COMPANIES

The *Arbitration Rules* of CIETAC and CMAC relate specifically to disputes arising from international economic and trade transactions. It is important to note that the legal person coming into existence as a result of an equity joint venture and possibly as the result of a contractual joint venture and a wholly-owned foreign enterprise will be considered to be Chinese legal persons. Consequently, for the purposes of *Contract Law* and other related economic laws, these entities, when dealing with other Chinese entities, will be dealt with on the basis of the principles of domestic laws relating to those areas.

CHN ¶70-134   RULES OF NATURAL JUSTICE

A characteristic of Chinese arbitration is that conciliation may be conducted in conjunction with arbitration. Conciliation may take place either before the arbitration or during the arbitration subject to the consent of both the parties. In both cases, the arbitrator may take on the role of conciliator at any time and if the conciliation takes place before arbitration, the conciliator may then be appointed as an arbitrator in the arbitration.

CHN ¶70-135   STATUS OF FOREIGN LAWYERS

See CHN ¶70-025 and CHN ¶70-304.

The *Arbitration Rules* specifically allow foreign lawyers to consult in the arbitration.

CHN ¶70-141   ASSISTANCE FROM OUTSIDE JURISDICTIONS

The *Arbitration Rules* of CIETAC and CMAC provide that the Arbitration Commission maintains a panel of arbitrators. The arbitrators are selected and appointed from amongst Chinese and foreign persons with special knowledge and practical experience in international economics and trade, science and technology, law and other fields. Until 1988, only Chinese nationals were allowed to be on the panel. There are now 158 non-Mainland Chinese nationals on the panel of CIETAC arbitrators.

The *Arbitration Rules* provide that the arbitral tribunal may consult experts or appoint appraisers for the clarification of special questions relating to the case. Such experts and appraisers may be Chinese or foreign organisations or citizens. The appointment of experts is not done directly by the parties to the arbitration, but by the arbitral tribunal unless otherwise agreed between the parties.

CHN ¶70-142   LANGUAGE OF PROCEEDINGS

The *Arbitration Rules* provide that the Chinese language is the official language of the Arbitration Commission. Either the Arbitration Commission may provide an interpreter or those who are not familiar with Chinese or the parties may bring their own interpreter. The secretariat of the Arbitration Commission, where it deems necessary, may ask the parties to translate documents into Chinese or hand in translation copies in Chinese of documents and other evidentiary materials.

Under the amended arbitration rules which took effect on June 1994, international disputes may be settled in languages other than Chinese. In doing so, companies would be less inclined to go to courts in other countries.

CHN ¶70-143   CONFIDENTIALITY OF PROCEEDINGS

Article 36 of the *Arbitration Rules* provides that "the arbitration tribunal shall not hear cases in open sessions. If both parties request hearings in open sessions, the arbitration tribunal shall decide thereon".

The proceedings of the arbitral tribunal are confidential unless the parties otherwise agree.

CHN ¶70-135

CHN ¶70-144 SPECIAL PROCEDURES FOR CERTAIN DISPUTES

Maritime

Arbitrations relating to maritime matters are dealt with by CMAC in accordance with its rules. The Maritime Arbitration Commission takes cognisance of a dispute upon the written application of one of the disputing parties and in accordance with such written arbitration agreement as concluded between the parties either prior or subsequent to the arising of the dispute (Art 3). The following items must be specified in the application for arbitration (Art 4):

- the name and address of the plaintiff and those of the defendant;
- the claim of the plaintiff and the facts and evidence upon which the claim is based; and
- the name of an arbitrator chosen by the plaintiff from among the members of CMAC or a statement authorising the chairman of CMAC to appoint the arbitrator for the plaintiff.

When submitting an application for arbitration, the plaintiff shall pay a sum equivalent to 1% of the amount of the claim as a deposit for the arbitration fee. The award given by CMAC is final and neither party shall bring an appeal for revision before a court of law or any other organisation.

CHN ¶70-145 ARBITRATION IN THIRD COUNTRY

In most cases, parties are free to decide whether they will arbitrate in China or the country of the other party or in a third country. Chinese parties are reluctant to agree to arbitration in the country of the foreign party and often the parties will decide upon arbitration in a third country. Until now, it has been relatively common to nominate Sweden as a third country in which arbitration may take place. In Sweden, arbitration is conducted at the Arbitration Institution of the Stockholm Chamber of Commerce, in accordance with its rules. There is a historical preference to specify arbitration in Sweden as a result of a previous agreement of longstanding currency between the Soviet Union and the United States of America that any dispute arising between parties to contractual relations of those two nations would be referred to arbitration in Stockholm. This preference has continued to the present. However, Chinese parties are prepared to accept other third countries as a place for arbitration. Issues such as the cost and inconvenience of geographical arbitration in Sweden are now being considered more, when determining an acceptable third country in which to arbitrate.

CONCILIATION, MEDIATION AND ALTERNATIVE DISPUTE RESOLUTION

Alternative methods of dispute resolution .... CHN ¶70-201

International conventions CHN ¶70-202

Appointment of conciliators and mediators .... CHN ¶70-203

Special rules governing proceedings .... CHN ¶70-204

Basis of jurisdiction ..... CHN ¶70-205

Enforcement of settlement .... CHN ¶70-211

Right of representation .. CHN ¶70-212

Choice of applicable law . CHN ¶70-213

Courts' power of intervention .... CHN ¶70-214

Confidentiality of proceedings .... CHN ¶70-215

Special rules for foreign participation .... CHN ¶70-221

Provisions in contract for forms of dispute resolution .. CHN ¶70-222

Restrictions on types of disputes for conciliation, etc. .... CHN ¶70-223

Disadvantages of conciliation, etc. .... CHN ¶70-224

Joint methods of dispute resolution .... CHN ¶70-225

CHN ¶70-201   ALTERNATIVE METHODS OF DISPUTE RESOLUTION

Although there is theoretically a distinction between conciliation and mediation, the distinction is not clearly drawn and often the terms are used interchangeably.

China has a highly developed system of alternative dispute resolution which operates both independently and in conjunction with the formal dispute resolution mechanisms such as arbitration and litigation. All forms of conciliation/mediation are based on the principles of voluntariness of the parties, the prerequisite of establishing the facts, distinguishing right from wrong and ensuring fairness and reasonableness.

CHN ¶70-202   INTERNATIONAL CONVENTIONS

In 1987, the Beijing Conciliation Centre was set up within CCPIT to conciliate international commercial and maritime disputes involving foreign parties. The Beijing Conciliation Centre has agreed to cooperate in conciliation with the Beijing/Hamburg Conciliation Centre to resolve international commercial and maritime disputes. They have formulated the *Beijing/Hamburg Conciliation Rules*. Such cooperation agreements were reached with American Arbitration Association and London International Arbitration Board.

CHN ¶70-201

CHN ¶70-203   APPOINTMENT OF CONCILIATORS AND MEDIATORS

The Beijing Conciliation Centre has a panel of conciliators from which the parties may choose. The conciliations run in conjunction with either arbitration or litigation, the arbitrators are selected according to CIETAC or CMAC Rules in the case of arbitration or the judge assigned to the matter respectively will act concurrently as conciliator. Neighbourhood committees established under local government bodies also do mediation work. Members of the neighbourhood committee are appointed and operate within the scope of the Mediation Committee Rules. However, disputes involving foreign parties seldom come before a mediation committee as the main function of the mediation committee is to mediate domestic and small household disputes.

CHN ¶70-204   SPECIAL RULES GOVERNING PROCEEDINGS

The Beijing/Hamburg Conciliation Centre operates under the *Beijing/Hamburg Conciliation Rules*.

CHN ¶70-205   BASIS OF JURISDICTION

Both parties to a dispute must voluntarily submit to conciliation/mediation. The *Code of Civil Procedure* requires that a judge attempts to mediate matters before the court, but the court will be unable to act as mediator unless both parties consent to submit the dispute to mediation.

CHN ¶70-211   ENFORCEMENT OF SETTLEMENT

The *Code of Civil Procedure* provides that where parties to litigation successfully conciliate their dispute, the court will issue a conciliation statement in the terms of their agreement. Such a conciliation statement has the same legal effect as a judgment made by the court and a party may apply to the court for enforcement.

Where parties to arbitration before either CIETAC or CMAC successfully conciliate their dispute, the rules of arbitration provide that those bodies shall make an award in accordance with the contents of the settlement agreement between the parties. Therefore, the conciliation agreement will be embodied in and enforceable as an arbitration award. Conciliation and mediation agreements which are otherwise concluded have contractual force. Compliance with these types of conciliation or mediation awards can be enforced by an action for breach of contract.

CHN ¶70-212   RIGHT OF REPRESENTATION

In the case of conciliation during litigation, legal representatives represent the parties under the provisions of the *Code of Civil Procedure*, the *Arbitration Rules* of CIETAC and CMAC are applicable in relation to legal representation for conciliation during arbitration matters.

The rules of the Beijing Conciliation Centre allow Chinese or foreign lawyers to accompany the parties during face-to-face conciliation or to represent the parties during those meetings.

CHN ¶70-213   CHOICE OF APPLICABLE LAW

Procedural and substantive rules for conciliation/mediation will be determined by the rules of the forum in which the conciliation is held, ie court-ordered mediation will be conducted according to the procedure set out in the *Code of Civil Procedure*, arbitration according to CIETAC or CMAC rules and conciliation in the Beijing Conciliation Centre according to the rules promulgated by that Centre.

CHN ¶70-214   COURTS' POWER OF INTERVENTION

In accordance with the provisions of the *Code of Civil Procedure*, all civil matters before the People's Court often go through a mediation/conciliation process. Conciliation agreements reached through other means will come before the People's Court where one of the parties is seeking to enforce the terms of the agreement. If a ''definite error'' is found when a conciliation statement is brought before the People's Court for enforcement, an appeal may be made to the Judicial Committee of the court which heard the case or an appeal may be made to the People's Court at the next higher level. Conciliation agreements embodied in documents other than courts judgment or arbitration commissions' arbitration awards have not enforceability in China today.

CHN ¶70-215   CONFIDENTIALITY OF PROCEEDINGS

The confidentiality or otherwise of conciliation or mediation proceedings will depend upon the forum for holding the conciliation; the proceedings in the People's Courts are open unless otherwise provided but arbitration proceedings are confidential (CIETAC Rules, Art 25).

CHN ¶70-221   SPECIAL RULES FOR FOREIGN PARTICIPATION

Where conciliation takes place in an arbitration forum, the rules of CIETAC and CMAC are specifically directed towards disputes with a foreign element. The rules of the Beijing Conciliation Centre are also specifically directed toward disputes which contain a foreign element.

CHN ¶70-222   PROVISIONS IN CONTRACT FOR FORMS OF DISPUTE RESOLUTION

It is not necessary to include a conciliation/mediation clause in a contract to be able to seek to resolve a dispute between the parties should one arise. In practice, Chinese parties usually require the inclusion of a dispute resolution clause which seeks first to resolve any disputes by amiable negotiation and, only when that process fails, to resort to more formalised dispute resolution processes. In the interests of expediency and certainty, parties should consider their requirements regarding notification of a dispute and time limits to be placed upon the informal dispute resolution process. As with arbitration, provision should be made concerning an award of costs to be made. There is no rule of thumb in China that the costs follow the award.

CHN ¶70-223 RESTRICTIONS ON TYPES OF DISPUTES FOR CONCILIATION, ETC

A Chinese court does not conciliate matters which are brought against administrative departments of the Chinese government relating to the administrative treatment of economic disputes. A distinction is drawn between international and domestic dispute resolution in all cases except in the matters brought before the People's Court.

CHN ¶70-224 DISADVANTAGES OF CONCILIATION, ETC

Apart from time delay, there are no structural disadvantages to undergoing alternative dispute resolution procedures. In fact, most parties will seek to resolve any disputes arising first by conciliation/mediation. Many disputes do not reach the stage of formal conciliation/mediation but are resolved on an informal basis with the assistance of a concerned third party. For example, the Foreign Investment Commission in Shanghai is involved in the settlement of disputes between Chinese and foreign parties before the dispute is referred to more formal dispute resolution procedures.

CHN ¶70-225 JOINT METHODS OF DISPUTE RESOLUTION

In theory, conciliation proceedings should precede arbitration. The conciliator may then act as an arbitrator in those proceedings and should not attempt to conciliate again after conciliation has failed and the arbitral proceedings have commenced. In practice, conciliation is pursued simultaneously with arbitration and the arbitrator frequently changes back and forth to the role of a conciliator.

FRAMEWORK FOR DISPUTE RESOLUTION

International conventions CHN ¶70-301

Recognised arbitration
  centres .... CHN ¶70-302

Internationally acceptable
  arbitrators .... CHN ¶70-303

Availability of local
  advisers .... CHN ¶70-304

CHN ¶70-301   INTERNATIONAL CONVENTIONS

China is a party to the New York Convention on the Recognition and Enforcement of Foreign Arbitral Awards. China has entered into several bilateral agreements on judicial assistance under Art 262 of the *Code of Civil Procedure*. China has entered into such agreements with France, Poland, Belgium and Germany. These agreements relate to service of documents and taking of evidence and the recognition and enforcement of the decisions made by foreign courts or arbitral bodies.

CHN ¶70-302   RECOGNISED ARBITRATION CENTRES

See CHN ¶70-101.

CHN ¶70-303   INTERNATIONALLY ACCEPTABLE ARBITRATORS

The two Arbitration Commissions maintain panels of arbitrators which consist of both Chinese and foreign arbitrators.

CHN ¶70-304   AVAILABILITY OF LOCAL ADVISERS

In dispute resolution proceedings, with the exception of those brought before the People's Court, parties are permitted to be represented by foreign lawyers. Foreign lawyers do not have the standing to appear in the People's Courts and in those matters a Chinese lawyer is required to represent the foreign party.

POSITION OF GOVERNMENT

Status of government	**CHN ¶70-401**	**Enforcement of orders** ..	**CHN ¶70-403**
Choice of forum	**CHN ¶70-402**	**International conventions**	**CHN ¶70-404**

CHN ¶70-401   STATUS OF GOVERNMENT

The Chinese government has a strict view of sovereign immunity. However, in commercial matters, it is of the view that commercial consequences of the activities of government agencies should apply. Consequently, an increasing number of bodies are becoming registered as legal entities under the provisions of SAIC or are creating corporate vehicles under government department. The *General Principles of the Code of Civil Procedure* provides that such entities are considered as independent legal persons with limited liability and liable for their own profits and losses when they fulfil the requisite legal requirements.

CHN ¶70-301

CHN ¶70-402   CHOICE OF FORUM

General considerations on choice of forum apply. When making a decision on the choice of forum, consideration should be given to the question of enforcement of any judgment obtained. See CHN ¶70-001, CHN ¶70-014, CHN ¶70-023, CHN ¶70-024 and CHN ¶70-102.

CHN ¶70-403   ENFORCEMENT OF ORDERS

China has entered into a number of bilateral investment protection agreements which set out protection against, and procedures for, compensation for expropriation and nationalisation of investments in China. China has entered into investment insurance agreements with both Canada and the United States, whereby a government agency established for the purpose insures and compensates for political risks and losses. After payment by the insurance agency, it is subrogated to the rights of the insured and may proceed against the Chinese government for recovery.

CHN ¶70-404   INTERNATIONAL CONVENTIONS

The Chinese government has acceded to the Multilateral Investment Guarantee Agency (MIGA) Convention.

Regulation of Local Finance

Identification of sources ....CHN ¶75-001

Control of financing ....CHN ¶75-101

Terms of financing ....CHN ¶75-201

Legal securities for finance ....CHN ¶75-301

IDENTIFICATION OF SOURCES

Types of local financial institutions ....CHN ¶75-001

How do financial institutions raise and supply finance? ....CHN ¶75-002

Methods used to access international capital markets ....CHN ¶75-003

Specialised institutions for investment and development ....CHN ¶75-004

Specialised institutions for financing exports ....CHN ¶75-005

Local and foreign equity-loan ratios ....CHN ¶75-011

CHN ¶75-001   TYPES OF LOCAL FINANCIAL INSTITUTIONS

China has issued several sets of Provisions regulating financial institutions: the *People's Bank of China (PBOC) Administration of Financial Institutions Provisions*, effective 9 August 1994; the PRC *Commercial Banking Law*, effective 1 July 1995; the PRC *Administration of Foreign Investment Financial Institutions Regulations*, effective 1 February 2002; and the *Guideline of Commercial Bank Internal Control*, effective 7 September 2002.

The *PBOC Administration of Financial Institutions Provisions* applies to domestic financial institutions engaged in financial activities within China. It stipulates the role of PBOC and its branches in regulating the financial sector. The PRC *Commercial Banking Law* is designed to standardise the commercial behaviour of the banks, to give them sufficient autonomy and to provide control over the fiduciary duties of bank officers/ directors.

The PRC *People's Bank of China Law* was promulgated and made effective on 18 March 1995 by the National People's Congress (NPC). The law designates PBOC as China's central bank empowered to formulate and implement monetary policies and macroeconomic control and to administer and supervise the banking industry of China as well as supply and issue money. The law also aims to strengthen control in the financial sector and to protect the interests of depositors respectively.

Major banking institutions

- Industrial and Commercial Bank of China;
- Bank of China;
- China Construction Bank;
- Agricultural Bank of China;
- Bank of Communications;
- China Merchants Bank;
- Huaxia Bank;
- Minsheng Bank;
- Everbright Bank;
- CITIC Industrial Bank;
- Pudong Development Bank;
- Shenzhen Development Bank; and
- Shanghai Bank.

Foreign financial institutions (FFIs)

Foreign banks and other foreign financial institutions are governed by the *Administrative Rules of the People's Republic of China governing Foreign-Funded Financial Institutions* and its detailed implementation rules, both of which became effective from 1 February 2002, and thus replaced those previous rules promulgated in 1994. These Rules have incorporated relevant commitments made by China in its WTO accession agreements.

On 8 July 2002, the *Administrative Measures of Representative Offices in China of Foreign Financial Institutions*, which repeals the *Administration of Representative Offices in China of Foreign Financial Institutions Procedures*, was effective as of 8 July 1996. The Administrative Rules apply to representative offices in China of FFIs registered outside China and also FFIs registered in Hong Kong, Macao and Taiwan. The procedures detail the requirements for setting up a representative office, the management of representative offices, closing such offices and penalties for acts in violation of the procedures. The procedures also provide that if a FFI has set up five or more representative offices in China, then it can apply to set up a general representative office.

The PBOC is the authority in charge of administering foreign financial institutions. The following types of financial institutions are covered by the new law:

- banks holding foreign capital which have their head office in China (referred to as "foreign investment banks");
- branches of foreign banks;
- banks formed as equity joint ventures between foreign and Chinese financial institutions (referred to as "joint venture banks");
- finance companies holding foreign capital which have their head office in China (referred to as "foreign investment finance companies"); and

- finance companies which are formed as equity joint ventures between foreign and Chinese financial institutions (referred to as "joint venture finance companies").

Preconditions have been set out for establishing a FFI including minimum capital requirements according to the type of institution being set up. Other preconditions include minimum total assets and that a representative office must have been maintained for more than two years. Foreign banks may operate in China through a representative office, a branch or by participation in a joint venture. Bank representative offices are the most common but they are not permitted to engage in direct business operations, only in a liaison capacity.

On 3 January 2003, PBOC promulgated the *Large and Suspicious Renminbi Payment Transactions Reporting Administrative Procedures* (the "Procedures") and the *Financial Institutions Anti-money Laundering Provisions* (the "Provisions") which became effective on 1 March 2003. The Procedures strengthen supervision of renminbi payment transactions and standardise the reporting procedures thereof in the aim of preventing the payment and settlement facilities of financial institutions from being used to launder funds (Art 1). Financial institutions shall integrate anti-money laundering mechanisms into their organisation, and appoint one or more staff who will be responsible for recording, analysing and reporting large and suspicious transactions (Art 6). Large transactions include:

- a single transfer of RMB1 million or more between the accounts of legal persons, other organisations or individually-owned household businesses;
- a single cash transaction of RMB200,000 or more (including deposits, withdrawals, cash transfers, money orders and cashier's cheques); and
- transfers of RMB200,000 or more between two accounts of an individual or an organisation (Art 7).

The Procedures also list a wide range of financial activities that shall be considered suspicious, including:

- transactions in a frequency or of an amount that obviously do not accord with the account holder's scope of business; and
- a noticeable increase in transactions with bank accounts in regions where drug trafficking, smuggling and terrorism are frequent (Art 8).

Financial institutions shall establish a client database for recording pertinent data, including registered capital, scope of business, principle senders and recipients of funds, and daily average account transaction amounts (Art 10). Financial institutions should report large or suspicious transactions to the People's Bank of China or its branches (Art 16). When the financial institution discovers a transaction that is clearly related to illegal activity, it should immediately notify public security authorities (Art 18).

The Provisions mainly provide that financial institutions are required by law to assist and cooperate with judicial authorities, customs and taxation authorities in investigating, freezing or withholding account funds (Art 6). In conformity with the provisions of the People's Bank, financial institutions shall set up a sound anti-money laundering internal control mechanism (Art 8). This will include establishing a specialised department to handle anti-money laundering, or designating an already established department to handle the task (Art 9). The Provisions also require that financial institutions demand and record client identification (Art 10 and 11). When a financial institution suspects that a large or suspicious transaction may be linked to criminal activity, it should promptly notify the local public security department (Art 16). Account and transaction records shall be kept for a minimum of five years (Art 17). The Provisions provide for a fine of up to RMB30,000 for actions breaching the Provisions.

On 5 November 2002, the China Securities Regulatory Commission (CSRC) and PBOC jointly promulgated the *Administration of Securities Investments in China by Qualified Foreign Institutional Investors Tentative Procedures* which became effective on 1 December 2002. The Procedures open the A share and domestic bond markets to foreign investment for the first time. There are restrictions on the size (measured in percentages and monetary terms) of investments made by qualified foreign institutional investors (QFIIs). The monetary limits are set out in the *Administration of Foreign Exchange for Securities Investments in the PRC by QFIIs Tentative Provisions* issued on 28 November 2002 and effective 1 December 2002 (the "QFII Forex Provisions"). These provide that the minimum investment limit that has to be applied for by a QFII is US$50 million, while the maximum is US$800 million.

The Implementing Regulations specify that the percentage of shares held by a single QFII in a single listed company cannot exceed 10% of the total A shares in that company and similarly the aggregate percentage of shares held by all QFIIs in a single listed company must not exceed 20% of the total A shares in that company. However, these percentages are subject to "adjustment" by CSRC. Under the Implementing Regulations, shares held by a QFII or by two or more QFIIs collectively at the end of each trading day that are in excess of the 10% or 20% cap, respectively, must be resold in the market following the issue of a "sell down" notice. The sell down notice is sent by the relevant stock exchange to the QFII's securities trading company and custodian, and requires the QFII to reduce its shareholding to below the shareholding cap. The timing is slightly curious, as the obligation is on the QFII to sell down within five trading days of receipt of the sell down notice, but it is unclear what happens if the custodian and securities company fail to pass on the notice to the QFII. Where the collective cap is breached, the excess shares must be resold on a "last in first out" principle unless, within those five trading days, another QFII has voluntarily reduced its shareholding in the listed company so that the aggregate shareholding falls below the collective cap. In this event only, the original QFII may then apply to the relevant stock exchange to maintain its original shareholding in the listed company.

On the aggregate percentage of shares held by all QFIIs in any single listed company reaching 16% of the A shares in that company, and thereafter on any further increases of 2%, the relevant stock exchange is required to publish the number of shares and the corresponding shareholding held by each QFII in the listed company on the relevant stock exchange's website at the end of that trading day. Investments made by QFIIs still have to comply with the Foreign Investment Industrial Guidance Catalogue, so one cannot use the scheme to skirt round equity caps under WTO commitments or to invest in "prohibited" category companies. There is however a question mark as to whether, and to what extent, QFII shares count towards the "foreign investment percentage" cap in industries where WTO commitments or other foreign investment.

On 17 December 2002, PBOC issued the *Issues Relevant to the Application by Commercial Banks for Engaging in the Custody Business of Domestic Securities Investments by Qualified Foreign Institutional Investors Circular* (the "Circular") in order to facilitate the implementation of the 1 December 2002 *Administration of Securities Investments in China by Qualified Foreign Institutional Investors Tentative Procedures* (the "QFII Tentative Procedures"). The Circular specifies the requirements and procedures regarding the ways that a commercial bank can apply to PBOC for permission to undertake a custodian business for domestic securities investments by QFIIs.

On 10 April 2003, PBOC issued the *Administration of Renminbi Bank Settlement Accounts Procedures* (the "Procedures"), which comes into effect on 1 September 2003. Part Two of the Procedures sets out the eligibility, procedures and requirements for opening of bank settlement accounts, namely:

- "basic deposit account" for daily transfer, settlement and cash receipt and payment (Art 11);
- "general deposit account" for loans or other settlement needs (Art 12);
- "specific deposit account" for the funds with specific purposes for exclusive administration and uses according to laws, administrative regulations and rules (Art 13);
- "provisional deposit account" for funds for temporary needs and used within a prescribed term (Art 14); and
- "personal deposit account" for natural persons for investment, consumption and settlement purposes (Art 15).

The bank shall verify the bank account opening documents and report the same to the local PBOC branch for approval or record filing (Art 28). Part Three sets out the uses and operations of these accounts. Settlement accounts cannot be leased out, lent or used for credit borrowing (Art 45). Part Four deals with the amendment to or cancellation of bank settlement accounts. If a circumstance specified in Art 49 arises, or if the account is dormant for a year and there is no outstanding payment, it shall be cancelled.

On 8 December 2003, the China Banking Regulatory Commission promulgated the *Administration of Investment and Equity Participation in Chinese-invested Financial Institutions by Offshore Financial Institutions Procedures*. The procedures set forth the criteria for investment and equity participation in Chinese invested financial institutions by overseas financial institutions. Investment and equity participation shall be made in monetary funds. The investment and equity participation proportion in a Chinese funded financial institution by a single foreign financial institution shall not exceed 20%. In case the aggregate investment and equity participation proportion in a non-listed Chinese funded financial institution by more than one offshore financial institution amounts to or exceeds 25%, the non-listed financial institution shall be treated as a foreign invested financial institution.

On 24 October 2003, the China Banking Regulatory Commission issued the *Further Opening of Renminbi Services to Foreign-invested Financial Institutions Notice*. Under the Notice, from 1 December 2003, foreign invested financial institutions may apply to engage in Renminbi services in Jinan, Fuzhou, Chengdu and Chongqin.

Non-bank financial institutions

Trust and investment companies

Trust and investment companies are regulated under the *Rules for the Control of Trust and Investment Companies of the People's Republic of China* (promulgated by PBOC on 10 January 2001 and replacing those provisional rules promulgated in 1986) and the *Provisional Measures of Administration of Money Trust of Trust and Investment Companies* became effective 8 July 2002. On 5 June 2002, PBOC issued the *Administration of Trust and Investment Companies Procedures*. The Procedures are a revision of the previous law promulgated in January 2001. The new Procedures make some changes with regard to the trust and investment company's use of its own property and trust property. The particulars on liquidation and standardisation of existing businesses in the previous law have been omitted from the new Procedures. Subject to meeting certain minimum paid-up equity and reserve requirements, trust and investment companies are permitted to manage mutual funds and engage in other trust-related business; engage in leasing, surety and guaranty business, make direct investments, and provide financial consultancy services.

Major trust and investment corporations include the China International Trust and Investment Corporation (CITIC) and Shanghai International Trust Corporation (SITCO).

Rural or city credit cooperatives

Originally operating as units in the countryside to provide credit assistance to individuals, small cooperatives or businesses, credit cooperatives became so popular in the cities that relevant regulations were promulgated since 1986 to regulate their activities. Again, like the trust and investment companies, credit cooperatives are required to satisfy certain regulatory requirements, such as minimum paid-up capital, before they may be granted a business licence. Credit cooperatives operate exclusively on the domestic banking scene and are not open to foreigners. More recently, many city credit cooperatives and even some rural ones have been restructured into commercial banks, usually named "(Name of Area) Commercial Bank", such as Beijing City Commercial Bank, Nanjing City Commercial Bank and Shanghai City Commercial Bank (which was the precedent of the Bank of Shanghai).

The Administration of Auto Finance Companies Procedures provide the non-bank financial enterprise legal persons to engage in providing loans to automobile purchasers and seller within the territory of China. The Procedures came into effective on 3 October 2003. The Procedures set forth the establishing requirements and the business scope as well as the regulation of such companies. It includes the following parts:

- Part One: General Provisions;
- Part Two: Establishment of, Change in and Termination of Organizations;
- Part Three: Scope of Business and Regulation;
- Part Four: Legal Liability; and
- Part Five: Supplementary Provisions.

Stock exchange

There are only two officially recognised securities exchanges in China:

- the Shanghai Securities Exchange; and
- the Shenzhen Stock Exchange.

The *Provisional Regulations on the Administration of the Issuing and Trading of Stocks* (the "National Securities legislation") governs the issuing and trading of shares in the PRC and was passed by the State Council on 22 April 1993. China launched a trial national inter-bank market in January 1996 to link commercial banks and credit offices in the country to one single network. The market has helped to stabilise interest rates, allow lending and borrowing of local renminbi currency between domestic banks and allow enterprises to gain increased access to loans and credits. Since 1998, certain foreign investment banks have been permitted to participate.

The PRC *Securities Law* was adopted on 29 December 1998 and came into effect on 1 July 1999.

The *Securities Law* is applicable to the issuing and marketing of the stocks, company bonds and other securities legally recognised by the State Council, and stipulates on matters such as principles of the issuing and marketing of the securities, purchase of listed companies and organisations related to administration, issuing and marketing of securities.

The Law stipulates that the securities regulatory department of the State Council should set up a verification committee to lawfully examine the stock issuing. Experts from other departments will be engaged to examine and verify the applications, and vote on a resolve.

The Law outlines obligations for issuers and underwriters to ensure the information disclosed to the public during the issuing is accurate (Art 63).

The (LEGREF) PRC Securities Investment Funds Law, promulgated on 28 October 2003, applies to public sale of fund shares to raise capital for securities investment funds that are managed by fund managers, kept in trust by custodians and put into securities investment activities by investing in a portfolio of assets for the benefit of fund share holders. The Law comprises 12 parts as following:

- Part One: General Provisions;
- Part Two: Fund Managers;
- Part Three: Fund Custodians;
- Part Four: Raising of Capital by Funds;
- Part Five: Transactions of Fund Shares;
- Part Six: Pruchase and Redemption of Fund Shares;
- Part Seven: Operation and Information Disclosure of Fund;
- Part Eight: Changes to and Termination of Fund Contracts and Settlement of Fund Assets;
- Part Nine: Rights and Interests of Holders of Fund Shares and the Exercise Thereof; and

- Part Ten: Regulation;
- Eleven: Legal Liability Part; and
- Part Twelve: Supplementary Provisions.

CHN ¶75-002   HOW DO FINANCIAL INSTITUTIONS RAISE AND SUPPLY FINANCE?

Raising finance

Funds are raised mainly via savings deposits (including foreign currency deposits), interest on loans, issuing State Treasury bonds and from a variety of financial services including business consultancy services. More recently, domestic banks have shown a great interest in the adoption of a shareholding system, and have been seeking listing of their shares on domestic or foreign stock exchanges. Currently, listed Chinese banks include Shenzhen Development Bank, Pudong Development Bank, Minsheng Bank, China Merchants Bank and Xingye Bank.

Supplying finance

Funds are supplied in the form of loans, letters of credit, other credit facilities and provision of trust services and leases.

CHN ¶75-003   METHODS USED TO ACCESS INTERNATIONAL CAPITAL MARKETS

Subject to approval by CSRC, companies incorporated in the PRC can list their shares on Hong Kong and other foreign stock markets. As of May 2003, there are 781 companies having their shares listed abroad, including on the stock exchanges in Hong Kong, New York, Singapore and London. Regulations controlling such shares are governed mainly by the relevant foreign stock market regulations. For example, the issue and trading of H shares on the Stock Exchange of Hong Kong are governed primarily by the new chapter 19A of the listing rules of the Hong Kong Exchange.

CHN ¶75-004   SPECIALISED INSTITUTIONS FOR INVESTMENT AND DEVELOPMENT

In 1994, as part of China's reform of its financial systems, the following policy-oriented banks were set up to take over those policy-oriented lending and related businesses from domestic commercial banks:

The State Development Bank of China

The State Development Bank of China is primarily responsible for the policy lending businesses in support of key construction projects of the country, which were previously handled by the China Construction Bank.

The Agricultural Development Bank of China

The Agricultural Development Bank of China is primarily responsible for the examination and approval of state funds utilised in support of agriculture, which were previously handled by the Agricultural Bank of China.

The Ex-import Bank of China

The Ex-import Bank of China is primarily responsible for the promotion and support of China's export and import businesses, which were previously the responsibility of the Bank of China.

CHN ¶75-005   SPECIALISED INSTITUTIONS FOR FINANCING EXPORTS

Most export sales contracts executed between Chinese sellers and foreign buyers provide for payment by an irrevocable and transferable letter of credit opened by the foreign buyer's bank. In the past, the opening bank had to be a correspondent bank of the Bank of China, and the advising bank in China was normally the local branch of the Bank of China. Currently, other banks are also engaged in the business of letters of credit.

CHN ¶75-011   LOCAL AND FOREIGN EQUITY-LOAN RATIOS

There are no regulatory requirements covering local and foreign debt-to-equity ratios.

Foreign investment enterprises wishing to borrow funds from a Chinese or foreign bank is regulated under the *Measures on Loans for Foreign Investment Enterprises*. Under these measures, borrowers are required to provide a guarantee or a mortgage of property as security for the loan. The *Provisional Regulations of Shanghai Municipality on Renminbi Mortgage Loan Administration* provide that the amount of the mortgage loan may not exceed 90% of the current cash value of the mortgaged property. The current cash value differs according to the type of property. In the case of state bonds, financial bonds and fixed-term deposit certificates, the current cash value may not exceed face value. For all other properties, the loan may not exceed 80% of the face value or net book value.

The Regulations are applicable to mortgages granted by Chinese legal persons (including Chinese enterprises, Chinese-foreign joint ventures and wholly foreign-owned enterprises) and individual Shanghai residents.

CONTROL OF FINANCING

Criteria for regulation of
   sources of loan finance . CHN ¶75-101

Manner in which sources of
   loan finance controlled . CHN ¶75-102

Regulations covering raising of
   local equity capital .... CHN ¶75-103

Manner of regulating raising of
   local equity capital .... CHN ¶75-104

Self-regulation by credit and
   financial institutions ..... CHN ¶75-105

Methods used for raising
   capital .... CHN ¶75-111

Taxation of dividends or
   interest to non-
   residents .... CHN ¶75-112

CHN ¶75-101   CRITERIA FOR REGULATION OF SOURCES OF LOAN FINANCE

The *Commercial Loans Measures* stipulates that all international commercial borrowings by PRC organisations must be approved by the relevant authority. The PBOC has delegated the authority to examine and approve loans to the State Administration of Foreign Exchange (SAFE) and applications for loan approval are to be made directly with SAFE. Loan agreements which are not approved are rendered void.

The *Commercial Loans Measures* distinguishes between short, medium and long-term loans. If the terms of a loan are less than one year, the loan is characterised as short term. Where the term is longer than a year, the loan is regarded as medium or long term.

The proceeds for medium and long-term loans must be used for importing advanced technology facilities or for projects which have the ability to generate foreign exchange. Short-term loans are controlled by SAFE through an overall quota system. A branch of bank seeking to borrow can apply through its head office to SAFE head office for approval of a short-term loan. The provincial and municipal branches of SAFE carry out supervision and management of short-term loans sought by bank branches within their area. The proceeds for short-term loans must be used as working capital required by export businesses and cannot be used for any specific investment item or for fixed asset acquisition.

Borrowers of international commercial loans are required to report annually to SAFE on the use of the loan proceeds during the previous year, and the benefits derived from the loans.

Lending to foreign investment enterprises

Foreign enterprises need not comply with the *Commercial Loans Measures* but must apply the *Foreign Debt Registration Measures* which states that foreign borrowings must be registered with SAFE.

Foreign investment enterprises are permitted to borrow funds from either a foreign bank or from the Bank of China or another Chinese bank. On 7 April 1987, the Bank of China issued the *Measures on Loans for Foreign Investment Enterprises* stating that

CHN ¶75-101

loans may be granted to foreign investment enterprises to finance construction and business operations. Priority is given to export-oriented enterprises and technologically advanced enterprises.

Loans may be made in RMB, US$, GBP, HK$ or any other convertible currencies accepted by the Bank of China. Under the Measures, borrowers are required to provide a guarantee or a mortgage of property as security for the loan. A security arrangement must be backed by a mortgage agreement which must be certified by a Chinese notary public. Insurance of the mortgaged property must be purchased with the People's Insurance Company of China (PICC).

On 28 September 1998, PBOC issued the *Circular on Enhancing the Management of Foreign Exchange Secured RMB Loans of Domestic Financial Institutions.*

With the view of enhancing the risk control and standardising the activities of Chinese-funded banks in granting RMB loans by way of foreign exchange pledge and foreign exchange guarantees granted by foreign-invested banks, the Circular stipulates that when granting RMB loans to Chinese-funded entities within China, the designated Chinese-funded foreign exchange banks within China shall not accept any foreign exchange guarantees from foreign-invested banks and offshore entities, nor should they accept the "account-opening certificate of domestic entities for fixed deposit", or any foreign exchange promissory notes, bills of exchange, checks, bonds, stocks or any other security instruments for the RMB loans.

Moreover, when designated Chinese-funded foreign exchange banks within China grant to foreign-invested enterprises RMB loans secured by foreign exchange and foreign exchange guarantees of foreign-invested banks, the prerequisite is that such secured RMB loans shall only be granted by the head office of the aforesaid designated foreign exchange banks or their authorised branch banks.

CHN ¶75-102   MANNER IN WHICH SOURCES OF LOAN FINANCE CONTROLLED

On 1 August 1991, PBOC approved the *Measures for Administration of the Taking Out of International Commercial Loans by Organisations within China* (the "Commercial Loans Measures"). These measures sought to increase the central government's control over foreign exchange borrowings by Chinese enterprises. This was achieved mainly by introducing restrictions on the authority of Chinese enterprises to borrow abroad.

Borrowings by organisations resident in the PRC from institutions outside the PRC are governed by the Commercial Loans Measures. The regulations also apply to borrowings by PRC organisations from wholly foreign-owned or joint venture capital, which are situated in China.

The Commercial Loans Measures stipulates that all international commercial borrowings by PRC organisations must be approved by the relevant authority. PBOC has delegated the authority to examine and approve loans to SAFE. Loan agreements which are not approved are rendered void.

Borrowings by foreign enterprises

Foreign borrowings must be registered with SAFE pursuant to the *Provisional Measures for Statistics on and Monitoring of Foreign Debt*. The Commercial Loans Measures does not apply to foreign investment enterprises within the PRC seeking direct international commercial borrowings. However, the regulations do confirm the continued applicability of foreign debt registration requirements.

Reporting

Borrowers of international commercial loans are required to report annually to SAFE on the use of the loan proceeds during the previous year and the benefits derived from the loans.

CHN ¶75-103   REGULATIONS COVERING RAISING OF LOCAL EQUITY CAPITAL

- The *Provisional Regulations on the Administration of the Issuing and Trading of Stocks* (the "National Securities Regulations").
- The Shanghai Stock Exchange is regulated by the China Securities Regulatory Commission (CSRC).
- The Shenzhen Stock Exchange is also regulated by CSRC.

CHN ¶75-104   MANNER OF REGULATING RAISING OF LOCAL EQUITY CAPITAL

The *Provisional Regulations on the Administration of the Issuing and Trading of Stocks* (the "National Securities Regulations") was passed by the State Council on 22 April 1993. The regulations govern the eligibility and procedures for a company issuing public shares. There are also two sets of regulations governing share trading in the Shanghai and Shenzhen stock exchanges, which set out procedural aspects of listings and public offerings on the stock exchanges. In cases of conflict, the National Securities Regulations will prevail.

A shares

A shares are registered shares issued by enterprises operating within the PRC which have only been allowed to be owned or traded by PRC citizens on domestic stock markets. On 5 November 2002, CSRC and PBOC jointly issued the *Provisional Rules on the Administration of Securities Investment by Qualified Foreign Institutional Investors*, which allows QFIIs, by meeting various requirements and procedures, to invest in China's domestic A share market through a stated approved custodian bank. This may change as China is pushing ahead with plans to open its domestic A share markets to foreign investors. A shares are denominated in renminbi and are sold and purchased in renminbi.

B shares

B shares are registered shares which were offered exclusively to foreign investors until 2001 when domestic investors were permitted to participate. They are denominated

CHN ¶75-103

in renminbi but traded in foreign currencies. CSRC is charged with the responsibility for approving B shares issues.

CHN ¶75-105 SELF-REGULATION BY CREDIT AND FINANCIAL INSTITUTIONS

Self-regulation amongst financial institutions takes second place to regulation by the authorities. The PRC *Commercial Banking Law* came into effect on 1 July 1995 to standardise the commercial behaviour of banks as the lack of legal restrictions led some commercial banks to engage in real estate and stock speculation disregarding the country's credit policy.

On 11 April 2000, the State Council publicised the *Opinion on Further Strengthening the Administration of Overseas Bond Issues of the State Development and Planning Commission and the People's Bank of China*. The Opinion defines the term ''Overseas Bond Issue'', stipulates the conditions that a native entity intending to issue bond overseas should satisfy and the examination of the Overseas Bond Issue.

The People's Bank of China introduced the *Joint Stock Commercial Bank Corporate Governance Guideline* and *Joint Stock Commercial Bank Guideline of Independent Director and Outside Supervisor System* on 4 June 2002, in an effort to strengthen and modernise the internal control and corporate governance of commercial banks.

CHN ¶75-111 METHODS USED FOR RAISING CAPITAL

The main methods most often used are:

- loan financing; and

- raising of local equity capital.

CHN ¶75-112 TAXATION OF DIVIDENDS OR INTEREST TO NON-RESIDENTS

The *Notice of State Administration of Taxation concerning Taxation of Income from Stock (Share Right) Transactions and Dividends received by Foreign Investment Enterprises, Foreign Enterprises and Foreign Nationals* states that exemptions shall apply to the following:

- A foreign enterprise who receives the net income from B shares or overseas shares transferred to it from an enterprise in China;

- A foreign enterprise who receives income in the form of dividends from the enterprise within Chinese territory which issued the said B shares or overseas shares; and

- Profit (dividends) received by a foreign investor from a foreign investment enterprise and dividends and bonuses distributed to a foreign national by a sino-foreign joint equity enterprise.

TERMS OF FINANCING

Customary terms for lending or
  investing money .... CHN ¶75-201

Flexibility of customary terms
  for lending or investing
  money .... CHN ¶75-202

Interest rates .... CHN ¶75-203

Covenants, financial ratios and
  security interest .... CHN ¶75-204

Local arrangements concerning
  currency exchange and
  rates .... CHN ¶75-205

Which law governs
  financing? .... CHN ¶75-211

CHN ¶75-201 CUSTOMARY TERMS FOR LENDING OR INVESTING MONEY

Under the *Measures on loans for Foreign Investment Enterprises*, priority is given to export-oriented enterprises and technologically advanced enterprises. Borrowers are also required to provide a guarantee or a mortgage of property as security for the loan. Insurance of the mortgaged property must also be purchased from PICC.

Loans by joint ventures from the Bank of China are governed by the *Provisional Regulations for Providing Loans to Joint Ventures using Chinese and Foreign Investment by the Bank of China* (the "Loan Regulations"). The Loan Regulations requires borrowers to have opened a deposit account with the Bank of China or a bank approved thereby and to be creditworthy and well managed. Loan applications must have been approved by the joint venture's board of directors and secured through the pledge of a collateral or the provision of a guarantee.

The latter form of security is the one most often used. As to the type of guarantee, the Bank of China generally prefers either an unconditional and irrevocable letter of guarantee from each party's parent company or a bank guarantee arranged by such parent companies in accordance with the ratio of the parties' contributions to the venture's registered capital.

The Loan Regulations specifies three types of loans that are available from the Bank of China, namely:

- working capital loans;
- accounts receivable financing; and
- loans for the purchase of fixed assets.

These loans may be granted in either renminbi or a foreign currency and must be repaid in the currency in which they are denominated. Interest on foreign currency loans is payable in the currency in question. The *Provisional Lending Principles* promulgated and made effective on 27 July 1995 were issued by PBOC. The rules on loans set forth the Principles intended to bring local lending activities in line with national monetary policies by providing guidelines for the supervision and quality of loans, procedures for loan recovery, lending procedures, terms and conditions for loans and non-payment. Under the Principles, borrowers who are not natural persons must undergo annual examination and approval of their borrowing record by the local administration of industry and commerce prior to applying for new loans. Furthermore, lenders will be permitted to issue ratings for borrowers according to the borrower's financial condition, capital structure, performance and development outlook; the principles prohibit lending and borrowing among enterprises.

On 8 January 2003, the State Development Planning Commission, the Ministry of Finance and the State Administration of Foreign Exchange (SAFE) promulgated the *Foreign Debt Administration Tentative Procedures*, which became effective on 1 March 2003. The Procedures are formulated with a view to strengthening the administration of foreign debts, regulating the acts of borrowing foreign debts, enhancing the benefit of utilisation of foreign debt funds, and guarding against the risk from foreign debts. Based on the types of debts, foreign debts shall be classified under the categories of loans of foreign governments, loans of international financial institutions and international commercial loans. Based on the repayment liability, foreign debts shall be classified under the categories of sovereign foreign debts and non-sovereign foreign debts. Part two regulates foreign debt borrowing and external security. Article 15 provides the borrowing of medium and long-term international commercial loans by domestic Chinese-invested enterprises shall be approved by the State Development Planning Commission. Article 20 provides that domestic institutions shall not provide any security for foreign institutions not of a business nature. Part three regulates the utilisation of foreign debt funds. Part four provides the repayment of foreign debts and risk management.

CHN ¶75-202   FLEXIBILITY OF CUSTOMARY TERMS FOR LENDING OR INVESTING MONEY

Lending or investing money strictly adheres to the governing regulations.

CHN ¶75-203   INTEREST RATES

The rate of interest on renminbi loans from the Bank of China is that determined by PBOC. The rate of interest on foreign currency loans from the Bank of China is set by the said bank but subject to approval by PBOC. The latter rate is usually quite close to the London Inter-Bank Offered Rate (LIBOR). Interest on overdue payments of principal and interest on loans from the Bank of China is charged at a rate of 20% to 50% over and above the original interest rate.

CHN ¶75-204   COVENANTS, FINANCIAL RATIOS AND SECURITY INTERESTS

Borrowers are required to provide a guarantee or a mortgage of property as security for a loan. A security arrangement must be backed by a ''mortgage arrangement'' which must be certified by a Chinese notary public. Insurance of the mortgaged property must be purchased with PICC.

The Bank of China has also instituted a special program whereby foreign currencies may be used as mortgage security for renminbi loans. The program is governed by the *Provisional Measures of the People's Bank of China on Foreign Exchange Secured Renminbi Loans for Foreign Investment Enterprises* and limited to Chinese foreign joint ventures (both equity and cooperative) and wholly foreign-owned enterprises within China.

CHN ¶75-205   LOCAL ARRANGEMENTS CONCERNING CURRENCY EXCHANGE AND RATES

The *Administrative Regulations on Domestic Foreign Exchange Accounts* was promulgated by PBOC on 7 October 1997 to standardise the opening and use of foreign exchange accounts and strengthen supervision and management of foreign exchange accounts in accordance with the *Rules of the People's Republic of China on Foreign Exchange Control* and the *Administrative Regulations on Foreign Exchange Settlements, Sales and Payments*. The Regulations set out in detail the specific purposes for which foreign exchange accounts may be opened and the types of foreign exchange accounts which may be opened. Purposes range from income of foreign nationals, foreign exchange earned overseas from contract projects and foreign exchange of foreign investment enterprises within approved limits (Art 6). Foreign investment enterprises have separate approval procedures when opening an account and its Foreign Exchange Registration Certificate for a foreign investment enterprise will be annotated with details of the account, including transaction limits (Art 12). Only individuals (foreign nationals) may open foreign exchange cash accounts (Art 9).

Restrictions on remittances and account transfers involving foreign exchange are outlined provisionally by SAFE. The *Provisional Administrative Regulations on Domestic Allocation and Transfer of Foreign Exchange* promulgated on 25 September 1997 that in stipulated business transactions, receipts and other evidentiary material be submitted to the bank handling the relevant foreign exchange transaction before the transaction can proceed. Agency export trade revenue, overseas insurance claim payments and foreign exchange loans fall within the scope of the Regulations.

The *Administrative Regulations Regarding Foreign Exchange Accounts Outside China*, promulgated on 12 December 1997 (effective 1 January 1998), applies to the opening, use and cancellation of foreign exchange accounts outside China. SAFE and its branches are the administrative authorities which govern and supervise foreign exchange accounts outside China, of Chinese entities and individuals.

The following domestic organisations may open foreign exchange accounts outside China:

- those having regular petty income from abroad;
- those having regular petty expenditure abroad;
- those engaged in contract project engineering work abroad;
- those issuing valuable securities abroad; and
- those having other particular business requirement for an overseas account.

The Regulations set out the documents and information which have to be submitted to SAFE when applying for approval to open foreign exchange accounts. Within 30 days after opening a foreign exchange account abroad, domestic organisations must provide SAFE with the name of the foreign bank with which the account is opened and the name of the account. Each quarter, accounting information must be provided to SAFE. If an offshore foreign exchange account is terminated, SAFE must be notified and the balance in the account must be remitted back to China.

CHN ¶75-211   WHICH LAWS GOVERNS FINANCING?

Chinese law does not require the parties to a Chinese-foreign economic contract to submit their disputes for arbitration before Chinese arbitral bodies. The parties are free to choose arbitration in either China or in some other country. Provisions relating to governing laws usually provide for the law of the lender's country to be the governing law. Loan agreements invariably contain clauses for dispute resolution which is agreed between the parties involved.

LEGAL SECURITIES FOR FINANCE

Security interests in	Recognised forms of security
property .... CHN ¶75-301	rights .... CHN ¶75-401
	Security rights .... CHN ¶75-501

CHN ¶75-301   SECURITY INTERESTS IN PROPERTY

Article 5 of the *Provisional Regulations of Shanghai Municipality on Renminbi Mortgage Loan Administration* (the "RMB Mortgage Regulations") outlines the types of property that may be used as security for loans:

- buildings and fixtures;
- land use rights;
- machinery, equipment, transportation equipment;
- finished products, raw materials;
- stocks, bonds, negotiable instruments, bills of lading;
- warehouse receipts, savings deposit certificates, etc; and
- other property transferable for value.

The PRC *Secured Interests Law*, effective 1 October 1995, gives creditors and investors greater flexibility and protection by providing a more expanded choice of security interests. In the case of a mortgage, the debtor or a third party's property may be used as security for the debt without physical possession of the property by the creditor. The law places a cap on the amount of the secured debt which is not permitted to be higher than the value of the mortgaged property (Art 35). The new concept of a mortgage which is up to a maximum amount allows a mortgage to be taken over property to secure a series of debts over a certain period of time up to a specified ceiling (Art 59).

Only property listed in Art 34 may be mortgaged; the list includes various moveable and immoveable property including state-owned property. Some types of property such as land ownership rights and welfare facilities cannot be mortgaged (Art 37).

In certain cases, prior consent is required before property may be mortgaged. For example, where jointly-owned property is used as security, consent from the other owners is necessary. Even with such consent, the mortgagor is entitled to mortgage only his own share of the property. Registration is mandatory for mortgages on property referred to in Art 42 and in order for the mortgage contract to be made legally effective. Such a system to register mortgage interests is a marked development for lenders.

CHN ¶75-401   RECOGNISED FORMS OF SECURITY RIGHTS

The usual form of security rights is by way of mortgage or guarantee. For buildings and land use rights, the recognised form of security is by way of a mortgage. Article 8 of the RMB Mortgage Regulations provides that they are only mortgageable if a relevant certificate of ownership or certificate of land use rights is presented. All mortgages must be registered with the Municipal Registry.

For renminbi loans, foreign currencies may be mortgaged. The applicable currencies are: the US$, the Japanese yen, the HK$, the Deutschemark and the Pound Sterling. Fixed assets such as machinery and equipment must also be mortgaged. For state-owned enterprises, they must obtain approval from the relevant government authorities before mortgaging its fixed assets.

Guarantees are the most common form of security arrangement for foreign bank lending in China.

Security Rights

Can subject property be readily identified? ....CHN ¶75-501

Can borrower's interest be readily identified? ....CHN ¶75-502

Formalities for creation of security ....CHN ¶75-503

Priority of security interests .CHN ¶75-504

Number of security interests against one property ....CHN ¶75-505

Floating securities over classes of assets ....CHN ¶75-511

Securities for further advances ....CHN ¶75-512

Is the continuing interest of the borrower recognised and protected? ....CHN ¶75-513

Retention of possession by borrower ....CHN ¶75-514

Realisation of security by lender ....CHN ¶75-515

Transferability of lender's security ....CHN ¶75-521

Forms of personal security ...CHN ¶75-522

Acceptable securities ....CHN ¶75-523

Charges for registration of securities ....CHN ¶75-524

Tax implications and choice of security ....CHN ¶75-525

CHN ¶75-501   CAN SUBJECT PROPERTY BE READILY IDENTIFIED?

The various types of property subject to security are readily identified through registration. The mortgage register is available for public inspection.

CHN ¶75-502   CAN BORROWER'S INTEREST BE READILY IDENTIFIED?

Borrower's interest may be readily identified in the case of securities which have to be registered. For example, mortgage of land use rights at the Municipal Registry.

CHN ¶75-503   FORMALITIES FOR CREATION OF SECURITY

Mortgages

In order to register a mortgaged property, the following documents must be lodged with the appropriate registry:

- the principal loan agreement;
- the mortgage document; and
- the ownership or leasehold certificate of the mortgaged property.

For mortgages of other property, registration is voluntary but non-registration will prevent the mortgagee from claiming against third parties.

Land and land use rights

The State Council promulgated the *Provisional Measures on Administration of Land Use Rights* which states that a land user wanting to mortgage land use rights must present the relevant State land use certificate of approval, certificate of title to buildings and other attachments on the land and other legal certificates to the local municipal or county people's government land management authority, together with a written application.

Both parties to the mortgaging of land use rights shall sign a land use rights mortgage contract and within 60 days of signing, the land user shall pay the land use rights transfer fee and carry out procedures to register the land use right transfer. When carrying out registration procedures, it shall be necessary to present the following:

- state land use certificate of approval;
- land use rights transfer contract;
- land use rights mortgage contract; and
- other documents considered necessary by the authorities.

Under the *Guangdong ETDZ on the Compensatory Transfer and Assignment of Land Use Rights*, when applying to use land use rights as a mortgage on a loan, the following must be submitted to the financial institution:

- a copy of the transfer or assignment contract;
- the land use certificate; and
- status report on the development and operation of the land.

The bank or financial institution must then apply for registration of the mortgage within 30 days after entering the mortgage loan contract. Non-registered mortgages will be deemed invalid. The registration must be cancelled when the mortgage expires. During the term of the mortgage, the mortgagor is prohibited from re-mortgaging and from disposing already mortgaged land use rights without the prior approval of the mortgagee.

The *Regulations of the Shenzhen Special Economic Zone on Land Management* stipulates that the parties to a mortgage must enter into and register the mortgage contract. The *Regulations on Mortgage Loan Administration in Shenzhen Special Economic Zone* specifies that the following must be included in the contract:

- names of the mortgagee and mortgagor;
- the purpose of the loan;
- the amount and currency of the loan;
- duration and interest rate;
- liabilities upon breach of contract; and
- the date and place for signing the contract.

The Shanghai regulations require the same terms as the Shenzhen regulations including the following:

- name of the debtor's bank and account number;
- the nature of ownership and current cash value of the collateral;
- the mortgage ratio;

CHN ¶75-503

- the method of recovering the mortgaged property; and
- the required insurance coverage and payment of proceeds in the event of loss or damage to the collateral.

Guarantees

The formal requirements for creating an enforceable guarantee are set out in Art 13 to 15. The agreement must be in writing and must include provisions on the type and amount of the secured debt, the term for the payment of the debt by the debtor, the form, scope and term of the guarantee and other matters agreed between the parties. The guaranteed document may guarantee a single debt or a series of debts.

The consent of the guarantor is required if the debtor wishes to assign the debt to a third party or if the alterations are made to the principal agreement. By contrast, a lender may assign its rights under the principal agreement without the consent of the guarantor. Certain individuals and bodies are prohibited from acting as guarantors including state authorities, branches of enterprises and social organisations.

On 28 June 2000, SAFE issued a *Notice with respect to the Limitation of Authority Approving Enforcement of Foreign Guarantees* (the "Notice"). In accordance with the Notice, the enforcement to foreign beneficiaries of substantial illegitimate guarantees which is required but fails to be approved by SAFE or its branches, shall be approved by SAFE; the enforcement of procedural improper guarantees, which fail to register in SAFE or its branches, is permitted by local SAFE branches on the basis of penalty measures.

Other mortgageable properties

The Shenzhen and Shanghai regulations also apply for other properties in that region. Since the regulations apply only to these regions, they have limited relevance to mortgages in other parts of China.

The *Provisional Measures of the People's Bank of China on Foreign Exchange Secured Renminbi Loans for Foreign Investment Enterprises* provides that the applicants must submit details of the source and amount of foreign exchange funds to SAFE. A formal loan application must then be filed with PBOC. Upon examination and approval, the bank and the applicant will sign a loan contract.

In the case of a Chinese-foreign equity or cooperative joint venture using his shares or rights as security, approval of the venture is required, evidenced by a certificate from the board of directors. Similarly, where a party mortgages imported goods and materials which require a special customs permit, approval from the Customs is required.

The *Administration of the Provision of Security to Foreign Entities by Domestic Institutions Inside China Procedures* came into effect on 1 October 1996. The procedures apply to the provision of security to foreign entities by domestic institutions in China such as letters of guarantee, letters of credit and bills of exchange. The procedures forbid the security provider to give any security to foreign entities in the form of a lien or cash deposit. If the security provider wishes to extend the duration of security, SAFE approval is required 30 days before the maturity of the debt.

CHN ¶75-504   PRIORITY OF SECURITY INTERESTS

The general rule is that registered mortgages take a priority over unregistered mortgages and registered mortgages are ranked in order of registration. Under the *Measures of Shanghai Municipality on the Compensatory Transfer of Land Use Rights*, priority among mortgages is determined on a first to register basis (Art 38). If the mortgagor fails to perform its obligations or becomes insolvent during the term of the contract, the mortgagee will have the right to dispose of the collateral according to the law and the mortgage contract.

In the case of liquidation proceedings, priority is given to a creditor secured by property over general creditors. Property rendered to the creditor as security may be appropriated by that creditor only, to the extent that its value does not exceed the amount of the secured liabilities.

Unsecured debts may be repaid out of the debtor enterprise's assets only after the following expenses have been paid in the following priority order:

- winding up expenses;
- employees' wages and labour insurance fees; and
- taxes owed by the enterprise to the government.

When the bankrupt enterprise's assets are insufficient to satisfy all claims with the same degree of priority, the claims are settled proportionally.

CHN ¶75-505   NUMBER OF SECURITY INTERESTS AGAINST ONE PROPERTY

Further security interests cannot be created without the mortgagee's consent. Without such consent, such actions shall be deemed invalid.

CHN ¶75-511   FLOATING SECURITIES OVER CLASSES OF ASSETS

There are no regulations providing for the possibility of creating a floating security over a class of assets of the borrower.

CHN ¶75-512   SECURITIES FOR FURTHER ADVANCES

Further advances can be secured provided the mortgaged property exceeds the loan amount. Under the Shanghai Regulations, the amount of mortgage loan may not exceed 90% of the current cash value of the mortgaged property. The current cash value differs according to the type of property. In some cases, the loan may not exceed 80% of the face value or net book value.

CHN ¶75-513   IS THE CONTINUING INTEREST OF THE BORROWER RECOGNISED AND PROTECTED?

A mortgagor may not sell, transfer by deed or by will, lease or give away the mortgaged property without the written consent of the mortgagee. The lender (mortgagee) may not sell the mortgaged property free of the borrower's interest unless the mortgagee fails to repay the principal and interest as provided in the contract.

CHN ¶75-514   RETENTION OF POSSESSION BY BORROWER

The party in possession of the mortgaged property is required to safeguard the property. Where damage to the property occurs while in the possession of the mortgagor, a new security on similar property is required if no insurance indemnification is available. If damage occurs while possessed by the mortgagee, he is liable to compensate the mortgagor. A mortgagor may not sell, transfer by deed or by will, lease or give away the mortgaged property without the written consent of the mortgagee.

CHN ¶75-515   REALISATION OF SECURITY BY LENDER

Following default by the borrower, secured lenders have three options for realising mortgages, pledges of moveable property and liens. They are: converting the security to value, auction and sale.

A mortgagee may dispose of the mortgaged property in the following circumstances:

- there is a failure to repay the principal and interest of the loan as provided in the contract;
- there is no heir or inheritor upon the mortgagor's death; or
- the mortgagor becomes bankrupt.

The mortgaged property may be disposed of by auction, by assignment and, where applicable, by cashing the property. Where the mortgagor defaults, the mortgagee is entitled to dispose of the property and enjoys a priority right to the repayment of the loan. Mortgaged property is not available to general creditors in the event of bankruptcy, except to the extent that the value of the mortgaged property exceeds the loan amount.

CHN ¶75-521   TRANSFERABILITY OF LENDER'S SECURITY

See CHN ¶75-515.

CHN ¶75-522   FORMS OF PERSONAL SECURITY

Personal security by way of guarantees and foreign currencies are available and in use.

CHN ¶75-523   ACCEPTABLE SECURITIES

The PRC *Secured Interests Law*, effective 1 October 1995, provides creditors and investors with more choice of security interests than currently exists under legislation. There are five types of security interests available to lenders under the law:

- personal guarantees;
- mortgages;
- pledges;
- liens; and
- cash deposits.

All the forms of security interests covered by the law, other than cash deposits, may be used to secure the repayment of the underlying loan as well as items such as interest, liquidated damages, compensatory damages and the costs of realisation.

Implemented since 12 August 2000, the *Official Reply of the Supreme Court Regarding the Issue Whether a Guarantor Should Be Responsible for a Creditor's Increased Interest Loss due to a Wrong Judgment* stipulates that since a creditor's increased interest loss is not in the scope of a guarantee, the guarantor should not be responsible for the same (referring to Art 21 of the *Security Law*).

CHN ¶75-524   CHARGES FOR REGISTRATION OF SECURITIES

Registration charges vary on the type of security. In 1991, the fee for mortgage registration of land was RMB80. In the Shenzhen province, registration fees are set by the Shenzhen City Pricing Administration and approved by the City People's Government. Upon expiration of the mortgage, the mortgagor and mortgagee are obliged to cancel the registration.

CHN ¶75-525   TAX IMPLICATIONS AND CHOICE OF SECURITY

The choice of security is not affected by tax implications.

Movement of Goods (Transport and Shipping)

Laws relating to inward and outward transport .... CHN ¶80-001

Laws relating to movement and storage of goods .... CHN ¶80-002

International conventions .... CHN ¶80-003

Laws relating to movement of dangerous substances .... CHN ¶80-004

Arrest of vessels, etc .... CHN ¶80-005

Regulation of shipbuilding industry .... CHN ¶80-011

Laws relating to shipping register .... CHN ¶80-012

CHN ¶80-001   LAWS RELATING TO INWARD AND OUTWARD TRANSPORT

The *Maritime Law of the People's Republic of China* was adopted on 7 November 1992 by the 28th Session of the Standing Committee of the 7th National People's Congress. It was formulated in order to improve ocean shipping and relations between vessels, to safeguard the legal rights and interests of parties concerned and to accelerate the development of ocean-shipping transportation, economics and trade.

CHN ¶80-002   LAWS RELATING TO MOVEMENT AND STORAGE OF GOODS

The following legislation is applicable to the movement and storage of goods and/or persons into, out of, and/or within China by all modes of transport:

- the *Regulations of the People's Republic of China on International Ocean Shipping Industry*;

- the *Law of the People's Republic of China on Food Hygiene* (Art 30 and 31);

- the *Regulations on Administration of the International Freight Transport Agency Industry*;

- the Administration of Foreign-invested International Freight Forwarding Agencies Procedure;

- the Supplementary Provisions of Administration of Foreign-invested International Freight Forwarding Agencies Procedure;

- the *Law of the People's Republic of China on the control of Foreigners entering and leaving the country*;

- the *Maritime Law of the People's Republic of China*;

- the *Regulations for the Trial Implementation of Control of Quality Control Permits for Mechanical and Electrical products for Export* (Art 16);

- the *State Council Decision to improve non-ferrous metals control* (Art 7); and

- the *Law of the People's Republic of China on the Administration of Drugs*.

CHN ¶80-003   INTERNATIONAL CONVENTIONS

International conventions relating to the movement of goods and/or persons into/out of and/or within China by all modes of transport are as follows:

- Convention against establishing illicit traffic in narcotic drugs and psychotropic substances — 25 October 1989;

- Convention on illicit import of cultural property — 28 November 1989;

- Convention on the control of transboundary movements of hazardous wastes and their disposal;

- Protocol to 1961 Narcotic Drugs Convention — 23 August 1985; and

- Universal Postal convention and general regulations of UPU — 23 January 1985.

CHN ¶80-004   LAWS RELATING TO MOVEMENT OF DANGEROUS SUBSTANCES

The following legislation governs the movement of dangerous substances and the pollution of the environment:

- the *Marine Environmental Protection Law of the People's Republic of China*;

- the *Regulations of the People's Republic of China Controlling the Prevention of Pollution of Sea Areas by Vessels*;

- the *Regulations of the People's Republic of China Concerning the Control of the Dumping of Wastes at Sea*;

- the *Law of the People's Republic of China on the Administration of Drugs* (Art 26 to 28);

- the *Regulations Governing Supervision and Control of Vessels of Foreign Registry Sailing in the Yangtze River*; and

- the *Maritime Traffic Safety Law of the People's Republic of China* (Art 32 and 33).

CHN ¶80-005   ARREST OF VESSELS, ETC

The *Law of Special Procedure for Maritime Litigation* came into effect on 1 July 2000. Prior to or during litigation, a claimant of maritime rights may ask a maritime court of law to impound the ship concerned, in order to preserve his right to exercise the right of claim. The term "maritime rights of claim" refers to the right of payment claim which is related to or has resulted from matters concerned with an ocean shipping vessel's construction, transaction, charterage, transport undertakings, operations and rescue, as well as ownership, occupancy right, right of mortgage, priority compensation, etc.

CHN ¶80-011   REGULATION OF SHIPBUILDING INDUSTRY

China is currently the third largest shipbuilder in the world. There are no laws on shipbuilding. The shipbuilding contract is usually governed by the terms of the contract between the builder and the owner. In the event of a dispute, it would be referred to the economic contract arbitration commission for resolution.

Some of the shipbuilding companies that carry on business in China are as follows:

- China State Shipbuilding Corporation;
- Jiang Nan Shipbuilding Company;
- Shanghai Ship Company (West Branch);
- Shanghai Ship Company (East Branch);
- Donghai Ship Company;
- QiuXin Ship Company;
- Hu Tong Ship Company; and
- Zhong Hua Ship Company.

CHN ¶80-012   LAWS RELATING TO SHIPPING REGISTER

The *People's Republic of China Vessel Registration Regulations* was promulgated on 2 June 1994 and became effective on 1 January 1995.

The Regulations applies to boats and ships of owners domiciled in China. It governs the registration of ownership and mortgage of boats and ships, nationality, procedures for altering and cancelling vessel registration amongst other things. It also lays out the penalties for violation of the Regulations.

The Regulations provides that boats and ships may not possess dual nationality and that vessels registered in foreign countries may not acquire Chinese nationality where the original nationality registration of such boats and ships has not been terminated or cancelled.

On 14 May 2002, the Ministry of Communications issued the *Implementation of the (International Maritime Transport Regulations) Notice*, which became effective on the same day. The Notice requires foreign international shipping companies that sign bills of lading and otherwise undertake to transport cargoes or collect transport fees within China without having vessels enter Chinese ports to obtain the qualification for no-vessel shipping business. In particular, companies that use rented vessels or feeder vessels to transport cargoes from a Chinese port to a foreign port for transhipment to the company's vessels (Art 1) must undertake this requirement. Foreign shipping companies and no-vessel common carriers that engage in cargo transport to or from Chinese ports shall designate a contact organisation in China (Art 2).

Foreign no-vessel common carriers without a branch organisation in China shall delegate a qualified local no-vessel common carrier to act as an agent in the issue of bills of lading (Art 3). Sino-foreign joint venture no-vessel common carriers can apply for qualification in the following two ways: the joint venture company itself applies for the qualification for no-vessel common carrier; or the joint venture company may apply as the branch organisation of the foreign no-vessel common carrier (Art 4). Foreign no-vessel common carriers can apply through the provincial department in charge of communications where their designated contact organisation is located. The municipal communications authorities in Dalian, Qingdao, Xiamen and Shenzhen are allow to accept applications as well.

On 20 June 2002, MOFTEC issued the *Notice on Issues Related to the Launch of Pilot Projects for the Establishment of Foreign-Invested Logistics Enterprises* (the ''New FIE Logistics Notice''). The regulations state that a Pilot Logistics FIE may engage in part or all of the following areas:

- International logistics services:
    - providing import/export and related services, including import/export of goods for self-use (*ziying*) as well as acting as an agent for the import/export of other parties goods;
    - acting as an agent for export-processing enterprises (*chukou jiagong qiye*); and
    - acting as an agent for the international transportation of goods including the import and export of goods by sea, air and land.
- Third-party logistics services:
    - transportation of normal goods by road, warehousing (*cangchu*), loading and discharge (*zhuangxie*), light goods processing (*jiagong*), packaging (*baozhuang*), allocation and delivery (*peisong*) and the relevant information processing and consulting services;
    - acting as an agent for the domestic transportation of goods; and
    - using computer networks for the management of transportation and logistics businesses.

On 11 December 2002, MOFTEC promulgated the *Administration of Foreign-invested International Freight Forwarding Agencies Procedures*. The Procedures are formulated in accordance with the state laws and regulations concerning foreign-invested enterprises and the PRC *Administration of the International Freight Forwarding Agency Business Provisions* in order to promote the healthy development of the international freight forwarding agency business in China, and to regulate the establishment and operational conduct of foreign-invested international freight forwarding agencies. The Procedures provide the establishment requirements of a FIE forwarding agency, business scope, and procedure for the agency to establish a subsidiary.

INSURANCE

Introduction ....CHN ¶85-000
Use of state-owned or resident brokers ....CHN ¶85-001
Classes of insurance underwriters ....CHN ¶85-002
Available range of insurance ....CHN ¶85-003
Insurance required for financing arrangements ......CHN ¶85-004
Compulsory insurance ....CHN ¶85-011
Insurance of local employees ....CHN ¶85-012
Legislation affecting choice of insurance
    company ....CHN ¶85-013
Application for insurance payments ....CHN ¶85-014
Product liability insurance ....CHN ¶85-021

CHN ¶85-000 Introduction

Prior to the introduction of economic reforms in the late 1970s, the state ultimately bore the risks of most hazards against which insurance would normally be sought in other countries. Moreover, extensive social welfare schemes covered the needs of individuals. The PRC *Insurance Law* came into effect on 1 October 1995 and regulates all insurance activities in China.

The 1985 regulations deal with the establishment of an insurance enterprise, the role of the People's Insurance Company of China (PICC) and various restrictions on the activities of insurers in China. Much of the activity of Chinese insurers relates to property insurance. These matters are dealt with in the *Regulations of the People's Republic of China on Contracts of Property Insurance* which took effect on 1 September 1983. The legislative framework is also provided by the articles of association of PICC.

With China's accession to the World Trade Organisation (WTO), its insurance sector is facing enormous changes. A series of milestone regulations has been introduced during the recent two years by the PRC State Council and the China Insurance Regulatory Commission (CIRC):

- the *Administration Regulations of Insurance Company* on 1 March 2000 (replaces the *Provisional Regulations Governing the Management of Insurance Enterprises* on 1 April 1985);

- the *Provisional Administration Measures of Part-time Insurance Agent* on 4 August 2000;

- the *Administration Regulations of Insurance Assessing Bodies* on 16 November 2001;

- the *Administration Regulations of Insurance Brokerage Company* on 16 November 2001;

- the *Administration Regulations of Insurance Agency* on 16 November 2001;

- the *Administration Measures of Insurance Company Marketing Service Department* on 1 February 2002;

- the *People's Republic of China Administration Regulations of Foreign-Invested Insurance Company* on 30 November 2001;

- the *Amendments to the Administration Regulations of Insurance Company* on 15 March 2002; and

- the amendments to *PRC Insurance Law* adopted by the Standing Committee of 9th National People's Congress on 28 October 2002.

- the *Fulfillment of Relevant WTO Accession Commitments Notice issued by CIRC* on 11 December 2003 allows foreign-invested property insurance companies to engage in all non-life insurance businesses other than statutory insurance. Another five cities, Fuzhou, Xiamen, Ningbo, Shenyang and Wuhan are open to the outside for insurance business.

- the *Administration of Insurance Companies Provisions issued by CIRC* on 13 May 2004, which replaces the *Administration Regulations of Insurance Company* and the *Amendments to the Administration Regulations of Insurance Company*. The Provisions consist of seven parts covering insurance organisations, insurance business operations, insurance clauses, insurance premium rates, insurance funds and solvency of insurance companies, and supervision and inspection;

- the *Administration of Foreign-invested Insurance Companies Regulations Implementing Rules* issued by CIRC on 13 May 2004. The Rules elaborate on the terms mentioned in the *People's Republic of China Administration Regulations of Foreign-Invested Insurance Company* and give details on the requirements and procedures for the establishment of branches and sub-branches of foreign-invested insurance companies.

CHN ¶85-001   Use of state-owned or resident brokers

Until 1988, there was only one major insurance company, PICC; PICC currently has a market share of 80%. As of August 2002, there were 53 insurance companies nationwide, out of which over 20 are foreign-invested insurance companies or branches of foreign insurance companies. Thus, a new insurance system with the state-owned insurance companies at its centre, co-existing and competing with many other insurance companies, has begun to take shape. At the same time, exchanges and cooperation between the Chinese and international insurance markets have been strengthened.

Foreign insurance companies are not permitted to operate directly in China, although they may establish branches, joint ventures and wholly foreign-owned enterprises according to relevant laws and regulations.

CHN ¶85-002   Classes of insurance underwriters

The PRC *Insurance Law*, which came into effect on 1 October 1995, applies to all insurance activities carried out within China. Under this law, insurance companies are required to choose between general and life insurance as their mainstream commercial business activity. Companies engaging in marine insurance are also governed by the PRC *Maritime Law*. The law requires companies to take the form of either a company limited by shares or a wholly state-owned company and to have the following requirements:

- articles of association complying with the law and the national company law;

- minimum registered capital of RMB200 million;
- senior management staff with professional knowledge and work experience;
- a sound organisational structure and management system; and
- business offices and related facilities that satisfy the required standard.

CIRC issued the *Provisions for the Establishment of Reinsurance Companies* on 17 September 2002 (the ''Reinsurance Provisions''), and they became effective on that same day.

CHN ¶85-003 Available range of insurance

Today, many insurance companies handle over 280 kinds of insurance coverage both at home and abroad, and the industry is gradually approaching the business range common in the international insurance industry.

PICC has widened the range of insurance it provides, as follows:

- cargo transport;
- property;
- investment (political risk);
- industrial property;
- construction and installation projects;
- construction all risks insurance;
- means of transportation;
- fire;
- personal accident;
- foreign goods and machinery on exhibition;
- automobile;
- aircraft;
- erection all risks (EAR); and
- life.

CHN ¶85-004 Insurance required for financing arrangements

For foreign enterprises, they are permitted to borrow funds from a bank. However, their security arrangement must be backed by insurance of the mortgaged property, among other things, and purchased from PICC.

CHN ¶85-011 Compulsory insurance

Under the *Regulations on the Labour Administration of Enterprises with Foreign Investment* promulgated on 11 August 1994, a joint venture is required to have social insurance covering pension, unemployment, medical treatment, work-related injury, childbirth, etc; as well as social insurance premium fully paid on time to the social insurance institution in accordance with the standards specified by the local government. According to the *Provisional Regulations on Unemployment Insurance Funds of State-Owned Enterprises*, an employer is required to contribute an amount equal to 1% of the total basic wages of its employees. In the case of state-owned enterprises, such contributions are deducted automatically each month from the bank account of the employer.

Under the *Labour Insurance Regulations of the People's Republic of China*, a participating state-owned enterprise is required to contribute on a monthly basis a specified percentage of its payroll to a labour insurance fund. This contribution may not be deducted from an employee's wages.

CHN ¶85-012   Insurance of local employees

The system of social insurance was introduced by the *Labour Insurance Regulations of the People's Republic of China* amended on 2 July 1953. Under the *Labour Insurance Regulations*, a participating state-owned enterprise is required to contribute on a monthly basis a specified percentage of its payroll to a labour insurance fund.

The labour insurance fund was intended to cover medical expenses and compensation or allowances payable to the employee or his relatives in case of illness, injury, disability or death of the employee, whether or not related to his work. Maternity treatment, maintenance of dependants and retirement benefits were also covered by labour insurance.

Since the reform of the urban economic system in 1984, the reform of the social security system with pension insurance as the mainstay has been carried out step by step. The Ministry of Labour and Social Security is responsible for comprehensive administration of social insurance work across the nation, including pension insurance, medical insurance, unemployment insurance, employment injury insurance and maternity insurance for urban enterprises, government organisations and institutions as well as pension insurance in the rural areas.

Pension

China has actively promoted and perfected the method of combining social overall planning with individual accounts, and set up a unified basic pension insurance system for staff and workers of enterprises.

In March 1995, the State Council promulgated the *Circular on Deepening Pension Insurance System Reform for Enterprise Workers* which adopted the principle of combining social pooling with individual accounts in pension insurance, and proposed two approaches for localities as reference. The *Decisions on the Unification of the Basic Pension Insurance for Enterprise Workers* promulgated by the State Council in July 1997 and the *Regulations on Social Insurance Contributions Collection and Payment* promulgated by the State Council in January 1999, have laid down the framework for the current pension insurance system. According to these regulations, contribution rate for enterprises are determined by provincial government, normally no more than 20% of their total payrolls.

Unemployment

Under the *Unemployment Insurance Regulation*, urban employees and employers are required to pay unemployment insurance premium, generally to a local social insurance agency. According to the *Unemployment Insurance Regulation*, effective 22 January 1999, an employer is required to contribute an amount equal to 2% of the total basic wages of its employees, and an employee is required to contribute an amount equal to 1% of his basic wages. Rural contracted employees recruited by urban enterprises and institutional organisations are not required to contribute to the employees' portion of unemployment insurance.

Medical

In December 1998, the State Council promulgated the *Decisions on the Development of Medical Insurance System for Urban Employees* which initiated the national medical insurance system reform for urban employees in early 1999 and reinstated the new system by end 1999 to replace systems of the public medical care and labour insurance medical care.

Under the new system, all urban enterprises, state organs, institutions, associations, private non-enterprise units and their employees shall participate in the medical insurance scheme. The medical cost shall be shared by the employers and individuals: employers shall pay a contribution equivalent to 6% of their payrolls while individuals shall contribute 2% of their wages.

CHN ¶85-013   Legislation affecting choice of insurance company

The Administration of Insurance Companies Provisions which came into effect as of June 15 2004 regulates the choice of insurance companies by reference to which companies are licensed to carry on business in China and the various restrictions on the activities of insurers in China. The Regulations also provides for the requirement and procedures to establish an insurance enterprise or branch office in China, as well as various aspects of the operation of insurance companies, such as use of insurance premiums, reinsurance and governmental supervisions, etc.

From 1 January 2003, the amended *PRC Insurance Law* took effect and applies to all insurance activities within China. These include the activities of joint ventures and wholly foreign-owned enterprises. Only insurance companies set up under the law may engage in commercial insurance business. The China government has adhered to the following amendment principles when it amended the law. Legislators kept firmly in mind the following three overriding themes while drafting all 38 items included in this amendment:

- sustained reform and development of the China insurance industry;
- strengthened supervision and regulation of the industry; and
- standardised regulations on insurance enterprises and business operations.

The new *Insurance Law* both meets the requirements mandated by China's accession to the WTO and gives adequate consideration to the interests of insurance consumers. It will nevertheless be quite hard-pressed to deal with the challenges that will arise after the full opening of China's insurance market. Therefore, this amendment may best be considered an interim measure practices. The law contains many important rules applying to the operations of insurance companies after their establishment, one of which is that a company may not engage in property and personal insurance at the same time.

Article 107 of the amended law stipulates that only the insurance policy clauses and premium rates for policy-mandated insurance and new types of life insurance products need pre-approval from insurance regulatory authorities, while clauses and rates for insurance products of all other types are to be reported to such authorities merely for filing on the record. Thus, by this amendment, insurance companies in China have finally been given the legal prerogatives of free-market product development and price competition. The amended *Insurance Law* clearly stipulates that an individual life insurance agent shall represent only a single company, the new law places no restrictions on the number of insurance companies that an incorporated agency may serve.

Article 105 of the amended *Insurance Law* makes a slightly looser restriction in stipulating that insurance funds shall not be used to establish securities business organisations or to establish enterprises beyond the realm of insurance, while retaining a clause permitting the State Council to stipulate appropriate investment vehicles for insurance funds in addition to the traditionally accepted bank deposit or purchase of government or financial bonds. The 20% compulsory reinsurance requirement has been deleted from the new *Insurance Law*, however, reinsurance is still required out of a certain percentage of the insurance premium as provided in China's WTO commitments. Moreover, asset of insurance company can be used to invest in securities operation companies or other insurance enterprises.

Insurance companies shall be required to choose between general and life insurance as their mainstream commercial business activity.

CHN ¶85-014   Application for insurance payments

This varies on the type of insurance taken out. For example, for industrial property insurance — when applying for compensation, an insured shall provide a detailed list of the damaged items of insured property together with such documents as necessary, account books, receipts and official documents. The insurer shall promptly decide whether compensation is warranted under the insurance policy. Compensation shall be paid immediately upon agreement between the insurer and the insured on the amount to be paid.

The PRC *Insurance Law*, as amended on 28 October 2002, provides a safeguard for policy holders and investors in that it requires insurance companies to deposit 20% of their registered capital with designated banks and contribute to an industry-wide fund as a backup measure for companies faced with large payouts (Art 79).

A policy which makes death a condition of the payment of insurance is void if the written consent of the insured party to the policy and the amount insured has not been obtained. The right to claim compensation or payment of insurance money expires after five years in the case of life insurance and two years in the case of property insurance and ocean cargo shipping insurance.

CHN ¶85-021   Product liability insurance

Product liability insurance is under development in China. The usual method of such cover is via China's *Product Quality Law of the People's Republic of China* which took effect on 1 September 1993. While the law mainly emphasises compliance with explicit written control standards, it also creates a general duty on manufacturers and retailers not to manufacture or sell defective goods.

Producers are liable to pay compensation if a defective product causes physical injury or damage to property. Penalties for non-compliance with state or industry standards include fines, directives to cease production of the non-complying products as well as confiscation of both the products and the illegal income. Enterprises may also have their business licence revoked and be subject to criminal prosecution (Art 37).

Recently, major insurance companies, such as PICC and China Pacific Property Insurance Company, have expanded their scope of business activities to include product liability insurance.